Recommended by **Teachers**
Trusted by **Toppers**

All in One

POLITICAL SCIENCE
Class 12

EVERYTHING YOU NEED TO SCORE

- Simplified Theory
- NCERT & Other Important Questions
- CBQs; MCQs, A-R, Case Based
- Board Questions Upto 2025
- Sample Question Papers

CBSE Exams 2026

Authors
Pooja Sharma
Divyanshi Jain

arihant
SUCCESS AND NOTHING LESS

arihant
SUCCESS AND NOTHING LESS

ARIHANT PRAKASHAN
(School Division Series)

ADMINISTRATIVE & PRODUCTION OFFICES

Regd. Office

'Ramchhaya' 4577/15, Agarwal Road, Darya Ganj, New Delhi -110002
Tele: 011- 47630600, 43518550; Fax: 011- 23280316

Head Office

Kalindi, TP Nagar, Meerut (UP) - 250002, Tel: 0121-7156203, 7156204

SALES & SUPPORT OFFICES

Agra, Ahmedabad, Bengaluru, Bareilly, Chennai, Delhi, Guwahati, Hyderabad, Jaipur, Jhansi, Kolkata, Lucknow, Nagpur & Pune.

PO No : TXT-XX-XXXXXXX-X-XX

Published By Arihant Publications (India) Ltd.

For further information about the books published by Arihant, log on to www.arihantbooks.com or e-mail at info@arihantbooks.com

Follow us on

PRICE ₹425.00

PRODUCTION TEAM

Publishing Managers
Mahendra Singh Rawat & Keshav Mohan

Cover Designer
Salman Shaikh

Inner Designer
Ankit Tyagi

Project Head
Monika Bhasin

Page Layouting
Chintoo Kumar

Proof Reader
Pravesh Bhagrwal, Anurag Vashist

Index *cum* Study Planner

PART A : Contemporary World Politics

		Studied	Revised	Exam ready
1. The End of Bipolarity	**1-25**			
The Soviet System	1-3	☐	☐	☐
Gorbachev and the Disintegration	3-5	☐	☐	☐
Shock Therapy in Post-Communist Regimes	5-6	☐	☐	☐
Tensions and Conflicts	6-7	☐	☐	☐
New Entities in World Politics	7-8	☐	☐	☐
India's Relations with Russia and Other Post- Communist Countries	8-9	☐	☐	☐
Mind Map	10	☐	☐	☐
NCERT Folder	11-13	☐	☐	☐
Exam Pattern Questions	13-24	☐	☐	☐
Self Assessment Test	25	☐	☐	☐
2. Contemporary Centres of Power	**26-49**			
European Union	26-28	☐	☐	☐
Association of South East Asian Nations (ASEAN)	28-29	☐	☐	☐
The Rise of the Chinese Economy	29-31	☐	☐	☐
Japan and South Korea as Emerging Powers	31-32	☐	☐	☐
Mind Map	33	☐	☐	☐
NCERT Folder	34-37	☐	☐	☐
Exam Pattern Questions	37-48	☐	☐	☐
Self Assessment Test	49	☐	☐	☐
3. Contemporary South Asia	**50-74**			
Political Background of South Asian Countries	50-51	☐	☐	☐
Democratisation in South Asia	51-53	☐	☐	☐
India Pakistan Conflict	53-54	☐	☐	☐
India and Its Neighbours	54-57	☐	☐	☐
Mind Map	58	☐	☐	☐
NCERT Folder	59-61	☐	☐	☐
Exam Pattern Questions	62-73	☐	☐	☐
Self Assessment Test	74	☐	☐	☐
4. International Organisations	**75-98**			
Need of International Organisations	75-78	☐	☐	☐
India and the UN Reforms	79-80	☐	☐	☐
The UN in Unipolar World	80-82	☐	☐	☐
Mind Map	83	☐	☐	☐
NCERT Folder	84-87	☐	☐	☐
Exam Pattern Questions	87-97	☐	☐	☐
Self Assessment Test	98	☐	☐	☐
5. Security in Contemporary World	**99-118**			
Traditional Notion of Security: External	99-100	☐	☐	☐
Traditional Notion of Security: Internal	100-101	☐	☐	☐
New Sources of Threats	101-103	☐	☐	☐
Co-operative Security	103	☐	☐	☐
India's Security Strategy	103	☐	☐	☐
Mind Map	104	☐	☐	☐
NCERT Folder	105-107	☐	☐	☐
Exam Pattern Questions	108-117	☐	☐	☐
Self Assessment Test	118	☐	☐	☐

		Studied	Revised	Exam ready
6. Envioronment and Natural Resources	**119-137**			
Environmental Concerns in Global Politics	119-120	☐	☐	☐
Protection of Global Commons	120-122	☐	☐	☐
India's Stand on Environmental Issues	122-123	☐	☐	☐
Resource Geopolitics	123-124	☐	☐	☐
Indigenous Peoples and their Rights	124	☐	☐	☐
Mind Map	125	☐	☐	☐
NCERT Folder	126-127	☐	☐	☐
Exam Pattern Questions	127-136	☐	☐	☐
Self Assessment Test	137	☐	☐	☐
7. Globalisation	**138-154**			
Concept of Globalisation	138-139	☐	☐	☐
Consequences of Globalisation	139-140	☐	☐	☐
India and Globalisation	140-141	☐	☐	☐
Mind Map	142	☐	☐	☐
NCERT Folder	143-144	☐	☐	☐
Exam Pattern Questions	145-153	☐	☐	☐
Self Assessment Test	154	☐	☐	☐
PART B : Politics in India Since Independence				
1. Challenges of Nation -Building	**155-181**			
A New Nation State	155-156	☐	☐	☐
Partition : Displacement and Rehabilitation	156-157	☐	☐	☐
Integration of Princely States	158-160	☐	☐	☐
Re-organisation of States	160-162	☐	☐	☐
Mind Map	163	☐	☐	☐
NCERT Folder	164-166	☐	☐	☐
Exam Pattern Questions	167-180	☐	☐	☐
Self Assessment Test	181	☐	☐	☐
2. Era of One-Party Dominance	**182-201**			
Challenge of Building Democracy	182-183	☐	☐	☐
Congress Dominance in the First Three General Elections	183-186	☐	☐	☐
Emergence of Opposition Parties	186-188	☐	☐	☐
Mind Map	189	☐	☐	☐
NCERT Folder	190-191	☐	☐	☐
Exam Pattern Questions	191-200	☐	☐	☐
Self Assessment Test	201	☐	☐	☐
3. Politics of Planned Development	**202-216**			
Political Contestation	202-203	☐	☐	☐
The Early Initiatives of Planning Commission	204-205	☐	☐	☐
Mind Map	206	☐	☐	☐
NCERT Folder	207-208	☐	☐	☐
Exam Pattern Questions	208-215	☐	☐	☐
Self Assessment Test	216	☐	☐	☐
4. India's External Relations	**217-239**			
International Context	217-219	☐	☐	☐
Peace and Conflict with China	220-222	☐	☐	☐
Wars and Peace with Pakistan	222-224	☐	☐	☐
India's Nuclear Policy	224-225	☐	☐	☐

		Studied	Revised	Exam ready
Mind Map	226	☐	☐	☐
NCERT Folder	227-229	☐	☐	☐
Exam Pattern Questions	229-238	☐	☐	☐
Self Assessment Test	239	☐	☐	☐
5. Challenges to and Restoration of the Congress System	**240-262**			
Challenges of Political Succession	240-241	☐	☐	☐
Fourth General Elections, 1967	242-244	☐	☐	☐
Split in the Congress	244-245	☐	☐	☐
Presidential Election, 1969	245-246	☐	☐	☐
The 1971 Election and Restoration of Congress	246-247	☐	☐	☐
Mind Map	248	☐	☐	☐
NCERT Folder	249-251	☐	☐	☐
Exam Pattern Questions	252-261	☐	☐	☐
Self Assessment Test	262	☐	☐	☐
6. The Crisis of Democratic Order	**263-287**			
Background to Emergency	263-265	☐	☐	☐
Declaration of Emergency	265-267	☐	☐	☐
Politics after Emergency	268-271	☐	☐	☐
Mind Map	272	☐	☐	☐
NCERT Folder	273-276	☐	☐	☐
Exam Pattern Questions	276-286	☐	☐	☐
Self Assessment Test	287	☐	☐	☐
7. Regional Aspirations	**288-315**			
Region and the Nation	288-289	☐	☐	☐
Jammu and Kashmir	289-293	☐	☐	☐
Punjab	293-294	☐	☐	☐
The North-Eastern	295-298	☐	☐	☐
Accommodation and National Integration	298-300	☐	☐	☐
Mind Map	301	☐	☐	☐
NCERT Folder	302-304	☐	☐	☐
Exam Pattern Questions	305-314	☐	☐	☐
Self Assessment Test	315	☐	☐	☐
8. Recent Developments in Indian Politics	**316-339**			
Context of the 1990s	316-317	☐	☐	☐
Era of Coalitions	317-319	☐	☐	☐
Political Rise of Other Backward Classes	319-320	☐	☐	☐
Communalism, Secularism, Democracy	320-321	☐	☐	☐
Emergence of a New Consensus	322-324	☐	☐	☐
Mind Map	325	☐	☐	☐
NCERT Folder	326-328	☐	☐	☐
Exam Pattern Questions	328-338	☐	☐	☐
Self Assessment Test	339	☐	☐	☐
Project Work	**341-361**			
Sample Question Paper (1-3)	**365-380**			
CBSE Examination Paper 2025	**381-388**			

One Book- Endless Features

to Help you Succeed

In this Chapter

At the start of each chapter, all the topics of the chapter have been listed, so that students may know what they are going to study.

01

CHAPTER

Part A Contemporary World Politics

The End of Bipolarity

This chapter deals with the reasons and consequences of the disintegration of the USSR. It also explores the relationship of India with the USSR and its successor Russia.

YOUR STUDY GOALS

1.1 The Soviet System
1.2 Gorbachev and the Disintegration
1.3 Shock Therapy in Post-Communist Regimes
1.4 Tensions and Conflicts
1.5 New Entities in World Politics
1.6 India's Relation with Russia and Other Post-Communist Countries

YOUR PRACTICE GOAL

- Objective Type Questions (43 Qs ; MCQs, A-R, Statements, Matching, Passage Based)
- Subjective Questions (10 VSAs, 9 SAs, 10 LAs, 1 Picture Based, 1 Map Based)

The concept of Bipolarity[1] and its end has significant implications on the global order. Starting from the fall of the Berlin Wall, various historical events led to the collapse of the Soviet system.

This collapse resulted into many important changes in the world politics including end of Cold War, unification of divided Germany, replacement of communist government with the liberal democratic government and private ownership.

The Berlin Wall was built in 1961. It symbolised the division between the capitalist and the communist world. It was broken by the people on 9th November 1989. This marked the unification of Germany and the beginning of the end of the communist bloc.

Quick Test

To assess your step by step learning of chapters quick test questions are incorporated in between the theory.

Quick Test 1

1. What was the objective of the socialist revolution of Russia?
2. Which type of party system was prevalent in the Soviet system?
3. Which country did the Soviet Union invade in 1979?
4. Who was the last leader of the Soviet Union who helped in the unification of Germany?

Complete Theory in Each Chapter

Each chapter has complete, easy to understand and simplified theory covering latest syllabus. Theory is developed in such a way that it is suitable for all types of learners.

1.1 The Soviet System

- The Union of Soviet Socialist Republics (USSR) emerged after the Socialist Revolution in Russia, in 1917. The Socialist Revolution was influenced by the ideals of socialism and the need for **egalitarian society**[2]. Thus, this system tried to abolish the institution of private property and promoted a society based on principles of equality.

1 **Bipolarity** It is a world order where two countries hold most of the global economic, military and cultural influence.
2 **Egalitarian society** It believes that all people are equally important and should have the same rights and opportunities in life.

One Book- Endless Features

to Help you Succeed

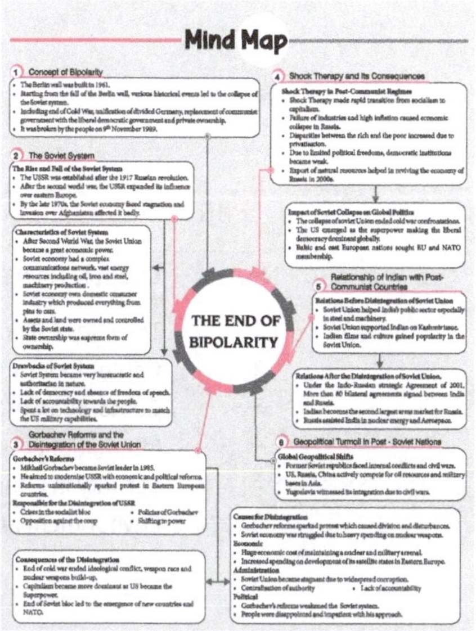

Mind Map

A quick revision visual tool for the complete chapter.

NCERT Folder

Intext Questions

1. I am amazed! How could so many sensitive people all over the world admire a system like this? (Pg. no. 4)

Ans. Many sensitive people all over the world admire the Soviet system due to the following reasons
- It was formed with the objective of creating an egalitarian society.
- It ensured a minimum standard of living for all citizens and the government subsidised basic necessities including health, education, childcare and other welfare schemes.
- The Soviet Union was self-reliant, which produced everything from pins to cars to meet their needs.

2. I heard someone say "The end of the Soviet Union does not mean the end of socialism". Is that possible? (Pg. no. 8)

Ans. Yes, it is possible that the end of the Soviet Union does not mean the end of socialism. Socialism is an ideology, whereas the Soviet Union was a state based on the ideology of socialism. Socialist ideas like economic equality, welfare state, etc. are still popular and relevant. The Soviet Union collapsed due to many reasons and not just because of socialism. So, its end is not the end of socialism.

- Nationalism is very broad in nature and emphasises language and culture. Secessionism is basically limited to political autonomy.
- Nationalism tries to secure rights for people. It may demand a new nation or seek greater autonomy within the current political framework. Secessionism tries to separate from the country that they are part of.

There is a very thin difference between secessionism and nationalism. Nationalism can take the form of secessionism and secessionism can take the form of nationalism. Secessionist leaders are celebrated as heroes of the nation, if they succeed. However, if they fail, they are blamed for challenging the existing political structure.

5. Make a list of the similarities between India and the USSR in their political and economic ideologies. (Pg. no. 11)

Ans. Similarities between India and the USSR in their political ideologies are as follows
- Both opposed colonialism and imperialism.
- Both embraced socialist principles in their political ideologies.
- Both established a welfare state, which allowed the state intervention to ensure equality.

Similarities between India and the USSR in their

NCERT Folder

To make students completely understand NCERT books, solutions of all the NCERT exercises have been given in each chapter in NCERT Folder. Accuracy, detailing and simplicity of solution are the major features of this section.

Self Assessment Test

At the end of the chapter, these unsolved questions are for practice and assessment of students. By practising these questions students can assess their preparation level for the chapter.

SELF ASSESSMENT TEST

Objective Type Questions

1. Who was the successor of Lenin?
   (a) Leonid Brezhnev (b) Boris Yeltsin
   (c) Joseph Stalin (d) Mikhail Gorbachev
2. Which of these republics joined the CIS in 1993?
   (a) Armenia (b) Georgia
   (c) Uzbekistan (d) Tajikistan
3. Consider the following statement about the Berlin Wall and choose the correct option(s).
   I. The Berlin Wall symbolised the division between the capitalist and the communist world.
   II. It was built in 1965.
   III. The wall was more then 150 km long and it stood for 28 years.

   Codes
   (a) I and II (b) II and III
   (c) I and III (d) Only II

SAMPLE QUESTION PAPER 1

A Highly Simulated Sample Question Paper for CBSE Class XII Examination

POLITICAL SCIENCE

General Instructions

1. The question paper consists of five sections (A, B, C, D and E) with 30 questions in total.
2. All questions are compulsory.
3. Question numbers 1-12 are multiple choice questions of one mark each.
4. Question numbers 13-18 are of 2 marks each. Answers to these questions should not exceed 50-60 words each.
5. Question numbers 19-23 are of 4 marks each. Answers to these questions should not exceed 100-120 words each. There is an internal choice in two of the 4 marks questions
6. Question numbers 24-26 are passage, cartoon and map-based questions. Answer accordingly.
7. Question numbers 27-30 are of 6 marks each. Answers to these questions should not exceed 170-180 words.
8. There is an internal choice in 6 marks questions.

Time : 3 hours **Max. Marks : 80**

SECTION A

1. Identify and choose the incorrect pair (1)
   (a) Lal Bahadur Shastri - Jai Jawan Jai Kisan
   (b) Indira Gandhi - Garibi Hatao
   (c) Syndicate - A group of powerful opposition leaders against Indira Gandhi
   (d) Grand Alliance - Formed by all non-Congress parties

4. Which country is not considered as a part of South-Asia region? (1)
   (a) Afghanistan (b) Myanmar
   (c) China (d) Sri Lanka

5. Which of the following term is all about who gets what, when, where and how? (1)
   (a) Globalisation (b) Privatisation
   (c) Resources geopolitics

Sample Question Papers

To make students practice of examination in real sense, there are 3 Sample Question Papers at the end. All these Sample Questions Papers are exactly prepared on the latest syllabus & pattern of examination.

Latest Course *Structure*

PART A : Contemporary World Politics

No.	Chapter Name	Marks Alloted
1	The End of Bipolarity	6
2	Contemporary Centres of Power	6
3	Contemporary South Asia	6
4	International Organisations	6
5	Security in Contemporary World	6
6	Environment and Natural Resources	6
7	Globalisation	4
	TOTAL	40

PART B : Politics in India since Independence

No.	Chapter Name	Marks Alloted
1	Challenges of Nation-Building	6
2	Era of One-Party Dominance	4
3	Politics of Planned Development	2
4	India's External Relations	6
5	Challenges to end Restoration of the Congress System	4
6	The Crisis of Democratic Order	4
7	Regional Aspirations	6
8	Recent Developments in Indian Politics	8
		40
	TOTAL	80

PART A : Contemporary World Politics

1. The End of Bipolarity

Topics to be focused

a) The Soviet System
b) Gorbachev and the disintegration
c) Causes and Consequences of disintegration of Soviet Union
d) Shock Therapy and its Consequences
e) New entities in world politics
- Russia
- Balkan States
- Central Asian States

f) India's relations with Russia and other post-communist countries

2. Contemporary Centres of Power

Topics to be focused

a) European Union
b) Association of South east Asian Nations
c) Rise of China as an economic power
d) Japan and South Korea as emerging powers

3. Contemporary South Asia

Topics to be focused

a) Military and Democracy in Pakistan and Bangladesh
b) Monarchy and Democracy in Nepal
c) Ethnic Conflict and Democracy in Sri Lanka
d) India-Pakistan Conflicts
e) India and its Neighbours
f) Peace and Co-operation

4. International Organizations

Topics to be focused

a) Meaning and importance of International Organisations
b) Evolution of the UN
c) Structure and function of International Organisations
d) Principal Organs of UN
e) Reform of the UN after Cold War
f) Reform of Structures, Processes and Jurisdiction of the UN
g) India and the UN Reforms
h) Key Agencies: IMF, World Bank, WTO, ILO, IAEA.
i) NGO: Amnesty International, Human Rights Watch.
j) Implications and Future of International Organisations

5. Security in the Contemporary World

Topics to be focused

a) Meaning and Type of Security.
b) Traditional concept of Security
c) Non-tradition notions of Security.
d) New Sources of Threats
e) Co-operative Security
f) India's Security strategy

6. Environment and Natural Resources

Topics to be focused

a) Environmental Concerns
b) Global Commons
c) Common but differentiated Responsibilities
d) India's Stand on Environment Issues
e) Environmental Movements
f) Resource Geopolitics
g) Rights of Indigenous peoples

7. Globalisation

Topics to be focused

a) Concept of globalisation
b) Causes and Consequences of globalisation
c) India and globalisation
d) Resistance to globalisation
e) India and resistance to globalisation

PART B : Politics in India Since Independence

1. Challenges of Nation Building

Topics to be focused

a) Challenges for the new Nation.
  - Three Challenges.

b) Partition: Displacement and Rehabilitation.
  - Consequences of Partition.

c) Integration of Princely States.
  - The problem
  - Government's approach
  - Hyderabad
  - Manipur

d) Reorganisation of States.

2. Era of One-Party Dominance

Topics to be focused

a) Challenge of building democracy.

b) Congress dominance in the First Three General Elections.
  - Nature of Congress dominance
  - Congress as social and ideological coalition.
  - Tolerance and management of Factions

c) Emergence of opposition parties.

3. Politics of Planned Development

Topics to be focused

a) Political contestation.
  - Ideas of Development
  - Planning
  - Planning Commission

b) The Early Initiatives
  - The First-Five Year Plan.
  - Rapid Industrialisation.

4. India's External Relations

Topics to be focused

a) International Context

b) The Policy of Non-Alignment.
  - Nehru's role
  - Distance from two camps.
  - Afro Asian Unity

c) Peace and conflict with China
  - The Chinese Invasion, 1962
  - War and Peace with Pakistan
  - Bangladesh War, 1971

d) India's Nuclear Policy.

5. Challenges to and Restoration of the Congress System

Topics to be focused

a) Challenges of Political Succession
  - From Nehru to Shastri
  - From Shastri to Indira Gandhi

b) Fourth General Election, 1967
  - Context of the Election.
  - Non Congressism
  - Electoral Verdict
  - Coalitions
  - Defections

c) Split in the Congress
  - Indira Vs. the Syndicate
  - Presidential Election, 1969

d) The 1971 Election and Restoration of Congress
  - The outcome and after
  - Restoration?

6. The Crisis of Democratic Order

Topics to be focused

a) Background to Emergency.
   - Economic Context.
   - Gujarat and Bihar Movements
   - Conflict with Judiciary

b) Declaration of Emergency
   - Crisis and response
   - Consequences

c) Lessons of the Emergency.

d) Politics after Emergency.
   - Lok Sabha Elections 1977
   - Janata Government
   - Legacy

7. Regional Aspirations

Topics to be focused

a) Region and the Nation
   - Indian Approach
   - Areas of Tension
   - Jammu and Kashmir
   - Roots of the Problem
   - External and Internal disputes
   - Politics since 1948
   - Insurgency and After
   - 2022 and Beyond

b) Punjab
   - Political Context
   - Cycle of Violence
   - Road to Peace

c) The North East
   - Demand for autonomy
   - Secessionist Movements
   - Movements against outsiders
   - Assam and National Integration.

8. Recent Developments in Indian Politics

Topics to be focused

a) Context of 1990s

b) Era of Coalition
   - Alliance Politics

c) Political rise if the Backward Classes
   - Mandal Implemented
   - Political Fallouts

d) Communalism, Secularism and Democracy.
   - Ayodhya Dispute
   - Demolition and after

e) Emergence of New Consensus

f) Lok Sabha Elections 2004

g) Growing Consensus

01 CHAPTER

This chapter deals with the reasons and consequences of the disintegration of the USSR. It also explores the relationship of India with the USSR and its successor Russia.

The End of Bipolarity

YOUR STUDY GOALS

1.1 The Soviet System
1.2 Gorbachev and the Disintegration
1.3 Shock Therapy in Post-Communist Regimes
1.4 Tensions and Conflicts
1.5 New Entities in World Politics
1.6 India's Relation with Russia and Other Post-Communist Countries

YOUR PRACTICE GOAL

- Objective Type Questions (43 Qs ; MCQs, A-R, Statements, Matching, Passage Based)
- Subjective Questions (10 VSAs, 9 SAs, 10 LAs, 1 Picture Based, 1 Map Based)

The concept of **Bipolarity**[1] and its end has significant implications on the global order. Starting from the fall of the Berlin Wall, various historical events led to the collapse of the Soviet system.

This collapse resulted into many important changes in the world politics including end of Cold War, unification of divided Germany, replacement of communist government with the liberal democratic government and private ownership.

> The Berlin Wall was built in 1961. It symbolised the division between the capitalist and the communist world. It was broken by the people on 9th November 1989. This marked the unification of Germany and the beginning of the end of the communist bloc.

1.1 The Soviet System

- The Union of Soviet Socialist Republics (USSR) emerged after the Socialist Revolution in Russia, in 1917. The Socialist Revolution was influenced by the ideals of socialism and the need for **egalitarian society**[2]. Thus, this system tried to abolish the institution of private property and promoted a society based on principles of equality.

1 **Bipolarity** It is a world order where two countries hold most of the global economic, military and cultural influence.

2 **Egalitarian society** It believes that all people are equally important and should have the same rights and opportunities in life.

- The makers of Soviet system gave priority to the state and the institution of the party. The Soviet political system was centred around the Communist Party. No other political party was allowed by the state. In terms of economy, everything was planned and controlled by the state.
- After the Second World War the East European countries liberated by the Soviet Army from the fascists forces after the Second World War, came under the control of the USSR. The political and economic system same as USSR was followed in these countries. This group of countries was called the **Second World** or the **Socialist bloc**. These countries were held together by the **Warsaw Pact** led by USSR. The USSR was the leader of the bloc.

Characteristics of Soviet System

The characteristics of Soviet system are discussed below

- After the Second World War, the Soviet Union became a great economic power. At that time the economy of USSR was more developed than the rest of the world except USA.
- It had a complex communications network, vast energy resources including oil, iron and steel, machinery production and a transport sector which connected its remotest areas with efficiency.
- It also had its own domestic consumer industry which produced everything from pins to cars. Although there was a difference in their quality as compared to the Western capitalist countries.
- A minimum standard of living was assured for all the citizens under the Soviet system. Basic necessities like health, education, childcare and other welfare schemes were subsidised by the government.
- Assets and land were owned and controlled by the Soviet state (Soviet Government). Thus, state ownership was supreme form of ownership.

Drawbacks of Soviet System

There were some drawbacks in Soviet system. These were as follows

- The Soviet system became very bureaucratic and authoritarian in nature. It became difficult for its citizens to express their problems.
- Lack of democracy and absence of freedom of speech discouraged the people to express their disagreements against the government.
- The Soviet system was based on one party system represented by Communist Party which had tight control over all the institutions. There was lack of accountability towards the people.
- The party refused to fulfill the needs and aspirations of the people in fifteen different republics in order to manage their own affairs including their cultural affairs. Russia dominated everything and people from other republics felt neglected and suppressed.
- The Soviet Union spent a lot on technology and infrastructure to match the US military capabilities. The Soviet Union lagged behind the West in technology, infrastructure for example, transport, power and most importantly, in fulfilling the political and economic aspirations of citizens.
- The Soviet system was weakened after the Afghanistan invasion in 1979 as its productivity and technology fell miserably behind that of West. It led to shortages in all consumer goods. Food import increased every year. The Soviet economy turned stagnant in the late 1970's.

Leader of the Soviet Union

Vladimir Lenin (1870-1924) He was the founder of the Bolshevik Communist Party and leader of the Russian Revolution of 1917. He was an outstanding theoretician and practitioner of Marxism and a source of inspiration for communists all over the world.

Joseph Stalin (1878-1953) He led the Soviet Union during its consolidation (1924-53). He began rapid industrialisation and forcible collectivisation of agriculture. He was held responsible for the Great Terror of the 1930s, authoritarian functioning and elimination of rivals within the party.

Nikita Khrushchev (1894-1971) He was the leader of the Soviet Union (1953-64). He criticised Stalin's leadership style and introduced some reforms in 1956 and suggested 'peaceful coexistence' with the West. He was involved in suppressing popular rebellion in Hungary and in the Cuban Missile Crisis.

Leonid Brezhnev (1906-82) He was the leader of the Soviet Union (1964-82) who proposed Asian Collective Security System. He was involved in suppressing a popular rebellion in Czechoslovakia and in invading Afghanistan.

Mikhail Gorbachev (1931-2022) He was the last leader of the Soviet Union (1985-91). He withdrew Soviet troops from Afghanistan and Eastern Europe and helped in the unification of Germany. He ended the Cold War and was blamed for the disintegration of the Soviet Union because of his polices of perestroika re-structuring and glass most (openners).

Boris Yeltsin (1931-2007) He was the first elected President of Russia (1991-1999). He joined the critics of Gorbachev and left the Communist Party and led the protests against the Soviet regime in 1991. He played a key role in dissolving the Soviet Union and was blamed for hardships suffered by Russians in their transition from communism to capitalism.

Quick Test 1

1. What was the objective of the socialist revolution of Russia?
2. Which type of party system was prevalent in the Soviet system?
3. Which country did the Soviet Union invade in 1979?
4. Who was the last leader of the Soviet Union who helped in the unification of Germany?

1.2 Gorbachev and the Disintegration

- Mikhail Gorbachev of the Communist Party of Soviet Union became General Secretary in 1985. He favoured reforms in the USSR as it would keep USSR ahead from the Western powers and maintaining an edge over the information and technological revolutions. His decisions to maintain normal relations with the West, democratise and reform the Soviet Union had some other effects.

  Series of events were responsible for the disintegration of USSR. Some of them are discussed below

  - **Crises in the Socialist Bloc** People in many East European countries which were part of Soviet bloc started protest against their own governments and USSR. Due to the lack of intervention of USSR at the right time, Communist Governments in the second world collapsed one after another.
  - **Policies of Gorbachev** Gorbachev identified the economic and political problems of USSR and started a series of reforms, with the intention to revive economy. This was a deviation from the communist policies and was more associated with the market economy. Many communist leaders opposed these reforms and they started a coup in 1991. By then people experienced freedom and did not want the old style rule of the Communist Party.

- **Opposition Against the Coup** Boris Yeltsin, who won popular election in Russian Republic, protested against the coup and centralised the control of USSR.
- **Shift of Power** Power began shifting from Soviet Union's Central authority to Republics, especially in the European regions which were part of the Soviet Union, which started seeing themselves as sovereign states. In December 1991, under yeltsin's leadership republics like Russia, Ukraine and Belarus emerged powerful and declared that Soviet Union was disbanded. The Communist Party of the Soviet Union was banned. Capitalism and democracy were adopted as the foundation of the post-Soviet republics.

- Russia, Belarus and Ukraine decided to end the 1922 treaty that created the USSR. They established the **Commonwealth of Independent State** (CIS).
- The declaration of the USSRs disintegration and the formation of the CIS came as a surprise to the other republics especially the Central Asian ones. To address their exclusion, they were made founding members of CIS.
- The members of the CIS were Russia, Belarus, Ukraine, Armenia, Azerbaijan, Moldova, Kazakhstan, Kyrgyzstan, Tajikistan, Turkmenistan and Uzbekistan. Georgia joined the CIS in 1993.
- Russia emerged as the successor state of the Soviet Union. It also inherited the UN Security Council seat. All the international treaties and commitments of the Soviet Union were accepted by Russia. It emerged as the only nuclear state of the post-Soviet space and it carried out some nuclear disarmament measures with the US. The old Soviet Union was thus dead and buried.

Causes for Disintegration

Some of the reasons which are mainly responsible for the disintegration of Soviet Union are discussed below

Economic

- The Soviet economy used much of its resources in maintaining a nuclear and military arsenal and the development of its satellite states[3] in Eastern Europe and within the Soviet system, which led to huge economic burden.
- The economy of the Soviet Union became stagnant which led to severe consumer shortages and distrust in the system. Ordinary citizens also became aware of the economic advancement of the West.

Administration

- The administration of the Soviet Union became stagnant due to widespread corruption, the unwillingness to allow more openness in governance and the centralisation of authority. There was lack of accountability.
- The party bureaucrats gained more privileges than ordinary citizens. People did not feel connected with the system and with the rulers.

Political

- Gorbachev's reforms weakened the Soviet System. There were sections of Soviet society which felt that Gorbachev should have acted more quickly. They were disappointed and impatient with his approach. Others, especially members of Communist Party felt that their power and privileges were eroding and Gorbachev was acting too quickly. In this 'tug of war', Gorbachev lost support on all sides.
- The most immediate cause was the rise of nationalism and the desire for sovereignty within various republics including Russia and the Baltic Republics (Estonia, Lativa and Lithuania), Ukraine, Georgia. Nationalism was stronger in Russia, the Baltics, Ukraine and Georgia as compared to regions of Central Asia. This was because people in these areas felt alienated from the Central Asians and from each other. They also resented the economic burden of supporting poorer regions.

3 **Satellite states** It is a country that is formally independent, but is under the control or influense of another country in terms of politics, economics or military.

Consequences of Disintegration

Some of the consequences which emerged after the collapse of Soviet Union are discussed below

End of Cold War Confrontations

It led to the end of Cold War confrontations. Basically, the ideological dispute related to socialism and capitalism was over. This further led to end of arms race and accumulation of nuclear weapons.

Change in Power Dynamics of World Politics

- As power equation in the world politics changed, it left only two possibilities i.e. unipolar system or multipolar system that would dominate the world. As a result, the US became the sole superpower which was supported by the capitalist system. This made the capitalist system as the dominant economic system globally. Liberal democracy emerged as the best way to organise politics.
- Institutions like the World Bank and International Monetary Fund became powerful advisors to all these countries since these institutions gave them loans for their transition to capitalism.

Emergence of New Countries

- The end of Soviet bloc led to the emergence of many new countries. All these countries had their own independent choices. For example, the Baltic and East European countries wanted to be a part of European Union and become part of the **North Atlantic Treaty Organisation** (NATO).
- The Central Asian countries wanted to take advantage of their geographical location and continue their close ties with the West, the US, China and others. Thus, the international area witnessed many new players each with their own identity, interests, economic and political difficulties.

1.3 Shock Therapy in Post-Communist Regimes

- Shock Therapy is a model of transition from an authoritarian socialist system to a democratic capitalist system. This model was used in Russia, Central Asia and East Europe with the help of the World Bank and the IMF.
- Though the direction and features were quite similar, but shock therapy varied in intensity and speed amongst the former second world countries.
- Each of these countries was required to make a complete shift to a capitalist economy.

  Following are the features of shock therapy
  - It meant that private ownership was to be the dominant form of economic ownership.
  - Privatisation of state assets and corporate ownership patterns were to be immediately brought in.
  - Collective farms were to be replaced by private farming and capitalism in agriculture.
  - This transition ruled out any **alternate** or **third-way**, other than state-controlled socialism or capitalism.
  - For promoting international trade, these countries adopted free trade regime and foreign direct investment.
  - End of the trade alliances among the countries of the Soviet bloc. Now these countries started their trade relations with Western countries directly.

Consequences of Shock Therapy

The shock therapy administered in 1990s did not fulfill the expectations of the people rather it had several adverse effects, which were as follows

Destruction of Economy

- The shock therapy weakened the economies of these countries. For example, about 90 per cent Russian industries were put up for sale to private individuals and companies. All citizens were given vouchers to participate in the sales but most of them sold these vouchers in the black market for the sake of money.
- This restructuring was carried out through market forces and not by government-directed industrial policies. Hence valuable industries were undervalued and sold at very less prices. Thus this was called the largest garage sale in history.

Decline of Russian Currency and Imports of Food

People lost all their savings due to high rate of inflation and sudden fall in the value of ruble. The disintegration of collective form system compelled Russia to import food. Due to all of these reasons, the real GDP of Russia in 1999 was less than what it was in 1989.

End of Welfare State

The end of old system of social welfare including the withdrawal of government subsidies led to increase in poverty, change in the status of the middle class and migration of intellectual class.

Inequality

The private mode of production and ownership resulted into inequality between the rich and the poor. The shock therapy also gave rise to many mafias who started controlling many economic activities in post-Soviet states.

Lack of Democratic Institutions

- The Constitution of all the Post-Soviet countries were drafted in a hurry. Most of them had features like a strong executive, weak Parliaments and a lack of judicial independence. In Central Asia, the Presidents had great powers, and many of them became very authoritarian. For example, the Presidents of Turkmenistan and Uzbekistan appointed themselves to power first for ten years and then extended it for another ten years.
- Most of these economies, especially Russia, started reviving in 2000, after ten years of their independence. The reason for the revival of their economies was the export of natural resources like oil, natural gas and minerals. Azerbaijan, Kazakhstan, Russia, Turkmenistan and Uzbekistan are major oil and gas producers. Other countries gained because of the oil pipelines that cross their territories for which they earned rent. Some amount of manufacturing restarted.

1.4 Tensions and Conflicts

Most of the former Soviet republics are prone to conflicts and many have had civil wars and insurgencies. Growing involvement of outside powers made situation more complicated.

Facts Related to Tensions and Conflicts

Some facts related to tensions and conflicts in these republics are as follows

- **Secessionist Movements**[4] In Russia, two republics, **Chechnya and Dagestan,** have had violent secessionist movements. Moscow's violent method of dealing with the Chechen rebels have led to many human rights violations but failed to deter the aspirations for independence.
- **Sectarian Conflicts** In Central Asia, Tajikistan witnessed a Civil War that went on for ten years till 2001. The region as a whole has many sectarian conflicts.

4 **Secessionist Movements** It is a political effort by a group to become as an independent country by separating from a country.

- In Azerbaijan's province of Nagorno-Karabakh, some local Armenians want to secede and join Armenia.
- In Georgia, the demand for independence came from two provinces, resulting in a civil war.
- There are movements against the existing regimes in Ukraine, Kyrgyzstan and Georgia.
- Countries and provinces are fighting over river waters. All this led to instability, making life difficult for the ordinary citizen.

Reasons for Tensions and Conflicts

Reasons for tensions and conflicts in these areas were as follows

- **Regions with Vast Hydrocarbon Resources** The Central Asian Republics are areas with vast Hydrocarbon resources, which brought them economic benefit. Central Asia has also become a zone of competition between outside powers and oil companies.
- **Establishment of Military Bases** The Central Asian region is next to Russia, China, Afghanistan and Pakistan and close to West Asia.
- After 11th September, 2001, the US wanted military bases in the region and paid the governments of all Central Asian states to hire bases and to allow airplanes to fly over their territory during the wars in Afghanistan and Iraq.
- However, Russia perceives these states as its Near Abroad and believes that they should be under Russian influence.
- China has interests here because of the oil resources and the Chinese have begun to settle around the borders and conduct trade.
- In Eastern Europe, **Czechoslovakia** split into two independent countries i.e. Czechs and Slovaks. But the most severe conflict took place in the Balkan republics of Yugoslavia.
- After 1991, it broke apart with several provinces like Croatia, Slovenia and Bosnia and Herzegovina declaring independence. Ethnic Serbs opposed this and a massacre of non-Serb Bosnians was followed. The NATO intervention and the bombing of Yugoslavia followed the inter-ethnic civil war.

Quick Test 2

1. When did Mikhail Gorbachev become General Secretary of the Communist Party?
2. Which event led to the end of Cold War?
3. How was Russian currency affected by the shock therapy?
4. Which Central Asian country has witnessed a civil war after the shock therapy?

1.5 New Entities in World Politics

Russia

Russia is the largest country in the world. It came into existence after the disintegration of the USSR. After the disintegration it had faced various socio-economic and political challenges but its vast natural resources, above all oil and gas, helped Russia to recover fast.

Central Asian States

Central Asia is also known as Middle Asia. It is a region of Asia that stretches from the Caspian sea in the West to Western China and Mongolia in the East and from Afghanistan and Iran in the South to Russia in the north. It includes the former Soviet republics of Kazakhstan, Kyrgyzstan, Tajikistan, Turkmenistan and Uzbekistan.

Balkans States

The Balkans also known as the Balkan Peninsula, is a geographical area in South-Eastern Europe with various geographical and historical definitions. The region takes its name from the Balkan mountains that stretch throughout the whole of Bulgaria.

It contains many countries, including Romania, Moldova, Bulgaria, Greece, Albania and the independent states of the former Yugoslavia–Serbia, Croatia, Slovenia, North Macedonia, Bosnia and Herzegovina, and Montenegro–but there is no universal agreement on the region's components.

1.6 India's Relations with Russia and other Post-communist Countries

India's Relations with Russia and other Post-Communist States

Before Disintegration

Even before the emergence of Russia in the world politics, India had maintained a multi-dimensional relationship with the **USSR** discussed as below

- **Economic** The Soviet Union assisted India's public sector companies by giving aid and technical assistance for steel plants like Bhilai, Bokaro, Visakhapatnam and machinery plants like Bharat Heavy Electricals Ltd., etc. It also accepted Indian currency for trade when India was short of foreign exchange.
- **Political** The Soviet Union supported India's positions on the Kashmir issue in the UN. It also supported India during its major conflicts, especially during the war with Pakistan in 1971. India too supported Soviet foreign policy in some crucial but indirect ways.
- **Military** India received most of its military hardware from the Soviet Union at a time when few other countries were willing to part with military technologies. The Soviet Union entered into various agreements allowing India to jointly produce military equipment.
- **Culture** Hindi films and Indian culture were popular in the Soviet Union. A large number of Indian writers and artists visited the USSR.

After Disintegration

- After the disintegration of the USSR, India has maintained good relations with all the post-communist countries. But the strongest relations are still those between Russia and India. Indo-Russian relations are deeply rooted in a history of trust and common interests.
- Hindi film songs and Indian heroes are very popular in Russia and many post-Soviet countries. More than 80 bilateral agreements have been signed between India and Russia as part of the **Indo-Russian Strategic Agreement** of 2001.
- India benefits from Russia in areas like energy, Kashmir terrorism, nuclear aid space programmes and relations with China. Russia in turn, gains from this relationship as India is its **second largest arms market** with a significant portion of India's military equipment sourced from Russia. Both nations continue to collaborate on various scientific and technological projects.

Arab Spring in the 21st Century

- The Arab Spring was a series of anti-government protests, uprisings and armed rebellions that spread across the Middle East in 2010. The 21st century witnessed the emergence of new developments for democracies and democratisation in West Asian countries.
- The Arab Spring emerged in Tunisia where the struggle against corruption, unemployment and poverty was started by the people. This protest later turned into a political movement because the people blamed autocratic dictatorship as a cause for existing problems.

- Then, the demand for democracy that started in Tunisia spread throughout the Muslim-dominated Arab countries in West Asia. The rule of Hosni Mubarak, who had been in power in Egypt since 1979 also collapsed as a result of the massive democratic protests.
- In addition, the influence of Arab Spring was also visible in Yemen, Bahrain, Libya and Syria where similar protests by the people led to democratic awakening throughout the region.

Quick Test 3

1. Why Russia is an important partner of India?
2. When was the Strategic Agreement signed between India and Russia?
3. Where was the Arab Spring started?
4. Name any two steel plants of India which were established with the assistance of Russia.

TIMELINE

Timeline of Disintegration of the Soviet Union.

1985 March	Mikhail Gorbachev elected as the General Secretary of the Communist Party of the Soviet Union; appoints Boris Yeltsin as the head of the Communist Party in mascow.
1988 June	Independence movement begins in Lithuania later spreads to Estonia and Latvia.
1989 Ocotber	Soviet Union declares that Warsaw pact members are free to decide their own futures.
1989 November	Berlin Wall falls
1990 February	Gorbachev permits multi-party politics
1990 March	Lithuania declares its independence
1991 June	Yeltsin becames the President of Russia
1991 August	Coup against Gorbachev by the Communist Party hardliners.
1991 September	3 Baltic republics of Estania, Latuia and Lithuania became the UN members.
1991 December	Establishment of CIS
25th December 1991	Gorbachev resigns as the President of the Soviet Union, the end of the Soviet Union.

Mind Map

THE END OF BIPOLARITY

1 Concept of Bipolarity

- The Berlin wall was built in 1961.
- Starting from the fall of the Berlin wall, various historical events led to the collapse of the Soviet system.
- Including end of Cold War, unification of divided Germany, replacement of communist government with the liberal democratic government and private ownership.
- It was broken by the people on 9th November 1989.

2 The Soviet System

The Rise and Fall of the Soviet System

- The USSR was established after the 1917 Russian revolution.
- After the second world war, the USSR expanded its influence over eastern Europe.
- By the late 1970s, the Soviet economy faced stagnation and invasion over Afghanistan affected it badly.

Characteristics of Soviet System

- After Second World War, the Soviet Union became a great economic power.
- Soviet economy had a complex communications network, vast energy resources including oil, iron and steel, machinery production .
- Soviet economy own domestic consumer industry which produced everything from pins to cars.
- Assets and land were owned and controlled by the Soviet state.
- State ownership was supreme form of ownership.

Drawbacks of Soviet System

- Soviet System became very bureaucratic and authoritarian in nature.
- Lack of democracy and absence of freedom of speech.
- Lack of accountability towards the people.
- Spent a lot on technology and infrastructure to match the US military capabilities.

3 Gorbachev Reforms and the Disintegration of the Soviet Union

Gorbachev's Reforms

- Mikhail Gorbachev became Soviet leader in 1985.
- He aimed to modernise USSR with economic and political reforms.
- Reforms unintentionally sparked protest in Eastern European countries.

Responsible for the Disintegration of USSR

- Crises in the socialist bloc
- Policies of Gorbachev
- Opposition against the coup
- Shifting to power

Consequences of the Disintegration

- End of cold war ended ideological conflict, weapon race and nuclear weapons build-up.
- Capitalism became more dominant as US became the Superpower.
- End of Soviet bloc led to the emergence of new countries and NATO.

Causes for Disintegration

- Gorbachev reforms sparked protest which caused division and disturbances.
- Soviet economy was struggled due to heavy spending on nuclear weapons.

Economic

- Huge economic cost of maintaining a nuclear and military arsenal.
- Increased spending on development of its satellite states in Eastern Europe.

Administration

- Soviet Union became stagnant due to widespread corruption.
- Centralisation of authority
- Lack of accountability

Political

- Gorbachev's reforms weakened the Soviet system.
- People were disappointed and impatient with his approach.

4 Shock Therapy and Its Consequences

Shock Therapy in Post-Communist Regimes

- Shock Therapy made rapid transition from socialism to capitalism.
- Failure of industries and high inflation caused economic collapse in Russia.
- Disparities between the rich and the poor increased due to privatisation.
- Due to limited political freedoms, democratic institutions became weak.
- Export of natural resources helped in reviving the economy of Russia in 2000s.

Impact of Soviet Collapse on Global Politics

- The collapse of soviet Union ended cold war confrontations.
- The US emerged as the superpower making the liberal democracy dominant globally.
- Baltic and east European nations sought EU and NATO membership.

5 Relationship of Indian with Post-Communist Countries

Relations Before Disintegration of Soviet Union

- Soviet Union helped India's public sector especially in steel and machinery.
- Soviet Union supported Indian on Kashmir issue.
- Indian films and culture gained popularity in the Soviet Union.

Relations After the Disintegration of Soviet Union.

- Under the Indo-Russian strategic Agreement of 2001, More than 80 bilateral agreements signed between India and Russia.
- Indian becomes the second largest arms market for Russia.
- Russia assisted India in nuclear energy and Aerospace.

6 Geopolitical Turmoil in Post - Soviet Nations

Global Geopolitical Shifts

- Former Soviet republics faced internal conflicts and civil wars.
- US, Russia, China actively compete for oil resources and military bases in Asia.
- Yugoslavia witnessed its integration due to civil wars.

NCERT Folder

Intext Questions

1. I am amazed! How could so many sensitive people all over the world admire a system like this? (Pg. no. 4)

Ans. Many sensitive people all over the world admire the Soviet system due to the following reasons

- It was formed with the objective of creating an egalitarian society.
- It ensured a minimum standard of living for all citizens and the government subsidised basic necessities including health, education, childcare and other welfare schemes.
- The Soviet Union was self-reliant, which produced everything from pins to cars to meet their needs.

2. I heard someone say "The end of the Soviet Union does not mean the end of socialism". Is that possible? (Pg. no. 8)

Ans. Yes, it is possible that the end of the Soviet Union does not mean the end of socialism. Socialism is an ideology, whereas the Soviet Union was a state based on the ideology of socialism. Socialist ideas like economic equality, welfare state, etc. are still popular and relevant. The Soviet Union collapsed due to many reasons and not just because of socialism. So, its end is not the end of socialism.

3. I can see the shock. But where is the therapy? Why do we talk in such euphemisms? (Pg. no. 9)

Ans. The phrase 'shock therapy' describes the harsh transition from socialism to capitalism. The therapy here refers to economic reforms, but these reforms caused economic collapse, poverty and inequality. Hence we talk about it in euphemism because it hides the painful truth of these drastic changes.

4. What is the difference between nationalism and secessionism? If you succeed, you are celebrated as a nationalist hero and if you fail you are condemned for crimes of secessionism. (Pg. no. 10)

Ans. Nationalism refers to the desire by a group of people who share the same ethnic group, culture, language, etc. to form an independent country. Secessionism refers to the efforts by a group to become an independent country by separating from a country.

Differences between nationalism and secessionism are as follows

- Nationalism emerges due to the belief of collective belonging of people, whereas secessionism emerges due to political dissatisfaction due to negligence.
- Nationalism is very broad in nature and emphasises language and culture. Secessionism is basically limited to political autonomy.
- Nationalism tries to secure rights for people. It may demand a new nation or seek greater autonomy within the current political framework. Secessionism tries to separate from the country that they are part of.

There is a very thin difference between secessionism and nationalism. Nationalism can take the form of secessionism and secessionism can take the form of nationalism. Secessionist leaders are celebrated as heroes of the nation, if they succeed. However, if they fail, they are blamed for challenging the existing political structure.

5. Make a list of the similarities between India and the USSR in their political and economic ideologies. (Pg. no. 11)

Ans. Similarities between India and the USSR in their political ideologies are as follows

- Both opposed colonialism and imperialism.
- Both embraced socialist principles in their political ideologies.
- Both established a welfare state, which allowed the state intervention to ensure equality.

Similarities between India and the USSR in their economic ideologies are as follows

- Both adopted the path of the planned economy by five-year plans.
- Both ensured a strong presence of public sector entepriseѕ.
- Both focused on the welfare of citizens and ran various government welfare schemes and programmes.

Exercise

1. Which among the following statements that describe the nature of Soviet economy is wrong?

(i) Socialism was the dominant ideology

(ii) State ownership/control existed over the factors of production

(iii) People enjoyed economic freedom

(iv) Every aspect of the economy was planned and controlled by the state

Ans. (iii) People enjoyed economic freedom

2. Arrange the following in chronological order. **CBSE 2024**

(i) Soviet invasion of Afghanistan

(ii) Fall of the Berlin Wall

(iii) Disintegration of the Soviet Union
(iv) Russian Revolution

Ans. (iv) Russian Revolution (1917)
(i) Soviet invasion of Afghanistan (1979-1989)
(ii) Fall of Berlin Wall (1989)
(iii) Disintegration of the Soviet Union (1991)

3. Which among the following is not an outcome of the disintegration of the USSR?
(i) End of the ideological war between the US and USSR
(ii) Birth of CIS
(iii) Change in the balance of power in the world order
(iv) Crisis in the Middle East

Ans. (iv) Crisis in the Middle East

4. Match the following

A. Mikhail Gorbachev	1. Successor of USSR
B. Shock Therapy	2. Military Pact
C. Russia	3. Introduced Reforms
D. Boris Yeltsin	4. Economic Model
E. Warsaw	5. President of Russia

Ans. A-3, B-4, C-1, D-5, E-2

5. Fill in the blanks.
(i) The Soviet political system was based on .... ideology.
(ii) .... was the military alliance started by the USSR.
(iii) .... Party dominated the Soviet Union's political system.
(iv) .... initiated the reforms in the USSR in 1985.
(v) The fall of the .... symbolised the end of the Cold War.

Ans. (i) socialist (ii) Warsaw Pact
(iii) Communist (iv) Mikhail Gorbachev
(v) Berlin Wall

6. Mention any three features that distinguish the Soviet economy from that of a capitalist country like the US.

Ans. The three features that distinguish the Soviet economy from that of a capitalist country like the US were as follows
(i) In the Soviet Union state ownership was the dominant form of ownership. Land and productive assets were owned and controlled by the Soviet state, whereas in capitalist countries like US there was private ownership of means of production.
(ii) The Soviet state ensured a minimum standard of living for all citizens and the government subsidised basic necessities including health, education, childcare and other welfare schemes. While in capitalist countries like US, the demand and supply were determined by the market forces.
(iii) The Soviet economy focused upon the equality of wealth and emphasised equitable distribution of wealth. On the other hand in capitalist countries like US, state was not responsible for maintaining economic equality.

7. What were the factors that forced Gorbachev to initiate the reforms in the USSR?
***Or* Explain any six factors that forced Gorbachev to initiate reforms in the Soviet Union.**

Ans. The factors that forced Gorbachev to initiate the reforms in the USSR are
(i) To keep the USSR informed of the information and technological revolutions which were taking place in West.
(ii) To normalise the relationships with that of the West.
(iii) To democratise and reform the Soviet Union.
(iv) To reform the administrative system by which the ordinary people were exempted from the privileges.
(v) To end the feeling of negligence among the people belonging to the region other than Russia.
(vi) The Soviet economy became stagnant because of low productivity and shortages of all consumer goods. Thus, to bring the economy back an track, Gorbachev initiated the reforms.

8. What were the major consequences of the disintegration of the Soviet Union for countries like India?
***Or* What were the consequences of the disintegration of USSR?** **Diksha App**
***Or* Explain any four consequences of the disintegration of the Soviet Union.** **CBSE 2025**

Ans. The major consequences of the disintegration of the Soviet Union for countries like India were as follows
(i) It gave end to Cold War confrontations and to the ideological disputes between the two superpowers.
(ii) Military alliance of Soviet countries were abolished and demand arose for world peace and security.
(iii) The vision of multipolar world was shared and discussed where a group of countries could play a crucial role in world politics.
(iv) Central Asian republics comprising Tajikistan, Azerbaijan, Georgia, Armenia and Kazakhstan were left open for bilateral agreements to be concluded in the field of mineral and energy resources for the upgradation of their economy.
(v) Many East European countries, Baltic nations and Balkan states were liberalised and most of them became part of the trade alliances of the West and NATO.
(vi) Many new countries emerged with the independent aspirations and choices. The idea of liberal democracy surfaced as a way to organise political life.

9. What was shock therapy? Was this the best way to make a transition from communism to capitalism?

Or **Can Shock Therapy be called the best way to make transition from authoritarian socialist system to liberal capitalist system after the disintegration of Soviet Union? Explain.** **CBSE 2025**

Ans. Shock therapy was the process of transition from an authoritarian socialist system to a democratic capitalist system, that was influenced by the World Bank and the IMF. Shock therapy is not considered as the best way to make a transition from communism to capitalism because

- The economies were ruined and there was disaster upon the people of the entire region of the past-Soviet countries.
- The large state controlled industrial complex almost collapsed in Russia. The valuable industries were undervalued and sold at throw away prices.
- The value of the Russian currency 'Ruble' declined.
- Due to high rate of inflation people lost all their savings.
- Russia started to import food as the collective farm system disintegrated and people were left without food security.
- With no alternatives in its place the old trading structure broke down.
- Large sections of the people were put into poverty due to the withdrawal of the government subsidies.

10. Write an essay for or against the following proposition. "With the disintegration of the second world, India should change its foreign policy and focus more on friendship with the US rather than with traditional friends like Russia".

Ans. India should not change its foreign policy and focus more on friendship with US, but India is required to maintain healthy relations with Russia because India has experienced a long bond of mutual trust, interests and popular perceptions with Russia in the following manner.

(i) Russia and India share a vision of multipolar world order i.e. co-existence of several world powers internationally, collective security, greater regionalism, democratisation of decision-making through bodies like the UN.

(ii) More than 80 bilateral agreements have been signed between India and Russia as a part of the Indo-Russia Strategic Agreement of 2001.

(iii) India has been benefitted from its relationhip on the issues like Kashmir, energy supplies, sharing information on international terrorism, access to Central Asia and balancing its relation with China.

(iv) Russia is also important for India's nuclear security and assisting India's space industry.

(v) Co-operation with Russia and republics of Kazakhstan, Turkmenistan in the form of partnership and investment in oil fields has also benefitted India.

(vi) Russia is also benefitted from India as India is the second largest arms market for Russia. Indian military gets most of its hardware from Russia.

(vii) Russia and India have collaboration on various scientific projects also.

Exam Pattern Questions

Objective Type Questions

Multiple Choice Questions (MCQs)

1. In which year the Berlin Wall was built?

(a) 1960 (b) 1961 (c) 1965 (d) 1955

2. Which one of the following statements about the Berlin Wall is incorrect?

(a) It symbolised the division between the capitalist and the communist world.
(b) It was built immediately after the Second World.
(c) It marked the unification of the two parts of Germany.
(d) It was broken by the people on 9th November, 1989.

3. The Union of Soviet Socialist Republics (USSR) came into being after the Socialist Revolution in Russia in **CBSE 2020**

(a) 1914 (b) 1917
(c) 1939 (d) 1991

4. Which one of the following statements was not a feature of the Soviet system? **CBSE Term I 2021**

(a) A minimum standard of living was ensured to all citizens.
(b) The Soviet Government subsidised the basic necessities.
(c) There was no unemployment.
(d) People had the right to property.

5. Which among the following statements about Soviet system is not true? CBSE 2020

(a) The Soviet Union had complex communication.
(b) It had a complex machinery production system and transport sector that connected its remotest areas with efficiency.
(c) It had a domestic consumer industry that produced everything from pins to cars.
(d) Soviet Union disintegrated in 1992.

6. Which one of the following was not a weakness of the Soviet Union? CBSE Term I 2021

(a) The Communist Party was not accountable to the people.
(b) There was rampant corruption in the Soviet Union.
(c) The party bureaucracy had many more privileges than an ordinary citizen had.
(d) Gorbachev initiated reforms in USSR.

7. Which of the following statement given below is/are correct about the Soviet leader Vladimir Lenin?

(a) He was the outstanding theoretician and practitioner of marxism.
(b) He began rapid industrialisation and forcible collectivisation of agriculture.
(c) He proposed Asian Collective Security System.
(d) He was the first elected President of Russia.

8. The Communist Party staged an abortive coup in August 1991, against which Soviet leader?

(a) Boris Yeltsin (b) Mikhail Gorbachev
(c) Leonid Brezhnev (d) Joseph Stalin

9. Which three major republics of the USSR declared in 1991 that the Soviet Union was disbanded? CBSE Term I 2021

(a) Lithuania, Georgia and Kyrgyzstan
(b) Russia, Latvia and Uzbekistan
(c) Russia, Ukraine and Belarus
(d) Russia, Estonia and Turkmenistan

10. Why did Russia become the successor of USSR? CBSE 2020

(a) Russia led the formation of CIS.
(b) It inherited the Soviet seat in the UN.
(c) It was the largest republic.
(d) Boris Yeltsin was more charismatic than Gorbachev.

11. Identify the group of countries that had been part of the Soviet Union before its disintegration.

(a) Tajikistan, Azerbaijan, Armenia
(b) Armenia, West Germany, Azerbaijan
(c) Poland, East Germany, Norway
(d) Norway, Hungary, Romania

12. Which one among the following is a cause of disintegration of the Soviet Union? CBSE Term I 2021

(a) Inability of the Soviet system to correct its own mistakes.
(b) Over aspirations of the people.
(c) Rapid economic development.
(d) Superiority of the Soviet system over Western capitalism.

13. Which event marked the end of communism in the Soviet Union? CBSE 2024

(a) Cuban Missile Crisis
(b) Rise of new world order
(c) Disintegration of the Soviet Union
(d) Rise in US economy

14. Politically which notion emerged as the best way to organised political life?

(a) Socialism (b) Liberal democracy
(c) Capitalism (d) None of these

15. Which one of the following was NOT a consequence of disintegration of the USSR?

(a) Many new states emerged.
(b) Russia emerged as a new superpower.
(c) Power relations in world politics changed.
(d) The capitalist system emerged as the winner.

16. Shock therapy is a phenomenon associated with .... CBSE 2020

(a) Central Asian conflicts in Tajikistan and Azerbaijan.
(b) New International Economic Order.
(c) US plans to root out communism.
(d) Stabilising the Russian currency against the US dollar.

17. The main engines of change in the East European countries post disintegration of USSR was brought by……… . Diksha App

(a) Foreign Direct Investment
(b) Financial Aids
(c) Inflation Rates
(d) All of the above

18. The collapse of the Soviet Union was followed by Shock Therapy. Which of the following statements is NOT correct about Shock Therapy? CBSE SQP 2024

(a) The transition involved a breakup of the existing trade alliances among the countries of the Soviet bloc.
(b) Shock therapy involved a drastic change in the external orientation of these economies.
(c) FDI and free trade were to be the main engines.
(d) The Eastern capitalist states guided and controlled the development of the region.

19. Which one of the following was not a consequence of shock therapy in Russia? CBSE Term I 2021

(a) The collective farm system disintegrated.
(b) It brought ruin to the economy and disaster upon the people.
(c) The whole large scale state controlled industrial complex almost collapsed.
(d) The system of social welfare got strengthened.

20. The Presidents of which Central Asian Republics appointed themselves to power first for ten years and then extended their term for another ten years? **CBSE 2024 C**

(a) Kyrgyzstan and Kazakhstan
(b) Ukraine and Azerbaijan
(c) Turkmenistan and Uzbekistan
(d) Tajikistan and Kazakhstan

21. The movement 'Arab Spring' that began in 2010 later turned into which type of movement?

(a) Social movement
(b) Religions movement
(c) Political movement
(d) Economic movement

22. The Arab Spring was a struggle against what? **CBSE 2020**

(a) Unemployment (b) Corruption
(c) Poverty (d) All of these

23. Which one of the following states is not a Baltic Republic?

(a) Estonia (b) Ukraine
(c) Latvia (d) Lithuania

24. The Arab Spring did not transcend which of the following countries? **CBSE 2020**

(a) Tunisia (b) Libya
(c) Iran (d) Yemen

25. The result of Arab Spring was .... **CBSE 2020**

(a) removal of autocratic dictatorship
(b) socialists system
(c) post Cold War
(d) capitalist system

26. The disintegration of Soviet Union was one of the most important events that altered the global geopolitics after the Second World War. Consider the following statement(s) in this regard and choose the correct one/(s).

I. A coup took place in 1991 that was encouraged by communist party hardliness.
II. Boris Yeltsin emerged as a national hero in opposing this coup.
III. In December 1991, under the leadership of Yeltsin, Russia, Ukraine and Belarus three major republics of the USSR, declared that the Soviet Union was disbanded.

Codes

(a) I and III (b) Only I
(c) I and II (d) I, II and III

27. Soviet system which came into being after Socialist Revolution in 1917 was very powerful, but disintegrated in 1991 due to the following given reasons.

I. One party system.
II. Russian dominance over other 15 republics of USSR.
III. Non-recognition of cultural affairs of people residing in these republics.

Codes

(a) I and II
(b) Only II
(c) I, II and III
(d) II and III

28. Arrange the following events in chronological order **CBSE 2024 C**

I. Gorbachev became the General Secretary of Communist Party of the Soviet Union.
II. Russia, Ukraine and Belarus declared that the Soviet Union is disbanded.
III. Russian Revolution.
IV. Fall of the Berlin Wall.

Choose the correct option

(a) III, I, IV, II (b) III, II, I, IV
(c) III, I, II, IV (d) III, IV, I, II

29. The statements given below are related to shock Therapy. Choose the option that represents only the true statements. **CBSE Term I 2021**

I. The value of the Ruble, the Russian currency, declined due to shock therapy.
II. Shock therapy strengthened communism.
III. Shock therapy reduced the prices of goods.
IV. Shock therapy destroyed the old system of social welfare.

Codes

(a) I and II (b) II and III
(c) I, II and III (d) I and IV

30. Arrange the following in chronological order.

I. The Soviet invasion of Afghanistan
II. Disintegration of the USSR
III. Socialist Revolution in Russia
IV. Indo-Russian Strategic Agreement—2001

Codes **CBSE 2024**

(a) I, II, III, IV
(b) III, I, II, IV
(c) I, IV, II, III
(d) I, IV, III, II

31. Match List I with List II. Select the correct answer from the codes given below.

	List I	List II
A.	Mikhail Gorbachev elected as the General Secretary of the Communist Party.	1. 1991
B.	Russian Parliament declared its independence from the Soviet Union.	2. 1988
C.	Independence movement began in Lithunia.	3. 1985
D.	Three Baltic republics Estonia, Latvia and Lithuania become republics.	4. 1990

Codes

	A	B	C	D		A	B	C	D
(a)	3	4	2	1	(b)	3	2	1	4
(c)	1	2	3	4	(d)	4	3	2	1

32. Identify and write the incorrect pair.
(a) Vladimir Lenin- Russian Revolution
(b) Joseph Stalin- Great Terror of the 1930s
(c) Nikita Khruschev- Successor of Lenin
(d) Leonid Brezhnev- Asian Collective Security System

33.

This picture symbolised the division between .... and .... world.
(a) capitalist and communist (b) communist and socialist
(c) socialist and capitalist (d) socialist and consumerist

34. Given below are two statements

Statement I The Central Asian Republics are areas with vast Hydrocarbon resources.

Statement II Central Asia has also become a zone of competition between outside powers and oil companies.

In the light of above statements, choose the correct answer from the options given below
(a) Both Statement I and Statement II are true.
(b) Both Statement I and Statement II are false.
(c) Statement I is true, but Statement II is false.
(d) Statement I is false, but Statement II is true.

35. Given below are two statements

Statement I After the disintegration of the USSR, India has maintained good relations with all the post-communist countries.

Statement II More than 80 bilateral agreements have been signed between India and Russia as part of the Indo-Russian Strategic Agreement of 1995.

In the light of above statements, choose the correct answer from the options given below
(a) Both Statement I and Statement II are true.
(b) Both Statement I and Statement II are false.
(c) Statement I is true, but Statement II is false.
(d) Statement I is false, but Statement II is true.

Assertion-Reason Questions

Directions (Q. Nos. 36-39) In the questions given below, there are two statements marked as Assertion (A) and Reason (R). Read the statements and choose the correct option.

Codes
(a) Both A and R are true and R is the correct explanation of A.
(b) Both A and R are true, but R is not the correct explanation of A.
(c) A is true, but R is false.
(d) A is false, but R is true.

36. Assertion (A) The Soviet Union had become stagnant in an administrative and political sense as well.

Reason (R) The Soviet system was based on the ideology of socialism. **CBSE Term I 2021**

37. Assertion (A) In December 1991, under the leadership of Yeltsin, Russia, Ukraine and Georgia, three major republics of the USSR, declared that the Soviet Union was disbanded.

Reason (R) The rise of nationalism led to various protests in post-Soviet republics. **CBSE SQP 2024**

38. Assertion (A) The Soviet Union and Communism collapsed in 1991.

Reason (R) The internal weaknesses of the Soviet political and economic institutions failed to meet the aspirations of the Soviet people. **CBSE Term I 2021**

39. Assertion (A) The old system of social welfare in the Soviet Union automatically got destroyed.

Reason (R) The withdrawal of government subsidies pushed large sections of the people into poverty. **CBSE Term I 2021**

Passage Based Questions

40. Study the following passage carefully and answer the questions that follow

The Soviet system, however, became very bureaucratic and authoritarian, making life very difficult for its citizens. Lack of democracy and the absence of freedom of speech stifled people who often expressed their dissent in jokes and cartoons. Most of the institutions of the Soviet state needed reform: the one-party system represented by the Communist Party of the Soviet Union had tight control over all institutions and was unaccountable to the people. The party refused to recognise the urge of people in the fifteen different republics that formed the Soviet Union to manage their own affairs including their cultural affairs.

Although, on paper, Russia was only one of the fifteen republics that together constituted the USSR, in reality Russia dominated everything and people from other regions felt neglected and often suppressed.

(i) The Soviet system was based on the ideology of ....

(a) socialism (b) capitalism
(c) liberalism (d) idealism

(ii) Which of these statements is incorrect about the Soviet economy?

(a) The Soviet Union had a domestic consumer industry.
(b) The Soviet economy was more developed than the US.
(c) The Soviet Government run various welfare schemes.
(d) The Soviet Union produced everything from pins to cars.

(iii) Which of these republics was accepted as the successor of the USSR?

(a) Belarus (b) Ukraine
(c) Russia (d) Armenia

(iv) Which of these founded the Communist Party who ruled the USSR?

(a) Karl Marx
(b) Joseph Stalin
(c) Fidel Castro
(d) Vladimir Lenin

41. Study the following passage carefully and answer the questions that follow.

Shock therapy also involved a drastic change in the external orientation of these economies. Development was now envisaged through more trade and thus a sudden and complete switch to free trade was considered essential. The free trade regime and foreign direct investment (FDI) were to be the main engines of change. This also involved openness to foreign investment, financial opening up or deregulation and currency convertibility.

(i) Which of these organisations influenced the 'shock therapy'?

(a) European Union
(b) North Atlantic Treaty Organisation
(c) World Bank
(d) African Union

(ii) Which of these was the objective of the 'shock therapy'?

(a) Development of science and technology in the post-communist regimes
(b) Disarmament of the US
(c) Establishment of democratic capitalist system in the post-communist regimes
(d) Equal distribution of natural resources among nations

(iii) Which two problems were faced by Russia due the 'shock therapy'?

42. Study the following passage carefully and answer the questions that follow

"The Collapse of Communism was followed in most of these countries by a painful process of transition from an authoritarian socialist system to a democratic capitalist system. The model of transition in Russia, Central Asia and East Europe that was influenced by the World Bank and the IMF came to be known as 'Shock Therapy'. Shock therapy varied in intensity and speed amongst the second world countries, but its direction and features were quite similar". **CBSE Term I 2021**

(i) Which of the following incidents has been quoted as the 'Collapse of Communism'?

(a) Gorbachev's failure to get the desired results through his reforms.
(b) Disintegration of the Soviet Union.
(c) The Soviet Union had become stagnant in administration.
(d) People were not satisfied with the Soviet system and government lost popular backing.

(ii) Which one of the following countries was popular for its Democratic Capitalist System?

(a) United States of America (b) Russia
(c) Cuba (d) East Germany

(iii) Which one of the following was not a consequence of 'Shock Therapy'?

(a) The rate of inflation rose high.
(b) The value of 'Ruble', the Russian currency declined.
(c) The collective form system got strengthened and food security was ensured.
(d) The old system of social welfare was systematically destroyed.

(iv) Choose the option that is a feature of communism.

(a) Multi-party system
(b) State controlled economy
(c) Special Economic Zones (SEZ)
(d) Privatisation of industries and agriculture

43. **Study the following passage carefully and answer the questions that follow**

India has maintained good relations with all the post communist countries. But the strongest relations are still those between Russia and India. India's relations with Russia are an important aspect of India's foreign policy. Indo-Russian relations are embedded in a history of trust and common interests and are matched by popular perceptions. Indian heroes from Raj Kapoor to Amitabh Bachchan are household names in Russia and many post Soviet countries. One can hear Hindi film songs all over the region and India is part of the popular memory.

(i) How many agreements were signed between India and Russia as part of the Indo-Strategic Agreement of 2001?

(a) 10 agreements
(b) More than 80 agreements
(c) More than 95 agreements
(d) 150 agreements

(ii) Russia and India share a vision of a ……….. world order.

(a) unipolar (b) bipolar
(c) tripolar (d) multipolar

(iii) Discuss the military and cultural relationship of India and the USSR in brief.

Answers

1. (b) 1961
2. (c) It marked the unification of the two parts of Germany.
3. (b) 1917
4. (d) People had the right to property.
5. (d) Soviet Union disintegrated in 1992.
6. (d) Gorbachev initiated reforms in USSR.
7. (a) He was the outstanding theoretician and practitioner of marxism.
8. (b) Mikhail Gorbachev
9. (c) Russia, Ukraine and Belarus
10. (b) It inherited the Soviet seat in the UN
11. (a) Tajikistan, Azerbaijan, Armenia
12. (a) Inability of the Soviet system to correct its own mistakes.
13. (c) Disintegration of the Soviet Union
14. (b) Liberal democracy
15. (b) Russia emerged as a new superpower.
16. (d) Stabilising the Russian currency against the US dollar.
17. (a) Foreign Direct Investment
18. (d) The Eastern capitalist states guided and controlled the development of the region.
19. (d) The system of social welfare got strengthened.
20. (c) Turkmenistan and Uzbekistan
21. (c) Political movement
22. (d) All of these
23. (b) Ukraine
24. (c) Iran
25. (a) removal of autocratic dictatorship
26. (d) I, II and III
27. (c) I, II and III
28. (a) III, I, IV, II
29. (d) I and IV
30. (b) III, I, II, IV
31. (a) 3 4 2 1
32. (c) Nikita Khruschev-Successor of Lenin
33. (a) capitalist and communist
34. (a) Both Statement I and Statement II are true.
35. (c) Statement I is true, but Statement II is false.
36. (b) Both A and R are true, but R is not the correct explanation of A.
37. (c) A is true, but R is false.
38. (a) Both A and R are true and R is the correct explanation of A.
39. (a) Both A and R are true and R is the correct explanation of A.
40. (i) (a) socialism
    (ii) (b) The Soviet economy was more developed than the US.
    (iii) (c) Russia
    (iv) (d) Vladimir Lenin
41. (i) (c) World Bank
    (ii) (c) Establishment of democratic capitalist system in the post-communist regimes
    (iii) The two problems faced by Russia due to the 'shock therapy' were
    - The collective farm system disintegrated leaving people without food security and Russia started to import food.
    - The value of the ruble, the Russian currency, declined dramatically. The rate of inflation was so high that people lost all their savings.
42. (i) (b) Disintegration of the Soviet Union.
    (ii) (a) United States of America
    (iii) (c) The collective form system got strengthened and food security was ensured.
    (iv) (b) State controlled economy

43. (i) (b) More than 80 agreements
(ii) (d) multipolar
(iii) India and the USSR enjoyed a strong military and cultural relationship.
- **Military Relationship** India received most of its military hardware from the Soviet Union at a time when few other countries were willing to part with military technologies. The Soviet Union entered into various agreements allowing India to jointly produce military equipment.
- **Cultural Relationship** Hindi films and Indian culture were popular in the Soviet Union. A large number of Indian writers and artists visited the USSR.

Subjective Questions

Very Short Answer Type Questions

1. What do you mean by the 'Second World'?

Ans. After the Second World War, the East European countries that the Soviet army had liberated from the fascist forces came under the control of the USSR. The political and the economic systems of all these countries were modelled after the USSR. This group of countries was called the Second World or the 'socialist bloc'.

2. State any two features of the Soviet system.

Or **Which were the two important features of the Soviet system?**

Or **Mention any two characteristics of the Soviet political system.**

Or **Describe any two features of Soviet system.**

Ans. The two features of the Soviet system were
(i) The Soviet system was based on state welfarism, where the state was engaged in mass production to meet the needs of the people.
(ii) The Communist Party of Soviet Union (CPSU) controlled the government and dominated the political decision-making.

3. The Soviet economy was more developed than the rest of the world except for the US after the end of the Second World War. Substantiate the statement with any one example.

Ans. After the end of the Second World War, the Soviet economy had developed a complex communication network and vast energy resources including oil, iron and steel. It had a domestic consumer industry that produced everything from pins to cars. However, Soviet goods lacked quality in comparison to Western goods.

So, it is true that Soviet economy was more developed than the rest of the world after the end of the Second World War.

4. Highlight any one major distinction between the Soviet economy and the capitalist economy.

Ans. The Soviet system was based on the principles of equality and planned economy controlled by the state. Whereas in capitalist economy, private ownership is dominant. Land and productive assets are owned and controlled by the capitalists.

5. How is the political system of India different from the USSR? Give any two points. Competency Based Que

Ans. The political system of India is different from India due to following reasons
(i) **Multiparty System** In India, there are multiple political parties. In the USSR, there was only one political party, the Communist Party.
(ii) **Lack of Civil Liberties** In India there is democracy where people enjoy civil liberties like freedom of speech and expression. In the USSR, civil liberties were severely restricted.

6. Why did the Soviet Union disintegrate? Highlight any two arguments in support of your answer.

Or **Mention any two main reasons for the collapse of the Soviet Union.**

Ans. The two main reasons for the collapse of the Soviet Union were
(i) The Soviet political and economic institutions had developed internal weaknesses which dissatisfied the people.
(ii) The administration of the Soviet Union became stagnant due to rampant corruption and lack of accountability of government towards the citizens.

7. How was the US benefitted by the Soviet disintegration?

Ans. The Soviet Union's disintegration benefitted the united states in several ways including
(i) With the disintegration of the USSR the cold war ended and the US became the sole super power.
(ii) The capitalist economy became dominant economic system globally and post Soviet states were ready to open their economies for international trade.

8. Discuss the position of Russia in the international domain after the disintegration of the Soviet Union.

Ans. Russia was accepted as the successor state of the Soviet Union. It inherited the Soviet seat in the UN Security Council. Russia accepted all the international treaties and commitments of the Soviet Union. It took over as the only nuclear state of the post-Soviet space and carried out some nuclear disarmament measures with the US.

9. Explain any two consequence of shock therapy. CBSE 2024 C

Ans. The two consequence of shock therapy are

(i) **End of Welfare State** The end of old system of social welfare including the withdrawal of government subsidies resulted into increase in poverty, change in the states of the middle classes and migration of intellectual class.

(ii) **Inequality** The private mode of production and ownership resulted into inequality between the rich and the poor. The shock therapy also gave rise to many mafias who started controlling many economic activities in post-Soviet states.

10. Give any two social causes that led to Arab Spring.

Ans. Following are the two social causes that led to the Arab Spring

(i) The demand for political freedom and removal of economic inequalities.

(ii) The media and internet made the transmission of information and news throughout the world thereby spreading the movement.

Short Answer Type Questions

1. Why did the Soviet system became so weak and Soviet economy stagnanted?

Ans. The Soviet system became so weak and Soviet economy stagnated because of the following reasons

- The internal weakness of the Soviet political and economic institutions, which failed to meet the aspirations of the people were responsible for the collapse of the system.
- Economic stagnation for many years led to severe shortage and downfall of consumers and made the Soviet system questionable.
- The use of large amount of its resources in maintaining nuclear and military arsenal and the development of its satellites in Eastern Europe and within the Soviet system led to the weakness of the economy.
- At the same time, the ordinary citizens had the knowledge of rapid advancement of West and their disparities with the system of the West came as a political and psychological shock.

2. "Soviet Union's disintegration was the consequence of many different factors". Justify the statement CBSE SQP 2024 Competency Based Que

Ans. "Soviet Union's disintegration was the consequence of many factors". This statement can be justified by the following points

- Economic stagnation for many years led to severe consumer shortages and a large section of Soviet society began to doubt and question the system and to do so openly.
- The administration of the Soviet Union became stagnant due to widespread corruption, the unwillingness to allow more openness in government and the centralisation of authority in a vast land. People feel disconnected with the rulers and the government.
- The reforms of Gorbachev loosened the administrative system. His reforms met with opposition by communist leaders who initiated a coup.
- Another reason was the rise of nationalism and the desire for sovereignty with various republics including Russia and the Baltic Republics, Ukraine and Georgia.

3. 'Most former Soviet republics had tensions and conflicts'. Support the statement with examples. CBSE SQP 2024

Ans. 'Most former Soviet republics had tension and conflicts.' This statement can be supported by the following examples

- **Russia** In Russia, two republics, Chechnya and Dagestan, have had violent secessionist movements. Moscow's method of dealing with the Chechen rebels and indiscriminate military bombings has led to many human rights violations but failed to deter the aspirations for independence.
- **Central Asia** In Central Asia, Tajikistan witnessed a civil war that went on for ten years till 2001. The region as a whole has many sectarian conflicts. In Azerbaijan's province of Nagorno-Karabakh, some local Armenians want to secede and join Armenia. In Georgia, the demand for independence has come from two provinces, resulting in a civil war. There are movements against the existing regimes in Ukraine, Kyrgyzstan and Georgia.

4. Differentiate between the Capitalist and the Socialist models of development.

Ans. Difference between the Capitalist and the Socialist models of development are as follows

Capitalist Model	Socialist Model
In this model, means of production can be owned by the individual which means state ownership is absent here.	The Socialist model favours state ownership of means of production and individual ownership is prohibited.
The main motive of this model is to extract maximum profit from the market.	The main motive of this model is the social welfare of the masses.
It doesn't recognise the principle of equality and widens the gap between rich and poor.	It upholds and recognises the principle of equality and seeks to create an egalitarian society.
Production is carried out on demand and supply basis.	The socialist model is based on mass production with no profit motive.

5. Why does the Central Asia play an important role in world politics?

Ans. The Central Asian Republics are areas with vast hydrocarbon resources, which have brought them economic benefit. Central Asia has also become a zone of competition between outside powers and oil companies. The region is next to Russia, China, Afghanistan and Pakistan and close to West Asia. After 11th September 2001, the US wanted military bases in the region and paid the governments of all Central Asian states to hire bases and to allow airplanes to fly over their territory during the wars in Afghanistan and Iraq. However, Russia perceives these states as its 'Near Abroad' and believes that they should be under Russian influence. China has interests here because of the oil resources and the Chinese have begun to settle around the borders and conduct trade.

6. What is the relationship between India and Russia? **CBSE 2023**

Ans. India has maintained good relations with all the post-communist countries, but the strongest relations are still these between Russia and India.

- Indo-Russian relations are a significant aspect of India's foreign policy.
- Russia and India share a vision of multipolar world order i.e. co-existence fo several world powers internationally.
- More than 80 bilateral agreements have been signed between India and Russia as a part of Indo-Russia Strategic Agreement of 2001.
- India has benefitted from its relationship on the issue like Kashmir, energy supplies, sharing information on international terrorism, access to Central Asia and balancing its relation with China.
- Russia and India have collaborated on various scientific projects also.

7. Explain any four conditions that helped the Soviet Union to become a superpower after the Second World War. **CBSE 2025**

Ans. After the Second World War, the Soviet Union emerged as a superpower due to several key factors

- The USSR had the world's largest army and developed nuclear weapons by 1949, which made it a key player in global military affairs. Its advanced defense industry and space programmes like the launch of Sputnik in 1957, showcased its technological strength.
- The Soviet Union's centrally planned economy allowed rapid industrialisation. State-controlled industries focused on heavy machinery, steel and energy production, that enabled its economic growth and self-sufficiency.
- After the Second World War, the USSR established communist governments in Eastern European countries like Poland, East Germany and Hungary. These countries became part of the Soviet bloc which strengthened its global position.
- The Cold War rivalry with the United States positioned the USSR as the leader of the socialist world and helped to gain support from countries in Asia, Africa and Latin America.

8. What do you mean by Arab Spring? Mention any four causes of Arab Spring.

Ans. The Arab Spring was a series of pro-democracy uprisings that developed largely in the Muslim countries, including Tunisia, Morocco, Syria, Libya, Egypt and Bahrain. The event in these nations generally began in the spring of 2011, which led to the name Arab Spring.

The various causes of Arab Spring are as follows

- The rise in the global crisis, such as the downfall in the oil prices during 2008-09.
- The rise in the price of food leading to food crisis gave rise to the political unrest especially in poor countries.
- Increase in unemployment especially among the youths and females were one of the most important causes behind Arab Spring.
- The demand for political freedom and removal of economic inequalities was one of the major cause behind Arab Spring.

9. "The Arab Spring was a series of anti-government protests, uprisings and armed rebellions that spread across the Middle East in 2010". Justify the statement. **CBSE 2023**

Ans.
- The Arab spring emerged in Tunisia where the struggle against corruption, unemployment and poverty was started by the people. Then, the demand for democracy that started in Tunisia spread throughout the

Muslim-dominated Arab countries in West Asia. Honi Mubarak, who had been in power in Egypt since 1979 also collapsed as a result of the massive democratic protests.

- In addition, the influence of Arab Spring was also visible in Yemen, Bahrain, Libya and Syria where similar protests by the people led to democratic awakening throughout the region. The global crises played an important role in the rising of the Arab Spring. The rise in food prices, fall in oil prices, and increasing unemployment contributed to the Arab Spring. Self immolation of Mohamed Bouazizi, a street hawker of Tunisia gave a sudden rise to the Arab Spring.

Long Answer Type Questions

1. Highlight any three positive and three negative features each of the Soviet system in the Soviet Union.

Or **Explain Soviet way of life prior to its disintegration.** **Diksha App**

Ans. The three positive features of the Soviet system were

(i) The Soviet economy was more developed than the rest of the world except the US. It had a complex communication network, vast energy resources, machinery production and a transport system that connected its remotest areas.

(ii) A minimum standard of living for all citizens was ensured by the Soviet state and the government subsidised basic necessities including health, education, child care and other welfare schemes.

(iii) State ownership was given more importance. Land and productive assets were owned and controlled by the Soviet state.

The three negative features of the Soviet system were

(i) The Soviet system was very bureaucratic and authoritarian in nature. It turned the life of the people into disorder. Authoritarianism meant the absence of democracy and freedom of speech which angered the people.

(ii) Soviet economy witnessed economic stagnation for a long time which led to the market failure, when demand failed to meet supply in the market for consumer goods.

(iii) State treasury had spent a huge fortune on building and maintaining nuclear arsenals and in developing its satellite states in East Europe and within the Soviet system. It turned into a large economic burden for the Soviet system.

2. Examine characteristics of the Soviet system during 1971-1991.

Ans. Following are the characteristics of the Soviet system during 1971-1991

(i) The USSR was only a federation on paper. In reality it didn't embrace the features of a federal system. The fifteen republics were denied autonomy and there was centralisation of power around Russia.

(ii) The Communist Party of the Soviet Union (CPSU) controlled the government and dominated the political decision-making. It strengthened the principle of democratic centralism which meant lack of dissent on the decisions of the upper party bodies. Thus, single party system was the norm.

(iii) The Soviet economy was state owned and state planned where state was the owner of the means of production thus, there was absence of private property.

(iv) The Soviet system was characterised by a complex communication network with vast energy resources like oil, iron and steel. The state had a vast network of transportation to manufacture or transport goods to remotest areas.

(v) The Soviet system was based on state welfarism where the state was engaged in mass production to meet the needs of the people.

3. Why did the Soviet Union, the second most powerful country in the world, suddenly disintegrate? Explain any six reasons.

Or **Explain any six reasons responsible for the disintegration of the USSR.**

Or **Explain any four factors that were responsible for the disintegration of the USSR.**

Ans. For answer refer to text under the heading 'Causes for Disintegration' on page no. 4.

4. What were the consequences of the disintegration of the USSR? **Diksha App**

Or **Describe any four consequences of the disintegration of the Soviet Union.**

Ans.
- It meant the end of Cold War confrontations. The ideological dispute over whether the socialist system would beat the capitalist system was not an issue any more.
- Power relations in world politics changed. The end of the Cold War left open only two possibilities: either the remaining superpower would dominate and create a unipolar system or different countries or groups of countries could become important players in the international system, thereby bringing in a multi-polar system where no one power could dominate.
- The end of the Soviet bloc meant the emergence of many new countries. All these countries had their own independent aspirations and choices. Thus, the international system saw many new players emerge, each with its own identity, interests and economic and political difficulties

5. Explain the Soviet way of life prior to its disintegration. **Diksha App**

Ans.
- The Soviet economy during the time was then more developed than the rest of the world except for the US.

- It had a complex communications network, vast energy resources including oil, iron and steel machinery production and a transport sector that connected its remotest areas with efficiency.
- It had a domestic consumer industry that produced everything from pins to cars, though their quality did not match that of the Western capitalist countries.
- The Soviet state ensured a minimum standard of living for all citizens and the government subsidised basic necessities including health, education, childcare and other welfare schemes. There was no unemployment.
- State ownership was the dominant form of ownership: land and productive assets were owned and controlled by the Soviet state.

6. Describe any four changes that occured in world politics after the end of Cold War. **CBSE 2024**

Ans. Some changes in world politics after the end of the Cold War include

(i) With the end of the Cold War, the ideological battle was resolved. The capitalism became victorious. As a result the dominance of free market economic system emerged dominant system.

(ii) The disintegration of the USSR resulted into an unipolar world with the United States as the sole super power.

(iii) Rapid rise of global trade and various international economic organisations. The expansion of global trade enabled countries to build economic links and become reliant.

(iv) Reduction in the production of nuclear arms and focus was shifted on the promotion of democracy.

7. Explain any four reasons responsible for the economic stagnation in the Soviet Union? **CBSE 2025**

Ans. The economic stagnation of the Soviet Union was driven by several structural and policy-related factors such as

Centralisation of the Bureaucracy The Soviet economy was controlled by a highly centralised planning system, which led to inefficiency, delays in decision-making and widespread corruption. The lack of flexibility hindered innovation and adaptation to new economic challenges.

Lack of Incentives Since industries were state-owned and profits were not a motive, workers and managers had little motivation to improve productivity or introduce technological advancements. This led to a decline in efficiency and innovation.

Heavy Military Expenditure A significant portion of the Soviet budget was allocated to defense and the arms race with the United States. This diverted resources away from essential sectors like education, health care and consumer goods, which resulted in economic imbalance and a decline in the standard of living.

Collectivisation of Agriculture The collectivisation of agriculture resulted in inefficiencies, low productivity and frequent food shortages. State-controlled farms lacked motivation to maximise output. As a result, the Soviet Union was forced to import grain despite having vast agricultural land.

8. Describe the consequences of the 'shock therapy'.

Or **What were the consequences of the 'shock therapy'? Describe.**

Ans. For answer refer to text under the heading 'Consequences of Shock Therapy' on page no. 6.

9. Discuss the multi-dimensional relationship between India and USSR during the Cold War years. **Diksha App**

Ans. During the Cold War era, India and the USSR enjoyed a special relationship which led critics to say that India was part of the Soviet camp. It was a multi-dimensional relationship

- **Economic** The Soviet Union assisted India's public sector companies at a time when such assistance was difficult to get. It gave aid and technical assistance for steel plants like Bhilai, Bokaro, Visakhapatnam and machinery plants like Bharat Heavy Electricals Ltd., etc. The Soviet Union accepted Indian currency for trade when India was short of foreign exchange.
- **Political** The Soviet Union supported India's positions on the Kashmir issue in the UN. It also supported India during its major conflicts, especially during the war with Pakistan in 1971. India too supported Soviet foreign policy in some crucial but indirect ways.
- **Military** India received most of its military hardware from the Soviet Union at a time when few other countries were willing to part with military technologies. The Soviet Union entered into various agreements allowing India to jointly produce military equipment.
- **Culture** Hindi films and Indian culture were popular in the Soviet Union. A large number of Indian writers and artists visited the USSR.

10. "India has maintained good relations with Russia after the end of 1st Cold War". Justify the statement with four examples. **CBSE 2024**

Ans. For answer refer to text under the heading 'India's Relations with Russia and other Post-Communist States' on page no. 8.

Picture Based Question

1. Study the given cartoon and answer the questions that follow.

(i) What does the above image depict?
(a) Crowd gathered to criticise the government for pollution.
(b) Protest for anti religious issues by making boundary walls.
(c) Disintegration of the two regions of a country.
(d) Breaking of Berlin Wall.

(ii) What does the wall symbolise?
(a) Division between capitalist and communist world
(b) Symbol of World War 1st
(c) Symbol of homage to martyred soldiers
(d) Parliament building wall

(iii) The wall belongs to ....
(a) USSR
(b) USA
(c) UK
(d) Germany

(iv) What is the motive of the people regarding the wall as shown in the image given above?
(a) To build the wall
(b) To break the wall
(c) Beautification of the wall
(d) Declaring the wall as the symbol of war

Ans. (i) (d) Breaking of Berlin Wall.
(ii) (a) Division between capitalist and communist world
(iii) (d) Germany
(iv) (b) To break the wall

Map Based Question

1. In the given map of central, Eastern Europe and commonwealth of independent state, four countries are marked as A, B, C and D. Identify them with the help of information given below and write their correct names in your answer book along with their respective serial number and alphabet concerned.

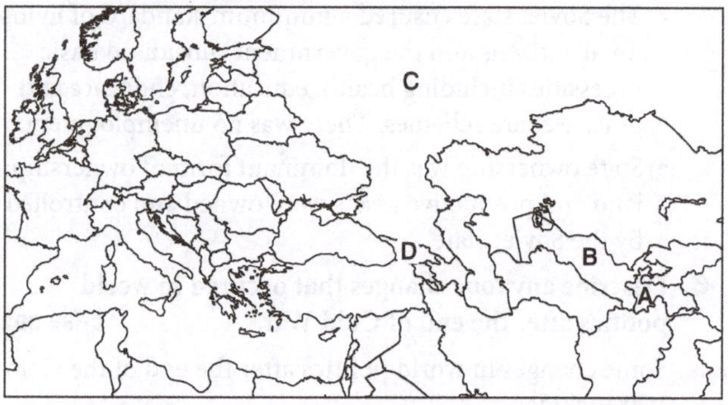

Sr. No. of the Information Used	Alphabet Concerned	Name of the State
(i)		
(ii)		
(iii)		
(iv)		

(i) A country that witnessed a civil war that went for ten years.
(ii) Major oil and gas producer.
(iii) A country which took over the USSR seat in the UN.
(iv) A state where demand for independence came from two provinces that resulted in a Civil War.

Ans.

Sr. No. of the Information used	Alphabet Concerned	Name of the Country
(i)	A	Tajikistan
(ii)	B	Uzbekistan
(iii)	C	Russia
(iv)	D	Georgia

SELF ASSESSMENT TEST

Objective Type Questions

1. Who was the successor of Lenin?
   (a) Leonid Brezhnev
   (b) Boris Yeltsin
   (c) Joseph Stalin
   (d) Mikhail Gorbachev
2. Which of these republics joined the CIS in 1993?
   (a) Armenia
   (b) Georgia
   (c) Uzbekistan
   (d) Tajikistan
3. Consider the following statement about the Berlin Wall and choose the correct option(s).
   I. The Berlin Wall symbolised the division between the capitalist and the communist world.
   II. It was built in 1965.
   III. The wall was more then 150 km long and it stood for 28 years.
   Codes
   (a) I and II
   (b) II and III
   (c) I and III
   (d) Only II

Very Short Answer Type Questions

4. "The Soviet Union had become stagnant in an administrative and political sense as well". Explain the statement. **Competency Based Que**
5. Which two options did the post-colonial regimes have as per the 'shock therapy'?
6. How people were affected by the 'shock therapy' in the post-colonial regimes?

Short Answer Type Questions

7. Write any four characteristics of the Soviet System after the Second World War.
8. Give a short account of collapse of communism in East Europe.
9. Explain any two reasons for the disintegration of the Soviet Union.
10. Analyse the characteristics of the political system evolved after the disintegration of USSR.
11. Can you consider Mikhail Gorbachev as solely responsible for the disintegration of the Soviet Union? Justify your opinion. **Competency Based Que**

Long Answer Type Questions

12. Elucidate the reasons necessary for the reforms in USSR.
13. Describe the major changes in the world that occurred due to the disintegration of the Soviet Union.
14. Discuss in brief about the conflicts in Central Asia.
15. How did the 'shock therapy' prove disastrous for Russia? Explain.
16. "India's relations with Russia are embedded in a history of trust and common interests". Support the statement with any three arguments. **Competency Based Que**

02

CHAPTER

After the end of biopolar structure of world politics in the early 1990s new centers of power emerged in the form of European Union (EU) and the Association of South East Asian Nation (ASEAN) in Asia.

Contemporary Centres of Power

▼ **YOUR STUDY GOALS**

2.1 European Union

2.2 Association of South East Asian Nations (ASEAN)

2.3 The Rise of the Chinese Economy

2.4 Japan and South Korea as Emerging Powers

▼ **YOUR PRACTICE GOAL**

- Objective Type Questions (33 Qs ; MCQs, A-R, Statements, Matching, Passage Based)
- Subjective Questions (16 VSAs, 10 SAs, 6 LAs, 4 Picture Based, 2 Map Based)

2.1 European Union

- After World War II, European leaders faced the 'Question of Europe'.
- They debated whether Europe should return to old rivalries or be rebuilt on new principles for better international relations.
- The war destroyed many assumptions and structures that had shaped European states' relationships.
- By 1945, European countries were dealing with economic ruin and the collapse of the systems that had previously defined Europe.
- Under the **Marshall Plan,** America extended massive financial help for reviving Europe's economy.

Marshall Plan

- The Organisation for European Economic Co-operation (OEEC) was established in 1948 to channel aid to the West European states.
- It became a forum where the Western European states began to co-operate on trade and economic issues.

- Further, **NATO** was created by the US to provide collective security. **The Council of Europe,** established in 1949, was another step forward in political co-operation.

- Formation of **European Economic Community (EEC)** in 1957, marked a significant step towards economic integration. This process acquired a political dimension with the creation of the **European Parliament.**
- **European Union (EU)** was established in 1992. It aimed for a common foreign and security policy, justice and home affairs co-operation on justice and home affairs and to have a single currency.

Evolution of EU

- The European Union has evolved over time from an economic union to a political union.
- The EU has started to act more like a nation state. Though, it failed to adopt a Constitution, it has a flag, anthem, founding date and currency. It also follows a common foreign and security policy. The EU has expanded its areas of co-operation and membership especially from the Soviet bloc.
- Some countries are hesitant to give up their national powers to the EU and there are reservations about including certain new members.

EU's Influence

- **Economic Influence** The EU has a large GDP and a significant share of world trade. The European Union GDP is projected to be approximately $19.35 trillion in the year 2024. Its currency, Euro can pose a threat to the dominance of the US Dollar. Its share of world trade is much larger than that of the United States. Its economic power gives it influence over its closest neighbours as well as that in Asia and Africa. It also functions as an important bloc in international organisations such as the World Trade Organisation (WTO).

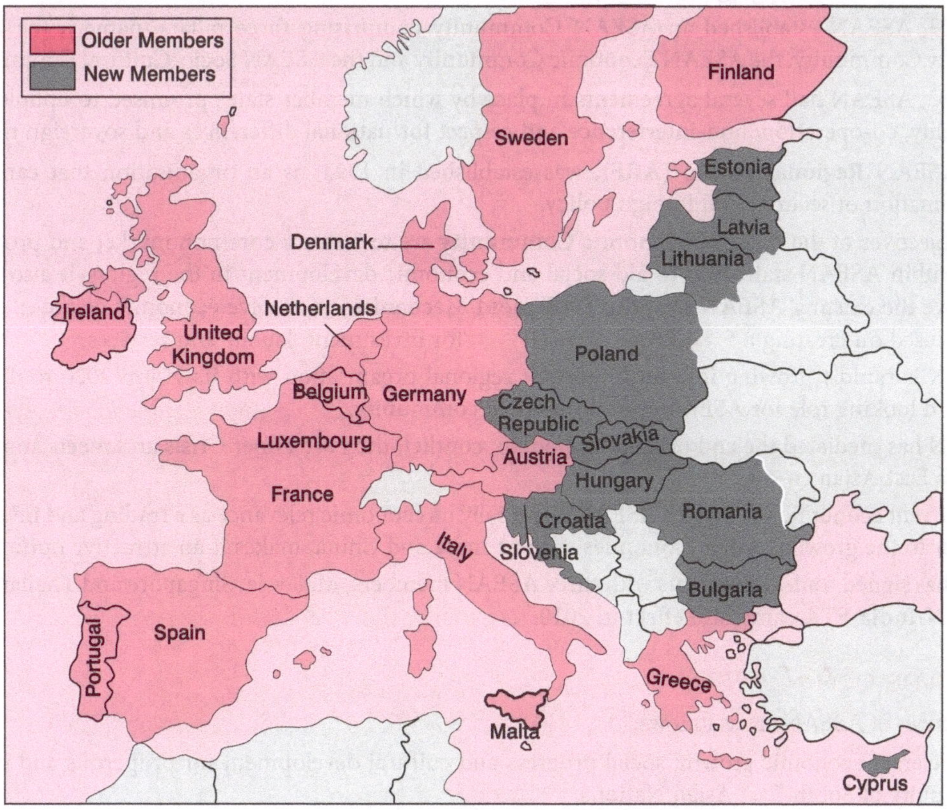

▲ *European Union Map*

- **Political and Diplomatic Influence** France, a member country of the EU holds permanent seat on the UNSC. The EU includes several non-permanent members of the UNSC. This EU has given a voice in international organisations like the UN and can influence US policies.

- **Military Influence** The EU has the second-largest combined armed forces in the world. Its total spending on defence is second after the USA. One of the member states of EU, France, has nuclear arsenals of approximately 335 nuclear warheads. It is also the world's second most important source of space and communications technology.
- **Supranationalism**[1] The EU can intervene in economic, political and social areas. But in many areas, its member states have their own foreign relations and defence policies that often differ with each other. This limits the EU's role in foreign relations and defence.

2.2 Association of South East Asian Nations (ASEAN)

- During the Second World War, the South East Asian region suffered economic and political consequences of colonialism, both European and Japanese. After the war, it faced problems of nation building, poverty and economic backwardness.
- To deal with these problems, ASEAN was formed in **1967** by five countries of the region -**Indonesia, Malaysia, the Philippines, Singapore and Thailand** — by signing the **Bangkok Declaration.**
- Later, Brunei Darussalam, Vietnam, Lao PDR, Myanmar (Burma) and Cambodia joined ASEAN taking its strength to ten.
- ASEAN countries have celebrated what has become known as the **'ASEAN Way'**, which is a form of interaction that is informal, non-confrontationist and co-operative. The respect for national sovereignty is critical to the functioning of ASEAN.
- In 2003, ASEAN established an ASEAN Community comprising three pillars, namely, the ASEAN Security Community, the ASEAN Economic Community and the ASEAN Socio-Cultural Community.
- By 2003, ASEAN had several agreements in place by which member states promised to uphold peace, neutrality, co-operation, non-interference and respect for national differences and sovereign rights.
- The **ASEAN Regional Forum (ARF),** was established in 1994, as an organisation that carries out co-ordination of security and foreign policy.
- The objectives of the **ASEAN Economic Community** are to create a common market and production base within ASEAN states and to aid social and economic development in the region. It also aims to improve the existing **ASEAN Dispute Settlement Mechanism** to resolve economic disputes. ASEAN has focused on creating a **Free Trade Area (FTA)**[2] for investment, labour and services.
- ASEAN is rapidly growing into an important regional organisation with its vision 2020 to define an outward looking role for ASEAN in international community.
- ASEAN has mediated the end of the Cambodian conflict, the East Timer Crisis and meets annually to discuss East Asian co-operation.
- The current economic strength of ASEAN, especially its economic relevance as a trading and investment partner to the growing Asian economies such as India and China, makes it an attractive option.
- India has signed trade agreements with three ASEAN members, Malaysia, Singapore and Thailand. The **ASEAN-India FTA** came into effect in 2010.

Objectives of ASEAN

The objectives of ASEAN are as follows

- To accelerate economic growth, social progress and cultural development for properous and peaceful community of South-East Asian Nations.
- To promote regional peace and stability through abiding respect for justice and the rule of law and the principles of the United Nations.

1 **Supranationalism** The state or condition of transcending national boundaries, authority or interests.
2 **Free Trade Area** It is a group of countries that have agreed to mutually lower or eliminate trade barriers for trade within the area.

- To promote active collaboration and mutual assistance on matters of common interests in the economic, social, cultural, technical scientific and administrative fields.

Quick Test 1

1. Which organisation was established under the Marshall Plan?
2. Why was NATO created by the US?
3. What is ASEAN Way?
4. Define European Union.

2.3 The Rise of the Chinese Economy

- China has been the fastest growing economy in Asia. It is projected to overtake the US as the world's largest economy by 2040. Its economic integration into the region makes it the driver of East Asian growth, thereby giving it enormous influence in regional affairs.
- Under the leadership of **Mao**, its economy was based on the **Soviet model.** The model was to create a state-owned heavy industries sector from the capital accumulated from agriculture.
- Due to shortage of foreign exchange, China decided to substitute imports by domestic goods. This model allowed China to use its resources to establish the foundations of an industrial economy on a large scale.
- This model helped China build an industrial economy, provide jobs, improve education and health care and grow by 5.6 percent yearly. However, population growth made it insufficient.
- A crisis similar to the USSR was also faced by China, its industrial production was not growing fast enough, international trade was minimal and per capita income was very low.
- The Chinese leadership took major policy decisions in the 1970s. China ended its political and economic isolation with the establishment of relations with the United States in 1972.
- **Premier Zhou Enlai** proposed the 'four modernisations' in the field of agriculture, industry, science and technology and military in 1973.
- By 1978, the then leader **Deng Xiaoping** announced the **'Open Door' policy**[3] and economic reforms in China. The policy was to generate higher productivity by investments of capital and technology from abroad. China opened its economy step by step. The **privatisation** of agriculture in 1982 was followed by the privatisation of industry in 1998. Trade barriers were eliminated only in **Special Economic Zones (SEZs)** where foreign investors could set up enterprises.
- The Chinese economy, including both industry and agriculture, grew at a faster rate. It became the most important destination for **Foreign Direct Investment (FDI)**[4]. It has large foreign exchange reserves that allow it to make big investments in other countries. China's accession to the WTO in 2001 has been a futher step in its opening to the outside world. China is also facing multiple challenges like unemployment, inequality, environmental degradation and corruption.

India-China Relations

- After the independence of India and China, both were expected to shape the future of Asia. The slogan of **'Hindi-Chini bhai-bhai'** was popular. However, Chinese aggression on the Indian border has spoiled that hope.
- Soon after independence, both states were involved in differences arising from the Chinese takeover of Tibet in 1950 and the final settlement of the Sino-Indian border. China and India were involved in a border conflict in 1962 over territorial issues in **Arunachal Pradesh** and in the **Aksai Chin region of Ladakh.**

3 Open Door Policy A statement of principles initiated by the United States in 1899 and 1900. It advocates for equal trading rights for all nations in China.

4 FDI An investment made by a company or an individual in one country into business interests located in another country.

- Diplomatic relations between the two countries degraded until 1976. Thereafter, relations between the two countries began to improve slowly. A series of talks to resolve the border issue were also initiated in 1981.
- **Rajiv Gandhi's** visit to China in December 1988 provided the room for an improvement in India–China relations. Since then both governments have taken measures to contain conflict and maintain 'peace and tranquility' on the border.
- They have also signed agreements on cultural exchanges and co-operation in science and technology and opened four border posts for trade.
- India–China trade is growing at 30 per cent per year since 1999 Bilateral trade between India and China has increased from $ 338 million in 1992 to more than $ 84 billion in 2017.
- More recently, both countries have agreed to co-operate with each other in areas such as bidding for energy deals abroad.
- China's military relations with Bangladesh and Myanmar were viewed as hostile to Indian interests in South Asia.
- Increasing transportation and communication links, common economic interest should help to establish a positive and sound relationship between India and China.
- Indian and Chinese leaders and officials visit Beijing and New Delhi with greater frequency.
- Currently India-China faces issues like, border disputes, China-Pakistan economic corridor and China's support to Pakistan in UN against India's move to counter terrorism.

Nations as Emerging Powers

After the disintegration of Soviet Union, some of the nations emerged as Global power in 21st century. For example, Russia emerged as a strong successor of USSR, India and Israel emerged as powerful and important nations in 21st century and China can be seen as strong emerging economic power since 1978.

Russia

- Even before the disintegration of Soviet Union Russia has been its largest part. Russia emerged as the strong successor of USSR (Union of Soviet Socialist Republic), after the dissolution of the Soviet Union in late 1980's and the early 1990's.
- Russia has emerged as one of the powerful country in the global world as it has vast reserves of nature resources, minerals and gases. In addition, Russia is a nuclear state with a huge stock of sophisticated weapons. It is also a permament member of the UN Security Council, called **P-5**

Economic Model of Russia

- Russia's economy is a mixed and transitional economy of upper-middle income, with vast natural resources, particularly oil and natural gas.
- It is Europe's fifth-largest economy, the world's eleventh-largest economy by nominal GDP and the world's sixth-largest economy by purchasing power parity.

India

- India has emerged as an important global power in the 21st century. The world is experiencing the power and rise of India in a multidimensional way.
- With the population of 135 crores the economic, cultural, strategic position of the country is very strong.

Economic Model of India

- From an economic perspective, targeting the goal of a $ 5 trillion economy by 2024-25, a competitive huge market, an ancient inclusive culture with 200 million people of Indian Diaspora spreading across the globe impart distinct meaning and salience to India as a new centre of power in 21st century.

- The military of India is self sufficient with indigenous nuclear technology making it another nuclear power from a strategic perspective. Projects like **Make in India** sets another milestone in Indian economy. Therefore, all these changes are making India an important power in the present world.

Israel

- Israel has also emerged as one of the most powerful nations in the 21st century in terms of science and technology, defense and intelligence. Israel has reached to the new heights of global political standing by virtue of its indomitable defense prowess, technological innovations, industrialisation and agricultural development, despite of its location situated in the middle of the burning politics of West Asian countries.
- Israel being a small Jewish-Zionist nation is placed in the contemporary global politics in general and the Arab-dominated West Asian politics in particular.

Economic Model of Israel

- Israel's economy is a well-developed free-market economy that is technologically advanced. After the United States, it has the world's second-largest number of start-up enterprises.
- Its top exports include cut diamonds, high-tech equipment and pharmaceuticals. Crude oil, foodstuffs, raw materials and military equipment are among the country's main imports.

Quick Test 2

1 Under whose leadership China became independent in 1949?
2 China followed which economic model initially?
3 When did China liberalise its economy?
4 Mention any one challenge in India-China relationship.
5 Russia's GDP is currently at which position?

2.4 Japan and South Korea as Emerging Powers

Both Japan and South Korea have emerged as significant global powers in recent times. Each has its own strengths and weaknesses.

Japan

- Japan has a reputation for making high-technology products. Japan has very few natural resources and imports most of its raw materials. Even then it progressed rapidly after the end of the Second World War.
- Famous Japanese brands include as Sony, Panasonic, Canon, Suzuki, Honda, Toyota, Mazda.
- Japan became a member of the **Organisation for Economic Co-operation and Development (OECD)** in 1964. In 2017, it is the third largest economy in the world. It is the only Asian member of the G-7. It is the eleventh most populous nation in the world.
- It is the **second largest contributor** to the regular budget of the UN, contributing almost 10 per cent of the total.
- Although Japan's military expenditure is only one per cent of its GDP, it is the seventh largest in the world.

South Korea

- The Korean peninsula was divided into **South Korea (Republic of Korea)** and North Korea (Democratic People's Republic of Korea) at the end of the Second World War along the **38th Parallel**.

- South Korea emerged as a center of power in Asia. Between the 1960s and the 1980s, it rapidly developed into an economic power, which is termed as Miracle on the Han River.
- South Korea became a member of the OECD in 1996. In 2017, its economy was the eleventh largest in the world and its military expenditure was the tenth largest.
- According to the Human Development Report 2016, the HDI rank of South Korea is 18. The major factors responsible for its high human development include successful land reforms, rural development, extensive human resources development and rapid equitable economic growth.
- The South Korean brands such as Samsung, LG and Hyundai have become renowned in India. Numerous agreements between India and South Korea signify their growing commercial and cultural ties.

TIMELINE

Timeline of European Integration

1951 April	Six west European countries, France, West Germany, Italy, Belgium, the Netherlands and Luxembourg sign the Treaty of Paris establishing the European Coal and Steel Community (ECSC).
1957 March 25th	These six countries sign the Treaties of Rome establishing the European Economic Community (EEC) and the European Atomic Energy Community (Euratom).
1973 January	Denmark, Ireland and the United Kingdom join the European Economic Community (EEC).
1979 June	First direct elections to the European Parliament.
1981 January	Greece joins the EEC.
1985 June	The Schengen Agreement abolishes border controls among the EEC members.
1986 January	Spain and Portugal join the EEC.
1990 October	Unification of Germany.
1992 February 7th	The Treaty of Maastricht was signed establishing the European Union (EU).
1993 January	European Economic Community (EEC) was renamed the European Community (EC).
1995 January	Austria, Finland and Sweden join the EU.
2002 January	Euro, the new currency, was introduced in the 12 EU members.
2004 May	Ten new members, Cyprus, the Czech Republic, Estonia, Hungary, Latvia, Lithuania, Malta, Poland, Slovakia and Slovenia join the EU.
2007 January	Bulgaria and Romania join the EU. Slovenia adopts the Euro.
2009 December	The Lisbon Treaty came into force.
2012	The EU is awarded the Nobel Peace Prize.
2013	Croatia becomes the 28th member of the EU.
2016	Referendum in Britain, 51.9 per cent voters decide that Britain exit (Brexit) from the EU.

Mind Map

CONTEMPORARY CENTRES OF POWER

1 Formation of the European Union

Global Influence of the European Union

- "Marshall Plan" was introduced by the US to revive European economy.
- The Organisations for European Economic Co-operation (OEEC) was established in 1948 under this plan.
- `The European Union becomes economically and politically influential over time.
- Internal disturbances and 'Euroskepticism' hinder the EU's ability to unify foreign and defense policies.

2 The Formation and Rise of ASEAN

The Role of ASEAN in Southeast Asia's Development and Geopolitics.

- Association of South East Asian Nations (ASEAN) was founded in 1967.
- Its objectives include promoting economic growth, peace and regional stability.
- An ASEAN community was established in 2003 having 3 pillars - Security, economic and socio cultural.
- The ASEAN Regional Forum (ARF) was established in 1994.
- The ASEAN - India Free Trade Agreement come into effect in 2010.

3 The Rise of the Chinese Economy

Rise of China and Economic Transformation

- China's economic success since 1978 has contributed to its rise as a global power.
- China is projected to become the largest economy by 2040.
- In 1970s, China began reforms with the "open door" policy.
- Agriculture was gradually privatised and Special Economic Zones (SEZs) were created.
- Employment and social welfare was assured to all.

Challenges After Economic Reforms

- Sudden economic rise has caused inequality and unemployment.
- Environmental degradation and corruption have increased.
- Working conditions for women became worst.

4 India-China Relations

India - China Relations Post Cold War

- India and China were influential powers in Asia before Western imperialism.
- The slogan of 'Hindi Chini bhai-bhai' was popular.
- Chinese aggression in 1962 border conflict strained relations.
- Diplomatic relation between the two countries degraded until 1976.

India - China Relations: From Tensions to Trade Growth.

- Rajiv Gandhi's visit to China in 1988 improved peace and border tranquility.
- Bilateral trade has grown from $ 338 million in 1992 to $ 84 billion in 2017.
- Indian and China adopted similar policies in WTO.
- China military relations with Bangladesh and Myanmar were viewed as hostile to India.
- India and China leaders and officials visit both countries frequently.
- Recently India and China are facing issue like border disputes.

5 Japan and South Korea as Emerging Powers

Japan

- Making high technology products.
- Second largest contributions to UN budget.
- In 2017, it was third largest economy in the world.

South Korea

- At the end of the Second World War along the 38th parallel.
- Korean peninsula was divided into South and North Korea.
- South Korea became a member of the OECD in 1996.
- Its economy is the 11th largest in the world in 2017 and its military expenditure is the 10th largest.
- Korean brands are renounced in India such as Samsung, LG and Hyundai.

ASIMO, the world's most advanced humanoid robot, walking with a person while holding hand.

Leaders release postal stamps to commemorate silver jubilee of India and ASEAN partnership in New Delhi on 25th January 2018.

NCERT Folder

Intext Questions

1. Locate the ASEAN members on the map. Find the location of the ASEAN secretariat. (Pg. no. 20)

Ans. The ASEAN members are shown in the map below.

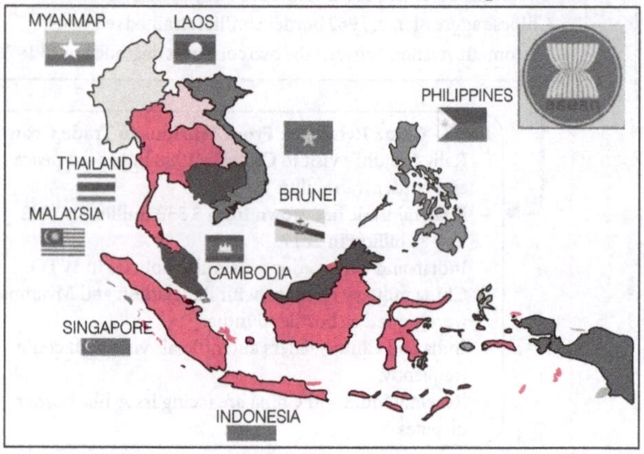

The ASEAN secretariat is located in Jakarta, Indonesia.

2. Who are the members of the ASEAN Regional Forum (ARF)? (Pg. no. 21)

Ans. The ASEAN Regional Forum (ARF) has 27 members, including the 10 members states of the Association of South East Asian Nations (ASEAN) and 16 other countries.

The ASEAN member states include Brunei, Cambodia, Indonesia, Laos, Malaysia, Myanmar, Philippines, Singapore, Thailand and Vietnam. Other members of ARF are Australia, Bangladesh, Canada, China, Democratic People's Republic of Korea, European Union, India, Japan, Mongolia, New Zealand, Pakistan, Papua New Guinea, Republic of Korea, Russia, Sri Lanka and Timor-Leste.

3. Chinese President XI Jinping paid a visit to India in 2019. Prime Minister Narendra Modi visited China in 2018. Find out about the agreements signed during their visits (Pg. no. 25)

Ans. Although no formal agreements were signed during the Chinese President XI Jinping's visit to India in 2019, the discussions between the two leaders resulted in the following outcomes

- The two leaders decided to establish a High-Level Economic and Trade Dialogue mechanism with the objective of achieving enhanced trade and commercial relations.
- The two leaders decided to designate 2020 as year of India-China cultural and people to people exchanges.
- The two leaders decided that 70 activities will be organised to celebrate the 70th anniversary of the establishment of India-China relations in 2020.

When Prime Minister Narendra Modi visited China in 2018, no agreements were inked, nor any announcements made at the summit, since the focus of the two leaders was to take stock of and further strengthen bilateral relationships as well as the strategic and long term partnership between India and China.

Exercise

1. Arrange the following in chronological order.

(a) China's accession to WTO (b) Establishment of the EEC
(c) Establishment of the EU (d) Birth of ARF

Ans. (b) Establishment of EEC (c) Establishment of the EU
(d) Birth of ARF (a) China's accession to WTO

2. The 'ASEAN Way'

(a) Reflects the lifestyle of ASEAN members.
(b) A form of interaction among ASEAN members that is informal and co-operative.
(c) The defence policy followed by the ASEAN members.
(d) The road that connects all the ASEAN members.

Ans. (b) A form of interaction among ASEAN members that is informal and co-operative.

3. Which of the following nations adopted an 'Open Door' policy?

(a) China (b) South Korea (c) Japan (d) USA

Ans. (a) China

4. Fill in the blanks

(i) The border conflict between China and India in 1962 was principally over .... and .... region.

Ans. Aksai Chin, Arunachal Pradesh

(ii) China entered into bilateral relations with .... (a major country) in 1972.

Ans. USA

(iii) .... Plan influenced the establishment of the Organisation for European Economic Co-operation in 1948.

Ans. Marshall

(iv) ARF was established in the year ....

Ans. 1994

(v) .... is the organisation of ASEAN that deals with the security.

Ans. ASEAN Regional Forum (ARF)

5. What are the objectives of establishing regional organisations?

Ans. The objectives of establishing regional organisations are discussed below

(i) To promote regional peace and stability based on rule of law.

(ii) To develop the countries politically so that they can have an impact on the decision-making process at the global level.

(iii) To accelerate economic growth of the native or indigenous forces by establishing co-operation and consensus.

6. How does geographical proximity influence the formation of regional organisations?

Ans. The geographical proximity influences the formation of regional organisations in the following ways

- It affects the parameters of security of all countries in particular regions by similar forces. Thus, the organisations are created mainly for security reasons.
- It promotes rise in some socio-cultural problems that leads to the formation of treaties between the countries like the formation of ASEAN.
- The economic issues also affects the merger of countries so that they can handle the economic problems of the respective regions by coalition of interests through an organisation like the European Union.

7. What are the components of the ASEAN Vision 2020?

Ans. The components of the ASEAN Vision 2020 are as follows

- To enhance the position of ASEAN countries at the global level.
- To resolve the conflicts in the geographical areas of the respective countries.

8. Name the pillars and the objectives of the ASEAN Community.

Or "ASEAN took steps to establish an ASEAN Community on the basis of its three pillars". Explain the importance fo these three pillars. **CBSE 2025**

Ans. The three pillars of ASEAN Community are

- ASEAN Security Community
- ASEAN Economic Community
- ASEAN Socio-Cultural Community

The objectives of the ASEAN Community are as follows

- To accelerate economic growth through social progress and cultural development.
- The territorial disputes should not escalate into armed confrontations.
- To promote regional peace and stability based on the rule of law.
- To establish dispute settlement mechanism for resolving economic disputes.
- Free Trade Areas will be created for investments, labour and services.

9. In what ways does the present Chinese economy differs from the command economy?

Ans. The present Chinese economy differs from the command economy in the following ways

- The command economy was based upon the notions of communism whereas the present economy is based on the capitalist notions.
- The command economy relied on the state-controlled assets while the present economy is based on the ideas of free-market economy.
- The command economy resulted in stagnation while the present economy led to remarkable economic growth.

10. How did the European countries resolve their post-Second World War problem? Briefly outline the attempts that led to the formation of the European Union.

Ans. After the Second World War, the European states confronted the ruin of their economies along with the destruction of assumptions and structure on which Europe had been founded. European countries resolved their post-Second World War problems in the following manner

- Under the Marshall Plan, the USA provided financial help to revive European economy.
- The US also created a new collective security structure under NATO.
- Under the Marshall Plan, the organisation for European Economic Co-operation was established in 1948 to extend co-operation on trade and economic issues among the Western European states.
- European Union was founded in 1993 for a common foreign security policy, co-operation on justice and home affairs and creation of a single currency.

The attempts that led to the formation of European Union are as follows

- The Council of Europe was established in 1949 for political co-operation.
- The process of economic integration of European capitalist countries led to the formation of European Economic Community in 1957.
- The collapse of Soviet Union put Europe on a fast track and resulted in the formation of European Union in 1992.

11. What makes European Union a highly influential regional organisation?

Or Explain any four factors that make European Union a strong organisation? **CBSE Term II 2022**

Or European Union is a highly influential organisation". Justify the statement with any four suitable arguments. **CBSE 2020**

Or Explain any three factors responsible for the European to be a highly influential regional orgnisation. **CBSE 2025**

Ans. European Union is a highly influential organisation due to the following reasons

Economic Influence of EU

- EU is the world's second biggest economy with a GDP of more than $17 trillion in 2016, next to the United States of America.
- Its currency Euro can pose a threat to the dominance of US dollar. EU's share of world trade is much larger than that of US.
- It has an economic influence over its closest neighbours as well as in Asia and Africa.

Political and Diplomatic Influence of EU

- The EU also has political and diplomatic influence as France, a member state holds permanent seat in the UN Security Council with several non-permanent members.
- The EU is enabled to influence some US policies such as the current US position on Iran's Nuclear Programme.
- Its diplomacy, economic investment and negotiations have been effective as in the case of its dialogue with China on human rights and environmental degradation.

Military Influence of EU

- EU's combined armed forces are the second largest in the world and also come second after the total spendings of US in defence.
- Britain and France as EU members also possess nuclear arsenal of 550 nuclear warheads. It is also the world's second most important source of space and communication technology.
- EU is able to intervene in economic, political and social areas. But in many areas member states have their own foreign and defence policy that are often at odds with each other.

12. The emerging economies of China and India have great potential to challenge the unipolar world. Do you agree with the statement? Substantiate your arguments. **Competency Based Que**

Ans. Yes, I agree with the statement that both India and China have great potential to challenge the unipolar world on the following grounds

- The New Economic policies of India and China have broken their economies from stagnation.
- In China, the creation of Special Economic Zones led to a phenomenal rise in the Foreign Trade. On the other hand, India is being seen as an important emerging global power in the 21st century from a strategic perspective as it is self-sufficient with indigenous nuclear technology.
- Both the countries are important destinations for Foreign Direct Investments.
- At the global level also both India and China has adopted similar policies in WTO to deepen their integration with the world economy as a challenge to a unipolar world.

13. The peace and prosperity of countries lay in the establishment and strengthening of regional economic organisations. Justify this statement. **Competency Based Que**

Ans. Regional Economic Orginisations promote peace, prosperity and stability among member nations. Economic co-operation reduces conflicts and strengthens diplomatic relations.

Organisations like EU and ASEAN help maintain peace and prosperity.

ASEAN and VISION 2020

- ASEAN is expanding its global role and encouraging conflict resolution through negotiations.
- The ARF co-ordinates security and foreign policy for regional stability.

EU

- It is founded on principles of common foreign and security policy.
- It expanded by integrating new members, especially from the Soviet bloc, ensuring stability and growth.

14. Identify the contentious issues between China and India. How could these be resolved for greater co-operation? Give your suggetions.

Or **Explain any two contentious issues between China and India. Suggest any to measures to resolve these issues for greater co-operation.** **CBSE 2025**

Ans. The contentions issues between China and India are

- In 1950, China annexed Tibet which removed a historical buffer between two countries. Initially, India didn't oppose it openly, but later it resented this issue when information regarding Tibetan culture suppression came up.
- Dalai Lama, the Tibetan spiritual leader sought and obtained political asylum in India in 1959. China opposed this move by declaring that India is supporting anti-China activities.
- China and India were involved in a border conflict in 1962 over competing territorial claims principally in Arunachal Pradesh and in the Aksai Chin region of Ladakh. The conflict of 1962, in which India suffered military reverses, had long-term implications for India–China relations.

These issues can be resolved for greater co-operation.

Although attempts have been made to normalise relations between the two nations by signing border pacts and agreements and with the visits of dignitaries, both nations need to again look into their strategies, revive cordial relations and collectively tread on the path of development.

The following important suggestions can be made to improve relations between India and China.

- India and China must accelerate the pace of economic co-operation between the two nations.
- Both the countries must discover innovative and pragmatic strategies for resolving the long-standing border dispute.
- The countries must enter into bilateral agreements on trade and encourage greater cultural exchange and interaction.
- Both the countries must join hands to fight challenges confronting the world, such as terrorism, environmental degradation, etc.

Exam Pattern Questions

Multiple Choice Questions (MCQs)

1. In which year, the Organisation for European Economic Co-operation was established?

(a) 1949 (b) 1948 (c) 1945 (d) 1957

2. Name the countries which resisted Maastricht Treaty.

(a) Britain and France (b) France and USA
(c) Germany and Britain (d) Denmark and Sweden

3. The first direct elections to European Parliament were held in the year

(a) January, 1981 (b) June, 1979
(c) June, 1985 (d) January, 1993

4. Two member countries of European Union are .... **CBSE 2020 Modified**

(a) Japan and China
(b) Australia and Mauritius
(c) Poland and Czech Republic
(d) Indonesia and Malaysia

5.

The given picture is the flag of which International Organisation?

(a) ASEAN (b) European Union (EU)
(c) BRICS (d) SAARC

6. Which of the following refers to America's massive financial help for reviving Europe's economy? **Diksha App**

(a) Brexit (b) Marshall Plan
(c) Euro (d) American dollar

7. Which among the following statements about the objectives for the establishment of the European Union is false?

(a) To provide a common foreign policy
(b) Creation of a single currency
(c) Establishment of a common market
(d) Co-operation on justice and home affairs

8. The 'ASEAN Way' is form of interaction that is .... **CBSE 2024**

(a) formal (b) confrontationist
(c) co-operative (d) provocative

9. Which one of the following countries is not a founder-member of ASEAN? **CBSE 2024**

(a) Singapore (b) Thailand
(c) Myanmar (d) Indonesia

10. In 2003, ASEAN agreed to establish an ASEAN community comprising of how many pillars?

(a) Three (b) Two (c) Five (d) Four

11. Name the country whose foreign policy did not give much attention to ASEAN during Cold War.

(a) China (b) Indonesia
(c) India (d) Thailand

12. Bangkok Declaration is related to which of the following?

(a) SAARC (b) BRICS
(c) EU (d) ASEAN

13. Two founder members of ASEAN are .... and .... **CBSE 2020 Modified**

(a) Australia, China (b) Indonesia, Malaysia
(c) Mauritius, Myanmar (d) Cambodia, Vietnam

14. The circle shown in the ASEAN flag symbolise .... **CBSE 2020 Modified**

(a) unity of ASEAN as it represents ten members of South-East Asian countries.
(b) disintegration of South-East Asian countries.
(c) political and social stability of ASEAN member countries.
(d) None of the above

15. Select the country which signed the Bangkok Declaration. **Diksha App**

(a) Philippines (b) Myanmar
(c) Cambodia (d) Vietnam

16. Which one among the following objectives for the formation of ASEAN is incorrect?

(a) A forum of interaction among the ASEAN members.
(b) To create a defence policy to be followed by its members.
(c) To create a common market in the region.
(d) To stop territorial disputes.

17. Rajiv Gandhi visit to China in December 1988 provided the impetus for an improvement in India-China relations. Mark the option which does not validate the statement. Diksha App

(a) Both government have taken measures to maintain peace and tranquility on the board.
(b) Both have signed agreement on cultural exchanges.
(c) Both agreed to sign Simla Agreement.
(d) Opened more border posts for trade.

18. Choose the option which does not specify characteristics of Chinese economy after inception of the PRC in 1949. Diksha App

(a) China chose to sever its links with the capitalist world
(b) State-owned heavy industries sector.
(c) China decided to substitute imports by domestic goods.
(d) Trade barriers were eliminated in Special Economic Zones.

19. Which of the following statement(s) is/are correct with regard to the European Union?

I. The EU over the time has turned from economic union to a political one.
II. The attempt to EU to have its own Constitution failed.
III. It has its own flag, anthem, founding date and currency.

Codes
(a) Only I (b) Only II
(c) Only III (d) All of these

20. Consider the following and arrange them in correct sequence.

I. ASEAN Vision
II. European Union
III. European Economic Community
IV. 'Open Door' Policy

Codes
(a) II, I, IV and III (b) III, IV, II and I
(c) I, II, III and IV (d) II, IV, I and III

21. In which year did China annex Tibet?

(a) 1950 (b) 1954
(c) 1960 (d) 1962

22. Match the following

List I (organisations)	List II (Establishment year)
A. ASEAN	1. 1967
B. EU	2. 1994
C. ASEAN Regional Forum	3. 1992

	A	B	C		A	C	D
(a)	1	2	3	(b)	3	2	1
(c)	1	3	2	(d)	2	3	1

23. Statement I The conflict of 1962, in which India suffered military reverses, had long-term implications for India-China relations.

Statement II Diplomatic relations between the two countries were downgraded until 1976.

In the light of above statements, choose the correct answer from the options given below

(a) Both Statement I and Statement II are true.
(b) Both Statement I and Statement II are false.
(c) Statement I is true, but Statement II is false.
(d) Statement I is false, but Statement II is true.

24. Statement I The ASEAN-India FTA came into effect in 2010.

Statement II During the Cold War years Indian foreign policy did not pay adequate attention to ASEAN.

In the light of above statements, choose the correct answer from the options given below

(a) Both Statement I and Statement II are true.
(b) Both Statement I and Statement II are false.
(c) Statement I is true, but Statement II is false.
(d) Statement I is false, but Statement II is true.

Assertion-Reason Questions

Directions (Q. Nos. 25-29) In the questions given below, there are two statements marked as Assertion (A) and Reason (R). Read the statements and choose the correct option.

Codes

(a) Both A and R are true and R is the correct explanation of A.
(b) Both A and R are true, but R is not the correct explanation of A.
(c) A is true, but R is false.
(d) A is false, but R is true.

25. Assertion (A) The Organisation for European Economic Co-operation (OEEC) was established in 1948.

Reason (R) It was established to channel aid to the West European State.

26. **Assertion** (A) The European Union has significant global influence in various domains, including diplomacy, economics and military power.

Reason (R) The EU's combined armed forces are the second largest in the world and it is the second most important source of space and communications technology.

27. **Assertion** (A) ASEAN has evolved beyond its original focus as primarily an economic association.

Reason (R) The ASEAN Regional Forum (ARF) was established in 1994 to co-ordinate security and foreign policy among member states.

28. **Assertion** (A) In 1978, Deng Xiaoping announced the 'Open Door' policy and economic reforms in China.

Reason (R) 'Open Door' policy was to generate higher productivity by investments of capital and technology from abroad.

29. **Assertion** (A) The relation between India and China has taken a downslide recently due to border disputes and China's support for Pakistan.

Reason (R) Border disputes, the China-Pakistan Economic Corridor, and China's support to Pakistan in the UN against India have led to deteriorating relations.

Passage Based Questions

30. **Study the following passage carefully and answer the questions that follow.**

America extended massive financial help for reviving Europe's economy under what was called the 'Marshall Plan'. The US also created a new collective security structure under NATO. Under the Marshall Plan, the Organisation for European Economic Co-operation (OEEC) was established in 1948 to channel aid to the West European States. It became a forum where the Western European States began to cooperate on trade and economic issues. The Council of Europe, established in 1949, was another step forward in political co-operation. The process of economic integration of European capitalist countries proceeded step by step leading to the formation of the European Economic Community (EEC) in 1957.

(i) **What was the 'Marshall Plan'?**

(a) Health aid given by the US.
(b) Economic aid given by the US.
(c) Military help given by the US.
(d) Financial aid given by the US.

(ii) **Which organisation became a forum where the Western European States began to co-operate on trade and economic issues?**

(a) Organisation for European Political Co-operation
(b) Organisation for European Economic Co-operation
(c) Organisation for European Military Co-operation
(d) None of the above

(iii) **Mention the factors on which EU was established?**

31. **Study the following passage carefully and answer the questions that follow.**

ASEAN was and still remains principally an economic association. While the ASEAN region as a whole is a much smaller economy compared to the US, the EU and Japan, its economy is growing much faster than all these. This accounts for the growth in its influence both in the region and beyond. The objectives of the ASEAN Economic Community are to create a common market and production base within ASEAN states and to aid social and economic development in the region. The Economic Community would also like to improve the existing ASEAN Dispute Settlement Mechanism to resolve economic disputes. ASEAN has focused on creating a Free Trade Area (FTA) for investment, labour and services. The US and China have already moved fast to negotiate FTAs with ASEAN.

(i) **Which of the following is the objective of ASEAN Economic Community?**

(a) To create common market and production based activities within ASEAN states itself.
(b) To aid social and economic development.
(c) To indulge the countries in Foreign Direct Investments.
(d) Both (a) and (b)

(ii) **How ASEAN Economic Community would resolve economic disputes?**

(a) By improving the existing ASEAN dispute settlement mechanism.
(b) By discussing the matter with the countries.
(c) By negotiating the FTA.
(d) None of the above

(iii) **During the Cold War years Indian foreign policy did not pay adequate attention to ASEAN. Critically analyse.** **Competency Based Que**

32. **Study the following passage carefully and answer the questions that follow.**

After the inception of the People's Republic of China in 1949, following the communist revolution under the leadership of Mao, its economy was based on the Soviet model. The economically backward communist China choose to sever its links with the capitalist world. It had little choice but to fall back on its own resources and, for a brief period, on Soviet aid and advice. The model was to create state-owned heavy industries sector from the capital accumulated from agriculture. As it was short of foreign exchange that it needed to buy technology and goods on the world market, China decided to substitute imports by domestic goods.

(i) The economy of China was based on .... model.

(a) Soviet (b) Socialist

(c) Communalist (d) Mixed Economy

(ii) Which among the following is the strength of Chinese economy?

(a) Land Mass (b) Population

(c) Regional location (d) All of these

(iii) The capital accumulated from agriculture was to be used to create ....

(a) tourism industry (b) manufacturing industry

(c) agriculture industry (d) heavy industries

(iv) Why China decided to substitute imports by domestic goods?

(a) To provide job to its citizens.

(b) Because of shortage of foreign exchange.

(c) Because China wanted to grow its domestic industry.

(d) None of the above

33. Study the following passage carefully and answer the questions that follow.

Rajiv Gandhi's visit to China in December 1988 provided the impetus for an improvement in India–China relations. Since then both governments have taken measures to contain conflict and maintain 'peace and tranquility' on the border. They have also signed agreements on cultural exchanges and co-operation in science and technology, and opened four border posts for trade. With India–China trade growing at 30 per-cent per year since 1999, a more positive perspective on relations with China has emerged.

(i) Which of the following events led to a shift in the initial positive relations between India and China after their independence?

(a) The independence of India from Britain.

(b) The Chinese takeover of Tibet in 1950.

(c) The signing of the Sino-Indian border agreement.

(d) India's adoption of the "Hindi-Chini bhai-bhai" slogan.

(ii) What was the slogan 'Hindi-Chini bhai-bhai' primarily associated with?

(a) India's efforts to gain support from other countries.

(b) The resolution of territorial disputes between India and China

(c) China's support for India during the Korean War.

(d) The initial hope for peaceful co-operation between India and China after their independence.

(iii) How did China's policy change in the 1970s affect its relations with India?

(a) China became more ideologically driven and aggressive towards India.

(b) China began to prioritise military confrontation over diplomacy.

(c) China adopted a less ideological approach, focusing on improving relations with India.

(d) China abandoned efforts to resolve border issues with India.

(iv) What role do both India and China aspire to play in the world since the end of the Cold War?

(a) They seek to dominate the global military sphere.

(b) They wish to play a major role in the Asian economy and politics.

(c) They aim to reduce their global influence and focus on regional matters.

(d) They wish to align exclusively with Western powers in global decision-making.

Answers

1. (b) 1948
2. (d) Denmark and Sweden
3. (b) June, 1979
4. (c) Poland and Czech Republic
5. (b) European Union (EU)
6. (b) Marshall Plan
7. (c) Establishment of a common market
8. (c) co-operative
9. (c) Myanmar
10. (a) Three
11. (c) India
12. (d) ASEAN
13. (b) Indonesia, Malaysia
14. (a) unity of ASEAN as it represents ten members of South-East Asian countries.
15. (a) Philippines
16. (b) To create a defence policy to be followed by its members.
17. (c) Both agreed to sign Simla Agreement.
18. (d) Trade barriers were eliminated in Special Economic Zones.
19. (d) All of these
20. (b) III, IV, II and I
21. (a) 1950
22. (c) 1 3 2

23. (a) Both Statement I and Statement II are true.
24. (a) Both Statement I and Statement II are true.
25. (a) Both A and R are true and R is the correct explanation of A.
26. (a) Both A and R are true and R is the correct explanation of A.
27. (b) Both A and R are true, but R is not the correct explanation of A.
28. (a) Both A and R are true and R is the correct explanation of A.
29. (a) Both A and R are true and R is the correct explanation of A.
30. (i) (d) Financial aid given by the US.
(ii) (b) Organisation for European Economic Co-operation
(iii) EU was established on following factors
(a) Co-operation on justice
(b) Creation of single currency
(c) Common foreign policy
31. (i) (d) Both (a) and (b)
(ii) (a) By improving the existing ASEAN dispute settlement mechanism.
(iii) During the Cold War, India's foreign policy prioritised non-alignment and relations with major powers, neglecting ASEAN. This oversight stemmed from ideological differences, India's focus on South Asia and ASEAN's perceived alignment with the West. Consequently, India missed opportunities for economic co-operation and regional influence. However, this approach also allowed India to maintain strategic autonomy and avoid entanglement in Southeast Asian conflicts. Post-Cold War, India recognised its oversight and began actively engaging with ASEAN.
32. (i) (a) Soviet (ii) (d) All of these
(iii) (d) heavy industries
(iv) (b) Because of shortage of foreign exchange.
33. (i) (b) The Chinese takeover of Tibet in 1950.
(ii) (d) The initial hope for peaceful co-operation between India and China after their independence.
(iii) (c) China adopted a less ideological approach, focusing on improving relations with India.
(iv) (b) They wish to play a major role in the Asian economy and politics.

Subjective Questions

Very Short Answer Type Questions

1. Mention the major challenges faced by Europe after Second World War.

Ans. The major challenges faced by Europe after Second World War were as follows
- It shattered many assumptions and structures on which European states maintained their relations.
- The European states confronted the ruin of economies and the destructions on which Europe had been founded.

2. What led the formation of the European Union?

Ans European Union was formed after the end of the Cold War. After the collapse of USSR, European Union was formed to consolidate the process of reviving the shattered economies of European countries and to get massive US financial help under the Marshall Plan.

3. Which four common symbols make the European Union look like a nation state? CBSE 2022

Or **Highlight any two factors that establish European Union as a nation state.** CBSE Term II 2022

Ans. Factors such as having its own flag, anthem, founding date and currency, make the EU look like a nation state.

4. What are the odds which limit the ability of EU?

Ans. European Union is a supranational organisation but in many areas its member states have their own foreign relations and defence policies that are often at odds as
- British Prime Minister Tony Blair supported the US's Iraq invasions and many new members made US-led 'coalition of willing' while Germany and France opposed it.
- Denmark and Sweden have resisted the Maastricht Treaty and the adoption of Euro.

5. Name any four member countries of the European Union. CBSE Term II 2022

Ans. The four member countries of the European Union are
(i) Austria (ii) Belgium (iii) Romania (iv) Latvia

6. In the European Union flag, what does the symbol of 'Twelve gold stars in a circle' signify? Competency Based Que

Or **What does the circle with golden stars on the European Union flag stands for?** Competency Based Que

Ans. The circle stands for solidarity and peace among the people of Europe. It contains twelve golden stars which symbolises perfection, completeness and unity.

7. Highlight the purpose of 'Marshall Plan'. CBSE Term II 2022

Ans. Marshall Plan was a plan under Mr. George C. Marshall, US Secretary. Under this plan America extended huge financial help for reviving Europe's economy. New collective security structure was created under NATO by the US.

Under Marshall Plan, Organisation for European Economic Co-operation (OEEC) was created in 1948 to help West European States. It acted as a platform where the West European States began to co-operate on trade and economic issues.

8. Explain the term Euroskepticism? Diksha App

Ans. Euroskepticism refers to the criticism or skepticism towards the European Union (EU) and its policies, often questioning the benefits of EU membership. It encompasses concerns about national sovereignty, perceived bureaucratic overreach and economic disparities among member states. Euroskeptic sentiments can lead to calls for reforms, reduced integration or even withdrawal from the EU, as seen in the Brexit movement.

9. Mention the agreements signed between India and ASEAN.

Ans. The agreements signed between India and ASEAN are as follows

- India signed Free Trade Areas (FTAs) with two ASEAN members i.e. Singapore and Thailand.
- India is trying to sign FTA with ASEAN itself.

10. When was the ASEAN Regional Forum (ARF) established? What were its main objectives?

Ans. The ASEAN Regional Forum (ARF) was established in 1994.

The main objectives of ASEAN were as follows

- To accelerate economic growth and through that social progress and cultural development.
- To promote regional peace and stability based on the rule of law and the principles of the United Nations Charter.

11. Name any four countries that established 'ASEAN'. CBSE Term II 2020

Ans. The four countries that established 'ASEAN' are

(i) Indonesia (ii) Malaysia
(iii) Singapore (iv) Thailand

12. State any two objectives of ASEAN. CBSE 2024

Ans. Two key objectives of ASEAN (Association of South-East Asian Nations) are

(i) **Promote Economic Growth** ASEAN aims to accelerate economic growth, social progress and cultural development among its member countries, fostering regional stability.

(ii) **Ensure Regional Peace** It strives to maintain peace, security and stability in the region by promoting active collaboration and mutual assistance on matters of common interest.

13. Comprehend ASEAN Vision 2020. Diksha App

Ans. ASEAN Vision 2020 is a strategic framework adopted in 1997, outlining the goals for the future of the Association of South-East Asian Nations. It aims to achieve a stable, prosperous and highly competitive region with equitable economic development and reduced poverty. The vision emphasises enhanced co-operation in various sectors, including trade, culture and security, to foster regional integration and solidarity.

14. Mention any two steps taken by China to improve its economy.

Ans. The two steps taken by China to improve its economy are

(i) Deng Xiaoping in 1978, announced 'Open Door' policy. This aimed at generation of high productivity by investments of capital and technology from abroad.

(ii) Privatisation of agriculture and industry was done.

15. Give any two reasons why regionally and globally China has become an economic power to reckon with.

Ans. Regionally and globally China has become an economic power to reckon with as

(i) The integration of China's economy has considerable influence on trade partners.

(ii) Adjustments through economic considerations have been made with Japan, US, ASEAN and Russia. Its investments and help in American, African and Latin states have helped it to project itself a major global player for developing states.

16. Analyse any two differences between India and China which led to a military conflict in 1962. CBSE 2024

Ans. Two key differences that led to the 1962 military conflict between India and China were as follows

(i) **Border Disputes** The primary issue was the disagreement over the Aksai Chin and Arunachal Pradesh regions. China claimed these areas as its own, while India considered them part of its territory.

(ii) **Political Tensions** India's support for Tibet's autonomy and its granting of asylum to the Dalai Lama strained relations, escalating tensions between the two nations.

Short Answer Type Questions

1. Mention any four common features of European Union.

Ans. The four common features of EU are as follows

(i) EU's share of world trade is much larger than that of US allowing it to be more assertive in trade disputes with US and China.

(ii) It has evolved from economic union to political one. It has its own flag, anthem, founding date and currency.

(iii) Its economic power gives it influence over its closest neighbours and on Asia and Africa. It also functions as an important bloc in international economic organisation such as WTO.

(iv) EU has political, economic, diplomatic and military influence. GDP of EU is slightly larger than that of US.

2. How can the Euro pose a danger to the US dollar?

Ans. European Union has a great economic influence in the world market including the market of United States. Euro is the currency of EU.

Euro can pose a danger to US dollar through following ways

- The EU is the world's biggest economy with GDP of more than $ 17 trillion in 2016 next to that of the United States of America.
- Share of EU in world trade is much larger than that of US and this is the reason why EU can be more assertive in trade disputes with US and China. Economic power of EU provides great influence over Asia, Africa and its close neighbours.
- Many countries have joined EU who are directly linked with US and carry Dollar as their currency. These countries can take up economic programmes which are against interest of US.

3. Assess the economic importance of the European Union.

Or **Analyse the role of the European Union as a supranational organisation with the help of examples.** **CBSE 2024**

Ans. The role of the European Union (EU) as a supranational organisation can be analysed through the following points

- **Economic Integration** The EU enables free movement of goods, services, capital and people within its single market, boosting trade and economic growth.
- **Common Currency** The Euro, used by 19 member states, enhances economic co-ordination and reduces exchange rate fluctuations.
- **Legislative Power** The EU Parliament and European Court of Justice hold authority over national laws in certain areas, ensuring uniform policies.
- **Social and Political Co-operation** The EU promotes shared standards on human rights, environmental regulations and foreign policy, fostering regional stability.

4. Interpret the economic, political, diplomatic and military influence of European Union. **Diksha App**

Or **Analyse any four factors that make the European Union an influential regional organisation.** **CBSE 2024**

Ans. The influence of the European Union (EU) can be interpreted in the following points

- **Economic Influence** The EU boasts one of the world's largest economies, with a single market facilitating free trade and investment among member states, enhancing economic stability.
- **Political Influence** The EU promotes democratic values and human rights, shaping governance standards both within and outside its borders.
- **Diplomatic Influence** As a unified entity, the EU conducts collective diplomacy, engaging in international negotiations on issues like climate change, trade agreements and global security, amplifying its voice on the world stage.
- **Military Influence** While lacking a standing army, the EU co-ordinates defense policies through the Common Security and Defense Policy (CSDP), enabling joint crisis management and peacekeeping missions, thus contributing to regional security.

5. What are the objectives of ASEAN Economic Community?

Or **Describe any three objectives of the ASEAN.** **CBSE 2024 C**

Ans. The objectives of ASEAN Economic Community are as follows

- To create common market and production based activities within ASEAN.
- To aid social and economic development.
- To resolve economic disputes.
- To create Free Trade Areas for investment, labour and services.
- To accelerate economic growth through social progress and cultural development.

6. Explain any two causes which led to the formation of ASEAN.

Ans. The causes which led to the formation of ASEAN were as follows

(i) The South-East Asian Nations suffered the economic and political consequences of repeated colonialisms before and during the Second World War.

(ii) The end of the Second World War confronted problems of nation building, the ravages of poverty and economic backwardness and the pressure to align with one great power or another during the Cold War.

Hence, South-East Asian countries established the association for South East Asian nations in order to solve the issues of South-East Asian countries.

7. What were the objectives behind the formation of the ASEAN in 1967?

Ans. Association of South-East Asian Nations (ASEAN) was created in 1967 with the following objectives

- **Primary Objective** It was to increase economic growth, which will result in social progress and cultural development of the ASEAN. Thus, this objective was related to economic, cultural and social perspectives.
- **Secondary Objective** Under United Nation Charter, principles and rules of law have been stated. So, the secondary objective of ASEAN nations was to promote stability and regional peace based upon those rules and principles.

8. What were the two major policy decisions taken by the Chinese leadership in the 1970s?

***Or* Describe any four new economic policies of China to make it grow at a faster rate.**

***Or* Explain the new economic policies of China since 1978.**

Ans. China's economic success has been linked to its rise as a great power. The major policy decisions regarding new economic policies of China were as follows

(i) China ended its political and economic isolation with the establishments of relations with the United States in 1972.

(ii) Four modernisations (agriculture, industry, science and technology and military) were proposed by the Premier Zhou Enlai in 1973.

(iii) Den Xiaoping declared the 'Open Door' policy and rapid economic reforms in China. It was meant to generate higher productivity by investments of capital and technology from other countries.

(iv) The privatisation of agriculture in 1982 was followed by the privatisation of industry in 1998.

(v) The trade barriers were eliminated only in Special Economic Zones (SEZs) where foreign investors could set up enterprises.

9. In spite of improvement in the Chinese economy, there have been negative consequences affecting the people of China. Mention any four such consequences.

***Or* Highlight any four drawbacks in the changed Chinese economic system.**

***Or* Why did the people of China not receive the benefits of the reforms whereas its economy had improved dramatically? Explain giving any two reasons.** **CBSE 2024**

Ans. Even though the Chinese economy has improved dramatically, there have been negative consequences affecting the people of China. The four negative consequences or drawbacks in the changed Chinese economic system are as following

(i) The benefits of the reforms have not been equally received. Approximately 100 million people are still unemployed.

(ii) Female employment and conditions of work are as bad as in Europe of the 18th and 19th centuries.

(iii) Corruption and environmental degradation have increased.

(iv) There has been rise in economic inequality between rural and urban residents and coastal and inland provinces.

10. Suggest any two measures to improve Indo-China relations. **CBSE 2024**

Ans. To improve Indo-China relations, the following two measures can be suggested

(i) **Bilateral Dialogue and Diplomatic Engagement** Regular high-level diplomatic talks should be conducted to resolve border disputes, enhance mutual trust and address strategic concerns. Establishing open channels for dialogue can help in de-escalating tensions and avoiding conflicts like the one in 1962.

(ii) **Economic and Trade Co-operation** Strengthening economic ties through trade agreements, joint investments and collaborations in sectors like technology and infrastructure can foster interdependence. Enhancing people-to-people contact through cultural exchanges, educational programmes and tourism will also help build goodwill and improve bilateral ties.

These steps can contribute to long-term peace and stability between India and China.

Long Answer Type Questions

1. Evaluate the effectiveness of the European Union as the most prominent regional organisation. **CBSE SQP 2024**

Ans. The effectiveness of the European Union as the most prominent regional organisation can be evaluated on the following basis

- It has its own flag, anthem, founding date and currency.
- It has a forum of foreign and security policy in its dealings with other nations.

- The EU is the world's biggest economy with a GDP of more than $12 trillion in 2005 slightly larger than that of the United States.
- Its share of world trade is much larger than that of the United States. Its economic power gives it influence over its closest neighbours as well as in Asia and Africa.
- It plays an important role in international economic organisations such as the World Trade Organisation.
- It has political and diplomatic influence. One of its member-France is a permanent member of the UN Security Council. Some of its members are non-permanent members of the UN Security Council. Its use of diplomacy, economic investments and negotiations rather than coercion have been more effective in dialogue with China on human rights and environmental degradation.
- Its military power is the second largest in the world. Britain and France have nuclear arsenals.
- It is the world's second most important source of space and communication technology.

2. Describe the process of evolution of the European Union from an economic union to an increasingly political one. **CBSE 2024**

Or **Evaluate any three major factors responsible for making the European Union a political force from an economic force.** **Competency Based Que**

Or **Explain the process of evolution of the European Union from an economic union to an increasingly political one.** **CBSE 2023**

Ans. The evolution of the European Union (EU) from an economic union to an increasingly political one can be described in the following steps

- **Formation as an Economic Union (1951-1957)** The EU began as the European Coal and Steel Community (ECSC) in 1951, focusing on economic Co-operation to prevent conflict. In 1957, the Treaty of Rome established the European Economic Community (EEC) and the European Atomic Energy Community (EURATOM), focusing on creating a common market.
- **Expansion of Economic Integration (1986)** The Single European Act (1986) aimed at creating a fully integrated single market by removing trade barriers, standardising regulations and enabling the free movement of goods, services, capital and people.
- **Political Integration (1992)** The Maastricht Treaty (1992) transformed the EEC into the European Union, introducing political elements like a common foreign and security policy, and deeper political Co-operation between member states.
- **Further Political Union (2009)** The Lisbon Treaty (2009) increased the EU's political influence by creating positions like the President of the European Council and enhancing the powers of the European Parliament, strengthening its role in global politics, diplomacy and security.

This evolution reflects a shift from economic co-operation to a more comprehensive political union.

3. ASEAN is rapidly growing into a very important regional organisation. Justify the statement. **CBSE 2024 Competency Based Que**

Ans. ASEAN (Association of South East Asian Nations) is rapidly growing into a very important regional organisation due to the following factors

- **Economic Growth and Integration** ASEAN countries collectively form one of the fastest-growing economic regions. Through initiatives like the ASEAN Free Trade Area (AFTA) and the ASEAN Economic Community (AEC), member states have enhanced trade and economic integration, making ASEAN a key player in the global economy.
- **Strategic Geopolitical Importance** Situated in a region critical for global trade routes, ASEAN nations are pivotal in regional stability and security. ASEAN plays a central role in balancing relations between major powers like the U.S., China and India, making it a crucial forum for diplomacy.
- **Cultural and Social Co-operation** ASEAN promotes cultural exchange, tourism and education among its members, enhancing people-to-people connections. Programmes such as the ASEAN Socio-Cultural Community (ASCC) focus on shared regional identity and social development.
- **Political Influence** ASEAN's diplomatic platform, such as the ASEAN Regional Forum (ARF), allows member states to address security issues collectively. Its role in promoting peace and stability in South East Asia, including dispute resolution in the South China Sea, elevates its political influence globally.

4. Explain with suitable arguments that Japan is emerging as a new alternate centre of power. **CBSE 2025**

Ans. Japan is emerging as an alternate centre of power due to its economic growth, technological advancement and increasing global influence.

After World War II, Japan focused on economic development and became the second-largest economy by the 1980s. Its advanced industries, particularly in automobiles and electronics have made it a global leader.

After its defeat in World War II, Japan adopted a peaceful development strategy and focused on economic reconstruction under US guidance. By the 1980s, it became the second-largest economy in the world. Japan's success was driven by industrial growth, technological innovation and a strong work ethic. Its automobile and electronics industries became globally dominant and it became a major player in international trade organisations like the G7 and WTO.

Although Japan's Constitution restricts military expansion, it has maintained strong security ties with the United States. It has modernised its Self-Defense Forces (SDF) and actively participates in international peacekeeping missions. Japan has also played a significant role in maintaining security in the Asia-Pacific region, especially in countering China's growing influence. Its involvement in the Quad (with the US, India and Australia) highlights its strategic importance in regional and global affairs.

Japan's influence is further strengthened by its cultural and diplomatic initiatives. It is known for its contributions to global education, technology and sustainable development. Through foreign aid, economic co-operation and active participation in international organisations, Japan has established itself as an emerging centre of power in world politics.

5. Highlight any three steps taken by China to improve its economy. **CBSE Term II 2022**

Ans. China has been growing as an economic power since 1978. It is estimated to overtake US as the world's largest economy by 2040. It has enormous regional influence due to its economic integration into the region.

Factors like population, landmass, resources, regional location and political influence adds to its power along with a strong economy.

Following are the factors responsible for rise of the Chinese economy

- Major policy decisions were taken in the 1970's by the Chinese leadership. China ended its political and economic isolation with US in 1972.
- Premier Zhou Enlai proposed 'four modernisations' i.e. agriculture, industry, science and technology and military in 1973. Later in 1978, Deng Xiaoping announced the 'Open Door' policy and economic reforms in China.
- 'Open Door' policy was to generate higher productivity by investments of capital and technology from abroad. Market economy was adopted and their economy was opened step by step.
- Agriculture sector was privatised in 1982 followed by privatisation of industry in 1998. Trade barriers were eliminated in Special Economic Zones (SEZs) where enterprises were set by the foreign investors.
- State plays a dominant role in setting up a market based economy in China.

6. Support with arguments that South Korea is emerging as a new alternative centre of power. **CBSE SQP 2024**

Ans. The fact that South Korea is emerging as a new alternative centre of power can be supported through following arguments

- Between the 1960s and the 1980s, it rapidly developed into an economic power, which is termed as "Miracle on the Han River".
- Signaling its all-around development, South Korea became a member of the OECD in 1996.
- In 2017, its economy was the eleventh largest in the world and its military expenditure was the tenth largest.
- According to the Human Development Report 2016, the HDI rank of South Korea is 18. The major factors responsible for its high human development include "Successful reforms, rural development, extensive human resources development and rapid equitable economic growth".
- Other factors are export orientation, strong redistribution policies, public infrastructure, development, effective institutions and governance.
- The South Korean brands such as Samsung, LG and Hyundai have become renowned in India. Numerous agreements between India and South Korea signify their growing commercial and cultural ties.

Picture Based Questions

1. Study the picture given below and answer the questions that follow

Choose the most appropriate option

(i) What event is referenced in the cartoon?

(a) The signing of the Treaty of Rome.

(b) The failure of the European Union's initiative to draft a common Constitution.

(c) The expansion of the European Union to include new member states.

(d) The formation of the European Parliament.

Ans. (b) The failure of the European Union's initiative to draft a common Constitution.

(ii) In what year did the European Union's initiative to draft a common Constitution fail, as referred to in the cartoon?

(a) 2003 (b) 2004 (c) 2005 (d) 2007

Ans. (a) 2003

(iii) What does the circle of gold stars on the European Union flag represent?

(a) The economic power of Europe.
(b) Solidarity and harmony between the peoples of Europe.
(c) The military strength of the European Union.
(d) The number of founding EU member states.

Ans. (b) Solidarity and harmony between the peoples of Europe.

(iv) What is the symbolic meaning of the number twelve in the context of the European Union flag?

(a) It symbolises perfection, completeness and unity.
(b) It symbolises the number of political leaders in Europe.
(c) It represents the number of stars in the EU flag.
(d) It represents the twelve largest European economies.

Ans. (a) It symbolises perfection, completeness and unity.

2. Observe the picture given below and answer the following questions.

(i) In which year the bipolar structure of world politics ended? What became clear for America's dominance? Which two associations of nations emerged in Europe and Asia?

(ii) What is indicated by the first picture?

(iii) What is being indicated by the second picture?

Ans. (i) The bipolar structure of world politics ended in 1990.

It became clear that alternative centres of political and economic power could unite against America's dominance.

Thus, in Europe, the European Union (EU) and in Asia, the Association of South-East Nations (ASEAN) have emerged as forces to reckon with.

(ii) The first picture here represents the beginning of the history of Red China (or Communist China). 'The Socialist Road is the Broadest of All' represents the ideology that guided China during its early phase after the revolution took place in China in 1949.

It tells that China's economy will become the largest economy of the world by 2040 because it prepared Soviet model of economy and always keeps capitalist ideas submissive to the same.

(iii) The second photograph is that of the city of Shanghai. This new and beautiful city is the symbol of China's new economic power.

3. Based on the image provided, here are four multiple-choice questions (MCQs) along with their answers

(i) What is the primary subject depicted in the cartoon?

(a) The rise of Western nations
(b) The growing competition from East Asian nations
(c) Economic decline in Europe
(d) Political struggles in Asia

Ans. (b) The growing competition from East Asian nations

(ii) What does the burning pile labeled 'competition' most likely symbolise?

(a) A new political movement
(b) Challenges faced by the West due to East Asian economic growth
(c) Environmental issues
(d) Cultural conflicts between East and West

Ans. (b) Challenges faced by the West due to East Asian economic growth

(iii) **What might the phrase "We'll have to get used to it" imply?**

(a) Resistance to change
(b) Acceptance of a new economic reality
(c) Hope for the future
(d) Denial of competition from East Asia

Ans. (b) Acceptance of a new economic reality

(iv) **Which global phenomenon does the cartoon most likely comment on?**

(a) The Cold War
(b) The rise of Asian economies in the global market
(c) The end of colonialism
(d) The beginning of space exploration

Ans. (b) The rise of Asian economies in the global market

4. Observe the cartoon given below and answer the following questions.

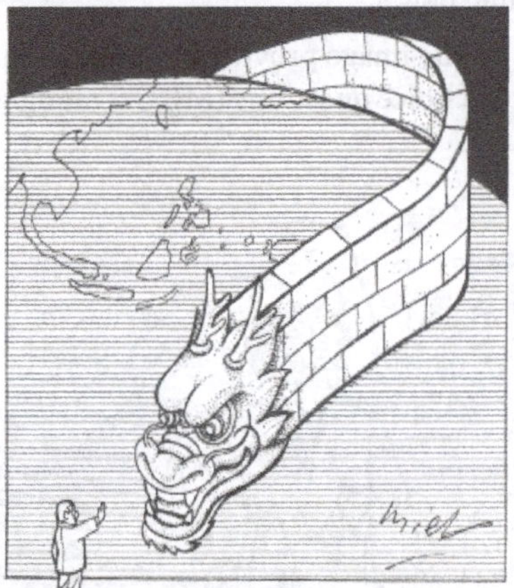

(i) **Where does the cartoon place the related country in the international power politics?**

(ii) **What message does this cartoon convey to the world?**

(iii) **Assess the strength of China on the basis of the cartoon.**

Ans. (i) The cartoon depicts the economic rise of China.

(ii) China adopted communism according to communist ideology. Capitalist exploited working class, that is why for a very long period China was cut off from capitalist world.

But after 1978, China ended its isolation and developed its relation with America. The message of this policay was conveyed to the world.

(iii) The cartoon shows the economic rise of China. It shows China's power to control the economic situation of South East Asia.

It also depicts that China is fast becoming a superpower and it has strength like its great wall.

Map Based Questions

1. In the given political outline map of Europe, four member countries of the European Union have been marked as A, B, C and D. Identify them with the help of information given below and write their correct names in your answer book along with their respective serial numbers and the alphabet concerned.

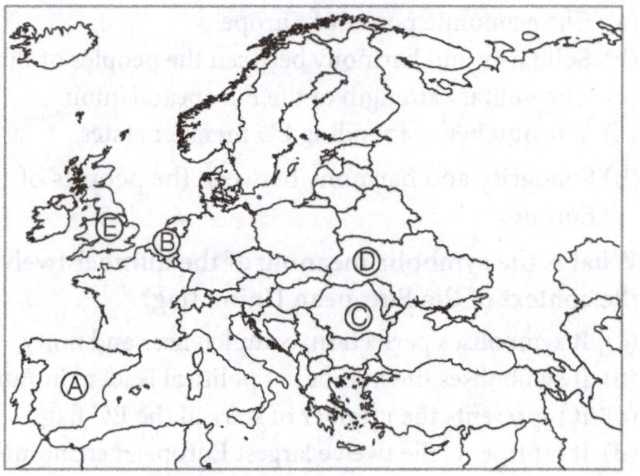

(i) **An older member of the European Union located between Portugal and France.**

(ii) **An older member of the European Union located near Netherlands and France.**

(iii) **Two new members of the European Union.**

(iv) **Locate the member which recently exited from BREXIT.**

Ans. (i) Spain (A) (ii) Belgium (B)
(iii) Bulgaria (C) and Romania (D) (iv) Britain (E)

2. In the given political outline map of the European Union, identify and write the names of four old members marked as A, B, C and D and four new members marked as P, Q, R and S in your answer book.

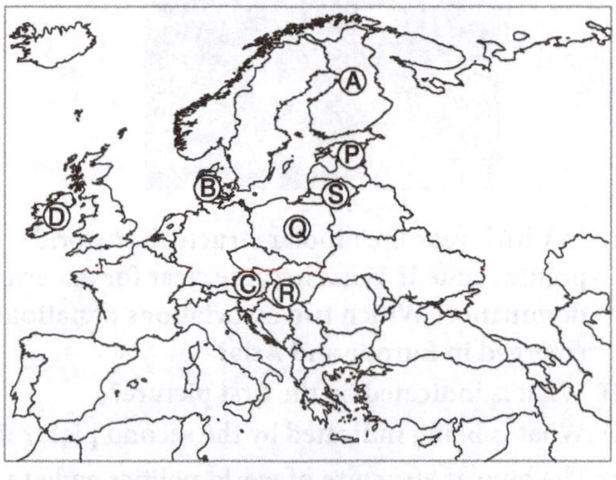

Ans. (i) Old members of European Union are

A-Finland B-Denmark C-Austria D-Ireland

(ii) New members of European Union are

P-Estonia Q-Poland R-Hungary S-Lithuania

SELF ASSESSMENT TEST

Objective Type Questions

1. For what purpose the council of Europe was established?
   (a) Economic integration (b) Security (c) Political co-operation (d) Trade development
2. Arrange the following in correct sequence.
   I. ASEAN Regional Forum II. Unification of Germany
   III. OEEC IV. European Union
   Codes
   (a) I, II, IV and III (b) II, IV, I and III (c) III, II, IV and I (d) IV, III, II and I
3. Consider the following statement(s) with regard to ASEAN community. Mark the correct option(s).
   (a) The ASEAN community has established three pillars.
   (b) It aims to uphold the regional or cultural sovereignty of the people.
   (c) It was established in 2004.
   (d) Both (a) and (b)
4. In the European flag circle of .... stars stands for ....
   (a) silver, harmony and peace (b) bronze, solidarity and Co-operation
   (c) gold, solidarity and harmony (d) copper, peace and solidarity

Very Short Answer Type Questions

5. What was 'Marshall Plan'?
6. What led to the formation of European Union?
7. What was the purpose behind ASEAN?
8. What was 'Open Door' policy of China?
9. Describe the challenges of India-China relations.

Short Answer Type Questions

10. What are the factors responsible for the rule of Chinese economy?
11. What do you know about 'Bangkok Declaration'?
12. State the components of ASEAN Vision 2020.
13. China will soon become world's largest economy. Critically analyse.

Long Answer Type Questions

14. Discuss the role of European Union as a supranational organisation.
15. Define ASEAN. What steps should be taken to strengthen it?
16. Elucidate the pillars of ASEAN.
17. Describe the challenges faced by EU in the current world.

03

CHAPTER

This chapter deals with the domestic politics of South Asian countries. It also explores India's relationship with its neighbours in the context of conflicts and co-operation.

Contemporary South Asia

▼ **YOUR STUDY GOALS**

3.1 Political Background of South Asian Countries
3.2 Democratisation in South Asia
3.3 India Pakistan Conflict
3.4 India and Its Neighbours

▼ **YOUR PRACTICE GOAL**

- Objective Type Questions (35 Qs; MCQs, A-R, Statements, Matching, Passage based)
- Subjective Questions (11 VSAs, 11 SAs, 8 LAs, 5 Picture Based, 1 Map Based)

South Asian region include countries like **India**, **Sri Lanka**, **Nepal**, **Bangladesh**, **Bhutan**, **Pakistan** and **Maldives**. These countries have witnessed many conflicts among themselves such as border disputes, water sharing disputes, etc.

China is an important **part** but is not considered to be a part of the region. South Asia stands for diversity in every sense and yet constitutes one geopolitical space[1].

The large Himalayas in the North and the vast Indian Ocean, the Arabian Sea and the Bay of Bengal in the South, West and East respectively provide a natural separation to the region. This is largely responsible for the **linguistic**, **social and cultural** distinctiveness of the sub-continent.

3.1 Political Background of South Asian Countries

- **India** and **Sri Lanka** have established and maintained democracy since independence.
- **Pakistan** began the post-Cold War period with successive democratic government under **Benazir Bhutto** and **Nawaz Sharif** but suffered a military overtake in 1999. It has been run by a civilian government again since 2008.

1 Geopolitical space It refers to the association of countries who are bound with each other geographically and their interests are also interlinked with each other.

- **Nepal** was under the Constitutional monarchy till 2006. In 2008, the monarchy was abolished and Nepal emerged as a democratic republic[2].
- **Bhutan** became a Constitutional monarchy in 2008. Later, it emerged as a multi-party democracy.
- **Bangladesh** has experienced both civilian and military rule, however it was able to maintain the democracy since the post-Cold War era.
- **Maldives** was a sultanate till 1968 after which it turned into republic with Presidential form of government. Mult-party system was introduced here in 2005. The Maldivian Democratic Party (MDP) dominates the political affairs.

3.2 Democratisation in South Asia

- A recent survey of the attitudes of the people in the five big countries of the region showed that there is widespread support for democracy in all these countries. People view democracy positively and support the institutions of representative democracy.
- They prefer democracy over any other form of government and think that democracy is suitable for their country.

Military and Democracy in Pakistan

- After Pakistan framed its first Constitution, **General Ayub Khan** took over the administration of the country and soon got himself elected.
- Popular dissatisfaction against the rule of Ayub Khan led to a military takeover under **General Yahya Khan.**
- Under Yahya's rule, **Bangladesh War** was fought in 1971, leading to formation of Bangladesh as an independent country. After this, an elected government was formed under **Zulfikar Ali Bhutto** from 1971-77.
- Later, Bhutto government was removed by **General Zia-ul-Haq** in 1977.
- General **Zia-uI-Haq** faced the **Pro-democracy Movement** from 1982, resulting in formation of elected government under **Benazir Bhutto in 1988** which lasted till 1999.
- In 1999, **Prime Minister Nawaz Sharif** was removed by the army under **General Pervez Musharraf** and in 2001, he elected himself as the **President**. Since 2008, democratically elected leaders have been ruling Pakistan.

Factors Responsible for Pakistan's Failure in Building a Stable Democracy

- The **social dominance of the military, clergy and landowning aristocracy** has led to the frequent overthrow of elected governments in Pakistan.
- Pakistan's conflict with India has made the pro-military group more powerful.
- The **lack of international support** for democratic rule in Pakistan has further encouraged the military to continue its dominance.
- The United States and other Western countries have encouraged the military **authoritarian rule** in the past for their own reasons like the fear of 'global Islamic terrorism' and concerns over Pakistan's nuclear weapons falling into the wrong hands.

Democracy in Bangladesh

- Bangladesh was a part of Pakistan from 1947 to 1971. It was known as the **East Pakistan**. It consisted of the partitioned areas of **Bengal** and **Assam** from British India.

---

2 **Republic** Political system where head of the state is an elected person.

- Soon after the partition they began protests against the **unfair treatment** of Bengali culture and language. They demanded **fair representation in the administration** and a fair share in political power.
- In 1970 elections, **Awami League** led by **Sheikh Mujibur Rahman** won all the seats in East Pakistan and secured a majority in the proposed Constituent Assembly. But the government dominated by the West Pakistani leadership refused to call the assembly and Sheikh Mujib was arrested.
- Under the military rule of **General Yahya Khan**, the Pakistani army tried to suppress the mass movement of the Bengali people. This led to a large scale migration into India.
- The government of India supported the demand of the people of East Pakistan for their independence and helped them financially and militarily. This resulted in a war between **India** and **Pakistan** in December 1971. In December 1971, Pakistani forces surrendered in East Pakistan and Bangladesh was formed as an independent country.
- Bangladesh drafted its **Constitution** declaring faith in secularism, democracy and socialism.

Internal Conflicts in Bangladesh

- In 1975, the Constitution was amended to shift from the **Parliamentary to Presidential** form of government by **Sheikh Mujibur Rahman**. He abolished all the political parties except his own Awami League. He was assassinated in a **Military Uprising in 1975**.
- The new military rule, **Ziaur Rahman**, formed his own Bangladesh National Party. He won the elections of 1979 but later he was also assassinated. Then, the military took over under **L. General H.M. Ershad**.
- The people started pro-democracy protests, as a result of which Ershad was forced to allow political activity on a limited scale. He was later elected as President for five years. Mass public protests made Ershad step down in 1990.
- Elections were held in 1991, since then representative democracy based on multi-party elections has been working in Bangladesh.

Monarchy and Democracy in Nepal

- Nepal was a **Hindu Kingdom** and became a **Constitutional monarchy** in modern period. The King of Nepal retained control over the government and restricted expansion of democracy with the help of army.
- The political parties demanded more transparent and accountable government time to time. The King accepted the demand for new **democratic Constitution** in 1990. However, democratic government had a short and troubled duration.
- The **Maoists** of Nepal were successful in spreading their influence during 90's in many parts of Nepal. Maoist believed in armed revolts against the monarch and the ruling elite. This resulted in violent conflicts between the Maoist guerrillas and the armed forces of the King. For some time, there was a triangular conflict among the monarchist forces, the democrats and the Maoists. The King dismissed the government and abolished the Parliament in 2002, thus it ended even limited democracy that existed in Nepal.
- In April 2006, a massive country wide **pro-democracy** protest was witnessed. A non-violent movement was initiated by the **Seven Party Alliance** (SPA), the Maoists and social activists.

Democratic Transition in Nepal

- Nepal formed a **Constituent Assembly** to prepare the country's Constitution.
- The Maoist organisations agreed to put their armed struggle on hold. They desired that the Constitution include significant social and economic transformation programmes. It was opposed by all the **SPA**[3] **parties**.

3 **SPA** It is an alliance of seven parties in Nepal which also demanded an end to monarchy.

- Maoists were also deeply suspicious of the Indian Government and its role in Nepal's future.
- In the year 2008, Nepal became a democratic republic after abolishing the monarchy. The **new Constitution** was adopted by Nepal in 2015.

Ethnic Conflicts and Democracy in Sri Lanka

- Sri Lanka got its independence in 1948 and since then it has retained its democracy. But it faced a serious challenge due to ethnic conflict leading to the demand for secession by one of the regions.
- After independence, politics in Sri Lanka (then known as Ceylon) was dominated by majority of **Sinhala community**. They were hostile to Tamils who had migrated from India to Sri Lanka and settled there. Sinhalese were not ready to give any concessions to Tamils as they were of the opinion that Sri Lanka belongs only to Sinhalese. The neglect of Tamil concerns led to militant **Tamil nationalism**.
- From 1983, the **Liberation Tigers of Tamil Eelam** (LTTE)[4], the militant organisation, was fighting an armed struggle against the army of Sri Lanka. LTTE demanded **'Tamil Elam'** or separate country for the Tamilians of Sri Lanka.
- The Sri Lankan problem involves people of Indian origin so there was pressure on the Indian Government from the Tamil people in India to protect the interest of Tamils in Sri Lanka. In 1987, the Government of India for the first time got directly involved in the Sri Lankan's Tamil problem.
- India signed an **accord** with Sri Lanka and sent troops to stabilise relations between the Sri Lankan government and the Tamils. The Indian army got into a fight with the LTTE. The presence of Indian troops was also not liked by the Sri Lankans.
- They saw this as an attempt by India to interfere in the internal affairs of Sri Lanka. In 1989, the **Indian Peace Keeping Force (IPKF)**[5] was pulled out of Sri Lanka. Finally, the armed conflict came to an end, as the **LTTE** was defeated in **2009**.
- In spite of the conflict, Sri Lanka has registered considerable economic growth and recorded high levels of human development. Sri Lanka was one of the first developing countries to successfully control the rate of growth of population and to liberalise the economy.
- It had the highest per capita **Gross Domestic Product** (GDP) for many years right through the civil war[6]. Despite the ravages of internal conflict, it has maintained a democratic political system.

Quick Test 1

Which two countries have maintained democracy since independence?
Name the country that was under the Constitutional monarchy till 2006.
Why did India sent troops to Sri Lanka?

3.3 India Pakistan Conflict

The post-Cold War era has not meant the end of conflicts and tensions in South Asia. There are some very crucial conflicts of an international nature.

Kashmir Issue

- After the partition, both the countries got involved in a conflict over the claim for Kashmir. Wars between India and Pakistan in 1947-48 and 1965 failed to settle the matter. It resulted in the division of the province into **Pakistan-occupied Kashmir (POK)** and the Indian province of Jammu and Kashmir divided by the **Line of Control**. In 1971, India won a decisive war against Pakistan but the Kashmir issue remained unsettled.

4 LTTE It is a militant organisation which fought for the establishment of separate state for Tamil people in Sri Lanka.
5 Indian Peace Keeping Force It was sent by India in Sri Lanka to support the demand of Tamils.
6 Civil war It refers to war between citizens of the same country.

Water Sharing Issue Between India and Pakistan

- India and Pakistan also have had problems over the sharing of river waters.
- Until 1960, they were locked in a fierce argument over the use of the rivers of the Indus basin. Eventually, in 1960, with the help of the **World Bank**, India and Pakistan signed the **Indus Waters Treaty** which has survived to this day in spite of various military conflicts in which the two countries have been involved.
- There are still some minor differences about the interpretation of the Indus Waters Treaty and the use of the river waters. The two countries are not in agreement over the demarcation line in **Sir Creek** in the Rann of Kutch. India and Pakistan are holding negotiations on all these issues.

Arms Race Between India and Pakistan

- India's conflict with Pakistan is also over strategic issues like the control of the **Siachen Glacier** and over acquisition of arms. The arms race between the two countries assumed a new character with both states acquiring nuclear weapons and missiles.
- In 1998, India conducted nuclear explosion in **Pokhran**. Pakistan responded within a few days by carrying out nuclear tests in the **Chagai Hill**.
- Since then India and Pakistan seem to have built a military relationship in which the possibility of a direct and full scale war has declined. But both the governments continue to be suspicious of each other.
- The Indian Government has blamed the Pakistan Government for violence by helping the **Kashmiri militants** with arms, training, money and protection to carry out terrorist strikes against India, and for aiding the pro-Khalistani militants with arms and ammunitions during the period 1985-1995.
- Pakistan spy agency, **Inter-Services Intelligence (ISI)**, is alleged to be involved in various anti-India campaigns in India's North-East, operating secretly through Bangladesh and Nepal. It blames the Indian Government and its security agencies for inciting trouble in the provinces of Sindh and Baluchistan.

Efforts Towards Peace and Co-operation

India and Pakistan are holding negotiations over many issues. Some of the efforts towards peace between both the countries are discussed below

- **Confidence building measures** has been signed between both the countries to minimise the tensions in terms of security.
- **Social activities** and prominent personalities collaborated to develop friendly atmosphere.
- Number of bus routes has been opened up between the countries. Trade between India and Pakistan had increased and visas had been more easily granted.
- **Samjhauta Express**, was started in July 1976 to improve people-to-people connect between the two countries after the Simla Agreement.
- Finalising of **Kartarpur corridor** has shown a narrow ray of hope for starting of talks between India and Pakistan after the **2019 Pulwama terror attack**.

3.4 India and Its Neighbours

India and Bangladesh

- There are few differences prevailing between the Governments of India and Bangladesh over sharing of rivers water of the Ganga and the Brahmaputra. Further, the Governments of India has been unhappy with Bangladesh due to the following reasons
  - Illegal immigration of Bangladeshi people.
  - Bangladesh's support for anti-India Islamic fundamentalist groups.
  - Bangladesh's refusal to allow Indian troops to move through its territory to North-Eastern India.

- Bangladesh decision not to export natural gas to India or allow Myanmar to do so through Bangladeshi territory.
- Bangladeshi Governments have felt that the Indian Government behaves like a regional bully over the sharing rivers water, encouraging rebellion in the Chittagong Hill Tracts, trying to extract its natural gas and being unfair in trade.
- The two countries could not resolve their boundary dispute for a long while.

Efforts Towards Peace and Co-operation

- Both the countries co-operate on many issues despite their differences. Economic relations have improved considerably in the last 20 years.
- Bangladesh is a part of **India's Look East Policy** (Act East since 2014) that wants to link up with South-East Asia through Myanmar.
- Both India and Bangladesh have co-operated regularly on disaster management and environmental issues.
- In 2015, they exchanged certain enclaves. Efforts are to broaden the areas of co-operation further by identifying common threats and being more sensitive to each other's needs.

India and Nepal

- India and Nepal has developed a cordial and special relationship.The treaty between the countries allows the citizens of the two countries to travel and work in other country without visas and passports. Despite this special relationship, the government of both the countries had trade-related disputes in the past.
- The Indian Government expressed displeasure at the relationship between China and Nepal and at the Nepal Government for not taking action against anti-Indian elements.
- Indian security agencies see the Maoist movement in Nepal as a growing security threat, given the rise of Naxalite groups in various Indian states from Bihar in the North to Andhra Pradesh in the South.
- Many leaders and citizens in Nepal think that the Indian Government interferes in its internal affairs and is preventing Nepal from getting easier access to the sea through Indian territory.

Efforts Towards Peace and Co-operation

- Despite differences, trade, scientific co-operation, common natural resources, electricity generation and interlocking water management grids hold the two countries together. India and Nepal relations are fairly stable and peaceful.

India and Sri Lanka

- The Government of India and Sri Lanka are mostly indulged in dispute over ethnic conflict in the island nation. The Indian leaders find it difficult to remain neutral when the Tamils are politically unhappy and are being killed. After the military intervention of 1987, the Indian Government has developed a policy of non-interference with Sri Lanka's internal troubles.

Efforts Towards Peace and Co-operation

The steps and policies which have further strengthened the ties between the two countries are as follows

- Free Trade Agreement
- Post-tsunami reconstruction in Sri Lanka

India and Bhutan

- India and Bhutan enjoy a special relationship and does not have any major conflict.
- The effort of the Bhutanese Government to eliminate the guerrillas and militants from **North-East India** has proved to be helpful to India.
- India is involved in big **hydroelectric projects** in Bhutan and remains its biggest source of development aid.

India and Maldives

- India has a good relationship with the island nation of Maldives.
- India supported Maldives on its request, in November 1988, when some Tamil Sri Lankan soldiers attacked Maldives, the Indian Air Force and Navy quickly reacted against the invasion.
- India also contributed towards the island economic development, tourism and fisheries.

SAARC(South Asian Association for Regional Co-operation)

- SAARC is a major regional initiative by the South Asian states to evolve cooperation through multilateral means.
- It was founded in **1985**.
- Members of SAARC: India, Pakistan, Nepal, Bhutan, Bangladesh, Sri Lanka, Maldives, Afghanistan.
- Unfortunately, due to persisting political differences, SAARC has not had much success.

SAFTA(South Asian Free Trade Agreement)

- The agreement was signed in **2004** and came into effect on 1st January, 2006.
- SAARC members signed the **South Asian Free Trade Agreement** (**SAFTA**) which promised the formation of a free trade zone for the whole of South Asia. The agreement also aims at lowering trade tariffs.
- But some of India's neighbours fear that SAFTA is a way for India to **'invade'** their markets and to influence their societies and politics through commercial business and a commercial presence in their countries.
- India thinks that there are real economic benefits for all from SAFTA and that a region that trades more freely will be able to co-operate better on political issues.

Role of USA and China in the South Asian Region

- China and the United States remain key player in South Asia politics.

China

- Sino-Indian relations have improved significantly in the last 10 years, but China's strategic partnership with Pakistan remains a major irritant.
- India and China have come closer due to the demands of development and globalisation. They have increased their economic ties since 1991.

USA

- American involvement in South Asia has rapidly increased ofter the Cold War.
- The US has maintained good relation with India and Pakistan since the Cold War ended.
- Economic reforms and liberal economic policies in India and Pakistan have led to greater American involvement in the region.
- The large South Asia communities in the US, along with the region's big population and markets, give America an added stake in the future of regional security and peace.

Quick Test 2

1. Name any two wars fought between India and Pakistan over Kashmir.
2. Which organisation helped India and Pakistan to sign Indus Water Treaty?
3. How did Bhutan help India?
4. When was SAARC founded?

TIMELINE

1947	India and Pakistan emerge as independent nations after the end of British rule.
1948	Sri Lanka (then Ceylon) gains independence; Indo-Pak conflict over Kashmir.
1954-55	Pakistan joins the Cold War military blocs-SEATO and CENTO.
1960	India and Pakistan sign Indus Water Treaty.
1962	Border conflict between India and China.
1965	Indo-Pak War; UN India-Pakistan observation mission.
1966	India and Pakistan sign the Tashkent Agreement; Six point proposal of Sheikh Mujibur Rahman for greater autonomy to East Pakistan.
1971 March	Proclamation of independence by leaders of Bangladesh.
1971 August	Indo-Soviet Treaty of friendship signed for 20 years.
1971 December	India-Pak War; Liberation of Bangladesh.
1972 July	India and Pakistan sign Simla Agreement.
1974 May	India conducts nuclear test.
1976 May	Pakistan and Bangladesh establish diplomatic ties.
1985 December	South Asian leaders sign the SAARC charter at the first summit in Dhaka.
1987	Indo-Sri Lanka accord; IPKF operation in Sri Lanka.
1988	India sends troops to the Maldives to fall a coup attempt by mercenaries. India and Pakistan signed the agreement not to attack nuclear installations and facilities of each other.
1988-91	Democracy restoration in Pakistan, Bangladesh and Nepal.
1996 December	India and Bangladesh sign the Farakka Treaty for sharing of the Ganga's water.
1998 May	India and Pakistan conduct nuclear tests.
1998 December	India and Sri Lanka sign the Free Trade Agreement (FTA).
1999 February	Indian Prime Minister Vajpayee undertakes bus journey to Lahore to sign a peace declaration.
1999 June-July	Kargil conflict between India and Pakistan.
2001 July	Vajpayee-Musharraf Agra Summit unsuccessful.
2004 January	SAFTA signed at the 12th SAARC Summit in Islamabad.
2007 January	Afghanistan joins SAARC.
2014 November	The 18th SAARC Summit in Kathmandu, Nepal.

Mind Map

CONTEMPORARY SOUTH ASIA

1 Introduction to South Asia

Political Background of South Asian Countries

- South Asia consists of seven countries including India.
- Himalayas and sea's create natural isolation.
- China is important region but it is not the part of South Asia.
- Largely responsible for the linguistic, social and cultural distinctiveness of the sub-continent.

2 A Political Background of South Asian Countries

- India and Sri Lanka have established and maintained democracy.
- Pakistan began the post-Cold War period with successive democratic government.
- Nepal was under the Constitutional monarchy and emerged as a democratic republic in 2008.
- Bhutan emerged as a multi-party democracy.
- Bangladesh has experienced both civilian and military rule.
- Maldives turned into republic with presidential form of government.

3 Democratisation in South Asia

- A recent survey of the attitudes of the people in the five big countries of the region.
- People view democracy positively and support the institutions of representative democracy.
- They prefer democracy over any other form of government and think that democracy is suitable for their country.

Military and Democracy in Pakistan

- General Ayub Khan took administrative control of Pakistan after first Constitution.
- Bangladesh War was fought in 1971 under General Yahya's rule.
- Zulfikar Bhutto led an elected government from 1971 to 1977.
- In 1999, Prime Minister Nawaz Sharif was removed by the army under General Pervez Musharraf.
- Since 2008, democratically elected leaders have been ruling Pakistan.

Democracy in Bangladesh

- In 1971, East Pakistan broke away from Pakistan and emerged as Bangladesh.
- In 1970, Awami league led by Sheikh Mujibur Rahman formed government.
- Bengali people protested and demanded a fair representation in political power.
- In 1975, Sheikh Mujibur Rahman shifted the Constitution from parliamentary to Presidential form.
- Elections were held in 1991 after the nation-wide mass protests.

Monarchy and Democracy in Nepal

- In April 2006, a massive country wide pro-democracy protests were held in Nepal.
- A non-violent movement was started by the Seven Party Alliance.
- In 2008, Nepal became a democratic republic.
- In 2015 it adopted a new Constitution.

Ethnic Conflicts and Democracy in Sri Lanka

- After Independency, politics in Sri Lanka was dominated by the Sinhala community.
- From 1983, militant organisation the Liberation Tigers of Tamil Eelam (LTTE) demanded a separate country 'Tamil Eelam'.
- India signed an accord with Sri Lanka and sent army to fight LTTE.
- In 2009, LTTE was defeated and armed conflict came to an end.

5 India and Its Neighbours

India and Bangladesh

- India and Bangladesh have had issues like river water sharing, illegal immigrants, etc.
- Bangladesh refused Indian troops to move through its territory.
- Bangladesh is a part of India's 'Look East' policy.
- In 2015, both the countries exchanged certain enclaves.

India and Nepal

- India and Nepal has a cordial relationship.
- The citizens of the two countries can work in each other country without visa.
- Indian security agencies see the Maoist movements in Nepal as a growing security threat.

India's Relations with Sri Lanka, Myanmar and Bhutan

- After the military intervention in 1987, Indian and Sri Lanka adopted a non-interference policy.
- India has strong ties with Bhutan, especially in security and hydroelectric projects.
- Indian has close relations with Maldives, and it offers military aid and economic help.

Regional Co-operation and American Involvement in South Asia.

- In 1985, SAARC was formed to improve regional co-operation.
- SAFTA agreement was signed in 2004 aimed to lower trade tariffs.
- American involvement in the Asia increased after the Cold War.

4 India - Pakistan Conflicts

Kashmir and Border Conflicts

- After the 1947 War, Kashmir was divided into two parts.
- Government of Pakistan claimed part of Kashmir.
- In 1960, India and Pakistan signed the Indus Water Treaty with the help of World Bank.
- In 1998, India conducted a nuclear test in Pokhran which sparked tensions between both nations.

NCERT Folder

Intext Questions

1. Identify some features common to all the South Asian countries but different from countries in West Asia or Southeast Asia. (Pg. no. 30)

Ans. Some common features to all the South Asian countries

- There is geographical proximity among all the countries of South Asia.
- Indo Aryan language is spoken amongst the south Asian countries.
- Common cultural heritage like art, dance etc.

South Asian countries are different from countries of West Asia or Southeast Asia.

- South Asian countries differ from West Asia in their monsoon climate, agriculture and Indo-Aryan languages, whereas West Asia is arid and semitic-speaking. Compared to Southeast Asia's tropical rains and Austronesian languages, South Asia has a colonial history, diverse religions like Hinduism and Buddhism, and a distinct, spice-rich cuisine.

2. Is there a fixed definition of these regions? Who decides that? (Pg. no. 30)

Ans. There is no universally fixed definition of the regions in Asia, including South Asia, West Asia and Southeast Asia. The definitions may vary based on different criteria, such as geographical, cultural, political or historical factors. The definitions of regions are generally decided by scholars and researchers. International organisations like the UN, the World Bank, etc. also decide the definition of these regions for their research and development work.

3. If Germany can be reunited, why can't the people of India and Pakistan at least travel more easily to each other's country? (Pg. no. 33)

Ans. Yes, people of India and Pakistan can travel to each other country easily of both countries have cordial relations. A number of bus routes have been opened up between the two countries. Visas had been granted more easily. However, in the recent times, the situation has changed due to bad relations between India and Pakistan.

4. Let's know more about Bangladesh's Grameen Bank. Can we make use of the idea to reduce poverty in India? (Pg. no. 35)

Ans. Grameen Bank, founded by Muhammad Yunus in Bangladesh, pioneered microcredit, offering small loans to the rural poor, especially women, to encourage entrepreneurship. This model helped millions escape poverty by enabling small-scale businesses and self-sufficiency.

Application in India

India, with its vast rural population, could replicate this by expanding microfinance initiatives, empowering women, fostering local entrepreneurship and reducing dependence on traditional, inaccessible banking systems.

5. Discussion on Kashmir sounds like a property dispute between the rulers of India and Pakistan. What do the Kashmiris feel about it? (Pg. no. 38)

Ans. People of Kashmir have seen wars between India and Pakistan and experienced its effects since 1947. Some Kashmiris are with India, whereas some have sympathy for Pakistan. Kashmiri militiants supported by Pakistan use violent methods to meet the goal of separation of India from Pakistan. However, most of the Kashmiris feel sad due to the lack of peace and development due to conflict between two nations.

6. Why is it that every one of our neighbours has a problem with India? Is there something wrong with our foreign policy? Or is it just our size? (Pg. no. 39)

Ans. Neighbours of India have a problem with India. This is due to historical, political and economic reasons. For example, India has territorial disputes with Pakistan, whereas it has problems with Bangladesh on issues like water sharing, illegal immigration, etc. India also has a troubled relationship with China. However, there is nothing wrong with Indian foreign policy. Neither size is the reason. India has maintained very cordial relations with Bhutan and the Maldives. It also took several efforts to normalise relations with Nepal, Sri Lanka, Bangladesh and Pakistan. It is necessary to consider that the view and attitude of neighbouring countries is also important to maintain a cordial relationship.

7. If the chapter, on US was called 'US hegemony' why is this chapter not called 'Indian hegemony'? (Pg. no. 41)

Ans. The term 'hegemony' refers to an international system which is dominated by a sole superpower. The collapse of the Soviet Union left the world with only one single power, the United States of America. India is considered a major power in South Asia and the world. But India is not considered as the sole superpower. Neither India affects world politics so deeply as the US does. So, this chapter is not called 'Indian hegemony'.

8. Every association seems to have emerged for trade. Is trade more important than people-to-people relations? (Pg. no. 42)

Ans. Trade is not more important than people-to-people relations. But trade is a way to strengthen people-to-people relations. Trade gives opportunities to people to get some benefit from the cordial relationship between two countries. It fulfills the needs of countries and increases the trust and co-operation among them. So, every association seems to have emerged from trade. Trade helps in the economic growth of countries and also help in people-to-people relations.

Exercise

1. Identify the country.

(i) The struggle among pro-monarchy, pro-democracy groups and extremists created an atmosphere of political instability.

(ii) A landlocked country with multi-party competition.

(iii) The first country to liberalise its economy in the South Asian region.

(iv) In the conflict between the military and pro-democracy groups, the military has prevailed over democracy.

(v) Centrally located and shares borders with most of the South Asian countries.

(vi) Earlier the island had the Sultan as the head of state. Now, it's a republic.

(vii) Small savings and credit co-operatives in the rural areas have helped in reducing poverty.

(viii) A landlocked country with a monarchy.

Ans. (i) Nepal (ii) Bhutan
(iii) Sri Lanka (iv) Pakistan
(v) India (vi) Maldives
(vii) Bangladesh (viii) Nepal

2. Which among the following statements about South Asia is wrong?

(i) All the countries in South Asia are democratic.

(ii) Bangladesh and India have signed an agreement on river-water sharing.

(iii) SAFTA was signed at the 12th SAARC Summit in Islamabad.

(iv) The US and China play an influential role in South Asian politics.

Ans. (i) All the countries in South Asia are democratic is the wrong statement.

3. What are some of the commonalities and differences between Bangladesh and Pakistan in their democratic experiences?

Ans. Commonalities between Bangladesh and Pakistan are as follows

- There is majority of Muslim population in both countries.
- There have been military take over in both countries from time to time.
- There have been pro-democracy movements in both the countries.

Differences between Bangladesh and Pakistan are as follows

- The US and Western countries have encouraged military's authoritarian rule in Pakistan in the past for their own interest. It is not so in case of Bangladesh.
- Pakistan is a nuclear power state but Bangladesh is not.
- In Pakistan, military, clergy and land-owning aristocrats dominated socially to overthrow elected governments whereas in Bangladesh, the leaders and their party members dominated for the same.

4. List three challenges to democracy in Nepal.

Ans. The three challenges to democracy in Nepal are as follows

(i) Some sections in Nepal who believe that a nominal monarchy is necessary for Nepal to retain its link with the past.

(ii) Maoists who wanted the Constitution to include the radical programmes of social and economic restructuring.

(iii) Differences between Maoists and the SPA.

5. Name the principal players in the ethnic conflict in Sri Lanka. How do you assess the prospects of the resolution of this conflict?

Ans. The principal players in the ethnic conflict in Sri Lanka are the Sinhala community and Tamils who had migrated from India to Sri Lanka and settled there. The Sinhala nationalists are in majority and they do not want to give any concessions to Tamils who are in minority. This has led to militant Tamil nationalism and the LTTE has been fighting an armed struggle with Sri Lankan army since 1983. Their demand is of Tamil Eelam or a separate country for the Tamils of Sri Lanka.

However, the prospects of the resolution of this conflict is possible by the following ways

- The Government of Sri Lanka should provide the fundamental and basic rights to the Tamil population Constitutionally and uphold the principle of democracy.
- It should also provides special status to the Tamil province for their rejuvenation and maintain peace in the province and the country.

6. Mention some of the recent agreements between India and Pakistan. Can we be sure that the two countries are well on their way to a friendly relationship?

Ans. The following are the agreements between India and Pakistan

- The two countries have agreed to undertake confidence building measures to reduce the risk of war.
- A number of bus routes have been opened up between he two countries.
- A train service has started operating between two countries.

No doubt, efforts are being made to have a durable peace but there is little possibility of friendly relationship because Kashmir continues to be the main problem between the two countries.

Pakistan is also responsible for terrorist activities in India such as Bombay blasts. Such actions on the parts of Pakistan are obstacles in the way of friendly relations between the two countries.

Therefore, the two countries are not well on their way to a friendly relationship.

7. Mention two areas each of co-operation and disagreement between India and Bangladesh.

Or **Explain any two points of co-operation as well as confrontation each between India and Bangladesh.**

Ans. Two areas of co-operation are as follows

(i) Bangladesh is a part of India's Look East Policy that wants to link up with South-East Asia through Myanmar.

(ii) On disaster management and environmental issues, the two states have co-operated regularly.

Two areas of disagreement are as follows

(i) Dispute over sharing of the Ganga and the Brahmaputra rivers water.

(ii) The Indian Government has been unhappy with Bangladesh's denial of illegal immigration to India.

8. How are the external powers influencing bilateral relations in South Asia? Take any one example to illustrate your point.

Ans. China and United States are the external power that who play an important role in influencing bilateral relations in South Asia.

- The United States has worked as a moderator in Indo-Pakistan relations.
- Economic reforms and liberal economic politics in both the countries have increased the American participation.
- The South Asian diaspora are working in USA and this gives America added stake in the future of regional security and peace.

9. Write a short note on the role and the limitations of SAARC as a forum for facilitating economic co-operation among the South Asian countries.

Ans. **Role of SAARC in Economic Co-operation**

- **Promotes Regional Trade** through initiatives like SAFTA (South Asian Free Trade Area).
- **Encourages investment** and infrastructure development.
- **Facilitates dialogue** on economic issues among member states.
- **Supports poverty reduction** through regional projects.

Limitations of SAARC

- **Political tensions,** especially between India and Pakistan, hinder co-operation.
- **Low Intra-regional trade** despite agreements like SAFTA.
- **Slow decision-making** and weak enforcement of policies.
- **Economic disparities** among member countries create unequal benefits.

10. India's neighbours often think that the Indian government tries to dominate and interfere in the domestic affairs of the smaller countries of the region. Is this a correct impression?

Ans. No, this is not a correct impression. India has never wanted to dominate or interfere in the domestic affairs of the smaller countries of the region. India thinks that there are real economic benefits for all, if all the countries lift up trade barriers. India believes that trade relations will remove the suspicion in the minds of every country.

Exam Pattern Questions

Objective Type Questions

Multiple Choice Questions (MCQs)

1. Which country is considered as a part of South-Asia region?

(a) Indonesia (b) Myanmar
(c) China (d) Sri Lanka

2. Which one of the following countries is not included in 'South Asia'? **CBSE 2024**

(a) Bangladesh (b) China
(c) Bhutan (d) Maldives

3. Name the party that dominates the political affairs of Maldives.

(a) Maldivian Dictatorship Party
(b) Maldivian Democratic Party
(c) Maldivian People's Party
(d) Maldivian Majority Party

4. Who took the administration after Pakistan framed its first Constitution?

(a) General Zia-ul-Haq
(b) General Yahya Khan
(c) General Parwez Musharraf
(d) General Ayub Khan

5. Which two countries signed Indus Water Treaty with the World Bank as negotiator?

(a) India and Bangladesh (b) India and Pakistan
(c) India and Afghanistan (d) India and Nepal

6. Name the party which won 1970s election under Sheikh Mujibur Rahman.

(a) Awami League
(b) Jatiya Party
(c) Bangladesh Nationalist Party
(d) Bangladesh People's League

7. In which year the King of Nepal dismissed the government and abolished the Parliament?

(a) 2000 (b) 2003 (c) 2002 (d) 2004

8. Which one of the following statements about the ethnic conflict in Sri Lanka is false? **CBSE 2024**

(a) Politics in Sri Lanka favoured the Sinhalese.
(b) Interests of Tamils were neglected.
(c) LTTE was supported by the SAARC countries.
(d) The Sri Lanka ethnic problem involved the Sinhalese and the Tamils.

9. Which one of the following developing countries was the first to successfully control the rate of growth of population? **CBSE 2024**

(a) India (b) Pakistan
(c) Nepal (d) Sri Lanka

10. Which one of the following statements about India's relations with Pakistan is incorrect? **CBSE Term I 2021**

(a) India and Pakistan signed the Indus Water Treaty which has survived in spite of various military conflicts.
(b) India and Pakistan worked together to restore people have to their families.
(c) India and Pakistan have signed a treaty of friendship to work against terrorism.
(d) India and Pakistan signed the Taskhent Agreement in 1966.

11. Which one pair of countries from the following is held together because of common natural resources, electricity generation and interlocking water management grids? **CBSE Term I 2021**

(a) India and Nepal (b) India and Bangladesh
(c) India and Sri Lanka (d) India and Myanmar

12. Identify the issue where the Government of India and Bangladesh have difference.

(a) Disaster management
(b) Environmental issues
(c) Export of natural gas
(d) India's act East policy

13. Which of the following events made the South Asian region a sudden focus of global attention after the cold war period? **CBSE 2025**

(a) Bangladesh War of 1971
(b) Ethnic conflict of Sri Lanka
(c) India and Pakistan both became nuclear power
(d) Kargil conflict between India and Pakistan

14. With which country does India have a treaty that allows the citizens of the two countries to travel to and work in the other country without visas and passports? **CBSE Term I 2021**

(a) Bangladesh (b) Sri Lanka
(c) Nepal (d) Israel

15. **Which one of the following factors has strengthened relations between India and Sri Lanka?** **CBSE Term I 2021**
(a) Ethnic conflict in Sri Lanka.
(b) Free trade agreement with Sri Lanka.
(c) India's peace keeping force.
(d) India's attitude towards Tamils in Sri-Lanka.

16. **The SAARC is a major .... initiative by South Asian states to evolve mutual co-operation.** **CBSE 2024**
(a) political (b) military
(c) international (d) regional

17. **Choose the incorrect statement.**
(a) Sheikh Mujibur was assassinated in the year 1975.
(b) Zulfikar Ali Bhutto was removed by General Zia-ul-Haq in 1977.
(c) Let. Gen. H.M. Ershad step down in Bangladesh in 1990.
(d) General Perwez Musharraf removed Prime Minister Nawaz Sharif in 2000.

18. **Arrange the following rulers of Pakistan in the chronological order as per the period of their rule.** **CBSE 2024**
I. General Zia-ul-Haq
II. Benazir Bhutto
III. General Musharraf
IV. Zulfikar Ali Bhutto
Codes
(a) IV, I, II, III (b) I, III, II, IV
(c) IV, III, II, I (d) I, II, III, IV

19. **Arrange the following correct sequence.**
I. Sri Lanka agains independence.
II. Democracy restoration in Pakistan, Bangladesh and Nepal.
III. Proclamation of independence by leaders of Bangladesh.
IV. Pakistan joins the Cold War military blocs. SEATO and CENTO.
Codes
(a) I, III, IV, II (b) II, III, IV, I
(c) I, III, II, IV (d) I, IV, III, II

20. **Arrange the following correct sequence.**
I. South Asian Free Trade Agreement came into force.
II. IPKF operation in Sri Lanka.
III. India and Bangladesh signed Farakka Treaty.
IV. India's nuclear test in Pokhran.
Codes
(a) I, II, III, IV (b) II, III, IV, I
(c) IV, I, II, III (d) III, II, IV, I

21. **Choose the correct statements about India's relations with Nepal.** **CBSE Term I 2021**
I. India and Nepal enjoy a very special relationship.
II. India does not interfere in the internal affairs of Nepal.
III. India has always helped Nepal during natural disasters.
IV. Citizens cannot travel to the other country without visas.
Codes
(a) I, II and IV (b) I, III and IV
(c) I, II and III (d) II, III and IV

22. **Select the correct statements.**
I. Bangladesh was a part of Pakistan from 1947 to 1991.
II. India and Bhutan have had complex relationship.
III. China and the USA influence the South Asian politics.
IV. India and Pakistan signed the Simla Agreement in 1972.
Codes
(a) I and II (b) I and III
(c) I and IV (d) III and IV

23. **Identify the country which has all the four features.** **CBSE Term I 2021**
I. It is a part of India's Look East Policy.
II. It came into existence with India's help.
III. Its border touches the border of India.
IV. It is a secular and democratic country.
Choose the correct option
(a) Myanmar (b) Nepal
(c) Bhutan (d) Bangladesh

24. **Identify and write the incorrect pair.**
(a) Indus Water Treaty-1960
(b) Tashkent Agreement-1966
(c) Simla Agreement-1972
(d) Indo-Soviet Treaty of Friendship- 1999

25. **Match the List-I with the List-II correctly.** **CBSE 2024**

	List-I		List-II
A.	The first country to lieberalise its economy in the South Asian region.	1.	Maldives
B.	Earlier this country had the Sultan as its head of state. Now, it is a republic.	2.	Sri Lanka
C.	A land locked country.	3.	Pakistan
D.	In the conflict between the military and the pro-democracy groups, the military had prevailed over democracy in this country	4.	Nepal

Codes

	A	B	C	D
(a)	3	1	2	4
(b)	2	1	3	4
(c)	2	1	4	3
(d)	4	2	3	1

26. Match the List I with the List II correctly.

List I	List II
A. Nepal	1. MDP
B. Bangaldesh	2. SPA
C. Pakistan	3. Awami League
D. Maldives	4. Muslim League

Codes

	A	B	C	D		A	B	C	D
(a)	2	3	4	1	(b)	1	4	3	2
(c)	2	4	3	1	(d)	4	2	1	3

27. Given below are two statements **CBSE 2025**

Statement I Nepal was a Hindu kingdom in the past and then a Constitutional monarchy in the modern period for many years.

Statement II The struggling pro-democracy forces achieved their first major victory in 2006, when the king was forced to restore the house of representatives.

Options
(a) Both Statement I and Statement II are true.
(b) Both Statement I and Statement II are false.
(c) Statement I is true, but Statement II is false.
(d) Statement I is false, but Statement II is true.

28. Given below are two statements **CBSE 2025**

Statement I The Maldives was a sultanate till 1965, it was transformed into a republic with a presidential form of government .

Statement II The Maldivian Democratic Party dominates the political affairs of the island and it won the 2018 elections.

Options
(a) Both Statement I and Statement II are true.
(b) Both Statement I and Statement II are false.
(c) Statement I is true, but Statement II is false.
(d) Statement I is false, but Statement II is true.

Assertion-Reason Questions

Directions (Q. Nos. 29-31) In the questions given below, there are two statements marked as Assertion (A) and Reason (R). Read the statements and choose the correct option.

Codes
(a) Both A and R are true and R is the correct explanation of A.
(b) Both A and R are true, but R is not the correct explanation of A.
(c) A is true, but R is false.
(d) A is false, but R is true.

29. **Assertion** (A) People of South Asia prefer democracy to any other type of administration and believe that democracy is the most appropriate form of the government for their country.

Reason (R) Democracy is the system of government by the whole population or all the eligible members of the state.

30. **Assertion** (A) The domocratic set up of Sri Lanka was disturbed by the ethnic conflict by the Sinhalese and Tamil people.

Reason (R) Sinhalese people were the largest ethnic group of Sri Lanka.

31. **Assertion** (A) The post-Cold War era has not meant the end of conflicts and tensions in the South Asia region.

Reason (R) There are many conflicts on various issues among the South Asian Regions. **CBSE 2024**

Passage Based Questions

32. **Study the following passage carefully and answer the questions that follow.**

Nepal's transition to democracy is not complete. At the moment, Nepal is undergoing a unique moment in its history because it is moving towards the formation of a Constituent Assembly that will write the Constitution for Nepal. Some sections in Nepal still think that a nominal monarchy is necessary for Nepal to retain its link with the past. The Maoist groups have agreed to suspend armed struggle. They want the Constitution to include the radical programmes of social and economic restructuring. All the parties in the SPA may not agree with this programme. The Maoists and some other political groups are also deeply suspicious of the Indian Government and its role in the future of Nepal.

(i) Why it is said that Nepal is undergoing a unique movement in its history?
(a) As it is moving towards the formation of Constituent Assembly that will write the Constitution.
(b) As it is moving towards uncivilised protests and movement.
(c) Due to nominal monarchy in Nepal.
(d) None of the above

(ii) What is the desire of Maoist groups in Nepal?
(a) The have agreed to suspend armed struggle.
(b) They want the Constitution to include the radical programmes of social and economic restructuring.
(c) They were deeply suspicious on the intentions of Indian Government.
(d) Both (a) and (b)

(iii) Why were some political parties suspicious in Nepal?

(a) Political groups were deeply suspicious regarding the role of Indian Government in the future of Nepal.
(b) Because they were against the democratic set-up.
(c) Because they were suspicious regarding the social restructuring.
(d) All of the above

(iv) In the above passage, SPA stands for ....

(a) State Party Alliance (b) Seven Party Alliance
(c) Static Party Alliance (d) Six Party Alliance

33. Study the following passage carefully and answer the questions that follow.

The lack of genuine international support for democratic rule in Pakistan has further encouraged the military to continue its dominance. The United States and other Western countries have encouraged the military's authoritarian rule in the past for their own reasons. Given their fear of the threat of what they call 'global Islamic terrorism' and the apprehension that Pakistan's nuclear arsenal might fall into the hands of these terrorist groups, the military regime in Pakistan has been seen as the protector of Western interests in West Asia and South Asia.

(i) What is the hurdle of democracy in Pakistan?

(a) It has no experience of any regular democracy.
(b) Democracy did not get any solid footing and development.
(c) Due to circumstances, military rule is regarded as the best option in Pakistan.
(d) All of the above

(ii) Why did the Western countries encourage the military to continue its dominance in Pakistan?

(a) As they fear that global Islamic terrorism may become active.
(b) Military regime in Pakistan has been the protector of the Western interest in West Asia and South Asia.
(c) As it was benefitting the Western countries.
(d) Both (a) and (b)

(iii) Which among the following initiative must be taken by the citizens of Pakistan in establishing democracy?

(a) They must play an active role in establishing democracy.
(b) The citizens of Pakistan should use their courage and intellect for fighting for democracy.
(c) Military rule must be discouraged and benefits of democracy must be encouraged.
(d) Both (a) and (b)

(iv) Military rule is regarded as the best option in Pakistan because ....

(a) democracy was never developed and encouraged in Pakistan.
(b) due to huge military popularity of on the citizens.
(c) due to fear and enemity among the citizens.
(d) None of the above

34. Study the following passage carefully and answer the questions that follow.

Despite the mixed record of the democratic experience, the people in all these countries share the aspiration for democracy. A recent survey of the attitudes of the people in the five big countries of the region showed that there is widespread support for democracy in all these countries. Ordinary citizens, rich as well as poor and belonging to different religions, view the idea of democracy positively and support the institutions of representative democracy. They prefer democracy over any other form of government and think that democracy is suitable for their country. These are significant findings, for it was earlier believed that democracy could flourish and find support only in prosperous countries of the world.

(i) Which of the following is a broader implication of widespread support for democracy in countries with varying economic status?

(a) Democracy is less likely to succeed in countries with high income inequality.
(b) Democratic values can gain support even in economically diverse societies.
(c) Democracy requires high levels of economic development to thrive.
(d) Only economically advanced countries can maintain democratic institutions.

(ii) What does the support for democracy across different religious and economic groups suggest about democratic ideals?

(a) Democracy is largely a political ideal for wealthy, secular societies.
(b) Democratic principles have universal appeal across various social groups.
(c) Democracy thrives only in homogenous societies.
(d) Religious differences prevent widespread support for democracy.

(iii) What can be inferred about the role of economic prosperity in supporting democracy?

35. Study the following passage carefully and answer the questions that follow.

In spite of the many conflicts, the states of South Asia recognise the importance of co-operation and friendly relationship, among themselves. The South Asian Association for Regional Co-operation (SAARC) is a major regional initiative by the South Asian states to evolve co-operation through multilateral means. It began in 1985. Unfortunately, due to persisting political differences, SAARC has not had much success. SAARC members signed the South Asian Free Trade Agreement (SAFTA) which promised the formation of a free trade zone for the whole of South Asia.

(i) Which of the following was the primary goal of establishing South Asian Association for Regional Co-operation (SAARC)?
(a) To create a unified military force.
(b) To enhance mutual support.
(c) To develop a common currency.
(d) To only resolve territorial disputes among member states.

(ii) What was the main objective of the South Asian Free Trade Agreement (SAFTA)?
(a) To create safer environment for investment.
(b) To establish free and fair market place.
(c) To form chamber of South Asian Association of Commerce.
(d) To promote business through cultural ties.

(iii) Explain the significance of SAARC in South Asia and the factor which led to the limited success of SAARC.

Answers

1. (d) Sri Lanka 2. (b) China
3. (b) Maldivian Democratic Party
4. (d) General Ayub Khan 5. (b) India and Pakistan
6. (a) Awami League 7. (c) 2002
8. (c) LTTE was supported by the SAARC countries.
9. (d) Sri Lanka
10. (c) India and Pakistan have signed a treaty of friendship to work against terrorism.
11. (a) India and Bangladesh 12. (c) Export of natural gas
13. (c) India and Pakistan both became nuclear power
14. (c) Nepal
15. (b) Free trade agreement with Sri Lanka.
16. (d) regional
17. (d) General Perwez Musharraf removed Prime Minister Nawaz Sharif in 2000.
18. (a) IV, I, II, III 19. (d) I, IV, III, II
20. (b) II, III, IV, I 21. (c) I, II and III
22. (d) III and IV 23. (d) Bangladesh
24. (d) Indo-Soviet Treaty of Friendship-1999
25. (c) 2 1 4 3 26. (a) 2 3 4 1
27. (a) Both Statement I and Statement II are true.
28. (d) Statement I is false, but Statement II is true.
29. (a) Both A and R are true and R is the correct explanation of A.
30. (b) Both A and R are true, but R is not the correct explanation of A.
31. (b) Both A and R are true, but R is not the correct explanation of A.
32. (i) (a) As it is moving towards the formation of Constituent Assembly that will write the Constitution.
(ii) (b) They want the Constitution to include the radical programmes of social and economic restructuring.
(iii) (a) Political groups were deeply suspicious regarding the role of Indian Government in the future of Nepal.
(iv) (b) Seven Party Alliance
33. (i) (d) All of the above (ii) (d) Both (a) and (b)
(iii) (d) Both (a) and (b)
(iv) (a) democracy was never developed and encouraged in Pakistan.
34. (i) (b) Democratic values can gain support even in economically diverse societies.
(ii) (b) Democratic principles have universal appeal across various social groups.
(iii) Economic prosperity is not a necessary condition for supporting democracy. People in both wealthy and less economically developed nations demonstrate strong support for democratic values. This challenges the traditional belief that democracy thrives only in prosperous societies, suggesting that democratic ideals can resonate with citizens regardless of their country's economic status.
35. (i) (b) To enhance mutual support.
(ii) (b) To establish free and fair market place.
(iii) SAARC promotes regional co-operation and development among South Asian nations, fostering economic, social and cultural collaboration. Its significance lies in creating platforms like SAFTA for trade and regional unity. However, political tensions, especially between India and Pakistan, have hindered progress, limiting SAARC's effectiveness in achieving its goals.

Subjective Questions

Very Short Answer Type Questions

1. Name any four countries that are included in 'South Asia'. **CBSE Term II 2022**

Ans. Countries that are included in 'South Asia' are

(i) India (ii) Pakistan (iii) Nepal (iv) Sri Lanka

2. Show with the help of any two examples the interference of military in the administration of Pakistan. **CBSE Term II 2022**

Ans. Two examples of interference of military in administration of Pakistan are as follows

(i) There was dissatisfaction against. General Ayub Khan's administration of the country. This gave way to a military takeover under General Yahya Khan.

(ii) General Pervez Musharraf took the command in 1999 and removed PM Nawaz Sharif. General Pervez Musharraf got himself elected as the President in 2001.

3. Which political party won all the seats in the 1970 elections in East Pakistan and under whose leadership? **CBSE 2024**

Ans. In the 1970 elections in East Pakistan, the Awami League won all the seats. The party, led by Sheikh Mujibur Rahman, secured an overwhelming victory by winning 160 out of 162 seats. This victory gave the Awami League a clear mandate, setting the stage for the demand for greater autonomy and eventually leading to the independence of Bangladesh.

4. Why did the people of East Pakistan region resent the domination of West Pakistan? Explain the reason. **CBSE 2024**

Ans. The people of East Pakistan resented the domination of West Pakistan due to political, economic and cultural disparities. They felt marginalised, as power and resources were concentrated in the West. Language discrimination, particularly against Bengali, further fueled their grievances. The lack of political representation and unequal development led to a strong desire for autonomy, ultimately culminating in the push for independence.

5. Explain any two reasons for protests by the people of East Pakistan against West Pakistan prior to the creation of Bangladesh. **CBSE 2024 C**

Ans. Reasons for Protests by the People of East Pakistan Against West Pakistan were as follows

- **Marginalisation of Bengali Culture and Language** Imposition of Urdu over Bengali led to protests as it undermined East Pakistan's cultural identity.
- **Lack of Fair Representation** East Pakistan faced under-representation in administration and politics despite having a larger population.

6. Describe the role of Government of India in the ethnic struggle of Sri Lanka.

Ans. The role of Government of India in the ethnic struggle of Sri Lanka is as follows

- It has tried to negotiate with the Sri Lankan Government on different occasions.
- In 1987, the Indian Government signed an accord with Sri Lanka and sent troops to stabilise relations between the Sri Lankan Government and the Tamils. However Indian Peace Keeping Force did not achieve its objective and was pulled out of Sri Lanka in 1989.

7. Suggest any two measures to have good relations with Pakistan.

Or **Suggest any two measures to improve relations between India and Pakistan.** **CBSE 2019, 2023**

Ans. Two measures to have good relations with Pakistan are as follows

(i) Pakistan must stop helping the terrorist.

(ii) Cultural delegates from both the countries must visit each other frequently.

8. What is Indus River Water Treaty? Mention its significance also.

Ans. Indus River Treaty is a treaty signed between India and Pakistan by the mediation of World Bank in 1960 over the issue of sharing rivers of the Indus basin.

The treaty is still significant as it has survived despite many military conflicts between the two countries.

9. What kind of relationship India has with Maldives?

Ans. India and Maldives shares a warm and cordial relationship. In November, 1988, when some Tamil mercenaries from Sri Lanka attacked the Maldives, the Indian Air Force and Navy reacted quickly to the Maldives request to help to stop the invasion.

India has also contributed towards the island's economic development, tourism and fisheries.

10. Describe any two problems between India and Pakistan. **CBSE Term II 2022**

Ans. Two problems between India and Pakistan are as follows

(i) The conflict over Kashmir is the major problem and reason for many wars that took place in the past.

(ii) Strategic issues are also evident among these countries like the control of the Siachen Glacier and over acquisition of arms.

11. Comprehend the significance of SAFTA. Diksha App

Ans. The South Asian Free Trade Area (SAFTA) aims to enhance regional trade and economic co-operation among South Asian countries. By reducing tariffs and trade barriers, SAFTA promotes economic integration, boosts intra-regional trade and fosters development.

Its significance lies in creating a more competitive market, leadership and facilitating collaboration among member states for sustainable economic growth.

Short Answer Type Question

1. South Asia stands for diversity in every sense and yet constitutes one geopolitical space. Justify the statement. CBSE Term II 2022

Ans. Yes, South Asia stands for diversity in every sense and yet constitutes one geopolitical space because

(i) The mighty Himalayas in the North and the vast Indian Ocean, the Arabian Sea and the Bay of Bengal in the South-West and East respectively provide a natural insularity to the region which is largely responsible for the linguistic, social and cultural distinctiveness of the sub-continent.

(ii) Though the various countries in South Asia do not have the same kind of political systems but still democracy has become an accepted norm in this region.

2. "Democracy is an accepted norm in the entire region of South Asia". Explain the statement. CBSE Term II 2022

Ans. Democracy is becoming the first choice of the people of South Asia. According to a survey conducted, the results show that all the five countries in the South Asia region supports democracy. People belonging to different religions, ordinary citizens, rich as well as poor, all view the idea of democracy positively and support the institutions of representative democracy.

For instance

(i) Nepal has transformed into a democracy from monarchy.

(ii) Sri Lanka and India have successfully operated a democratic system since their independence from the British.

(iii) Bhutan transformed from monarchy to democracy.

(iv) Maldives evolved from sultanate to republic with a Presidential form along with Multi-Party system.

Thus, it can be concluded that, "Democracy is an accepted norm in the entire region of South Asia".

3. Analyse any two reasons for the problems that India has with its smaller neighbours. CBSE 2024 C

Ans. Two reasons for the problems that India has with its smaller Neighbours are as follows

(i) **Water Sharing Disputes** Differences over sharing the waters of Ganga and Brahmaputra create tensions with neighbors like Bangladesh.

(ii) **Security Concerns** Issues like illegal immigration, support for anti-India groups, and refusal to co-operate on troop movement in critical areas heighten mistrust.

4. Describe any four consequences of Bangladesh war of 1971.

Ans. The consequences of Bangladesh war of 1971 are as follows

(i) India supported the demand of East Pakistan financially and militarily.

(ii) The war of 1971 made Pakistani forces to surrender in East Pakistan.

(iii) Bangladesh was formed as an independent country.

(iv) Bangladesh drafted its Constitution declaring faith in secularism, democracy and socialism.

5. "Nepal and India enjoy a very special relationship that has very few parallels in the world". Justify the statement with any three suitable arguments.

Ans. Nepal and India share a very special relationship that can be illustrated with three suitable examples as follows

(i) A treaty between the two countries allows the citizens of the two countries to travel and work in the other county without visas and passports.

(ii) Nepal being a landlocked country enjoys easier access to sea through Indian territory for the purpose of trade and commerce with other nations.

(iii) Both countries share together trade, scientific co-operation, common natural resources, electricity generation and interlocking water management grids.

6. State the democratic transition in Nepal.

Or **Explain the process of transition from monarchy to democracy in Nepal.** CBSE Term II 2022

Ans. Nepal's democratic transition is nearly complete as it has experienced a once-in a lifetime event by forming a Constituent Assembly to draft the country's Constitution. Some people in Nepal believed that a nominal monarchy was required for Nepal to maintain its historical past. The Maoist organisations agreed to put their armed struggle on hold. They desired that the Constitution include significant social and economic transformation programmes.

These programmes were opposed by all the SPA's parties. The Indian Government and its role in Nepal's future were also viewed with suspicion by the Maoists and other political organisations. In the year 2008, Nepal became a democratic republic after abolishing the monarchy. A new Constitution was adopted by Nepal in 2015.

7. Highlight any two reasons for the ethnic conflict in Sri Lanka. **CBSE Term II 2022**

Ans. Reasons for the ethnic conflict in Sri Lanka are stated below

(i) Sinhalese people were the largest ethnic group of Sri Lanka and after the independence, this group dominated the politics of the state.

Tamils were the people who had migrated from India to Sri Lanka and settled there. According to Sinhala nationalists, Sri Lanka should not give concessions to Tamils as this state belongs only to Sinhala's.

(ii) The neglect of Tamils concerns and interests resulted in militant Tamil nationalism. The militant organisation Liberation Tigers of Tamil Eelam (LTTE) was working since 1983 onwards with the army of Sri Lanka. This demanded for a separate country belong to Tamil people. The North-Eastern parts of Sri Lanka were controlled by LTTE.

8. "Despite the mixed record of democratic experiences, the people of South Asian countries share the aspiration for democracy." Justify the statement with two suitable arguments. **CBSE 2025**

Ans. The statement highlights that despite challenges in democratic governance, the people of South Asian countries continue to aspire for democracy. This can be justified with the following arguments

Struggles for Democratic Rights In South Asia, people have consistently fought for democracy, even in countries with a history of military or authoritarian rule. For example, in Pakistan, despite military interventions, the public has repeatedly pushed for democratic elections. Similarly, in Nepal, mass movements led to the establishment of democracy in 1990 and again in 2006 after the monarchy was abolished.

High Voter Participation and Democratic Movements Countries like India, Bangladesh and Sri Lanka have witnessed high voter turnout, showing people's strong belief in democratic participation. Even in nations facing political instability, such as Myanmar and the Maldives, citizens have actively supported democratic reforms. The demand for free and fair elections, civil rights and accountable governments reflects the deep-rooted aspiration for democracy in the region.

9. How does India's relationship with Bhutan benefit both countries?

Ans. India and Bhutan share a special relationship with no major conflicts between them. Bhutan has helped India by removing guerrillas and militants from North-Eastern India operating in its territory, ensuring greater security for India. India is also involved in large-scale hydroelectric projects in Bhutan, which contribute to the country's energy development. Additionally, India remains Bhutan's largest source of development aid, supporting its growth and infrastructure. This close co-operation strengthens both nations, ensuring mutual benefits in areas such as security, energy and economic development.

10. "India enjoys a very special relationship with Bhutan". Support the statement with two examples. **CBSE 2024 C**

Ans. India enjoys a very special relationship with Bhutan. Following two examples support the statement

(i) **Development Co-operation through Hydroelectric Projects** India is actively involved in building large hydroelectric projects in Bhutan, which are crucial for Bhutan's economic development. Additionally, India is Bhutan's largest source of development aid, reflecting the strong economic ties between the two nations.

(ii) **Support in Regional Security** Bhutan has been instrumental in helping India maintain regional security by taking decisive steps to eliminate guerrillas and militants operating in North-East India. This cooperation strengthens the strategic relationship between the two countries.

11. "SAARC has taken a major regional initiative in South Asian States to evolve co-operation through multilateral means". Justify the statement with two examples. **CBSE 2024**

Or **How is the South Asian Association for Regional Cooperation (SAARC) a major regional initiative by South Asian states to evolve co-operation through multilateral means? Assess.** **CBSE 2025**

Ans. The South Asian Association for Regional Co-operation (SAARC), established in 1985, aims to strengthen co-operation through multilateral efforts.

- One example is the South Asian Free Trade Area (SAFTA) agreement, signed in 2004 and implemented in 2006. This agreement promotes regional economic co-operation by reducing trade tariffs among SAARC countries.
- Another example is the shared interest in addressing regional challenges such as poverty, environmental issues and security. It demonstrates that despite political tensions, co-operation for mutual benefit continues to be a priority in South Asia.

Long Answer Type Questions

1. Explain the factors responsible for Pakistan's failure in building a stable democracy. Describe any two pro-democracy factors present in Pakistan which can pave the way for establishing a lasting democratic set-up over there. CBSE 2024

Or **Why could democrary not succeed in Pakistan. Analyse any three reasons?** CBSE 2022 Term II

Ans. Pakistan does not have a good experience with democracy. Several factors contributed to failure in building a stable democracy in Pakistan.

They are as follows

- There was always social dominance of military, clergy and landowning aristocracy which resulted in downfall of democratic government and existence of military government.
- Due to Pakistan's conflict with India, pro- military groups in Pakistan got strengthened.
- According to these pro-military groups, political parties and democracy is defective and there is a chance of harm to the security of Pakistan by narrow minded parties and disorganised democracy. And this way, justification for army's stay in power is provided. Lack of international support has been there in Pakistan for democratic rule.
- US and some Western countries moved Pakistan towards authoritarian rule for their own benefits. Military rule in Pakistan is supposed to be the protector of Western interests in West Asia, South Asia as 'Global Islamic Terrorism' and nuclear arsenal can only be controlled by military.

2. Explain the ethnic conflict in Sri Lanka and any two consequences of it. CBSE 2019

Ans. The democratic setup of Sri Lanka was disturbed by the ethnic conflict among the Sinhalese and Tamil origin people.

The bone of contention was the region of Ceylon which was represented by the majority Sinhala group. They opposed the migration and settlements of Tamilians from India in their region. According to the group, Sri Lanka was only for Sinhala people and not for Tamils. This attitude of Sinhala people led to the establishment of Liberation Tigers of Tamil Eelam (LTTE), a militant organisation, which desired for a separate country.

The consequences of ethnic conflict led to the following situations

(i) There was a pressure on the Government of India by the Tamils of Indian origin to intervene in the matter. Hence, the Government of India tried to negotiate with the Government of Sri Lanka on Tamil's question. But direct involvement was in the year 1987. India conceded to send troops to Sri Lanka for the protection of relations between Tamils and Sri Lankan Government. Eventually, the Indian troops got into a fight with LTTE.

(ii) The presence of Indian troops was not liked by many Sri Lankans and hence in 1989, the Indian Peace Keeping Force (IPKF) pulled out of Sri Lanka without attaining its objective.

3. Discuss some of the conflicts and issues between India and Pakistan which are of an international nature.

Ans. Some of the conflicts and issues between India and Pakistan of an international nature are discussed below

- A conflict over Kashmir is the major issue between both the countries. The Pakistani Government claimed that Kashmir belonged to it. Wars between India and Pakistan in 1947-48 and 1965 failed to solve the issue. In 1971, India won a decisive war against Pakistan but the Kashmir issue remain unsettled.
- Conflicts related to strategic issues are also visible among these countries like the control of Siachen Glacier and over acquisition of arms. Suspicious nature of both the governments led to border disruptions especially in the Kashmir region.
- The Indian Government also believes that Pakistan had aided the pro-Khalistani militants with arms and ammunitions during the period of 1985-1995.
- Both countries also have problems related to sharing of Indus river waters. With the help of World Bank in 1960, both countries negotiated over this issue. The two countries are not in agreement over the demarcation line in Sir Creek in the Rann of Kutch. With this dispute, the issue of usage of resources in the area adjoining Sir Creek is related.

4. Explain India's changing relationship with Pakistan.

Ans. India's relationship with Pakistan has evolved over the years, marked by periods of hostility and efforts at reconciliation. Recent efforts towards peace and co-operation highlight both challenges and opportunities for improving ties

- **Confidence-Building Measures** Agreements have been signed between the two nations to reduce tensions, particularly in the area of security, indicating mutual efforts to stabilise relations.
- **People-to-People Connections** Social activities and collaborations by prominent personalities have been instrumental in fostering a friendly atmosphere.
- **Transportation Links** The opening of multiple bus routes and initiatives like the Samjhauta Express (1976) after the Simla Agreement have helped improve people-to-people connections.

- **Trade Relations** Trade between the two parts of Punjab has seen significant growth, supported by easier visa policies, boosting cross-border economic interactions.
- **Kartarpur Corridor** The finalisation of this corridor, especially post the 2019 Pulwama terror attack, has provided a hope for dialogue and reconciliation.

India's relationship with Pakistan remains complex, influenced by historical, political and security concerns. While initiatives like the Kartarpur Corridor signify progress, challenges such as terrorism and cross-border tensions continue to test the path to sustainable peace.

5. Despite their differences, India and Bangladesh do co-operate on many issues. What are the key areas of their collaboration?

Ans. India and Bangladesh, despite historical differences, have found common ground in several areas of co-operation. Over the past 20 years, economic relations between the two countries have grown significantly. Bangladesh is an important partner in India's Look East (now Act East) Policy, aiming to strengthen connectivity with Southeast Asia through Myanmar. The two countries also work closely on disaster management and environmental issues, sharing expertise and resources for mutual benefit. In 2015, India and Bangladesh exchanged certain enclaves, a significant step in resolving border disputes. Furthermore, both countries have made efforts to identify common security threats, such as terrorism and climate change, and work together on addressing them.

6. Not all conflicts in South Asia are between India and its neighbours. Justify the statement with the help of examples.

Ans. Not all conflicts in South Asia are between India and its neighbors. For example, Nepal and Bhutan have had disagreements over the migration of ethnic Nepalese into Bhutan, which has created tensions. Similarly, Bangladesh and Myanmar have faced issues regarding the migration of Rohingyas, leading to disputes between the two countries. Bangladesh and Nepal have also had differences over the management and sharing of Himalayan river waters, a key issue in the region. While India does have its own conflicts with its neighbors, the region's complex geography often makes India a central player in most of these disputes. However, the conflicts involving Nepal, Bhutan, Bangladesh and Myanmar demonstrate that tensions in South Asia are not limited to India's relations alone.

7. Describe any two factors responsible for the economic growth in Sri Lanka despite the internal conflicts. **CBSE 2024**

Ans. Two factors responsible for Sri Lanka's economic growth despite internal conflicts are as following

(i) **Tourism and Export Economy** Sri Lanka has capitalised on its natural beauty and cultural heritage to attract tourism, generating significant revenue. Additionally, the country is a major exporter of tea, textiles and rubber, contributing to its economic stability and growth, even during times of conflict.

(ii) **Foreign Remittances and Investments** A large Sri Lankan diaspora, particularly in the Middle East, has sent remittances back home, boosting the economy. Additionally, foreign investments in infrastructure, aided by political stability after the civil war, have fueled growth in sectors like construction, services and transport.

8. Describe the circumstances that led to the Bangladesh War in 1971. **CBSE 2024**

Ans. The Bangladesh War of 1971 was sparked by rising tensions between East and West Pakistan. East Pakistan (now Bangladesh) felt marginalised, as political power and economic resources were concentrated in West Pakistan. The situation worsened when the Awami League, led by Sheikh Mujibur Rahman, won the 1970 elections but was denied power. In response, Pakistan's military launched a brutal crackdown in East Pakistan in March 1971, leading to widespread atrocities. This triggered a popular uprising, with millions of refugees fleeing to India. India supported the independence movement and after a brief war between India and Pakistan, East Pakistan became the independent nation of Bangladesh in December 1971.

Picture Based Questions

1. Study the given cartoon and answer the questions that follow.

(i) Who are the two leaders shown in the cartoon?

(a) Narendra Modi and Nawaz Sharif
(b) Dr. Manmohan Singh and General Pervez Musharraf
(c) Atal Bihari Vajpayee and Benazir Bhutto
(d) Indira Gandhi and General Zia-ul-Haq

Ans. (b) Dr. Manmohan Singh and General Pervez Musharraf

(ii) What could be the two issues discussed by the leaders?

(a) Climate change and economic trade agreements
(b) Kashmir and terrorism
(c) Water disputes and border infrastructure
(d) Tourism and cultural exchanges

Ans. (b) Kashmir and terrorism

(iii) What was the outcome of their discussion?

(a) Both nations signed a trade deal
(b) No agreement was reached, and talks were discontinued
(c) Conflicts were to be resolved peacefully, and transport services were resumed
(d) A new border fencing initiative was launched

Ans. (c) Conflicts were to be resolved peacefully, and transport services were resumed

(iv) Which transport services were agreed to be resumed between India and Pakistan after the talks?

(a) Roadways and waterways
(b) Bus, train and air services
(c) Air services and shipping routes
(d) Highways and metro services

Ans. (b) Bus, train and air services

2. Observe the cartoon given below and answer the questions that follow.

(i) What does the cartoon primarily represent?

(a) General Pervez Musharraf's foreign policy initiatives
(b) The dual role of General Pervez Musharraf as President and Army General of Pakistan
(c) The economic challenges faced by Pakistan
(d) The relationship between Pakistan and India

Ans. (b) The dual role of General Pervez Musharraf as President and Army General of Pakistan

(ii) Which Prime Minister of Pakistan was removed by General Musharraf in a military coup?

(a) Benazir Bhutto (b) Nawaz Sharif
(c) Imran Khan (d) Yousaf Raza Gillani

Ans. (b) Nawaz Sharif

(iii) What does the phrase "I'm always good at calculations" in the cartoon represent?

(a) Musharraf's expertise in mathematics
(b) Musharraf's intention to balance foreign relations
(c) Musharraf's desire to control Pakistan militarily and administratively
(d) Musharraf's focus on economic calculations

Ans. (c) Musharraf's desire to control Pakistan militarily and administratively

(iv) Why did General Musharraf combine military and administrative power in Pakistan?

(a) To improve economic growth
(b) To gain international recognition
(c) To strengthen his hold on power as President
(d) To foster peace with neighboring countries

Ans. (c) To strengthen his hold on power as President

3. Observe the cartoon given below and answer the questions that follow.

(i) Interpret the role of two key players who are also interested in the region.

(ii) Is there any commonality between their perspective?

(iii) What does the second cartoon represent?

Ans. (i) China and USA are the two key players in the region. Sino-Indian relations have improved significantly during the last ten years. As shown in the cartoon, two leaders from India and China are exchanging agreements regarding trade, commerce and economy. It is being resented by Pakistan who wants China to stick to 'Core' issues (border issue) with India.

(ii) Both China and USA wants to have economic ties i.e. trade and commerce in the region in this age of liberalisation and globalisation.

(iii) Second cartoon represents the role of USA in South Asian region. The US has good relations with both India and Pakistan and therefore work as a moderator in India-Pakistan relations. In the cartoon, the US has been shown as a reference in tennis match between India and Pakistan.

4. Study the cartoon given below related to Sri Lanka and answer the questions that follow. **CBSE 2024**

(i) Tiger represents which community as shown in the cartoon?
(ii) Which community does the lion shown in the cartoon represent?
(iii) What did the balancing act at by Rajapakshe aims at? Explain

Ans. (i) Tiger shown in the cartoon represents Tamil community.
(ii) Lion shown in the cartoon represents Sinhalese community.
(iii) Rajapakshe action aims at balancing the problem of Sinhalese and Tamils so as to avoid Civil War.

5. **Study the given cartoon and answer the questions that follows.**

(i) What is the likely reason for the group of people walking away from the SAARC summit in the cartoon?
(a) They have lost interest in the discussions.
(b) Political tensions between member states.
(c) The summit was canceled due to a natural disaster.
(d) The members have already agreed on key issues.

Ans. (b) Political tensions between member states.

(ii) Which of the following countries is not represented at the SAARC table in the cartoon?
(a) Afghanistan (b) Maldives
(c) Bangladesh (d) Sri Lanka

Ans. (a) Afghanistan

(iii) According to the image, which country's relations with Pakistan have been a major hurdle for SAARC's progress?
(a) Nepal (b) Bhutan
(c) India (d) Bangladesh

Ans. (c) India

(iv) What message is the cartoonist likely conveying about the effectiveness of SAARC Summits?
(a) SAARC Summits are well-attended and productive.
(b) SAARC Summits face challenges due to member disagreements.
(c) SAARC Summits primarily focus on cultural exchange.
(d) SAARC Summits are focused on economic development.

Ans. (b) SAARC Summits face challenges due to member disagreements.

Map Based Question

1. **In the given outline map of South Asia, five countries have been marked as A, B, C, D and E. Identify them on the basis of the information given below and write their correct names in your answer book with their respective serial number of the information used and the alphabet concerned as per the following format.**

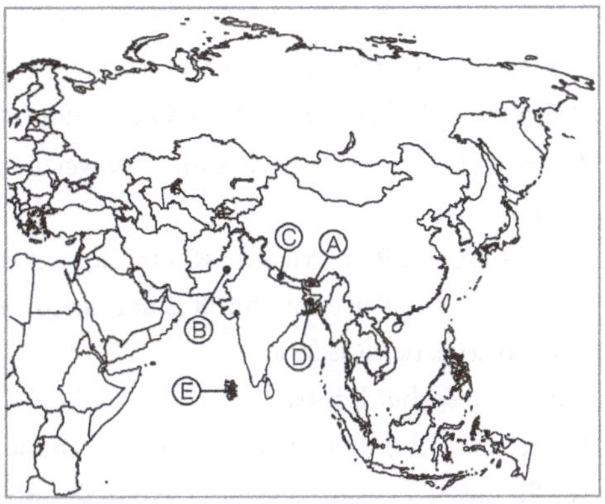

Sr. No. of the Information Used	Alphabet Concerned	Name of the Country
(i)		
(ii)		
(iii)		
(iv)		
(v)		

Information used

(i) The country has experienced both civilian as well as military rule.
(ii) Democracy was restored in this country in 2006.
(iii) This country is still a monarchy.
(iv) The Parliament of this country voted unanimously to introduce multi-party system in June, 2005.
(v) This country is a part of India's 'Look East Policy via Myanmar'.

Ans.

Sr. No. of the Information used	Alphabet Concerned	Name of the Country
(i) The country has experienced both civilian as well as military rule	B	Pakistan
(ii) Democracy was restored in the country in 2006.	C	Nepal
(iii) This country is still a monarchy.	A	Bhutan
(iv) The Parliament of this country voted unanimously to introduce multi-party system in June, 2005.	E	Maldives
(v) This country is a part of India's 'Look East Policy through Myanmar'.	D	Bangladesh

SELF ASSESSMENT TEST

Objective Type Questions

1. Which two countries have a democratic system since their independence from British?
   (a) Bhutan and Pakistan (b) Sri Lanka and Nepal (c) India and Sri Lanka (d) Pakistan and Bangladesh
2. **Assertion** (A) Pakistan has instable democratic history.
   Reason (R) There military is more powerful than the democratically elected government.
   Codes
   (a) Both A and R are true and R is the correct explanation of A.
   (b) Both A and R are true, but R is not the correct explanation of A.
   (c) A is true, but R is false.
   (d) A is false, but R is true.
3. Which one of the following statements about ethnic conflict in Sri Lanka is false?
   (a) Politics in Sri Lanka openely favoured the Sinhalas.
   (b) Interests of Tamil were neglected.
   (c) Liberation Tigers of Tamil Elam were supported by all the SAARC countries.
   (d) There was no political equality in Sri Lanka.
4. It is one of the first developing countries to successfully control the population growth. Identify the country being referred to here.
   (a) Nepal (b) Bhutan (c) Sri Lanka (d) Pakistan
5. What is a significant challenge to Sino-India relations, despite their improvement in recent years?
   (a) China's strategic partnership with Pakistan (b) China's economic showdown
   (c) India's growing ties with the US. (d) The territorial disputes between India and Nepal

Very Short Answer Type Questions

6. Why South Asian countries prefer democracy as a form of government?
7. Why military rule is regarded as the best option in Pakistan?
8. Which community dominates the politics of Sri-Lanka?
9. When was the sultanate abolished from Maldives?
10. How has Bhutan assisted India in dealing with militants?

Short Answer Type Questions

11. Mention any three efforts towards peace and co-operation between India and Pakistan.
12. Highlight the issues in India-Bangladesh relation.
13. How has the United States been involved in South Asia after the Cold War?
14. Why do some neighbouring countries have concerns about SAFTA?

Long Answer Type Questions

15. What are the common problems of South Asian Countries? Elaborate.
16. Write a brief account of India's relationship with Sri Lanka.

04 CHAPTER

After the fall of Soviet Union, there was the discussion over the role of international organisations. In the emerging world there was a need for the re-organisation of international organisations to deal with new challenges like rise of US power.

International Organisations

▼ **YOUR STUDY GOALS**

4.1 Need of International Organisations
4.2 India and the UN Reforms
4.3 The UN in Unipolar World

▼ **YOUR PRACTICE GOAL**

- Objective Type Questions (39 Qs ; MCQs, A-R, Statements, Matching, Passage Based)
- Subjective Questions (17 VSAs, 5 SAs, 7 LAs, 2 Picture Based, 1 Map Based)

4.1 Need of International Organisations

- International organisations are not the solution to everything, but they play a key role.
  - It help countries co-operate to make better living conditions for all.
  - It enables countries to discuss issues and find peaceful solutions.
  - It helps with matter of war and peace.
  - It helps in dealing with global issues like global warming.
  - In today's world **United Nation (UN)** is the most important international organisation. It represents the hope of humanity for peace and progress. International organisation is not a **super state**[1] with authority over its members. It is created by the countries by agreeing among themselves.
- However, various events like Lebanon crises of 2006 revealed the ineffectiveness of United Nation Organisation (UNO).

1 **Super state** It refers to state superior to other states.

International Manefary Fund [IMF]

- It is an international organisation that oversees and regulate International Financial Institutions.
- It has 190 members.
- Member countries do not enjoy an equal say.
- G7 members have 41.29 per cent of vote share of IMF.
- India has 2.64 per cent vote share.

Evolution of the United Nations (UN)

- After the **First World War,** countries decided to create international organisation to deal with conflicts. This resulted in the formation of **League of Nation**. However, league could not prevent the **Second World War** (1939-45) .
- After the Second World War, UN was formed in **1945** as a successor to the League of Nations.
- UN was formed by signing of the **United Nations Charter**[2] by 51 states.

Objectives of United Nations (UN)

The main objectives of the United Nations are as follows

- To prevent international conflicts.
- To facilitate the co-operation among states.
- To stop conflicts between states escalating into war.
- To limit the extent of hostilities in the war.
- To bring countries together to improve the prospects of socio-economic development all over the world.

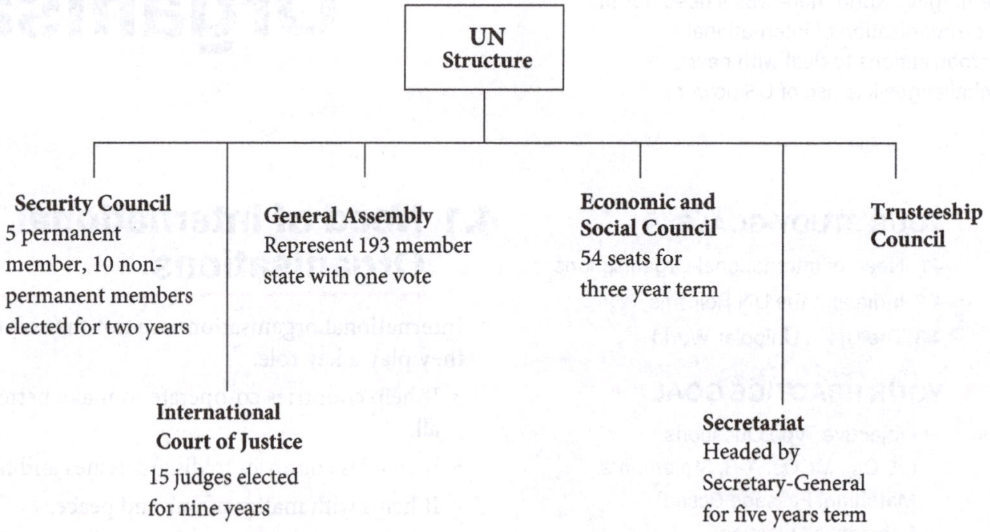

▲ *Structure of UN*

Members of United Nations (UN)

- By 2011, the UN had 193 member states.
- Five permanent members of UN Security Council are: US, UK, China, France, Russia.
- Non-permanent members of UNSC cannot be re-elected immediately after completing a term of two years. They do not have any Veto Power.

Special Power of Permanent Members

The Veto Power allows as permanent member of the UNSC to block a decision by voting against it. Even if all other permanent and non-permanent members support a decision, a single negative vote for any permanent member can stop the decision.

2 **United Nations Charter** It is the Constitution of UN to deal with the objectives of the UN.

Secretary-General of UN

Secretary-General is the UN's most visible public figure, and the representative head.

Antonio Guterres

- Antonio Guterres is the current Secretary-General of the UN. He is the ninth Secretary-General of the UN.
- He became Secretary-General on 1st January, 2017.
- Guterres was the Prime Minister of Portugal from 1995 to 2002.
- He served as the UN High Commissioner for Refugees from 2005 to 2015.

Changes in the World After the Cold War

After the Cold War, following changes have occurred in the world

- The Soviet Union has collapsed.
- The US has emerged as the strongest power.
- The relationship between Russia and US is much more co-operative.
- China is emerging as great power and India is also growing rapidly.
- The economies of Asia are growing at high rate.
- Membership of UN has increased.
- World is facing new set of challenges like genocide, civil war, terrorism etc.

Reforms in UN

- Reforms and improvements are essential for any organisation to adopt to the changing world and the UN is no exception.
- Two basic kind of reforms needed by the UN are as follows

Reform of the Structure and Processes of UN

- In 1992, the UN General Assembly adopted the resolution reflecting three main issues over the reform of the UN Security Council (UNSC)
  - The UNSC no longer represent the contemporary political realities.
  - Its decisions reflect only Western values and interests and are dominated by few powers.
  - It lacks equitable representation.
- On 1st January, 1997, UN General Secretary **Kofi Annan** proposed criteria for inclusion of new permanent and non-permanent members of the UNSC. The new member should be
  - A major economic power.
  - A major military power.
  - A substantial contributor to the UN budget.
  - Big nation in terms of its population.
  - A nation that respects democracy and human rights.
  - A country that would make the council more representative of the world's diversity in terms of geography, economic systems and culture.
  - Review of the issues that fall within the jurisdiction of the organisation.
  - There are differences on the issues to be given greater priority within the jurisdiction of the UN.
  - Some countries and experts wanted the organisation to play a greater or more effective role in peace and security missions, while others wanted its role to be confined to development and humanitarian works such as, health, education, environment, population control, human rights, gender and social justice.

Major contributors to the UN regular budget for 2019

No.	Member State	%	No.	Member State	%
1	USA	22.0	12	Australia	2.2
2	China	12.0	13	Spain	2.1
3	Japan	8.5	14	Turkey	1.3
4	Germany	6.0	15	Netherlands	1.3
5	UK	4.5	16	Mexico	1.2
6	France	4.4	17	Saudi Arabia	1.1
7	Italy	3.3	18	Switzerland	1.1
8	Brazil	2.9	19	Argentina	0.9
9	Canada	2.7	20	Sweden	0.9
10	Russia	2.4	21	India	0.8
11	Republic of Korea	2.2			

Reforms in Jurisdiction of the UN

- In 2005, UN meeting was held in which it was decided to take following steps to make the UN more relevant to the changing world
  - Creation of a Peacebuilding Commission.
  - Acceptance of the responsibility of the International Community in case of failures of national governments to protect their own citizens from atrocities.
  - Establishment of a Human Rights Council (operational since 19th June, 2006).
  - Agreements to achieve the Millennium Development Goals (MDGs).
  - Condemnation of terrorism in all its forms and manifestations.
  - Creation of a Democracy Fund.
  - An agreement to wind up the Trusteeship Council.

World Bank

- It was created in **1944** during the Second World War.
- Its activities are focused on the developing countries.
- It works for human development, agriculture and rural development, environmental protection, infrastructure and governance.
- It provides loans and grants to the member-countries.
- It exercises enormous influence on the economic policies of developing countries.
- It is often criticised for setting the economic agenda of the poorer nations, attaching tough conditions to its loans and forcing free market reforms.

Quick Test 1

1 Which organisation was established as the successor to the league of nations.?
2 How many countries signed the UN Charter?
3 Name the two permanent member of UN.
4 How many member states are part of UN?
5 Who is ninth Secretary-General of UN?

4.2 India and the UN Reforms

- India has supported the restructuring of the UN.
- India supports a stronger role for the UN in fostering development and co-operation among states.
- It believes that a strengthened and revitalised UN is desirable in a changing world.
- According to India, development should be a central focus of the UN, as it is crucial for maintaining international peace and security.

Concerns about the Security Council

- The composition of the (UNSC) has remained mostly unchanged, while the membership of the UN General Assembly has grown. India believes the static nature of the Security Council has weakened its representative character.
- An expanded Security Council with broader representation would gain greater support from the global community.
- India argues that developing country should have more role in decision-making of UNSC as its decisions directly impacts them.

India's Proposal for UNSC Expansion

- India supports an increase in both permanent and non-permanent members of the Security Council.
- The Council's activities have expanded in last few years and its success depends on global political support.
- India argues for the inclusion of more developing countries in the Security Council.

India's Bid for Permanent Membership

- India aspires to become a permanent member of a re-structured UNSC.
- Justifications for India's claim includes the following
    - India is the **most populous country,** representing almost 20 per cent of the global population.
    - It is the **largest democracy** in the world.
    - India has participated in all the initiatives of the UN.
    - India has played a significant role in UN **peacekeeping**[3].
    - India's **economic growth** adds to its claim for a permanent seat.
    - India has also made the regular financial contributions to the UN and has never failed on its payment.
    - India is aware that permanent membership of the Security Council also has symbolic importance. This greater status is an advantage to a country in the conduct of its foreign policy.

Challenges to India's Bid

- Some countries like **Pakistan**, oppose India's inclusion due to their troubled relationship.
- Concerns about **India's nuclear capabilities** and its disputes with Pakistan are cited as potential problems.
- There are calls for other emerging powers such as Brazil, Germany, Japan and South Africa to also be considered for permanent seats.

3 **Peacekeeping** It is a mechanism for restoring peace and security by sending UN controlled troops in the affected areas.

- Africa and South America are **currently un-represented** in the permanent membership, leading to demands for their inclusion.

  Given these concerns, it may be difficult for India or other countries to become permanent members of the UNSC in the near future.

World Trade Organisation [WTO]

- It is an international organisation which sets the rules for global trade.
- It was set up in 1995 as the successor to the General Agreement on Trade and Tariffs (GATT) created after the Second World War.
- It has 164 members (as on 29th July, 2016).
- All decisions are taken unanimously.

IAEA

- The International Atomic Energy Agency (IAEA) was established in 1957.
- It aims to implement US President Dwight Eisenhower's 'Atoms for Peace' proposal.
- It seeks to promote the peaceful use of nuclear energy and to prevent its use for military purposes.
- IAEA teams regularly inspect nuclear facilities all over the world to ensure that civilian IAEA reactors are not being used for military purposes.

5.3 The UN in Unipolar World

After the collapse of the Soviet Union, the US became the dominant superpower without any serious rivals. Many countries hope that UN reforms could help the organisation manage a world dominated by the US, acting as a balance against US dominance.

- The question is whether the UN can balance US dominance.
- The UN could help maintain dialogue between the US and the rest of the world.
- The goal is to prevent the US from acting unilaterally without considering other countries.

Influence of the US in the UN

- The US is the **largest financial contributor** to the UN, giving it substantial leverage.
- The **UN headquarters** is located in the US, further boosting American influence.
- The US has many **nationals** in key positions within the UN bureaucracy.
- The US **Veto Power** on the Security Council allows it to block decisions it opposes, ensuring it has a say in shaping the UN's actions.
- It influences the selection of the UN Secretary-General.

UN in Unipolar World

- While the UN can not directly challenge US power, it still plays a role in bringing the US and the rest of the world into discussions on global issues.
- Despite frequent criticism of the UN, US leaders recognise the value of the organisation in addressing global challenges and promoting dialogue among 190+ nations.
- The UN provides a platform for the rest of the world to express opposition to certain US policies and influence compromises.

- Although, it is rare for the global community to be united against the US, the UN creates space for discussions and adjustments to American policies. Despite its flaws, the UN is essential for maintaining global co-operation.
- As inter-dependence among nations increases, especially through technology, the UN's role in managing global issues will become even more important.
- Governments and people will need to continue using and supporting international organisations like the UN to address shared global challenges.

Amnesty International

- Amnesty International is an NGO that campaigns for the protection of human rights all over the world.
- It promotes respect for all the human rights in the Universal Declaration of Human Rights.
- It prepares and publishes reports on human rights.
- It focuses on the misconduct of government authorities.

Human Rights Watch

- Human Rights Watch is an international NGO involved in research and promoting human rights.
- It is the largest International Human Rights Organisation in the US.
- It helped in building international coalitions like the campaigns to ban landmines, to stop the use of child soldiers and to establish the International Criminal Court.

UN Agencies

The UN has various structures and agencies. The conflicts between the states are discussed both in General Assembly and Security Council. Many agencies deal with the social and economic issues such as the World Health Organisations (WHO), United Nations Development Programme (UNDP), United Nations Human Rights Commission (UNHRC), United Nations High Commission for Refugees (UNHCR), United Nations Children's Fund (UNICEF) and the United Nations Educational, Scientific and Cultural Organisation (UNESCO) among others.

Some of the UN key agencies are discussed below

UNESCO

- The United Nations Educational, Scientific and Cultural Organisation (UNESCO) was established on 4th November, 1946. Its headquarter is located in Paris, France.
- It is a special body of the United Nations whose main objective is to promote education, natural science, society and anthropology, culture and communication. During past several years, the special work done by UNESCO has been to promote literacy, technical and educational training and independent media, etc. all across its member nations.

Objectives of UNESCO

The objectives of UNESCO are as following

- To access quality of education for everyone
- To actively provide the knowledge of science and policies for sustainable development.
- To address the challenges, whether it be social or ethical.
- It attempts to build a culture of peace in diversity and intercultural dialogue of harmony.
- To establish knowledge societies with the help of information and communication.

UNICEF

- The United Nations International Children's Emergency Fund (UNICEF) was created by the UN general assembly during its first session in 1946 to help the emergency needs of the children in post was Europe. In 1950, its programme was extended to provide long-range benefits to children of all developing countries. Later on its name was changed to United Nations Children's Fund.
- However, its acronym UNICEF continued. UNICEF is governed by 36-member Executive Board. It has its headquarter in New York and has more than 200 officers in developing countries. It has been working successfully in almost all 193 countries of the world.

Objectives of UNICEF

The main objectives of UNICEF are

- To look after children's welfare especially in developing countries.
- To provide people with low cost community based services in maternal and child health, nutrition and immunisation, etc.
- It also helps and encourages the work that promote children's health and better life in all parts of the world.

International Labour Organisations (ILO)

- The International Labour Organisation (ILO) was founded in 1919, its constitution forming part of the Treaty of versaillies. The ILO became the first specialised agency of the UN in 1946.
- The ILO is the only 'Tripartite' UN agency. It brings together representatives of governments, employers and workers to jointly shape policies and programmes. This unique arrangement gives the ILO an edge in incorporating 'real world' knowledge about the employment and work.
- The ILO is devoted to advancing opportunities for women and men to obtain decent and productive work in conditions of freedom, equity, security and human dignity.

  Its main aims are to
  - promote rights at work
  - encourage decent employment opportunities
  - enhance social protection
  - strengthen dialogue in handling work related issues.
- The ILO helps in the creation of decent jobs and the kinds of economic and working conditions that give working people and business people a stake in lasting peace, prosperity and progress.

Objectives of ILO

There are four principle strategic objectives of ILO which are as follows

(i) To promote and realise standards and fundamental principles and rights at work.
(ii) To create greater opportunities for women and men to secure decent employment.
(iii) To enhance the coverage and effectiveness of social protection for all.
(iv) To strengthen tripartism and social dialogue.

Quick Test 2

1 When did India joined the UN?
2 Is India a permanent UNSC member?
3 What is UN peacekeeping force?
4 On the basis of which proposal was the IAEA established?

Mind Map

INTERNATIONAL ORGANISATIONS

1 Need of International Organisations

Evolution of the United Nations (UN)
- UN was formed in 1945 after the world war II.
- On October 30, 1945, India joined the UN.
- The UN has 193 member states.
- The US, The UK, Russia, China and France are the permanent members of the UNSC.

Special Power to Permanent Member
- Veto Power allows a permanent member to reject a proposal.
- Even of all other permanent and non-permanent member support a decision.

UN Structure
- **Security Council** 5 permanent member, 10 non- permanent member elected for two years.
- **General Assembly** Represent193 member state with one vote.
- **Economic and Social Council** 54 members elected for three year term.
- **Trusteeship Council**
- **International Court of Justice** 15 judges elected for nine years term.
- **Secretariat** Headed by Secretary-General for five years term.

Changes in the World After the Cold War
- The Soviet Union has collapsed.
- US has emerged as the strongest power.
- The Economics of Asia are growing at high rate.
- Membership of UN has increased.
- World is facing new set of challenges.

Reforms Demanded in the UN
- After the Cold War structural and jurisdictional reforms were introduced in the UN.
- A criteria should be fixed for the inclusion of permanent and non-permanent members of the UNSC.
- Peace Building Commission and Human Rights Council were set up.

Jurisdiction of the UN
- Creation of a Peace Building Commission.
- Agreements to achieve the Millennium Development Goals.
- Condemnation of terrorism in all its forms and manifestations.
- Creation of a Democracy Fund.

2 India and the UN Reforms

India's Push for UNSC Reform
- India supported the UNSC reforms with development as the main agenda.
- India supported an increase in the number of permanent and non-permanent members.
- India claimed to become a permanent member of the UNSC.
- India's presence is crucial in UN for maintaining international peace and security.

Concerns About the Security Council
- The membership of the UN General Assembly has grown.
- India believes that static nature of the Security Council has weakened its representative character.
- An expanded Security Council with broader representation would gain greater support.
- India argues that developing country should have more role in decision-making of UNSC.

India's Bid for Permanent Membership
- Most Populous country.
- Largest democracy.
- Economic growth.
- Major role in peacekeeping mission.

Challenges to India's Bid
- Some countries have objected to India's claim like Pakistan.
- India's nuclear capabilities.
- Calls for other emerging powers such as Brazil, Germany, Japan also be considered for permanent seats.

3 The UN in the Unipolar World

Unipolar World and the Influence of the US
- The US became the dominate superpower after the collapse of Soviet Union.
- As a result, UN lost its ability to directly challenge US power.
- As interdependence increases the UN's role will become more important.

UN in Unipolar World
- UN provides platform to modify US attitude and policies.
- UN provides a platform also to the rest of the world.

Influence of the US in the UN
- Largest financial contributor.
- UN headquarters.
- US Veto Power in Security Council.
- Selection of UN Secretory-General.

Ban kimoon, UN Secretary-General, launches UN @70 to celebrate the 70th anniversary in, New Delhi in 2015.

NCERT Folder

Intext Questions

1. Make a list of issues or problems that cannot be handled by any one country and require an international organisation. (Pg. no. 47)

Ans. The list of global issues or problems that cannot be effectively handled by any one country alone and require international organisations is given below

- **Climate Change** The global nature of climate change means that no single country can address it on its own. International agreements, such as the Paris Agreement, are essential in this direction.
- **Pandemics and Global Health Crises** Infectious diseases like COVID-19 require international co-ordination for prevention, response, vaccine distribution and information sharing. Organisations like the World Health Organisation (WHO) play a critical role in this area.
- **Terrorism** Terrorism crosses national borders and international co-operation is needed for intelligence sharing, counter terrorism efforts and preventing the financing of terrorist groups.
- **Refugee and Migration Crises** Large-scale migration due to conflict, persecution or economic hardship requires international frameworks for protection, re-settlement and co-operation of resources. The United Nations High Commissioner for Refugees (UNHCR) is one such organisation.
- **Human Rights Protection** Human rights abuses often occur across borders and international organisations like the United Nations and various Non-Governmental Organisations (NGOs) work together to promote and protect Fundamental Human Rights globally.

2. Search for at least one news item about the activities of each of the UN agencies. (Pg. no. 50)

Ans. News items about the activities of UN agencies are as follows

- **World Health Organisation (WHO)** The WHO has announced that Mpox will continue to be classified as a Public Health Emergency of International Concern (PHEIC), citing a resurgence in cases and the virus's ongoing geographic spread.
- **United Nations Development Programme (UNDP)** The UNDP released a press release about boosting energy efficiency in Belarus' small-town housing sector.
- **United Nations Human Rights Commision (UNHRC)** The UNHRC in South Sudan visited Addis Ababa to discuss transitional justice with the African Union.
- **United Nations High Commission for Refugees (UNHCR)** The UN refugee agency (UNHCR) has launched a $10 billion appeal for 2025 to meet critical needs and implement sustainable solutions for millions of refugees, displaced persons and stateless people worldwide.
- **United Nations International Children's Emergency Fund (UNICEF)** UNICEF and the World Health Organisation (WHO) launched an emergency polio vaccination campaign in September, reaching nearly 60,0000 children under 10 years old.
- **United Nations Educational, Scientific and Cultural Organisation (UNESCO)** UNESCO, the Brazilian government and the United Nations launched the global initiative for information integrity on climate change at the G20 Leaders' Summit. The initiative aims to strengthen research and measures to address dis-information about climate change.

3. Find out about the Sustainable Development Goals (SDGs). (Pg. no. 55)

Ans. To bring sustainable development to the mainstream, the United Nations (UN) launched the 2030 Agenda for Sustainable Development and SDGs. This universal, integrated and transformative agenda aims to spur actions that will end poverty and build a more sustainable world over the next 15 years.

There are 17 goals and 169 specific targets to be achieved by 2030. Reaching the goals requires action on all fronts governments, businesses, civil society and people everywhere all have a role to play. SDGs are not legally binding.

The 17 goals under the Sustainable Development Goals are as follows

(i) End poverty in all its forms everywhere.
(ii) End hunger, achieve food security and improved nutrition and promote sustainable agriculture.
(iii) Ensure healthy lives and promote well being for all at all stages.
(iv) Ensure inclusive and equitable quality education and promote lifelong learning opportunities for all.
(v) Achieve gender equality and empower all women and girls.
(vi) Ensure availability and sustainable management of water and sanitation for all.

(vii) Ensure access to affordable, reliable, sustainable and modern energy for all.

(viii) Promote sustained, inclusive and sustainable economic growth, full and productive employment and decent work for all.

(ix) Built resilient infrastructure, promote inclusive and sustainable industrialisation and foster innovation.

(x) Reduce inequalities within and among countries.

(xi) Make cities and human settlements inclusive, safe, resilient and sustainable.

(xii) Ensure sustainable consumption and production pattern.

(xiii) Take urgent actions to combat climate change and its impact.

(xiv) Conserve and sustainably use the oceans, seas and marine resources.

(xv) Protect, restore and promote sustainable use of terrestrial ecosystems, sustainably managed forests, combat desertification and halt and reverse land degradation and halt biodiversity loss.

(xvi) Promote peaceful and inclusive societies for sustainable development, provide access to justice for all and build effective, accountable and inclusive institutions at all levels.

(xvii) Strengthen the means of implementation and revitalise the global partnership for sustainable development.

Exercise

1. Mark correct or wrong against each of the following statements about the Veto Power.

(a) Only the permanent members of the Security Council possess the Veto Power.

(b) It's a kind of negative power.

(c) The Secretary-General uses this power when not satisfied with any decision.

(d) One veto can stall a Security Council resolution.

Ans. (a) Correct (b) Correct
(c) Wrong (d) Correct

2. Mark correct or wrong against each of the following statements about the way the UN functions.

(a) All security and peace related issues are dealt with in the Security Council.

(b) Humanitarian policies are implemented by the main organs and specialised agencies spread across the globe.

(c) Having consensus among the five permanent members on security issues is vital for its implementation.

(d) The members of the General Assembly are automatically the members of all other principal organs and specialised agencies of the UN.

Ans. (a) Correct (b) Correct (c) Correct (d) Wrong

3. Which among the following would give more weightage to India's proposal for permanent membership in the Security Council?

(a) Nuclear capability.

(b) It has been a member of the UN since its inception.

(c) It is located in Asia.

(d) India's growing economic power and stable political system.

Ans. (d) India's growing economic power and stable political system.

4. The UN agency concerned with the safety and peaceful use of nuclear technology is

(a) The UN Committee on Disarmament

(b) International Atomic Energy Agency

(c) UN International Safeguard Committee

(d) None of the above

Ans. (b) International Atomic Energy Agency

5. WTO is serving as the successor to which of the following organisations?

(a) General Agreement on Trade and Tariffs

(b) General Arrangement on Trade and Tariffs

(c) World Health Organisation

(d) UN Development Programme

Ans. (a) General Agreement on Trade and Tariffs

6. Fill in the Blanks

(i) The prime objective of the UN is ....

Ans. to maintain peace and security

(ii) The highest functionary of the UN is called ....

Ans. Secretary-General

(iii) The UN Security Council has .... permanent and .... non-permanent members.

Ans. five, ten

(iv) .... is the present UN Secretary-General .

Ans. Antonio Guterres

7. Match the principal organs and agencies of the UN with their functions.

Principal Organs and Agencies	Functions
A. Economic and Social Council	1. Oversees the global financial system.
B. International Court of Justice	2. Preservation of international peace and security.
C. International Atomic Energy Agency	3. Looks into the economic and social welfare of the member countries.

D. Security Council	4. Safety and peaceful use of nuclear technology.
E. UN High Commission for Refugees	5. Resolves disputes between and among member countries.
F. World Trade Organisation	6. Provides shelter and medical help during emergencies.
G. International Monetary Fund	7. Debates and discusses global issues.
H. General Assembly	8. Administration and co-ordination of UN affairs.
I. World Health Organisation	9. Providing good health for all.
J. Secretariat	10. Facilitates free trade among member countries.

Ans. A-3, B-5, C-4, D-2, E-6, F-10
G-1, H-7, I-9, J-8

8. What are the functions of the Security Council?

Ans. The main functions of the Security Council is to maintain peace and security in the world. Some of the other functions are discussed below

- To investigate any dispute or situation which might lead to international conflicts.
- To recommend methods of adjusting such disputes or the terms of settlement.
- To formulate plans for the establishment of a system to regulate armaments.
- To determine the existence of a threat to the peace or act of aggression and to recommend what action should be taken.
- It can apply economic sanctions also to stop any aggression.

9. As a citizen of India, how would you support India's candidature for the permanent membership of the Security Council? Justify your proposal.
Competency Based Que

Ans. As the citizen of India, we should support India's candidature for the permanent membership of the Security Council. India rightly deserves a permanent seat, as it fulfills almost all the criteria laid down by the UN. These criteria are as follows

- India is the second most populous country of the world comprising one-fifth of the world population that too of multi-cultural diaspora.
- It is the world's largest democracy and upholds the democratic ideals.
- It has emerged as potential economic power in the world with a stable political system.
- India supports the initiatives taken up by the UN.
- It has also made regular financial contributions to the UN and never faltered on its payments.

Thus, all these factors justify India's claim to a permanent seat in the UN Security Council.

10. Critically evaluate the difficulties involved in implementing the suggested reforms to reconstruct the UN.
Competency Based Que

Ans. Many difficulties are involved in implementing the suggested reforms to reconstruct the UN which are as follows

- There is lack of representation especially in Asia, Africa and Latin America. The countries in these continents are not represented equally like the developed countries in the UN.
- The current composition of the UN Security Council represents the post-World War II realities and thus is not in pace with the changing balance of power in the world.
- There is lack of adequate membership criteria as well as conditions for membership in the UN. There are no parameters in the UN Security Council for considering the countries for permanent membership.
- There is a dominance of permanent members of UN who use their Veto Power which further deteriorate the process of reform and restructuring of UN.

11 Though the UN has failed in preventing wars and related miseries, nations prefer its continuation. What makes the UN an indispensable organisation?
Competency Based Que

Ans The following facts makes the UN an indispensable organisation for maintaining the world peace

- Interdependence and globalisation is not possible without the international organisation such as the UN.
- To enforce co-operation on the issues of poverty, unemployment, environmental degradation, crime rate etc.

  Thus, it works for the co-operation and protection of basic rights and conditions for survival.
- To provide financial assistance to developing countries to stabilise economy all over the world, the UN and its specialised agencies are always required.
- The UN works as a forum to solve any international dispute among nations and sort out the problem in best possible way. It is the only organisation which consists of 193 member states.

Hence, though the UN has failed in preventing related wars and miseries, despite this the nations require its continuation due to above mentioned reasons to promote international peace and security.

12. 'Reforming the UN means restructuring of the Security Council'. Do you agree with this statement? Give arguments for or against this position. CBSE 2024 Competency Based Que

Ans. Yes, I agree with the statement because Security Council plays a crucial role in functioning of the UN. In today's scenario power equations have been changed with the disintegration of USSR and many new countries are entering into the UN.

- The UN Charter has given a privileged position to permanent members to bring stability all over the world. This position remains the same and no one is allowed to enter. Permanent member enjoy veto power to be placed in a valuable position.
- Permanent members category is from industralised developed country which should be balanced by enhancing representation from developing countries to become either permanent or non-permanent members.

Exam Pattern Questions

Objective Type Questions

Multiple Choice Questions MCQs

1. How many founder states signed the UN Charter in 1945?
(a) 45 (b) 51 (c) 52 (d) 56

2. UN was established with the objective to…… CBSE 2024
(a) boost trade among the member states.
(b) prevent international conflict and facilitate co-operation among member states.
(c) provide help at the time of war.
(d) help the member states in formation of military alliances.

3. The United Nations was established……… CBSE Term I 2021
(a) after the First World War
(b) after the disintegration of the USSR
(c) before the Second World War
(d) after the Second World War

4. The main objective of the United Nations is to……… CBSE Term I 2021
(a) control the big powers to exploit small countries
(b) check population growth
(c) prevent international conflicts
(d) manufacture medicines

5. Which one of the following is not a principal organ of the United Nations? CBSE Term I 2021
(a) Security Council
(b) World Bank
(c) International Court of Justice
(d) General Assembly

6. Which one of the following organs of the United Nations has been suspended since 1994?
(a) General Assembly
(b) Trusteeship Council
(c) Economic and Social Council
(d) Secretariat

7. Given the contemporary realities of the, world how can the UN play a more important role?
(a) By being more assertive about human rights violations and calling for change.
(b) By letting the regional powers take change.
(c) By indulging US-China to resolve disputes.
(d) By being proactive and sending peacekeeping forces to resolve territorial disputes.

8. How many UN members were there by 2011?
(a) 180 (b) 195 (c) 193 (d) 190

9. From the following statements related to the United Nations Organisation, choose the one which is NOT true? CBSE Term I 2021
(a) It does not have authority over its member states.
(b) It is a sovereign body.
(c) It was created by and responds to its member states.
(d) The UN came into being when states agreed to its creation.

10. Which one of the following criterion was NOT proposed for new permanent and non-permanent members of the UN Security Council?
(a) Should be a substantial contributor to the UN debates.
(b) Should be a major economic power.
(c) Should be a major military power.
(d) Should be a nation that respect democracy.

11. Which one of the following statements does not justify India's claim to be a permanent member of the UN Security Council? CBSE Term I 2021
(a) India is the world's largest democracy.
(b) India is the second most populous country.
(c) India has won two battles against Pakistan.
(d) India makes regular contributions to the United Nations.

12. **Which of the following statements about the United Nations is incorrect?**
(a) The UN was founded as a successor to the League of Nations.
(b) It was established in 1946.
(c) Its primary objective is to prevent international conflict.
(d) It was intended to bring countries together.

13. **The United Nations Children's Fund (UNICEF) was created by ....**
(a) UN Development Council
(b) UN Development Group
(c) UN Security Council
(d) UN General Assembly

14. **Identify the main function of the UNICEF.** CBSE Term I 2021
(a) To promote efficient conditions of social justice and work.
(b) To collect emergency funds for children.
(c) To promote education and science.
(d) To create safety, parity and self-respectful conditions for both women and children.

15. **What is 'Amnesty International'?** CBSE 2020
(a) Nuclear Safety Organisation
(b) Government Organisation
(c) Non-Government Organisation
(d) Human Development Organisation

16. **Who is the head and most visible figure of UN?**
(a) President of the UNGA
(b) UN Secretary-General
(c) Head of the Security Council
(d) Director General of UNESCO

17. **Which UN agency focuses on the welfare of children?**
(a) UNESCO (b) UNICEF
(c) UNHRC (d) UNDP

18. **How much is the tenure of the judges in the International Court of Justice?**
(a) Five years
(b) Seven years
(c) Nine years
(d) Ten years

19. **The countries which used WTO to advance its own interest are ....**
(a) USA (b) European Union
(c) Japan (d) All of these

20. **Which of the following changes occured after the Cold War?** Competency Based Que
(a) The Soviet Union Collapsed
(b) The US became the strongest power
(c) Growth of major military power
(d) Both (a) and (b)

21. **Which of the following statements are true about the steps to be taken to make the UN more relevant as recommended by heads of all the member states who met in September 2005 to celebrate the 60th anniversary of the UN?** CBSE Term I 2021
I. Creation of a Peace Building Commission.
II. Creation of Democracy Fund.
III. Making no war zones.
IV. Condemnation of terrorism in all its forms.
Choose the correct option
(a) I and II (b) I, II and III
(c) I, II and IV (d) II, III and IV

22. **Choose the number of incorrect argument/arguments as far as India's claim to a permanent seat in the Security Council is concerned** CBSE 2020
I. India has made financial contributions to the UN and always faltered on its payments.
II. India has emerged as an economic power on the world stage.
III. India has participated in virtually all of the initiatives of the United Nations.
IV. India's role in the United Nations' peacekeeping force is a long and substantial one.
Codes
(a) I is incorrect.
(b) II and III are incorrect.
(c) II, III and IV are incorrect.
(d) All are incorrect.

23. **Arrange the following events in chronological order**
I. Establishment of the World Bank
II. Establishment of the WTO
III. Establishment of the UNO
IV. Establishment of the IAEA CBSE 2024
Choose the correct option
(a) I, III, IV, II (b) II, I, III, IV
(c) III, II, I, IV (d) III, I, IV, II

24. **Arrange the following in the chronological order of their establishment.** CBSE 2020

I. The World Trade Organisation	**1995**
II. Amnesty International	**1961**
III. League of Nations	**1920**
IV. World Bank	**1944**

Choose the correct option
(a) III, IV, II and I (b) IV, III, II and I
(c) II, III, IV and I (d) I, II, III and IV

25. **Arrange the following in chronological order of their formation.** CBSE 2025
I. The World Trade Organisation.
II. World Bank

III. The International Atomic Energy Agency
IV. United Nations Organisation

Codes

(a) I, II, III, IV (b) IV, I, III, II
(c) II, IV, III, I (d) III, I, II, IV

26. Match the following.

List I (Organisations)	List II (Headquarters)
A. Human Rights Watch	1. An organ of the United Nations
B. International Monetary Fund	2. An agency of the United Nations
C. World Health Organisation	3. An international organisation that oversees financial institutions
D. General Assembly	4. An international NGO

Codes **CBSE 2025**

	A	B	C	D		A	B	C	D
(a)	3	1	4	2	(b)	4	1	2	3
(c)	4	3	2	1	(d)	2	4	3	1

27. Given below are two statements

Statement I UN General Assembly members have one vote each.

Statement II Some of the member of UN General Assembly have Veto Power in UNSC.

In the light of above statements, choose the correct answer from the options given below

(a) Both Statement I and Statement II are true
(b) Both Statement I and Statement II are false.
(c) Statement I is true, but Statement II is false.
(d) Statement I is false, but Statement II is true.

28. Given below are two statements.

Statement I IMF have 191 members.

Statement II India is not a part of IMF.

In the light of above statements, choose the correct answer from the options given below.

(a) Both Statement I and Statement II are true.
(b) Both Statement I and Statement II are false.
(c) Statement I is true, but Statement II is false.
(d) Statement I is false, but Statement II is true.

29.

The message that this picture gives is .... **CBSE Term I 2021**

(a) de-nuclearisation of the world is the need.
(b) use of military power to control the world.
(c) colonisation of the world is not to be appreciated.
(d) All of the above

30. Study the logo given below and carefully answer the question that follows **CBSE Term I 2021**

Name the organisation to which this 'logo' belongs.

(a) United Nations Organisation
(b) World Health Organisaiton
(c) International Labour Organisation
(d) All of the above

Assertion-Reason Questions

Directions (Q. Nos. 31-35) In the questions given below, there are two statements marked as Assertion (A) and Reason (R). Read the statements and choose the correct option.

Codes

(a) Both A and R are true and R is the correct explanation of A.
(b) Both A and R are true, but R is not the correct explanation of A.
(c) A is true, but R is false.
(d) A is false, but R is true.

31. **Assertion** (A) The case for reform of the UN Security Council has widespread support.

Reason (R) The Security Council no longer represents contemporary political realities, reflects only Western values, and is dominated by a few powers.

32. **Assertion** (A) All members of the UN have one vote. However, the permanent members can vote in a negative manner. **CBSE Term I 2021**

Reason (R) The developing world consists of countries at many different levels of development.

33. **Assertion** (A) The main privilege of the five permanent members of the UN Security Council is the 'Veto Power'.

Reason (R) The UN Charter gave the permanent members a privileged position to bring about the stability in the world. **CBSE Term I 2021**

34. **Assertion** (A) India supports an increase in the number of both permanent and non-permanent members of the UN Security Council.

Reason (R) India itself is not interested to be a permanent member of the UN Security Council.

35. **Assertion** (A) The membership of the UN Security Council was expanded from 11 to 15 in 1965.

Reason (R) Number of permanent members of the Security Council was changed. **CBSE Term I 2021**

Passage Based Questions

36. **Study the passage given below carefully and answer the questions that follow**

United Nation Organisation was set up through the signing of the United Nations Charter by 51 states. It tried to achieve what the League could not between the two world wars. The UN's objective is to prevent international conflict and to facilitate co-operation among states. It was founded with the hope that it would act to stop the conflicts between states escalating into war and, if war broke out, to limit the extent of hostilities. Furthermore, since conflicts often arose from the lack of social and economic development, the UN was intended to bring countries together to improve the prospects of social and economic development all over the world. By 2011, the UN had 193 member states. These included almost all independent states. In the UN General Assembly, all members have one vote each. In the UN Security Council, there are five permanent members. These are: the United States, Russia, the United Kingdom, France and China.

(i) Which of the followings are the objectives of UN?

(a) To prevent international conflict.
(b) To facilitate co-operation among states.
(c) To stop the conflicts between states escalating into war.
(d) All of the above

(ii) What is the primary goal of establishing UN?

(a) To bring military reforms.
(b) To resolve country's political problem.
(c) To improve the prospects of social and economic development all over the world.
(d) All of the above

(iii) Describe the structure of the UN Security Council?

37. **Study the passage given below carefully and answer the questions that follow**

By 2011, the UN had 193 member states. These includeed almost all independent states. In the UN General Assembly, all members have one vote each. In the UN Security Council, there are five permanent members. These are: the United States, Russia, the United Kingdom, France and China.

These states were selected as permanent members as they were the most powerful immediately after the Second World War and they constituted the victory in the war.

(i) Which of the following country is not a permanent member of UN Security Council?

(a) China (b) France (c) Vietnam (d) USA

(ii) The permanent members of the UNSC were part of which historical event?

(a) Cold War (b) World War I
(c) World War II (d) Enlightenment

(iii) Why only some states are part of permanent membership in the UN Security Council?

(a) Because these states were independent at the time of Second World War.
(b) Because they were the most powerful countries immediately after the Second World War and they also emerged victorious.
(c) Because these countries were colonial powers.
(d) None of the above

(iv) Wars and peace differences between member states of US are discussed in .... and ....

(a) General Assembly (b) Security Council
(c) WHO (d) Both (a) and (b)

38. **Study the passage given below carefully and answer the questions that follow** **CBSE 2020**

Reform and improvement are fundamental to any organisation to serve the needs of a changing environment. The UN is no exception. In recent years, there have been demands for reform of the world body. However, there is little clarity and consensus on the nature of reform. Two basic kinds of reforms face the UN: reform of the organisation's structures and processes and a review of the issues that fall within the jurisdiction of the organisation.

(i) What is the main focus of the discussions regarding the reform of the UN Security Council?

(a) Changes to the veto power of permanent members.
(b) The functioning of the Security Council and its representation.
(c) The structure of the General Assembly.
(d) The improvement of peace keeping operations.

(ii) Which of the following regions is mentioned in the proposals for increasing the Security Council's membership?

(a) Asia, Africa and South America
(b) Europe and North America
(c) The Middle East and Oceania
(d) Australia and Eastern Europe

(iii) Why is there a demand to increase the membership of the UN Security Council?

39. **Study the passage given below carefully and answer the questions that follow** **CBSE 2020**

The UN is an imperfect body, but without it the world would be worse-off. Given the growing connections and links between societies and issues-what we often call 'interdependence'-it is hard to imagine how more than seven billion people would live together without an organisation such as the UN technology promises to increase planetary interdependence and therefore, the importance of the UN will only increase.

Peoples and governments will have to find ways of supporting and using the UN and other international organisation in ways that are consistent with their own interests and the interests of the International Community more broadly.

(i) **Which of the following are the limitations of the United Nations that make it an imperfect body?** **Competency Based Que**

(a) US stands as the only superpower after the disintegration of USSR and the UN cannot check the US powers.
(b) The single largest contributor of UN is the US which increases the influence of US over the UN.
(c) The UN provides an arena in which it is possible to modify US attitudes and policies.
(d) Both (a) and (b)

(ii) **How would the world would be worse off, if there were no United Nations?** **Competency Based Que**

(a) The UN provides an arena in which it is possible to modify US attitudes and policies.
(b) The UN represents all the countries from each continent of the world.
(c) The UN provide a space within which arguments against specific US attitudes and policies are heard and compromises and concessions are shaped.
(d) Both (a) and (c)

(iii) **Which one of the following is the example of Planetary Interdependence?**

(a) Technology
(b) Trade
(c) Globalisation
(d) International Community Interests

(iv) **How can UN work in favour of meeting interests of International Community?** **Competency Based Que**

(a) By providing them equal representation.
(b) Peoples and governments will have to find ways of supporting and using the UN effectively.
(c) By disregarding the aspects provided by the US at the international level.
(d) None of the above

Answers

1. (b) 51
2. (b) prevent international conflict and facilitate co-operation among member states.
3. (d) after the Second World War
4. (c) prevent international conflicts
5. (b) World Bank
6. (b) Trusteeship Council
7. (a) By being more assertive about human rights violations and calling for change.
8. (c) 193
9. (b) It is a sovereign body.
10. (a) Should be a substantial contributor to the UN debates.
11. (c) India has won two battles against Pakistan.
12. (b) It was established in 1946.
13. (d) UN General Assembly
14. (b) To collect emergency funds for children.
15. (c) Non-Government Organisation
16. (b) UN Secretary-General
17. (b) UNICEF
18. (c) Nine years
19. (d) All of these
20. (d) Both (a) and (b)
21. (c) I, II and IV
22. (a) I is incorrect.
23. (a) I, III, IV, II
24. (a) III, IV, II and I
25. (c) II, IV, III, I
26. (c) 4 3 2 1
27. (a) Both Statement I and Statement II are true.
28. (b) Both Statement I and Statement II are false.
29. (b) use of military power to control the world.
30. (a) United Nations Organisation
31. (a) Both A and R are true and R is the correct explanation of A.
32. (b) Both A and R are true, but R is not the correct explanation of A.
33. (a) Both A and R are true and R is the correct explanation of A.
34. (c) A is true, but R is false.
35. (c) A is true, but R is false.
36. (i) (d) All of the above
(ii) (c) To improve the prospects of social and economic development all over the world.

(iii) The United Nations Security Council (UNSc) consists of 15 members 5 permanent members (P5) with Veto Power—China, France, Russia, the United Kingdom, and the United States—and 10 non-permanent members elected for two-year terms. The UNSC is responsible for maintaining international peace and security, making decisions on conflict resolution, sanctions and military action.

37. (i) (c) Vietnam (ii) (c) Would War II

(iii) (b) Because they were the most powerful countries immediately after the Second World War and they also emerged victorious.

(iv) (d) Both (a) and (b)

38. (i) (b) The functioning of the Security Council and its representation.

(ii) (a) Asia, Africa and South America

(iii) There is a demand to increase the Security Council's membership, both permanent and non-permanent, to make the council more representative of modern global politics. The goal is to reflect the growing political influence of regions like Asia, Africa and South America, which are currently under-represented in the council's decision-making processes.

39. (i) (d) Both (a) and (b)

(ii) (d) Both (a) and (c)

(iii) (a) Technology

(iv) (b) Peoples and governments will have to find ways of supporting and using the UN effectively.

Subjective Questions

Very Short Answer Type Questions

1. State any two objectives of the UN.

Ans. The objectives of the UN are

(i) To maintain international peace and security.

(ii) To facilitate co-operation among member countries by avoiding conflicts and war.

2. Why are international organisations like the UN required?

Or **Why do we need organisations like the UN?**

Or **Mention any two advantages of having international organisation in the world.**

Ans. We need organisations like UN to

- Resolve the conflicts and differences among the nations.
- Prescribe rules, regulations and mechanisms for co-operation to avoid mistrust and mis-management.

3. List any four principal organs of the UN.

Or **Name any four main organs of the United Nations.**

Ans. The four principal organs of the UN are

(i) The General Assembly

(ii) The Security Council

(iii) International Court of Justice

(iv) Economic and Social Council

4. How many member countries have got Veto Power in the UN Security Council and why?

Ans. All the five permanent member countries of the UN Security Council have got Veto Power. The UN Charter gave the permanent members a privileged position to bring about stability in the world after the Second World War.

5. What is meant by Security Council? Mention its composition.

Ans. Security Council is one of the principal organs of UNO. It consists of five permanent members and ten non-permanent members. The permanent members have the 'Right to Veto' and the other members are elected for a term of two years.

6. Why do only the five permanent members of the Security Council have right to veto?

Ans. All the members of the UN have one vote. But right to veto is given only to permanent members because permanent members can vote in a negative manner so that even if all the permanent and non-permanent and members vote for a particular decision, any permanent member's negative vote can hold the decision.

7. Give any two reasons why Veto Power of permanent members of Security Council cannot be abolished.

Ans. Veto Power of permanent members of Security Council cannot be abolished because

(i) No permanent member would agree to do this.

(ii) To maintain the interest of big powers in functioning of UN, Veto Power is significantly important and without active participation of the permanent powers, the UN itself will become irrelevant.

8. Give any two arguments of some countries, which oppose the inclusion of India in UNSC as a permanent member.

Ans. Arguments of countries which oppose India's inclusion as permanent member in UNSC are

(i) The conflict between India and Pakistan will make India ineffective as a permanent member.

(ii) With India's inclusion in UNSC, prominent member countries like Brazil, Germany, Japan, South Africa will demand for their inclusion too.

9. Mention any two reforms in the UN after the Cold War.

Ans. The UN was restructured and reformed after the Cold War on following two basis

(i) Reform of the organisation's structures and processes.

(ii) Review of the issues that fall under the jurisdiction of the UN.

10. How has the static composition of the Security Council harmed its representative character? **Competency Based Que**

Ans. The static composition of the Security Council has harmed its representative character because of the following reasons

- It doesn't represent Africa, South America and even doesn't adequately represent Asia.
- A large population of the world is not represented. It makes the Security Council non-democratic in character.

11. List out the specialised agencies of UN which deals with social and economic issues.

Ans. The specialised agencies of UN are World Health Organisation (WHO), United Nations International Children's Emergency Fund (UNICEF), United Nations Educational, Scientific and Cultural Organisation (UNESCO), United Nations Development Programme (UNDP), International Labour Organisation (ILO) and United Nations Environment Programme (UNEP).

12. Mention any two functions of WHO.

Ans. The two functions of WHO are as follows

- Providing leadership on matters critical to health and engaging in partnerships where joint action is needed.
- Monitoring the health situation and addressing health trends.

13. How is the International Court of Justice composed? Where is it based?

Ans. The International Court of Justice consists of fifteen judges who are elected for nine years by absolute majority in both the General Assembly and the Security Council. It is based in the Hague, Netherlands.

14. Mention any two functions of World Bank.

Ans. The functions of World Bank are

(i) It works for human development (education, health).

(ii) It provides loans and grants to member states.

15. List any two functions of the General Assembly of the UN.

Ans. Two functions of the General Assembly of the UN are

(i) To discuss and make recommendations on any issue under the ambit of the UN Charter.

(ii) To maintain international peace and security.

16. Mention any two basic concerns about the reforms related to the processes and restructing of the UNO.

Ans. The two basic concerns about the reforms related to the processes and restructing of the UNO are

(i) To increase the number of permanent and non-permanent members of Security Council.

(ii) US and other Western countries want improvements in the UN's budgetary procedures and its administration.

17. Explain any two complaints related to the UN Security Council reflected in the resolution passed by the UN General assembly in 1992. **CBSE 2024**

Ans. In 1992, the UN General Assembly expressed concerns about the Security Council's lack of transparency and its decision-making processes, which many felt were dominated by a few powerful nations. Council had limited representation and the existing structure did not adequately reflect the geopolitical realities of the post-Cold War world, leaving many nations marginalised.

Short Answer Type Questions

1. State the two main expectations on the basis of which the United Nations was formed in 1945. Mention any two organs and agencies each of the UN.

Or **State any two advantages of international organisation like UNO** **CBSE 2024**

Ans. Two expectations on the basis of which the United Nations was formed in 1945 were

(i) To prevent international conflicts and to facilitate co-operation among states. It was also expected to limitise situation of war between states. It is intended to bring countries together to improve the prospects of social and economic development.

(ii) To promote respect for human rights, dignity and freedom.

Two organs of the UN are the General Assembly and the Security Council and two agencies of the UN are World Health Organisation (WHO) and United Nations Development Programme (UNDP).

2. Describe any four criteria proposed in 1997 for new permanent and non-permanent members of the UN Security Council. **CBSE 2024**

Ans. In 1997, several criteria were proposed for new permanent and non-permanent members of the UN Security Council which are as follows

(i) **Geographical Representation** New members should reflect the diverse regions of the world, ensuring equitable representation from Africa, Asia, Latin America and Europe.

(ii) **Contribution to Peace and Security** Candidates should demonstrate a commitment to maintaining international peace and security, actively participating in peace keeping and conflict resolution efforts.

(iii) **Economic and Political Influence** Nations considered for permanent membership should possess significant economic power and political influence, enabling them to contribute meaningfully to global governance.

(iv) **Adherence to International Norms** Prospective members should uphold principles of the UN Charter, including respect for human rights, rule of law and commitment to multilateralism, fostering a co-operative international environment.

3. Suggest any six steps since 2005 to make the United Nations more relevant in the changing context.

Ans. In September 2005, the UN celebrated its 60th anniversary and leaders decided to make it more relevant in the changing context by following steps

(i) Creation of Peace Building Commission.

(ii) Acceptance of the responsibility of the International Community in case of failures of National Government to protect their own citizens from atrocities.

(iii) Establishment of Human Rights Council.

(iv) Agreement to achieve Millennium Development Goals.

(v) Condemnation of Terrorism in all its forms and manifestations.

(vi) Creatrion of a Democracy Fund.

(vii) An agreement to wind up the Trusteeship Council.

4. What is the full form of WTO? When was it set up? How does it function?

Ans. The full form of WTO is World Trade Organisation which sets the rules for global trade. It is an international organisation. WTO replaced GATT (General Agreement on Trade and Tariffs) in 1995.

It includes 164 members. Major economic powers such as EU, US and Japan have managed to use the WTO to work in favour of them. The developing countries complain about its non-transparent procedures and it being influenced by big powers.

5. "After the end of the Cold War, the United Nation is working in accordance with the changed realities of the world". Justify the statement with six arguments. CBSE SQP 2025

Ans. The UN was established in 1945 immediately after the Second World War. After the Cold War, some of the changes that have occurred are as follows

(i) The Soviet Union has collapsed. The US is the strongest power.

(ii) China is fast emerging as a great power and India also is growing rapidly.

(iii) The economies of Asia are growing at an unprecedented rate.

(iv) Many new countries have joined the UN.

(v) A whole new set of challenges confronts the world (genocide, civil war, ethnic conflict terrorism, nuclear proliferation, climate change, environmental degradation, epidemics).

(vi) In accordance to these changes, the UN has considered Reforms of structure and processes especially of the Security Council.

Long Answer Type Questions

1. 'The United Nations was not created to take humanity to heaven, but to save it from hell'. Support the statement with relevant examples. CBSE SQP 2025

Or **Explain the relevance of United Nation in contemporary world.** CBSE 2024 C

Ans. The above statement can be supported with the following examples

- The UN is an imperfect body, but without it the world would not work properly. International organisations are not the answer to everything, but they are important.
- They help with matters of war and peace. They also help countries co-operate to make better living conditions for us all.
- Countries have conflicts and differences with each other. That does not necessarily mean they must go to war to deal with their antagonisms. They can, instead, discuss contentious issues and find peaceful solutions. The role of an international organisation can be important in this context.
- An international organisation is not a super-state with authority over its members. Once created, it can help member states resolve their problems peacefully.
- There are issues that are so challenging that they can only be dealt with when everyone works together. Disease is an example. Some diseases can only be eradicated if everyone in the world co-operates in inoculating or vaccinating their populations. Or take global warming and its effects; international organisations can help produce information and ideas about how to co-operate.
- It can provide mechanisms, rules and a bureaucracy, to help members have more confidence that costs will be shared properly, that the benefits will be fairly divided.

2. Trace the evolution of the United Nations since its establishment in 1945. How does it function with the help of its structures and agencies?

Ans. The United Nations was established in 1945 after the end of Second World War as a successor to the League of Nations. The United Nations Charter was signed by 51 States. The basic aim was to achieve what League of Nations was not able to achieve during the two World Wars. The other objectives of the UN are as follows

- Prevention of conflicts and facilitating co-operation among nations.
- To stop conflicts among states resulting into war and if it takes the shape of war, then to limit the effects of war.
- To reduce the reasons of conflict by bringing the countries together for improving social and economic development all over the world.

The UN Structures and Agencies

The UN includes many different structures for dealing with different issues. The issues relating to war and peace and differences between member states are dealt by discussion in General Assembly as well as in the Security Council.

The other issues such as social and economic are dealt by a number of agencies which include

- World Health Organisation (WHO)
- United Nations International Children's Emergency Fund (UNICEF)
- United Nations Educational, Scientific and Cultural Organisation (UNESCO)

3. What is the major difference in the privileges given to its permanent and non-permanent members?

Ans. The selection of the permanent members were on the basis of their being powerful immediately after the Second World War and they being the victors in the war.

There is the major difference in the privileges given to the permanent and non-permanent members.

- The UN Charter gave the permanent members a privileged position to bring about stability in the world. After the Second World War the main privileges enjoyed by the permanent members are

(i) Permanency (ii) Veto Power

- The non-permanent members are elected only for two years at a time and cannot be re-elected immediately after completing two years. They are elected in a manner that they represent all continents of the world.
- The non-permanent members do not have the Veto Power. When decisions are taken by Security Council, voting is done.
- All members have one vote. But the permanent members can vote in a negative manner so that even if all other permanent and non-permanent members vote for a particular decision, any permanent member's negative vote can stall the decision. This negative Vote is the veto.

4. Describe the two basic reforms of the UN on which almost everyone agrees that they are necessary after the Cold War.

Ans. As reform and improvement are fundamental to any organisation, there have been demands for changes in the UN from different countries.

The nature of reforms that are desired are of two types

(i) Reform of the organisation's structure and processes.

(ii) Review of the issues that fall within the jurisdiction of the organisation.

The major area of structural reform was the functioning of the Security Council. This covers increasing the number of permanent and non-permanent members of the UN Security Council so as to show in better way the realities of present world politics. Whereas, the proposed increment should be from Asia, Africa and South America. The another area of reform for the UN was its budgetary procedures and its administration.

When the areas of jurisdiction are taken, some states and experts wish that the UN should have more role in peace and security missions whereas others wish to restrict the UN's role in development and humanitarian work like health, education, environment, population control, human rights, gender and social justice.

5. Which three complaints related to the UN Security Council were reflected in the resolution passed by the UN General Assembly in 1992? Describe any three criterias that have been proposed for new permanent members of the Security Council.

Or **Describe any six criterias for the new membership of Security Council as suggested after 1997.**

Ans. In 1992, with a view to bring reforms in the UN Security Council, a resolution was adopted by the UN General Assembly.

The resolution was about following three main complaints

(i) The Security Council is not adequately representing the present political realities.

(ii) Decisions by Security Council are re-flective of Western values and interests and dominance by a few powers.

(iii) The representation is not on an equitable basis.

In view of re-organisation, the UN Secretary-General, Kofi Annan initiated an inquiry into the ways of reformation of the UN on 1st January, 1997.

After the years of inquiry, following criterias have been suggested for the permanent and non-permanent members of Security Council. Six criterias for new membership of Security Council suggested after 1997 are

(i) It should be a major economic power.
(ii) A major military power.
(iii) A substantial contributor to the UN budget.
(iv) A big nation in terms of its population.
(v) A nation that respects democracy and human rights.
(vi) A country that would make the council more representative of the world's diversity in terms of geography, economic system and culture.

6. Describe the composition of UNSC and the suggested reforms to make it more relevant.

Or **"The Security Council lacks equitable representation". In the light of the above statement. Explain the need for restructuring the United Nations.** **CBSE 2024 C**

Ans. Composition of UNSC

(i) **Permanent Members (P5)**
- China, France, Russia, the United Kingdom and the United States.
- Each holds Veto Power, allowing them to block any substantive resolution.

(ii) **Non-Permanent Members**
- 10 members elected by the General Assembly for two-year terms.
- Represent different regions: Africa, Asia-Pacific, Latin America, Western Europe and others.

(iii) **Voting Structure**
- Requires 9 out of 15 votes to pass a resolution, but any P5 member's veto can block it.

Suggested Reforms

(i) **Expansion of Membership** Increase the number of permanent and non-permanent members to reflect current global power dynamics. Include emerging powers like India, Brazil, Germany and Japan (G4 nations).
(ii) **Abolition or Limitation of Veto Power** Reduce or limit the P5's Veto Power to prevent deadlock on critical global issues.
(iii) **Improved Regional Representation** Include more countries from Africa, Latin America and other under-epresented regions in both permanent and non-permanent categories.
(iv) **Greater Transparency** Increase accountability and inclusiveness in decision-making processes.

7. Explain the grounds on the basis of which India seeks to become a permanent member of the UN Security Council.

Ans. India seeks permanent membership in the UN Security Council based on several grounds

(i) **Demographic Significance** As the world's most populous democracy, India represents a significant portion of the global population, deserving a voice in decision-making processes that affect all nations.
(ii) **Economic Growth** India's rapid economic development and status as one of the largest economies position it as a key player in global economic governance, warranting a permanent seat.
(iii) **Contributions to Peace-keeping** India is one of the largest contributors to the UN peace-keeping missions, demonstrating its commitment to international peace and security, thereby justifying its inclusion in the Security Council.
(iv) **Commitment to Multilateralism** India advocates for a multipolar world and a rules-based international order, aligning with the UN's principles and promoting co-operation among nations.
(v) **Geopolitical Stability** India's strategic location in South Asia and its role in regional stability make it essential for addressing regional conflicts and global security challenges.
(vi) **Support for Reform** India actively supports reforms in the UN system, advocating for more inclusive representation, thus aligning with broader calls for change within the International Community.

Picture Based Questions

1. Observe the picture given below and answer the following questions.

(i) **Which organisation is represented by the above logo? When did this organisation formally established?**
(ii) **What is made in this logo or the emblem? When did India join it? What is seen around the world map given in the emblem and what is being signified by them?**
(iii) **What is considered the most important organ among the principal organs of the UN? How many members are there in it?**

Ans. (i) This is the logo of the United Nations. The UNO was formally established on 24th October, 1945.
(ii) The logo or emblem has a world map. India joined the UN on 30th October, 1945. The world map has olive branches around it. These branches signifies world peace.

(iii) The Security Council is considered the most important organ among the principal organs of the United Nations. It has 15 members in all. Out of them, 5 members are permanent with veto rights and other ten members are elected by the General Assembly or the UN for two years.

2. Study the given cartoon and answer the questions that follow. **CBSE 2025**

(i) What does the cartoon depict?

(a) Influence of UNO on the World

(b) Influence of USA on UNO

(c) Relevance of UNO

(d) Influence of USA on the World

Ans. (b) Influence of USA on UNO

(ii) What message is given by the cartoon ?

(a) If UN fails then the US can control the world by its military power.

(b) Economic superiority of US

(c) Veto power of permanent members of UN

(d) US is the largest

Ans. (a) If UN fails then the US can control the world by its military power.

(iii) Why this cartoon is not relevant today?

(a) UN has become more powerful.

(b) Many new powerful international organisations have emerged.

(c) Countries are not having faith in UN.

(d) Now many new centres of power have emerged.

Ans. (b) Many new powerful international organisations have emerged.

(iv) What is the primary objective of UNO?

(a) To foster economic ties of the developed nations

(b) To promote international peace and co-operation

(c) To eradicate terrorism

(d) To promote health care

Ans. (b) To promote international peace and co-operation

Map Based Question

1. Study the given map of the world and answer the following questions in your answer book.

(i) Identify and name the countries marked as A, B, C and D respectively.

(ii) Write the names of the following UN Secretary-Generals with the the names of the countries they belonged to

(a) Dag Hammarskjold (b) Kurt Waldheim (c) Boutros Boutros-Ghali (d) Kofi Annan

Ans. (i) A- Sweden, B- Ghana, C-Austria, D- Egypt

(ii) (a) Dag Hammarskjold-Sweden

(b) Kurt Waldheim-Austria

(c) Boutros Boutros-Ghali-Egypt

(d) Kofi Annan-Ghana

SELF ASSESSMENT TEST

Objective Type Questions

1. UN Secretary-General Antonio Guterres was the Prime Minister of which Country?

(a) Portugal (b) UK (c) France (d) Japan

2. Human Right Council is operational since which year?

(b) 2001 (b) 2006 (c) 2012 (d) 2009

3. Arrange in Sequence

I. India joins the UN. II. The Second World War.

III. Humanitarian Cisis in Darfur, Sudan. IV. League of Nations.

Codes

(a) IV, II, I and III (b) I, II, III and IV (c) III, I, II and IV (d) IV, I, II and III

4. The Trusteeship Council was suspended on ....

(a) 1st November, 1994 (b) 1st September, 1994

(c) 1st December, 1995 (d) 1st November, 1995

5. Choose the wrong statement

(a) UNICEF was established in 1946 by the UN General Assembly.

(b) Its main task is to collect emergency funds for natural disasters.

(c) It is working in almost 193 countries.

(d) It's headquarter is in New York, United States.

Very Short Answer Type Questions

6. What is Veto Power?

7. What is the objective of WHO?

8. Suggest any two major changes to improve the functioning of the Security Council.

9. Suggest any one measure that should be taken to make WTO more acceptable to the developing countries.

Short Answer Type Questions

10. When was the United Nations Organisation established? What were its aims?

11. Write a short note on the functions of UNSC.

12. Give two suggestions for the reform of the structures and processes of the UNs.

13. List any four principle organs of the UN.

Long Answer Type Questions

14. Discuss the aims and programmes of UNESCO.

15. Discuss the main organs of the UN. Also discuss their functions.

16. What is the need for expansion of Security Council?

17. Write a short note on Human Rights Watch.

05

CHAPTER

Security is the major component of human life. Almost all the countries of the world have the same concern on the subject of the safety of their citizens.

▼ **YOUR STUDY GOALS**

5.1 Traditional Notion of Security : External

5.2 Traditional Notion of Security : Internal

5.3 New Sources of Threats

5.4 Co-operative Security

5.5 India's Security Strategy

▼ **YOUR PRACTICE GOAL**

- Objective Type Questions (31 Qs ; MCQs, A-R, Statements, Passage Based)
- Subjective Questions (14 VSAs, 5 SAs, 8 LAs, 4 Picture based)

Security in Contemporary World

5.1 Traditional Notion of Security: External

- Things which threaten the **core values** are known as security issue. Here **core values** refer to those issues which could do larger damage if not addressed properly.
- Various nations of security are classified under two groups traditional and non-traditional.
  - In traditional view, a country's biggest threats come from outside. This is because there is no central world authority to control actions.
  - In world politics, no single authority rules over all nations. So, each country must take care of its own security.
- According to traditional conception of security, military threats are the greatest danger to the country. If a country takes military action against another country, then it is threatening the core values of sovereignty[1], independence and territorial integrity.
- There are three choices with the government in response to the threat of war which are as follows
  - (i) To surrender.
  - (ii) To prevent the other side from attacking by ensuring that the cost of war would be unbearably high.
  - (iii) To defend itself when war begins.

1 Sovereignty It refers to supreme authority within the state.

- Governments may choose to surrender in war, but they won't openly state it as their policy. Therefore, the first component of traditional security policy which focuses on preventing war is known as **deterrence**. The second component which focuses on limiting or ending war is known as **defense**.

Balance of Power

- It is the third component of traditional security. In this situation, countries observe that some nations are larger and stronger, which can indicate potential future threats. Even if a neighboring country doesn't openly plan an attack, its strength might suggest that it could become aggressive later.
- To maintain a favorable balance of power, countries often focus on building up military strength, along with economic and technological power, as these support military capabilities.

Alliance Building

- The fourth component of traditional security is a coalition where a group of countries work together to defend against any military attack based on their national interest. Coalitions are formed to increase their collective power.

  For example, the US supported the Islamic militants in Afghanistan against the Soviet Union in the 1980s, However it later attacked them when Al Qaeda- (a group of Islamic militants) led by Osama Bin Laden launched a terrorist attack on America on 11th September, 2001.

5.2 Traditional Notion of Security: Internal

- After the Second World War, the Cold War started and newly independent countries of Europe faced new kinds of challenges. They feared being attacked by other powers like the US, USSR or their former colonial rulers.
- Newly independent countries of Asia and Africa faced different challenges from that of Europe. They were concerned about the military conflicts with neighbouring countries and also the internal military conflicts.
- Another internal challenge for the countries were **separatist movements**[2] which lead to **civil wars**[3] within the country. Internal wars now make up more than 95 per cent of all armed conflicts fought anywhere in the world.

Traditional Security and Co-operation

- It is now an almost universally accepted view that countries should only go to war for the right reasons, either for self-defence or to protect other people from genocide. Force should be used only after all other alternatives have failed.
- Traditional view of security involves the three forms of co-operation- **disarmament, arms control and confidence building.**
  - **Disarmament** It requires all states to give up certain kinds of weapons. For example, the 1972 **Biological Weapons Convention (BWC)** and the 1997 **Chemical Weapons Convention (CWC)** banned the production and possession of these weapons. More than 155 states acceded to the BWC and 193 states acceded of the CWC. US and Soviet Union did not want to give up nuclear weapons, so they pursued arms control.
  - **Arms Control** It regulates the acquisition or development of weapons. The Anti-ballistic Missile (ABM) Treaty in 1972 tried to stop the United States and Soviet Union from using ballistic missiles as a defensive shield to launch a nuclear attack. Other arms control treaties includes the Strategic Arms Limitations Treaty II or SALT II, the Strategic Arms Reduction Treaty (START) and the Nuclear Non-Proliferation Treaty (NPT) of 1968.

2 **Separatist Movements** Separatism may be defined as an instance of political disintegration.

3 **Civil wars** It is a war between opposing groups of citizens of the same country or nation.

Nuclear Non-Proliferation Treaty (NPT) of 1968.

- It is an arms control treaty which regulates the **acquisition of nuclear weapons.**
- Those countries that had tested and manufactured nuclear weapons before 1967 were allowed to keep their weapons and those that had not done so were to give up the right to acquire them.
- The NPT did not abolish nuclear weapons; rather, it limited the number of countries that could have them.

- **Confidence Building** It is a process in which countries share ideas and information with their rivals. They tell each other about their military intentions and plans to some extent. It is the process designed to ensure that rivals do not go to war through misunderstanding or misperception.

Quick Test 1

1. Which component of traditional security policy focuses on preventing war?
2. What are countries likely to focus on to maintain a favorable balance of power?
3. What is the main goal of alliance building in traditional security?
4. In the 1980s, the US supported which group in Afghanistan against the Soviet Union?
5. Which treaty regulated the acquisition of nuclear weapons in 1968?

Non-Traditional Notions

Non-traditional security means 'not just the security of the state but also individuals or communities or indeed of all human kind'. Non-traditional views of security are also referred to as 'human security' or 'global security'.

Human Security

- **Human Security** Prioritises the protection of people from internal violence. While state security and human security can mean the same thing, a secure state does not always mean secure individuals.
- Foreign attacks are not the only threat, more people have been harmed by their own governments than by foreign armies in the last 100 years.
- The goal of human security is to protect individuals, but there are different views on what threats to focus on.
- **Narrow View of Human Security** Focuses on violent threats like internal conflicts, as emphasised by former UN Secretary-General Kofi Annan.
- **Broad View of Human Security** Includes hunger, disease and natural disasters, which cause more deaths than war, genocide and terrorism combined.

Global Security

- It refers to security from the global nature of threats like global warming, International Terrorism and health epidemics like AIDS.
- No country can solve these problems alone. In some cases, one country may have to bear most of the burden of a global issue like environmental degradation.

5.3 New Sources of Threats

The non-traditional conceptions-both human security and global security focus on the changing nature of threats of security.

Terrorism

- Terrorism refers to **political violence** that targets civilians deliberately and indiscriminately.
- International Terrorism involves the citizens or territory of more than one country.

- Terrorists aim to change the political context that they don't like by force or threat of force.
- Cases of terrorism involve hijacking planes or planting bombs in trains, cafes etc.
- There could be three broad meanings of Terrorism
  - A systematic use of terror, often violent, especially as a means of coercion.
  - These are violent acts which are intended to create fear (terror); are perpetrated for a religious, political or ideological goal and deliberately target or disregard the safety of non- combatants or civilians.
  - Terrorism is defined as acts of unlawful violence and war.

Human Rights

- Human rights refer to basic rights of human beings. They are classified into three types.
  - **Political Rights** Such as freedom of speech and assembly.
  - **Economic** and **Social rights.**
  - The right of colonised people of **ethic** and **indigenous minorities.**

Global Poverty

- Half of the population growth is happening in six countries: India, China, Pakistan, Nigeria, Bangladesh and Indonesia. The population in the poorest countries is expected to triple in the next 50 years, while many rich countries will see a decline.
- High **per capita income**[4] and low population growth make rich states or rich social groups get richer, whereas low incomes and high population growth reinforce each other to make poor states and poor groups get poorer.
- This disparity contributes to the gap between Northern and Southern countries. In the South, some countries have controlled population growth and increased incomes, while others have not. This has increased differences between them.

Migration

Poverty in the global South has caused **large-scale migration** to the North for better economic opportunities, creating political tensions.

- Conflicts, especially in the global South, have produced millions of refugees. For example, from 1990-1995, 93 wars in 70 countries caused 55 lakh deaths and widespread displacement.
- Whole communities have been forced to migrate because of generalised fear of violence or due to the destruction of livelihood, identities and living environments.

Terms Related to Migration

- **Migrants** leave their home countries voluntarily for better opportunities.
- **Refugees** flee due to war, natural disasters or persecution.
- **Internally Displaced People** (IDP) those who flee but stay within their country (For example, Kashmiri Pandits in the 1990s).

Health Epidemics

- Diseases like HIV-AIDS, SARS, bird flu and COVID-19 spread across countries due to migration, business and travel.
- Epidemics affect global health and poor regions, especially regions like Africa, which struggle with diseases like HIV-AIDS due to the high cost of treatments.

4 **Per capita income** It is a measure of the average income earned by each person in a given population or geographic region.

- New diseases like Ebola and COVID-19, along with drug-resistant forms of older diseases like tuberculosis and malaria, continue to pose global health threats.
- Animal epidemics like mad cow disease and bird flu have caused significant economic losses, showing how global interdependence requires international co-operation.
- To be considered a security problem, an issue must threaten the existence of a group or state, though the nature of the threat may vary.
- For example, the Maldives is threatened by global warming and rising sea levels, while HIV-AIDS is a major threat in Southern Africa, particularly in Botswana. In 1994, the Tutsi tribe in Rwanda faced a threat to its existence due to mass killings by the Hutu tribe. This shows that both traditional and non-traditional security issues vary based on local contexts.

5.4 Co-operative Security

- Non-traditional security requires international co-operation to deal with threats.
- Co-operation can be **bilateral, regional, continental or global**. It depends on the nature of the threats and the willingness and abilities of countries to respond. Co-operation also involves variety of other national and international organisations like, **UN, WHO, World Bank, IMF** etc.
- Co-operative security may involve the use of force as a last resorts. The International Community may have to sanction the use of force to deal with governments that kill their own people. It may also involve use of violence against international terrorists and those who support them.

5.5 India's Security Strategy

India's security strategy has four broad components. These components are as follows

- The first component is **strengthening its military capabilities** because India has been involved in conflicts with Pakistan in 1947-48, 1965, 1971 and 1999 and China in 1962. India's nuclear test in 1974 and in 1998 was justified on the grounds of national security.
- The second component is **strengthening of international norms and institutions** to protect its security interests. India's first Prime Minister Jawaharlal Nehru supported the cause of Asian solidarity, decolonisation, disarmament and the UN as a forum in which international conflicts could be resolved.
- India also advocated for a fair **New International Economic Order** (NIEO) and used non-alignment to maintain peace outside the superpower blocs. Additionally, Indian troops have participated in the UN peacekeeping missions to support global security efforts.
- The third component is **meeting the security challenges within the nation** like militancy in the areas of Nagaland, Kashmir etc. India has **democratic political system** which allows different communities to freely express their grievances.
- Final component of India's security strategy has been to develop its economy in such a way that brings many people out of poverty and prevents large economic inequalities. There is a pressure to combine economic growth with human development.

Quick Test 2

1. When did India conduct its Nuclear Test?
2. Name the three types of Human Rights.
3. Define Migration.
4. Who are referred to as refugees?

Mind Map

SECURITY IN THE CONTEMPORARY WORLD

1 Traditional Notion of Security: External

Components of Security and Balance of Power
- Various notions of security are classified into two groups-traditional and non-traditional.
- According to traditional conception of security, military threats are the greatest danger.
- The third component of traditional security policy is the Balance of Power.

Coalition and Alliance Building
- To maintain Balance of Power, Countries focus on military strength.
- Alliance building is the fourth component of traditional security.
- Coalition refers to a group of states co-ordinating to defend against military attacks.
- For example, the US supported the Islamic militants in Afghanistan against Soviet Union.

2 Traditional Nation of Security: Internal

Cold Wars Internal Conflicts and Global Security
- From the late 1940s, some newly independent countries became members of Cold War alliances.
- These countries faced security challenges from both neighbour and internal conflicts.
- During 1946 and 1991, the number of civil wars increased.
- Internal wars make up more than 95% of armed conflicts.

3 Traditional Security and Co-operation

Disarmament Control in Global Security
- The US and Soviet Union forced on disarmament of nuclear weapons.
- The 1972 Biological weapons convention and chemical weapons convention of 1997 banned the production of certain types of weapons.
- The US and Soviet Union did not want to give up the nuclear weapons.

Arms Control and Nuclear Weapons Regulation
- Arms control regulates the acquisition or development of weapons.
- The Anti Ballistic Missile Treaty 1972 aimed to prevent the US and Soviet Union from using ballistic missiles.
- US and Soviet Union signed arms control agreements like SALT -II and START.
- Nuclear Proliferation Treaty restricted nuclear weapons acquisition.

Confidence Building
- Process of countries share ideas and information with their rivals.
- Process designed to ensure that rivals do not go to war through misunderstanding.

4 Non Traditional Nation

Human Security
- It refers to protection of communities and individuals from violence.
- It is a broad concept which includes hunger, diseases, natural disaster, etc.

Global Security
- It refers to security from global threats like global warming, terrorism and health epidemics.
- No country can solve these problems alone.

5 New Sources of Threats

Terrorism and Human Rights
- It is a type of political violence that targets innocent citizens.
- Hijacking planes, planting bombs are some cases of terrorism.
- Human rights refers to basic rights of human beings.
- It include political, economical and social rights.

Global Poverty and Migration
- High income and low population growth make states rich.
- Low incomes and high population growth make states poor.
- Migrants are those who leave voluntarily for better opportunities.
- Internally displaced people are those who flee but stay within country.

Health Epidemics
- Diseases like AIDS, SARS spread globally due to migration, tourism and business operations.
- By 2003, 4 crore people were infected with HIV-AIDS worldwide.
- Animal epidemics also causes economic losses.

6 Co-operative Security

Co-operation and Non-traditional Security
- Non traditional security requires international co-operation.
- Co-operation can be regional, continental or global.
- It also involves variety of national and international organisations like UN, WHO, etc.
- It may also involve use of violence against international terrorism.

NCERT Folder

Intext Questions

1. Take a map of Africa and plot various threats to the people's security on that map. (Pg. 74)

Ans.

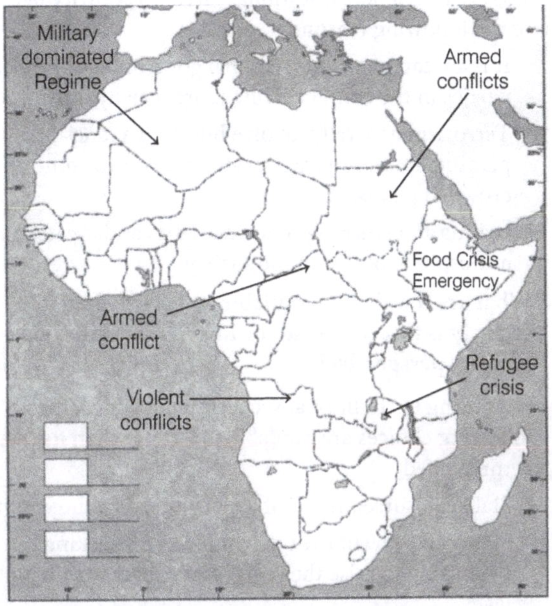

2. Compare the expenditure by the Indian Government on traditional security with its expenditure on non-traditional security. (Pg. 77)

Ans. The expenditure by the Indian Government on traditional security and non-traditional security differs in terms of focus and allocation.

Expenditure on Traditional Security

- Traditional security focuses primarily on defense and military preparedness. This includes expenditure on the Indian Armed Forces, including the Army, Navy and Air Force.
- The budget for traditional security also covers defense procurement, infrastructure for defense operations and maintaining border security.
- The expenditure on traditional security often takes up a significant portion of the national budget, given India's strategic concerns, its proximity to neighboring countries with complex security dynamics and its military capabilities.

Expenditure on Non-Traditional Security

- Non-traditional security refers to a broad range of issues that are not directly related to military conflict but still impact the nation's security. This includes areas like environmental protection, public health, economic stability, human security and cyber security.
- Expenditure on non-traditional security includes investments in disaster management, healthcare (including fighting pandemics), climate change adaptation, food security, poverty alleviation and countering terrorism and cyber crime.
- The focus on non-traditional security is growing in India, as the country faces challenges like natural disasters, climate change, infectious diseases and rising unemployment.

Exercise

1. Match the terms with their meaning.

	List I (Terms)		List II (Meaning)
(i)	Confidence Building Measures (CBMs)	(a)	Giving up certain types of weapons.
(ii)	Arms Control	(b)	A process of exchanging information on defence matters between nations on a regular basis.
(iii)	Alliance	(c)	A coalition of nations meant to deter or defend against military attacks.
(iv)	Disarmament	(d)	Regulates the acquisition or development of weapons.

Ans.

	List I (Terms)		List II (Meaning)
(i)	Confidence Building Measures (CBMs)	(b)	A process of exchanging information on defence matters between nations on a regular basis.
(ii)	Arms Control	(d)	Regulates the acquisition or development of weapons.
(iii)	Alliance	(c)	A coalition of nations meant to deter or defend against military attacks.
(iv)	Disarmament	(a)	Giving up certain types of weapons.

2. Which among the following would you consider as a traditional security concern/non-traditional security concern/not a threat?

(a) The spread of chikungunya/dengue fever.

(b) Inflow of workers from a neighbouring nation.
(c) Emergence of a group demanding nationhood for their region.
(d) Emergence of a group demanding autonomy for their region.
(e) A newspaper that is critical of the armed forces in the country.

Ans. (a) Non-traditional (b) Non-traditional
(c) Traditional (d) Not a threat
(e) Not a threat

3. What is the difference between traditional and non-traditional security? Which category would the creation and sustenance of alliances belong to?

Or **Differentiate between the traditional and the non-traditional notions of security.**

Ans. The difference between traditional and non-traditional security are as follows

Traditional Security	Non-traditional Security
Traditional notion is concerned with the use of military, war, balance of power and alliance building.	It goes beyond military by threatening the conditions necessary for human survival.
It is concerned with the states and its governing institutions.	It covers broad aspects of security i.e. hunger, diseases, etc.
It is confined to states only by thinking of internal and external threats.	It covers not only the state but also individuals or human kind.
Its main focus is on force only to achieve the target.	It comprises co-operation, hence it protects human or global security.

The creation and sustenance of alliances belong to traditional notion of security.

4. What are the differences in the threats that people in the Third World face and those living in the First World face?

Ans. The differences in the threats that people in the Third World face and those living in the First World face are as follows

- The Third World countries face the threats not only from outside their borders, from neighbours, but also from within the country. They quarrell over borders and territories or control over people and populations of all of these simultaneously.
  On the other hand, most of the First World countries, particularly the powerful Western European countries, faced no serious threats from groups or communities living within those borders. These countries faced threats only from outside their borders.
- New states of the Third World face threats from separatist movements which wanted to form an independent country. Sometimes such movements get help from neighbouring countries. There were no such threats in the First World countries.

5. Is terrorism a traditional or non-traditional threat to security? **Competency Based Que**

Ans. Terrorism is a non-traditional threat to security because of the following reasons

- It is a weapon against national government or other parties in the conflict civilians are usually terrorised.
- Terrorism generally involve hijacking planes or planting bombs in trains, cafes, markets or other crowded places.
- It aims at disturbing state's activities and creates an atmosphere of fear in the society.

6. What are the choices available to a state when its security is threatened, according to the traditional security perspective? **Competency Based Que**

Ans. According to traditional security perspective, the following choices are available to a state when its security is threatened

- State can surrender itself against the attacking country.
- State can prevent the other side from attacking by promising to raise the costs of war to an unacceptable level.
- State can defend itself when war actually breaks out so as to deny the attacking country its objectives. It can also turn back to defeat the attacking forces altogether.

7. What is 'Balance of Power'? How could a state achieve this?

Or Explain 'Balance of Power' as a component of traditional security policy. How could a state achieve this balance?

Ans.
- The 'Balance of Power' is one of the third components of traditional security policy. It means that all countries are not equally powerful, bigger and stronger.
- This is a clue to who might be a threat in the future. Governments are therefore, very sensitive to the 'Balance of Power' between their country and other countries.
- States achieve this by working hard to maintain a favourable 'Balance of Power' with other countries with whom they have differences and with those they had issues in the past.
- This is the reason that every country put their main emphasis to enhance military power along with economic and technological power which provide the basis for the same and help to maintain the 'Balance of Power' around the world.

8. What are the objectives of military alliances? Give an example of a functioning military alliance with its specific objectives.

Ans. The objectives of military alliances are as follows

- To form alliances with other countries to increase their effective power of the state.
- These alliances are based on national interest which changes according to the changing circumstances.
- Another objective of military alliance is to maintain Balance of Power in a region.

For example, USA supported the Islamic militants in Afghanistan to harm USSR in 1980s, but later attacked them when Al-Qaeda launched terrorist attack against USA on 9/11.

9. Rapid environmental degradation is causing a serious threat to security. Do you agree with the statement? Substantiate your arguments.

Ans. Yes, I agree with the statement because in some situations one country may have to disproportionately bear the brunt of a global problem such as environment degradation which causes a serious threat to security.

For example, due to global warming, a sea-level rise of 1.5-2.0 metre would flood 20 per cent of Bangladesh, inundate most of Maldives and threaten nearly half the population of Thailand. Since these problems are global in nature, international co-operation is vital and more attention is needed at global level.

It led to increase in non-traditional threats like global diseases which are mainly caused due to air and water pollution. Further, it also led to economic security threat to the countries in the form of affecting the ecological tourism and marine life.

10. Nuclear weapons as deterrence or defence have limited usage against contemporary security threats to states. Explain the statement. **Competency Based Que**

Ans. The contemporary security threats to states are terrorism, violation of human rights, global poverty, large scale migration to seek a better life, health epidemics and so on.

Nuclear weapons as deterrence or defence have limited usage against these threats because these threats require co-operation rather than military confrontation. Military forces may be used against terrorism but not for alleviating poverty or to control health epidemics.

These threats need co-operation at the regional, continental and global level. It depends on the nature of the threats and willingness and ability of countries to respond.

11. Looking at the Indian scenario, what type of security has been given priority in India, traditional or non-traditional? What examples could you cite to substantiate the argument?

Ans. In India, both traditional and non-traditional security have gained attention, but non-traditional security issues have increasingly been prioritised. For instance, concerns over terrorism, cyber threats and climate change have prompted the government to enhance its focus on non-traditional security measures.

The National Cyber Security Policy (2013) illustrates efforts to combat cyber threats, while initiatives like the National Disaster Management Authority address environmental challenges. Additionally, India's engagement in regional co-operation, such as the South Asian Association for Regional Co-operation (SAARC), emphasises collaborative approaches to non-traditional security issues, reflecting a shift in strategic priorities.

12. Read the cartoon below and write a short note in favour or against the connection between war and terrorism depicted in this cartoon. **Competency Based Que**

Ans. The cartoon represents the close relationship between war and terrorism. We find that terrorism has been the main cause of wars fought during the last one decade. It was due to terrorist attack on World Trade Centre, USA fought the war in Afghanistan. Similarly, it was due to terrorist attack on Indian Parliament in the year 2001, that India and Pakistan came very close to war.

Many a times the relations betweeen the two countries are very tense due to the terrorist activities supported and aided by Pakistan into India. The terrorist activities in Jammu and Kashmir also have brought the two countries near war. So, it can be concluded that, yes, there is a close relationship between war and terrorism.

Exam Pattern Questions

Objective Type Questions

Multiple Choice Questions

1. What do you understand by traditional security?
(a) It deals with the use or threat of use of the military.
(b) The major focus is on the use of military force.
(c) In this force is both principal threat to security and means to achieve security.
(d) All of the above

2. Which of the following are the components of traditional security?
(a) Deterrence, Defence (b) Balance of Power
(c) Alliance Building (d) All of these

3. Arms Control is an important measure of traditional security as ....
(a) It regulates the acquisition or development of weapons.
(b) It prevents the military action.
(c) It is concerned with preventing a war like situation.
(d) It co-ordinates actions to defend against military attacks.

4. 'Disarmament' requires all states to .... CBSE 2024 C
(a) give up certain kinds of weapons
(b) regulate the acquisition or development of weapons
(c) share information about arms with rivals
(d) co-ordinate their actions to deter or defend against military attack

5. .... is a coalition of states that co-ordinate their actions to deter or defend against military attack.
(a) Traditional security (b) Non-traditional security
(c) Alliance (d) Military power

6. Balance of Power requires countries to .... CBSE 2024
(a) give up certain kinds of weapons.
(b) regulate acquisition and development of weapons.
(c) co-ordinate their actions to defend against military attack.
(d) maintain a favourable balance with other countries.

7. A process in which the countries share ideas and information with their rivals is called .... CBSE 2024
(a) Alliance Building (b) Arms Control
(c) Confidence Building (d) Balance of power

8. The non-traditional concept of security focuses on which among the following?
(a) Human Security (b) Global Security
(c) Defence (d) Both (a) and (b)

9. Poverty in South Asia has led to a problem of ....
(a) migration (b) insecurity
(c) terrorism (d) over-population

10. When did the idea of global security emerge?
(a) 1990 (b) 1992 (c) 1991 (d) 1995

11. Which of the following statement(s) is/are incorrect about terrorism?
(a) Terrorism refers to political violence that targets civilians.
(b) Terrorism involves hijacking planes or planting bombs in trains, cafes, markets and crowded places.
(c) Attack on World Trade Centre in America on 11th September, 2000 threatened the people.
(d) Most of the terror attacks in the past have occured in the middle East, Europe, Latin America and South Asia.

12. Consider the following statement and choose the correct option(s) about the threats to human rights.
(a) These can be political rights like freedom of speech and assembly.
(b) Economic and social rights.
(c) Right of colonised people of ethnic and indigenous minorities.
(d) All of the above

13. Health epidemics are spread through .... across the countries.
(a) migration (b) business and tourism
(c) military operations (d) All of these

14. Which one of the following is not considered as a new source of threat to security ? CBSE 2024
(a) Terrorism (b) Hijacking of planes
(c) Use of drones (d) War

15. People who flee their homes but remain within national borders are called .... CBSE 2024
(a) Fugitives (b) Migrants
(c) Internally displaced people
(d) Indigenous people

16. People who seek better economic opportunities abroad are called .... CBSE 2024
(a) Immigrants (b) Migrants
(c) Refugees (d) Non-Residents

17. People who flee from war, natural disaster or political persecution are called .... **CBSE 2024 C**

(a) Fugitives (b) Expatriates
(c) Refugees (d) Migrants

18. Arrange the following in correct sequence.

I. Chemical Weapons Convention.
II. Non-Proliferation Treaty.
III. Biological Weapons Convention.
IV. Strategic Arms Reduction Treaty.

Codes

(a) III, IV, II and I (b) II, IV, III and I
(c) II, IV, I and III (d) II, III, IV and I

19. Which countries or regions have historically faced the most terror attacks ?

(a) Middle East and Europe
(b) Latin America and South Asia
(c) North America and Australia
(d) Both (a) and (b)

20. What did the ABM Treaty allow both the US and Saoviet Union to do?

(a) Deploy an unlimited number of ballistic missiles.
(b) Deploy a very limited number of defensive systems.
(c) Completely eliminate nuclear weapons.
(d) Share nuclear technology with other countries.

21. Choose the correct statement.

(a) The NPT was an Arms Control Treaty which regulated the acquisition of nuclear weapons.
(b) The Anti Ballistic Missile Treaty in 1972 tried to stop the US and Soviet Union from using ballistic missiles as defence shield.
(c) Non-traditional nations of security go beyond military threats to include a wide range of threats affecting the condition of human existence.
(d) All of the above

22. Study the given cartoon and answer the questions that follows.

What does the above cartoon mention?

I. Massive expenditure on defence
II. Attack on the citizens
III. Money spent on wars

Choose the correct codes

(a) I and II (b) II and III
(c) I and III (d) All of these

23. **Statement I** Co-operative security may involve the use of force as a last resort.

Statement II Co-operation may be bilateral, regional, continental or global.

In the light of above statements, choose the correct answer from the options given below

(a) Both Statement I and Statement II are true.
(b) Both Statement I and Statement II are false.
(c) Statement I is true, but Statement II is false.
(d) Statement I is false, but Statement II is true.

24. **Statement I** Terrorism refers to political violence that targets civilians deliberately and indiscriminately.

Statement II Terrorists aim to change the social context that they don't like by force or threat to force.

In the light of above statements, choose the correct answer from the options given below

(a) Both Statement I and Statement II are true.
(b) Both Statement I and Statement II are false.
(c) Statement I is true, but Statement II is false.
(d) Statement I is false, but Statement II is true.

Assertion-Reason Questions

Directions (Q. Nos. 25-28) In the questions given below, there are two statements marked as Assertion (a) and Reason (R). Read the statements and choose the correct option.

Codes

(a) Both A and R are true and R is the correct explanation of A.
(b) Both A and R are true, but R is not the correct explanation of A.
(c) A is true, but R is false.
(d) A is false, but R is true.

25. **Assertion** (A) In the traditional view of security, more threat to a country's security comes from outside its borders.

Reason (R) The international system is rather a brutal arena in which there is no central authority capable of controlling behaviour.

26. **Assertion** (A) Traditional security accepts confidence building as a means of avoiding voilence.

Reason (R) Confidence building is a process in which countries share ideas and information wtih their rivals.

27. **Assertion** (A) Migration is the movement of human resources from one state to another due to some particular reasons.

Reason (R) Poverty in South has prompted large scale migration to the North in search of a better life.

28. **Assertion** (A) An alliance is a coalition of states that co-ordinate their actions to deter or defend against military attack.

Reason (R) Countries form alliances to increase their effective power relative to another country or alliance.

Passage Based Questions

29. Study the passage given below and answer the questions that follow.

All proponents of human security agree that its primary goal is the protection of individuals. However, there are differences about precisely what threats individuals, should be protected from. Proponents of the 'narrow' concept of human security focus on violent threats to individuals.

(i) Which type of security is the main concern of 'human security'?

(a) Security of integrity rights and self-respect of human beings along with their life, dignity and honour.
(b) Security of property rights of an individual.
(c) Security from violence and inhuman activities.
(d) None of the above

(ii) What would be included under the 'broad' concept of human security?

(a) It encompasses economic security and threats to human dignity.
(b) It includes threats like hunger, disease and natural disaster that kill more people than war.
(c) It includes global disparity on the basis of finance.
(d) Both (a) and (b)

(iii) Which among the following are the threats from which individuals should be protected?

(a) Terrorism and Income Inequality
(b) Global Poverty
(c) Human Rights Violation
(d) All of the above

(iv) What would be included under the 'narrow' concept of human security?

(a) Violent threats to individuals (b) Economic security
(c) Income inequality (d) Poverty

30. Study the passage given below and answer the questions that follow.

Globally, this disparity contributes to the gap between the Northern and Southern countries of the world. Within the South, disparities have also sharpened, as a few countries have managed to slow down population growth and raise incomes while others have failed to do so. For example, most of the world's armed conflicts now take place in sub-Saharan Africa, which is also the poorest region of the world. At the turn of the 21st century, more people were being killed in wars in this region than in the rest of the world combined.

(i) What are the reasons for disparity in the Southern countries of the world?

(a) Population of several countries have increased rapidly.
(b) Per capita income in these countries is below the expectation.
(c) High ethnic-disparities
(d) Both (a) and (b)

(ii) In what ways are the Northern countries of the world different from the Southern countries?

(a) High per capita income in these countries
(b) Low population growth
(c) Political stability
(d) Both (a) and (b)

(iii) How has disparity between Northern and Southern countries contributed to global conflicts, particularly in sub-Saharan Africa?

31. Study the passage given below and answer the questions that follow.

The US and Soviet Union signed a number of other arms control treaties including the Strategic Arms Limitations Treaty II or SALT II and the Strategic Arms Reduction Treaty (START). The Nuclear Non-Proliferation Treaty (NPT) of 1968 was an Arms Control Treaty in the sense that it regulated the acquisition of nuclear weapons: those countries that had tested and manufactured nuclear weapons before 1967 were allowed to keep their weapons and those that had not done so were to give up the right to acquire them. The NPT did not abolish nuclear weapons; rather, it limited the number of countries that could have them.

(i) What was the intention behind regulation of NPT?

(a) To limit the number of countries that could have nuclear weapons.
(b) To increase the number of countries that could have nuclear weapons.
(c) To abolish the countries from having nuclear weapons.
(d) None of the above

(ii) Why NPT was an Arms Control Treaty?

(a) It regulated the acquisition of nuclear weapons to protect the world from large scale destruction.
(b) It had tested and manufactured nuclear weapons.
(c) It abolished the acquisition of nuclear weapons to save the world.
(d) All of the above

(iii) What was the purpose of the Nuclear Non-Proliferation Treaty (NPT) of 1968, and how did it regulate nuclear weapons?

Answers

1. (d) All of the above 2. (d) All of these
3. (a) It regulates the acquisition or development of weapons.
4. (a) give up certain kinds of weapons
5. (c) Alliance
6. (c) co-ordinate their actions to defend against military attack.
7. (c) Confidence Building 8. (d) Both (a) and (b)
9. (a) migration 10. (a) 1990
11. (c) Attack on World Trade Centre in America on 11th September, 2000 threatened the people.
12. (d) All of the above 13. (d) All of these
14. (b) Hijacking of planes
15. (c) Internally displaced people
16. (b) Migrants
17. (c) Refugees
18. (d) II, III, IV and I
19. (d) Both (a) and (b)
20. (b) Deploy a very limited number of defensive systems
21. (d) All of these
22. (d) All of these
23. (a) Both Statement I and Statement II are true.
24. (a) Both Statement I and Statement II are true.
25. (a) Both A and R are true and R is the correct explanation of A.
25. (b) Both A and R are true, but R is not the correct explanation of A.
26. (b) Both A and R are true, but R is not the correct explanation of A.
28. (a) Both A and R are true and R is the correct explanation of A.
29. (i) (a) Security of integrity rights and self-respect of human beings along with their life, dignity and honour.
   (ii) (d) Both (a) and (b)
   (iii) (d) All of the above
   (iv) (a) Violent threats to individuals
30. (i) (d) Both (a) and (b)
   (ii) (d) Both (a) and (b)
   (iii) The disparity between Northern and Southern countries has worsened inequalities, with some Southern nations advancing while others struggle. Sub-Saharan Africa, the poorest region, faces the greatest challenges. At the start of the 21st century, most global armed conflicts occurred there, leading to more deaths than in the rest of the world combined.
31. (i) (a) To limit the number of countries that could have nuclear weapons.
   (ii) (a) It regulated the acquisition of nuclear weapons to protect the world from large scale destruction.
   (iii) The Nuclear Non-Proliferation Treaty (NPT) of 1968 aimed to regulate the spread of nuclear weapons. It allowed countries that had tested and manufactured nuclear weapons before 1967 to retain them, while preventing other nations from acquiring nuclear arms. The treaty didn't eliminate nuclear weapons but limited the number of countries possessing them.

Subjective Questions

Very Short Answer Type Questions

1. Highlight any two threats to a country's security as per the traditional notion of security.

Ans. Two threats as per the traditional notion of security are

(i) Military threats which endangers the core values of sovereignty, independence and territorial integrity.

(ii) 'Balance of Power' which means some countries are bigger and stronger than other countries.

2. Which are the two forms of co-operative security as per its traditional notion?

Ans. The two forms of co-operative security as per its traditional notion are

(i) Disarmament (ii) Confidence building

3. What is the relationship between traditional security and co-operation?

Ans. Traditional security is closely related with co-operation as it recognises the need for co-operation to limit violence. This limit directly relates to both means and ends of the war. It has been universally accepted that countries should go to war for the genuine reasons, say self-defence as to protect other people from genocide.

4. Explain the traditional concept of security.

***Or* What is the traditional notion of security?**

Ans. The traditional notion of security implies 'national security' covering both the external and internal threats.

The external threats has four main components like, Military threats, Threat of war, 'Balance of Power' and Alliance building.

Whereas, the internal threat is concerned with maintaining internal peace and order in the societies. Apart from this in traditional security, there is recognition that co-operation in limiting voilence is possible. And these limits relate both to the ends and the means of war.

5. How is 'Balance of Power' a component of traditional security? **CBSE 2024**

***Or* What is 'Balance of Power'?**

Ans. 'Balance of Power' refers to the maintenance of balance of military power in comparison to a neighbouring country.

The governments have to be very careful regarding balance of power between nations, as at some point of time in future any government can opt to be aggressive.

6. What is meant by the Non-traditional notion of security?

Ans. Non-traditional notion of security implies human security and global security. It goes beyond military threats to include a wide range of threats and dangers affecting the conditions of human existence.

Non-traditional security covers not just the state but also individuals or communities or indeed all of human kind.

7. Highlight the main reason that led to the emergence of the idea of global security. **CBSE 2020**

Ans. The idea of global security emerged in the 1990's in response to the global nature of threats such as global warming, international terrorism and health hazards like AIDS, Bird Flu, Swine Flu, etc. No country can resolve these problems alone.

In these global problems, international co-operation is vital, although it is difficult to achieve. Sometimes one country may face disproportionately the problems such as environmental degradation like Bangladesh, Maldives, Thailand, etc. Their problems should be tackled comprehensively.

8. Explain the meaning of 'Global Security'. **CBSE 2024**

Ans. Global security refers to the collaborative efforts of nations, organisations and institutions to ensure the safety, stability and peace of the international community. It encompasses protecting against threats such as terrorism, warfare, cyber attacks and climate change. Global security also includes arms control, conflict resolution and addressing economic and humanitarian crises, aiming to promote worldwide peace and co-operation.

9. Which sort of weapon both the superpowers did not want to give up under the concept of disarmament?

Ans. Disarmament requires all states to give up certain kinds of weapon i.e. the 1972 Biological Weapons Convention (BWC) banned the production and possession of these weapons.

Despite this, the US and Soviet Union were not ready to give-up the weapons of mass-destruction namely, nuclear weapons.

10. Highlight any two sources of threats being faced by the third world countries. **CBSE 2020**

Ans. The two new sources of threats being faced by the third world countries are

(i) **Terrorism** is a new source of threat which is faced by third world countries. It refers to political violence that targets civilians deliberately and indiscriminately.

(ii) **Health Epidemic** refers to HIV-AIDS, Bird Flu, Swine Flu, SARS (Severe Acute Respiratory Syndrome), etc. It can rapidly spread across the third world countries through migration, tourism etc.

11. Explain the difference between refugees and migrants. **CBSE 2020**

Ans. The difference between refugees and migrants is as follows

- Refugees are forced to abandon their homes and move across borders. They go through immense sufferings.
- On the other hand, migrants make a conscious choice to leave their country to seek a better life elsewhere. They plan their own travel and are free to return home at any time.

12. How has the strengthening of international norms and international institutions helped India protect its security interests? Explain. **Competency Based Que CBSE 2024**

Ans. The strengthening of international norms and institutions has helped India protect its security interests by promoting multilateral co-operation, ensuring global peace and combating terrorism. India's participation in organisations like the United Nations (UN) and adherence to international treaties has enhanced its diplomatic leverage, supported nuclear non-proliferation and facilitated defense collaborations, safeguarding its national security and strategic interests.

13. **'Terrorism is a new threat to security'. Support the statement.** CBSE 2024 Competency Based Que

Ans. Terrorism is a new threat to security because it goes beyond national borders, targeting civilians and governments alike, creating widespread fear and instability. Unlike traditional warfare, terrorism involves non-state actors using asymmetric tactics, including bombings, cyber attacks and kidnappings. It threatens global peace, disrupts economies and challenges national security by exploiting vulnerabilities, requiring co-ordinated international efforts to counter.

14. **'Nuclear weapons as deterrence or defense have limited usage against contemporary security threats to states'. Explain the statement.** SQP 2024 Competency Based Que

Ans. Nuclear weapons have limited effectiveness against modern security threats due to their changing nature. Today's challenges often involve non-state actors, cyber warfare, terrorism and climate change-threats that nuclear deterrence cannot address. The use of nuclear weapons against these threats is impractical and disproportionate. Additionally, the global consequences of nuclear warfare make their use highly undesirable, reducing their utility as a credible defense or deterrent in most contemporary scenarios.

Short Answer Type Questions

1. **What is meant by alliance building as a component of traditional security policy? What are its advantages?**

Or **What do you understand about alliance building? Explain its various advantages?** Diksha App

Ans. Alliance building is the fourth element of traditional security policy. An association or an alliance is a partnership of states which co-ordinate with each other to deter and defend against military attack.

Advantages of alliance building as a component or traditional security policy are as follows

- Most alliances are made in written treaties and are based on a fairly clear identification that makes the threat.
- Alliances are formed based on national interest and can change when national interests change. Countries form alliances to increase their effective power relative to another country or alliance.

2. **What are the Non-traditional notions to security?**

Ans. Non-traditional notions to security includes a wide range of threats affecting the conditions of human existence. It focuses on human security and global security.

(i) **Human Security** It refers to protection of people more than the protection of states. Here, state does not mean secure people. For example, more people have been killed by their own governments rather than by the foreign armies in the last 100 years.

(ii) **Global Security** The idea of global security came up in the 1990s in response to the global nature of threats like global warming, international terrorism and health epidemics like AIDS and Bird Flu, etc.

Therefore, it cannot be resolved by a single country rather a comprehensive effort of all countries is required to deal with such issues.

3. **What is the primary goal of human security ? Explain the difference between the narrow and broad concepts of human security.** Diksha App; CBSE 2024

Ans. The primary goal of human security is to protect individuals' rights and welfare, ensuring their safety from chronic threats such as violence, poverty and disease.

The narrow concept of human security focuses on safeguarding individuals from direct threats like armed conflict, terrorism and crime, emphasising physical safety. It often aligns with traditional security measures, prioritising state security and law enforcement.

In contrast, the broad concept encompasses a wider array of factors affecting human well-being, including economic stability, social equity, environmental sustainability and access to basic needs like education and health care. This perspective recognises that true security involves addressing the root causes of insecurity, fostering a holistic approach to human dignity and development.

4. **Explain any three components of the Indian security strategy.** Diksha App; CBSE 2024

Ans. India's security strategy has three main components.

(i) **Military Strength** India has strengthened its military due to past conflicts with Pakistan (1947, 1965, 1971, 1999) and China (1962). Surrounded by nuclear-armed nations, India conducted nuclear tests in 1974 and 1998 to safeguard national security.

(ii) **International Co-operation** India promotes peace and stability by supporting the UN. non-alignment, and global agreements like the Kyoto Protocol. It advocates for fair policies on nuclear weapons and economic development, ensuring equal rights for all countries.

(iii) **Internal Security** India faces internal challenges from separatist groups in Nagaland, Mizoram, Punjab and Kashmir. It maintains national unity through democracy, allowing diverse communities to voice concerns and share political power.

5. **Co-operative security may involve the use of force as a last resort. Analyse.** Competency Based Que

Ans. Co-operative security emphasises collaboration among states to enhance mutual safety and stability through dialogue, diplomacy and shared resources. While the primary goal is conflict prevention and resolution, the use of force may be considered as a last resort when diplomatic efforts fail. In such cases, co-operative security frameworks—like collective defense arrangements (e.g., NATO)—can authorise military intervention to address aggression or restore peace. This approach underscores the importance of multilateral co-operation, where member states work together to respond to threats in a manner that is proportional and justified. By prioritising peaceful solutions, co-operative security aims to minimise the need for force while maintaining the capability to act decisively when necessary.

Long Answer Type Questions

1. Distinguish between the internal and external notion of traditional security.

Ans. Difference between the internal and external notion of traditional security are as follows

Internal Notion	External Notion
Although internal security was a part of the concerns of the governments historically, however, it was not given much importance.	Mostly when we talk of security in traditional conception, it is about external security wherein greatest threats is from another country.
Internal security mainly concerned with maintaining internal peace and order and protecting the country from separatist threats within.	External notion of security is concerned with protecting sovereignty, independence and territorial integrity from military threats of another country.
Under internal notion of traditional security, security policy of states is either suppression of separatist demands or adjustment of their demands.	Under external notion, security policy are deterrence, defence, balance of power and alliance building.
Internal wars and conflicts now make up more than 95 per cent of all armed conflicts fought anywhere in the world.	Although, external security threats still have been major concern for governments, however frequency of war between countries has been reduced greatly now.
Internal security problems and threats can be regulated by acknowledged central authority that is government.	In case of external security conflicts, war and threats, there is no acknowledged central authority that stands above everyone else. UNO authority is only to the extent that member state allows.

2. Describe any three new sources of threat to security.

Ans. New sources of threat to security are as follows

(i) **Terrorism** It refers to political violence that targets civilians deliberately and indiscriminately.
International terrorism involves the citizens of territory of more than one country.
Civilian targets are usually chosen to terrorise the public and to use the unhappiness of the public as a weapon against the governments or other parties in conflict. Terrorism involve hijacking planes or planting bombs in trains, cafes, markets and other crowded places.

(ii) **Threats to Human Rights** Since the 1990s, developments such as Iraq's invasion of Kuwait, the genocide in Rwanda and the Indonesian military's killing of people in East Timor have led to a debate that the UN should interfere to stop human abuses or not. However, debates and discussions are taking place for the implementation of laws against the violation of the human rights by the UN.

(iii) **Global Poverty** It signifies a condition present in the states ranging from low incomes to less economic growth.
It is another source of insecurity, as the world population will reach to 1000 crore within 25 years. Currently, half of the world's population growth occurs in just six countries i.e. India, China, Pakistan, Nigeria, Bangladesh and Indonesia.
While the population of the poorest countries are expected to triple in the next 50 years, the population of rich countries will experience population decrease in that period. High per capita income and low population growth make rich state get richer, while the low incomes and hight population growth make them poorer.
This disparity contributes to the gap between the Northern and Southern countries of the world.

3. Explain any three security challenges faced by the newly independent countries of Asia and Africa after the Second World War. **CBSE 2024, 2025**

Ans. After the Second World War, newly independent countries in Asia and Africa faced several significant security challenges such as

(i) **Political Instability** Many of these nations emerged from colonial rule without stable political structures, leading to internal conflicts and power struggles. Ethnic and tribal divisions often flared into violence, as various groups vied for control, resulting in civil wars and prolonged unrest. Countries like Nigeria and Sudan experienced severe internal strife rooted in these divisions.

(ii) **Territorial Disputes** The arbitrary borders drawn during colonialism often grouped disparate ethnic communities together, leading to territorial disputes both within and between nations. For instance, the partition of India and Pakistan in 1947 triggered violent conflicts over Kashmir, with lasting geopolitical tensions that continue today.

(iii) **Cold War Dynamics** The global rivalry between the United States and the Soviet Union during the Cold War further complicated security. Newly independent states often found themselves pressured to align with one of the superpowers, leading to proxy wars, foreign interventions and de-stabilisation. Countries such as Vietnam and Afghanistan became battlegrounds for these larger geopolitical conflicts, severely affecting their sovereignty and security.

These challenges significantly hindered nation-building efforts and contributed to ongoing regional instability.

4. What is meant by global poverty? Suggest any two ways to reduce disparity between the poor and the rich at the global level.

Or **How is global Poverty a new source of threat to security in the contemporary world? Explain.** **CBSE 2024 C**

Ans. Global poverty is another source of insecurity.

High per capita income and low population growth make rich state or rich social groups get richer, whereas low incomes and high population growth reinforce each other to make poor states and poor groups get poorer.

Globally, this disparity contributes to the gap between the Northern and Southern countries of the world. Poverty in the South has also been causing large-scale migration to seek a better life and economic opportunities.

Two ways to reduce disparity between the poor and the rich at the global level are as following

(i) **Quality Education** Provides children knowledge and life skills they need to realise their full potential. Education is a means through which employable skills are imparted. To remove poverty globally, governments must ensure quality education to each and every child. Education is liberating force which liberate the people from poverty suppression, exploitation, etc.

(ii) **Economic and Social Security** To overcome poverty, communities around the world must be provided economic and social securities they need to thrive. Government across the globe must extend basic health care, education, housing, pension, disability insurance, survivor benefits and unemployment insurance to the families living under poverty.

5. Explain any three differences between the Traditional and Non-traditional notions of security.

Competency Based Que, CBSE 2025

Ans. Security is a fundamental concern for nations, but its understanding has evolved over time. Traditional security mainly focuses on military aspects, while non-traditional security addresses broader concerns that impact the well-being of individuals and societies. Below is a detailed comparison of these two notions

Aspect	Traditional Security	Non-Traditional Security
Focus	Traditional security is centered around protecting the sovereignty and territorial integrity of a nation. It primarily deals with military threats and external aggression from other countries.	Non-traditional security includes a wide range of threats that are not necessarily military in nature, such as economic instability, terrorism, environmental degradation, cyber threats and pandemics.
Nature of Threats	The threats in traditional security are mostly external, involving wars, border disputes, military conflicts and arms races between nations. The primary concern is the defense of the state.	The threats in non-traditional security can be both internal and external. These include climate change, organised crime, economic crises, refugee crises, human rights violations and diseases like COVID-19.
Approach to Security	The approach relies on military preparedness, strategic alliances, deterrence policies and arms buildup. Governments invest in defense forces, nuclear weapons and military technology to maintain security.	The approach is more comprehensive and involves international co-operation, economic policies, environmental conservation, public health measures and social development programmes to address security concerns.

6. Explain any three reasons for spending more on traditional security than on non-traditional security by India. **CBSE 2024**

Ans. India's emphasis on spending more on traditional security compared to non-traditional security is influenced by several factors as following

(i) **Geopolitical Tensions** India faces significant threats from neighboring countries, particularly Pakistan and China. The historical conflicts and ongoing border disputes necessitate a strong military presence and capabilities. This focus on conventional military readiness is deemed essential for deterrence and defense, leading to higher allocations for defense spending

(ii) **Asymmetric Warfare and Terrorism** India is increasingly targeted by non-state actors and terrorist organisations, particularly in regions like Jammu and Kashmir. While non-traditional security aspects such as counter terrorism are important, the immediate response to armed threats often requires military capabilities. Consequently, resources are diverted towards enhancing intelligence, surveillance and combat readiness to address these pressing security concerns.

(iii) **Resource Allocation and Prioritisation** Traditional security is often prioritised in budget allocations due to its direct impact on national sovereignty and territorial integrity. Government priorities focus on ensuring a robust military force capable of addressing conventional threats, while non-traditional security issues, such as environmental concerns or cyber threats, may receive comparatively less funding despite their growing importance.

This focus reflects a pragmatic approach to addressing the most immediate security challenges faced by the nation.

7. Explain health epidemics and terrorism as the two new source threat under the non-traditional sources of threat to security. **CBSE 2025**

Ans. For answer refer to text under th heading 'New Sources of Threats' on page no. 99-100.

8. Suggest the type of security that India should prefer to fight threats like poverty and epidemics? **CBSE 2025**

Ans. India should prioritise non-traditional security to effectively combat challenges like poverty and epidemics. Unlike traditional security, which focuses on military threats, non-traditional security encompasses human security, economic stability, public health and environmental protection.

Poverty in India is a complex issue that cannot be resolved through military strategies. Instead, the government must focus on economic policies, social welfare programmes, job creation and education to uplift vulnerable populations. Initiatives like Skill India, MGNREGA and financial inclusion schemes can help reduce poverty and improve the quality of life.

Similarly, epidemics like COVID-19 have demonstrated the importance of robust health care infrastructure. India needs better public health systems, medical research and disease surveillance mechanisms to prevent and manage future outbreaks. Strengthening institutions like ICMR, WHO collaborations and Ayushman Bharat can ensure nationwide health care coverage.

Moreover, addressing these challenges requires international co-operation, technological advancements and social welfare policies rather than military force. By focusing on non-traditional security, India can create a resilient society where economic and health-related threats are minimised, leading to sustainable national development.

Picture Based Questions

1. Observe the cartoon given below and answer the following questions.

(i) What does the cartoon represents?

(ii) What does the pigeon and man with goods symbolises?

(iii) What message does the cartoon convey?

Ans. (i) The cartoon represents the movement of peace keeping force i.e. pigeon (white) a symbol of peace and an army personnel is flying it.

(ii) Pigeon symbolises peace and a man with goods to maintain peace at a place where threat has occured.

(iii) The cartoon conveys message that the peace keeping forces are also supposed to bear arms to initiate peace.

2. Study the given cartoon and answer the questions that follow.

(i) What is the main cause of concern for the big powers as shown in the image above?

(a) New countries with nuclear weapon threatening the supremacy of big powers.

(b) Increasing pollution and global warming.

(c) Illiteracy in the increasing population.

(d) Small countries not accepting the hegemony of big powers.

Ans. (a) New countries with nuclear weapon threatening the supremacy of big powers.

(ii) Which are the two countries shown walking in the image given above?

(a) Pakistan and South Korea (b) Iran and North Korea
(c) Russia and Pakistan (d) China and North Korea

Ans. (b) Iran and North Korea

(iii) The meeting shown in the image is related to ....

(a) nuclear power countries (b) biggest carbon emitters
(c) declaration of world peace (d) controlling global warming

Ans. (a) nuclear power countries

(iv) Why do small countries want to join the big powers in the club membership?

(a) Security, prestige, dominance.
(b) Want to contribute to save environment.
(c) Want to be like developed economy like USA.
(d) To export domestic products for huge profit.

Ans. (a) Security, prestige, dominance.

3. Study the cartoon and answer the questions that follow.

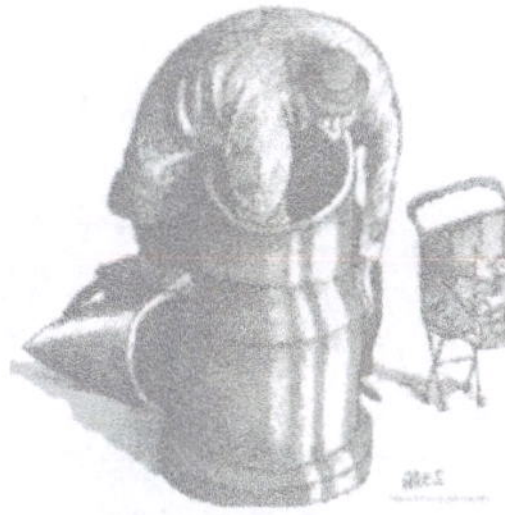

(i) What does the image primarily symbolise regarding arms in Third World countries?

(a) The growing importance of arms control in developed countries.
(b) The heavy military burden and arms proliferation affecting developing nations.
(c) The industrialisation and technological advancement of Third World countries.
(d) The peaceful co-existence of arms production in underdeveloped regions.

Ans. (b) The heavy military burden and arms proliferation affecting developing nations.

(ii) In the context of international relations, what might the cartoon suggest about the priorities of Third World nations?

(a) They prioritise defense spending over essential needs like food and healthcare.
(b) They have balanced both military and economic development successfully.
(c) They are global leaders in arms control initiatives.
(d) They have minimal military involvement and focus mainly on diplomacy.

Ans. (a) They prioritise defense spending over essential needs like food and healthcare.

(iii) What does the contrast between the large weapon and the nearby cart with basic supplies signify?

(a) The balance between economic growth and military preparedness in Third World nations.
(b) The disconnect between the arms industry and everyday survival needs in underdeveloped regions.
(c) The technological advancement in arms manufacturing in developing countries.
(d) The integration of military spending into everyday life.

Ans. (b) The disconnect between the arms industry and everyday survival needs in underdeveloped regions.

(iv) How does the image critique global arms proliferation in relation to Third World countries?

(a) It shows that Third World countries benefit from arms trading.
(b) It emphasises how arms proliferation negatively impacts basic human needs and development in these nations.
(c) It portrays Third World countries as aggressors in global conflicts.
(d) It advocates for more arms production in developing countries to ensure their security.

Ans. (b) It emphasises how arms proliferation negatively impacts basic human needs and development in these nations.

4. Observe the cartoon given below and answer the following questions.

(i) What does the cartoon represents?
(ii) Is it different from our country?
(iii) What message does this cartoon convey?

Ans. (i) The cartoon represents the US's massive expenditure of defence and lack of money for peace related issues.

(ii) Yes, it is different from our country as our country spends the major part in defence but also spends a lot on peaceful initiations and makes efforts to find out a peaceful solution first.

(iii) This cartoon conveys message that the countries are ready to spend on military rather than on department of peace.

SELF ASSESSMENT TEST

Objective Type Questions

1. The Anti-Ballistic Missile Treaty came up in the year ....

   (a) 1962 (b) 1968 (c) 1972 (d) 1973

2. Which of the following is the form of co-operation as per the Traditional Security?

   (a) Alliance-Building (b) Disarmament (c) Deterrence (d) Defence

3. What regulates acquisition of weapons?

   (a) Disarmament (b) Arms Control (c) Confidence Building (d) Balance of Power

4. Traditional concept of security includes

   (a) Only External (b) Only Internal

   (c) Both Internal and External (c) Security as Confidence Builders

Very Short Answer Type Questions

5. Briefly describe traditional views of security.
6. What is meant by human security?
7. What is global security?
8. What is disarmament?
9. Explain how separatist movements can be threat to security of the country.

Short Answer Type Questions

10. Mention any four components of traditional security.
11. Discuss the differences in security challenges faced by the newly independent countries of Asia and Africa.
12. Discuss confidence building measures as a means of avoiding violence.
13. Alliance making is a part of collective security. Critically analyse.

Long Answer Type Questions

14. In the traditional view of security, most threats to a country's security come from outside its orders. Justify the statement.
15. Discuss the common criterion for an issue to qualify as a security problem.
16. What are the different proponents of human security?
17. Enumerate the components of traditional security and co-operation.
18. Explain how refugees can threaten the security of the country.

06

CHAPTER

Environment and Natural Resources

Environmental concerns play a key role in world politics. Since the 1960s, various movements have emerged to protect nature. Common property resources, like forests and fisheries, require collective management. Global commons, such as oceans and the atmosphere, demand international co-operation. India has actively participated in climate discussions and conservation efforts.

YOUR STUDY GOALS

6.1 Environmental Concerns in Global Politics
6.2 Protection of Global Commons
6.3 India's Stand on Environmental Issues
6.4 Resource Geopolitics
6.5 Indigenous People and their Rights

YOUR PRACTICE GOAL

- Objective Type Questions (31 Qs ; MCQs, A-R, Statements, Matching, Passage Based)
- Subjective Questions (9 VSAs, 5 SAs, 5 LAs, 3 Picture Based)

6.1 Environmental Concerns in Global Politics

- The world's cultivable area is no longer expanding, and much of the agricultural land is losing fertility. Grasslands are over-grazed, fisheries over-harvested, and water bodies are polluted, limiting food production.
- The United Nations Development Programmes (UNDPs) 2016 Human Development Report states that 663 million people lack safe water, and 2.4 billion lack sanitation, leading to over three million child deaths each year.
- Natural forests, which stabilise the climate, moderate water supplies and support biodiversity, are being cut down. This displaces people and causes habitat loss.
- A steady decline in the total amount of ozone in the Earth's stratosphere (ozone hole) is posing threats to ecosystems and human health.
- While the open sea is relatively clean, coastal pollution is rising due to land-based activities, harming marine life.
- These issues aren't just natural phenomena; they have political consequences. Environmental degradation requires global action as no single government can solve them.

Environment: A significant Issue of Global Politics

- The Club of Rome, a global think tank, published a book in 1972 entitled **Limits to Growth.** It explained the potential depletion of the Earth's resources against the rapidly growing world population.
- International agencies, such as the United Nations Environment Programme (UNEP), began holding international conferences and promoting detailed studies to get a more co-ordinated and effective response to environmental problems.
- The importance of environmental issues in global politics became more clear during the United Nations Conference on Environment and Development in Rio de Janeiro, Brazil, in June 1992. This was also called the **Earth Summit**.
  - The Earth Summit was attended by 170 states, thousands of NGOs and many MNCs.
- **1987 Brundtland Report, Our Common Future,** had warned that traditional patterns of economic growth were not sustainable in the long term. This was especially true considering the demands of the South for further industrial development.
- First world countries[1] (referred to as **'Global North'**) are concerned about the global warming and ozone depletion. While third world countries[2] called as **'Global South'** are anxious to address the relationship between economic development and environmental management.
- The **Rio Summit** produced conventions dealing with climate change, biodiversity, forestry and recommended a list of development practices called **'Agenda 21'**.
- There was a consensus on combining economic growth with ecological responsibility. This approach to development is commonly known as 'sustainable development'. Some critics argued that Agenda 21 focused more on economic growth than on protecting the environment.

6.2 Protection of Global Commons

- 'Commons' are those resources which are not owned by anyone but rather shared by a community. This includes common place like a park or a river. There are many agreements for co-operation on global commons like 1959 Antarctic Treaty, the 1987 Montreal Protocol and the 1991 Antarctica Environmental Protocol. However the major issue is achieving the consensus on common environmental agendas.
- There are some areas or regions of the world which are located outside the sovereign jurisdiction of any one state. They therefore require common governance by the international community. These are known as **res communis humanitatis** or global commons. They include the Earth's atmosphere, Antarctica, the ocean floor and outer space.

Antarctica

Antarctica covers 14 million square kilometers, making up 26 per cent of the world's wilderness. It holds 90 per cent of terrestrial ice and 70 per cent of freshwater. The region includes 36 million square kilometers of ocean. It has few plants and animals including (e.g. microscopic algae, fungi and lichen), marine mammals, fish and hordes of birds. It has a productive marine ecosystem, with krill at the center of the food chain. Antarctica helps to maintain the global climate and provides important data on greenhouse gases and temperatures from ice cores.

There are disputes over ownership. Countries like the UK, Argentina, Chile, Norway and others claim sovereignty, while many believe Antarctica is part of the global commons, not owned by any country. Despite these claims, rules for environmental protection have been established. Since 1959, the region has been limited to scientific research, fishing and tourism, but waste and oil spills still harm parts of it.

1 First world countries It refers to industrialised nations with advanced economies.
2 Third world countries It refers to countries that are poor or developing.

- A key issue in environmental problems is reaching agreement based on unclear scientific evidence and timelines. The discord of the ozone hole in the 1980s showed both the opportunities and risks of global environmental issues.
- Similarly, the use of outer space highlights how North-South inequalities affect management. The main concern is that technology and industrial development benefit some more than others.

Common but Differentiated Responsibilities

- The developed countries of the North want to talk about the environment as it is now. They believe that everyone should share equal responsibility for protecting it.
- The developing countries of the South feel that much of the ecological degradation in the world is caused by the industrial development undertaken by the developed countries. If they have caused more degradation, they must also take more responsibility for undoing the damage now.
- The developing countries are in the process of **industrialisation period**[3] and they must not be subjected to the same restrictions, which apply to the developed countries. Thus the special needs of the developing countries must be taken into account in the development, application and interpretation of rules of International Environmental Law.
- This argument was accepted in the **Rio Declaration at the Earth Summit** in 1992. It is called the principle of **'common but differentiated responsibilities'**.
- According to the Rio Declaration, countries should co-operate to protect and restore the Earth's ecosystem. It acknowledges that all countries have a shared responsibility, but different countries have different levels of contribution to environmental damage.
- Developed countries recognise their larger role due to the pressure their societies place on the environment and their greater technological and financial resources.
- The **1992 United Nations Framework Convention on Climate Change** (UNFCCC) also provides that the parties should act to protect the climate system on the basis of equity and in accordance with their **common but differentiated responsibilities** and respective capabilities.
- The parties to the convention agreed that the largest share of historical and current global emissions of greenhouse gases has originated in developed countries.
- It was also accepted that per capita emissions in developing countries are still relatively low. China, India and other developing countries were, therefore, exempted from the requirements of the **Kyoto Protocol**.

Kyoto Protocol

- The protocol was agreed to in 1997 in Kyoto in Japan, based on principles set out in UNFCCC.
- It sets targets for industrialised countries to reduce their greenhouse gas emissions. Certain gases, like carbon dioxide and methane, contribute to global warming, which can harm life on the Earth. The protocol is based on guidelines from the UNFCCC.

Common Property Resources

- Common property is a resource shared by a group, where members have rights and duties to use and take care of it.
- Through mutual understanding and centuries of practice many village communities in India have defined member rights and responsibilities.
- Factors such as privatisation, agriculture intensification, population growth and ecosystem degradation have caused common property to degrade in size, quality and availability to the poor in the world.

3 **Industrialisation period** It is believed to be causing today's global warming and climate change.

Quick Test 1

1. What is Agenda 21?
2. What does the decline in the ozone layer pose a danger to?
3. When did awareness about environmental degradation and its consequences on economic growth arise as a political issue?
4. When was the Brundtland commission report released?

6.3 India's Stand on Environmental Issues

- India signed and ratified the **1997 Kyoto Protocol** in August 2002.
- India, China and other developing countries were exempt from the requirements of the Kyoto Protocol because their contribution to the emission of greenhouse gases during the **industrialisation period** was not significant.
- Critics of the Kyoto Protocol argue that eventually, countries like India and China, along with other developing nations will become some of the biggest contributors to greenhouse gas emissions.
- At the G-8 meeting in June 2005, India pointed out that the per capita emission[4] rates of the developing countries are a tiny fraction of those in the developed world.
- Following the principle of common but differentiated responsibilities, India is of the view that the major responsibility of curbing emission rest with the developed countries which have accumulated emissions over a long period of time.
- Based on the principle of 'common but differentiated responsibilities', India believes developed countries should take the lead in reducing emissions.
- India prioritises economic and social development for developing countries. It also opposes binding emission commitments for industrialising nations like itself, Brazil and China, as it goes against the UNFCCC spirit. By 2030, India's emissions will still be less than half the world average.
- India is engaged in global efforts with programs like the National Auto-fuel Policy for cleaner fuels, the **Energy Conservation Act (2001)** for energy efficiency, and the **Electricity Act (2003)** promoting renewable energy.
- India is also adopting clean coal technologies and importing natural gas. India ratified the **Paris Agreement in 2016** and has one of the largest renewable energy programmes.
- At the Earth Summit in 1997, India noted a lack of progress in providing financial resources and clean technologies to developing nations. India calls on developed countries to act immediately and urges SAARC countries to adopt a unified stance on global environmental issues.

Sacred Groves in India

Sacred groves in India are protected for religious reasons, dedicated to deities or spirits. They help preserve biodiversity, ecology and cultural diversity. These groves, ranging from small clumps to large forests, have spiritual value. Many temples originated from them. Preservation is driven by religious regard.

However, human settlement and new forest policies are threatening these groves. Conflicts arise when control is shared between the state and local communities with different goals.

Environmental Movements: One or Many

- Environmental movements are diverse and raise new ideas about protecting the environment. It is within social movements that new forms of political action are born.
- Forest movements in countries like Mexico, Brazil, India and others face major challenges. Deforestation continues despite decades of activism, and forest destruction has increased in the last decade.

4 **Per Capita Emission** It refers emissions of an average person in a country or region.

- The minerals industry, through global economic liberalisation, causes environmental damage by extracting minerals, polluting water and displacing communities.
- In the Philippines, many groups campaigned against the Western Mining Corporation (WMC), an Australian-based multi-national. There is also strong opposition to the company in Australia, due to anti-nuclear sentiments and support for indigenous rights.
- Anti-dam movements oppose mega-dam projects, focusing on sustainable river management and protecting rivers. The first anti-dam movement in the North was in the 1980s, focused on saving the Franklin river in Australia. Today, mega-dam construction is rising in countries like Turkey, Thailand, South Africa, Indonesia and China.
- India has led anti-dam movements, with the **Narmada Bachao Andolan** being one of the most well-known. Non-violence is a key principle in these movements.

6.4 Resource Geopolitics

- Resource geopolitics is about who controls resources and how they are accessed. Resources have played a key role in European power expansion and global rivalries. Western countries have focused on trade, war and power, especially with overseas resources and sea navigation.
- From the 17th century, securing timber for navies was a major priority for European powers. During both World Wars, the need for a steady supply of strategic resources, especially oil, became even more important.
- During the Cold War, countries used military forces, stockpiling, and supporting friendly governments to secure resources. They also worked with multi-national companies and made international agreements.
- Traditional Western strategic thinking focused on securing access to important resources, especially oil in the Gulf and minerals in Southern and Central Africa, as these could be threatened by the Soviet Union.
- After the Cold War ended and the Soviet Union collapsed, concerns about securing resources, especially radioactive materials, still influence government and business decisions. However, oil remains the most crucial resource in global strategy.

Oil

- The global economy relied on oil for much of the 20th century as a portable and indispensable fuel. The immense wealth associated with oil generates political struggles to control it. The history of petroleum is also the history of war and struggle.
- West Asia, specifically the Gulf region, accounts for about 30 per cent of global oil production. But it has about 64 per cent of the planet's known reserves. This makes it the only region capable of meeting a significant rise in oil demand.
- **Saudi Arabia** has a quarter of the world's oil reserves and is the largest producer. Iraq has the second-largest reserves and since parts of Iraq are still unexplored, its actual reserves could be much larger.
- Major consumers like the United States, Europe, Japan, and increasingly India and China, are far from this crucial region.

Water

- Water is a crucial resource that is important to global politics. Regional variations and the increasing scarcity of fresh water in some parts of the world point to the possibility of disagreements over shared water resources.
- Some commentators on world politics have referred to **'water wars'** to describe the possibility of violent conflict over this life-sustaining resource.
- Countries sharing rivers often have disagreements. A common issue is when upstream countries cause pollution, overuse water for irrigation, or build dams, which can reduce or harm the water quality for downstream countries. Sometimes, countries use force to protect or take control of freshwater resources.

- Examples of violence include those between Israel, Syria and Jordan in 1950s and 1960s over attempts by each side to divert water from the Jordan and the Yarmuk rivers. It also includes recent threats between Turkey, Syria and Iraq over the construction of dams on the Euphrates river.
- A number of studies show that countries that share rivers — and many countries do share rivers — are involved in military conflicts with each other.

6.5 Indigenous Peoples and their Rights

- The UN defines indigenous people as those people whose ancestors lived in a country before people of other culture and ethnicity arrived and took over. Today, they continue to follow their own traditions and customs, rather than the laws of the countries they are now part of.
- There are about 30 crore indigenous people worldwide, including in India. Indigenous people fight for recognition and equal rights globally.
- They live in regions like Central and South America, Africa, India (where they are called Tribals), Southeast Asia and Oceania, including Australia and New Zealand. Many of these lands were originally inhabited by Polynesian, Melanesian and Micronesian peoples.
- They often use the phrase **since times immemorial** to refer to their long-standing presence on their lands. The identity and survival of indigenous societies are tied to the land and its ecosystems. Losing their land means losing not just their homes but also their economic resources, which is the greatest threat to their survival.
- In India, indigenous people are referred to as **Scheduled Tribes** who constitute nearly **8 per cent** of the population. They depend on the cultivation of land for their subsistence.
- Most indigenous populations in India depend on cultivation for their livelihood, except for small groups of hunters and gatherers. For centuries, they had free access to land for cultivation. However, with the arrival of British colonial rule, the land once freely used by Scheduled Tribe communities was taken over by outside forces.
- Although they enjoy Constitutional protection in political representation, they have not received much of the benefits of development in the country. In fact they have paid a huge cost for development since they are the single largest group among the people displaced by various developmental projects since independence.
- Issues related to the rights of the indigenous communities have been neglected in domestic and international politics for very long.
- In the 1970s, increased interconnections among indigenous leaders from different countries led to a growing sense of shared concerns and common experiences. The **World Council of Indigenous Peoples** was formed in 1975. The council became subsequently the first of 11 indigenous NGOs to receive consultative status in the UN.

Quick Test 2

1. When was the first anti-dam movement started?
2. When was the World Council of Indigenous people formed?
3. Who are referred to as Scheduled Tribes?
4. When did India sign the Kyoto Protocol?

Mind Map

ENVIRONMENT AND NATURAL RESOURCES

1 Environmental Concerns in Global Politics

- Agriculture land is shrinking and losing fertility.
- Billions lack clean water and sanitation across world causes child deaths.
- Forest are disappearing, harming the climate and habitats also.
- Ozone hole and pollution threatens life on the earth.

Environment: A Significant Issue of Global Politics

- The club of Rome published 'Limits to Growth' book in 1972 to warn about resources depletion.
- UNEP promotes global environmental action.
- The 1992 Earth Summit focused on sustainable development.
- The Brundtland Report called growth unsustainable.
- The Rio summit produced a list of development practices called Agenda 21.
- Consensus on combining economic growth with ecological responsibility.

2 Protection of Global Commons

- Commons are shared resources like Parks and rivers.
- Global commons includes the atmosphere, Antarctica oceans and outer space.
- Antarctica treaty, Montreal protocol aims to protect the global commons.
- Outer space use expose North-South inequality in use.
- Environment agreement struggles due to unclear scientific evidences.

3 Common But Differentiated Responsibilities

- This means countries share environmental duties but with varying levels.
- Developing countries of the South feel that much of the ecological degradation in the world is caused by the industrial development under the developed countries.
- This principle was adopted in 1992 in Rio declaration.
- According to the Rio Declaration, countries should co-operate to protect and restore the Earth's ecosystem.
- The largest share of historical and current global emissions of greenhouse gases has originated in developed countries.
- Developing countries were exempted from strict emission targets of Kyoto protocols.
- Kyoto protocol set targets for industrialised countries to reduce GHG emission.
- The protocol is based on guidelines of the UNFCCC.

4 Common Property Resources

- Common property resources are shared with defined rights and responsibilities.
- Indian village communities have long managed these resources through mutual agreement.
- Privatisation of agriculture and population growth have degraded the natural resources.
- Industrialisation contributes to global warming and climate change.

5 India's Stand on Environmental Issues

- India ratified the Kyoto protocol in August 2002 but was exempted from emission cuts.
- Critics say India and china will become major emitter in future.
- India believes that developed nations should lead in emission reduction.
- India focuses on economic growth and support renewable energy based solutions.

6 Resource Geopolitics

- Resource geopolitics is about who controls resources and how they are accessed.
- Securing timber for navies was a major priority for European powers in 17th century.
- Europeans worked with multi-national companies and made international agreements to grab resources.
- Traditional Western strategic thinking was focused on securing access to important resources.
- After the Cold War the Soviet Union get collapsed, concerns about resource supply were raised.

Oil

- The history of petroleum is also the history of war and struggle.
- Global economy is relied on oil for much of the 20th century as a portable and indispensable fuel.
- Iraq has the second-largest reserves and some parts of Iraq are still unexplored.
- Major consumers like the United States, Europe, Japan, and increasingly India and China, are far from this crucial region.

Water

- Water is a crucial resource that is important to global politics.
- World politics have referred to 'water wars' to describe the possibility of violent conflict over this life-sustaining resource.
- Countries sharing rivers often have disagreements.
- Sometimes, countries use force to protect or take control of freshwater resources.

7 Indigenous Peoples and Their Rights

- There are about 30 crore indigenous people worldwide, including in India.
- They live in regions like Central and South America, Africa, India.
- Obvious threat of indigenous people is loss of land which also means the loss of an economic resource base.
- Issues related to the rights of the indigenous communities have been neglected in domestic and international politics for very long.
- Increased interconnections among indigenous leaders from different countries.
- They (World Council for Indigenous People) became subsequently the first of 11 indigenous NGOs to receive consultative status in the UN.

NCERT Folder

1. Which among the following best explains the reason for growing concerns about the environment?

(i) The developed countries are concerned about protecting nature.

(ii) Protection of the environment is vital for indigenous peoples and natural habitats.

(iii) The environmental degradation caused by human activities has become pervasive and has reached a dangerous level.

(iv) None of the above

Ans. (iii) The environmental degradation caused by human activities has become pervasive and has reached a dangerous level.

2. Mark correct or wrong against each of the following statements below that describe the Earth Summit.

(i) It was attended by 170 countries, thousands of NGOs and many MNCs.

(ii) The summit was held under the aegis of the UN.

(iii) For the first time, global environmental issues were firmly consolidated at the political level.

(iv) It was a summit meeting.

Ans. (i) Correct (ii) Correct (iii) Correct (iv) Correct

3. Which among the following are true about the global commons?

(a) The Earth's atmosphere, Antarctica, the ocean floor and outer space are considered as part of the global commons.

(b) The global commons are outside sovereign jurisdiction.

(c) The question of managing the global commons has reflected the North-South divide.

(d) The countries of the North are more concerned about protection of the global commons than the countries of the South.

Ans. (a) True (b) True

(c) True (d) False

4. What were the outcomes of the Rio Summit?

Ans. The outcomes of the Rio Summit are as follows

- The Rio Summit produced conventions dealing with climate change, bio-diversity, forestry and recommended a list of development practices called Agenda 21.
- It gave the concept of sustainable development to be combined with economic growth and ecological responsibility.

5. What is meant by global commons? How are they exploited and polluted?

Ans. The areas or regions of the world which are located outside the sovereign jurisdiction of any one state and require common governance by the international community are known as global common. They include the Earth's atmosphere, Antarctica, the ocean floor and outer space.

These areas are exploited and polluted due to the following reason

(i) Vague scientific evidences, their lack of consensus on common environmental issues.

(ii) The inequalities between North-South and their exploitative activities and competition lack proper management area out space.

(iii) The Earth's atmosphere and the ocean floor have also been affected by technological and industrial development.

6. What is meant by 'Common but differentiated responsibilities'? How could we implement the idea?

Ans. Common but Differentiated Responsibilities' (CBDR) is a principle in international environmental law recognising that all nations share responsibility for protecting the environment, but not equally. Developed countries have contributed more to environmental damage due to industrialisation. They must take greater responsibility for addressing it. Developing nations, st industrialising, should have fewer restrictions. Implementing CBDR requires financial and technological support from developed nations to help developing countries adopt sustainable practices. Global policies, such as the Kyoto Protocol, should set fair targets based on each nation's capacity. Co-operation and equitable burden-sharing are key to effective climate action.

7. Why have issues related to global environment protection become the priority concern of states since the 1990s?

Ans. Since the 1990s, global environmental protection has become a priority due to increasing threats like climate change, deforestation and pollution. Scientific reports warned of rising temperatures, biodiversity loss, and resource depletion, pushing nations to act. The 1992 Earth Summit and Rio Declaration emphasised sustainable development, while the Kyoto Protocol set emission reduction targets. Natural disasters, rising sea levels, and extreme weather events further highlighted the urgency.

Industrialised nations acknowledged their historical role in environmental damage, while developing countries demanded fair responsibilities. As environmental issues became linked to economic stability, human health, and security, international co-operation gained momentum.

8. Compromise and accommodation are the two essential policies required by states to save planet Earth. Substantiate the statement in the light of the ongoing negotiations between the North and South on environmental issues. Competency Based Que

Ans. Compromise and accommodation are the two essential policies to save planet Earth by the states but the states from North and South have different notions towards environmental issues

- The Northern states (Developed countries) are concerned with ozone depletion and global warming, whereas Southern states (Developing) want to address the relationship between economic development and environmental management.
- The developed countries of the North want to discuss the environmental issues as it stands today.
- The developing countries of the South feel that much of the ecological degradation in the world is created by developed countries through their industrial projects.
- Developed countries are supposed to take more responsibility since they cause more environmental degradation.
- The developing countries should be exempted from restrictions imposed on developed countries through various conventions since they are under process of industrialisation.
- The special needs of developing countries must be taken into consideration in the process of development, application and interpretation of rules of International Environmental Law.

Therefore, all the above mentioned provisions were accepted in the Earth Summit, 1992, while adopting common but differentiated responsibilities.

9. The most serious challenge before the states is pursuing economic development without causing further damage to the global environment. How could we achieve this? Explain with a few examples. Competency Based Que

Ans. The economic development without causing further damage to the global environment can be achieved by adopting the following approaches

- The approach to development should be of sustainable development i.e. economic growth with ecological responsibility.
- There should be more cooperation over the global commons i.e. the Earth's atmosphere, Antarctica, the ocean floor and outer space.
- There should be proper implementation and execution of Kyoto Protocol in achieving targets of greenhouse gas emissions.
- Forest clearing in the Third World which continues at an alarming rate must be stopped.
- The mineral industry's extraction of the Earth, use of chemicals and clearance of vegetation and other activities should be checked.
- The use of renewable resources should be encouraged.

Exam Pattern Questions

Objective Type Questions

Multiple Choice Questions (MCQs)

1. Which of the following is/are accounted as the major environmental problems across the globe?

(a) Forest depletion (b) Ozone depletion
(c) Overgrasing (d) Both (a) and (b)

2. Which among the following is/are the environmental issues that are concerned of global politics?

(a) The decline in the cultivable land throughout the world.
(b) Grasslands have been over-grazed and fisheries over-harvested.
(c) A steady decline in the total amount of ozone in the earth stratosphere.
(d) All of the above

3. What are the main causes of global warming?

(a) Deforestation
(b) Increased use of fossil fuels
(c) Increase intensive agriculture activities
(d) All of the above

4. The ozone hole is present in ....
(a) stratosphere (b) mesosphere
(c) troposphere (d) ionosphere

5. Which among the following are greenhouse gases?
(a) Methane (b) Carbon dioxide
(c) Hydro-fluoro Carbon (d) All of these

6. Statement I A steady decline in the total amount of ozone in the Earth's stratosphere poses a real danger to ecosystems and human health.
Statement II Although the open sea is relatively clean, the coastal waters are becoming increasingly polluted.
In the light of above statements, choose the correct answer from the options given below
(a) Both Statement I and Statement II are true.
(b) Both Statement I and Statement II are false.
(c) Statement I is true, but Statement II is false.
(d) Statement I is false, but Statement II is true.

7. This conference led to the establishment of a global action plan to promote sustainable development in 1992, Brazil. This is ....
(a) World Summit on Sustainable Development.
(b) UN Conference on Environment and Development.
(c) General Assembly Special Session on the Environment.
(d) UN Sustainable Development Summit.

8. Global common include the Earth's .... Antarctica, the ocean floor and the outer space.
(a) atmosphere (b) arctic region
(c) environment (d) lithosphere

9. Statement I 'Commons' are those resources which are not owned by anyone but rather shared by a community.
Statement II They include the Earth's atmosphere, Antarctica, the ocean floor and outer space.
In the light of above statements, choose the correct answer from the options given below
(a) Both Statement I and Statement II are true.
(b) Both Statement I and Statement II are false.
(c) Statement I is true, but Statement II is false.
(d) Statement I is false, but Statement II is true.

10. Which one of the following agency of the UN is related to environmental issues?
(a) UNDP (b) UNEP
(c) UNESCO (d) UNHRC

11. Which among the following is the first global treaty to explicitly address climate change?
(a) Montreal Protocol, 1987
(b) UN Framework Convention on Climate Change (UNFCCC), 1992
(c) Kyoto Protocol, 2005
(d) Paris Agreement, 2015

12. Which of the following statement(s) is/are correct about UNFCCC.
(a) It provides that parties should act to protect the climate system.
(b) It should be on the basis of equity.
(c) It is an international environment treaty adopted in 1992.
(d) All of the above

13. Which one of the following treaty is wrongly matched?
(a) Antarctic Treaty-1959 (b) Montreal Protocol-1987
(c) Kyoto Protocol - 1997
(d) Antarctic Environmental Protocol-1987

14. What was the purpose of Kyoto Protocol? Diksha App
(a) Preventing the emission of greenhouse gases to check global warning
(b) Preventing the water pollution
(c) Preventing the electronic pollution
(d) Preventing the air pollution

15. Choose the correct statement.
I. The Club of Rome, published a book in 1972 entitled Limits to Growth.
II. In 1987, Brundtland Report, Our Common Futures was published.
III. The Rio Summit produced conventions dealing with climate change, biodiversity forestry and recommended a list of development practices called Agenda 21.
IV. Common but differentiated responsiblities were declared at the Earth Summit in 1992.
Codes
(a) I and II (b) III and IV
(c) I, III and IV (d) All of these

16. Match the List-I correctly with List-II.

List I	List II
A. Antarctic Treaty	1. 1997
B. Montreal Protocol	2. 1991
C. Antarctic Environmental Protocol	3. 1987
D. Kyoto Protocol	4. 1959

Codes

	A	B	C	D		A	B	C	D
(a)	4	3	2	1	(b)	1	2	3	4
(c)	2	4	1	3	(d)	3	1	4	2

17. Arrange the following in chronological order of their formation CBSE SQP 2024
I. Energy Conservation Act
II. Paris Climate Agreement
III. The Electricity Act
IV. Montreal Protocol

Codes

(a) I, II, III, IV (b) II, IV, I, III
(c) IV, I, III, II (d) III, I, II, IV

18. **Match List I with List II and choose the correct option** **CBSE 2024**

	List I		List II
A.	Kyoto Protocol	1.	List of developmental practices
B.	Electricity Act	2.	Economic growth with ecological responsibility
C.	Agenda 21	3.	Aims to cut greenhouse gas emissions
D.	Sustainable Development	4.	Encourages use of renewable energy

Codes

	A	B	C	D
(a)	3	4	1	2
(b)	2	3	4	1
(c)	4	1	3	2
(d)	1	2	3	4

19. **Which of the following acts was passed to encourage the use of renewable energy?**

(a) The Energy Conservation Act of 2001
(b) The Electricity Act of 2003
(c) The Antarctic Treaty of 1959
(d) None of the above

20. **Which of the following fact is incorrect regarding the environmental movements?**

(a) Various organisation works in collaboration for addressing environmental concerns.
(b) These are diverse and powerful social movements with long-term visions.
(c) New forms of political action are reinvented within these movements.
(d) These movements are generally violent in nature.

21. **Given below are two statements.** **CBSE SQP 2024**

Statement I Resource geopolitics pertains to the allocation of resources during the cold war.

Statement II Oil is considered as the most important resource in global politics.

In the light of above statements, choose the correct answer from the options given below.

(a) Both Statement I and Statement II are true
(b) Both Statement I and Statement II are false.
(c) Statement I is true, but Statement II is false.
(d) Statement I is false, but Statement II is true.

22.

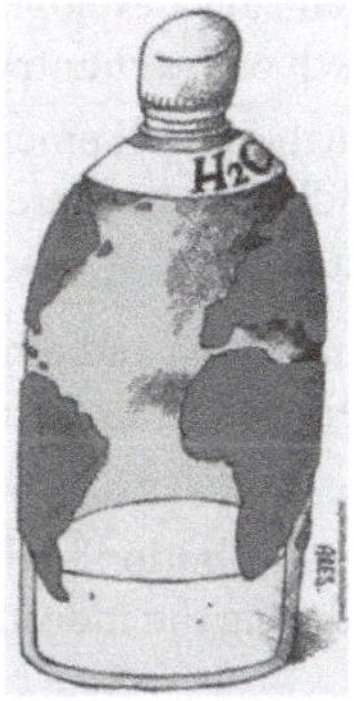

What message does the disproportionate focus on land in the image cowry about water?

(a) Water is plentiful easily accessible
(b) Water is being overlooked
(c) Water scarcity is a gearing concern
(d) water is as important as land

23. **Match List I with List II and choose the correct option** **CBSE 2024 C**

	List I		List II
A.	The Energy Conservation Act, India	1.	1975
B.	The Electricity Act, India	2.	1992
C.	Earth Summit	3.	2001
D.	World Council of Indigenous Peoples	4.	2003

Codes

	A	B	C	D		A	B	C	D
(a)	4	1	3	2	(b)	3	4	2	1
(c)	2	3	1	4	(d)	1	2	4	3

Assertion-Reason Questions

Directions (Q. Nos. 24-27) In the questions given below, there are two statements marked as Assertion (A) and Reason (R). Read the statements and choose the correct option.

Codes

(a) Both A and R are true and R is the correct explanation of A.
(b) Both A and R are true, but R is not the correct explanation of A.
(c) A is true, but R is false.
(d) A is false, but R is true.

24. **Assertion** (A) Global atmosphere is warming up.

Reason (R) The depletion of the stratospheric ozone layer has resulted in an increase in ultravoilet radiation reaching the Earth. **CBSE 2024**

25. Assertion (A) Sustainable development is essential for the economic growth of the country.

Reason (R) Sustainable development ensures that environment-friendly measures are adopted for carrying out the production process.

26. Assertion (A) India, China and other developing countries were exempted from the requirements of the Kyoto Protocol. **CBSE 2024**

Reason (R) Their contribution to the emissions of greenhouse gases during the industrialisation period was not significant.

27. Assertion (A) Oil continues to be the most important resource in global strategy.

Reason (R) The immense wealth associated with oil generates political struggles.

Passage Based Questions

28. Read the following passage carefully and answer the questions that follow.

The growing focus on environmental issues within the arena of global politics was firmly consolidated at the United Nations Conference on Environment and Development held in Rio de Janeiro, Brazil, in June 1992. The summit was attended by 170 states, thousands of NGOs and many multinational corporations. Five years earlier, the 1987 Brundtland Report, Our Common Future, had warned that traditional patterns of economic growth were not sustainable in the long term, especially in view of the demands of the South for further industrial development.

What was obvious at the Rio Summit was that the rich and developed countries of the First World, generally referred to as the 'Global North' were pursuing a different environmental agenda than the poor and developing countries of the Third World, called the 'Global South'. Whereas the Northern states were concerned with ozone depletion and global warming, the Southern states were anxious to address the relationship between economic development and environmental management.

(i) Which summit has been referred in the above passage?

(a) The Earth Summit
(b) Kyoto Protocol
(c) World Summit on Sustainable Development
(d) UN Sustainable Development Summit

(ii) Which of the following countries are known as Third World Countries?

(a) USA (b) UK
(c) India and South Africa (d) France

(iii) The environmental agenda of Global North is based on ....

(a) economic development
(b) environmental management
(c) ozone depletion and global warming
(d) climate awareness

(vi) Agenda 21 is related with which among the following?

(a) The Earth Summit (b) Kyoto Protocol
(c) Montreal Protocol (d) UNFCCC

29. Read the following passage carefully and answer the questions that follow

India is of the view that the major responsibility of curbing emission of greenhouse gases rests with the developed countries, which have accumulated emissions over a long period of time. India pointed out that the per capita emission rates of the developing countries are a tiny fraction of those in the developed world.

(i) Why were some developing countries exempted from the requirements of the Kyoto Protocol ?

(a) They were pioneers in developing eco-friendly technology.
(b) They were assisting some other countries to adopt clean technologies.
(c) They had already launched renewable energy programmes.
(d) Their contribution to emission of greenhouse gases was not significant.

(ii) India signed and ratified the Kyoto Protocol in

(a) August 2000 (b) August 2001
(c) August 2002 (d) August 2003

(iii) Which one of the following is an example of Global Commons ?

(a) The Great Barrier Reef (b) The Grand Canyon
(c) The Outer Space (d) The Sahara Desert

(iv) Why does India believe that developed countries should bear a greater responsibility for reducing greenhouse gas emissions?

30. Read the following passage carefully and answer the questions that follow

The question of indigenous people brings the issues of environment, resources and politics together. The UN defines indigenous populations as comprising the descendants of peoples who inhabited the present territory of a country at the time when persons of a different culture or ethnic origin arrived there from other parts of the world and overcame them. Indigenous people today live more in conformity with their particular social, economic and cultural customs and traditions than the institutions of the country of which they now form a part.

(i) Which of the following best describes the United Nations' definition of indigenous populations?
(a) People who have migrated to other parts of the world in search of better resources and opportunities.
(b) Descendants of people who inhabited a country before the arrival of different cultures or ethnic origins.
(c) Communities who have modernised and adapted to the institutions of the countries they live in.
(d) Tribes who settled in urban areas for employment and better living conditions.

(ii) What is the primary concern for indigenous people around the world?
(a) The need for modern technology to uplift their living standards.
(b) The loss of land, which also means the loss of an economic resource base.
(c) The desire to migrate and seek better resources in different countries.
(d) The need to integrate fully into the institutions of their countries.

(iii) Explain how indigenous people's struggles are connected to world politics.

31. Read the given passage carefully and answer the questions that follow **CBSE 2024 C**

'Commons' are those resources which are not owned by anyone but rather shared by a community. This could be a 'common room' or a 'community centre', a park or a river. Similarly, there are some areas or regions of the world which are located outside the sovereign jurisdiction of any one state and therefore require common governance by the international community. These are known as 'Global Commons'.

(i) Which one of the following aspects best describes the 'Global Commons' ?
(a) Resources only accessible for scientific research.
(b) Resources under the jurisdiction of a single nation.
(c) Resources located outside the governance of developed nations.
(d) Sovereign regions under the common governance of the international community.

(ii) The Rio Summit of 1992 is also known as ....
(a) Global Summit (b) Planet Summit
(c) The Earth Summit (d) World Summit

(iii) Why is international cooperation essential for managing the 'Global Commons' ?
Choose the most suitable option from the following
(a) Resources are abundant and self-replenishing.
(b) There are political benefits for sharing resources of other countries.
(c) Individual countries can manage their resources.
(d) The approach towards sustainable development is common for all.

(iv) Which of the following pair of countries was exempted from the requirements of the Kyoto Protocol ?
(a) China and Russia (b) China and India
(c) China and USA (d) India and France

Answers

1. (d) Both (a) and (b) **2.** (d) All of the above
3. (d) All of the above **4.** (a) stratosphere
5. (d) All of these
6. (a) Both Statement I and Statement II are true.
7. (b) UN Conference on Environment and Development.
8. (a) atmosphere
9. (a) Both Statement I and Statement II are true.
10. (b) UNEP
11. (b) UN Framework Convention on Climate Change (UNFCCC), 1992
12. (d) All of the above
13. (d) Antarctic Environmental Protocol-1987
14. (a) Preventing the emission of greenhouse gases to check global warning
15. (d) All of these **16.** (a) 4 3 2 1
17. (c) IV, I, III, II **18.** (a) 3 4 1 2
19. (b) The Electricity Act of 2003
20. (d) These movements are generally violent in nature.
21. (d) Statement I is false, but Statement II is true.
22. (c) Water scarcity is a growing concern.
23. (b) 3 4 2 1
24. (b) Both A and R are true, but R is not the correct explanation of A
25. (a) Both A and R are true and R is the correct explanation of A.
26. (a) Both A and R are true and R is the correct explanation of A.
27. (a) Both Assertion A and Reason R are true and Reason R is the correct explanation of the Assertion A.
28. (i) (a) The Earth Summit
(ii) (c) India and South Africa
(iii) (c) ozone depletion and global warming
(vi) (a) The Earth Summit
29. (i) (d) Their contribution to emission of greenhouse gases was insignificant.

(ii) (c) August 2002 (iii) (c) The Outer Space

(iv) India argues that developed countries have historically accumulated emissions over a long period, making them primarily responsible for the current levels of greenhouse gases. Additionally, the per capita emission rates of developing countries like India are significantly lower compared to those of developed nations.

30. (i) (b) Descendants of people who inhabited a country before the arrival of different cultures or ethnic origins.

(ii) (b) The loss of land, which also means the loss of an economic resource base.

(iii) Indigenous people's struggles are deeply connected with world politics because they often face challenges related to land rights, resource access and cultural identity. These issues frequently arise from historical colonisation and contemporary government policies that disregard their rights. Indigenous people around the world, including those in regions like South America, Africa, Southeast Asia and India, face common problems such as the loss of their ancestral lands and the economic base those lands provide.

31. (i) (d) Sovereign regions under the common governance of the international community.

(ii) (c) The Earth Summit

(iii) (d) The approach towards sustainable development is common for all.

(iv) (B) China and India

Subjective Questions

Very Short Answer Type Questions

1. Mention any two environmental issues that have become the concern of global politics.

Ans. The environmental issues which are causes of concern to the global politics are

- The cultivable land area is declining throughout the world and existing agricultural land is losing fertility. Grassland have been overgrased and fisheries over-harvested.
- Water bodies have suffered extensive depletion and pollution which severely restricted food production.

2. Explain any two outcomes of the 'Earth Summit' held in june 1992 in Rio de Janeiro. CBSE 2024

Or **State any two outcomes of the Rio Summit.** CBSE 2025

Ans. The Earth Summit in Rio de Janeiro (1992) led to two key outcomes which are as follows

(i) **Agenda 21** A comprehensive action plan for sustainable development worldwide, aiming to address environmental and social issues.

(ii) **Rio Declaration** This set of 27 principles emphasised the need for global co-operation on environmental protection and sustainable development, balancing economic progress with ecological conservation.

3. Analyse any two reasons as to why issues of environment and natural resources have become a part of world politics. CBSE 2024

Ans. Issues of environment and natural resources have become part of world politics due to

- **Global interdependence** Environmental challenges like climate change, deforestation and pollution transcend national borders. They require international co-operation for sustainable solutions.
- **Resource scarcity** The depletion of vital resources such as water, energy and minerals has led to competition and conflicts, pushing nations to address these issues collectively on global platforms.

4. What is UNFCCC?

Ans. The 1992, United Nations Framework Convention Climate Change (UNFCCC) provides that the parties should act to protect the climate system on the basis of equity and in accordance with the common but differentiated responsibility.

5. Is there any difference between the perspective adopted by the rich and the poor nations to protect the Earth at Rio-Summit? Competency Based Que

Ans. Yes, the rich and the poor nations adopted different perspectives to protect the Earth at Rio-Summit. These were

- The rich countries were called as Global North, whereas the poor countries were called Global South.
- Northern states showed concern with ozone depletion and global warming whereas Southern states showed concern for economic development and environmental management.

6. How environmental movements play a significant role in the society?

Ans. Environmental movements plays a significant role in the society in the following ways

- It helps to create awareness among the masses as more people become aware regarding the effects of human activities on the environment.

- These movements advocate for re-use and the recycling of non-biodegradable products such as plastics, obsolete electrical equipment and many others.

7. Name any four Greenhouse gases. **CBSE 2025**

Ans. Greenhouse gases (GHGs) are gases in the atmosphere that trap heat and contribute to global warming and climate change. Four major greenhouse gases are

- **Carbon Dioxide (CO_2)** Released from burning fossil fuels like coal, oil and gas, it is the primary cause of global warming.
- **Methane (CH_4)** Emitted from livestock, agriculture and landfills, it is more potent than CO_2 in trapping heat.
- **Nitrous Oxide (N_2O)** Produced from fertilisers, industrial activities and vehicle emissions.
- **Chlorofluorocarbons (CFCs)** Found in refrigerants and aerosol sprays, they damage the ozone layer and increase global warming.

8. What common interests do indigenous people share in world politics?

Ans. Indigenous peoples worldwide advocate for recognition, equality, cultural preservation, land rights and the acknowledgment of their identity and traditions. They seek to join the global community as equals while maintaining their unique heritage.

9. What challenges do downstream countries face in managing shared water resources?

Ans. Downstream countries often face reduced water availability and quality due to upstream actions, such as dam construction and pollution. These challenges lead to disputes, as downstream states rely on upstream co-operation to safeguard their water needs.

Short Answer Type Questions

1. "States have common but differentiated responsibilities towards environment". Analyse the statement giving suitable examples.

Or **"States have not only common, but differentiated responsibilities also". Support the statement with two suitable arguments.** **CBSE 2025**

Ans. The given statement is true due to the following reasons

- The developing countries feel that much of the environmental degradation in the world is the product of industrial development undertaken by the developed countries. If they have caused more degradation, they must also take more responsibility for undoing the damage.
- Developing countries are in the process of industrialisation and they must not be subjected to the same restrictions. They must be taken into account in the development application and interpretation of rules of international environmental law. This argument was accepted in the Rio Declaration at the Earth Summit in 1992 and is called 'common but differentiated responsibilities.'
- The 1992 United National Framework Conversation on Climate Change (UNFCCC) also provides that the states should act to protect the climate system on the basis of equality and in accordance with their common but differentiated responsibilities.

2. "The Indian Government is already participating in global efforts through a number of programmes related to environmental issues". Give any four examples to support the statement.

Or **Explain any three programmes initiated by the Government of India to protect and conserve the environment.** **CBSE 2024**

Ans. Initiatives undertaken by the Indian Government in global efforts through a number of programmes to check environmental degradation are

(i) India's National Auto Fuel Policy mandates cleaner fuels for vehicles. The Energy Conservation Act, passed in 2001, outlines initiatives to reform energy efficiency.

(ii) The Electricity Act of 2003, supports the use of renewable energy. Presently, India is importing natural gas and encouraging the adoption of clean coal technologies. It shows India's sincere efforts in this direction.

(iii) The Indian Government also started 'National Mission on Biodiesel'. Nearly, 11 million hectares of land is being used to produce biodiesel.

(iv) India has also one of the largest renewable energy programmes in the world.

3. Highlight any two threats to the survival of Indigenous people. **CBSE 2025**

Ans. Indigenous communities around the world face numerous challenges that threaten their survival and way of life. Two major threats are

Loss of Land and Resources One of the biggest challenges indigenous people face is the forcible acquisition of their land for industrial projects, mining, deforestation and urban development. Governments and corporations often prioritise economic development over indigenous rights which results in the displacement and loss of their traditional livelihoods. When they lose access to their land, they struggle to sustain their agricultural and hunting practices, which are deeply connected to their cultural identity.

Climate Change and Environmental Degradation Many indigenous communities live in forests, coastal areas and river basins which are highly vulnerable to climate change. Rising sea levels, deforestation and pollution disrupt their ecosystems. Natural disasters like hurricanes, floods and droughts disproportionately affect them as they lack adequate resources and government support.

4. Name any four global commons CBSE 2025

Ans. 'Global commons' are those resources which are not owned by anyone but rather shared by a community. Four major global commons are

- **The High Seas** These are parts of the oceans that do not fall under any country's territorial control and are crucial for marine biodiversity.
- **The Atmosphere** It is essential for life and is impacted by pollution and climate change, requiring global efforts for protection.
- **Antarctica** A continent governed by the Antarctic Treaty, which prohibits military activities and promotes scientific research.
- **Outer Space** It is regulated by international treaties to prevent conflicts and ensure peaceful exploration. Since these resources belong to all of humanity, sustainable management and international co-operation are necessary to prevent over-exploitation and environmental damage.

5. Suggest any four steps for the Indian Government to take to check the pollution and save the environment. CBSE 2025

Ans. The Indian Government can take several steps to control pollution and protect the environment.

- **Improving Public Transport** Expand and promote eco-friendly public transport like metro systems and electric buses to reduce vehicular emissions and traffic congestion.
- **Promotion of Renewable Energy** Encourage the use of solar, wind and hydro energy to reduce dependence on fossil fuels, which contribute to air pollution and climate change.
- **Industrial Waste Management** Implement strict regulations for industries to treat wastewater and hazardous waste before disposal.
- **Strengthening Environmental Laws** Enforce penalties for violations of environmental laws, conduct regular pollution audits and promote eco-friendly technologies in industries.

Long Answer Type Questions

1. Explain any three environmental concerns in global politics which no single government can address. CBSE 2024

Ans. Three key environmental concerns in global politics that no single government can address are

(i) **Climate Change** Rising global temperatures, melting ice caps, extreme weather events and rising sea levels are affecting every region of the world. Since greenhouse gas emissions from one country can impact the entire planet, climate change requires international collaboration. Agreements like the Paris Climate Agreement aim to limit global temperature rise, but their success depends on collective action by all nations.

(ii) **Biodiversity Loss** The rapid extinction of species and destruction of ecosystems due to deforestation, habitat loss and pollution is a global crisis. Biodiversity is vital for maintaining ecological balance and supporting human life, but no country can preserve it alone. International efforts, such as the convention on Biological Diversity, are necessary to protect endangered species and conserve habitats.

(iii) **Ozone Layer Depletion** The thinning of the ozone layer, caused by chemicals like CFCs, poses a global threat by increasing harmful ultraviolet radiation. The Montreal Protocol is a successful example of international co-operation to phase out these harmful substances, showing that global challenges require united efforts. Addressing these concerns requires shared responsibility and global governance.

2. Define climate change and discuss any three global initiatives on climate change in detail.

Ans. Climate change refers to a long-term change in the average weather patterns that have come to define the Earth's local, regional and global climates.

The global initiatives taken on climate change are discussed below

(i) **Montreal Protocol, 1987** It was a historical environmental accord that became a model for future diplomacy on the climate issue. Every country in the world eventually ratified the treaty, which required them to stop producing substances that damage the ozone layer, such as chlorofluorocarbons (CFCs). The protocol has succeeded in eliminating nearly 99 per cent of these ozone-depleting substances.

(ii) **UN Framework Convention on Climate Change (UNFCCC), 1992** It was ratified by 197 countries including the United States. It is also considered a landmark accord or a first global treaty to explicitly address climate change. It established an annual forum, known as the Conference of the Parties, or COP, for international discussions aimed at stabilising the concentration of greenhouse gases in the atmosphere. These meetings produced the Kyoto Protocol and the Paris Agreement.

(iii) **Kyoto Protocol, 2005** It was adopted in 1997 and came into force in 2005, which is the first legally binding climate treaty. It is an international agreement setting targets for industrialised countries to cut down their greenhouse gas emissions. China, India and other developing countries were exempted from the requirements of Kyoto Protocol.

3. What is the significance of Kyoto Protocol? Is India a signatory to this protocol?

Ans. The significance of Kyoto Protocol is stated in the points below

- Kyoto Protocol frames an action plan so as to reduce emission of greenhouse gases proportionately for Global North and Global South countries of the world.
- It had cleared the confusion regarding responsibilities of all countries belonging to Global North and Global South.
- United Nations Framework Convention on Climate Change (UNFCCC) has set out the principles and allocated different targets for preserving global common. It decided that Global North will provide Global South with financial and technological resources so as to meet existing commitments.
- India, China and other developing countries are exempted from the responsibility regarding reduction in greenhouse gas emissions.

Yes, India is a signatory to Kyoto Protocol.

4. In what ways has the principle of 'common but differentiated responsibilities' helped in addressing and overcoming the differences between the 'Global North' and 'Global South' over environmental issues? Explain. **CBSE 2024**

Ans. The principle of Common but Differentiated Responsibilities (CBDR) has been important in bridging the divide between the Global North(developed countries) and the Global South (developing countries) on environmental issues in several key ways

(i) **Acknowledgement of Historical Responsibility** CBDR recognises that industrialised nations have historically contributed more to environmental problems, such as climate change, due to their early and extensive use of fossil fuels.

(ii) **Equitable Burden Sharing** By differentiating responsibilities, CBDR ensures that developed countries take on greater commitments, such as higher emission reduction targets and more stringent environmental regulations. This reduces the pressure on developing countries, allowing them to focus on growth without bearing an undue burden.

(iii) **Financial and Technological Support** The principle has led to initiatives like the Green Climate Fund, where wealthier nations provide financial and technological assistance to developing countries. This support enables the Global South to implement sustainable practices, adapt to climate impacts and reduce emissions, fostering co-operation between both groups.

Overall, CBDR promotes fairness and co-operation, helping to overcome the historic distrust between the Global North and South on environmental issues.

5. Explain the role of environmental movements to meet the challenge of environmental degradation.

Ans. The role of environmental movements to meet the challenge of environmental degradation is very important. It is justified from the points below

- Some of the most significant responses to environmental challenges have come not from government but rather from groups of environmentally conscious volunteers around the world.
- The environmental movements are amongst the most vibrant, diverse and powerful social movements all over the world. These movements create new ideas and long-term visions. The forest movements of the South, in Mexico, Chile, Brazil, Malaysia, Indonesia, Continental Africa and India are facing lots of pressure. The process of forest clearing in the Third World Countries is on at an alarming rate, despite 30 years of environmental activism.
- In the Philippines, a big network of groups and organisations campaigned against the Western Mining Corporation. Vehement opposition to the company in its own country Australia is based on anti-nuclear sentiments and support for the basic rights of Australian indigenous peoples.
- Another group of movements are involved in struggles against mega-dams. In every country where mega-dams are being built, we find the environmental movements opposing the projects. Basically anti-dam movements are pro-river movements for more sustainable and equitable management of river systems and valleys. The Narmada Bachao Andolan is one of the best known of these movements.

Picture Based Questions

1. Observe the picture given below and answer the following questions.

(i) **In which year and where the Earth Summit was held?**
(ii) **What is being shown in the above pictures? What is the importance of forests for us?**
(iii) **Discuss the environmental concerns in global politics.**

Ans. (i) The Earth Summit on environment issues was held in Rio de Janeiro, Brazil (South America) in June, 1992.

(ii) A dense rain forest is shown above. These forests are being cut down relentlessly.

Forests stabilise the climate, moderate water supplies and harbour the biodiversity on land.

(iii) The Earth atmosphere, ocean floors, outer space and Antarctic region are global commons.

Any country in the world have no claim or coverage on these visible and invisible entities. As the regions described above are global commons, only world politics can get enforced rules and regulation for their conservation.

2. Study the given cartoon and answer the questions that follow.

(i) According to the picture given above what is the most important resource in global strategy?

(a) Automobile (b) Human Resource
(c) Arms and Weapons (d) Oil and Natural Resources

Ans. (d) Oil and Natural Resources

(ii) Identify the country shown in the uniform.

(a) USA (b) USSR
(c) UK (d) Japan

Ans. (a) USA

(iii) What does the above picture depicts?

(a) Military saving the citizens from foreign attacks
(b) The working of neo-colonialism
(c) Asking people to not getting outside their homes during war
(d) Attacking citizens

Ans. (b) The working of neo-colonialism

(iv) According to the image given above, why oil is given importance?

(a) Because it is good for health.
(b) It should be stored carefully for future use.
(c) It is a portable and indispensable fuel.
(d) It is used in industries.

Ans. (c) It is a portable and indispensable fuel.

3. Study the picture given below and answer the questions that follow **CBSE SQP 2024**

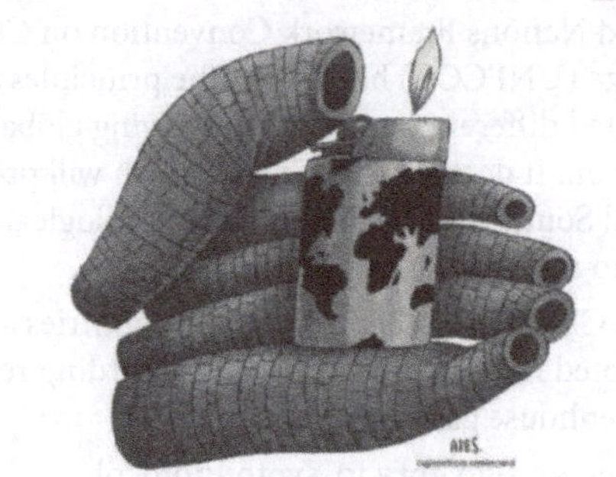

Choose the most appropriate option

(i) What does the lighter in the cartoon symbolise?

(a) The Earth being consumed as a source of fuel.
(b) The continents being burned for energy.
(c) The world being used up for power.
(d) The oceans being exploited for its resources.

Ans. (b) The continents being burned for energy.

(ii) Why are the fingers in the cartoon designed like chimneys?

(a) To represent humans are supporting the Earth.
(b) To show only humans are causing global warming.
(c) To show importance of chimneys in cleaning factories.
(d) To show importance of industrial revolution.

Ans. (d) To show importance of industrial revolution.

(iii) The main theme of the cartoon could be……… .

(a) the celebration of technological advancement
(b) the impact of deforestation on wildlife
(c) the role of industrial pollution in global warming
(d) the importance of reducing waste to save planet

Ans. (c) the role of industrial pollution in global warming

(iv) Thicker chimney has been shown on the push button of the lighter to show that ………… .

(a) only humans can stop pollution
(b) only developed countries contribute to pollution
(c) pollution can be curbed by shutting factories
(d) chimneys need to be made more efficient to save earth.

Ans. (a) only humans can stop pollution

SELF ASSESSMENT TEST

Objective Type Questions

1. Why are environmental concerns becoming increasingly important in global politics?
   (a) Due to loss of expansion and fertility
   (b) Due to lack of safe water and sanitation
   (c) Due to deforestation
   (d) All of these
2. What was the primary focus of the book 'Limits to Growth?
   (a) Advancing technology to solve environmental problems
   (b) Highlighting depletion of the Earth's resources due to population growth
   (c) Encouragcing industrial expansion
   (d) Criticsing international agencies
3. How many countries ratified the UN Framework Convention on Climate Change (UNFCCC), 1992?
   (a)120
   (b) 169
   (c)197
   (d) 193
4. Which of the following statement is incorrect regarding the Paris Agreement?
   (a) It requires all countries to set emissions-reduction pledges.
   (b) It aims to reach global net-zero emissions.
   (c) Countries set their own targets under this agreement.
   (d) There are different mechanisms to ensure the targets are met on time.

Very Short Answer Type Questions

5. What does UNEP stands for?
6. Why is conservation of natural resources vital for overall growth?
7. What criticism has been made regarding Agenda 21?
8. What was the primary concern of the Global South regarding the environment?

Short Answer Type Questions

9. Give any two environmental connection of global politics.
10. What was the Earth Summit?
11. What was the UN Sustainable Development Summit? When was it held?
12. Elaborate the relevance of Montreal Protocol, 1987.

Long Answer Type Questions

13. What did the Kyoto Protocol say about emissions from developed and developing countries?
14. What do you understand by Resource Geopolitics?
15. Indigenous people suffer the most from enivronmental degradation. Analyse.

07

CHAPTER

Globalisation is a concept which deals with flow of ideas, capital, commodities and people between countries. Globalisation is a multi-dimensional concept which has various political, economic and cultural effects.

Globalisation

YOUR STUDY GOALS

7.1 Concept of Globalisation
7.2 Consequences of Globalisation
7.3 India and Globalisation

YOUR PRACTICE GOAL

- Objective Type Questions (26 Qs ; MCQs, A-R, Statements, Passage Based)
- Subjective Questions (10 VSAs, 8 SAs, 3 LAs, 3 Picture Based)

7.1 Concept of Globalisation

- Globalisation[1] involves the movement of services, products, ideas, money and people across countries. It leads to inter-connectedness of the world. Globalisation includes the following
  - **Globalisation of Services** People work in different countries and provide services to clients they may never meet physically. They adapt to new languages and cultural norms.
  - **Movement of Commodities** Products manufactured in one country are sold in another, connecting markets across borders.
  - **Cultural and Social Changes** Exposure to different cultures leads to new opportunities. This leads to challenging of traditional norms and values, especially in areas like employment and gender roles.
- While globalisation has positive effects, such as increased opportunities and market access, it also has negative impacts.
- For example, some farmers committed suicide after their crops failed, despite buying expensive seeds from an MNC; retail shopkeepers in India fear losing their livelihoods if international companies open retail chains in the country. These examples show that globalisation isn't always beneficial.
- The impact of globalisation is uneven, with negative consequences felt more by vulnerable groups.

1 Globalisation It signifies integration of an economy with the economies of other countries under the process of free flow of trade and capital.

Causes of Globalisation

- Globalisation involves the flow of ideas, capital, goods and people across borders. While these flows have existed throughout history, today's globalisation is unique because of its scale and speed.
- **Technology** Technological inventions like the telegraph, telephone and microchip have made global communication faster and easier. Just as printing helped create nationalism, modern technology shapes how we view our personal and collective lives.
- Technological advances have made it easier for ideas, capital, commodities and people to move across the world. The speed of these flows can vary. For example, capital and commodities usually move faster and more widely than people across different regions.
- **Inter-connectedness** Globalisation happens because people are more aware of connections between different parts of the world. Events like the bird flu or tsunami show how problems in one place can affect others, regardless of borders.

Quick Test 1

1 What is the core element of globalisation?
2 What kind of flows are fundamental to globalisation?
3 What is unique about contemporary globalisation?
4 Can globalisation have negative impacts? Give an example.

7.2 Consequences of Globalisation

Political Consequences

There are three aspects in the political consequences of globalisation as follows

(i) **Globalisation weakens government power** The old welfare state is replaced by a **minimalist**[2] government that focuses mainly on law, order and security. It no longer handles welfare tasks like economic and social well-being. The market plays a bigger role in setting economic and social priorities. The rise of multinational companies also reduces governments' ability to make independent decisions.

(ii) **Globalisation doesn't always reduce state power** The state remains the main foundation of the political community. Rivalries between countries still matter and states continue to perform essential functions like law, order and security. While states may withdraw from some areas, they remain important.

(iii) **Globalisation can strengthen state power** New technologies help states gather more information about citizens, making it easier for them to govern. As a result, states become more powerful due to these technological advancements.

Economic Consequences

- Economic globalisation involves institutions like the IMF and WTO, which shape global economic policies.
- Globalisation leads to more economic exchanges, like trade, capital, people and ideas. Some exchanges are voluntary, while others are forced by powerful countries. Trade barriers have been reduced. Investors from rich countries can invest in poorer countries for better returns.
- Ideas, like internet services, spread easily. However, the movement of people is still limited by visa restrictions in developed countries. This is done to ensure that citizens of other countries cannot take away the jobs of their own citizens.

2 **Minimalist** It refers a government with a limited role in the lives of its citizens.

- The impact of globalisation is not the same everywhere. Countries with similar policies can have different outcomes.
- Critics are concerned about social justice. They argue that globalisation benefits only a small group and harms the poor. They want 'safety nets' to protect the vulnerable. Some argue safety nets don't work and demand an end to forced globalisation.
- Advocates of economic globalisation argue that it boosts growth and well-being for many people when there is deregulation. Greater trade allows countries to focus on what they do best.
- They believe globalisation is inevitable and avoiding it is unwise. Some moderate supporters are of the view that globalisation can be managed wisely. There is growing inter-dependence between governments, businesses and people worldwide because of globalisation.

Cultural Consequences

- Globalisation affects not just politics and the economy, but also our daily lives. It influences what we eat, drink, wear and think. It shapes our preferences.
- Some fear that globalisation threatens local cultures. This happens because it leads to a uniform culture which is called **cultural homogenisation**[3].
- Uniform culture is the spread of Western culture, particularly American. The popularity of goods like burgers and blue jeans is linked to the influence of the American lifestyle.
- The dominant culture leaves its mark on less powerful societies. The world starts to resemble the dominant culture's values. This is called the 'McDonaldisation' of the world, where cultures buy into the American dream. This is seen as harmful, especially for poorer countries, as it shrinks the diverse cultural heritage of the world.
- However, not all cultural effects of globalisation are negative. Cultures are not fixed; they are always changing.
- Some external influences can expand our choices. External influences can mix with local cultures without replacing them. For example, burgers don't replace traditional foods like masala dosa; they simply add to our choices. Blue jeans can be worn with traditional khadi kurtas, creating a new style.
- While globalisation leads to cultural homogenisation, it also creates **cultural heterogenisation**[4]. This means cultures become more distinct and unique.

Quick Test 2

1. What does economic globalisation involve?
2. Why do developed countries restrict migration?
3. What is 'McDonaldisation' of the world?
4. How can globalisation create cultural combinations? Give example.

7.3 India and Globalisation

- Globalisation has happened in different periods of history. The movement of capital, goods, ideas and people has been part of India's history for centuries.
- During British rule, India was a supplier of raw materials and a consumer of finished goods. After independence, India decided not to allow others to export to us, so our own producers could learn to make things. This policy of **protectionism**[5] created problems.

3 **Cultural Homogenisation** It refers to the rise of uniform culture or different cultural practices into one common culture.
4 **Cultural Heterogenisation** It leads to each culture becoming more different and distinctive.
5 **Protectionism** It is the principle or practice of protecting a country's own industry by taxing foreign goods.

- While some progress was made, important areas like health, housing and education were neglected. India's economic growth was slow.
- In 1991, due to a financial crisis and the need for faster growth, India started economic reforms. These reforms aimed to deregulate sectors like trade and foreign investment.

Resistance to Globalisation

- Left-wing critics argue that globalisation is part of global capitalism, which makes the rich richer and the poor poorer. They also believe that weakening the state reduces its ability to protect the poor.
- Right-wing critics fear the political, economic and cultural impacts of globalisation. They worry about the state's weakening power, and demand more self-reliance and protectionism in the economy. They fear that traditional cultures and values will be lost.
- There are several anti-globalisation movements that participate in global networks and oppose certain types of globalisation. They view it as a form of imperialism rather than opposing globalisation as a whole.
- There were widespread protests at the WTO ministerial meeting in seattle in 1999. The protests were held against the unfair trading practices by powerful states and the lack of attention to developing countries' interests.
- **World Social Forum (WSF)** is a global platform that brings together activists from various fields like human rights, environment, labour, youth and women's issues. They are opposed to neo-liberal globalisation.
- The first WSF was held in Porto Alegre, Brazil, in 2001, and the fourth one in Mumbai, India, in 2004. The most recent WSF meeting was held in Nepal in February, 2024.

India and Resistance to Globalisation

- Resistance has come from different groups in India. This includes
- **Left-wing protests** to economic liberalisation[6] are often voiced by political parties and forums like the Indian Social Forum.
    - Trade unions and farmer groups have protested against multinational companies entering India.
    - There also has been opposition to patents on plants like Neem by foreign firms.
- **Right-wing resistance** focuses on cultural issues, such as celebrating Valentine's day or Western-style clothing worn by girl students in schools and colleges.

Quick Test 3

1. What was India's economic approach after independence?
2. When did India start its economic reforms?
3. Who benefits the most from globalisation, according to left-wing critics?
4. Where was the first World Social Forum held?

6 **Economic Liberalisation** It signifies relaxation of government rules and regulation relating to activities in service and industrial sector.

Mind Map

GLOBALISATION

1 Concept of Globalisation

Concept of Globalisation
- Globalisation is the process of countries become more connected through the exchange of goods, services, ideas, etc.
- Items made in one country are sold in other.
- Exposure to new cultures lead to new opportunities.
- People work in different countries and provide services without meeting clients in person.

Causes of Globalisation
- Globalisation happens because of technology and inter-connectedness.
- Inventions like Telegraph, Telephone, Microchip have made communication faster and easier.
- People are aware of connections between different parts of the world like how problem in one place can effect others.

2 Consequences of Globalisation

Political Consequences
- Globalisation has changed the role of old welfare state to minimalist only.
- MNC reduces the independent decision-making of states.
- Globalisation strengthened the governance system in states by technology transfer.

Economic Consequences
- It involves institution like IMF and WTO plays crucial role in policy formation for strengthening of economic globalisation.
- More economic exchanges like trade, capital and ideas.
- Ideas like internet services, spread easily.
- Critics are concerned about social justice.

3 India and Globalisation

Resistance to Globalisation
- Left-wing critics agues globalisation increases inequality and weakens the state.
- Right-wing criticise for the less of political, economy and cultural control due to globalisation.
- Anti globalisation protest were held in 1999 against developed nation practices.
- World social forum fight against neo-liberal globalisation.
- WTO ministerial meeting was held in Seattle in 1999.
- The first WSF was held in Porto Alegre, Brazil in 2001 and fourth one in Mumbai.
- India in 2004 and the most recent WSF was held in Brazil in March 2018.

India and Resistance of Globalisation
- Left-wing protects economic liberalisations.
- Right-wing resistance focuses on cultural issues.
- Not all cultural effects of globalisation are negatively they are not fixed and always changing.
- Globalisation leads to cultural homogenisation because it spreads one uniform culture, which threatens the local cultural values.
- Cultural heterogenisation is the product of globalisation.

Globalisation in India

Globalisation is Here to Stay

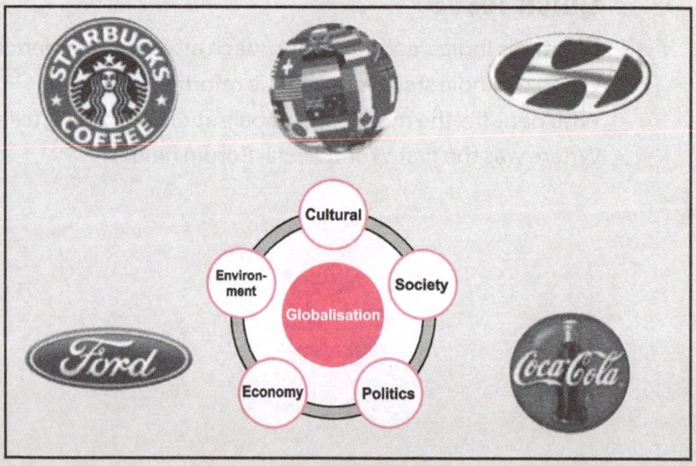

The Causes of Globalisation

NCERT Folder

1. Which of the statements are TRUE about globalisation?

(a) Globalisation is purely an economic phenomenon.
(b) Globalisation began in 1991.
(c) Globalisation is the same thing as Westernisation.
(d) Globalisation is a multi-dimensional phenomenon.

Ans. (d) Globalisation is a multi-dimensional phenomenon.

2. Which of the statements are TRUE about the impact of globalisation?

(a) Globalisation has been uneven in its impact on states and societies.
(b) Globalisation has had a uniform impact on all states and societies.
(c) The impact of globalisation has been confined to the political sphere.
(d) Globalisation inevitably results in cultural homogeneity.

Ans. (a) Globalisation has been uneven in its impact on states and societies.

3. Which of the statements are TRUE about the causes of globalisation?

(a) Technology is an important cause of globalisation.
(b) Globalisation is caused by a particular community of people.
(c) Globalisation originated in the US .
(d) Economic inter-dependence alone causes globalisation.

Ans. (a) Technology is an important cause of globalisation.

4. Which of the statements are TRUE about globalisation?

(a) Globalisation is only about movement of commodities.
(b) Globalisation does not involve a conflict of values.
(c) Services are an insignificant part of globalisation.
(d) Globalisation is about worldwide inter-connectedness.

Ans. (d) Globalisation is about worldwide inter-connectedness.

5. Which of the statements are FALSE about globalisation?

(a) Advocates of globalisation argue that it will result in greater economic growth.
(b) Critics of globalisation argue that it will result in greater economic disparity.
(c) Advocates of globalisation argue that it will result in cultural homogenisation.
(d) Critics of globalisation argue that it will result in cultural homogenisation.

Ans. (d) Critics of globalisation argue that it will result in cultural homogenisation.

6. What is worldwide inter-connectedness? What are its components?

Or **Analyse that globalisation is about world wide inter-connectedness.**

Competency Based Que CBSE Term II 2022

Ans. Globalisation is defined as worldwide inter-connectedness. Globalisation fundamentally means the flow of ideas, capital, commodities and people across different parts of the world. The crucial element is the 'worldwide inter-connectedness', that is created and sustained as a consequence of these constant flows. It is a multi-dimensional concept as it has political, economic and cultural manifestations and these must be adequately distinguished.

The impact of globalisation is vastly uneven because it affects some societies more than others and some parts of some societies more than others.

The major components of worldwide inter-connectedness, i.e. globalisation are

- **Technological Advancement** Technology remains an important factor with regard to globalisation. The technological inventions such as telegraph, telephone and the microchip has revolutionised communication between various global factors. Thus, technological advancements has been most significant component of worldwide inter-connectedness.
- **Free Flow of Capital and Investment** It has also been the key component of rising worldwide inter-connectedness. Flow of FDI across the world has transformed the world into a inter-connected global market.
- **Migration and Movement of People** It has also been responsible for growing worldwide inter-connectedness. Technological advancement has reduced the physical distances and increased the migration and movement of people from one country to another.
- **Sharing of Ideas and Knowledge** They have also countributed to increasing inter-connectedness. With technological advancement, ideas and knowledge are rapidly moving from one part to another parts of world.

7. How has technology contributed to globalisation?

Or **Evaluate the role of technology in globalisation.**

CBSE Term II 2022; Competency Based Que

Ans. Technology has contributed to globalisation in the following ways

- The technological inventions such as telegraph, telephone and the microchip has revolutionised communication between various global factors and hence invention of printing laid the basis for the emergence of nationalism. Thus, technology influences the way we think of our personal and collective lives.
- The transfer of capital goods and services is likely to be wider and quicker than the transfer of people across the various parts of the world.

- Technological advances has reduced the physical distances and increased inter-connectedness worldwide.

8. Critically evaluate the impact of the changing role of the state in the developing countries in the light of globalisation. Competency Based Que

Ans. The impact of the changing role of the state in the developing countries in the light of globalisation is discussed below

- State only plays a minimal role which includes core functions like maintenance of law and order as well as security.
- Globalisation has further restricted the role of state as it minimises the role of state in the economy. It reduces the state capacity and it is being dominated by the market forces.
- The position of state has also been relieved due to globalisation as it increases technological developments which help the state to run efficiently.
- Globalisation has impacted the way the state functions and set international standards that have to be adhered in order to keep up with the wave of economic growth through assistance from organisations such as World Bank and IMF.

The state has become more transparent and they are answerable to other governing bodies. The state still has influence.

9. What are the economic implications of globalisation? How has globalisation impacted on India with regard to this particular dimension? Competency Based Que

Or **Explain any two arguments given in favour of economic globalisation.** CBSE 2025

Ans. The economic implications of globalisation are as follows

- Economic globalisation gives more importance to institutions like the IMF and the WTO.
- It involves greater economic flows among different countries of the world.
- As the restrictions imposed by different countries have been reduced, so greater trade in commodities across the globe can be seen.
- It has led to the flow of ideas across national boundaries through internet and computer.
- Economic globalisation has also brought economic ruin for the weaker countries, especially for the poor within these countries.

Impact on India

Globalisation affected India economically, socially and culturally. After adopting New Economic Policy in 1991, India has removed restrictions on imports of goods. It also encouraged the investors to invest in India. Foreign Direct Investment to produce goods and services has increased, it has also enhanced foreign exchange reserves. India is also involved in trade and commerce with other nations. However, in India, resistance to globalisation has come from various quarters.

These are as follows

- Trade Unions of industrial workforce as well as social movements and farmer agitation against monopoly. MNCs are also some forms of resistance to globalisation.
- The acquiring of certain plants like Neem by American and European firms has also generated widespread opposition in India.

10. Do you agree with the argument that globalisation leads to cultural heterogeneity? Competency Based Que

Ans. Globalisation leads to cultural heterogeneity by promoting the exchange of ideas, traditions, and lifestyles across nations. As people interact through travel, trade, and digital communication, they adopt and adapt diverse cultural elements. Local traditions blend with global influences, creating unique cultural expressions. For example, food, fashion, and music often reflect a mix of global and regional styles.

However, globalisation does not erase cultural identities; instead, it encourages their evolution. While some fear cultural dominance by powerful nations, many societies reinterpret global trends in their own way. This continuous exchange enriches cultural diversity.

11. How has globalisation impacted on India and how is India in turn impacting on globalisation?

Ans. Globalisation affected India economically, socially and culturally. After adopting New Economic Policy in 1991, India has removed restrictions on imports of goods. It also encouraged the investors to invest in India. Foreign Direct Investment to produce goods and services has increased. It also enhanced foreign exchange reserves. After adopting globalisation, USA and European culture has spread in India. The food habit and dressing style is changing. Families are converting from joint to nuclear. Eating burgers and pizzas and wearing jeans have brought dramatic change in our lives.

Information technology and space technology have been enhanced after globalisation. India is also involved in trade and commerce with other nations.

However, in India, resistance to globalisation has come from various quarters.

These are as follows

- Trade Unions of industrial workforce as well as social movements and farmer agitation against monopoly. MNCs are also some forms of resistance to globalisation.
- The acquiring of certain plants like Neem by American and European firms has also generated widespread opposition in India.

Exam Pattern Questions

Objective Type Questions

Multiple Choice Questions (MCQs)

1. What do you mean by globalisation?
(a) Flow of ideas
(b) Flow of capital
(c) Commodities and people across the world
(d) All of the above

2. The process of integration of different countries is called ....
(a) privatisation (b) globalisation
(c) liberalisation (d) None of these

3. What are the ideas behind understanding the process of globalisation and its impact?
(a) Integration of production
(b) Integration of grass profits
(c) Integration of markets
(d) Both (a) and (c)

4. Institutional safeguards to minimise the negative effects of globalisation on those who are economically weak are known as .... CBSE 2025
(a) Welfare measures
(b) Social safety nets
(c) Economic liberalisation
(d) Voluntary services

5. Which of the following statements is not true regarding globalisation? Diksha App
(a) Technological advancement is the main cause of contemporary globalisation.
(b) Diseases and natural calamities don't respect national boundaries.
(c) In the contemporary world, people recognise inter-connectedness.
(d) All countries get equally benefited by globalisation.

6. Erosion of state capacity is related to .... globalisation.
(a) economical (b) cultural (c) social (d) political

7. Which of the following is not a political consequence of globalisation? Diksha App
(a) Globalisation has eroded state capacity.
(b) It affected the traditional concept of sovereignty adversely.
(c) It led the state to withdraw from many of its earlier welfare functions.
(d) It resulted in making the state irrelevant in the globalised world.

8. Statement I Globalisation results in an erosion of state capacity, that is, the ability of government to do what they do.

Statement II The entry and the increased role of multinational companies all over the world leads to a reduction in the capacity of governments to take decisions on their own.

In the light of above statements, choose the correct answer from the options given below
(a) Both Statement I and Statement II are true.
(b) Both Statement I and Statement II are false.
(c) Statement I is true, but Statement II is false.
(d) Statement I is false, but Statement II is true.

9. Statement I Globalisation is a multidimensional concept which has political, economic and cultural manifestations, and these must be adequately distinguished.

Statement II Globalisation does not emerge merely because of the availability of improved communications.

In the light of above statements, choose the correct answer from the options given below
(a) Both Statement I and Statement II are true.
(b) Both Statement I and Statement II are false.
(c) Statement I is true, but Statement II is false.
(d) Statement I is false, but Statement II is true.

10. Which among the following institutions play an important role in economic globalisation?
(a) World Trade Organisation
(b) World Bank
(c) International Monetary Fund
(d) All of the above

11. Which of the following statements is correct? Diksha App
(a) Globalisation is a new phenomenon that started only in the 1990s.
(b) The flow of labour is much easier than other flows.
(c) The flow of ideas, goods, capital, and people started much earlier in human history.
(d) All countries welcome the unrestricted flow of goods.

12. Choose the correct statement regarding positive impacts of globalisation.
I. There is increase in the volume of trade in goods and services.

II. Improved productive efficiency and healthy competition.

III. Now jobs are created in industries set up by multinational companies.

IV. There is less availability of investable funds in the form of Foreign Direct Investment.

Codes

(a) I and II (b) I, II and III
(c) I and IV (d) I, III and IV

13. What message does the cartoon convey?

(a) Effects of privatisation
(b) Effects of globlisation
(c) Effects of liberalisation
(d) Effects of commercialisation

14. Which of the following is/are true about Cultural Homogenisation?

(a) It refers to the rise of uniform culture of different cultural practices into one common culture.
(b) It is an important aspect of globalisation.
(c) It is viewed negatively as it leads to reduction in cultural diversity.
(d) All of the above

15. "McDonaldisation" doesn't refer to .... Diksha App

(a) the powerful influence of the American way of life
(b) cultural homogenisation
(c) cultural hegemony
(d) cultural heterogenisation

16. Which of the following statements is not true? Diksha App

(a) Protectionism is a hindrance on the path of free trade.
(b) Protectionism leads to the extension of favours to MNCs.
(c) Protectionism intends to benefit indigenous industries.
(d) Protectionism resulted in a low economic growth rate in India.

17. What is not true regarding the World Social Forum(WSF)? Diksha App

(a) Which campaigns in favour of policies of WTO.
(b) Opposes neo liberal globalisation.
(c) Comprises of human right activists, environmentalists, labour, youth, women from across the world.
(d) Highlights issues and concerns of indigenous people.

18. Which of the following statements is not true with respect to the resistance to globalisation in India? Diksha App

(a) Both left and right wing organisations resisted globalisation in India
(b) Farmers resisted the entry of MNCs.
(c) Industrial workers welcomed globalisation.
(d) Right-wing organisations resisted globalisation due to its cultural influences.

19. According to the rightist view in India, globalisation tends to ....

(a) benefit the weaker section of the society.
(b) divide the state into rich and poor.
(c) weakens the state.
(d) reduces political party competition.

20. Which of the following statements is not correct regarding the leftist critique of globalisation? Diksha App

(a) Contemporary globalisation makes the rich richer and the poor poorer.
(b) Reduces the capacity of the state to protect the interests of the poor.
(c) Globalisation gives excessive powers to the state, enhance its capacity.
(d) Globalisation in its present form serves the interests of the developed countries only.

Assertion-Reason Questions

Directions (Q. Nos. 21-23) In the questions given below, there are two statements marked as Assertion (A) and Reason (R). Read the statements and choose the correct option.

Codes

(a) Both A and R are true and R is the correct explanation of A.
(b) Both A and R are true, but R is not the correct explanation of A.
(c) A is true, but R is false.
(d) A is false, but R is true.

21. Assertion (A) Globalisation is the integration of economy of a country in the process of free flow trade and capital.
Reason (R) It has led to growth in all the countries.

22. Assertion (A) The entry and the increased role of multinational companies all over the world leads to a reduction in the capacity of governments to take decisions on their own.
Reason (R) The state continues to discharge its essential functions and consciously withdraws from certain domains from which it wishes to.

23. **Assertion** (A) In India, globalisation has led to setting up of foreign companies.

Reason (R) India realised the need for relating the Indian economy with the world by responding to 1991 financial crisis.

Passage Based Questions

24. Read the following passage carefully and answer the questions that follow.

While globalisation is not caused by any single factor, technology remains a critical element. There is no doubt that the invention of the telegraph, the telephone, and the microchip in more recent times has revolutionised communication between different parts of the world. When printing initially came into being it laid the basis for the creation of nationalism. So also today, we should expect that technology will affect the way we think of our personal but also our collective lives. **CBSE 2019 Modified**

(i) **Which of the following is the critical element of globalisation?**

(a) Capital (b) Technology
(c) Inter-connectedness (d) Market

(ii) **How has technology aided globalisation?**

(a) It has revolutionised communication between countries.
(b) It has created a gap between countries.
(c) It led to bonding among the powerful nations.
(d) None of the above

(iii) **On what basis we can say that globalisation is a multi-dimensional concept?**

(a) Because it is adopted in every nation.
(b) Because it has political, economic and cultural manifestations.
(c) Because it consists of different notions.
(d) All of the above

(iv) **Which of the following are the events or happenings that have a global impact?**

(a) Technological advancements like internet.
(b) Cultural homogenisation like adopting jeans in developing countries.
(c) Both (a) and (b)
(d) Can't say

25. Read the following passage carefully and answer the questions that follow.

At the most simple level, globalisation results in an erosion of state capacity that is, the ability of government to do what they do. All over the world, the old 'welfare state' is now giving way to a more minimalist state that performs certain core functions such as the maintenance of law and order and the security of its economic and social well-being. In place of the welfare state, it is the market that becomes the prime determinant of economic and social priorities.

(i) **Erosion of state here means ....**

(a) reduction in the role of state in society and economy.
(b) welfare state is being promoted in the society.
(c) market economy is being prevalent in the society.
(d) None of the above

(ii) **Why is the concept of welfare state giving way to a minimalist state?**

(a) As it performs according to the free market economy norms.
(b) As it performs only crucial functions like maintenance of law.
(c) As it is not providing welfare services to the poor people.
(d) All of the above

(iii) **How has the market become the prime determinant of social priorities?**

(a) State is making decision on the basis of market forces.
(b) Market is the prime determinant which influences the role of state.
(c) Market has been forcing the state in the decision making process for the society.
(d) All of the above

(iv) **Which of the following are the functions of welfare state?**

(a) To provide subsidies to the poor.
(b) To make welfare policies for the poor.
(c) To make policies for the benefit of private sector.
(d) Both (a) and (b)

26. Read the following passage carefully and answer the questions that follow.

Globalisation does not always reduce state capacity. The primacy of the state continues to be unchallenged basis of political community. The old jealousies and rivalries between countries have not ceased to matter in world politics. The state continues to discharge its essential functions (law and order, national security) and consciously withdraws from certain domains from which it wishes to. States continue to be important.

Indeed, in some respects state capacity has received a boost as a consequence of globalisation, with enhanced technologies available at the disposal of the state to collect information about its citizens.

(i) How do enhanced technologies enable the state to rule better?

(a) The state can collect important information about its citizens.

(b) State can keep surveillance on its people.

(c) State can generate welfare policies on the basis of data.

(d) Both (a) and (b)

(ii) Globalisation has given boost to the state capacity because ....

(a) it has made available advance technology to state to rule its people better.

(b) state has become more market centric in approach which is beneficial for the people.

(c) state has increased its welfare capacity through globalisation.

(d) None of the above

(iii) How has globalisation paradoxically strengthened state capacity while seemingly promoting inter-connectedness and borderless interactions?

Answers

1. (d) All of the above
2. (b) globalisation
3. (d) Both (a) and (c)
4. (b) Social safety nets
5. (d) All countries get equally benefited by globalisation.
6. (d) political
7. (d) It resulted in making the state irrelevant in the globalised world.
8. (a) Both Statement I and Statement II are true
9. (a) Both Statement I and Statement II are true
10. (d) All of the above
11. (c) The flow of ideas, goods, capital and people started much earlier in human history.
12. (b) I, II and III
13. (b) Effects of globlisation
14. (d) All of the above
15. (d) cultural heterogenisation
16. (b) Protectionism leads to the extension of favours to MNCs.
17. (a) Which campaigns in favour of policies of WTO.
18. (c) Industrial workers welcomed globalisation.
19. (c) weakens the state.
20. (c) Globalisation gives excessive powers to the state, enhance its capacity.
21. (c) A is true, but R is false.
22. (b) Both A and R are true, but R is not the correct explanation of A.
23. (a) Both A and R are true and R is the correct explanation of A.
24. (i) (c) Inter-connectedness

    (ii) (a) It has revolutionised communication between countries.

    (iii) (b) Because it has political, economic and cultural manifestations.

    (iv) (c) Both (a) and (b)
25. (i) (a) reduction in the role of state in society and economy.

    (ii) (b) As it performs only crucial functions like maintenance of law.

    (iii) (d) All of the above

    (iv) (d) Both (a) and (b)
26. (i) (d) Both (a) and (b)

    (ii) (a) it has made available advance technology to state to rule its people better.

    (iii) Despite globalisation's emphasis on inter-connectedness, states have maintained and even enhanced their power through technological advancements and selective engagement. Modern states utilise improved surveillance capabilities and information technologies to maintain control, while strategically choosing which areas to regulate or liberalise. This demonstrates that globalisation has transformed rather than diminished state authority.

Subjective Questions

Very Short Answer Type Questions

1. Mention any two benefits of globalisation.

Ans. Two benefits of globalisation are

(i) It provides job opportunities for the youth.

(ii) It provides the exchange of ideas, capital, commodities and people from one place to another.

2. What are flows in relation to globalisation? Describe any two flows related to globalisation? CBSE Term II 2022

Ans. Flows refers to the movement of ideas, capital, commodity and people from one part of world to another. The two flows related to globalisation are as following

(i) **Trade Flow** It takes place to satisfy material demands ranging from raw materials to finished goods.

(ii) **Information Flow** It is important for communication and power exchanges and symbolic exchanges.

3. What is meant by social safety nets?

Ans. Social safety nets refer to welfare measures implemented by states to provide social security to poor and weaker sections of society who are at the receiving end of economic development.

4. "Globalisation results in an erosion of state capacity". Justify the statement by giving any three arguments. Diksha App

Ans. Globalisation erodes state capacity as

- The welfare state is now giving way to a more minimalist state.
- The state is confined to certain core functions like maintaining law and order, and security to citizens.
- It withdraws from many of its earlier welfare functions.
- Market instead of state has become a prime determinant of economic and social priorities.

5. What is cultural homogenisation? Give an example to show that its consequences are not negative.

Ans. The rise of a uniform culture is known as homogenisation. It is mixing of one culture with another one.

The consequences of cultural homogenisation are not always negative, for e.g., jeans can even go well with khadi kurta. Now-a-days, Americans also wear jeans and kurta.

6. Give any two examples to show that globalisation has affected our food habits.

Ans. Two examples to show that globalisation has affected our food habits are as follows

(i) Now-a-days, the young people prefer burgers, hot dogs, fried chickens, etc.

(ii) They like to hang out in decorative and air-conditioned environment with variety of foods on their plates. The growing number of food restaurant chains offer different recipes at comparatively cheaper rates.

7. Mention any one problem created by protectionism.

Ans. Protectionism is practised by states to protect the economic and business interest of domestic industries, companies, traders, etc.

In long term, protectionism weakens the industry as without competition there will be no innovation, efficiency which may result in lower quality and expensive production. This makes it difficult for domestic product to compete with foreign product.

8. Highlight any two advantages of globalisation to India. CBSE Term II 2022

Ans. The two advantages of globalisation to India are as follows

(i) It provides the job opporunites for the youth.

(ii) It provides the exchanges of ideas, capital, commodities and people from one place to another.

9. Analyse any two reasons for the resistance to globalisation. Competency Based Que; CBSE Term II 2022

Or **What are the reasons behind resistance to contemporary globalisation?** Diksha App

Ans. Globalisation is resisted due to the following reasons

(i) The cultural globalisation would harm age old values of people while harming their traditional culture.

(ii) Leftist parties argue that contemporary globalisation represents a global capitalism that makes the rich richer and poor poorer.

(iii) Promotes western culture.

10. What is W.S.F.? What its purpose?

Ans. W.S. F. stands for World Social Forum. It is an international organisation camprising human rights activities, environmentalists labour leaders, woman activists, etc. who are opposed to neo-liberal globalisation.

Short Answer Type Questions

1. Explain any two positive and any two negative effects of globalisation.

Or Highlight any two positive effects of globalisation. CBSE 2024

Ans. Positive impacts of globalisation are as follows *(any two)*

(i) Increase in the volume of trade in goods and services.

(ii) It creates new job opportunities.

(iii) It raises standard of living.

(iv) It increases production, efficiency and healthy competition.

(v) It attracts foreign direct investment also.

Negative impacts of globalisation are as follows *(any two)*

(i) The foreign companies focus on their profit orientation projects only in place of social welfare.

(ii) It has widened income disparities by making the rich more richer and the poor more poorer.

(iii) Globalisation is also a reason for depletion of flora and fauna in country.

2. Explain any four factors responsible for the development of globalisation.

Or Define globalisation. Explain any three causes of globalisation.

Or What is globalisation? Highlight any three causes of globalisation.

Or Explain any two major causes of globalisation. CBSE 2025

Or Analyse any two causes of globalisation.

Ans. The following factors are responsible for globalisation are

(i) Technology is the most important element. The invention of the telegraph, the telephone and the microchip has revolutionised communication between various global factors. The technology has made it easier to exchange ideas, capital and commodities from one place to another. The transfer of capital and commodities is a major cause of globalisation.

(ii) The increased inter-connectedness has led to migration of people in search of economic opportunities. This in turn helps in the flow of investments across the world. This has initiated globalisation on a large scale.

3. How has technology contributed to globalisation? Explain.

Ans. Technology has contributed to globalisation in the following ways

- The technological inventions such as telegraph, telephone and the microchip has revolutionised communication between various global factors. The sharing of ideas, capital, commodities and people throughout the globe has been made possible only by technological advancement.
- The transfer of capital goods and services is likely to be wider and quicker than the transfer of people across the various parts of the world.
- Technological advances has reduced the physical distances and increased inter-connectedness worldwide.

4. Describe any three effects of globalisation on the economy of a country.

Or Mention any four economic consequences of globalisation. CBSE 2024

Or Explain any two economic consequences of globalisation. CBSE 2024

Ans. Following are the three effects of globalisation on the economy of a country *(any three)*

(i) Economic globalisation gives more importance to institutions like the IMF and the WTO.

(ii) It involves greater economic flows among different countries of the world.

(iii) As the restrictions imposed by different countries have been reduced, so greater trade in commodities across the globe can be seen.

(iv) It has led to the flow of ideas across national boundaries through internet and computer.

(v) Economic globalisation has also brought economic ruin for the weaker countries, especially for the poor within these countries.

5. Why do some economists describe economic globalisation as re-colonisation of the world?

Ans. Some economists describe economic globalisation as re-colonisation of the world because

- Consequences of globalisation favour the developed countries particularly USA, while there are increasing situation of unemployment, over exploitation of workers due to privatisation and relaxation in labour laws of the developing countries.
- Markets of developing countries are stocked with blue jeans of USA, toys of China, etc. In the same way as Indians were compelled to import garments during the period of colonisation.

6. Explain any four consequences of globalisation. CBSE 2024

Ans. Globalisation has brought significant consequences across various spheres as below

- **Economic Growth** It has expanded trade, investment and innovation, enabling countries to access global markets and technologies, boosting economic development.

- **Cultural Exchange** Globalisation facilitates the spread of ideas, values and cultures across borders, enriching societies through cultural diversity but also contributing to cultural homogenisation.
- **Job Creation and Displacement** It has created new employment opportunities, particularly in developing countries, through outsourcing and multinational corporations. However, it has also led to job losses in some regions due to shifting industries.
- **Environmental Impact** The expansion of industries and trade has increased resource extraction and pollution, contributing to global environmental issues like climate change and biodiversity loss, requiring international co-operation for solutions.

7. Analyse any two reasons for resistance to globalisation in India. CBSE SQP 2024

Or **Assess any three basics on which globalisation is being resisted in India.** Competency Based Que

Ans. Resistance to globalisation in India stems from several factors

- **Economic Inequality** Globalisation has led to uneven benefits, with wealth often concentrated in urban areas and among large corporations, while small-scale industries and rural communities face economic marginalisation. This disparity has led to opposition, as many feel left out of the economic gains globalisation promises.
- **Cultural Preservation** Globalisation is seen as a threat to India's rich cultural heritage. The influx of Western products, media and values is perceived as undermining traditional customs, languages and lifestyles. Many Indians fear that cultural homogenisation, driven by global forces, could erode the country's distinct identity, leading to efforts to resist foreign cultural influences in favour of protecting local traditions.

8. Explain the difference between cultural homogenisation and cultural heterogenisation. CBSE 2024

Ans. Cultural homogenisation and cultural heterogenisation are contrasting outcomes of globalisation.

Cultural homogenisation refers to the blending and unification of cultures, leading to increased similarities across societies. It often occurs through the global spread of dominant cultures, such as Westernisation, where popular culture, language and consumer habits become widely adopted, sometimes eroding local traditions.

In contrast, cultural heterogenisation emphasises the preservation and promotion of local cultures despite global influences. It highlights how globalisation can lead to a resurgence or strengthening of unique cultural identities, as local communities adapt global elements to fit their distinct traditions.

While homogenisation can create uniformity, heterogenisation allows diversity to flourish as cultures interact and integrate selectively with global trends, maintaining their distinctiveness.

Long Answer Type Questions

1. Explain any three benefits of globalisation with examples.

Or **Evaluate any three benefits of globalisation.** Competency Based Que; CBSE Term II 2022

Ans. The three benefits of globalisation are as follows

(i) **Economic Benefits**

(a) It involves greater economic flows among various countries.

(b) It has enhanced trade in commodities among countries.

(c) The restrictions on the imports and movement of capital have also been reduced.

(d) This has spread internet and computer related services across national boundaries.

(ii) **Technological Benefits** Technological equipments as telephone, internet, telegraph and microchip have contributed to globalisation.

(iii) **Political Benefits** States have received a boost under globalisation to become more powerful and strong.

2. Evaluate any three effects of globalisation on the role of state in developing countries? Competency Based Que; CBSE Term II 2022

Or **Analyse any two political consequences of globalisation.** CBSE 2024, SQP 2024

Or **Explain any two political consequences of globalisation.** CBSE 2025

Ans. Following are the effects of globalisation on the role of state in developing countries

(i) State only plays a minimal role which includes core functions like maintenance of law and order as well as security.

(ii) Globalisation has further restricted the role of state as it minimises the role of state in the economy. It reduces the state capacity and it is being completely dominated by the market forces.

(iii) The position of state has also been relieved due to globalisation as it increases technological developments which help the state to run efficiently.

(iv) Globalisation has impacted the way the state functions and set international standards that have to be adhered in order to keep up with the wave of economic growth through assistance from organisations such as World Bank and IMF. However, the state has become more transparent and even though they are answerable to other governing bodies, the state still has influence.

3. Evaluate the cultural consequences of globalisation. **CBSE 2019**

Or **Describe any two cultural consequences of globalisation.**

Or **Explain any four cultural consequences of globalisation.** **CBSE 2024 C**

Ans. Cultural consequences of globalisation affects our food, clothes and thinking. But sometimes external influence simply enlarge our choices and sometimes they modify our culture without overwhelming the traditional norms. The examples are

- The burger is no substitute for a masala dosa and therefore does not pose any real challenge.
- In the same way blue jeans can go well with a pure cotton khadi kurta. Here the outcome of outside influences is a new combination that is unique. This clothing combination has been exported back to the country that gave us blue jeans.
- The culture of the politically and economically dominant society leaves it imprint on a less powerful society. The society begins to behave like a dominant power which it wishes to be.
- This is dangerous not only for the poor countries but for the whole of humanity. It leads to the shrinking of the rich cultural heritage of the entire globe. So we can say that globalisation broadens our cultural outlook and promotes cultural homogenisation.

Picture Based Questions

1. Consider the picture given below and answer the questions that follow.

(i) What are the manifestation of globalisation?

(ii) So many Nepalese workers come to India to work. Is that globalisation?

(iii) Why do farmers commit suicide?

Ans. (i) Globalisation consists of political, economic and cultural manifestations.

(ii) Yes, coming of Nepalese workers to India is a kind of globalisation. They come to India for better livelihood.

(iii) There are various reasons for the suicide of farmers. The foremost reason is the debt trap in which they are engulfed by purchasing various inputs from MNCs, such as seeds, fertilisers, etc.

2. Study the given cartoon and answer the question that follow.

(i) The given picture is associated with globalisation. Identify the option which best signifies it.

(a) Flow and inter-connectedness of trade, idea, culture, technology among countries
(b) Studying of globes and maps of different regions
(c) Both (a) and (b)
(d) International organisation meetings

Ans. (a) Flow and inter-connectedness of trade, idea, culture, technology among countries

(ii) What does the cartoon comment?

(a) Child not eating and studying properly
(b) Impact of globalisation then and now
(c) Economic consequences of globalisation
(d) None of the above

Ans. (c) Economic consequences of globalisation

(iii) What is referred under the title 'Yesterday'?

(a) Poverty in developing countries
(b) Starving developing countries due to less economic growth
(c) Both (a) and (b)
(d) None of the above

Ans. (c) Both (a) and (b)

(iv) What message does the title 'Today' convey?
(a) Impact of globalisation in form of brain drain
(b) Less jobs in market
(c) Inefficient education system
(d) Less educated and skilled people now

Ans. (a) Impact of globalisation in form of brain drain

3. Study the given image and answer the following questions.

(i) Which of the following best represents a key feature of digital globalisation?
(a) Physical transportation of goods
(b) Data flows and digital platforms
(c) Traditional banking systems
(d) Local market restrictions

Ans. (b) Data flows and digital platforms

(ii) The digital economy has primarily transformed globalisation through ....
(a) reduced international trade
(b) increased tariff barriers
(c) enhanced digital connectivity and e-commerce
(d) recreased business communications

Ans. (c) enhanced digital connectivity and e-commerce

(iii) The rise of the digital economy in globalisation has led to ....
(a) decreased international competition
(b) slower business processes
(c) new forms of digital divide between nations
(d) reduced need for innovation

Ans. (c) new forms of digital divide between nations

(iv) Which of the following is a significant challenge associated with digital globalisation?
(a) Enhanced global cooperation
(b) Privacy and data security concerns
(c) Universal access to technology
(d) Increased local employment opportunities

Ans. (b) Privacy and data security concerns

SELF ASSESSMENT TEST

Objective Type Questions

1. Which of the following is incorrect about globalisation?
   (a) Globalisation will result in greater economic growth.
   (b) Globalisation will result in greater economic disparity.
   (c) Globalisation will result in cultural homogenisation according to some critics.
   (d) All of the above
2. Globalisation is a multi-dimensional concept having manifestations like ....
   (a) political (b) economic
   (c) cultural (d) All of these
3. Due to globalisation, culture of a country becomes more diverse and distinctive. This process is called ....
   (a) cultural complexity (b) cultural diversity
   (c) cultural homogenisation (d) cultural heterogenisation
4. Consider the following statement which is/are incorrect about the positive effect of globalisation?
   (a) It has widened income disparity.
   (b) It is also the reason for depletion flora and foura.
   (c) It has attracted private foreign capital investment.
   (d) Both (a) and (b)

Very Short Answer Type Questions

5. Mention about the two thrust areas of globalisation.
6. Why do developed countries restrict the movement of people across borders?
7. How does globalisation affect daily life and personal preferences?
8. Analyse the impact of globalisation on Indian society.
9. What concerns do critics from the political right have regarding globalisation?

Short Answer Type Questions

10. How does globalisation leads to cultural homogenisation?
11. Globalisation leads to cultural heterogenisation. Explain.
12. What led India to start economic reforms in 1991?

Long Answer Type Questions

13. Have do advocates of economic globalisation justify its benefits for the global economy?
14. How has technology contributed to globalisation?
15. Globalisation leads to shrinkage of rich cultural heritage. Critically analyse.

01 CHAPTER

This chapter explores the challenges India faced after independence, including the impact of partition, which caused violence and displacement. It also discusses the integration of Princely States into the Indian Union and the reorganisation of states based on language. These efforts helped strengthen national unity and democracy in the early years.

YOUR STUDY GOALS

1.1 A New Nation State
1.2 Partition : Displacement and Rehabilitation
1.3 Integration of Princely States
1.4 Re-organisation of States

YOUR PRACTICE GOAL

- Objective Type Questions (49 Qs ; MCQs, A-R, Statements, Matching, Passage Based)
- Subjective Questions (12 VSAs, 4 SAs, 9 LAs, 4 Picture Based, 1 Map Based)

Challenges of Nation-Building

1.1 A New Nation State

- After the British rule of nearly 200 years, India became independent nation state on the midnight of 14th-15th August, 1947. On the same night, **Jawaharlal Nehru**, the **first Prime Minister** of free India made a famous speech **tryst with destiny**[1] in a **special session of the Constituent Assembly**.
- During the national movement, it was decided that after the independence, India will work upon the following goals
  (i) Run the country through a **democratic** government.
  (ii) Government will work for the good of all, particularly **poor** and **socially disadvantaged** groups.

Challenges for the New Nation-state

- With the independence, India became a **nation-state** which was accompanied by the trauma of partition. Thus, **nation building**[2] was a difficult task for India.
- The nation building process in independent India broadly, faced **three** kinds of challenges.
  (i) **First challenge** was to accommodate and unite India. India had a vast geographical area with diverse cultures, languages and identities in every region.

---

1 **Tryst with Destiny** It is an expression that means making a secret agreement with something that is destined for us.

2 **Nation Building** It refers to the creation or development of a nation, especially one that has recently become independent.

(ii) **Second challenge** was to **establish the democracy** and comply to the following principles of the Constitution
- Parliamentary form of government
- Representative democracy
- Equal rights to the citizens including right to vote.

(iii) **Third challenge** was to **develop effective policies** for economic development and elimination of poverty. For the welfare of the society our Constitution has granted the following provisions
- Directive Principles of the State policy
- Protection to religious and cultural minorities.
- Development of the whole society rather than any one particular section.

1.2 Partition : Displacement and Rehabilitation

- Before the independence, **Muslim League** devised a two-nation theory[3]. According to this theory, there were two 'people', Hindus and Muslims in India. Thus, Muslim League demanded a separate Muslim nation which is Pakistan.
- The Congress strongly opposed this theory as well as the demand for Pakistan. But, factors like political competition between the Congress and the Muslim League along with the British interference led to the formation of Pakistan.
- Thus, British India was partitioned into two nation states-**India** and **Pakistan**.

Process of Partition

- British India was divided on the basis of religion. The places with higher Muslim majority would join Pakistan. The rest was to stay with India.
- This partition presented some difficulties which are given below
  - There was no single area with Muslim population in majority. Thus, Pakistan was created as **the West and East Pakistan**. These two areas were geographically apart from each other and separated by India in between.
  - There were some Muslim majority areas which did not want to join Pakistan. **Khan Abdul Gaffar Khan**, the leader from NWFP was also known as Frontier Gandhi. He strongly opposed the two nation theory. But, ultimately NWFP was merged with Pakistan.
  - Deepest trauma of partition came from the provinces of Bengal and Punjab. Inspite of being Muslim dominated areas, these areas also had a large number of non-Muslim population. These areas were to be divided into smaller levels like district. But their future was undecided even at the **midnight of 14th-15th** August.
- On both sides of the borders, unpredictable violence erupted against the religious communities who were in the minority. Many were forced to leave their homes at short notices because of partition. The violence took place as follows
  - Hindus and Sikhs in the areas of now Pakistan
  - Muslims on Indian side of Punjab, Bengal and some part of Delhi.

3 **Two Nation Theory** It is the idea that Hindus and Muslims in India are two distinct communities that cannot co-exist peacefully within a single state.

Jawaharlal Nehru and Muhammad Ali Jinnah on Minorities

We have a Muslim minority who are so large in numbers that they cannot, even if they want, go anywhere else. That is a basic fact about which there can be no argument. Whatever the provocation from Pakistan and whatever the indignities and horrors inflicted on non-Muslims there, we have got to deal with this minority in a civilised manner. We must give them security and the rights of citizens in a democratic state. If we fail to do so, we shall have a festering sore which will eventually poison the whole body politic and probably destroy it. **—Jawaharlal Nehru.**

We should begin to work in that spirit and in course of time all these angularities of the majority and minority communities, the Hindu community and the Muslim community - because even as regards Muslims you have Pathans, Punjabis, Shias, Sunnis and so on and among the Hindus you have Brahmins, Vaishnavas, Khatris, also Bengalees, Madrasis, and so on - will vanish. ... You are free; you are free to go to your temples, you are free to go to your mosques or to any other place of worship in this state of Pakistan. You may belong to any religion or caste or creed - that has nothing to do with the business of the state.

—Muhammad Ali Jinnah.

Consequences of Partition

- The year **1947** was the year of fear, violence, abrupt displacement, mass killings and brutal assault against humanity in the history due the partition.
- Cities like Lahore, Amritsar and Kolkata became the communal zones[4].
- People who were forced to leave their homes had to cross the borders. These people became refugees[5] in other country and had to live in **'refugee camps'**.
- Many were attacked, killed and abducted during journey women were forced to convert or killed for 'family honour'.
- Children were separated from their parents.
- Around 80 lakh people were forced to migrate across the new border. Between 5-10 lakh people were killed in partition related violence.
- Writers, poets and filmmakers had depicted the pain of partition in many novels, short-stories and movies. The partition was not only a land division, but it was a **'division of hearts'**. This was because people who had been living since ages together, were now divided.
- Partition also led to division of assets, properties political and administrative arrangements like chairs, tables, musical instruments, paper clips and even typewriters were divided too.

Faiz Ahmed Faiz

- Faiz Ahmed Faiz (1911-1984) was born in Sialkot and stayed in Pakistan after the partition.
- He was regarded as one of the greatest poets of South Asia in the 20th century.
- He was leftist and opposed the Pakistani regime and was imprisoned.
- His poetry collection includes: Naksh-e-Fariyadi, Dast-e-Saba and Zindan-Nama.

Amrita Pritam

- Amrita Pritam (1919-2005) was a prominent Punjabi poet and a fiction writer.
- After partition, she made Delhi, as her second home.
- She wrote and edited the Nagmani, a Punjabi magazine.

Quick Test 1

1. What was the name of the famous speech given by Jawaharlal Nehru?
2. What was the first challenge in the procees of nation building?
3. Which two states had the deepest trauma of the partition?
4. Name the cities which became the communal zones.
5. Where did the people had to live after crossing the borders during partition?

---

4 **Communal Zone** It is a place where a community of one religion is exploited by another religion based on their religion.

5 **Refugees** People who have been forced to leave their homes, cities or countries due to any war or social issues.

1.3 Integration of Princely States

- Before independence, British India was divided into **two** parts. These were as follows
  - **British Indian Provinces** which were directly ruled by the British.
  - **Princely States** which were ruled by the local Princes with some authority. These Princes accepted the British supremacy and this system was called as **Suzerainty or Paramountcy**[6] of the British Crown.

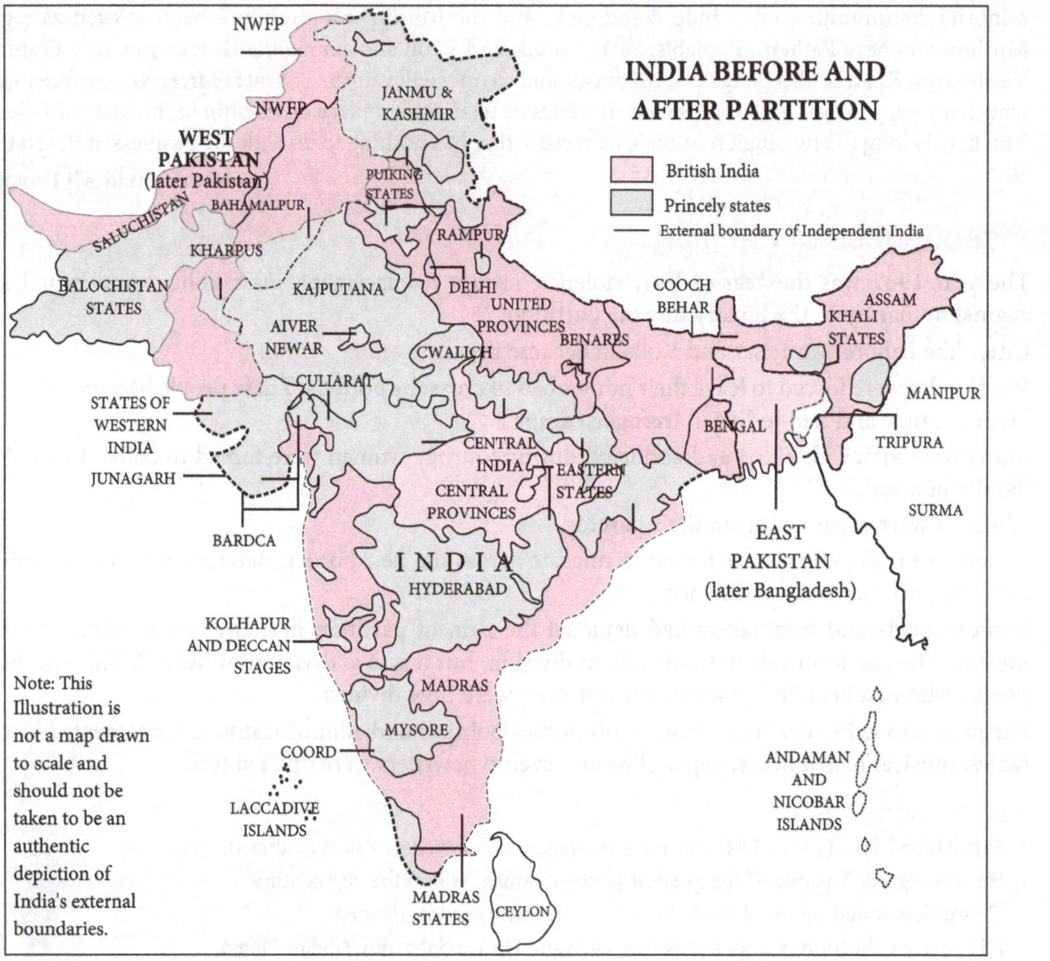

The Problem

- As per the **Mountbatten Plan,** British announced that after the independence, around 565 Princely States were free to join either state – India or Pakistan or they could remain free. This decision was left not to the people but to the princely rulers of these states.
- The **rulers of Travancore,** the **Nizam of Hyderabad** and **Nawab of Bhopal** announced to remain free. This made our intermediate government worried. Such legal independence of the Princely States would create many smaller countries in India.
- It was a very strange situation for our leaders to see India as a collection of so many small principalities or Princely States because India's aim was **self-determination** and **democracy**. In some of these Princely States, governments were running in a non-democratic manner, which was not accepted to our national leaders.

6 **Suzerainty or Paramountcy** It means the right of a country to partially control another country.

Government's Approach

Congress leaders never wanted the partition thus, the temporary government took a firm stance against the division of India into small principalities. To integrate these 565 Princely States into one union was a difficult task.

Role of Sardar Vallabhbhai Patel

- He was the Congress leader and took part in the Indian freedom movement.
- He was the first Deputy Prime Minister and Home Minister of free India. He was also the member of the Constituent Assembly.
- He has played important role in integration of Princely States with India.
- With his tactful diplomacy, he was successful in integrating the Princely States into the Indian Union.
- He took a hard hand against the Nizam of Hyderabad.
- It was his vision to see India as united, thus, he has been given the tribute of the tallest statue in the world-'Statue of Unity', which is located in Gujarat state.

- To carve a new nation state India, the interim government followed three considerations
  (i) Those Princely States who wanted to join the Indian Union.
  (ii) Giving some autonomy to the states with regional demands. The key idea was to accommodate the diversity.
  (iii) To demarcate the clear boundaries of the states and India as a nation.
- Many of the Princely States had signed the **Instrument of Accession** to join India. But accession of the Princely States of Junagarh, Hyderabad, Kashmir and Manipur was difficult than the rest of the states.

Junagarh

The issue of Junagarh was resolved as the plebiscite[7] took place in which people choose to join India.

Hyderabad

- Hyderabad state was the largest Princely State and had one of the richest leader, Nizam. The state of **old Hyderabad** included **the present day parts of Maharashtra, Karnataka and Andhra Pradesh**.
- The Nizam wanted an independent status for Hyderabad.
- He signed a 'Standstill Agreement'[8] with the government in November 1947, for a year while the negotiations with the Indian Government were going on.
- The peasantry in the Telangana region was particularly opposed to Nizam's oppressive rule and rose against him.
- The communists and the Hyderabad Congress were in the forefront of the movement.
- Women also joined the movement in large numbers.
- Nizam responded with its paramilitary force called Razakars.
- They raped, murdered and looted, targeting particularly the non-Muslims.
- The Indian Government made Nizam surrender with the **military action** in September 1948. Thus, the Princely State of Hyderabad was merged with Indian Union.

7 **Plebiscite** It means a vote by the people of a country or a region.

8 **Standstill Agreement** An agreement which was signed between the Indian Government and Princely States Rulers to include these states into the Indian Union.

Mahatma Gandhi's Sacrifice

- **Mahatma Gandhi** did not celebrate the Independence Day in 1947. He was busy in bringing peace in Kolkata where communal violence was going on.
- He began prayer meetings which attracted large crowds but soon, a violence errupted in Delhi.
- He went to Delhi. He was concerned that Muslims may reach their homes safely and they should stay with dignity as equal citizens. He was also against the due finances for Pakistan by our Indian Government. Thus, he also took his last fast.
- His efforts led to the reduction of communal tension and violence in Delhi. Muslims of Delhi and surrounding areas returned to their home safely. The government also paid the dues to Pakistan.
- However, his efforts were not liked by some people of both the communities.
- One day an extremist Nathuram Vinayak Godse killed him with three bullets on 30th January, 1948.
- Thus, the long struggle of truth, non-violence, justice and tolerance came to an end.

Manipur

- Before independence, Maharaja of Manipur **Bodhchandra Singh** and **the Government of India** signed the **'Instrument of Accession'**. It was signed on the condition that the internal autonomy of the state will be maintained.
- Under the pressure of people, in **June, 1948** elections were held in Manipur. Thus, Manipur was the **first** state to hold elections in June, 1948 on the basis of Universal Adult Franchise[9]. Manipur became the **Constitutional Monarchy**.
- In the legislative assembly of Manipur, there were sharp differences over the question of merger of Manipur with India. While the state Congress wanted the merger, other political parties were opposed to this. Manipur was merged into the Indian Union finally in **September, 1949**.

Quick Test 2

1. Which plan proposed that Princely States were free to join India or Pakistan?
2. Hho were Razakars?
3. Which agreement was signed by Nizam in 1947?
4. Name the first state which conducted the elections in June, 1948.

1.4 Re-organisation of States

- After India gained independence and integrated the princely states, a new challenge arose—how to divide the country into different states. This was not just about administration but also about ensuring that India's diverse languages and cultures were respected while maintaining national unity.
- During British rule, states were formed based on administrative convenience or the territories they controlled.
- However, the Indian freedom movement had always demanded states be created based on language. In 1920, the Indian National Congress even reorganised its internal structure based on linguistic divisions.
- After independence, leaders worried that forming states based on language could weaken national unity and shift focus from economic and social development. They decided to delay the issue, especially since the partition had already caused much tension.
- However, people across the country strongly demanded linguistic states.

9 **Universal Adult Franchise** It is a right of every adult citizen of a country to vote in elections without any discrimination.

The Visalandhra Movement

- The first major protest came from Telugu-speaking people in the Madras province, which included present-day Tamil Nadu, Andhra Pradesh, Kerala and Karnataka.
- They wanted a separate Andhra state. This movement, called the Visalandhra movement, was supported by most political leaders in the region.
- Potti Sriramulu, a Congress leader and a follower of Gandhi, went on an indefinite hunger strike to demand a separate Andhra state. After 56 days, he died, leading to massive protests, violence and police firing. Many people were injured, and some lost their lives. In response, several legislators resigned in protest.
- Seeing the growing unrest, Prime Minister Nehru announced the creation of Andhra Pradesh in December 1952.

Creation of Linguistic States

- The success of the Andhra movement inspired similar demands in other regions. In 1953, the government set up the State Re-organisation Commission to examine the issue.
- The commission recommended that states should be reorganised based on language. In 1956, the States Reorganisation Act was passed, creating 14 states and six union territories.
- Initially, leaders feared that linguistic states would divide the country. However, the opposite happened. Recognising regional languages and cultures helped strengthen national unity.
- It also made democracy more inclusive by allowing people from different regions to participate in politics, rather than just the English-speaking elite.
- More than 50 years later, linguistic states have become a key part of India's political structure. The decision to accommodate diversity helped maintain stability and strengthened India's democracy. It showed that accepting differences and respecting regional identities can make a nation stronger rather than weaker.

Potti Sriramulu

- He was a Gandhian worker who left his job to join Salt Satyagraha. He also participated in individual Satyagraha.
- He went on fast in 1946 demanding for temple opening for the Dalits in Madras province.
- He undertook a fast unto death from 19th October, 1952 demanding separate Andhra state. He died on 15th December, 1952 due to fast.

Creation of New States

- **Maharashtra** and **Gujarat** were carved out of the **Bombay province** in 1960 after a popular agitation.
- In **Punjab,** Hindi speaking and Punjabi speaking people demanded separate state. This could be fulfilled when territories of today's Haryana and Himachal Pradesh were separated from Punjab in 1966.
- **Meghalaya** was carved out of **Assam** in 1972. **Manipur** and **Tripura** too became separate states in 1972. **Arunachal Pradesh** and **Mizoram** were made states in 1987. **Nagaland** became a state in **1963**.
- Language was not solely responsible for the state formation. There were other reasons such as separate regional culture or complaints of regional imbalances in development.
- In the year 2000, three new states were formed **Chhattisgarh, Uttarakhand** and **Jharkhand**.
- **Telangana** has emerged as a new state on 2nd June, 2014.

- The formation of states that took place in later years is summarised below

S. No.	Original States	New States	Year
1.	Bombay	Maharashtra, Gujarat	1960
2.	Assam	Nagaland	1963
3.	Punjab	Haryana, Punjab, Himachal Pradesh	1966
4.	Assam	Meghalaya, Manipur, Tripura	1972
5.	Uttar Pradesh	Uttrakhand	2000
6.	Bihar	Jharkhand	2000
7.	Madhya Pardesh	Chhattisgarh	2000
8.	Andhra Pradesh	Telangana	2014

- Some regions are still demanding the separate states such as : Vidarbha in Maharashtra, Harit Pradesh in Western UP and Northern region of West Bengal.

Quick Test 3

1. On what basis were the boundaries of the Indian state territories drawn during the British period?
2. In which year was the State Re-organisation Commission appointed?
3. Who was the first Deputy Prime Minister of independent India?
4. Which Gandhian worker left his job to participate in Salt Satyagraha?
5. Where is the Vidarbha region located?

Mind Map

CHALLENGES OF NATION-BUILDING

1 A New Nation State

- India became independent nation state on the midnight of 14th–15th August 1947.
- Jawaharlal Nehru's famous tryst with destiny speech.

Challenges for the New Nation State

- Accommodate and Unite India.
- Establish the Democracy.
- Develop effective politics.

2 Partition: Displacement and Rehabilitation

Background

- Two Nation Theory.
- Political Competition (Congress Vs. Muslim League).
- British Interference.

Consequences of Partition

- Displacement and refugee crisis.
- Communal Violence.
- Division of hearts.
- Psychological Impact.

Process of Partition

- Division based on religion.
- Creation of West and East Pakistan.
- Violence against minorities (Hindus, Sikhs, Muslims).

3 Integration of Princely States

The Problem

- **Mountbatten Plan** 565 Princely States were free to join either state (India or Pakistan) or remain free.
- Some states announced to remain free (Travancore, Hyderabad and Bhopal).

Government's Approach

- Diplomacy and Negotiation.
- Instrument of Accession.

Accession of Junagarh, Hyderabad and Manipur

- **Junagarh** Plebiscite.
- **Hyderabad** Military action.
- **Manipur** Instrument of accession followed by elections in June 1948 and finally merging with Indian Union in September,1949.
- Re-organisation of states.

4 Re-organisation of States

Background

- Linguistic diversity in India.
- **Nagpur Session (1920)** INC promised to form states on the basis of linguistic principles.

Key Events

- Demand for Andhra Pradesh (Potti Sriramulu's fast).
- **Andhra Pradesh** 1st state to be created on language basis.
- State Re-Organisation Commission (1953).
- 14 new states and 6 union territories were created.

Creation of New States

- 1960: Maharashtra and Gujarat.
- 1963: Nagaland.
- 1966: Haryana, Punjab and Himachal Pradesh.
- 1972: Meghalaya, Manipur and Tripura.
- 2000: Uttarakhand, Jharkhand and Chhattisgarh.
- 2014: Telangana.

The Hindustan Times

END OF 200-YEAR-OLD BRITISH RULE IN INDIA

ROYAL ASSENT TO INDEPENDENCE BILL

BRIEF BUT COLOURFUL CEREMONY IN LORDS

Two Dominions Created

UNION'S RELATIONSHIP WITH RULERS

The Hindustan Times, 19 July 1947

A Train Full of Refugees in 1947

NCERT Folder

Intext Questions

1. Read the map and answer the following question (Pg. no. 20)

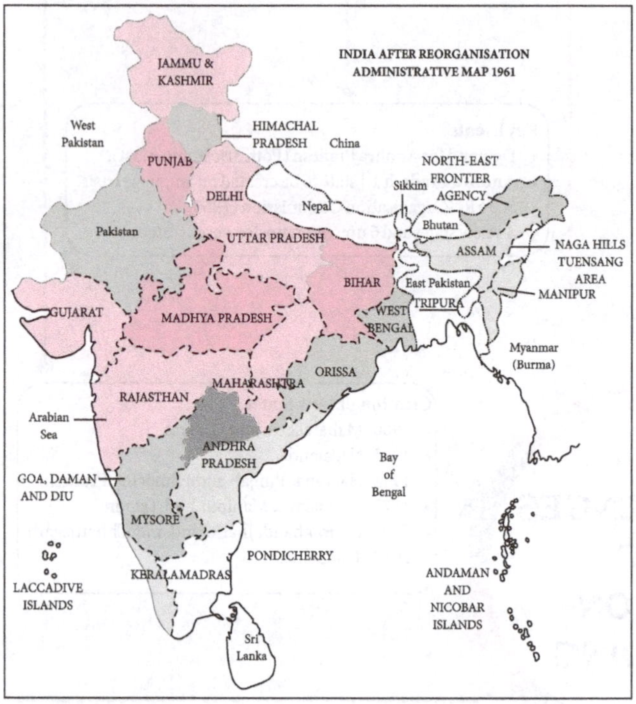

(i) Name the original state from which the following states were carved out

(a) Gujarat (b) Haryana
(c) Meghalaya (d) Chhattisgarh

(ii) Name two states that were affected by the partition of the country.

(iii) Name two states today that were once a union territory.

Ans. (i) **Gujarat** It was carved out of Bombay state in 1960.

Haryana It was carved out of Punjab in 1966.

Meghalaya It was carved out of Assam in 1972.

Chhattisgarh It was carved out of Madhya Pradesh in 2000.

(ii) **Punjab** It was divided between India and Pakistan, causing massive migration and violence.

West Bengal It was divided to create East Pakistan (now Bangladesh).

(iii) **Goa** It was a union territory until it became a state in 1987.

Himachal Pradesh It was a union territory before gaining statehood in 1971.

Exercise

1. Which among the following statements about the partition is incorrect?

(i) Partition of India was the outcome of the 'two-nation theory'.

(ii) Punjab and Bengal were the two provinces divided on the basis of religion.

(iii) East Pakistan and West Pakistan were not contiguous.

(iv) The scheme of partition included a plan for transfer of population across the border.

Ans. (iv) The scheme of partition included a plan for transfer of population across the border is the incorrect statement.

2. Match the principles with the instances.

List-I	List-II
A. Mapping of boundaries on religious grounds.	1. Pakistan and Bangladesh
B. Mapping of boundaries on grounds of different languages.	2. India and Pakistan
C. Demarcating boundaries within a country by geographical zones.	3. Jharkhand and Chattisgarh
D. Demarcating boundaries within a country on administrative and political grounds.	4. Himachal Pradesh and Uttarakhand

Ans. A → 2, B → 4, C → 1, D → 3

3. Here are two opinions

Bismay "The merger with the Indian state was an extension of democracy to the people of the Princely States".

Inderpreet "I am not so sure, there was force being used. Democracy comes by creating consensus".

What is your own opinion in the light of accession of Princely States and the responses of the people in these parts?

Ans. In my opinion, the merger of Princely States with the Indian Union was an extension of democracy to the people of the Princely States because rulers of these states suppressed the democratic rights of their people and ruled over the public in undemocratic manner.

Certainly, Inderpreet is also correct that force was used instead of consensus in some cases.

4. Take a current political map of India (showing outlines of states) and mark the location of the following Princely States.

(i) Junagarh (ii) Manipur (iii) Mysore (iv) Gwalior

Ans.

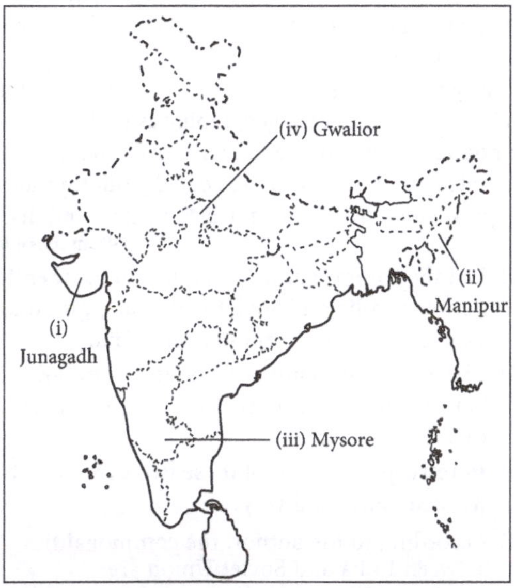

5. Read the following very different statements made in August, 1947.

"Today you have worn on your heads a crown of thorns. The seat of power is a nasty thing. You have to remain ever wakeful on that seat ...... you have to be more humble and forbearing ...... now there will be no end to your being tested". **— M.K. Gandhi.**

"...... India will awake to a life of freedom...we step out from the old to new........ we end today a period of ill fortune and India discovers herself again. The achievement we celebrate today is but a step, an opening of opportunity". **— Jawaharlal Nehru**

Spell out the agenda of nation building that flows from these two statements. Which one appeals more to you and why?

Ans. The statement of Gandhiji focuses on agenda before the nation to remain awake and cautious. He reminded the nation that power has a corrupting influence. India has to be kind and polite to its people and patient in exercising power to build nation.

Nehru in his statement spell out the agenda of establishing democracy, giving equal opportunity to people. He highlighted the new beginning of nation with new opportunities and challenges. And independence is a step towards opening the path of nation-building.

To me, both statements are appealing, however, the statement of Gandhiji is more appealing than Nehru as he reminded the nation to remain focused, awaken because power has corrupting influence and advices the nation to be kind and polite to the people.

6. What are the reasons being used by Nehru for keeping India secular? Do you think these reasons were only ethical and sentimental?

Or **Were there some prudential reasons as well?**

Ans. The main reasons for keeping India secular by Nehru were

- India after partition had considerable amount of Muslim minority population that needed accommodation.
- Providing rights and recognition to minorities will further help to strengthen our democratic system.
- It was essential to provide the minorities with citizenship status to strengthen the democratic polity of our country so that outbreak of conflict in the society is prevented.

The reasons provided by Pt. Jawaharlal Nehru were both ethical and prudential in nature.

- **Ethical reasons** The religious minorities in India is widely acknowledged by Pt. Jawaharlal Nehru and granting them rights also strengthened our democratic polity.
- The declaration of India as a secular nation would allow everyone to freely profess and propagate religion of their choice.
- Thus, it would form a basic foundation of our democratic system.

7. Bring out two major difference between the challenge of nation building for Eastern and Western regions of the country at the time of independence.

Ans. At the time of Independence, the challenges of nation-building were different in the Eastern and Western parts of India.

(i) **Partition and Refugee Crisis** In the West (mainly Punjab), Partition led to large-scale violence and the sudden movement of millions of people between India and Pakistan. In the East (Bengal), the refugee movement was slower but continued for many years, creating problems in resettling people.

(ii) **Border Issues and Conflicts** In the West, India had to fight a war with Pakistan over Kashmir in 1947-48. In the East, the border remained open, leading to constant migration. Later, in 1971, the Bangladesh Liberation War caused another refugee crisis.

8. What was the task of the States Re-organisation Commission? What was its most salient recommendation?

Ans. The State Re-organisation Commission was appointed in 1953 by Central Government to look into the matter of redrawing of internal boundaries of state.

The commission in its report accepted that states' boundaries should reflect the boundaries of different languages.

The State Re-organisation Act was passed in 1956 which led to the creation of 14 states and 6 union territories.

The most salient re-commendation was the formation of linguistic states i.e. re-organisation of states on the basis of their languages.

9. It is said that the nation is to a large extent an 'Imagined community' held together by common beliefs, history, political aspirations and imaginations. Identify the features that make India a nation.

Ans. A nation is defined as a group of people living in a common geographical area, sharing common history, language, religion, descent, ethnicity and culture. Features that make India a nation are as follows

- India is a land of immense diversities. It is multi-lingual, multi-religious, multi-cultural and multi-regional country. With all sorts of diversities, the country has maintained unity and integrity.
- There is unity amidst diversity. Despite all the crisis, political decay, chaos, instability changes and challenges, the country has retained its unity, integrity and nationhood.
- India as a nation is held together with same political aspirations which ensures democratic set-up based on Parliamentary form of government that inculcates political competition in a democratic framework.
- Indian society is based on welfare state i.e. on the principles of equality, freedom, protection to socially disadvantaged groups and religions, etc. There will be no discrimination on the basis of religion, race, sex or place of birth as per the Indian Constitution.

10. Read the following passage and answer the questions below.

"In the history of nation-building only the Soviet experiment bears comparison with the Indian. There too, a sense of unity had to be forged between many diverse ethnic groups, religious, linguistic communities and social classes. The scale-geographic as well as demographic was comparably massive. The raw material the state had to work with was equally unpropitious: a people divided by faith and driven by debt and disease".

—Ramachandra Guha

(i) List the commonalities that the author mentions between India and Soviet Union and give one example for each of these from India.

(ii) The author does not talk about dissimilarities between the two experiments. Can you mention two dissimilarities?

(iii) In retrospect, which of these two experiments worked better and why?

Ans. (i) According to the author, the commonalities between India and Soviet Union are

(a) Both witnessed same path of nation-building by and large.

(b) Both countries stand united despite having diverse ethnic groups, religious, linguistic communities and social classes.

(ii) The dissimilarities between both are

(a) Differences in nature of federation of both nation.

(b) Differences in the form of government and economic system.

(iii) Indian experiment worked better in establishing democracy and accommodating the diversity because citizens enjoy greater democratic rights and states have greater say in Indian federation than in Russian federation.

Exam Pattern Questions

Objective Type Questions

Multiple Choice Questions (MCQs)

1. **Which of the following challenges were faced by India after independence?**

(a) Accommodation and unity
(b) Establishing Democracy
(c) Development and well-being
(d) All of the above

2. **What was issued by the government from the following to mark the first Republic Day on 26th January, 1950?**

(a) Three journals (b) Three stamps
(c) Three magazines (d) Three pamphlets

3. **Who propounded 'Two-Nation Theory'?**

(a) Muhammad Ali Jinnah (b) Khan Abdul Gaffar Khan
(c) Nizam of Hyderabad (d) Maulana Abul Kalam Azad

4. **Which one of the following was not a reason for the partition of British India in 1947?**

CBSE Term I 2021

(a) The Two-Nation Theory
(b) The political aim of the Muslim league
(c) Integration of Princely States with India
(d) British policy to divide India

5. **Who advanced the 'Two-Nation Theory' that led to the partition of British India?** Diksha App, CBSE 2023

(a) Khan Abdul Guffar Khan
(b) Muslim League
(c) British Government
(d) Coungress Party

6. **Who was known as 'Frontier Gandhi'?** Diksha App

(a) Khan Abdul Gaffar Khan (b) Jawaharlal Nehru
(c) Sardar Vallabhbhai Patel (d) Dr. B.R. Ambedkar

7. **Who among the following leaders of the National Movement strongly opposed the Two-Nation Theory?**

CBSE Term I 2021

(a) Muhammad Ali Jinnah (b) Jawaharlal Nehru
(c) Mahatma Gandhi (d) Khan Abdul Gaffar khan

8. **Which of the following were the problems faced at the time of partition of India?**

(a) There was not single territory of Muslim majority areas in British India.
(b) Not all Muslim majority areas wanted to join Pakistan.
(c) The minorities on both sides of the border had no option except to leave their home at very short notice.
(d) All of the above

9. **Which of the following are the consequences of India's partition in 1947?** Competency Based Que; CBSE Term I 2021

I. Communal violence
II. Lakhs of people had to migrate from one place to another
III. Parliamentary system of government
IV. Re-organisation of states

Codes

(a) I and III (b) II and IV
(c) I and II (d) III and IV

10. **Which Princely State of India was the first to announce the remain as an independent state?**

(a) Mysore (b) Ajmer CBSE Term I 2021
(c) Gwalior (d) Travancore

11. **Which one of the following statements about the Princely States is false?** CBSE Term I 2021

(a) In all there were 565 Princely States at the time of Independence.
(b) All the 565 Princely States were legally free to become independent countries.
(c) Hyderabad's accession to India took place in 1948.
(d) The Nawab of Bhopal was eager to join the Constitutent Assembly.

12. **Consider the following statement(s) is/are incorrect about the accession of Hyderabad.** Competency Based Que

I. Nizam of Hyderabad signed the Instrument of Accession with India on the assurance of internal autonomy.
II. Nizam wanted an independent status for Hyderabad.
III. He signed Standstill Agreement in November with India.
IV. The peasantry, women and people of Hyderabad rose against oppressive rule of Nizam.

Codes

(a) Only I (b) Only IV
(c) Both I and II (d) Both II and III

13. **Choose the one which was NOT a Princely State of British India?**

(a) Mysore
(b) Hyderabad
(c) Bombay
(d) Manipur

14. **Which one of the following Princely States of India initially opposed joining the Indian Union?** CBSE 2024

(a) Baroda (b) Hyderabad
(c) Mysore (d) Gwalior

15. **Which of the following states initially refused to join the Indian Union?**

(a) Manipur (b) Kashmir
(c) Punjab (d) Both (a) and (b)

16. **Which group among the following options represents the three Princely States that resisted their merger with India?** CBSE Term I 2021

(a) Hyderabad, Bhopal, Jammu and Kashmir
(b) Junagarh, Gwalior, Mysore
(c) Junagarh, Hyderabad, Travancore
(d) Gwalior, Travancore, Bhopal

17. **The merger issue of Junagarh was resolved after ...... confirmed people's desire to join India. Choose the correct word to fill in the blank** CBSE Term I 2021

(a) election (b) public meeting
(c) plebiscite (d) compromise

18. **The rule is of most of the Princely States had agreed to become a part of the union of India ....**

(a) on 15th of August, 1947
(b) before 15th of August, 1947
(c) on 25th of January, 1950
(d) after 26th of January, 1950

19. **Given below are the two statements** Competency Based Que

Statement I Manipur and Kashmir were easily integrated into the Indian Union.

Statement II Hyderabad was accessed through the military action.

(a) Both Statement I and Statement II are true.
(b) Both Statement I and Statement II are false.
(c) Statement I is true, but Statement II is false.
(d) Statement I is false, but Statement II is true.

20. **Which one of the following leaders played an important role in the integration of Princely States with India?** CBSE 2020

(a) Pt. Jawaharlal Nehru (b) Sardar Vallabhbhai Patel
(c) C. Rajagopalachari (d) Dr. B.R. Ambedkar

21. **Razakars were the Paramilitary force of which of the following Nizam?** Diksha App

(a) Nizam of Hyderabad (b) Nizam of Manipur
(c) Nizam of Junagarh (d) Nizam of Jaipur

22. **Identify the part of independent India in which elections based on universal adult franchise were conducted for the first time.** Competency Based Que; Diksha APP

(a) Manipur (b) Jharkhand
(c) Hyderabad (d) Travancore

23. **Choose the statements that were the basis for drawing the state boundaries during the colonial rule in India.** Competency Based Que; CBSE Term I 2021

I. On administrative convenience.
II. To ensure the security of British India.
III. Simply coincided with the territories annexed by the British Government.
IV. Coincided with the territories ruled by the Princely States.

Codes

(a) I, II and III (b) I, III and IV
(c) II, III and IV (d) I, II and IV

24. **"Our leaders after independence, decided to postpone the formation of states on the basis of language". What was the basis of this thought? Choose the correct option.** Competency Based Que; Term I 2021

I. It would lead to disruption and disintegration.
II. They thought it would draw attention away from social and economic challenges that the country faced.
III. The fate of Princely States had not been decided.
IV. The memory of partition was still fresh.

Codes

(a) I and IV (b) I and II
(c) I, II and IV (d) All of these

25. **Which of the following is/are correct with regard to Vishalandhra movement?** Competency Based Que

I. It demanded that the Telugu speaking areas should be separated from Madras province.
II. The protest began in the areas of old Madras province which included present day Tamil Nadu, parts of Andhra Pradesh, Kerala and Karnataka.
III. The movement gathered momentum as a result of Central Government's vacillation.
IV. All of the above

Codes

(a) Only I (b) Only IV
(c) Both I and II (d) Both II and III

26. **How many states and union territories were created with the State Re-organisation Act which was passed in 1956?**

(a) 28 states 7 union territories
(b) 14 states 6 union territories
(c) 24 states 3 union territories
(d) 12 states 5 union territories

27. **From the following options, choose the set of states that belong to North-East India only.** CBSE 2023

(a) Assam, Manipur, Chhattisgarh
(b) Manipur, Tripura, Nagaland
(c) Jharkhand, Nagaland, Uttrakhand
(d) Manipur, Maharashtra, Mizoram

28. **Name the state from which Chhattisgarh was carved out.** **CBSE 2024**

(a) Uttar Pradesh
(b) Bihar
(c) Jharkhand
(d) Madhya Pradesh

29. **Which one of the following from the North-East had become a state before 1972?**

(a) Meghalaya (b) Manipur
(c) Tripura (d) Nagaland

30. **Identify and write the incorrect pair.** **Competency Based Que**

(a) Nagaland : 1967
(b) Gujarat : 1960
(c) Arunachal Pradesh: 1987
(d) Tripura : 1972

31. **Study the picture given below carefully and answer the question that follows.** **Competency Based Que**

The picture is related to which incident?

(a) Quit India Movement -1942
(b) First Independence Day of India - 15th August, 1947
(c) First Republic Day of India -26th January, 1950
(d) An election rally in 1952

32. **Study the following postal stamps carefully and answer the question that follows** **Competency Based Que**

Out of four challenges given below that India faced at the time of independence, three have been depicted on the given postal stamps. Choose the challenges that have NOT been depicted on the stamps.

(a) To make India an industralised nation
(b) To provide employment to the masses
(c) To become self sufficient in agriculture
(d) To promote cultural harmony

33. **Study the cartoon given below and answer the questions that follows** **Competency Based Que**

Which one of the following statements related to the cartoon is incorrect?

(a) The cartoon depicts the relation between the ruler and the ruled in the Princely States.
(b) Sardar Patel is asking the ruler to sign the Instrument of Accession.
(c) The cartoon depicts the Patel's effort to negotiate with the rulers of Princely States.
(d) Foreign affairs, defence and communication were the subjects under the control of Princely rulers.

34. **Arrange the following in sequence.** **Competency Based Que**

I. Formation of separate Andhra state
II. Nagpur Session of Congress
III. Appoints State Re-organisation Commission by Central Government
IV. Creation of state of Maharashtra and Gujarat

Codes

(a) I, II, III and IV
(b) II, I, III and IV
(c) I, II, IV and III
(d) III, IV, II and I

35. **Arrange the following in sequence.**

I. Mizoram and Arunachal Pradesh came into being.
II. State of Nagaland was created.
III. Territories of Haryana and Himachal Pradesh were separated from larger Punjab state.
IV. Creation of states-Chhattisgarh, Uttarakhand and Jharkhand. **Competency Based Que**

Codes

(a) IV, II, III and I
(b) II, III, I and IV
(c) IV, I, II and III
(d) IV, II, I and III

36. Match the facts given in list A with those in list B in the meaningful way.

	List-I		List-II
A.	Proponent of two-nation theory	1.	Jawaharlal Nehru
B.	Raised the demand for a separate state in 1952	2.	M.A. Jinnah
C.	Signed instrument of Merger in 1949	3.	Potti Sriramulu
D.	Announced the formation of a separate state in December 1952	4.	Maharaja Bodhchandra Singh

Codes

	A	B	C	D		A	B	C	D
(a)	2	3	4	1	(b)	1	2	3	4
(c)	4	1	2	3	(d)	3	4	2	1

37. Arrange the following in chronological order. **Competency Based Que**

I. **Formation of Maharashtra**
II. **Assassination of Mahatma Gandhi**
III. **Elections were held in Manipur**
IV. **Nizam entered into a Standstill Agreement with the government**

Codes

(a) IV, II, III, I (b) II, III, I, IV
(c) III, II, IV, I (d) I, III, IV, II

38. Match the following.

List I	List II
A. Standstill Agreement	1. 1949
B. Maharaja of Manipur signed Merger Agreement	2. 1972
C. State Re-organisation Act Passed	3. 1947
D. Major Re-organisation of states in North-East	4. 1956

Codes

	A	B	C	D		A	B	C	D
(a)	3	1	4	2	(b)	3	2	4	1
(c)	2	3	1	4	(d)	4	1	3	2

Assertion-Reason Questions

Directions (Q. Nos. 39-43) In the questions given below, there are two statements marked as Assertion (A) and Reason (R). Read the statements and choose the correct option.

Codes

(a) Both A and R are true and R is the correct explanation of A.
(b) Both A and R are true, but R is not the correct explanation of A.
(c) A is true, but R is false.
(d) A is false, but R is true.

39. Assertion (A) The idea of partition was very painful as well as it was difficult to be implemented.

Reason (R) One of the difficulty emerged was that "Not all Muslim, majority areas wanted to join Pakistan".

40. Assertion (A) Movement of the people of Hyderabad state against the Nizam's rule had gathered force and momentum. **CBSE Term I 2021**

Reason (R) Peasantry and women joined hands against the oppressive rule of the Nizam.

41. Assertion (A) The Prime Minister announced the formation of a separate Andhra state in December 1952.

Reason (R) Potti Sriramulu, a Congress leader went on an indefinite fast that led to his death after 56 days which caused unrest in Andhra region.

42. Assertion (A) Three new states, Chattisgarh, Uttarakhand and Jharkhand were created in 2000.

Reason (R) Language remain the sole basis of organisation of states.

43. Assertion (A) Major re-organisation of states took place in the North-East in 1972.

Reason (R) Nagaland became a state much earlier in 1963.

Passage Based Questions

44. Read the following passage carefully and answers the questions that follow. **CBSE Term I 2021**

Broadly, independent India faced three kinds of challenges. The first and the immediate challenge was to shape a nation that was united, yet accommodative of the diversity in our society.

India was a land of continental size and diversity. Its people spoke different languages and followed different cultures and religions. At that time it was widely believed that a country full of such kinds of diversity could not remain together for long. The partition of the country appeared to prove everyone's worst fears. There were serious questions about the future of India: Would India survive as a unified country? Would it do so by emphasising national unity at the cost of every other objective? Would it mean rejecting all regional and sub-national identities? And there was an urgent question: How was integration of the territory of India to be achieved?

(i) **What was the main reason for the immediate challenge of shaping India as a united nation just after independence?**

(a) India was a secular state.
(b) India became free after a long period of slavery.
(c) The British had drained out the mineral resources and ruined the active industries.
(d) India was a large sub-continent having multi-religious, diverse culture and various languages.

(ii) Which one of the following statements related to the partition of India in 1947 is incorrect?

(a) The partition paved the way for religious harmony between India and Pakistan.
(b) The partition of India was responsible for the largest and tragic transfer of population in human history.
(c) There were killings and atrocities on both sides of the border.
(d) Minorities on both sides of the border fled their homes to seek safe shelter in refugee camps.

(iii) Why was it believed that country like India which was full of diversities could not remain together for long?

45. Read the following passage carefully and answer the questions that follow.

We have a Muslim minority who are so large in numbers that they cannot, even if they want, go anywhere else. That is a basic fact about which there can be no argument. Whatever the provocation from Pakistan and whatever the indignities and horrors inflicted on non-Muslims there, we have got to deal with this minority in a civilised manner. We must give them security and the rights of citizens in a democratic state. If we fail to do so, we shall have a festering sore which will eventually poison the whole body politic and probably destroy it. Jawaharlal Nehru, letter to Chief Minister, 15th October, 1947.

(i) In spite of indignities and horrors inflicted on non-Muslims by Pakistan, Why Jawaharlal Nehru wanted to deal with the Muslim minority in a civilised way?

(a) Because Muslims were large in number.
(b) Because Muslims had no option to go anywhere even if they want to.
(c) Because Muslims were not represented as a minority section.
(d) Both (a) and (b)

(ii) Why this minority should be given the security and rights on the same footing as to all others in a democratic system?

(a) Because Indian Constitution didn't provide these rights equally.
(b) Because India is a democratic and secular country where all religions are treated equally.
(c) Because in India there is truly an equal opportunity to influence government by the minorities.
(d) All of the above

(iii) What kind of scenario will be envisaged if the Muslim minority is not provided security and rights?

46. Read the following passage carefully and answer the questions that follow. **CBSE Term I 2021**

On 14th-15th August, 1947, not one but two nation-states came into existence. India and Pakistan. This was a result of 'Partition', the division of British India into India and Pakistan. The partition was the outcome of 'Two-Nation Theory' advanced by the Muslim League. The Congress opposed this theory and the demand for Pakistan. But several political developments led to the decision for the creation of Pakistan.

(i) Which political leader demanded the partition of British India?

(a) Jawaharlal Nehru (b) Sardar Patel
(c) M. A. Jinnah (d) Khan Abdul Gaffar Khan

(ii) Choose the statement that correctly explains the 'Two-Nation Theory'.

(a) India consisted of two groups of people, Hindu and Muslims, hence two nations are required.
(b) Two separate nations should be formed to accommodate the leaders of Hindus and Muslims.
(c) One nation for Congress and other for Muslim League was demanded.
(d) Hindus should have a separate nation but Muslims could choose any one out of the two.

(iii) Which of the two states were bifurcated on the basis of religious majority?

(a) Gujarat and Punjab (b) Gujarat and Rajasthan
(c) Punjab and Bengal (d) Bengal and Gujarat

(iv) What among the following was not divided between India and Pakistan?

(a) Typewriters, books and musical instruments
(b) Liabilities
(c) Hearts of the people
(d) All of the above

47. Read the following passage carefully and answer the questions that follow. **CBSE 2024**

The interim government took a firm stance against the possible division of India into smaller principalities of different sizes. The Muslim League opposed the Indian National Congress and took the view that the states should be free to adopt any course they liked. Sardar Patel, India's Deputy Prime Minister and the Home Minister during the crucial period, immediately after Independence, played a historic role in negotiating with the rulers of Princely States in bringing most of them into the Indian Union.

(i) Which principle was followed for the division of British India at the time of partition in 1947?

(a) Principle of administrative control
(b) Principle of ethnic composition
(c) Principle of religious majorities
(d) Principle of equality

(ii) Who was the first Deputy Prime Minister of free India?

(a) Dr. B.R. Ambedkar (b) Sardar Patel
(c) V.K. Menon (d) Khan Abdul Gaffar Khan

(iii) **How many Princely States were there in British India at the time of independence ?**
(a) 556
(b) 566
(c) 655
(d) 565

(iv) **Which one of the following statements about the Princely States is not correct?**
(a) The Indian Government was ready to give autonomy to some regions.
(b) The ruler of Junagarh had decided to be part of independent India.
(c) Princely States covered one third of the land area of British Indian empire.
(d) Some of the Princely States clearly wanted to become part of the Indian Union.

48. Read the following passage carefully and answer the questions that follow.

The linguistic states underlined the acceptance of the principle of diversity. When we say that India adopted democracy, it does not simply mean that India... adopted the format of elections. The choice was larger than that. It was a choice in favour of recognising and accepting the existence of differences which could at times be oppositional. Democracy, in other words, was associated with plurality of ideas and ways of life.

(i) **Which of the following are the forms of diversity in the cultural life of people of India?**
(a) Linguistic diversity (b) Caste diversity
(c) Race diversity (d) Both (a) and (b)

(ii) **Which of the following examples shows that democracy in India is associated with plurality of ideas and acceptance of differences?**
(a) Religious tolerance and language adoption
(b) Political instability
(c) Separatist movements
(d) Protests and mass movements

(iii) **How role of elections help in strengthening democracy?**
(a) Due to elections, political equality is honoured.
(b) Elections boost social integrity.
(c) Elections are the instrument for peaceful transfer of power with consent.
(d) All of the above

(iv) **Which of the following is/are dicuobid between India and Pakistan?**
(a) General legal framework and Constitutional government
(b) Encompassing free and fair elections
(c) Maintenance of rule of law
(d) None of the above

49. Read the following passage carefully and answer the questions that follow.

The third challenge was to ensure the development and well- being of the entire society and not only of some sections. Here again the Constitution clearly laid down the principle of equality and special protection to socially disadvantaged groups and religious and cultural communities. The Constitution also set out in the Directive Principles of State Policy the welfare goals that democratic politics must achieve. The real challenge now was to evolve effective policies for economic development and eradication of poverty.

(i) **Which of the following are protected under the Constitution?**
(a) Religious minorities (b) Cultural minorities
(c) Both (a) and (b) (d) None of these

(ii) **Which of the following was included in the Constitution for the welfare of the society?**
(a) Fundamental Rights
(b) Right to Vote
(c) Directive Principles of the State Policy
(d) None of the above

(iii) **What was the real challenge in ensuring the development of the whole society ?**

Answers

1. (d) All of the above 2. (b) Three stamps
3. (a) Muhammad Ali Jinnah
4. (c) Integration of Princely States with India.
5. (b) Muslim League
6. (a) Khan Abdul Gaffar Khan
7. (d) Khan Abdul Gaffar Khan
8. (d) All of the above 9. (c) I and II
10. (d) Travancore
11. (d) The Nawab of Bhopal was eager to join the Constitutent Assembly.
12. (a) Only I 13. (c) Bombay
14. (b) Hyderabad 15. (d) Both (a) and (b)
16. (c) Junagarh, Hyderabad, Travancore
17. (c) plebiscite 18. (b) before 15th of August, 1947
19. (d) Statement I is false, but Statement II is true.
20. (b) Sardar Vallabhbhai Patel

21. (a) Nizam of Hyderabad
22. (a) Manipur
23. (b) I, III and IV
24. (c) I, II and IV
25. (b) Only IV
26. (b) 14 states 6 union territories
27. (b) Manipur, Tripura, Nagaland
28. (d) Madhya Pradesh
29. (d) Nagaland
30. (a) Nagaland: 1967
31. (b) First Independence Day of India - 15th August, 1947
32. (b) To provide employment to the masses
33. (b) Sardar Patel is asking the ruler to sign the Instrument of Accession.
34. (b) II, I, III and IV
35. (b) II, III, I and IV
36. (a) 2 3 4 1
37. (a) IV, II, III, I
38. (a) 3 1 4 2
39. (a) Both A and R are true and R is the correct explanation of A.
40. (a) Both A and R are true and R is the correct explanation of A.
41. (a) Both A and R are true and R is the correct explanation of A.
42. (c) A is true, but R is false.
43. (b) Both A and R are true, but R is not the correct explanation of A.
44. (i) (d) India was a large sub-continent having multi-religious, diverse culture and various languages.
    (ii) (a) The partition paved the way for religious harmony between India and Pakistan.
    (iii) (a) People were divided on the basis of religion.
    (b) The caste based division in the social life created hatred.
    (c) The British had already divided the people on various grounds.
45. (i) (d) Both (a) and (b)
    (ii) (b) Because India is a democratic and secular country where all religions are treated equally.
    (iii) If the Muslim minority is not provided security and rights, then following scenario will be envisaged
    (a) It may poison the whole Indian political system.
    (b) The democratic set-up will come to an end.
    (c) Instability will be there in the society
46. (i) (c) M. A. Jinnah
    (ii) (b) Two separate nations should be formed to accommodate the leaders of Hindus and Muslims.
    (iii) (c) Punjab and Bengal
    (iv) (d) All of the above
47. (i) (c) Principle of religious majorities
    (ii) (b) Sardar Patel
    (iii) (d) 565
    (iv) (b) The ruler of Junagarh had decided to be part of independent India.
48. (i) (d) Both (a) and (b)
    (ii) (a) Religious tolerance and language adoption
    (iii) (d) All of the above
    (iv) (d) None of the above
49. (i) (c) Both (a) and (b)
    (ii) (c) Directive Principles of the State Policy
    (iii) The real challenge was to evolve effective policies for economic development and eradication of poverty. These include poverty, unemployment and low productivity of the agriculture produce.

Subjective Questions

Very Short Answer Type Questions

1. What were the goals on which everyone agreed on the eve of independence?

Ans. Although, there were many voices and demands during national movement but there were two goals on which everyone agreed upon. These were as follows

(i) Our country shall be governed by a democratic government after independence.

(ii) Government will work for the welfare of all, particularly poor and socially disadvantaged groups of society.

2. Mention any two challenges that were faced by India just after independence?

Or **"Free India was born in very difficult circumstances". Justify the statement with any two suitable arguments.**

Competency Based Que; CBSE 2019

Ans. It is true that free India was born in very difficult circumstances as it had to face a number of challenges. The two challenges faced by India just after independence were as follows

(i) Challenge to shape a nation which is accommodative of the diversity in our society.

(ii) Challenge to establish democracy.

3. "The Constitution framers of India ensured development and well-being of the entire society and not only of some sections". Validate the statement with any two suitable arguments. **Competency Based Que; CBSE 2019**

Ans. The Constitution framers wanted development and well-being of the entire society and not only some sections. For this they agreed upon two things. These were as follows

(i) Our country shall be governed by a democratic government after independence.

(ii) Government will work for the welfare of all, particularly poor and socially disadvantaged groups of society.

4. What is meant by 'Two-Nation Theory'?

Ans. The 'Two-Nation Theory' means the cultural, political, religious, economic and social dissimilarities between the two major communities living in India; Hindus and Muslims. This theory gave rise to the demand of two separate countries/nations, one for Muslims (Pakistan) and one for Hindus (India).

5. "The idea of Pakistan might have appeared simple, but its creation presented many severe difficulties". Elucidate any two of them. **Competency Based Que; CBSE 2019**

Ans. The idea of Pakistan might have appeared simple but the creation of Pakistan presented many severe difficulties. These were

(i) There was no single territory of Muslim majority areas in British India. There were two areas of Muslim population viz, West and East Pakistan.

(ii) Lakhs of Hindus and Sikhs in the areas that are now in Pakistan and an equally large number of Muslims on the Indian side of Punjab and Bengal found themselves trapped.

6. Analyse the two political developments of 1940s that led to the decision for the creation of Pakistan.

Or **Analyse any two factors that led to the creation of Pakistan.** **CBSE 2019**

Ans. During 1940s in India, there were many political developments which led to the decision for the creation of Pakistan. These were

(i) The competition between the Congress and the Muslim League was taking place. The Congress wanted to make a nation that reflect democratic government, whereas the Muslim League propounded 'Two-Nation Theory' to gain power and status for minority community in politics i.e. Muslims.

(ii) The British were also playing their role of 'divide and rule' policy and accepted the 'Two-Nation Theory' for partition of India.

Thus, in 1947 the two-nation i.e. India and Pakistan came into existence.

7. Identify any two consequences of the Partition of India in 1947. **Competency Based Que**

Or **Highlight any two outcomes of partition or division of India into India and Pakistan.**

Ans. Two consequences of the partition of India in 1947 were the following

(i) There were killings and atrocities on both sides of the border.

(ii) Political division of the country led to the administrative failure.

8. What had been government's approach towards the integration of Princely States?

Ans. Government's approach towards the integration of Princely States was based on three considerations

(i) People of most of the Princely States wanted to be a part of the Indian Union.

(ii) Government was flexible to give autonomy to some regions for accommodating diversity.

(iii) In the back drop of partition, integration and consolidation of territorial boundaries of the country had become highest priority.

9. Explain the role played by Sardar Patel in the unification of Princely States in India.

Or **Mention the role of Sardar Vallabhbhai Patel towards India's integration.**

Ans. Sardar Patel played following roles in the unification of Princely States in India

(i) He got document of accession signed from the Princely States through diplomacy and negotiation.

(ii) He diplomatically brought the states of Hyderabad, Junagarh and Manipur through military action, plebiscite and Instrument of Accession respectively.

10. What was the Instrument of Accession and why was it important for the integration of Princely States?

Ans. The Instrument of Accession was a legal document signed by the rulers of Princely States to agree to become part of the union of India. It was important because it allowed India to peacefully integrate the territories of 565 Princely States after independence. Without this agreement, many Princely States could have chosen to remain independent or joined Pakistan, threatening the unity and integrity of India.

Leaders like Sardar Vallabhbhai Patel played a significant role in persuading the rulers to sign this document.

11. While the rest of the country was re-organised on linguistic lines in 1950s, why had Punjab to wait till 1966? Competency Based Que

Ans. Punjab had to wait until 1966 because of the following reasons

(i) There were two linguistic groups in Punjab: Hindi speaking and Punjabi speaking

(ii) Punjabi speaking people desired their own state but it was not granted in 1956.

(iii) Later in 1966, Haryana and Himachal Pradesh were finally separated from Punjab in 1966, and Punjab become a state.

12. Which states in India demand the separate and smaller states.

Ans. There are several regions in some parts of India which demand for separate and smaller states. These are as follows

(i) Vidarbha in Maharashtra

(ii) Harit Pradesh in the Western Uttra Pradesh

(iii) Northern region in West Bengal

Short Answer Type Questions

1. According to Mahatma Gandhi , the day of 15th August, 1947, was of both joy and sorrow.Why? Competency Based Que

Ans. Mahatma Gandhi called the day of 15th August, 1947, as a day of both join and sorrow because

(i) India became independent from the exploitative British rule after the long span of 200 years, thus, it was the end of the year of tyranny and colonialism. Therefore, it was the day of joy.

(ii) However, with the independence, India had to be partitioned also. During the partition there was so much violence in the name of religion, which was against the Gandhian principle of truth and non-violence.

(iii) Gandhi never wanted the partition for India and he always been a supporter of peace and communal harmony but such pain and trauma of partition has made him to say that it was a day of sorrow.

2. What was the approach of the Government of India towards the Princely States immediately after the partition of India in 1947?

Ans. At the time of India's independence, there were 565 Princely States. Immediately after partition, communal violence was at its culmination.

During that phase, the government's approach towards Princely States was guided by three considerations

(i) Firstly, the people of most of the Princely States clearly wanted to become part of the Indian Union.

(ii) Secondly, the government was prepared to be flexible in giving autonomy to some regions. The idea was to accommodate plurality and adopt a flexible approach in dealing with the demands of the regions.

(iii) Thirdly, in the backdrop of partition which brought into focus the contest over demarcation of territory, the integration and consolidation of the territorial boundaries of the nation had assumed supreme importance.

3. How did the state of Hyderabad became a part of the Indian Union after partition?

Ans. Hyderabad, the largest of the Princely States covered almost one-third part of South India. Nizam signed Standstill Agreement with the Government of India and state emerged as an independent state after India's independence.

Many movements took place in Hyderabad state specially in Telangana region where many peasants were victimised and oppressed by Nizam.

Nizam sent his paramilitary force, called Razakars. Razakars murdered, raped and looted particularly the non-Muslims.

Therefore, Central Government ordered the army to tackle the situation. On 13th September, 1948, Indian army marched in Hyderabad and on the 17th September, 1948, Hyderabad surrendered. This led to Hyderabad's accession to India.

4. How did the death of Potti Sriramulu lead to the state re-organisation on linguistic basis?

Ans. Potti Sriramulu was a renowned Gandhian activist and participated in Civil Disobedience Movement and also in individual Satyagraha. He left his job and joined all the movements throughout India. He undertook fast unto death for demanding a separate Andhra state from Madras province. His death raised the movement for separate Andhra Pradesh.

In Madras province, several legislators resigned their seats in protest. At last, the Prime Minister announced the formation of a separate Andhra Pradesh state. In December, 1952, the formation of Andhra Pradesh led to the struggle for making of other states on linguistic lines.

These struggles forced the government to appoint States Re-organisation Commission. Centre appointed States Re-organisation Commission in 1953, to look into the question of redrawing of the boundaries of states on linguistic basis.

Long Answer Type Questions

1. Highlight any three challenges faced by India after independence. CBSE 2023; Diksha App

Or **Describe any three major challenges that independent India faced immediately after independence.** CBSE 2024

Ans. Broadly India faced three challenges after the independence in 1947. These challenges are as follows

(i) First challenge was to accommodate and unite India. India had a vast geographical area with diverse cultures, languages and identities at every different region. At the time of independence, it was widely believed that any country with huge diversity cannot remain united for long time. Partition had made this fear true. Thus, to maintain the unity among such differences was a challenging task.

(ii) Another challenge was to establish the democracy. Although Indian Constitution has provided for the Parliamentary form of government. Everyone had been provided the equal voting rights to ensure the representative democracy. Each of the citizen was provided with equal Fundamental Rights also. But to strengthen the democracy, Constitution was not enough alone.

(iii) The third challenge was to ensure the development of the entire society rather than some sections. The Constitution has clearly laid down the principles of equality. It has also safeguarded the socially disadvantaged people. For the welfare of the society our Constitution has granted the following provisions

- Directive Principles of the State Policy
- Protection to religious and cultural minorities.

But, the real challenge now was to evolve effective policies for economic development and elimination of poverty.

2. Describe any three major difficulties that came in the way of the partition of British India in 1947. CBSE 2024

Or **Describe any three problems that were faced during the process of partition of British India.** CBSE 2024

Ans. The three major difficulties that came in the way of the partition of British India in 1947 are as follows

(i) **No Single Territory with Muslim Majority** British India was divided on the basis of religion. The places with higher Muslim majority would join Pakistan. There was no single area with Muslim population in majority. There were two places one in the east and other in the west which had Muslim majority.

Thus, Pakistan could not be created as a single territory. Pakistan was created as the West and East Pakistan separated by Indian territory in between.

(ii) **Not Everyone Willing to join Pakistan** There were some Muslim majority areas which did not want to join Pakistan. Khan Abdul Gaffar Khan (Frontier Gandhi) from North West Frontier Province (NWFP) strongly opposed the 'Two-Nation Theory' and Pakistan. But, ultimately NWFP was merged with Pakistan.

(iii) **Issues with Punjab and Bengal** Deepest trauma of partition came from the provinces of Bengal and Punjab. Inspite of being Muslim dominated areas, these had a large number of non-Muslim population. It was decided to divide these areas into smaller levels like district or even lower level. But this was delayed and undecided even at the 14th-15th midnight. It created a lot of confusion among the people whether they belong to India or Pakistan.

3. Analyse any six consequences of the partition of India in 1947.

Or **Assess any six consequences of the partition of British India in 1947.**

Or **Explain any three consequences of partition of British India in 1947.**

Or **Describe any four consequences of the partition of British India in 1947.**

Or **Describe the socio-economic effects of the partition of British India in 1947.** CBSE SQP 2024

Ans. The consequences of partition of India in 1947 are as follows

(i) **Division of Provinces** According to majority the implementation of partition was very difficult because there was no single belt of Muslims majority in British India. The concentration of Muslims were in Punjab which was in the West and Bengal which was in East. The problems lied in these areas as concentration of non-Muslims were more.

Therefore, it was decided that these two provinces would be separated according to the majority at the district or even lower level.

(ii) **Exploition of Minorities** There were problems with the minorities on both side of the borders. They were easily targeted and there was no option except to leave their own land and homes and go across the border.

This transfer is said to be most abrupt, largest and unplanned transfer known in the human history. There were killings and atrocities on both sides of border in the name of religion.

The minorities on both sides fled from their homes and often secured temporary shelter in refugee camps. Even they were not safe in refugee camp, so they travelled to the other side by all means i.e. railway, roads and by foot.

(iii) **Problem with Women** During this journey, women were often attacked and killed. Women were abducted and raped and also forcefully converted to other religion. Therefore, family members killed their girls and women.

(iv) **Problem with Refugee** Those who did manage to cross the border found that they had no home. For lakhs of these refugees, the country's freedom meant life in refugee camps, for months and sometimes for years.

(v) **Administrative Failure** There were competing political interests behind communal conflicts. The Muslim League was formed to protect the interests of the Muslims in colonial India. It was in the forefront of the demand for a separate Muslim nation.

Similarly, there were organisations which were trying to organise the Hindus in order to turn India into a Hindu nation. This situation led to administrative failure in the country.

(vi) **Distribution of Financial Assets** The financial assets and things like tables, chairs, typewriters, paper-clips, books and also musical instruments of the police band were divided. The employees of the government and the railways were also 'divided'. It was a violent separation of communities who had earlier lived together as neighbours.

4. Describe the role of Mahatma Gandhi to reduce communal violence that erupted in many parts of India at the time of the partition in 1947?

Ans. Mahatma Gandhi has played a key role in reducing communal violence that erupted in many parts of India at the time of the partition.

He did not participate in any of the Independence Day celebrations. He was in Kolkata in the areas where violence took place between the Hindus and Muslims. He was saddened by the communal violence and disheartened that the principles of Ahimsa (non-violence) and Satyagraha (active but non-violent resistance) were not being followed. He went on to convince the Hindus and Muslims to give up violence. His presence in Kolkata greatly improved the situation, and the coming of independence was celebrated in a spirit of communal harmony, with joyous dancing in the streets.

Gandhiji's prayer meetings attracted large crowds. But, this did not last. Riots erupted again. Thus, Gandhiji had to resort to a fast to bring peace.

He also moved to Delhi where violence took place at a larger scale. He under took a fast is 1948 again which turned out to be his last fast. His fast reduced the communal tension in Kolkata and Delhi. He worked so that all the Muslims could safely return to their homes.

He was killed by an extremist, Nathuram Vinayak Godse, who walked up to Gandhiji during his evening prayer in Delhi and fired three bullets at him, killing him instantly. He sacrificed his life to make the principles of truth, non-violence, justice and tolerance alive forever.

5. Describe the difficulties faced by India to get the merger of all the Princely States into the Union of India. **CBSE 2024**

Ans. There were following difficulties faced by India to get the merger of all the Princely States into the Union of India,

(i) Just before the independence it was announced by the British that with the end of their rule over India, paramountcy of the British crown over Princely States would also lapse. This meant that all these states, as many as 565 in all, would become legally independent. Thus, that all these states were free to join either India or Pakistan or remain independent if they so wished.

(ii) The decision was left with the rulers of these 565 Princely States to choose their freedom. Problem began when the ruler of Travancore announced that the state had decided on Independence. The next day similar announcement was made by the Nizam of Hyderabad. Other rulers like Nawab of Bhopal were also not willing to join the Constituent Assembly.

(iii) All these situations create a fear factor among national leaders. Such freedom to the rulers may create several smaller countries within India. Such division is against the principles of unity and integrity.

(iv) Also India at the time of independence aimed at the self determination and democracy. In most of the states, Rulers were running their government in a non-democratic manner. Thus, the idea of a Democratic country seemed to be bleak.

6. Describe the events that led to the merger of Hyderabad and Manipur with the Union of India. **CBSE 2019**

Or **Describe the events that led to the accession of the Hyderabad into the Union of India.** **CBSE 2024**

Ans. The events that led to the merger of Hyderabad and Manipur with the Union of India are discussed below

Manipur After the independence in 1947, Maharaja of Manipur Bodhachandra Singh, signed the Instrument of Accession with Indian Union on the assurance that the internal autonomy of Manipur would be maintained. Under the pressure of people of Manipur, Maharaja held the election in June, 1948 and state became a Constitutional monarchy. Thus, it could be said that Manipur was the first state to hold an election on the basis of universal adult franchise.

The legislators of the regional parties of Manipur did not want to merge with India but state Congress wanted to merge. Government of India pressurised the Manipur Maharaja and succeeded to do so.

Maharaja accepted the agreement and signed it without consulting the Legislative Assembly. As a result, Manipur was merged with the Union of India.

Hyderabad It was the largest of the Princely States that covered almost one-third part of South India. Nizam signed Standstill Agreement with the Government of India and the state emerged as an independent state after India's independence. Many movements took place in Hyderabad state specially in Telangana region where many peasants were victimised and oppressed by Nizam. Hyderabad Congress and the communits were at the forefront of such movement.

Nizam sent his para military force, Razakars. Razakars murdered, raped and looted particularly the non-Muslims. Therefore, Central Government ordered the army to tackle the situation. On 13th September, 1948, Indian army marched in Hyderabad and on the 17th September, 1948, Hyderabad surrendered.

This led to merger of Hyderabad with the Union of India.

7. Highlight the role of Sardar Vallabhbhai Patel to bring the Princely States into the Indian Union. Support your answer with the help of any three examples. **CBSE 2023**

Ans. Sardar Patel was India's Deputy Prime Minister and the Home Minister during the crucial period immediately following Independence. He played a historic role in discussing with the rulers of Princely States firmly but diplomatically and bringing most of the states into the Indian Union.

His pivotal role can be understood in the following examples

(i) He took a plebiscite in the state of Junagarh. People of Junagarh agreed to join the India thus, this issue resolved and Junagarh was integrated into the Union of India.

(ii) He took a firm stance to send the Indian army to curb the atrocities by the military of Nizam of Hyderabad. It was his strong intent that made people of Hyderabad free from the exploitation of the Nizam. Thus, Hyderabad was made united into the Indian Union by signing the instrument of accession with the Nizam.

(iii) He diplomatically convinced the Maharaja of Manipur to sign the Instrument of Accession into India. He made him agreed on the terms and conditions that Manipur would be maintaining its internal autonomy. Later on, successfully Maharaja of Manipur signed the merger document with Union of India.

Thus, it was the vision of Sardar Vallabhbhai Patel that made India a united country and he is remembered as the Iron Man of India.

8. How did the re-organisation of state take using example of Andhra Pradesh place in India after its independence? Explain.

Ans. After partition, the challenge was to draw the internal boundaries of the Indian states. The boundaries had to be drawn in a way so that the linguistic and cultural plurality of the country could be reflected without affecting the unity of the nation.

Indian National Congress and many leaders recognised the linguistic principle as recognisation of new state boundaries. But our leader further felt that carving out states on the basis of language might lead to disruption and disintegration and would draw attention away from other social and economic challenges that the country faced. For example, Protests began in the Telugu speaking areas of the old Madras province. The Vishalandhra Movement (the movement for a separate Andhra) demanded that the Telugu speaking area should be separated from the Madras province and be made into a separate Andhra province.

The movement gathered momentum. Potti Sriramulu, a Congress leader and a veteran Gandhian went on a indefinite fast that led to his death after 56 days. This caused great unrest and resulted in violent outbursts in Andhra region. Finally, the Prime Minister announced the formation of a separate Andhra State in December 1952.

New states formed after 1956 were

(i) This Commission led to the creation of 14 states and 6 union territories. Maharashtra, Gujarat, Punjab, Haryana, Himachal Pradesh, Tripura, Meghalaya, Arunachal Pradesh, Uttarakhand, Chattisgarh and Jharkhand are the new states formed after 1956.

(ii) Gujarat was formed out by Bombay; Haryana was formed out from Punjab; Himachal Pradesh was formed out from Punjab; Tripura, Meghalaya, Arunachal Pradesh were created from Assam and Uttarakhand from Uttar Pradesh, Chattisgarh from Madhya Pradesh and Jharkhand from Bihar. All of these were created in 2000.

9. "The accommodation of regional demands and the formation of linguistic states were also seen as more democratic". Justify the statement with any three suitable arguments. **Competency Based Que**

Or **Language has always played an imperiture role in uniting the country. Explain the statement in the context of challenges of nation building in India after independence.** **Competency Based Que; CBSE SQP 2024**

Ans. The accommodation of regional demands and the formation of linguistic states were also seen as more democratic due to the following reasons

(i) The States Re-organisation Commission was set up in 1953 by the Central Government to redraw the boundaries of the states.

(ii) The commission accepted that the boundaries of the state should reflect the boundaries of different languages. On the basis of this, the States Re-organisation Act was passed in 1956. This led to the creation of 14 states and 6 union territories.

(iii) In the early phase, it was felt that linguistic states may foster separation and create pressures on newly founded nation. But India considered democracy and federalism by making a favour to linguistic states. It was hoped that if the people accept the regional and linguistic claims of all regions, the threat of division and separatism would be reduced.

When linguistic states were formed, they

- Enhanced democratic practices.
- Reduced separatist activities by accepting the regional linguistic claims of all religions.
- Provided a uniform base to the nation and strengthened unity of nation.
- Promoted the principle of unity in diversity, a distinct feature of nation.

Therefore, the accommodation of regional demands and the formation of linguistic states were also seen as more democratic.

Picture Based Questions

1. Observe the picture given below carefully and answer the following questions.

These three stamps were issued in 1950 to mark the first Republic Day on 26 January 1950. What do the images on these stamps tell you about the challenges to the new republic? If you were asked to design these stamps in 1950, which images would you have chosen?

(i) What does the inscription "INAUGURATION JAN 26th, 1950" on the stamps signify?

(a) The day India became a republic
(b) The day India gained independence
(c) The day the Constitution was adopted
(d) The day Mahatma Gandhi was assassinated

Ans. (a) The day India became a republic

(ii) What is the common theme among the images on these stamps?

(a) Social equality and justice
(b) Economic prosperity and development
(c) Independence and sovereignty
(d) Cultural diversity and unity

Ans. (c) Independence and sovereignty

(iii) What does the plough and crop depict in the second stamp?

(a) Self-sufficiency in agriculture (b) Prosperity
(c) Poverty (d) Technology

Ans. (a) Self-sufficiency in agriculture

2. Observe the picture given below carefully and answer the following questions.

(i) What does this picture seek to represent?

(ii) What were the consequences of the partition?

(iii) Why did partition happen?

Ans. (i) This picture is of the people who were leaving their home during the partition.

(ii) Partition caused communal riots, massacres, murder and rape of women, and division of communities who had lived together as neighbours till that time.

(iii) Partition happened due to political competition between Congress and Muslim League together with British rule.

3. Observe the picture given below carefully and answer the following questions.

(i) Name the two people shown in the above cartoon. **Diksha App**

(a) Dr. B.R. Ambedkar and Maharaja of Manipur
(b) Sardar Vallabhbhai Patel and Maharaja of Manipur
(c) Mahatma Gandhi and Jawaharlal Nehru
(d) Jawaharlal Nehru and Sardar Vallabhbhai Patel

Ans. (b) Sardar Vallabhbhai Patel and Maharaja of Manipur

(ii) **Highlight the result of the efforts of the person shown in the picture above.** **Diksha App**

(a) The efforts of Sardar Vallabhbhai Patel got wasted and no Princely State was included in Indian Union.
(b) All the Princely States immediately signed the instrument of succession without any resistance.
(c) Most of the Princely States had non-democratic government, but by joining India, the people would get access to the rights and democracy through the efforts of Sardar Vallabhbhai Patel.
(d) All of the above

Ans. (c) Most of the Princely States had non-democratic government, but by joining India, the people would get access to the rights and democracy through the efforts of Sardar Vallabhbhai Patel.

(iii) **What are the different portfolios that the national leader is asking to take from the King?**

(a) Defence (b) External Affairs
(c) Communication (d) All of these

Ans. (d) All of these

(iv) **Whom do/es the man below the king represent?**

(a) Common People
(b) Kings and Queens
(c) Ministers
(d) None of these

Ans. (a) Common People

4. Observe the cartoon given below carefully and answer the questions that follow.

(i) **Who is the person in the centre of the cartoon?**
(ii) **What does the cartoon refer about?**
(iii) **How did India accommodate the demand of regional groups?**

Ans. (i) The person is the first Prime Minister of India Pt. Jawaharlal Nehru, who faced the first and foremost challenge of integration of Princely States and formation of linguistic states.

(ii) The picture refers the problem of re-organisation of states on linguistic basis with the fear of disintegration in the country.

(iii) India indentified and respected regional demands of the people and enhanced democracy by providing some automony to the states also.

Map Based Question

1. In the given political outline map of India, four states have been marked as (A), (B), (C) and (D). Identify these states on the basis of the information given below and write their correct names in your answer book along with the respective serial numbers of the information used and the concerned alphabets shown in the map as per the format that follows **CBSE 2025**

Sr. no. of the Information Used	Alphabet Concerned	Name of the State
(i)		
(ii)		
(iii)		
(iv)		

(i) **The Princely State whose ruler resisted its merger with India.**
(ii) **The State that was most affected by the partition of the country.**
(iii) **The State carved out from Madhya Pradesh.**
(iv) **The State that was formed in 1952.**

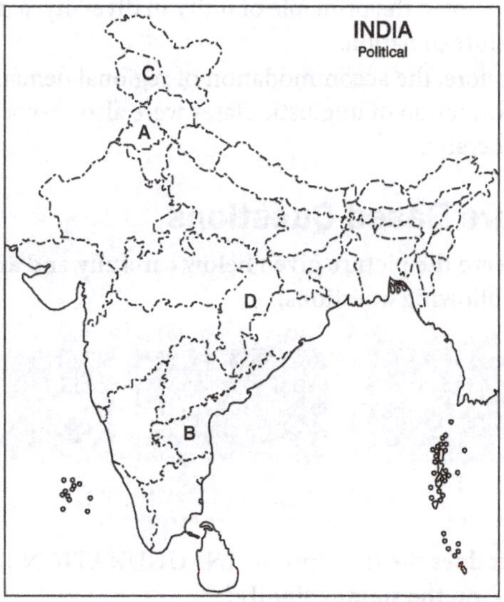

Ans.

Sr. no. of the Information Used	Alphabet Concerned	Name of the State
(i)	C	Jammu and Kashmir
(ii)	A	Panjab
(iii)	D	Chhattisgarh
(iv)	B	Andra Pradesh

SELF ASSESSMENT TEST

Objective Type Questions

1. When was the famous speech, 'Tryst with destiny' made by the first Prime Minister of the free India in a special session of the Constituent Assembly?
   (a) Morning of 14th August, 1947
   (b) Afternoon of 15th August, 1947
   (c) Midnight of 14th-15th August, 1947
   (d) Afternoon of 14th August, 1947
2. What was issued by the government from the following to mark the first Republic Day on 26th January, 1950? **Diksha App**
   (a) Three pamphlets
   (b) Three journals
   (c) Three newsletters
   (d) Three stamps
3. Which of the following statement about Sardar Vallabhbhai Patel is incorrect?
   (a) He did not play any role to integrate India.
   (b) He emerged as a major leader of the national movement.
   (c) He was not in favour of any compromise with the territorial integrity of India.
   (d) He was the first Deputy Prime Minister of independent India.
4. Arrange the following events in a correct sequence.
   I. Maharaja of Manipur signed Merged Agreement.
   II. Meghalaya carved out of Assam.
   III. Jharkhand was created as a new state.
   IV. Nagpur Session of Congress.
   (a) I, III, IV and II
   (b) IV, III, I and II
   (c) III, IV, II and I
   (d) IV, I, II and III

Very Short Answer Type

5. Enlist any two hurdles in the process of partition of India?
6. What is 'Instrument of Accession'?
7. Who was Sardar Patel?
8. How many states and union territories were created with the State Re-Organisation Act, which was passed in 1956? **Diksha App**

Short Answer Type Questions

9. Ensuring the development of the whole society and not of some sections was a challenge to newly independent India. Elaborate the statement with any two arguments. **Diksha App**
10. Differentiate between the British Indian Provinces and Princely States.
11. Why did the independence of small principalities or Princely States created difficult situation for India?
12. Why did the leader not carve out the new states on the basis of language immediately after independence? **Diksha App modified**

Long Answer type Questions

13. Explain any three steps taken by the government of India and Constitutional safeguards to strengthen the democracy in India.
14. Discuss the re-organisation of state in the context of State Re-organisation Commission.
15. Language did not however remain the sole basis of the organisation of state. Elucidate. **Competency Based Que**

02

CHAPTER

After India gained independence, its leaders faced a big challenge in building a strong democracy. In building a strong democratic nation they established a system of free and fair elections, which laid the foundation for India's strong democratic tradition.

Era of One-Party Dominance

YOUR STUDY GOALS

2.1 Challenge of Building Domocracy
2.2 Congress Dominance in the First Three General Elections
2.3 Emergence of Opposition Parties

YOUR PRACTICE GOAL

- Objective Type Questions (29 Qs ; MCQs, A-R, Matching, Passage Based)
- Subjective Questions (7 VSAs, 8 SAs, 5 LAs, 2 Picture Based, 2 Map Based)

2.1 Challenge of Building Democracy

- During the period when India got its independence, many other countries also gained freedom from the British Rule. Most of the countries chose the non-democratic path but India despite of difficult situations chose democracy. It was because the Indian freedom struggle was deeply committed to the **democratic path**.
- Indian Constitution was adopted on **26th November, 1949** signed on **24th January, 1950** and it came into the effect on **26th January, 1950**. The Constitution has laid down the rules to run a democratic country. With this India was all set to hold its first general elections[1] after independence.
- **The Election Commission of India** was set up in January 1950. **Sukumar Sen** became the **first Chief Election Commissioner**. But it was a mammoth task to conduct the elections for the huge population. The Election Commission of India faced the following challenges to hold free and fair elections.
  - Drawing the boundaries of electoral constituencies.
  - Prepare the list of electoral rolls. It was a huge task, and required a lot of time.
  - The names of nearly 40 lakh women's were not recorded in the list. Identifying these women was a challenging task.

1 General Elections It means an election in which all the eligible people of a country vote to choose a government.

- Most of the eligible votes were illiterate, so conducting the election needed special voting method.
- Large number of staff required.

- India's first election was unusual as it tested democracy in a poor, mostly illiterate country. Until then, democracy existed mainly in rich countries like those in Europe and North America, where most people were literate. Many European countries had not even given all women the right to vote. In this situation, India's choice of universal adult franchise was bold and risky.
- The elections had to be postponed twice and finally held from **October 1951 to February 1952.** The elections were referred as **1952 election** because most of the regions in India voted in the month of January 1952. It took six months for campaigning, polling, counting of votes.
- When the results were declared, even the losers accepted them as fair. India's election proved critics wrong. Observers worldwide were impressed. The 1952 election became a landmark, proving democracy could succeed even in conditions of poverty and low literacy.

Changing Methods of Voting

- Today, we use **Electronic Voting Machine (EVMs)** for selecting the candidates.
- EVMs were started to be used by the end of 1990s and by 2004, the entire country shifted to EVM.
- During the first general elections, it was decided to keep a box in each polling booth for each candidate. Each voter was given a blank ballot paper which they had to drop into the box of the candidate they wanted to vote for.
- After first two elections, ballot papers[2] were introduced. Ballot papers had the names and symbols of the candidates. Voters had to put a stamp on the name of candidate they wanted to vote for. This method worked for nearly forty years.

Maulana Abul Kalam Azad (1888-1958)

- His original name was Abul Kalam Ghulam Muhiyuddin Ahmed.
- He was the scholar of Islam, freedom fighter and the Congress leader.
- He supported the Hindu-Muslim unity.
- He oppossed the partition.
- He was the Education Minister in the first cabinet of free India.

2.2 Congress Dominance in the First Three General Elections

- The Indian National Congress won the first general elections as expected because it was the only party which was popular in the whole country. Congress won **364** out of **489** seats in the first Lok Sabha election. **Jawaharlal Nehru** emerged as the most popular and charismatic leader at that time.
- The Communist Party of India won only 16 seats and came next after congress.
- In state elections too, Congress did well except in **Travancore-Cochin (Today's Kerala part), Madras** and Odisha. Still, Congress formed the government in these states.
- Jawaharlal Nehru became the **Prime Minister** after the first general elections.
- **The Congress** maintained the same position in the **second** and **third** general elections as well as in state assembly elections. However, in Kerala CPI formed the coalition government[3]. Apart from this, the Congress controlled the national and all the State Governments.

2 Ballot Papers It means a slip of paper used to register a vote.

3 Coalition government Coalition government is formed by two or more different political parties, when no political party gets clear majority in the elections.

- The Congress Party's victory appeared larger due to the **First-Past-The-Post method**[4]. In 1952, Congress won 74 per cent of the seats with only 45 per cent of the votes. The Socialist Party, though the second-largest in votes with over 10 per cent, won less than 3 per cent of the seats. This happened because non-Congress votes were divided among many parties, allowing Congress to win more seats despite not having a majority of the total votes.

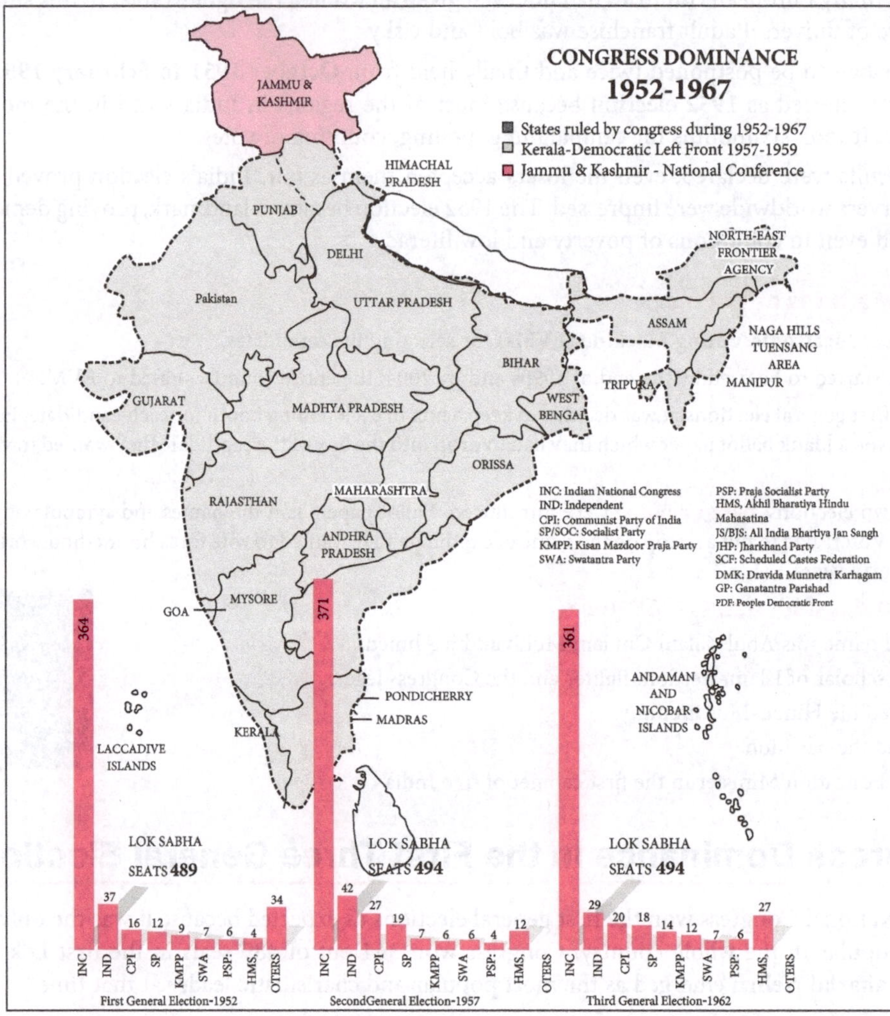

Rajkumari Amrit Kaur (1889-1964)

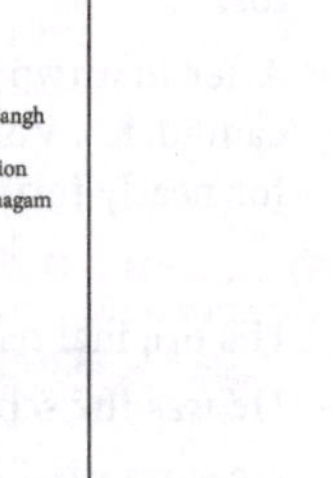

She was a Gandhian and a freedom fighter. She was Minister for Health in independent India's first ministry. She belonged to the royal family of Kapurthala.

Communist Victory in Kerala

For the very first time in the world, a Communist Party government had come to power in India through democratic elections in 1957 in the state of Kerala. The Communist Party of India won 60 of the 126 seats and also had the support of five independents. **E.M.S. Namboodiripad**, formed the government in Kerala. On losing the power in the state, the Congress Party began a **'liberation struggle'** against the elected government and imposed **Article 356** in Kerala. This decision was very controversial and cited as **misuse** of the Constitutional emergency powers.

4 **First-Past-The-Post-method** In this method, the party that gets more votes than the other tends to get win the elections on that seat.

Nature of Congress Dominance

- India is not the only country to have experienced the dominance of one party. But there is a crucial difference between other such countries and the India's experience.
- In other countries, the dominance of one party was ensured by compromising the democracy in the following ways
  - **China, Cuba** and **Syria** permits only **single party** system as per their **Constitution**.
  - **Countries** like **Myanmar, Belarus, Egypt** and **Eritrea** follow **one party** system due to **legal** and **military measures**.
  - Until a few years ago, **Mexico, South Korea and Taiwan** were also one party dominant states.
  - The democratic conditions of India distinguished the congress party of India from all these countries.
- The Congress dominance is somewhat similar to the **African National Congress** which it enjoyed in South Arica after the end of apartheid.
- Congress was able to enjoy the dominance because of the following reasons
  - Roots of Congress lie in the freedom struggle.
  - Already popular leaders in the freedom struggle were now contesting the elections thus, people found them more trustworthy.
  - Congress was a well-organised party. It had started its campaign as before other parties could even think of a strategy.
  - It was all-inclusive party that included the people from different sections.
- Thus, Congress had the **'first off the blocks[5]** advantage. This was because many parties were formed around or after independence, but Congress had an early advantage.

Rafi Ahmed Kidwai (1894-1954)

- He was the Congress leader from Uttar Pradesh.
- He was the Minister for Communications in the first ministry of free India.

Babasaheb Bhimrao Ramji Ambedkar (1891-1956)

He was the leader of the anti-caste movement, and the struggle for justice to the Dalit. He founded the Independent Labour Party. He was founder of the Scheduled Caste Federation. Dr. B.R. Ambedkar was also the Chairman of the **Drafting Committee** the Constituent Assembly. He was in Nehru's first cabinet after independence but, resigned in 1951 due to differences over Hindu Code Bill. He adopted Buddhism in 1956.

Quick Test 1

1. Who was the first Chief Election Commissioner?
2. What do you mean by a coalition government?
3. Why did Congress impose Article 356 in Kerala?
4. Which country has experienced a situation similar to Congress dominance in India?

Congress as Social and Ideological Coalition

- Congress emerged in 1885 as a pressure group for the newly educated, professional and commercial classes to a mass movement in the 20th century.
- In the beginning Congress began as a party dominated by the
  - English speaking
  - Upper caste
  - Upper middle-class
  - Urban elite

5 **First off the blocks** It means at the very beginning or from the very start.

- Gradually, its **social base** widened with every civil disobedience movement. It began including the following sections of society
  - Peasants
  - Industrialists
  - Urban dwellers
  - Villagers
  - Workers
  - Owners
  - Middle, lower and upper classes
  - Different castes
- The Congress has also accommodated the various ideologies under its platform like
  - Revolutionary
  - **Pacifist**[6]
  - **Conservative**[7]
  - Radical
  - Extremist
  - Moderate
  - **Right**[8]
  - **Left**[9]
- Thus, the Congress was a platform for wider social and ideological base.
- The Congress was transformed into a rainbow like social coaltion broadly representing India's diversity.

Tolerance and Management of Factions

The Congress could stand out as a strong party for such a long time because of the following reasons

- The coalition includes all those who join it and avoid any extreme position or ideology. Thus, it creates a balance on almost all issues. Such balance makes the opposition in difficulty to raise a valid criticism.
- There was a greater tolerance of the internal differences and different ambitions of various leaders inside the Congress. Even if any group inside the Congress was unhappy with the position of the party or with its share of power. It chose to remain in the Congress Party rather than to become an 'opposition'.
- These groups inside the party were called **factions**[10] most Congress state units had many factions. These factions held different ideologies, making Congress a **centrist party**[11].
- These factions are not actually involved in the authority or ruling of the nation. But, they do criticise the ruling party and worked as balancing mechanism within the ruling party.
- Thus, the Congress acted both as the **ruling party** as well as the **opposition**. That is why this period of Indian politics has been described as the **'Congress system'**.

2.3 Emergence of Opposition Parties

- India have many parties other than the Congress. Some of these even emerged before the First General Elections of 1952. Some of these played an important role in Indian politics of the country in 60s and 70s.
- Even if there was a very low representation of such opposition parties, but they played a principal role in criticising the policies and practises of Congress Party. This kept a system of **check** and **balance of power** within the Congress and providing a democratic alternative to the people.
- In the earlier years, there was a lot of mutual respect between the Congress leaders and the parties of opposition. For example, Jawaharlal Nehru was very fond of the Socialist Party and invited **Jayaprakash Narayan** to join his government. **Dr. B.R. Ambedkar** and **Syama Prasad Mukherjee** were also the opposition members which were included in the cabinet formed after independence.
- Thus, the first phase of democratic politics in our country was quite unique. The key role of the Congress in the freedom struggle gave an advantage to it against all the other political opposition parties.

6 **Pacifist** It means someone who believes in peace and opposes violence. Pacifists advocate for peaceful solutions to conflicts.
7 **Conservative** It is someone who is cautious about change and prefers to maintain the system as going on.
8 **Right** It generally the ideology to maintain the traditions and cultures as way towards modernisation and progress for a country. They also prefer free market approach.
9 **Left** It refers to the Ideologies that advocate for social and economic equality through welfare schemes.
10 **Faction** A political faction is a group of individuals within political party.
11 **Centrist Party** A centrist party holds a balance between the right and left political ideologies.

Syama Prasad Mukherjee (1901-1953)

- He was the leader of Hindu Mahasabha.
- He founded the Bharatiya Jana Sangh.
- He was the Minister in First Cabinet after independence but resigned in 1950 due to differences over relations with Pakistan.
- He was the member of Constituent Assembly.
- He was arrested during agitation against Kashmir policy and died during detention.

Socialist Party

- Socialist party was formed during the mass movement stage of the Indian National Congress in the pre-independence era. It was formed as the Congress Socialist Party in 1934 within the Congress.
- It was formed by the group of **young leaders** who wanted a more Radical[12] and Egalitarian[13] Congress due to the amendment of the Constitution within the Congress. Socialist were forced to form a separate Socialist Party in 1948.
- The socialist believed in the ideology of **democratic socialism**. They also criticised Congress for supporting capitalist and landlords while ignoring the workers and peasants. Some leaders, like Ram Manohar Lohia, moved away from the Congress and became critical of it when the Congress declared its goal to be a socialist pattern of society.
- Some leaders like **Asoka Mehta** advocated a limited co-operation within the Congress. The Socialist Party went through many **splits** and **reunions** leading to the formation of many other socialist parties. These included the following
  - Kisan Mazdoor Praja Party
  - The Praja Socialist Party
  - Samyukta Socialist Party
  - Parties in the contemporary India also trace their origin to the Socialist Party like Samajwadi Party, Rashtriya Janata Dal, Janata Dal, Janata Dal (Secular) and Janata Dal (United).

Acharya Narendra Deva (1889-1956)

- He was the freedom fighter and founding President of the Congress Socialist Party.
- He was active in peasants movement.
- After the independence he led the **Socialist Party** and later the **Praja Socialist Party**.

The Communist Party of India (CPI)

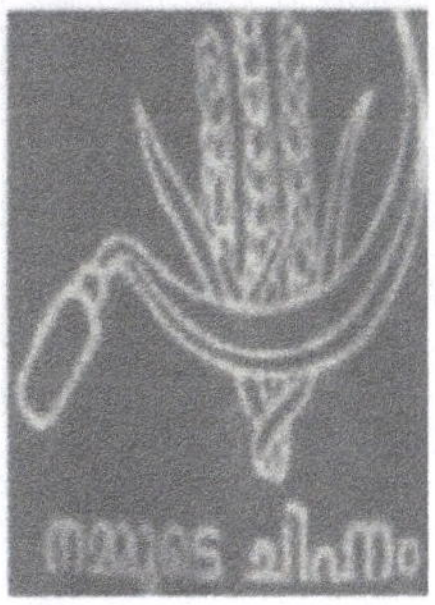

- In the early 1920s, Communist group influenced from the **Bolshevik revolution** in Russia and started advocating for **socialism** as a solution.
- From 1935, the Communist worked mainly within the Indian National Congress, but in 1941, they parted their ways.
- The Communist Party was more organised, unlike other non-Congress parties. But, it failed to generate popular support for their position during the uprising in Telangana.
- During the 1952 general election, CPI won **16 seats** and emerged as the **largest opposition party** with more concentrated support in **Andhra Pradesh, West Bengal, Bihar and Kerala.**
- **A.K. Gopalan, S.A. Dange, E.M.S. Namboodiripad, P.C. Joshi, Ajay Ghosh and P. Sundarayya** were among the notable leaders of the CPI.

---

12 Radical It means who want immediate changes like social or political.

13 Egalitarian It is the principle that all people are equal and deserve equal rights and opportunities.

A.K. Gopalan (1904-1977)

- He was the Communist leader from Kerala and worked for Congress initially.
- Later, he joined the Communist Party in 1939. After split in Communist Party in 1964, he joined CPI(M).

Bharatiya Jana Sangh (BJS)

- **Bharatiya Jana Sangh** was formed in **1951** by **Syama Prasad Mukherjee**. It finds its roots in the **Rashtriya Swayamsewak Sangh (RSS)** and the **Hindu Mahasabha** before independence.

- The **Jana Sangh** emphasised on the following ideals
  - One country, one culture and one nation.
  - Following Indian culture and traditions as way towards modernisation and progressive India.
  - Reunion of India and Pakistan to form **Akhand Bharat.**
- The party led the agitation to replace **English** with **Hindi**. It also opposed the **cultural** and **religious minorities** concessions.
- It advocated to develop **nuclear weapons** especially after **China** carried out its atomic tests in 1964.
- In the early years its support came mainly from the **urban areas** of **the Hindi speaking states** like Rajasthan, Madhya Pradesh, Delhi and Uttar Pradesh.
- The party's leaders included **Syama Prasad Mukherjee, Deendayal Upadhyaya and Balraj Madhok.** The **Bharatiya Janata Party** traces its roots to the **Bharatiya Jana Sangh.**

Deendayal Upadhyaya (1916-1968)

- He was the full-time RSS worker since 1942. He was the founder of Bharatiya Jana Sangh.
- He was the President of Bharatiya Jana Sangh.
- He initiated the concept of **integral humanism.**

Quick Test 2

1. Give any two ideologies accommodated under the Congress.
2. Whom did Jawaharlal Nehru invite to join the government?
3. Which revolution influenced the communist group of India?
4. Who was the founder of Jana Sangh?

Mind Map

ERA OF ONE-PARTY DOMINANCE

1 Challenges of Building Democracy

Indian Independence
- Gained freedom from British rule.
- Committed to democratic path.

Constitution of India
- Adoption -26th November, 1949.
- Signed- 24th January, 1950.
- Effective-26th January, 1950.

First General Election
- Conducted in 1951-52.
- Faced Challenges.

Challenges
- Drawing Electoral Boundaries.
- Preparing electoral roles.
- Identifying unrecorded women voters.
- Large number of illiterate voters-required special voting method.
- Large number of staff required.

2 Congress Dominance in the First Three General Elections

Election Results
- **First General Elections (1952)** Congress won 364 out of 489 seats.
- **Second and Third General Elections** Congress maintained its dominance.
- First-Past-The-Post method worked in favour of Congress.

Nature of Congress Dominance
- Different from other countries with One-Party Dominance e.g, China, Belanes etc .
- Similar to African National Congress Dominance in South Africa after the end of apartheid.

Congress as a Social and Ideological Coalition
- Initial Dominance English Speaking upper caste, upper –middle caste etc.
- Widening of Social Base, so included peasants, industrialists, urban dwellers, villages etc.
- Accommodating various ideologies revolutionary, pacifist consecutive etc.

Tolerance and Management of Factions
- Coalition avoided extreme positions or ideologies .
- Tolerance of internal difference .
- Factions worked as a balancing mechanism .

3 Emergence of Opposition Parties

Role of Opposition Parties
- Criticism of Congress policies provided a system of check and balance .
- Fostered leaders who later played significant role in shaping the nation .
- Initially there was mutual respects between Congress leaders and opposition parties .

Major Political Parties
Bhartiya Jana Sangh (BJS)
- Formed in 1951 by Syama Prasad Mukherjee .
- **Leaders** Syama Prasad Mukherjee, Deendayal Upadhyaya, Balraj Madhok .
- **Ideology** One country, One culture, One Nation.

Communist Party of India
- Influenced by Bolshevik revolution in Russia
- **Leaders** A.K. Gopalan, P.C. Joshi, Ajay Ghosh
- **Ideology** State control of Production, Support of labour rights .

Socialist Party
- **Formed** In 1934 as a group with in Congress.
- **Leaders** Jayaprakash Narayan, Ashok Mehta, S.M. Joshi , Rammanohar Lohia.
- **Ideology** Democratic Socialism.

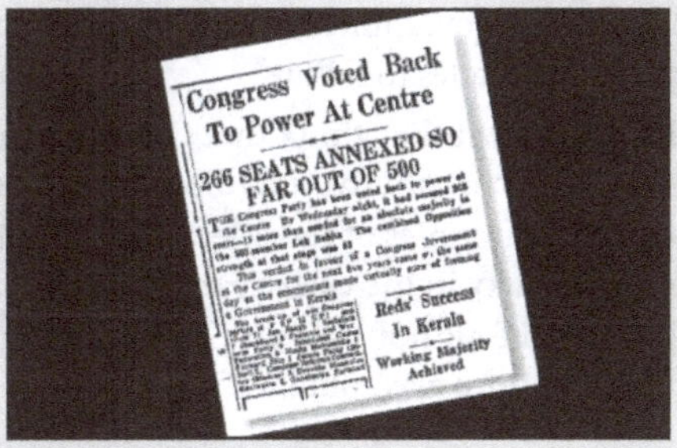
Congress Voted Back To Power At Centre

266 SEATS ANNEXED SO FAR OUT OF 500

Reds' Success In Kerala

Working Majority Achieved

Credit: The Hindu

Nehru's Cabinet after the Swearing

NCERT Folder

1. Choose the correct option to fill in the blanks.

(i) The First General Elections in 1952 involved simultaneous elections to the Lok Sabha and .... (The President of India/ State Assemblies/Rajya Sabha/The Prime Minister).

(ii) The party that won the second largest number of Lok Sabha seats in the first elections was the .... (Praja Socialist Party/Bharatiya Jana Sangh/ Communist Party of India/Bharatiya Janata Party).

(iii) One of the guiding principles of the ideology of the Swatantra Party was ...... (Working class interest/protection of Princely States/Economy free from State control/Autonomy of States within the Union).

Ans. (i) State Assemblies.

(ii) Communist Party of India.

(iii) Economy free from state control.

2. Match the following.

List I		List II	
A.	S.A. Dange	1.	Bharatiya Jana Sangh
B.	Syama Prasad Mukherjee	2.	Swatantra Party
C.	Minoo Masani	3.	Praja Socialist Party
D.	Asoka Mehta	4.	Communist Party of India

Ans. A → 4, B → 1, C → 2, D → 3

3. Four statements regarding one-party dominance are given below. Mark each of them as true or false.

(i) One-party dominance is rooted in the absence of strong alternative political parties.

(ii) One-party dominance occurs because of weak public opinion.

(iii) One-party dominance is linked to the nation's colonial past.

(iv) One-party dominance reflects the absence of democratic ideals in a country.

Ans. (i) True (ii) False (iii) True (iv) False

4. Take a political map of India (with state outlines) and mark.

(i) Two states where Congress was not in power at some point during 1952-67.

(ii) Two states where the Congress remained in power through this period.

Ans.

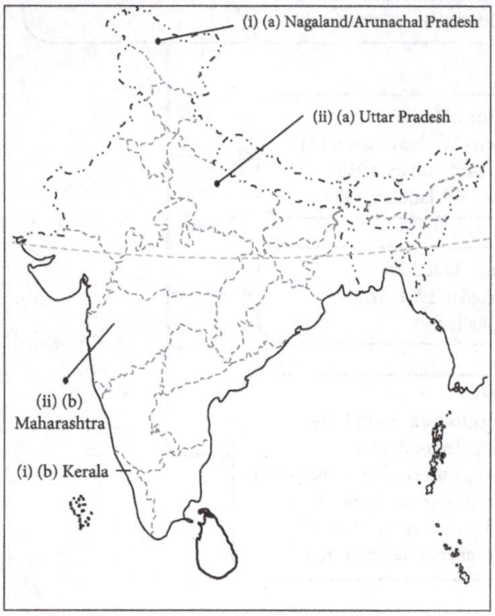

Ans. (i) (a) Nagaland

(b) Kerala

(ii) (a) Uttar Pradesh

(b) Maharashtra

5. Read the following passage and answer the questions below.

"Patel, the organisational man of the Congress, wanted to purge the Congress of other political groups and sought to make of it a cohesive and disciplined political party. He .... sought to take the Congress away from its all-embracing character and turn it into a close-knit party of disciplined cadres. Being a 'realist' he looked more for discipline than for comprehension. While Gandhi took too romantic view of 'carrying on the movement', Patel's idea of transforming the Congress into strictly political party with a single ideology and tight discipline showed an equal lack of understanding of the eclectic role that the Congress, as a government, was to be called upon to perform in the decades to follow". **—Rajni Kothari**

(i) Why does the author think that Congress should not have been a cohesive and disciplined party?

(ii) Give some examples of the eclectic role of the Congress Party in the early years.

(iii) Why does the author say that Gandhi's view about Congress future was romantic?

Ans. (i) Author thinks that Congress should not have been a cohesive and disciplined party because it will take away the inclusive nature of Congress which accommodated the different opinions, interest groups of society within itself. It will make the party a close-knit party of disciplined group.

(ii) In the early years, the Congress was called a social and ideological coalition representing the different and diverse, sometimes contradictory interest groups, caste group, religious and language groups. It also acted as a platform for numerous groups, interests like peasants and industrialists and even political parties to participate in national movement. Thus, Congress was rainbow coalition having different social and ideological groups.

(iii) According to the author, Gandhi's view about Congress future was romantic because he believed in its inclusive ideology and its ability to represent all sections of Indian society.

Exam Pattern Questions

Multiple Choice Questions (MCQs)

1. In which year was the Election Commission of India set up? CBSE 2024

(a) 1949 (b) 1950
(c) 1951 (d) 1952

2. The first Chief Election Commissioner of India was .... CBSE 2024

(a) S.L. Shakdhar
(b) Sukumar Sen
(c) K.V.K. Sundaram
(d) R.K. Trivedi

3. Why was the first draft of electoral rolls not accepted by the Election Commission? Diksha App

(a) These were not legible.
(b) These did not contain the name of senior citizens.
(c) These did not contain the name of lower castes.
(d) These did not contain the name of 40 lakh women voters.

4. Which method of voting was used in the first General Election? Diksha App

(a) Ballot boxes
(b) Ballot paper
(c) Electronic Voting Machines
(d) Computer aided machines

5. What was the outcome of the Indian general election of 1951?

(a) The election result were rejected.
(b) The election was declared unfair.
(c) The election proved the critics wrong and was widely accepted as fair.
(d) It led to the formation of a new government in another country.

6. The "Era of One-Party Dominance" in India refers to the period from .... CBSE SQP 2024

(a) 1952 to 1962 (b) 1977 to 1984
(c) 1989 to 1996 (d) 1998 to 2004

7. He was the founder of the Independent Labour Party in India and later founded the Scheduled Caste Federation. Identify the person. Competency Based Que

(a) Acharya Narendra Deva
(b) A.K. Gopalan
(c) Rafi Ahmed Kidwai
(d) Babasaheb Bhimrao Ramji Ambedkar

8. Which political party came to power in Jammu and Kashmir in 1952? CBSE 2024

(a) Indian National Congress
(b) Kashmir National Congress
(c) Communist Party of India
(d) National Conference

9. For the first time the Communist Party came to power through democratic elections in which state of India. CBSE 2024

(a) West Bengal
(b) Kerala
(c) Tripura
(d) Manipur

10. By which group of leaders, Congress Socialist Party was formed within the Congress?

(a) Group of old leaders who wanted conservative Congress.
(b) Group of young people leaders who wanted a more radical and egalitarian Congress.
(c) Group of young people leaders who wanted a more liberal and free market approach.
(d) None of the above

11. **Which of the following political parties in contemporary India trace their origin to the Socialist Party?**

(a) Samyukta Socialist Party (b) Samajwadi Party
(c) Janata Dal (Secular) (d) Both (b) and (c)

12. **Which among the following was not a leader of Socialist Party?** Diksha App

(a) Jayaprakash Narayan (b) Asoka Mehta
(c) S.M. Joshi (d) Syama Prasad Mukherjee

13. **Which political party was at the second place in winning the Lok Sabha seats in the first General Elections of India?** CBSE 2024

Or **Which one of the following political parties was the main opposition party in the first Lok Sabha?** CBSE 2024 C

(a) Socialist Party
(b) The Communist Party of India
(c) Bharatiya Jana Sangh
(d) Swatantra Party

14. **Bharatiya Jana Sangh was formed in which year?**

(a) 1950 (b) 1949 (c) 1951 (d) 1952

15. **Who was Deendayal Upadhyaya?** Diksha App

(a) Full time RSS worker
(b) Congress President
(c) Leader of Communist Party
(d) None of the above

16. **Identify the incorrect pair.** Competency Based Que

(a) Rajkumari Amrit Kaur-Health Minister
(b) Maulana Azad-Education Minister
(c) Dr. Ambedkar-Food Minister
(d) Syama Prasad Mukherjee- Cabinet Minister

17. **Consider the following statements about the Communist Party of India.**

I. It was influenced by Russian Bolshevik Revolution.
II. Soon after independence, the party encouraged violent uprisings in Telangana.
III. It was a well-oiled machinery.
IV. It was always satisfied with the nature of Indian independence.

Which of the above statement/(s) is /are correct ?

Codes

(a) Only I (b) III and IV
(c) Only IV (d) I, II and III

18. **Consider the following statements about the role of the Opposition parties in India during the Congress dominance period.** Competency Based Que

I. None of the opposition party existed before independence.
II. All the opposition parties were successful in gaining only a token representation in the Lok Sabha.

Which of the above statement/(s) is /are correct ?

(a) Only I (b) Only II
(c) Both I and II (d) Neither I nor II

19. **Arrange the following events in the chronological sequence.** Competency Based Que

I. The amendment of the Constitution to prevent its members from having a dual party membership.
II. The dismissal of the Communist government in Kerala under Article 356 of the Constitution.
II. Formation of Bharatiya Jana Sangh.
IV. Adoption of Buddhism by Dr. Ambedkar.

Codes

(a) II, III, IV, I (b) I, IV, III, II
(c) I, III, IV, II (d) II, III, I, IV

20. **Match the following questions.**

	List-I	List-II
A.	1957	1. Death of Syama Prasad Mukherjee
B.	1934	2. Kerala State Assembly Elections
C.	1953	3. India adopted its Constitution
D.	1949	4. Congress Socialist Party

Codes

	A	B	C	D		A	B	C	D
(a)	2	4	1	3	(b)	4	3	2	1
(c)	3	2	1	4	(d)	1	4	2	3

21. **Match the following.**

	List-I	List-II
A.	A.K. Gopalan	1. Minister for Communications in Free India
B.	Rafi Ahmed Kidwai	2. Founding President of the Congress Socialist Party
C.	Deendayal Upadhyaya	3. Communist Leader of Kerala
D.	Acharya Narendra Deva	4. Founding Member of the Bharatiya Jana Sangh

Codes

	A	B	C	D
(a)	1	2	4	3
(b)	2	4	3	1
(c)	3	1	4	2
(d)	2	1	3	4

Assertion-Reason Questions

Directions (Q. Nos. 22-26) In the questions given below, there are two statements marked as Assertion (A) and Reason (R). Read the statements and choose the correct option.

Codes

(a) Both A and R are true and R is the correct explanation of A.
(b) Both A and R are true, but R is not the correct explanation of A.
(c) A is true, but R is false.
(d) A is false, but R is true.

22. **Assertion** (A) Our leaders were conscious of the critical role of politics in any democracy.

Reason (R) They did not see politics as a problem; they saw it as a way of solving problems.

23. **Assertion** (A) The first general elections in India had to be postponed twice and were finally held from October 1951 to February 1952. **CBSE 2024**

Reason (R) It was no longer possible to argue that democratic elections could not be held in conditions of poverty or lack of education.

24. **Assertion** (A) The first general election in 1950 was held under very challenging conditions.

Reason (R) India had a large illiterate population, and there were issues in preparing the electoral rolls and symbols for the candidates.

25. **Assertion** (A) The Communist Party of India (CPI) formed the government in Kerala in 1957.

Reason (R)The CPI's government was the first Communist government in the world to come to power through democratic elections.

26. **Assertion** (A) Congress dominated Indian politics in the first three general elections (1952, 1957 and 1962).

Reason (R) Congress had inherited the legacy of the national movement and had a widespread organisation across the country.

Passage Based Questions

27. **Read the following passage and answer the questions given below**

India is not the only country to have experienced the dominance of one party. If we look around the world, we find many other examples of one-party dominance. But there is a crucial difference between these and the Indian experience. In the rest of the cases the dominance of one party was ensured by compromising democracy. In some countries like China, Cuba and Syria the Constitution permits only a single party to rule the country. **Delhi 2019**

(i) **Which political party dominated the political scene of India after independence?**

(a) Bharatiya Jana Sangh
(b) Indian National Congress
(c) Swatantra Party
(d) Communist Party of India

(ii) **Which of the following countries has also been one party dominant ?**

(a) Cuba (b) China
(c) United States of America
(d) both (a) and (b)

(iii) **How the one-party dominance in India is different from the one-party dominance in other countries?**

28. **Read the following passage and answer the following questions given below**

The Jana Sangh was different from other parties in terms of ideology and programmes. It emphasised the idea of one country, one culture and one nation and believed that the country could become modern, progressive and strong on the basis of Indian culture and traditions. The party called for a reunion of India and Pakistan in Akhand Bharat. The party was in forefront of the agitation to replace English with Hindi as the official language of India and was also opposed to the granting of concessions to religious and cultural minorities.

(i) **What was the Jana Sangh's vision for India's development?**

(a) Based on foreign influences and modern technology
(b) Rooted in Indian culture and traditions
(c) Focused on economic liberalisation and privatisation
(d) Prioritising social welfare and equality

(ii) **What was the Jana Sangh's stance on India-Pakistan relations?**

(a) Calling for a united Akhand Bharat
(b) Advocating for peaceful coexistence
(c) Supporting a separate homeland for minorities
(d) Promoting cultural exchange and co-operation

(iii) **In what way the ideology of Jana Sangh was different from other political parties?**

29. **Read the following passage and answer the following questions given below**

This coalition-like character of the Congress gave it an unusual strength. Firstly, a coalition accommodates all those who join it. Therefore, it has to avoid any extreme position and strike a balance on almost all issues. Compromise and inclusiveness are the hallmarks of a coalition. This strategy put the opposition in a difficulty. Anything that the opposition wanted to say, would also find a place in the programme and ideology of the Congress. Secondly, in a party that has the nature of a coalition, there is a greater tolerance of internal differences and ambitions of various groups and leaders are accommodated. The Congress did both these things during the freedom struggle and continued doing this even after independence. That is why, even if a group was not happy with the position of the party or with its share of power, it would remain inside the party and fight the other groups rather than leaving the party and becoming an 'opposition'.

(i) **What is the key characteristic of the Congress coalition that makes it difficult for the opposition to attack?**
(a) Extreme positions
(b) Lack of internal differences
(c) Compromise and inclusiveness
(d) Strong leadership

(ii) **What strategy did the Congress employ to put the opposition at a disadvantage?**
(a) Adopting extreme positions
(b) Ignoring the opposition's demands
(c) Focusing on internal unity
(d) Incorporating the opposition's ideas

(iii) **How did the coalition-like nature of Congress affect internal differences?**
(a) Internal differences were ignored.
(b) It led to the formation of many new parties.
(c) There was greater tolerance for internal differences and ambitions.
(d) It created more conflict between groups.

(iv) **What would happen when a group within the Congress was unhappy with the party's position?**
(a) They would leave the party and form a new opposition.
(b) They would fight with the opposition parties.
(c) They would leave the country.
(d) They would remain within the party and fight other groups internally.

Answers

1. (b) 1950
2. (b) Sukumar Sen
3. (d) These did not contain the name of 40 lakh women voters.
4. (a) Ballot boxes
5. (c) The election proved the critics wrong and was widely accepted as fair.
6. (a) 1952 to 1962
7. (d) Babasaheb Bhimrao Ramji Ambedkar
8. (d) National Conference
9. (b) Kerala
10. (b) Group of young people leaders who wanted a more radical and egalitarian Congress.
11. (d) Both (b) and (c)
12. (d) Syama Prasad Mukherjee
13. (b) The Communist Party of India
14. (c) 1951
15. (a) Full time RSS worker
16. (c) Dr. Ambedkar-Food Minister
17. (d) I, II and III
18. (b) Only II
19. (c) I, III, IV, II
20. (a) 2 4 1 3
21. (c) 3 1 4 2
22. (a) Both A and R are true and R is the correct explanation of A.
23. (b) Both A and R are true, but R is not the correct explanation of the A.
24. (d) A is false, but R is true.
25. (a) Both A and R are true and R is the correct explanation of A.
26. (a) Both A and R are true and R is the correct explanation of A.
27. (i) (b) Indian National Congress
(ii) (d) both (a) and (b)
(iii) In India one-party dominance is different from the one-party dominance in other countries because in India leaders have not compromised the principles of democracy.
India has been a multi-party electoral landscape and the Congress Party won India's elections in a fair and democratic manner.
28. (i) (b) Rooted in Indian culture and traditions
(ii) (a) Calling for a united Akhand Bharat
(iii) Unlike other political parties, Jana Sangh has emphasised on the ideals of one country, one culture and one nation. It has called for the reunion of India and Pakistan as the Akhand Bharat.
29. (i) (c) Compromise and inclusiveness
(ii) (d) Incorporating the opposition's ideas
(iii) (c) There was greater tolerance for internal differences and ambitions.
(iv) (d) They would remain within the party and fight other groups internally.

Subjective Questions

Very Short Answer Type Questions

1. Why was India's experiment with universal adult franchise described as "bold and risky"? Explain. Competency Based Que; CBSE 2024

Ans. India's experiment with universal adult franchise was described as "bold and risky" because of the following reasons

(i) India was a huge country with around 17crore eligible voters who had to elect about 3200 MLAs and 489 members of Lok Sabha. Thus, preparing electoral rolls and drawing of the delimitation boundaries was going to be a huge task for the election commission.

(ii) Also, the first general election was a big test of democracy because India was a poor and illiterate country. Even the prosperous democracies of Europe have not given the voting rights to all women.

2. Why did India's general elections of 1952 become a landmark in the history of democracy all over the world? Explain. Diksha App CBSE 2024

Ans. India's general election of 1952 became a landmark in the history of democracy all over the world because of the following reasons

(i) The level of participation during India's 1952 general election was highly encouraging as more than half of the eligible voters, turned out to vote. Even the election results were fairly accepted by the losers.

(ii) The Indian experiment had proved the critics wrong, and it was no longer possible for them to argue that democratic elections could not be held in the conditions of poverty or lack of education.

3. Explain the nature of Congress dominance after the independence in relation to democracy in other countries. CBSE Term II 2022

Ans. With the dominance of Congress, India was not the only country to have experienced of the dominance of one party. In some countries like China, Cuba and Syria also had a single party system. However India's case was unique in the sense that its democracy was not compromised unlike in other nations.

4. Explain the major difference of ideology between that of the Congress and the Bharatiya Jana Sangh.

Ans. The major difference of ideology between Congress and Bharatiya Jana Sangh was that Bharatiya Jana Sangh emphasised on one party country, one culture, one nation i.e. based on Hindu nation or Hindutva.

Whereas Congress formed ideological and social coalitions accommodating social diversities.

5. Did the prevalence of 'one-party dominance' in India affect the democratic nature of Indian politics? Express your opinion. CBSE SQP 2024

Or **"One-party dominance did not affect the very essence of Indian democracy. Justify the statement with any two arguments.** CBSE 2025

Ans. No, the prevalence of one-party dominance in India did not affect the democratic nature of Indian politics. It was because in India, many parties contested elections in the conditions of free and fair manner, but Congress managed to win elections democratically.

However, in some instances like Kerala elections in 1957, some decisions of Congress became controversial. But overall, the presence of the opposition parties played a crucial role in maintaining democratic character through their criticism and the process of checks and balance.

6. Explain the nature of the Congress Party as an ideological coalition during the freedom movement. CBSE 2024

Ans. Congress has evolved as an ideological coalition since 1885. It started with a pressure group for the newly educated and professional classes.

Gradually, it began accommodating the various ideologies of freedom movement, like revolutionary, pacifist, conservative, radical, extremist, moderate and all shades of right and left. Thus, the Congress has become a platform, for various ideologies during the freedom movement.

7. Explain the two commonly agreed-upon goals of the national movement which were achieved after independence. CBSE 2025

Ans. The two commonly agreed-upon goals of the national movement that were achieved after independence are

- **Democratic Government** India became an independent and sovereign nation with a democratic system based on universal adult franchise, that ensures equal political rights for all citizens.
- **Secularism** India adopted a secular Constitution which ensured freedom of religion and equal treatment to all religious communities.

Short Answer Type Questions

1. Keeping in mind the crucial role of politics in a democracy, which route did our national leaders decide to take in the newly independent India? Explain any two points. Competency Based Que; CBSE 2024

Ans. Our leaders chose the route of democracy for the newly independent India because

(i) Our leaders same politics as the way of solving problems rather than seeing it as a problem. They believe that there are always different policy alternatives to choose in the politics. There are different groups with different aspirations and to unite these differences on a national level was their first priority.

(ii) For our leaders, democratic politics was an answer because the purpose of political activity should be based on pursuing the public interest. That is why our leaders decided to take the democratic political route.

2. Trace the journey of the changing voting methods in India since the first general elections. Competency Based Que

Ans. During the first general elections, it was decided to place inside each polling booth a box for each candidate with the election symbol of that candidate. Each voter was given a blank ballot paper which they had to drop into the box of the candidate they wanted to vote for.

After the first two elections, this method was changed. Now the ballot paper carried the names and symbols of all the candidates and the voter was required to put a stamp on the name of the candidate they wanted to vote for.

Then, towards the end of 1990s, Electronic Voting Machine started to be used. By 2004, the entire country has been using Electronic Voting Machines.

3. How did the legacy of the freedom struggle contribute to the Congress Party's dominance in India?

Ans. The Congress Party's dominance in India can be largely attributed to its legacy as the inheritor of the national freedom struggle. Many of the prominent leaders who had led the fight for independence continued to contest elections as Congress candidates after independence. This association with the freedom movement gave Congress significant popularity and legitimacy among the people.

Congress was already a well-organised party with an extensive network at the grass-roots level, giving it a significant advantage over newer political parties that were formed only after independence. The party's historical connection to the struggle for independence helped cement its position as a national party with broad-based support.

4. The extent of the victory of the Congress was artificially boosted by our electoral system. Elucidate. Competency Based Que

Ans. The Congress emerged as the winner in the first three general elections but it did not get half of the total votes. For example in 1952, the Congress obtained 45 per cent of the total votes. But still it won 74 per cent of the seats. The Socialist Party which was the second largest party in terms of votes, secured more than 10 per cent of the votes all over the country. Despite of lesser votes, Congress emerged as the winner because of the first-past-the-post method followed in Indian election process. Thus, it is right to say that the extent of the victory of the Congress was artificially boosted by our electoral system.

5. Describe any four features of the Congress Party. CBSE 2020

Or **Explain any four reasons for the dominance of the Congress Party in the first three general elections.**

Ans. The main features of the Congress Party are

- The Congress Party inherited the legacy of the national movement. It was the only party to have an organisation spread all over the country.
- The Congress Party was supported by elites, educated business classes and middle classes people. It also got support from peasants for its socialist nature.
- The leadership of the Congress expanded beyond the upper caste and upper class professionals to agriculture based leaders with a rural orientation.
- The Congress was a 'platform' for numerous groups, interests and even political parties to take part in the national movement. Many organisations and parties with their own Constitution and organisational structure were allowed to exist within the Congress.

6. Describe any four features of the Communist Party of India. CBSE 2020

Ans. The four features of the Communist Party of India (CPI) are

(i) The Communist Party of India is inspired by the Bolshevik Revolution in Russia and advocated socialism as the solution to problems affecting the country.

(ii) Soon after independence, the party thought that the transfer of power in 1947 was not true independence and encouraged violent uprising in Telangana.

(iii) The basic question that troubled the party was the nature of Indian independence.

(iv) In 1951, the Communist Party abandoned the path of violent revolution and decided to participate in the approaching general elections.

7. Describe any four features of the ideology of the Bharatiya Jana Sangh. **CBSE 2020**

Ans. The Bharatiya Jana Sangh was formed in 1951. Its main features are

- The lineage of Bharatiya Jana Sangh can be traced back to the Rashtriya Swayamsevak Sangh (RSS) and the Hindu Mahasabha before independence.
- It was different from other parties in terms of ideology and programmes. It emphasised the idea of one country, one culture and one nation. It believed that the country could become modern, progressive and strong on the basis of Indian culture and traditions.
- The party called for a reunion of India and Pakistan in Akhand Bharat.
- The party was in forefront of the agitation to replace English with Hindi as the official language of India. It was opposed to the granting of concessions to religious and cultural minorities.

8. What was the relationship between Congress and opposition leaders in the early years after Independence?

Ans. In the early years after India gained independence, the relationship between Congress and opposition leaders was marked by mutual respect. Even though they belonged to different parties, leaders like Jawaharlal Nehru had a good relationship with opposition figures such as Dr. Ambedkar and Syama Prasad Mukherjee, who were included in the interim government. Nehru also invited socialist leaders like Jayaprakash Narayan to join his government.

This respect between political rivals was important for the smooth functioning of the government and for shaping India's early democratic politics. However, as time passed, this mutual respect began to fade as competition between parties grew more intense.

Long Answer Type Questions

1. 'Preparing for the first general election was a mammoth exercise'. Justify the statement with suitable arguments. **Competency Based Que**

Or **Highlight four problems before the election commission of India for holding first general elections.** **Diksha App**

Or **Why was holding of the first general election in 1952 a great challenge for the Election Commission of India? Explain.** **Competency Based Que; CBSE 2024 C**

Ans. For the Election Commission of India, the preparation of the first general election was a mammoth exercise because of the following reasons.

(i) India was a large country in terms of size and to draw the boundaries of the electoral constituency was a challenging task for the Election Commission of India.

(ii) It also required preparing the electoral rolls which would take a lot of time because nearly 40 thousand names of the women were not recorded in the list as they simply listed as 'wife of' or 'daughter of'.

(iii) At that time, there were 17 crore eligible voters who had to elect about 3200 MLAs and 489 members of the Lok Sabha.

(iv) On the head of it, only 15 per cent of these eligible voters were literate, thus training of the election officers and polling staff to conduct the election was also a challenging task.

2. The Congress Party succeeded in maintaing its dominance till 1967 explain the reason. **Diksha App**

Or **The period from 1952 to 1966 in Indian politics has been termed as an 'era of one-party dominance'. Do you agree? Explain any three factors that helped it in its dominance.** **Competency Based Que**

Or **Highlight any three major reasons for the dominance of Congress Party in the first three General Elections after independence.** **Delhi 2019**

Or **Explain any four reasons for the dominance of Congress Party in the first three General Elections in India.** **CBSE 2023**

Ans. The Congress Party succeed in maintaining its dominance till 1967 due to following reasons

(i) The roots of this extraordinary success of the Congress Party go back to the legacy of the freedom struggle. Congress was seen as inheritor of the national movement.

Many leaders who were in forefront of the struggle were now contesting elections as Congress candidates.

(ii) The Congress Party was supported by elites, educated business class and middle class people. It also got support from peasants because of its socialist nature.

(iii) It had many popular faces like Jawaharlal Nehru, C Rajagopalachari, Vallabhbhai Patel etc. Moreover, Jawaharlal Nehru was charismatic and very popular leader.

(iv) Congress worked at upper level as well as at grass-root level. Congress was popularised due to the participation in civil disobedience movement.

(v) During the period of Nehruji, Congress attained mass popularity.

(vi) The traditional loyalities made Congress a one-party dominance.

3. In what sense Congress played the role of the ruling party and the opposition party in the first decade of electoral competition?

Ans. Congress had played the role of ruling party for the following reasons

(i) Congress had a coalition-like character that gave it an unusual strength. It accommodated all ideologies that join it by avoiding any extreme positions. This strategy put the opposition in difficult situation to raise any issue.

(ii) It maintains the greater tolerance of internal differences. It managed the ambitions of various groups and leaders by keeping them happy through power sharing. Even if people did not share power, they remained in the party and formed groups called factions. These groups fought the other groups rather than leaving the party.

The Congress Party also played the role of opposition in the following manner

(i) The coalitional nature of the Congress Party tolerated and in fact encouraged various factions. Instead of being a weakness, internal factionalism became a strength of the Congress.

(ii) The factions took different ideological positions making the Congress appear as a grand centrist Party. Even, most of the state units of the Congress were made up of numerous factions.

(iii) The system of factions functioned as balancing mechanism within the ruling party. Political competition therefore took place within the Congress itself.

4. How did the Congress had the 'first off the blocks advantage'?

Ans. The Congress had the 'first off the blocks advantage' over the political parties because,

(i) The roots of the extraordinary success of the Congress Party go back to the legacy of the freedom struggle. Congress was seen as inheritor of the national movement. Many of the congress leaders were at the forefront of the freedom struggle.

(ii) The Congress has become a well organised party by time of independence. It could thus prioritise the strategy to start its campaign for the elections.

(iii) By the time of independence, Congress had become an organisational network and it was spread across the length and breadth of the whole country. It has reached to the lowest levels of the society.

(iv) Many other parties were formed only during the independence or after that. Congress however had been following the legacy of the national freedom struggle thus, it had the advantage of starting ahead from other political parties.

5. What is meant by opposition in a democratic system? Describe any two activities of the opposition during the first two Parliaments of 1952 and 1957.

Or **During the early years of independence, despite the fact that the opposition parties had a token representation, they played a crucial role in maintaining the democratic character of the system. How?** **Competency Based Que**

Or **List any four activities of the opposition during the Parliaments of 1952 and 1957.**

Or **Describe the role of opposition parties in the first phase of democratic politics in our country which was quite unique.** **All India 2019**

Ans. The opposition is the group of all the parties which do not support the ruling party on their policies and agenda. It is also generally viewed as the alternative government or 'government in waiting'.

At the time of independence, there were many opposition parties and after independence it increased, but it gained only token representation in the Lok Sabha and also in State Assemblies. Yet their presence played a crucial role in maintaining the democratic character of the system. The four activities of the opposition during the Parliament of 1952 and 1957 are as follows

(i) These opposition parties offered sustained and principled criticism of the policies and practices of the Congress Party. This phenomena indicated the check and balance of power of the Congress.

(ii) In 1957, in Kerala, Congress was defeated by CPI and made government, but after that Congress dismissed the Kerala Government under Article 356. It was criticised by the opposition leaders and said that it was the first instance of the misuse of Constitutional emergence powers.

(iii) In 1950, BJS was able to secure 3 seats and in 1957, it secured 4 seats. The party played the role of opposition and started agitation to replace English with Hindi as the official language and also advocated for the development of nuclear weapons.

(iv) The opposition parties prevented the resentment with the system from turning anti-democratic. These parties also groomed the leaders (young citizens) who wanted to shape the India as developed and powerful state.

Picture Based Questions

1. Observe the cartoon given below carefully and answer the questions that follow.

(i) What does the cartoon represent?
(ii) Who were the members of this committee?
(iii) Who have been shown sitting on the top?

Ans. (i) The cartoon represent the scenario of candidates seeking ticket for election from Election Committee of Congress which decide the candidates of the Congress for election.

(ii) The member of the Election Committee were Nehruji, Morarji Desai, Dr. B.C. Roy and Maulana Azad.

(iii) Morarji Desai, Nehru, Maulana Azad, D.P. Mishra, P.D. Tandon, Govind Ballabh Pant, Rafi Ahmed Kidwai, Dr. B.C. Roy, Kamaraj Nadar and Jagjivan Ram were shown sitting on the top.

2. Study the picture given below carefully and answer the questions that follow.

(i) What is the central theme of the cartoon depicted above?

(a) The struggle for votes between the Congress and the opposition.
(b) The significance of the strong and united government.
(c) The struggle for power between the government and the opposition.
(d) None of the above

Ans. (c) The struggle for power between the government and the opposition.

(ii) Whom do the sitting people represent?

(a) Opposition
(b) The Indian National Congress
(c) The common people
(d) The members of Nehru Cabinet

Ans. (d) The members of Nehru Cabinet

(iii) What does the tree signify here?

(a) The Government (b) The Country
(c) The Election Committee (d) All of these

Ans. (a) The Government

(iv) Identify the correct relationship between the government and the opposition in India during the period depicted in the given cartoon.

(a) It was very co-operative.
(b) The government was dominant and opposition was weak.
(c) It was characterised by constant conflict.
(d) It was very smooth and harmonious relationship.

Ans. (c) It was characterised by constant conflict.

Map Based Questions

1. In the given political outline map of India, two States have been marked as A and B. Identify these States on the basis of the information given below and write their correct names in your answer-book along with the respective serial number of the information used and the concerned alphabets given in the map as per the following format. CBSE Term II 2022

(i) The state where the CPI emerged as the winner democratically.

(ii) The region which is a union territory now and had National Conference during 1952 elections.

Sr. no. of the Information Used	Concerned alphabet in the map	Name of the State
(i)		
(ii)		

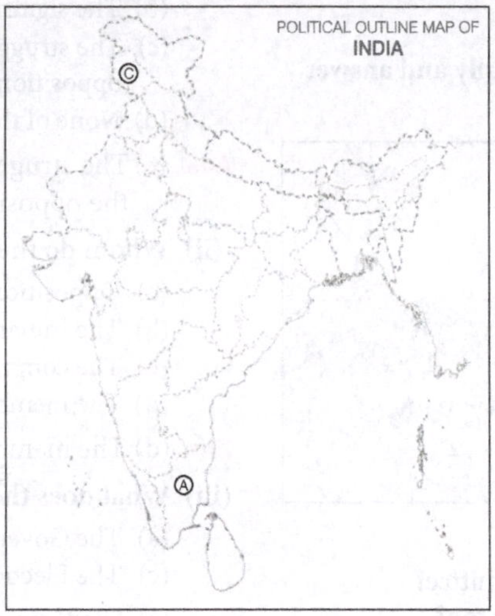

Ans.

Sr. no. of the Information Used	Alphabet Concerned	Name of the State
(i)	A	Kerala
(ii)	C	Jammu & Kashmir

2. In the given political outline map of India, two states have been marked as A and B. Identify these states on the basis of the information given below and write their correct names in the table.

(i) State where the Congress Party was not in power in first general elections.

(ii) State where the Congress Party remained in power between 1952-1962.

Sr. no. of the Information Used	Concerned alphabet in the map	Name of the State
(i)		
(ii)		

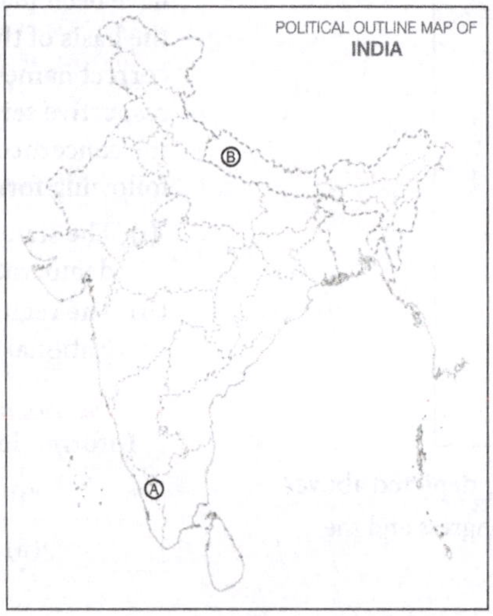

Ans.

Sr. no. of the Information Used	Alphabet Concerned	Name of the State
(i)	A	Kerala
(ii)	B	Uttar Pradesh

SELF ASSESSMENT TEST

Objective Type Questions

1. Constitution came into effect on which day?
   (a) 26th November, 1949 (b) 26th January, 1951 (c) 26th January, 1950 (d) None of these
2. Which of the following languages were used in the election boxes to show candidat's name during the 1st general elections?
   (a) English & Punjabi (b) Hindi & English (c) Urdu & Sindhi (d) Hindi & Punjabi
3. How many months were taken to complete the first general elections process?
   (a) 3 (b) 6 (c) 5 (d) 2
4. How did Congress respond after its defeat in 1957, Kerala assembly elections?
   (a) It accepted its defeat (b) It formed coalition government with the CPI.
   (c) It began a 'liberation struggle' (d) All of these
5. How was the ideology of communists different from the socialists?
   (a) It believed in the democratic socialism.
   (b) It believed in the violent overthrow of capitalism.
   (c) Both (a) and (b)
   (d) All of the above

Very Short Answer Type Questions

6. Explain 'First-Part The Post-method' used in Indian electoral system.
7. Why did Communist Party abandon the path of violent revolution during the first general elections?
8. What was the significance of the Communist Party's victory in Kerala in 1957 and how did the Congress Party react to it?

Short Answer Type Questions

9. How did Congress transform into a rainbow-like social coalition?
10. 'Inspite of low representation in the Lok Sabha, opposition parties play a role in mainstring the democratic character of Indian polity'. Comment. **Competency Based Que**

Long Answer Type Questions

11. How did the dominance of Congress Party in the first three general elections help in establishing a democratic set-up in India?
12. How did the ideological differences within the Indian socialist movement affect its political effectiveness and unity during the post-independence period?

03

CHAPTER

This chapter discusses the economic development challenges faced by independent India. It explains the key choices and strategies adopted by leaders in the first two decades, along with their achievements and limitations. It also explores why this strategy was later abandoned.

Politics of Planned Development

YOUR STUDY GOALS

3.1 Political Contestation

3.2 The Early Initiatives of Planning Commission

YOUR PRACTICE GOAL

- Objective Type Questions (29 Qs ; MCQs, A-R, Passage Based)
- Subjective Questions (12 VSAs, 5 SAs, 5 LAs, 1 Picture Based)

Development and planning are the most important aspects of any country to provide its citizens with the **socio-economic justice**. The meaning of development often differs from one section to another. When the demand for steel began growing in the world, our government took it as an opportunity for the investment and employment. **Odisha** has the largest reserves of iron ore. But many tribals were worried about their displacement from their home and livelihood due to mining.

Thus, it is necessary to plan the development according to every section of the society.

3.1 Political Contestation

After the independence, everyone agreed that the development of India should mean both economic growth as well as social and economic justice. It was decided that the questions of development cannot be left upon the businessmen, farmers or industrialists. Thus, the government would decide the path of development by considering the needs and requirement of all.

Left Vs. Right

- In parties, there are references of parties and groups with a left or right ideology.
- These ideologies are concerned with the groups or parties, regarding social change and the role of the state in effecting economic re-distribution.

Left often refers to those who favour the economy controlled by the state. They prefer that state should regulate the prices in the market.

Right refers to those who favour the free market competition. They believe that government should not un-necessarily interfere in the economy.

Ideas of Development

- During the first decade of independence, there was a lot of debate about the idea of development. For many people **West** is the standard for measuring development.
- It was believed that development means modernisation which is based on capitalism[1] and liberalism[2] where ideas of growth, material progress and scientific rationality shape the opinion of people.
- On the eve of the independence, India had two models of modern development which are as follows
  - **Liberal capitalist model** of USA and Europe
  - Socialist model[3] of USSR
- There were very less supporters of the American style capitalist developments. Most of the leaders from the Communist Party, Socialist Party and even Congress supported the Soviet model of development.
- But there were different views on the aims of development. Like some preferred the path of agricultural development and some prefer industrialisation. But the key objective was to remove the poverty and bring the **social** and **economic re-distribution** within the society by the government.

Planning

- Despite the various differences in the ideas of the development, there was a common goal that the idea of development cannot be left to the private sector.
- Leaders agreed on this common goal because many of the following events had led to the great economic damage
  - Great depression in Europe
  - The inter-war re-construction of Japan and Germany
- The Planning Commission was invented and some of the big industrialists got together in 1944 and drafted a proposal to set up a planned economy in the country. This proposal, was known as Bombay Plan.
- The Bombay Plan wanted the state to take major initiatives in industrial and other economic investment.
- Soon after the independence, **Planning Commission** came into being with the Prime Minister as its chairperson. The Planning Commission became one of the most influential and important machinery to decide the strategies, which India would adopt for its development.

Quick Test 1

1 Which state has the largest reserve of iron?
2 At the time of independence, how many models of development were available in India?
3 Which country did the socialist model belongs to?
4 Who proposed the Bombay Plan?

1 Capitalism Capitalism is a system where businesses own and control the means of production, such as factories and land and the prices are determined by supply and demands in a free market and the interference of government is very limited.

2 Liberalism It is a philosophy in which government do not interfere and every person has the right to freely pursue its goals.

3 Socialist model It is an economic and political system that aims to create a more equal society.

3.2 The Early Initiatives of Planning Commission

- Similar to the USSR, Planning Commission of India opted for **Five-Year Plans**. In these Five-Year Plans, Government of India prepare a document for all its income and expenses for the next five years.
- The budget was divided into two parts
  - **Non-Plan Budget** This budget was spent on routine items on a yearly basis.
  - **Plan Budget** This part of the budget was to be spent on a five year basis and as per the priority fixed by the plan.
- A Five-Year Plan allows the government to focus on the larger picture and make long term intervention in the economy.
- When the **First Five-Year Plan** was released in **December 1951,** there was a lot of excitement in the country. Many academics, journalist, farmers, politicians and government and private sector employees discussed and debated this document extensively.
- The **Second Five-Year Plan** was released in **1956** and it also gathered the similar excitement.
- The **Third Five-Year Plan** was released in **1961.**
- The **Fourth Five-Year Plan** was due to start in **1966**, but by this time, India was facing economic crisis. Thus, government decided to take a **'plan holiday'**.

Planning Commission

- Planning Commission was set up in March, 1950 by a simple resolution of the Government of India. It has an advisory role to draft the policies for the development of India.

NITI Aayog

- Hence, During his Independence Day speech on 15th August, 2014, Prime Minister Narendra Modi falked about the abolition of the Planning Commission.
- The Government of India replaced the Planning Commission with a new institution named NITI Aayog (National Institute for Transforming India). NITI Aayog was established on 1st January, 2015.
- To harmonise the interests of national security and economic policy and to prepare strategic and long term framework of policy and programme.

National Development Council (NDC)

- The NDC or Rashtiya Vikas Parishad is the apex body for decision creating and deliberations on development matters in India, presided over by the Prime Minister.
- It was set up on 6th August, 1952, under the chairmanship of India first Prime Minister Pandit Jawaharlal Nehru to strengthen and mobilise the effort and resources of the nalion in support of the Five-Year Plans made by Planning Commission.

The First Five-Year Plan

- The First Five-Year Plan took place from 1951 to 1956. According to one of the drafting member, **K.N. Raj**, India should move slowly towards the development in the first two decades. He believed that if India would develop very fast, then it may endanger the democracy.
- The First Five-Year plan, focused upon the following issues
  - **Agrarian Sector** It includes the investment in dams and irrigation. **Bhakra Nangal Dam** was proposed as an important project.
  - **Land Reform** The land distribution pattern in the country was identified as the main obstacle in the agriculture growth of the country. Thus, it was decided to carry land reforms.
  - **Save Money** The basic aim of the planners was to raise the level of national income, which could be possible only if the people saved more money than they spent.

- In the 1950s, spending was already very low, so it couldn't be reduced further. Planners tried to increase savings, but it was hard because the country had little capital compared to the number of workers. Savings did grow during the early plans, but not as much as expected. From the early 1960s to the early 1970s, savings started to drop.

The Second Five-Year Plan-Rapid Industrialisation

- The Second Five-Year Plan was drafted under the leadership of **P.C. Mahalanobis**.
- Before finalising the Second Year Plan, Congress passed a resolution held at Avadi, near Madras. It declared that the Congress has "**socialist pattern of society**" as its goal.
- The socialist pattern of society was reflected in the second plan. It includes
  - The government imposed tariffs on imports from the foreign countries, to protect the domestic industries. This helped both public and private sector industries to grow.
  - In this period, both **savings and investments increased,** which helped in the development of industries like: electricity, railway, steel, machineries and communication.
- This push, marked a turning point in the development of India.
- However, in terms of technology, India was not much developed. Therefore, India had to spend its foreign currency to buy technology from foreign countries. As more investment went to industry than agriculture, there was a risk of food shortage.
- With the idea of planning, government had tried hard to balance the agriculture and industrial sectors of the society. Critics saw an urban bias and felt industries were wrongly prioritised over agriculture. Some wanted focus on agriculture related industries.

P.C. Mahalanobis (1893-1972)

- He was a world famous scientist and statistician.
- He founded the Indian Statistical Institute in 1931.
- He played an important role in the preparation of the Second Five-Year Plan and supported the rapid industrialisation and active role of the public sector.

Quick Test 2

1. What were the two types of budgets?
2. Who preferred the slower economic growth for the first two decades to maintain Indian democracy ?
3. Which institution replaced the Planning Commission of India?
4. Who was P.C. Mahalanobis?

Mind Map

1 Development and Planning

- Meaning of development Differs from one section to another in a democracy.
- Development Encompasses economic growth with social and economic justice.
- Planning Balances economic growth with social and economic justice and ensures development benefits all sections of society.

2 Political Contestation

- India aimed for development balancing economic growth with social justice.
- Government decided development path through consultations and public approval.

Planning in India Bombay Plan (1944)
- Proposed a planned economy with state-led industrial investment.

Planning Commission
- Established soon after independence with the Prime Minister as chairperson.
- Played a crucial role in deciding India's development strategies.

Ideas of Development
It was believed that development means modernisation based on capitalism and liberalism.

Models of Development
- India had two models of development before it
  - Liberal Capitalist Model (USA and Europe).
  - Socialist Model (USSR).
- Most of the leaders in India supported the Soviet Model of development.

Aims of Development
There were different views on aims of development
- Agricultural development.
- Industrialisation.
- Poverty removal and social and economic redistribution.

POLITICS OF PLANNED DEVELOPMENT

3 Early initiatives of the Planning

Commission of India
Five-Year Plans
- Inspired by USSR model.
- Prepared document for income and expenses for next five years.

Budget divided into
- **Non-Plan Budget** Routine items, yearly basis.
- **Plan Budget** Five-year basis, priority-based.

First Five-Year Plan (1951-1956)
Key Focus Areas
- **Agrarian Sector** Investment in dams and irrigation (e.g., Bhakra Nangal Dam).
- **Land Reform** Addressing the obstacle of land distribution pattern in agriculture growth.
- **Saving Money** Raising national income through increased savings.

Second Five-Year Plan (1956)
Rapid Industrialisation
- Drafted under P.C. Mahalanobis' leadership.
- **Socialist Pattern of Society** Government-imposed tariffs to protect domestic industries.
- **Growth in Industries** Electricity, railway, steel, machineries and communication.

Nehru Addressing the Staff of the Planning Commission

The Hindustan Times

FIVE-YEAR PLAN PRESENTED TO PARLIAMENT

Rs 2,069 CRORES OUTLAY FOR VARIOUS PROJECTS

Blue-print For Increasing National Wealth

Discussion On Plan To Begin On Monday

DEVELOPMENT SCHEMES FOR DELHI

NEW HUDSON AUTOCYCLES

Source: The Hindustan Times
This news cutting is about presentation of the Five-Year Plan in Parliament

NCERT Folder

1. Which of these statements about the Bombay Plan is incorrect?

(a) It was a blueprint for India's economic future.
(b) It supported state-ownership of industry.
(c) It was made by some leading industrialists.
(d) It supported strongly the idea of planning.

Ans. (b) It supported state-ownership of industry.

2. Which of the following ideas did not form part of the early phase of India's development policy?

(a) Planning (b) Liberalisation
(c) Co-operative Farming (d) Self-sufficiency

Ans. (b) Liberalisation

3. The idea of planning in India was drawn from

I. The Bombay Plan.
II. Experiences of the Soviet bloc countries.
III. Gandhian vision of society.
IV. Demand by peasant organisations.

Codes

(a) II and IV (b) IV and III
(c) I and II (d) All of these

Ans. (d) All of these

4. Match the following

	List I		List II
A	Charan Singh	1.	Industrialisation
B	P.C. Mahalanobis	2.	Zoning
C	Bihar Famine	3.	Farmers
D	Posco plant	4.	Odisha

Ans. A → 3, B → 1, C → 2, D → 4

5. What were the major difference in the approach towards development at the time of independence? Has the debate been resolved?

Ans. The major differences in the approaches towards the idea of development after independence were mainly based on the lines of socialistic and capitalist tendencies.

These two models were outcome of the Cold War between the two world powers USA and USSR.

- Many people in India were impressed with the USSR and wanted India to adopt socialist model of development.
- This included members of Communist Party of India, Socialist Party and Nehru was also inspired by this model.
- Very few people supported the liberal-capitalist model of USA.

This reflected a broad consensus that had developed during the national movement.

The nationalist leaders were clear that the economic concerns of Government of India would have to be different from the narrowly defined commercial functions of the colonial government.

It was clear that the core focus of the development was agriculture, poverty alleviation and social and economic re-distribution.

There was a debate among them. For some, industrialisation seemed to be the preferred path and for others agriculture and particularly alleviation of poverty was the priority.

Yes, this debate was resolved by adopting the model of planning as the consensus for process of rebuilding economy. Thus, idea of Five-Year Plan on the USSR lines was adopted for the future economic strategy.

6. What was the major thrust of the First Five-Year Plan? In which ways did the Second Plan differ from the first one?

Ans. The First Five-Year Plan (1951-1956) sought to get economy of the country out of the cycle of poverty. K.N. Raj, a young economist involved in drafting the plan, emphasised that the fast rate of development might endanger democracy.

The major thrust of First Five-Year Plan were as follows

- It focused mainly on agrarian sector. Huge investment were made in large scale projects like Bhakhra Nangal Dam and irrigation projects.
- It also identified the pattern of land distribution and focused on land reform in India.
- It aimed to increase the level of national income.

The First Five-Year Plan differed from the Second Five Year Plan in following aspects

- The First Five-Year Plan focused on the agrarian sector while the Second Five-Year Plan focused on heavy industrialisation.
- The First Five-Year Plan had brought slow growth but Second Five-Year Plan wanted to bring about quick transformation in all possible directions.

7. Read the following passage and answer the questions below.

"In the early years of independence, two contradictory tendencies were already well advanced inside the Congress Party". On the one hand, the national party executive endorsed socialist principles of state ownership, regulation and control over key sectors of the economy in order to improve productivity and at the same time curb economic concentration. On the other hand, the National Congress government pursued liberal economic policies and incentives to private investment that was justified in terms of the sole criterion of achieving maximum increase in production.

—Francine Frankel

(i) What is the contradiction that the author is talking about? What would be the political implications of a contradiction like this?

(ii) If the author is correct, why is it that the Congress was pursuing this policy? Was it related to the nature of the opposition parties?

(iii) Was there also a contradiction between the central leadership of the Congress Party and its state level leaders?

Ans. (i) The author is talking about two contradictory views which existed inside the Congress Party. The national party executive endorsed socialist principles of state ownership, regulation and control over key industries.

While the Congress government pursued liberal economic policies and incentives to promote private investment.

It showed that the Congress Party did not have a unanimous view regarding the model to be adopted for development.

Therefore, mixed economy was adopted.

(ii) The Congress was pursuing this policy to accommodate and please both leftist and rightist oriented members of it.

Yes, it was also related to the nature of opposition parties because it wanted to be the representative of all ideological groups.

This is why Congress was called as a social and ideological coalition.

(iii) Yes, most of state units of the Congress were made up of numerous factions. These factions took different ideological positions from the central leadership.

The system of factions functioned as balancing mechanism within the Congress.

Exam Pattern Questions

Objective Type Questions

Multiple Choice Questions (MCQs)

1. Which two model of development India had adopted on the eve of independence?

(a) The Socialist model as in USSR.
(b) Gandhian model of development .
(c) The Liberal-capitalist model as in Europe and the USA.
(d) Both (a) and (c)

2. Why did India adopt planning?

(a) To bring socio-economic changes.
(b) To provide controlled and faster growth rate.
(c) To gain consensus by almost all sections.
(d) All of the above

3. India's planned economic development model was mainly inspired from .... Diksha App

(a) American style capitalist development model.
(b) Soviet model of development.
(c) Gandhian model of development
(d) None of the above

4. Which of the following is/are correct about the Bombay Plan?

(a) It was drafted in 1944.
(b) It was drafted by section of big industrialists.
(c) It wanted state to take major initiatives in industrial and other economic investments.
(d) All of the above

5. Which one of the following was formed for the planned development of India, just after independence? CBSE 2024

(a) Election Commission
(b) Planning Commission
(c) Shah Commission
(d) NITI Aayog

6. Planning Commission was set up by .... CBSE 2023

(a) Constitution of India
(b) President of India
(c) a resolution of Government of India
(d) the Constituent Assembly

7. **Planning Commission of India was replaced with NITI Aayog because ....** **CBSE 2021**
(a) it was becoming irrelevant to face the new challenges of development.
(b) it had become very old.
(c) it was totally based on socialist model.
(d) many states were not in favour of Planning Commission.

8. **Five-Year Plans were adopted by the Government of India as a policy of ....** **CBSE 2023**
(a) planned development
(b) mixed economy
(c) socialism
(d) industrialisation

9. **Who drafted the First Five-Year Plan?**
(a) K.C. Neogy (b) T.T. Krishnamachari
(c) K.N. Raj (d) J.C. Kumarappa

10. **Under whose leadership the Second Five-Year Plan was drafted?**
(a) P.C. Mahalanobis
(b) K.C. Neogy
(c) T.T. Krishnamachari
(d) Smt. Durgabai Deshmukh

11. **Which statement among the following is correct about the planning ideology of left wing?** **CBSE 2025**
(a) The Left supports a free-market economy.
(b) They support government policies which are for the benefit of poor sections.
(c) They do not want unnecessary intervention of government in the economy.
(d) They advocate for progressive policies.

12. **Who among the following appoints the vice chairperson of NITI Aayog?** **CBSE Term I, 2021**
(a) President of India
(b) Prime Minister of India
(c) Vice-President of India
(d) Lok Sabha Speaker

13. **Which one of the following statements about the Third Five-Year Plan is not correct?**
Competency Based Que; CBSE Term I, 2021
(a) It was significantly different from the Second Five-Year Plan.
(b) It was urban biased.
(c) Industry was given priority.
(d) There was hardly any focus on agriculture-based industries.

14. **Identify the correct pair.** **Competency Based Que**
(a) Planning Commission-1949
(b) First Five-Year Plan-1951
(c) Third Five-Year Plan-1980
(d) Fourth Five-Year Plan-1966

15. **The Forth Five-Year Plan in India was delayed and 'Plan-Holiday' was declared due to ....**
(a) political instability (b) economic crisis
(c) national disaster (d) international presence

16. **Which of the following was the key focus of Five-Year Plan.**
(a) Industrial
(b) Agrarian sector and land reform
(c) Expansion of foreign trade
(d) Development of technology

17. **Which one among the following statements NOT the objective of NITI Aayog?** **CBSE 2025**
(a) Provide a critical directional and strategic input to the development process of India
(b) Serve as a think tank of the government both at the centre and state level.
(c) Arrange funds for the implementation of developmental programmes.
(d) Seek to put an end to the slow and tardy implementation of the policies.

18. **Consider the following statements about the NITI Aayog.** **Competency Based Que; Modified CBSE 2021**
I. It was abolished because it became old.
II. The Prime Minister of India is the ex-officio chairperson of the NITI Aayog.
III. It replaced the Planning Commission.
IV. It was formed just after the independence.
Which of the above statement/s is/are correct?
(a) I and IV (b) II, IV
(c) II and III (d) All of these

19. **Consider the following statements about the Second Five-Year Plan.** **Competency Based Que; Modified CBSE 2021**
I. Huge allocations were made for large scale projects like the Bhakra Nangal Dam.
II. The government put tariffs on the imports.
III. It focused upon the rapid industrialisation.
IV. It was drafted under the leadership of P.C. Mahalanobis.
Which of the above statement/ s is/are correct?
(a) I and II (b) II and IV
(c) Only III (d) II, III and IV

20. **Arrange in sequence.** **Competency Based Que**
I. Abolition of Planning Commission
II. Formation of Planning Commission
III. Formation of NITI Aayog
IV. Release of First Five-Year Plan
Codes
(a) I, II, III and IV (b) II, I, III and IV
(c) II, IV, I and III (d) IV, III, II and I

21. **Indian statistical institute was set up in ....**
(a) 1930 (b) 1940
(c) 1931 (d) 1942

Assertion-Reason Questions

Directions (Q. Nos. 22-26) In the questions given below, there are two statements marked as Assertion (A) and Reason (R). Read the statements and choose the correct option.

Codes
(a) Both A and R are true and R is the correct explanation of A.
(b) Both A and R are true, but R is not the correct explanation of A.
(c) A is true, but R is false.
(d) A is false, but R is true.

22. **Assertion** (A) Industrialisation in Orissa has led to displacement of tribal communities.
Reason (R) Large-scale industries require vast areas of land, which were located in tribal regions.

23. **Assertion** (A) Industrialisation contributes to economic growth but harms the environment.
Reason (R) Industries consume natural resources and release pollutants into the air and water.

24. **Assertion** (A) NITI Aayog acts in the spirit of co-operative federalism.
Reason (R) It ensures equal participation of all states in the country. **CBSE Term I, 2021**

25. **Assertion** (A) The First Five-Year Plan addressed, mainly the agrarian sector including investment in dams and irrigation.
Reason (R) Agricultural sector was hit haldest by partition and needed urgent attention.

26. **Assertion** (A) The Second Five-Year Plan focused on only small industries.
Reason (R) It aimed to make India self-reliant by reducing dependence on foreign imports.

Passage Based Questions

27. **Read the passage given below carefully and answer the questions that follow.**
The Planning Commission of India opted for Five-Year Plan (FYP) like in the USSR. Five-Year Plan (FYPs) are centralised and integrated national economic programmes. Under this Government of India prepares a plan document for all its income and expenditure for the next five years. The budget of the Central and all the State Government was divided into two parts i.e. plan budget that is spent on priorities of next five years and non-plan budget that is spent on routine items on yearly basis. The draft of the First Five-Year Plans and the actual plan document was released in December, 1951.

(i) **Five-Year Plan was opted by the Planning Commission of India as it followed the model of ....**
(a) USA (b) United Kingdom
(c) USSR (d) China

(ii) **Plan budget of the government is defined as ......**
(a) budget which is allotted for priorities items of the nation.
(b) budget which is allotted for routine items of the nation.
(c) budget which is allotted for poverty alleviation.
(d) All of the above

(iii) **The First Five-Year Plan was implemented in ......**
(a) 1950 (b) 1951
(c) 1952 (d) 1953

(iv) **Why there is a need of Five-Year Plan?**
(a) For growth and development of the country.
(b) It helps in eradicating poverty.
(c) Helps to boost the economy through different measures.
(d) All of the above

28. **Read the passage given below carefully and answer the questions that follow.**
The socialist model followed in USSR. The leaders of the Communist Party of India and the leaders of Socialist Party like Nehru were deeply impressed by the Soviet model of development. The main reason to support this model was that the economic concerns of independent India would have to be different from colonial government. The tasks of poverty alleviation, social and economic re-distribution were regarded as the primary responsibility of the government.

(i) **The socialist model is based upon the principles of ....**
(a) socialism (b) liberal economy
(c) state controlled economy (d) Both (a) and (c)

(ii) **Why developing country like India supported the Soviet model of development?**
(a) Due to the economic concerns of newly independent India.
(b) Due to Soviet ideology of welfarism.
(c) Due to state intervention policies of Soviet Union.
(d) Due to people's pressure.

(iii) **What was considered as the primary responsibility of state?**

29. **Read the passage given below carefully and answer the questions that follow**
On the eve of independence, India had before it, two models of modern development: the liberal-capitalist model as in much of Europe and the US and the socialist model as in the USSR. You have already studied these

two ideologies and read about the 'Cold War' between the two super powers. There were many in India then who were deeply impressed by the Soviet model of development. These included not just the leaders of the Communist Party of India, but also those of the Socialist Party and leaders like Nehru within the Congress. There were very few supporters of the American style capitalist development.

(i) **Which country represented the liberal-capitalist model of development?**

(a) USSR (b) China
(c) Europe and the US (d) Japan

(ii) **What aspect of the Soviet model appealed to Indian leaders like Nehru?**

(a) Focus on capitalist growth.
(b) Rapid industrialisation and state-led development.
(c) Emphasis on free-market policies.
(d) Avoidance of economic planning.

(iii) **Why were there few supporters of the American-style capitalist model in India?**

Answers

1. (d) Both (a) and (c) 2. (d) All of the above
3. (b) Soviet model of development.
4. (d) All of the above 5. (b) Planning Commission
6. (c) a resolution of Government of India
7. (a) it was becoming irrelevant to face the new challenges of development
8. (a) planned development
9. (c) K.N. Raj
10. (a) P.C. Mahalanobis
11. (b) They support government policies which are for the benefit of poor sections.
12. (b) Prime Minister of India
13. (a) It was significantly different from the Second Five-Year Plan.
14. (b) First Five-Year Plan-1951
15. (b) economic crisis
16. (b) Agrarian sector and land reform
17. (c) Arrange funds for the implementation of developmental programmes.
18. (c) II and III
19. (d) II, III and IV
20. (c) II, IV, I and III
21. (c) 1931
22. (a) Both A and R are true and R is the correct explanation of A.
23. (a) Both A and R are true and R is the correct explanation of A.
24. (a) Both A and R are true and R is the correct explanation of A.
25. (a) Both A and R are true and R is the correct explanation of A.
26. (d) A is false, but R is true.
27. (i) (c) USSR
    (ii) (a) budget which is allotted for priorities items of the nation.
    (iii) (b) 1951
    (iv) (d) All of the above
28. (i) (d) Both (a) and (c)
    (ii) (b) Due to Soviet ideology of welfarism.
    (iii) The primary responsibility of state was poverty alleviation and socio-economic re-distribution in the society.
29. (i) (c) Europe and the US
    (ii) (b) Rapid industrialisation and state-led development.
    (iii) There were few supporters of the American-style capitalist model in India because, it was associated with exploitation and economic inequality. And India, as a newly independent country, needed strong government intervention to address poverty and ensure equitable resource distribution.

Subjective Questions

Very Short Answer Type Questions

1. Write the meaning and importance of economic planning in the Indian context.

Ans. Economic planning is a strategy to achieve the goal of economic development by pursuing a policy of planned economy. Planning always play a crucial role in the economic development of the country.

Planning opens new opportunities for development of people and also enhance the standard of living.

2. Name the two models of development before India on the eve of independence. **CBSE 2024**

Ans. On the eve of independence, there were two models of development

(i) Socialist model based in USSR

(ii) Liberal-capitalist model in USA

3. List two models of development and give reason for the model adopted by India. **CBSE SQP 2024**

Ans. The two models of development are the liberal-capitalist model in USA and the socialist model based in USSR.

India adopted the socialist model because of the following reasons

(i) Most of the leaders were impressed by the Soviet model of development.

(ii) The leaders were concerned about the elimination of poverty and to provide the socio-economic justice and it was found that the socialist model best suits this goal.

4. Differentiate between the capitalist and the socialist models of development.

Ans. The difference between the capitalist and socialist models of development is discussed below

Capitalist Model of Development	Socialist Model of Development
The capitalist economic model allows free market conditions to drive innovation and wealth creation.	The socialist based economy involves elements of centralised economic planning, utilised to ensure conformity and to encourage equality of opportunity and economic outcome.
Example of this model of development is USA.	Example of this model of development is USSR.

5. What appealed to Indian leaders about the Soviet model of development?

Ans. The Soviet model of development appealed to Indian leaders because it demonstrated rapid industrial growth through state-led planning. It showed how a nation could modernise its economy while ensuring social equality.

Leaders believed this approach could help India overcome poverty and underdevelopment. Nehru and others appreciated its focus on collective welfare rather than individual profit, making it a suitable choice for a diverse and economically backward country like India.

6. Describe any two objectives of planning in India.

Ans. Two objectives of planning in India are

(i) To ensure optimal utilisation of scarce resources.

(ii) To bring desired socio-economic changes rapidly.

7. In which year was 'NITI Aayog' constituted and which organisation did it replace? **CBSE 2024**

Ans. NITI Aayog was constituted in 2015 and it replaced Planning Commission of India.

8. Explain any two reasons for the formation of the NITI Aayog in place of the Planning Commission. **Competency Based Que; CBSE 2023**

Ans. The two reasons for the formation of the NITI Aayog in place of the Planning Commission are

(i) To evolve a shared vision of national development priorities, sectors and strategies with the active involvement of states.

(ii) To foster co-operative federalism through structured support initiatives and mechanisms with the states on a continuous basis, recognising that strong states make a strong nation.

9. How did the First Five-Year Plan address the issue of poverty and inequality?

Ans. The First Five-Year Plan addressed poverty and inequality by focusing on the agricultural sector, which employed the majority of the population. Investments were made in irrigation projects like the Bhakra Nangal Dam, to improve productivity.

The plan also emphasised land reforms to address unequal land distribution. By promoting food security and rural development, the plan aimed to uplift rural communities and reduce poverty.

10. Who was P.C. Mahalanobis?

Ans. P.C. Mahalanobis was a scientist and statistician of international repute and was also the founder of Indian Statistical Institute. He was architect of Second Five-Year Plan and supported rapid industrialisation and active role of the public sector.

11. Who was the main architect of the Second Five-Year Plan? What did the Second Five-Year Plan stress upon? CBSE 2024

Ans. World famous statistician, P.C. Mahalanobis was the main architect of the Second Five-Year Plan.

The Second Five-Year Plan stressed upon the structural transformation mainly in industrial sector. It focused upon the rapid industrialisation by protecting the domestic industries through taxation on imports from the foreign countries.

12. What were the main criticisms of India's Five-Year Plans?

Ans. While the Five-Year Plan contributed to India's development but they also faced several criticisms

- **Urban Bias** Industrialisation was prioritised over agriculture and neglected rural development.
- **Inefficiency** It failed to address regional and local needs.
- **Overemphasis on Public Sector** Private investment was restricted, which limited innovation and competition.
- **Environmental Neglect** Large projects like dams caused displacement and ecological damage.

Short Answer Type Questions

1. How does the term 'development' has different meaning for different sections? Explain with the help of examples. Competency Based Que

Ans. The term 'development' has different meanings for the different sections of the society in the following manner

(i) The iron mining may be an economic opportunity for the government and industries but it is a matter of concern for the tribal people living in that area.These tribal people might fear of displacement and loss of their livelihoods.

(ii) The idea of development sometimes refers to the western idea of modernisation which means to adopt new culture and discarding our own traditions and cultures.

2. Describe briefly the composition and any four functions of the Planning Commission of India.

Ans. Composition of Planning Commission are

- The Prime Minister of India is the Chairman of the commission.
- The commission has a Deputy Chairman.
- The Finance Minister and Planning Minister are the ex-officio members of the commission.
- The commission has four to seven full time expert members.

Four functions of the Planning Commission are

(i) To make an assessment of material, capital and human resources of the country and investigate the possibilities of augmenting them.

(ii) To formulate a plan for the most effective and balanced utilisation of the country's resources.

(iii) To determine priorities and to define stages in which the plan should be carried out.

(iv) To indicate the factors that retard economic development.

3. How was the Planning Commission of India set-up? Mention its scope of work.

Ans. The Planning Commission was set-up by a simple resolution passed by Government of India in March 1950. The Planning Commission has a advisory role and its recommendations become effective when government approves them.

The Planning Commission drafts the Five-Year Plan for India keeping all resources in mind, when it is drafted.

The Constitution of India has guaranteed certain Fundamental Rights to the citizens of India and enunciated certain Directive Principles of State Policy in particular that the state shall strive to promote the welfare of the people by securing and protecting a social order in which justice, social, economic and political shall direct its policy towards securing among other things.

The resolution which set-up the commission defined the scope of its work in the following terms

- That the citizen, men or women equally have the right to an adequate means of livelihood.
- That the ownership and control of the material resources of the community are so distributed as best to serve the common good.
- That the operation of the economic system does not result in the concentration of wealth and means of production to the common detriment.

4. What was early initiative taken by the Government of India under the planned economy?

Ans.
- Government of India established the Planning Commission in 1950. The Planning Commission of India opted for Five-Year Plan (FYP) on the similar grounds in USSR.
- The Government of India prepared a document plan which had all the income and expenses for the next five years.This budget included the expenditure for both the Central and the State Governments.

- The budget was divided into two parts-plan budget that will have routine expenses. The other was non-plan which will be fixed on yearly basis.

5. Analyse the key controversies regarding development strategies in the early years of Planned Economic developments in India. **Diksha App**

Ans. **Agriculture Vs. Industry**

- Many people emphasised that Five-Year Plans should give priority to agriculture and rural development. It would benefit the majority of the population.
- Others argued that only a rapid increase in industrial production can alleviate poverty, so the focus should be on the industrial sector.

Public Vs. Private Sector

- Under a mixed economy model, much of the agriculture, trade and industry was left in the Private hands and state-controlled key heavy industries. A mixed model like this was open to criticism by both the left and the right.
- Rightists argued that the private sector was not provided adequate space and stimulus to grow. The public sector created hurdles for private capital. Leftists criticised the development strategy for not spending significant amounts on public education and health care.

Long Answer Type Questions

1. What does the example of Orissa reveal about the complexities of development?

Ans. Orissa's case highlights that development is not a one-size-fits-all solution. While industrialisation brings economic growth, it also raises concerns about displacement, environmental damage and cultural loss. Different stakeholders such as government, industries, tribal communities and environmentalists have conflicting interests.

This example shows that development must balance economic progress with social and environmental sustainability. Policies must include

- Respect for tribal rights and livelihoods.
- Effective rehabilitation and compensation.
- Sustainable practices to minimise environmental harm.

The Orissa case emphasises the need for inclusive and participatory decision-making in development projects to ensure fairness and long-term success.

2. What do you understand by planning in economic sense? Give reasons why planning was adopted as a strategy for the Indian economic development.

Or **What were the major areas of consensus regarding the economic development model in India after independence?** **Diksha App**

Ans. Planning in economic refers to the process of making decisions about the allocation of resources to achieve specific objectives. It involves setting goals, identifying available resources and developing strategies to utilise those resources effectively.

Planning was adopted as a strategy for the Indian economic development because

- During the 1940s and 1950s, the idea of planning was widely supported as a process of re-building economy all over the world.
- Despite of great depression in Europe, the planned economy of Soviet experienced spectacular growth.
- Most of our nationalist leader, specially Nehru was influenced by the Soviet model of planning.
- Some of the big industrialists also drafted a proposal called Bombay Plan to propose the planning for economic growth.
- Thus planning emerged as the best suitable option for economic growth from left to right after independence.

3. Highlight any three features of the First Five-Year Plan. **CBSE 2023, 2024**

Ans. The three features of the First Five-Year Plan are as follows

(i) It addressed mainly the agriculture sector. The big scale projects like Bhakra Nangal Dam Project was decided to be launched. Huge money was allocated for such irrigation projects.

(ii) The idea of land reforms was identified necessary because it was felt that improper land distribution is the main cause of the poor condition of the agriculture. Thus, it was decided to carry the land reforms.

(iii) One of the basic aims of the planners was to raise the level of national income.

4. **How did the First Five-Year Plan differed from the Second Five-Year Plan?**

Ans.

First Five-Year Plan	Second Five-Year Plan
It was drafted by young economist, K.N. Raj.	It was drafted under the leadership of famous statistician and economist P.C. Mahalanobis.
It focused on the slower growth of Indian economy.	It focused on the faster growth of Indian economy.
It emphasised upon the growth of the agricultural sector.	It emphasised upon the growth of the industrial sector.
It proposed heavy investments in the irrigation and dam projects like the domestic industries Bhakra Nangal Dam.	It proposed to heavily invest in industries like steel, railway, machineries protect etc.
It carried out land reforms to improve agriculture.	It imposed tariffs on the imports to protect the domestic industries from foreign competition.

5. **Explain three major outcomes of planned economic development in India.** **Diksha App**

Ans. (i) During the First Five-Year plan, major irrigation projects were undertaken to improve the agriculture.

(ii) The land reforms also improved the agricultural growth in India. The savings of people also rose during the first phase of the planned development.

(iii) The protected environment of tariffs on foreign imports boosted the domestic industrial growth. It helped both public and private sector industries to grow.

(iv) The savings and investments were also growing during this period. Therefore industries like electricity, steel, machineries and communication could be developed in the public sector, thus, industrialisation marked a turning point in India's development.

(v) Despite of the development India had to face some problems. India had to spend its foreign exchange to buy technology from the global market.

Since the focus became more on the industrial investment, thus, agriculture received lesser investment which lead to the food shortage. Thus, planned development was sometimes criticised as 'urban bias'.

Picture Based Question

1. **Observe the picture given below and answer the following questions.**

(i) Choose the correct statement about the event that has been depicted in the above picture?

(a) Jawaharlal Nehru meeting the members of Constituent Assembly.
(b) Jawaharlal Nehru addressing his cabinet after the elections of 1951.
(c) Jawaharlal Nehru addressing the staff of Planning Commission.
(d) Jawaharlal Nehru meeting a delegate of businessmen.

Ans. (c) Jawaharlal Nehru addressing the staff of Planning Commission.

(ii) Why was planning adopted for Indian development strategy?

(a) It gained consensus from every section.
(b) It gained support as a process of re-building economy.
(c) Big industrialists also proposed to have planning.
(d) All of the above

Ans. (d) All of the above

(iii) The Planning Commission was replaced by NITI Aayog in ....

(a) 2014
(b) 2015
(c) 2016
(d) 2017

Ans. (b) 2015

(iv) Who was the Chairperson of Planning Commission?

(a) The President
(b) The Vice-President
(c) The Prime Minister
(d) The Speaker of Lok Sabha

Ans. (c) The Prime Minister

SELF ASSESSMENT TEST

Objective Type Questions

1. The Bombay Plan was proposed in ....

   (a) 1940 (b) 1942 (c) 1944 (d) 1945

2. Why did Nehru emphasise the need for a Planning Commission?

   (a) To regulate elections (b) To develop a centralised strategy for ecnomic growth

   (c) To strength military power (d) To manage educational policies

3. The Second Five-Year Plan emphasised upon ....

   (a) agriculture (b) heavy industries (c) foreign exchange (d) foreign direct investments

Very Short Answer Type Questions

4. What do you mean by left and right ideologies in an economy?
5. How is modernisation described ?
6. Differentiate between the 'plan' and 'non-plan' budget.

Short Answer Type Questions

7. The Planning Commission was not a sudden invention. Elucidate.
8. Why did the Government of India decide to take a 'Plan Holiday' During 1960s ?
9. Which type of industries began to flourish during the Second Five-Year Plan? Can you mention any one reason?
10. Write short note on NITI Aayog.

Long Answer Type Questions

11. "India should hasten slowly for the first two decades as a fast rate of development might endanger democracy". Justify the statement. **Competency Based Que**
12. What were the problems faced by India during rapid industrialisation? How did critics take these plans as an impact upon the national economy?
13. How did the first Two Five-Year Plan impact the Indian economy?

04

CHAPTER

This chapter introduces the foreign policy adopted by Jawaharlal Nehru during the Indian Independence. The chapter discusses about the various conflicts and peace agreements of India with its neighbours like Pakistan and China. It also highlights India's Nuclear Policy.

India's External Relations

YOUR STUDY GOALS

4.1 International Context
4.2 Peace and Conflict with China
4.3 Wars and Peace with Pakistan
4.4 India's Nuclear Policy

YOUR PRACTICE GOAL

- Objective Type Questions (37 Qs ; MCQs, A-R, Matching, Passage Based)
- Subjective Questions (8 VSAs, 10 SAs, 7 LAs 2 Picture Based)

4.1 International Context

- When India became independent, other countries also became free from the British rule. This period was very challenging because the world has witnessed a war and every country was trying to recover from the devastating effects of the war. The new countries which became independent were facing **twin challenges**. These twin challenges were welfare of the citizens of the country and to establish the democracy after such exploiting British rule.
- British had left many problems for the newly independent India like
  - Issue of partition
  - International disputes
  - Poverty
- This was the overall context in which India started participating in the world affairs as an independent nation state.
- Indian Government decided to conduct its foreign relations with an aim to respect the sovereignty of all other nations and to achieve security through maintaining the peace.
- Foreign policy of any nation is determined by both the **internal** and **external factors**. To pursue foreign policy, the developing countries consider the following factors
  - Moderate goals because they lack in resources.
  - Focus more on peace and development in their neighbourhood.

- Usually they are dependent upon the more powerful nations for their economy and security.
- Just after the **Second World War**, the whole world was being divided into the **two camps**, on the basis of aid or credit.
  - Under the United States and its Western country **allies**[1]
  - Under the Soviet Union
- India however, experimented with the policy of **Non-Aligned Movement**. This meant that India was not inclined to any of the above mentioned camps ideologically. India choose to pursue its national interests while maintaining the relations with any foreign country. This policy of non-alignment was challenged when **Cold War**[2] began.

The Policy of Non-Alignment

- Indian National Movement had inspired the liberation movements of many **Asian** and **African countries,** which were earlier British colonies. During the Second World War, **Netaji Subhash Chandra Bose** established the **Indian National Army (INA)** which proves that even before independence, our leaders had relations with the leaders of other colonies. They were united in their common struggle against colonialism and imperialism.
- Indian Foreign Policy was inspired by the similar goals of Indian freedom struggle. These goals were to fight against the **colonialism**[3] and **imperialism**[4]. Thus, while framing its foreign policy, India had to consider the following events that were happening at the time of its independence
  - Beginning of the Cold War between the two **superpowers**[5] the USSR and the US.
  - Establishment of the United Nations
  - Creation of the nuclear weapons
  - Emergence of the communist China
  - Beginning of decolonisation

Nehru's Role

- Being the Prime Minister as well as the Foreign Minister of independent India, **Jawaharlal Nehru** played a crucial role in setting the national agenda. He himself framed and implemented the foreign policy for the newly independent India from 1946-1964.
- The three **key objectives** of his foreign policy were as follows
  - To preserve India's sovereignty which had been earned through struggle against the British.
  - To protect the territorial integrity.
  - To promote rapid economic development.
- Nehru wanted to achieve these objectives through the strategy of non-alignment.
- There were some leaders like, Dr. Ambedkar and some political parties like, Bharatiya Jana Sangh and the Swatantra Party. These parties opposed communism and wanted India to follow pro-US foreign policy. But, Nehru followed a different approach in formulating foreign policy.

1 **Allies** It refers to the people, countries or groups that work on common goal. Here, it is referred to the countries that supported the US cause during the world war.

2 **Cold War** It is a state of political conflict (silent war), between the countries characterised by threats and propaganda. This ideology of Cold War existed in mid 1940s to the late 1980s between the capitalist US and socialist USSR.

3 **Colonialism** It is a practice when one country establishes the control over the territory of another country either through economic dominance or military.

4 **Imperialism** It is a political system in which a powerful country controls over other countries, which are not powerful.

5 **Superpower** During the Cold War, there were two dominant countries in terms of economic power and military strength. These countries were the US and the USSR.

The Constitutional Principles

Article 51 of the Indian Constitution lays down Directive Principles of State Policy on 'Promotion of international place and security'. The state shall endeavour to

- Promote international peace and security.
- Maintain just and honourable relations between nations.
- Foster respect for international law and treaty obligations in the dealings of organised people with one another.
- Encourage settlement of international disputes by arbitration.

Distance from Two Camps

- India wanted to advocate the idea of peace in the world by reducing Cold War tensions and by contributing human resources to the UN peacekeeping operations[6].
- It did not join any military alliance led by the US or the USSR. India remained non-aligned during the US led **North Atlantic Treaty Organisation** (NATO) and Soviet-led **Warsaw Pact**.
- India did face some difficulties due to its policy of non-alignment. When Britain attacked Egypt in 1956 over the **Suez Canal issue**, India strongly criticised it as a new form of colonialism. However, When Soviet Union entered into Hungary, it did not criticise the act publicly.
- Despite such as situation, India maintained its independent stand on many international issues events and could get assistance from both the sides of camps during the Cold War era.
- There were some problems in the **India-US relationship** during the 1950s. It was because when India was trying to convince other developing nations to follow the non-alignment, **Pakistan** joined the US camp. The US was not happy with India's non-alignment. It also disliked the growing partnership of India and Soviet.

Afro-Asian Unity

- Nehru considered the size, location and power potential of India, which played an important role in the world affairs especially, in **Asian affairs**. Under his leadership, India held the Asian Relations Conference in March 1947. He played a key role in promoting Asian unity during 1940s and 1950s. He established contacts with the newly independent African nations too.
- India also supported **Indonesian freedom** from **Dutch colonial rule** by convening an international conference in 1949. India strongly opposed racism, apartheid in South Africa and supported decolonisation.
- In 1955, the **Afro-Asian Conference** was held in Bandung, Indonesia which was also known as the **Bandung Conference**. This marked a new beginning of Afro-Asian relations and later led to the establishment of NAM[7] **(Non-Aligned Movement)** which was co-founded by Jawaharlal Nehru. The first summit of NAM was held in Belgrade in September 1961.

Quick Test 1

1. What were the twin challenges for the newly colonised countries?
2. Which factors determined the foreign policy of any nation?
3. Name the leaders and political parties that, wanted India to follow pro-US policy?
4. Which article of Indian Constitution focuses on promotion of International peace and security?
5. Where was first summit of NAM held?

6 UN Peacekeeping Operation UN peacekeeping operations are deployed by the United Nations to maintain or restore peace in areas affected by conflict.

7 NAM Non Alignment Movement which was initiated by Prime Minister Jawaharlal Nehru and other leaders like, Kwame Nkrumah from Ghana, to advance interests of developing countries in the context of Cold War.

4.2 Peace and Conflict with China

- Unlike Pakistan, India had began friendly relations with China. India was one of the first countries to identify the **Communist Government in China** after the Communist revolution in 1949.
- For many years, Chinese borders were guarded by **para-military forces** rather than army because Nehru felt that China would never become threat for India. However, **Sardar Vallabhbhai Patel** believed that China may show aggression in future towards India.
- Nehru was impressed with the **Chinese leader Zhou Enlai** who was coming out of the Western influence. He signed **Panchsheel Agreement** with Zhou Enlai on 29th April, 1954, in which they mentioned the five principles of peaceful co-existence.
- This marked the era of new friendship. Both the leaders visited each other's countries. They were welcomed and greeted by large crowds on both sides.

▲ *Principles of Foreign Policy of India*

The Chinese Invasion, 1962

- The friendly relations soured between India and China because of the following reasons
  - China annexed Tibet due to which the **buffer zone**[8] was abolished between the two nations. India opposed China when it came to know about the suppression of Tibetan culture by China. The Tibetan spiritual leader **Dalai Lama** took political **asylum**[9] in India in 1959. China accused India of allowing anti-China activities in its territory.
  - A **boundary dispute** occurred between India and China due to British territorial markings. The land which was claimed by India was not accepted by China. The main dispute occurred on the following regions
    - China claimed two areas of the Indian territory, one **Aksai-Chin** area in Ladakh region of Jammu and Kashmir.
    - Another **Arunachal Pradesh,** which was called **NEFA** (North Eastern Frontier Agency) at that time.
  - China occupied the Aksai-Chin area between 1957-59, and built strategic road in the region. Despite official talks, this issue could not be resolved.
  - China took the ill advantage of **Cuban Missile Crisis** between the two super powers and launched an attack on the disputed region of Indian territory in October, 1962.

8 **Buffer Zone** It refers to an area situated between two powerful rival countries. The buffer zone acts as a neutral zone and act as a barrier between the two countries preventing them from war.

9 **Asylum** It means the protection that a government gives to people, who have left their own country usually because they were in danger for political reasons.

- The first attack went for a week and Chinese forces captured some areas of Arunachal Pradesh. Then, **second wave of attack** came next month. Indian forces were trying to block the Chinese in the Western region, Chinese came inside the Eastern India till Assam plains.
- China itself declared a **unilateral ceasefire** and announced its army to withdraw to the point where they were before the attack.

▪ This invasion by China affected India in many ways which are as follows

- India's image as a sovereign nation was humiliated at the international level. India had to ask for the military assistance from Americans and British. The Soviet Union remained neutral during this conflict.
- Indian top army commanders resigned, including the then Defence Minister and a close associate of Nehru V.K. Krishna Menon.
- Nehru himself was humiliated as he was blamed for lack of military preparedness.

V. K. Krishna Menon (1897-1974)

He was a diplomat and minister. He was active in UK between 1934-47 in the Labour Party. Later he was appointed as the Defence Minister of India but resigned in 1962 after India-China War.

Sino-India Relations since 1962

In 1976 full diplomatic relations were restored between India and China. It took more than a decade to normalise the relations with China. **Atal Bihari Vajpayee** was the first top level leader to visit China in 1979 when he was External Affairs Minister. Later, Rajiv Gandhi became the first Prime Minister to visit China after Nehru. Since then, the emphasis is more on maintaining trade relations with China.

- This was the first time, **No-confidence motion** was passed in Lok Sabha against the Nehru government along with lot of debates in the Lok Sabha.
- Congress also lost some of the by-elections to Lok Sabha.
- The Chinese attack on the North-Eastern region alerted Indian authorities. This region was isolated and not much developed. Thus, considering its volatile location and situation, major re-organisation took place in North-Eastern region.
- **Nagaland** was given statehood. **Manipur** and **Tripura** got the right to elect their own legislative assemblies despite of being union territories.

▪ The political mood of the country also changed after the Chinese invasion. It not only affected the opposition but many parties too got split. The Sino-Indian conflict and the growing tension between China and USSR led to the division of Communist Party of India. The Pro-USSR faction remained within the **CPI** and Pro-China formed Communist Party of India (Marxist) **CPI(M)** in 1964.

▪ The CPI (M) leaders were also arrested for being Pro-China.

Tibet

- Tibet is a Plateau of Central Asian region. From time to time, China had claimed administrative control over Tibet.
- In 1950, it was captured by China. Large sections of Tibetan population opposed this capture. India also tried to convince China to recognise Tibet's claims for independence.
- Due to the **Panchsheel Agreement**, which was signed between China and India, India had to accept Chinese claim on Tibet.
- China assured India that Tibet will be given greater autonomy than any other Chinese region. But when Chinese atrocities against Tibetans increased, the spiritual leader of Tibet, **Dalai Lama** had to cross the border and take asylum in India.
- This created tension between China and India. Dalai Lama made Dharamshala in Himachal Pradesh as his home which is the largest Tibetan settlement in India. There are many Tibetan refugee settlements in India like in Delhi and Himachal Pradesh.
- Many of the political parties in India like Jana Sangh and Socialist Party supported the Tibetan independence.
- China claims that Tibet is an autonomous region, but is an integral part of China. Tibetans argue that this autonomy is not a true autonomy and in real sense, China wants to undermine the traditional religion and culture of Tibet.

India Israel Relations

India's Foreign Policy with Israel remained unexplored notwithstanding the two nations gaining independence from the British colonial rule in 1947 and 1948 respectively. Both countries share historical and cultural ties from the past. But the formal diplomatic relations developed between the two after the opening of Israeli Embassy in India in 1992.

The relations between the two democratic nations are further intensified with the visits of the two heads of government i.e. PM Narendra Modi to Israel in 2017 and PM Benjamin Netanyahu to India in 2018. The two nations have started co-operation in various fields like cultural exchange, security, defence, counter terrorism, space research, water, energy and agricultural development.

Multiple collaborative agreements were signed between Indian and Israel during Modi's visit. Like for instance, The Israel Space Agency and the Indian Space Research Organisation signed an agreement to foster partnership in the development of electric propulsion systems for small satellites, and creating systems to accurately measure the extreme conditions of outer space.

Quick Test 2

1. In which year Britain attacked Egypt?
2. Which independent region was a buffer state between India and China?
3. Who was the Defence Minister during 1962 Chinese invasion?
4. Which two union territories got the right to elect their own legislative assembly after 1962?
5. Who was Dalai Lama?

4.3 Wars and Peace with Pakistan

- Conflict with Pakistan soon began after independence when Proxy War[10] broke out between the armies of India and Pakistan in Jammu and Kashmir. The conflict was referred to the **United Nations** and thereafter, Pakistan became a critical issue with the US and then with China.
- The Kashmir Conflict did not prevent co-operation between the Governments of India and Pakistan.

10 Proxy War An indirect conflict between the two nations through a third party.

- Despite the Kashmir problem, leaders of India and Pakistan worked together to restore the women kidnapped during the partition. The **World Bank** mediated the **Indus Water Treaty** for water sharing between India and Pakistan. It has been one of the most successful water sharing treaty. It was signed by **Prime Minister Nehru** and **General Ayub Khan** in 1960.
- In 1965, Pakistan launched armed attacks in **Rann of Kutch** area of Gujarat. This turned into a serious armed conflict. After Gujarat, Pakistan attacked offensively in **Jammu Kashmir** in August-September. Pakistan did not get any local support and the then Prime Minister Lal Bahadur Shastri ordered the army for a counter-offensive attack upon Pakistani army on Punjab border. In this battle Indian army reached close to **Lahore**.
- Later this issue reached **UN** and the war came to an end. In January 1966, **Prime Minister Lal Bahadur Shastri** went to Tashkent for signing **Tashkent Agreement** with the General Ayub. This agreement was mediated by the Soviet Union.

Kargil Confrontation

- During 1999, Mashkoh, Dras, Kaksar and Batalik areas on Indian LOC side were illegally occupied by forces who claimed as Mujahideens.
- Indian forces reacted against this as they had a doubt about the involvement of Pakistani army. This led to a confrontation between the two countries. This was known as **Kargil Conflict**.
- The Kargil Conflict went on during May and June 1999.
- By 26th July 1999, India recovered many of the captured points.
- It was alleged later that **Pakistani Prime Minister** was unaware of these steps by the Pakistani military. Soon after this incident, Pakistan was overtaken by Army Chief General Pervez Musharraf.

Bangladesh War, 1971

- During 1970s, Pakistan faced its biggest internal crisis due to the split in elections results. In the west Pakistan, **Zulfikar Ali Bhutto** emerged as winner and in the Eastern part **Sheikh Mujibur Rahman** from Awami League Party emerged as the winner. But, the Pakistani rulers were not accepting the victory of Awami League. The Bengali population in East Pakistan voted against Zulfikar. They were treated as second class citizens by the Government of West Pakistan.
- Pakistan did not accept the democratic decision of the elections. Pakistani army arrested Sheikh Mujib ur Rahman and created a terrorising effect in East Pakistan.
- People thus started a struggle to liberate **'Bangladesh'** from Pakistan. India extended the help to around 80 lakh refugees of Eastern Pakistan. Pakistan accused India of conspiracy to break it up.
- US and China supported Pakistan. US President's adviser Henry Kissinger visited China through Pakistan secretly in July 1971.
- To counter the **US-Pakistan-China axis,** India signed 20-year **Treaty of Peace and Friendship with the Soviet Union.** It assured Soviet support in case of any attack.
- In **December 1971,** a full scale war broke out between India and Pakistan after months of diplomatic and military tensions. Pakistani aircrafts attacked Punjab and Rajasthan and the army moved to the Jammu and Kashmir region.
- India retaliated with an attack by the **army, navy** and **airforce** on both the borders i.e. Eastern and Western. With the support of local people, India succeded to surround Dhakha (in Eastern Pakistan) within 10 days. Around 90,000 Pakistani army soldiers had to surrender. Bangladesh became a free country.
- Later on 3rd July, 1972, Indira Gandhi signed **Simla Agreement** with Zulfikar Ali Bhutto to formalise the return of peace. The Third Plan (1961-66) was affected and it was followed by Three Annual Plans. Fourth Plan could be initiated only in 1969.

- After 1962, Indian Government allocated more funds to the defence sector in their budget. Although India had lesser resources but it went for defence modernisation in several ways
  - The Department of Defence Production was established in November 1962.
  - The Department of Defence Supplies was established in November 1965.
  - India's defence expenditure increased enormously after the wars.

Quick Test 3

1. What do Tibet people accuse China of ?
2. Who was the Prime Minister of India during 1965 India-Pakistani Conflict?
3. Which organisation mediated the Indus Water Treaty between India and Pakistan?
4. Which treaty was signed between India and Soviet Union?
5. Who was the counter part of Indira Gandhi during the siging of Simla Agreement?

4.4 India's Nuclear Policy

- Nehru always had faith in science and technology. Thus, a significant component of his industrialisation plans, was his nuclear programme which was initiated in late 1940s under the guidance of **Homi J. Bhabha.**
- India under took the first nuclear explosion in May 1974. India wanted to generate atomic energy for peaceful purposes. India was always against the nuclear weapons. Nehru, pleaded the superpowers for comprehensive nuclear disarmament. China conducted nuclear test in October 1964. The five nuclear weapon powers, the US, USSR, France, UK and China tried to impose **Nuclear Non-Proliferation Treaty** of 1968 on rest of the world.
- India always found Non-Proliferation Treaty (NPT) by the five permanent members of the United Nations Security Council as discriminatory. Therefore, India refused to sign the treaty and conducted its first nuclear test. It was termed as peaceful explosion as India has always claimed that it will use the nuclear power only for peaceful purposes. Indian domestic politics was already suffering when the nuclear test were carried out. Due to Arab-Israel War in 1973 entire world was affected due to increase in oil prices. It led to the inflation and even national railway strike.
- Despite of differences between the political parties, Indian Foreign Policy has always adhered to the protection of international boundaries and national integration.
- Therefore, during the decade of 1962-1971, when India faced 3 wars, when different political parties came to power from time to time, foreign policy has played only a limited role in party politics.

India's Nuclear Programme

- India has opposed the international treaties like **non-proliferation** because they are discriminatory. These treaties allow only few countries to have nuclear weapon.
- Thus, India opposed **NPT extension in 1995** and refused to sign the **Comprehensive Test Ban Treaty (CTBT).**
- India conducted a series of nuclear tests in May 1998, which aimed to demonstrate the power to use nuclear energy for military purposes.
- Pakistan also began to prepare for the nuclear tests which made Indian sub-continent a vulnerable region. Thus, international community imposed restrictions upon both Pakistan and India.
- India follows the doctrine of **credible minimum deterrence**. It professes the policy of **'no first use'**.

- India's nuclear policy has always been peace-oriented, whose clear impression is reflected in the present the policy of 'No First Use'. But as per the contemporary regional security challenges, the present government led by PM Narendra Modi held that the policy of no first use can be reviewed and changed in accordance to the regional and national security.
- In addition to this, India is committed to ensure its membership in the Nuclear Suppliers Group (NSG) and opposes the unjust nuclear treaties like CTBT and NPT.

Shifting Alliances in World Politics

- The period of 1977 witnessed a change in world politics. In India, the Janata Party government came to power in 1977. It announced that it will follow the policy of non-alignment and the tilt towards Soviet Union would be corrected. Therefore, India, started to improve her relations with China and US.
- After 1990, ruling parties were criticised for being Pro-US.
- India's Foreign Policy always see two questions. First one is India's stand with respect to Pakistan and another is India's relation with US.
- When USSR disintegrated in 1990, Russia continued to be an important friend of India. But due to Russia's economic failure, India had to shift its interest towards the US.
- India also tried to normalise its ties with Pakistan through cultural exchanges, movement of its citizens and economic co-operation.
- A train and bus service to also started between India and Pakistan. However, such efforts could not avoid the war in 1999. Even after the war, efforts to maintain peace have been going on.

Quick Test 4

1. When India under took the first nuclear explosion?
2. What is CTBT?
3. Name the doctrine professed by India as parts of its nuclear policy.

Mind Map

INDIA'S EXTERNAL RELATIONS

1 International Context

Post-Independence Challenges
- **Twin challenges** Welfare of citizens and establishing democracy.
- **Legacy of British Rule** Partition, international disputes, poverty.

Foreign Policy of India
- Foreign policy of any nation is determined by internal and external factors.
- Foreign policy of India was based on
  - Respect sovereignty of other nations.
  - Achieve security through peace.

Cold War Era and Non-Aligned Movement
- World divided into two camps: US and USSR.
- India maintained independence in international issues.

Non-Aligned Movement
- India adopted the policy of non-alignment.
- Not inclined to any ideological camp.
- Pursue national interests while maintaining relations.

Nehru's Role
- Prime Minister and Foreign Minister.
- Framed and implemented foreign policy (1946-1964).

Key Objectives of his Foreign Policy
- Preserve sovereignty.
- Protect territorial integrity.
- Promote rapid economic development.

Afro-Asian Unity
- Asian Relations Conference.
- Held in March 1947.
- Promoting Asian unity.

Afro-Asian Conference
- Held in Bandung, Indonesia (1955).
- Marked beginning of Afro-Asian relations.
- Led to establishment of Non-Aligned Movement (NAM).

2 Peace and Conflict with china

Early Relations
- India recognised Communist Government in China in 1950.
- Nehru and Zhou Enlai signed Panchsheel Agreement in 1954.
- Five principles of peaceful co-existence.

Border Disputes
- **Tibet** China annexed Tibet, abolished buffer zone.
- **Aksai-Chin** China occupied area in Ladakh region.
- **Arunachal Pradesh** China claimed area as its own.

1962 Chinese Invasion
- China launched attack on Indian territories.
- India's image humiliated internationally.
- Top army commanders resigned, including Defence Minister V.K. Krishna Menon.

Aftermath
- Full diplomatic relations were restored in 1976.
- Emphasis on maintaining trade relations.
- Reorganisation of North-Eastern region.

3 War and Peace with Pakistan

Early Conflicts
- Proxy War broke out in Jammu and Kashmir after independence.
- Conflict brought to the United Nations, making Pakistan a critical factor for India's relations with the US and China.

Key Agreements and Treaties

Indus Water Treaty (1960)
- Mediated by the World Bank for water sharing between India and Pakistan.
- Considered one of the most successful water sharing treaties.

Tashkent Agreement (1966)
- Mediated by the Soviet Union to end the Indo-Pakistani War of 1965.

Simla Agreement (1972)
- Formalised the return of peace after the Bangladesh War of 1971.

Treaty of Peace and Friendship (1971)
- 20-year treaty signed between India and the Soviet Union.
- Assured Soviet support to India in case of any attack.

Major Wars
- Indo-Pakistani War of 1965.
- Pakistan launched armed attacks in Rann of Kutch area of Gujarat.
- India counter-attacked by reaching close to Lahore.
- Tashkent Agreement signed in January 1966, mediated by the Soviet Union.

Bangladesh War of 1971
- Pakistan faced internal crisis due to split election results.
- India supported Bangladesh's liberation, leading to a full-scale war with Pakistan.
- India succeeded in surrounding Dhaka, leading to the surrender of 90,000 Pakistani soldiers.
- Simla Agreement signed in July 1972, formalising the return of peace.

Defence Modernisation

Department of Defence Production (1962)
- Established to modernise India's defence capabilities.

Department of Defence Supplies (1965)
- Established to improve defence supplies and logistics.

Increased Defence Expenditure.
- India increased its defence expenditure after the wars to modernise its military capabilities.

4 India's Nuclear Policy

India's Nuclear Doctrine
- **Credible Minimum Deterrence** India will never use nuclear weapons first.
- **No First Use** India will only retaliate to a nuclear attack.

Early Developments
- Initiated in late 1940s under Homi J. Bhabha's guidance.
- First nuclear explosion in May 1974.
- Aimed to generate atomic energy for peaceful purposes.

International Treaties and Agreements
- Nuclear Non-Proliferation Treaty (NPT).
- India refused to sign due to discriminatory nature.
- Allows only five countries to possess nuclear weapons.
- India opposed NPT extension in 1995.

Comprehensive Test Ban Treaty (CTBT)
- India refused to sign.
- Conducted nuclear tests in May 1998 to demonstrate military capabilities.

NCERT Folder

1. Write 'True' or 'False' against each of these statements.

(i) Non-alignment allowed India to gain assistance both from USA and USSR.

(ii) India's relationship with her neighbours has been strained from the beginning.

(iii) The Cold War has affected the relationship between India and Pakistan.

(iv) The Treaty of Peace and Friendship in 1971 was the result of India's closeness to USA.

Ans. (i) True (ii) False (iii) True (iv) False

2. Match the following.

	List I		List II
A.	The goal of India's Foreign Policy in the period 1950-1964.	1.	Tibetan spiritual leader who crossed over to India.
B.	Panchsheel Agreement	2.	Preservation of territorial integrity, sovereignty and economic development.
C.	Bandung Conference	3.	Five principles of peaceful co-existence.
D.	Dalai Lama	4.	Led to the establishment of NAM.

Ans. A-2 B-3 C-4 D-1

3. Why did Nehru regard conduct of foreign relations as an essential indicator of independence? State any two reasons with examples to support your reading.

Ans. Independent conduct of foreign policy shows that nation is free from fear and favour of any strong nation. This is why, Nehru decided to independently conduct its foreign policy without being influenced by US and USSR camps.

To Nehru, foreign policy was an essential indicator of independence because

(i) Independent foreign relation protect the sovereignty of nation in international system and can bring rapid economic development. Nehru pursued it in the form of NAM.

(ii) Independent foreign relation respect the sovereignty of all other nations and protect security through the maintenance of peace. This proposition also echoed in the Directive Principles of State Policy of our Constitution.

4. "The conduct of foreign affairs is an outcome of a two-way interaction between domestic compulsions and prevailing international climate". Take one example from India's external relations in the 1960s to substantiate your answer. Competency Based Que

Ans. India's Foreign Policy in the 1960s was shaped by both domestic needs and global conditions. A key example is India's relationship with the Soviet Union. After the 1962 war with China and worsening ties with the U.S., India sought Soviet support for defense and economic development.

Domestically, India needed military strength and economic aid, while internationally, the Cold War influenced alliances. The Soviet Union provided weapons and technological assistance, strengthening India's position. This shows how India's Foreign Policy balanced internal challenges with global power dynamics, demonstrating the two-way interaction between domestic needs and the international climate.

5. Identify any two aspects of India's Foreign Policy that you would like to retain and two that you would like to change, if you were to become a decision maker. Give reasons to support your position.

Ans. Two aspects of India's Foreign Policy that should be retained are

(i) NAM as the ideal foreign policy approach of India since the beginning should be retained even today because India should not be the part of any camp in world politics. Instead, it should keep friendly relations with all nations to promote world peace.

(ii) Even today, Afro-Indian unity must be maintained to protect the energy needs and security of the nation.

Two aspects that needed to be changed are as follows

(i) India must be assertive to protect its interest with neighbours.

(ii) India should attempt to be a strong economy and military power to exercise greater role in international politics.

6. Write short notes on the following.

(i) India's Nuclear Policy

(ii) Consensus in foreign policy matters

Ans. (i) India's Nuclear Policy

- India advocates no first use and reiterates India's commitment to global verifiable on non-discriminatory nuclear disarmament leading to a nuclear weapon free world.
- Pt. Nehru always promoted 'science and technology to build' a modern India, i.e. initiated nuclear programme in the late 1940s under the guidance of Homi J. Bhabha.
- India was against nuclear weapons, hence pleaded for nuclear disarmament with superpowers.

- India always considered NPT as discriminatory and refused to sign on it.
- Even India's first nuclear test in May 1974 was termed as a peaceful explosion and India argued to use nuclear power for peaceful purposes only.

(ii) **Consensus in Foreign Policy Matters** Although, there are minor differences among the political parties about how to conduct foreign relation, however the foreign policy's concerns are same for every political party which has come to the power since the independence. There is a limited role of politics over foreign policy.

There have been consensus among all the major political parties over national integration, protection of international boundaries and on the questions of national interest.

Since independence, we have dispute with Pakistan and China. But, whether it be Congress or BJP or coalition government, there has been consensus to maintain trade and cultural exchange and scientific co-operation with them.

7. India's Foreign Policy was built around the principles of peace and co-operation. But India fought three wars in a space of ten years between 1962 and 1971. Would you say that this was a failure of the foreign policy? Or would you say that this was a result of international situation? Give reasons to support your answer.

Competency Based Que

Ans. No, this was not a failure of foreign policy but this was the result of international situation.

- As India's Foreign Policy was based upon the international system of different ideologies presented by two blocs i.e. USA and USSR.
- There were barriers in the way of establishing a territorial integrity and sovereignty between India and China as well as between India-Pakistan which resulted in full scale wars.
- At the global level, it was necessary for India to protect its democratic and political nature this is the reason that led India to participate in the wars.
- To preserve its national interest was another factor which led India to participate in the wars.

8. Does India's Foreign Policy reflect her desire to be an important regional power? Argue your case with the Bangladesh war of 1971 as an example.

Ans. Bangladesh War 1971

In 1970, Pakistan's first general election produced a split verdict. Zulfikar Ali Bhutto's party won in the West-Pakistan, whereas Awami League led by Sheikh Mujibur Rahman won in East Pakistan. Pakistani rulers were not ready to accept this democratic verdict nor were ready to accept demand of federation by Awami League.

Instead, in 1971, they arrested Sheikh Mujibur and started terrorising the people of East Pakistan. People responded with strong movement to liberate Bangladesh from Pakistan.

India's Role during Bangladesh War

- India provided shelter to about 80 lakh Bangladeshi refugees and gave moral and material support to freedom movement in Bangladesh. Pakistan blamed India for conspiracy to break it up.
- US and China supported Pakistan. To counter the US-Pakistan-China axis, India signed a 20-year Treaty of Peace and Friendship with Soviet Union in August 1971. This treaty assured Soviet support to India in case of any attack.
- After months of diplomatic tension and military preparation, a full-scale war between India and Pakistan started in December, 1971. Pakistani air force attacked Punjab and Rajasthan and its army march to the Jammu and Kashmir front.
- India responded with counter attack involving the air force, navy and the army on both the Eastern and Western front. With the support of local population, Indian army within 10 days surrounded Dhaka from three sides. And Pakistani army of about 90000 had to surrender before Indian army. With this, Bangladesh became independent and India declared a unilateral ceasefire.

Thus, we can conclude from above given points that during the Bangladesh war of 1971, India's Foreign Policy reflect its desire to be an important regional power.

9. How does political leadership of a nation affect its foreign policy? Explain this with the help of examples from India's Foreign Policy.

Ans. Political leadership of a nation always affect its foreign policy. There are two examples given below

(i) **Foreign Policy of Nehru** Nehru was the main architect of foreign policy after independence. He had a deep knowledge of world affairs.

He was the main leader to advocate the unity of the Asian nations. The main elements of his foreign policy were as follows

- Non-Alignment Movement.
- Panchsheel Agreement.
- Not to join any of the two blocs (US and USSR).
- To promote the international peace and co-operation.
- Nuclear disarmament and promoting democratic relationship with overseas.

(ii) **Foreign Policy of Shastri and Indira Gandhi** India faced war during the period of Shastri and Mrs. Gandhi. Both maintained the integrity and sovereignty of the country.

The foreign policy of both was focusing on the peace and prosperous development of India as well as with neighbouring states. They both were favouring the concept of Nehru's Non-Aligned Movement and made good relations with Asian and African countries.

When Janta Party came into power in 1977, it focused on the NAM and followed the principles of NAM. This resulted in change in the Pro-USSR foreign policy. Since then, all government attempted to have better relation with US and China.

10. Read this passage and answer the questions below.

"Broadly, non-alignment means not tying yourself off with military blocs..... It means trying to view things, as far as possible, not from the military point of view, though that has to come in sometimes, but independently, and trying to maintain friendly relations with all countries". **—Jawaharlal Nehru**

(i) Why does Nehru want to keep off military blocs?

(ii) Do you think that the Indo-Soviet friendship treaty violated the principle of non-alignment? Give reasons for your answer.

(iii) If there were no military blocs, do you think Non-alignment would have been unnecessary?

Ans. (i) Nehru wanted to keep off military blocs because he sought to maintain friendly and peaceful relations with all the countries of the world. And wanted to chalk out a new path in the form of NAM for newly independent countries of Asia, Africa and Latin America.

(ii) No, the Indo-Soviet Friendship Treaty did not violate the principle of non-alignment because Indo- Soviet friendship treaty was to counter US-China axis through diplomacy. It was not a military alliance but a diplomatic alliance to protect its interest.

(iii) No, apart from maintaining distance from both US and USSR camps, NAM was also a platform for newly independent countries of Asia, Africa and Latin America to discuss the issue of decolonisation, disarmament, terrorism, economic co-operation etc.

Exam Pattern Questions

Objective Type Questions

Multiple Choice Questions (MCQs)

1. Which of the following statements is not correct with respect to the aim of India's foreign relations? **Diksha App**

(a) To respect the sovereignty of all other nations.
(b) To achieve security through maintenance of peace.
(c) To align with the capitalist block.
(d) Aims of India's foreign relations find an echo in the Directive Principles of State Policy.

2. Which of the following was one of the main concerns for India after its independence?

(a) Economic development through exports
(b) Peace and security through international alliances
(c) Poverty alleviation and international disputes
(d) Establishment of a nuclear weapon programme

3. Which one of the following was not a major objective of Jawaharlal Nehru's foreign policy?

Or **What was not the major focus of the foreign policy of the newly independent nations immediately after the Second World War?** **Diksha App**

(a) To preserve the hard earned sovereignty of India.
(b) To protect the territorial integrity of India.
(c) To make India a nuclear power.
(d) To promote rapid economic development.

4. Which of the following issues led to the attack on Egypt in 1956 by Britain? **CBSE SQP 2024**

(a) Suez Canal issue (b) Suzhou Canal issue
(c) Panama Canal issue (d) Bruges Canal issue

5. Why did India follow the policy of Non-Alignment during the Cold War era?

(a) To avoid becoming part of either the US-led NATO or the Soviet-led Warsaw Pact
(b) To support the US in the Cold War
(c) To form an alliance with China
(d) To promote military expansion

6. India made earnest effort for the early realisation of freedom of Indonesia from the colonial regime of the .... **CBSE 2024**

(a) British (b) French (c) Portuguese (d) Dutch

7. Which conference marked the zenith of India's engagement with the newly independent Asian and African nations? CBSE SQP 2024

(a) Malaysian Conference (b) Singapore Conference
(c) Bandung Conference (d) Egyptian Conference

8. What was the objective of the Bandung Conference 1952? Diksha App

(a) First NAM Summit
(b) Afro-Asian Unity
(c) Formation of South-East Treaty Organisation
(d) None of the above

9. Where was the Afro-Asian Conflence held in 1955. CBSE 2024 C

(a) Jakarta (b) Bandung
(c) Bali (d) Jawa

10. The first NAM Summit was held in CBSE 2024 set 2

(a) Cairo (b) Belgrade
(c) India (d) Indonesia

11. There was considerable unease in Indo-US relations during the 1950s because CBSE 2024 set I

(a) India had a growing partnership with the Soviet Union.
(b) The Soviet Union, invaded Hungary.
(c) India was not a member of NATO.
(d) India was a founder of NAM.

12. In which year did India and China sign the Panchsheel Agreement. CBSE 2024 C

(a) 1950 (b) 1952
(c) 1954 (d) 1956

13. In which year did China annex Tibet? CBSE 2024

(a) 1950 (b) 1954
(c) 1960 (d) 1962

14. In which of the following countries did the Dalai Lama obtain political asylum? CBSE 2024

(a) Nepal (b) Bhutan (c) India (d) Myanmar

15. Which one of the following statements related to Indo-China War (1962) is correct? Competency Based Que; CBSE 2020

(a) China could not cross the line of control.
(b) The Soviet Union remained neutral during the conflict.
(c) The Soviet Union helped China against India.
(d) The Chinese forces did not withdraw their troops back to earlier position.

16. Which one of the following statements about India-China relations is not correct? Competency Based Que; CBSE Term I 2021

(a) The slogan 'Hindi Chini Bhai Bhai' was popular for a brief while only.
(b) China took over Tibet in 1950.
(c) India opposed China's entry into the UN Security Council.
(d) China attacked India in 1962.

17. Which of the following parties split due to irreconcilable differences between the Pro-USSR and Pro-Chinese faction? Diksha App

(a) Communist Party of India
(b) Indian National Congress
(c) Bharatiya Jana Sangh
(d) Lok Dal

18. Indian Prime Minister Lal Bahadur Shastri in January 1966 signed the Tashkent Agreement with which General of Pakistan?

(a) Ayub Khan (b) Yahya Khan
(c) Muhammad Zia Ul Haq (d) Musa Khan

19. Identify the country which has all the four features

I. It is a part of India's 'Look East Policy'.
II. It came into existence with India's help.
III. Its border touches the border of India.
IV. It is a secular and democratic country.
Choose the correct option

Competency Based Que; CBSE Term I 2021

(a) Myanmar (b) Nepal
(c) Bhutan (d) Bangladesh

20. Which of the following statements is NOT TRUE with respect to Indo-Pak armed conflicts? Diksha App

(a) 1974 proxy war between India and Pakistan in Kashmir
(b) 1965 Pakistan launched an armed attack in the Rann of Kutch
(c) 1971 Bangladesh war
(d) 2000 Kargil Conflict

21. Which one of the following statements about India's relations with Pakistan is incorrect?

Competency Based Que; CBSE Term I 2021

(a) India and Pakistan signed the Indus Water Treaty which has survived inspite of various military conflicts.
(b) India and Pakistan worked together to restore people back to their families.
(c) India and Pakistan have signed a treaty of friendship to work against terrorism.
(d) India and Pakistan signed the Tashkent Agreement in 1966.

22. Simla Agreement, 1972 was signed between Indira Gandhi and ....

(a) Asif Ali Zardari
(b) Zulfikar Ali Bhutto
(c) Bilawal Bhutto
(d) Yahya Khan

23. NPT refers to Diksha App

(a) Nuclear Power Treaty
(b) Nuclear Proliferation Treaty
(c) Nuclear Non-proliferation Treaty
(d) None of the above

24. Identify the correct pair

I. Indus Water Treaty- World Bank

II. Tashkent Agreement- The US **Competency Based Que**

Codes

(a) Only I (b) Only II
(c) Both I and II (d) Neither I Nor II

25. Match the following.

List I		List II	
A.	Henry Kissinger	1.	Tibet
B.	Zhou Enlai	2.	US
C.	Ayub Khan	3.	China
D.	Dalai Lama	4.	Pakistan

Codes

	A	B	C	D		A	B	C	D
(a)	1	2	4	3	(b)	3	2	1	4
(c)	2	3	4	1	(d)	2	4	1	3

26. Which of the following statement (s) is/ are incorrect about the Bangladesh War, 1971? **Competency Based Que**

I. The war conditions led India signing a 20 years Treaty of Peace and Friendship with USA in 1971.

II. The Simla Agreement between Lal Bahadur Shastri and Zulfikar Ali Bhutto formalised the return of peace in July 1972.

III. US and China supported Pakistan.

IV. India retaliated the Pakistan army with an attack mainly using the air force, navy and the army.

Codes

(a) Only I (b) II and III (c) III and IV (d) Only IV

27. Choose the features of India's Nuclear Policy from the following **Competency Based Que; CBSE Term I 2021**

I. It is peace oriented

II. The policy of 'no first use' can be reviewed.

III. Supports the nuclear treaties like CTBT and NPT.

IV. Ensuring the membership in the Nuclear Supplier Group.

Choose the correct option

(a) I, III and IV (b) II, III and IV
(c) I, II and III (d) I, II and IV

28. Given below are two statements

Statement I Pakistan formed an elected government under the leadership of Zulfikar Ali Bhutto which lasted form 1971 to 1977.

Statement II The Zulfikar Ali Bhutto government was removed by General Pervez Musharraf in 1977.

Options

(a) Both Statement I and Statement II are true.
(b) Both Statement I and Statement II are false.
(c) Statement I is true, but Statement II is false.
(d) Statement I is false, but Statement II is true.

Assertion-Reason Questions

Directions (Q. Nos. 29-33) In the questions given below, there are two statements marked as Assertion (A) and Reason (R). Read the statements and choose the correct option.

Codes

(a) Both A and R are true and R is the correct explanation of A.
(b) Both A and R are true, but R is not the correct explanation of A.
(c) A is true, but R is false.
(d) A is false, but R is true.

29. **Assertion** (A) Nehru was a co-founder of the NAM.

Reason (R) The Foreign Policy of Independent India advocated the policy of non-alignment to reduce the cold war tensions.

30. **Assertion** (A) The creation of Bangladesh in 1971 marked a significant victory for India.

Reason (R) India provided support to the people of West Pakistan during their struggle for independence.

31. **Assertion** (A) India signed a Treaty of Peace and Friendship with the Soviet Union in 1971.

Reason (R) The treaty assured Soviet support to India in case of any external aggression.

32. **Assertion** (A) The Kargil Conflict in 1999 was a limited war between India and Pakistan.

Reason (R) The conflict remained confined to the Kargil region despite both nations having nuclear capabilities.

33. **Assertion** (A) India was opposed to the indefinite extension of NPT is 1995 and refused to sign NPT and CTBT both.

Reason (R) India considers these treaties to be discriminatory and is against the monopoly of five nuclear weapon powers. **CBSE Term I 2021**

Passage Based Questions

34. **Read the passage given below carefully and answer the questions that follow.**

What does independence consist of ? It consists fundamentally and basically of foreign relations. That is the test of independence. All else is local autonomy. Once foreign relations go out of your hands into the charge of somebody else, to that extent and in that measure you are not independent. **—Jawaharlal Nehru**

(i) **In the above passage, the statement was made at which place?**

(a) In the Constituent Assembly of India.
(b) In the Press Conference at his residence.
(c) In the public meeting at Rashtrapati Bhawan.
(d) None of the above

(ii) What is the symbol of independence of a nation?
(a) Maintaining peaceful relations with neighbours.
(b) By indulging in wars to show regional supremacy.
(c) Conduct of foreign relations.
(d) By signing peaceful treaties.

(iii) How India did maintain its independence in the Cold War period?

35. Read the passage given below carefully and answer the questions that follow.

Two developments strained this relationship. China annexed Tibet in 1950 and thus removed a historical buffer between the two countries. Initially, the Government of India did not oppose this openly. But as more information came in about the suppression of Tibetan culture, the Indian Government grew uneasy. The Tibetan spiritual leader, the Dalai Lama, sought and obtained political asylum in India in 1959. China alleged that the Government of India was allowing anti-China activities to take place within India.

(i) In the above passage 'historical buffer' means ....
(a) a country which prevents conflicts.
(b) a country lying between two rival or potentially hostile powers.
(c) an agreement between the countries.
(d) None of the above

(ii) Why didn't Government of India oppose the annexation of Tibet by China?
(a) Due to the Panchsheel Agreement signed between India and China.
(b) As it believed that it is the internal matter of China.
(c) China assured India that Tibet will be given greater autonomy.
(d) Both (a) and (c)

(iii) Why Indian Government grew uneasy over the Tibet Issue?
(a) As Tibetan culture was suppressed by China.
(b) Due to migration from Tibet to India.
(c) As India was unable to help Tibet.
(d) All of the above

(iv) How far it was justified on the part of India to grant political asylum to Dalai Lama and thousands of Tibetan refugees?
(a) As Dalai Lama was a known Tibetan Spiritual leader.
(b) India granted political asylum on humanitarian grounds.
(c) Dalai Lama had a political influence over India.
(d) As there were many followers in India who supported Dalai Lama.

36. Read the passage given below carefully and answer the questions that follow.

India conducted a series of nuclear tests in May 1998, demonstrating its capacity to use nuclear energy for military purposes. Pakistan soon followed, thereby increasing the vulnerability of the region to a nuclear exchange. The international community was extremely critical of the nuclear tests in the subcontinent and sanctions were imposed on both India and Pakistan, which were subsequently waived. India has opposed the international treaties aimed at non-proliferation.

CBSE 2023

(i) In which year did India conduct series of nuclear tests?
(a) 1971 (b) 1985 (c) 1992 (d) 1998

(ii) Identify the treaty that India refused to sign.
(a) Comprehensive Test Ban Treaty
(b) Simla Agreement
(c) Panchsheel Agreement
(d) Indus Water Treaty

(iii) In the beginning, India wanted to generate nuclear energy for__________
(a) peaceful purpose.
(b) making atomic bombs.
(c) competing with the super powers.
(d) ensuring its security.

(iv) Under whose guidance did India initiate its nuclear programme?
(a) C.V. Raman (b) Homi J. Bhabha
(c) A.P.J. Abdul Kalam (d) K. Kasturirangan

37. Read the passage given below carefully and answer the questions that follow.

Foreign policy is always dictated by ideas of national interest. In the period after 1990, Russia, though it continues to be an important friend of India, has lost its global pre-eminence. Therefore, India's Foreign Policy has shifted to a more Pro-US strategy. Besides, the contemporary international situation is more influenced by economic interests than by military interests. This has also made an impact on India's Foreign Policy choices. At the same time, Indo-Pakistan relations have witnessed many new developments during this period. While Kashmir continues to be the main issue between the two countries, there have been many efforts to restore normal relations.

(i) According to the passage, India's Foreign Policy shift after 1990 was primarily due to
(a) The decline of Russia's global influence.
(b) The increasing importance of economic interests.
(c) The need to improve relations with Pakistan.
(d) All of the above

(ii) The passage suggests that Indo-Pakistan relations have
(a) Deteriorated significantly since 1990.
(b) Remained unchanged since 1990.
(c) Improved significantly since 1990.
(d) Experienced both improvements and setbacks since 1990.

(iii) By what factor foreign policy is dictated?

Answers

1. (c) To align with the capitalist block.
2. (c) Poverty alleviation and international disputes
3. (c) To make India a nuclear power.
4. (a) Suez Canal issue
5. (a) To avoid becoming part of either the US-led NATO or the Soviet-led Warsaw Pact
6. (d) Dutch
7. (c) Bandung Conference
8. (b) Afro-Asian Unity
9. (b) Bandung
10. (b) Belgrade
11. (d) India was a founder of NAM.
12. (c) 1954
13. (a) 1950
14. (c) India
15. (b) The Soviet Union remained neutral during the conflict.
16. (c) India opposed China's entry into the UN Security Council.
17. (a) Communist Party of India
18. (a) Ayub Khan
19. (d) Bangladesh
20. (d) 2000 Kargil Conflict
21. (c) India and Pakistan have signed a treaty of friendship to work against terrorism.
22. (b) Zulfikar Ali Bhutto
23. (c) Nuclear Non-proliferation Treaty
24. (a) Only I
25. (c) 2 3 4 1
26. (c) III and IV
27. (d) I, II and IV
28. (c) Statement I is true, but Statement II is false.
29. (a) Both A and R are true and R is the correct explanation of A.
30. (c) A is true, but R is false.
31. (a) Both A and R are true and R is the correct explanation of A.
32. (a) Both A and R are true and R is the correct explanation of A.
33. (a) Both A and R are true and R is the correct explanation of A.
34. (i) (a) In the Constituent Assembly of India.
    (ii) (c) Conduct of foreign relations.
    (iii) India maintained its independence in the Cold War period by not by not joining either of the super blocs i.e. USA and USSR and adopting new path in the form of NAM.
35. (i) (b) a country lying between two rival or potentially hostile powers.
    (ii) (d) Both (a) and (c)
    (iii) (a) As Tibetan culture was suppressed by China.
    (iv) (b) India granted political asylum on humanitarian grounds.
36. (i) (d) 1998
    (ii) (a) Comprehensive Test Ban Treaty.
    (iii) (a) peaceful purposes.
    (iv) (b) Homi J. Bhabha
37. (i) (d) All of the above
    (ii) (d) Experienced both improvements and setbacks since 1990.
    (iii) Foreign policy is dictated by the ideas of national interests of any nation.

Subjective Questions

Very Short Answer Type Questions

1. Why did India not join either of the two camps during the Cold War?

Ans. India did not join either of the two camps of world during the Cold War because

(i) India wanted to separate itself from military blocs.

(ii) India wanted to preserve its sovereignty.

2. What was the purpose of the Bandung Conference?

Ans. This conference was held in 1955. It placed India on zenith to engage with the newly independent countries of Asia and Africa.

This conference further led to the establishment of Non-Alignment Movement.

3. What does Panchsheel imply?

Ans. The Panchsheel Agreement was signed by Zhou Enlai (Prime Minister of China) and Indian counterpart Pandit Nehru in 1954.

4. Why did Dalai Lama seek refuge in India?

Ans. When China annexed Tibet and tried to suppress its culture, the Tibetans rebelled. In return, Chinese forces crushed this rebellion, which worsened the situation. This led Dalai Lama flee to India and seek refuge.

5. Which two differences between India and China led to an army conflict in 1962?

Ans. Two differences between India and China which led to an army conflict in 1962 were

(i) India gave political asylum to the Tibetan leader Dalai Lama.

(ii) China's help to Pakistan against India.

6. Who signed the Tashkent Agreement and when?

Ans. Tashkent Agreement was signed between Lal Bahadur Shastri (Prime Minister of India) and General Ayub Khan (President of Pakistan) in 1966.

7. Which political party won all the seats in the 1970 elections in East Pakistan and under whose leadership? CBSE 2024

Ans. Awami League by Sheikh Mujibur Rahman won all the seats in 1970 elections in the East Pakistan.

8. Why did the people of East Pakistan resent the domination of West Pakistan? CBSE 2024

Ans. The people of East Pakistan resent the domination of West Pakistan because, the people of East Pakistan felt that they were treated as second class citizens by the ruler based in West Pakistan.

Short Answer Type Questions

1. List four Directive Principles of State Policy that aim to promote international peace and security. CBSE SQP 2024

Ans. Article 51 of the Indian Constitution lays down some Directive Principles of the State Policy that aim to promote the international peace and security. This states that The state shall endeavour to

(i) Promote international peace and security.
(ii) Maintain just and honourable relations between nations.
(iii) Foster respect for international law and treaty obligations in the dealings of organised people with one another.
(iv) Encourage settlement of international disputes by arbitration.

2. Suggest any two measures to improve Indo-China relations. CBSE 2024

Ans. India-China relations can be improved by the following measures

(i) By peacefully resolving the border issues. Conducting the high official talks regularly, avoiding any border clashes.
(ii) Working together on common goals, like trade, water, sharing, security and peace in the region.

3. Highlight the role of Jawaharlal Nehru in the foreign policy of India. CBSE 2024

Or Describe any two major objectives of Nehru's foreign policy.

Or Enumerate any two principles of Nehru's foreign policy.

Or Highlight any two contribution made by Jawaharlal Nehru to the foreign policy of India. CBSE 2024

Ans. Jawaharlal Nehru was the first Prime Minister and Foreign Minister of the newly independent India. He played the most important role in the formulation and implementation of India's Foreign Policy from 1946 to 1964, which can be summarised below

(i) The key objective of Nehru's foreign policy was to preserve the hard earned sovereignty, to protect territorial integrity and promote rapid economic development.
(ii) Nehru was to achieve these objectives through the strategy of non-alignment. He was against the principle of colonialism and he did not wanted to join any of the military block led by the two superpowers, the US and the USSR.
(iii) Despite of advices by other leaders like Dr. Ambedkar to join the US bloc, Nehru possessed a different way of foreign policy to achieve the aim of human security, peace and respect for all nations in the world.

4. Justify the 'policy of non-alignment' adopted by India, by giving any three arguments. Competency Based Que; CBSE 2024

Ans. (i) The Indian policy of non-alignment was inspired from its Indian freedom struggle. The entire freedom struggle of India was not an isolated process, but it was a long struggle against the colonialism and imperialism. Therefore, India wanted to maintain the policy of non-alignment to protect sovereignty of all other nations and maintain the security through peace.
(ii) India's independence was marked by the political, economic and military confrontation at the global level between the two superpowers. But India did not join any of these superpower rather it focused to maintain its independence on international issues.
(iii) Under the leadership of Jawaharlal Nehru, India played an important role in maintaining Afro-Asian unity as a policy of non-alignment for the newly decolonised counties.

5. Explain the circumstances that forced the Tibetans to leave China. Highlight India's role in helping the Tibetan refugees. Competency Based Que

Or What was the Tibet issue? How did it cause tension between India and China? Explain.

Or What was the Tibet issue? How did India help the Tibetan migrants to settle down?

Ans. China administrated Tibet since older times and wanted to control all its parts. China took control over Tibet in 1950. Tibet was good friend of India since history, therefore India insisted China to give independence to Tibet.

According to Panchsheel Agreement, India conceded China's claim over Tibet. China assured India that it will provide full autonomy. But these issues of Tibet led to war between China and India. When China supressed the revolt, spiritual leader of Tibet, Dalai Lama fled to India.

Dalai Lama wanted help from India and discussed the worsening condition of Tibet. Many Tibet refugees settled in India at places like, in Delhi and Dharamashala. The Tibetan people opposed this takeover of China and they settled in India. Thus, China invaded Indian Territory in 1962 which led to tensions between India and China.

6. How did China War of 1962 dirt India's image at home and abroad? Explain any four points. CBSE 2020

Or **Evaluate the impact of the Chinese invasion of 1962 in denting India's image at home and abroad.** Competency Based Que; CBSE 2019

Ans. The China War (1962) damage India's image at home and abroad in the following ways

(i) India had to approach the Americans and the British for military assistance to overcome the crises. The Soviet Union remained neutral during the conflict which caused a sense of national humiliation.

(ii) Jawaharlal Nehru was severely criticised for his naive assessment of the Chinese intentions and the lack of military preparedness.

(iii) Some of the top army commander either resigned or were retired which made the situation worse.

(iv) For the first time, Nehru's image suffered and a no-confidence motion against his government was moved and debated in the Lok Sabha.

7. Explain any two reasons for the popular struggle in East Pakistan (now Bangladesh) against West Pakistan during 1971. Competency Based Que

Or **Describe any two major issues of conflict between India and Pakistan leading to the war of 1971.**

Or **Describe the circumstances that led to the Bangladesh war in 1971.** CBSE 2020

Ans. Reasons for 1971 war/conflict are following

(i) In 1970, Pakistan had to face its biggest internal disturbance. The first general elections of Pakistan constructed a rift between West Pakistan and East Pakistan (now Bangladesh). Zulfikar Ali Bhutto's party won all the seats in West Pakistan but he lost in East Pakistan. Sheikh Mujibur Rahman's party Awami League swept through East Pakistan.

(ii) The Bengali people of East Pakistan had voted to protest against being treated as second class citizens over years by the government based in West Pakistan.

(iii) The Pakistani Government was not ready to accept this democratic judgement nor were they ready to accept the Awami League's demand for a federation.

(iv) In 1971, Pakistan army arrested Sheikh Mujibur Rahman and unleashed a reign of terror on East Pakistan. This started people's struggle to liberate Bangladesh from Pakistan.

(v) India had to bear 80 lakh refugees who fled from East Pakistan to take shelter. Hence, India had to extend moral and material support to the freedom struggle in Bangladesh.

Thus, full scale war broke out between India and Pakistan in 1971, when Pakistan attacked on Punjab and Rajasthan.

8. Explain any two reasons that led to National Jubilation (triumph) in India after the 1971 war with Pakistan. CBSE 2020

Ans. India started a war with Pakistan in December 1971 for the independence of Bangladesh. Pakistan army was forced to surrender and Bangladesh became a sovereign country. A decisive victory in the war led to National Jubilation because

(i) Most people in India saw this as a moment of glory and clear sign of India's growing military powers.

(ii) At that time, the Congress was in power and Indira Gandhi was the Prime Minister. Her popularity increased immensely and the people of India under the leadership of Indira Gandhi considered it to be their own victory against Pakistan.

9. Suggest any two measures to improve India's relation with Pakistan.

Ans. India-Pakistan relations can be improved by following measures

(i) **Confidence building measures**
- Talks between the high officials from to time.
- Resolving the borders disputes peacefully.

(ii) **Cultural Exchanges**
- Reviving the old ties of religion, culture between India and Pakistan.
- Training regular bus and train services to increase the people to people engagement.

10. Explain any four features of the India's Nuclear Policy. CBSE 2020

Or **Analyse the Nuclear Policy of India.** CBSE 2024 C

Ans. Some of the main features of the India's Nuclear Policy are

(i) Jawaharlal Nehru was against nuclear weapons, thus he emphasised on generating atomic energy only for peaceful purposes.

(ii) India is against the international treaties which aimed at non-proliferation as the five nuclear states (US, USSR, UK, France and China) are not restricted from proliferating nuclear weapons. The Nuclear Proliferation Treaty (NPT) denied right to peaceful nuclear explosions by non-nuclear states.

(iii) India's nuclear policy dependable on minimum nuclear deterrence proclaims 'no first use'.

(iv) This policy reaffirms India's commitment to global, verifiable and non-discriminatory nuclear disarmament leading to a nuclear weapons free world.

Long Answer Type Questions

1. "Adoption of the policy of non-alignment and advancing national interest proved a tight rope walk for newly independent countries". Justify this statement by giving any three arguments.

Competency Based Que; Diksha App

Ans. (i) India and some other Afro-Asian countries became independent during the era of world war, which was immediately followed by Cold War era. Thus it was natural for these countries to take some tough decisions in order to adhere to the principles of non-alignment. India did not join any military block, led by the two superpowers, USA and the USSR.

(ii) But when the international context changed these non-aligned countries had to compromise the principle of non-alignment to advance their national interest. When Britain attacked on Suez Canal, India criticised publicly. However, it did not criticise the USSR when it invaded Hungary because of its national interests.

(iii) Some of the newly independent countries like Pakistan join the US bloc when India was trying to convince the other developing countries to follow the policy of non-alignment.

However, India played a key role in following the policy of non-alignment by promoting Afro-Asian unity through various NAM Summit.

2. "The foreign policy of Independent India has pursued the dream of a peaceful world." Support your answer with any three suitable arguments.

Competency Based Que; CBSE 2024, 2025

Or **Describe the contribution of Jawaharlal Nehru which helped in shaping properly the foreign policy of India.**

Or **Mention the objectives of Nehru's foreign policy. What was the strategy through which he wanted to achieve them?**

Ans. India formulated its foreign policy with an aim to respect the sovereignty of all other nations and to achieve security through the maintenance of peace.

The major principles of India's Foreign Policy are

(i) **Non-Alignment** It means not to join any of the power blocks or enter into military alliance, having an independent foreign policy and working for peaceful co-existence. Non-alignment stands for disarmament, development, decolonisation, democratisation of international organisations, protection of the environment, etc.

(ii) **Panchsheel** It is a guideline in our relation with other countries that was signed between India and China in 1954. Its five principles are

- Respect for each other's territorial integrity and sovereignty
- Mutual non-aggression
- Mutual non-interference in each other's internal affairs
- Equality and mutual benefit
- Peaceful co-existence

(iii) **Opposition to Colonialism** Since we have been the victims of colonial rule and exploitation, we stand for the right of self-determination and anti-imperialism. We supported the cause of freedom of the colonies of Africa and Asia, as colonialism is a violation of Fundamental Human Rights.

India co-operated with Indonesia in its efforts for freedom and also supported the freedom struggles in Malaya, Algeria, Tansia and Namibia, etc. India's concern for Bangladesh and of Iraq's invasion of Kuwait reflects our opposition to colonialism.

3. Explain the role played by India in maintaining Afro-Asian unity.

Or **Examine the efforts taken by Jawaharlal Nehru for the promotion of Afro-Asian unity.**

Or **"India played an important role in maintaining Afro-Asian Unity". Support the statement with three suitable examples.** **CBSE 2025**

Ans. Efforts taken by Jawaharlal Nehru for the promotion of Afro-Asian unity is as follows

- Due to India's size, location and power potential, Nehru dreamt of major role for India in world affairs specially in Asia.
- Under Nehru's leadership, India made contact with other newly emerged independent nations of Asia and Africa.
- During the 1940s and 1950s, Nehru advocated with great enthusiasm to support the Asian unity. Under his leadership, India hosted the Asian relations conference in March 1947, five months before India's independence.
- India was a staunch supporter of decolonisation and firmly opposed racism, partiaularly apartheid in South Africa.
- The Afro-Asian Conference known as the Bandung Conference was held in 1955.
- The Bandung Conference marked the climax of India's engagement with newly independent Asian and African nations.

4. "India was a staunch supporter of the decolonisation process and firmly opposed racism". Support the statement with any three suitable arguments. Competency Based Que; CBSE 2024

Ans. India was a staunch supporter of the decolonisation process as

- The Indian national movement was not an isolated process. It was a part of worldwide struggle against the principle of colonialism and imperialism. Indian freedom struggle, inspired, many other colonies in Asia and Africa.
- India was connected with these countries even before its independence. In fact, India made the earnest effort for the liberation of Indonesia from Dutch colonial regime by convening an international conference in 1949. India made serious efforts to oppose racism, specially apartheid in South Africa.
- It was in this backdrop, that India convened Bandung Conference in Indonesian city of Bandung to mark a new era of the friendship of Afro- Asian unity.

5. Describe the areas of conflict in India-China relation. Diksha App

Ans. India has began its relation in a friendly manner with China. Prime Minister Nehru had a good faith with Chinese President and they also signed a Panchsheel Agreement in 1954, which was aimed at mutual respect of sovereignty for both of the nations. However, tension buildup after sometime. Following are the areas of conflict between India-China relation

- China had captured the Tibet autonomous region, which was a historical buffer between India and China. When India came to know about the suppression of Tibetan culture by Chinese Government, India became uneasy.
  Though China had assured India that autonomy of Tibet would be restored, but the Tibetan spiritual leader Dalai Lama had sought to, take political asylum in India in 1959. China blamed India of allowing anti-Chinese activities on its soil.
- There were boundary disputes between India and China. The dispute was because of the western and eastern end of the long border between the two countries. China claimed two areas which lie completely in the Indian territory. The first area is the Aksai-Chin area in the Ladakh region of Jammu and Kashmir. The second area is in the state of Arunachal Pradesh, which was then called the NEFA (North Eastern Frontier Agency).
- Between 1957 and 1959, China occupied the Aksai-Chin area in India. China began to built a strategic road on this despite a very long discussion between the top leaders. This issue could not be resolved and small border issues also took place between the two armies.
- Then, in October 1962, China launched a massive invasion attack on both the Western and Eastern borders of India. When it attacked for the first time, it went for one week and Chinese forces captured some important areas in Arunachal Pradesh.
- The second attack came next month when Indian forces were trying to block the Chinese March on Western front of Ladakh. The Chinese army entered till the Assam planes in India. However, this conflict ended when China itself cleared its troop to withdraw to the point where they were originally before they invasion.

6. Explain the areas of tension in Indo-Pakistan. Diksha App

Or **Evaluate the relationship between India and Pakistan with the help of example.** Competency Based Que; CBSE 2023

Ans. India and Pakistan had many areas of tension just after the independence. There have been several incidents of war and peace between the two countries which are described below

- The main dispute between India and Pakistan is in the Kashmir region. During 1947, a proxy war broke out between the two armies. Pakistan since then has emerged a critical factor in India's relation with the US and then with China, the same Kashmir issue also reached to the United Nations, however, solution has not been found out till yet.
- A more serious conflict between the armies began in 1965, when Pakistan launched army attacks in the Rann of Kutch of Gujarat. It was followed by a bigger offensive attack in Jammu and Kashmir during 1965 September. The then Prime Minister Lal Bahadur Shastri ordered army troops to launch a counter-offensive attack on the Punjab border.
- During 1971, India supported Bangladesh in its liberation struggle. In 1971, Pakistani Air Force attacked Punjab and Rajasthan, which India retaliated with Air Force, navy and army on both the Western and Eastern front India captured Dhaka within 10 days and made around 90,000 army troops of Pakistan to surrender. Bangladesh was finally made an independent country.
- Another conflict emerged when Pakistani army troops in the disguise of Mujahideens, illegally occupied some of the LOC areas (Mashkoh, Dras, Kaksar and Batalik) in Indian side. India recovered all of its illegally captured points by 26th July, 1999. This conflict was known as Kargil Conflict.
- Despite of all these tensions, India and Pakistan time to time had tried to build peace and improve their trade relations.

7. Why did India not sign the Nuclear Non-proliferation Treaty? **Diksha App**

Ans. India did not sign the Nuclear Non-proliferation Treaty because

- India has always put faith in science and technology for rapidly building a modern India. It has started its nuclear programme which was a key component of its industrialisation process. India aimed to develop atomic energy for peaceful purposes.
- India has been urging the superpowers for not using the nuclear weapons, but the five permanent members of UN Security Council have been increasing their nuclear weapons. These superpowers have been preventing other countries to increase their nuclear power.
- India found it discriminatory when these five permanent members of UN Security Council tried to impose the Nuclear Non-proliferation Treaty in 1968 on rest of the world.
- According to this treaty, only selective countries can have nuclear power. India is strictly against such international treaties and found it the monopoly of the five nuclear weapon powers.
- Thus, India opposed to the NPT extension in 1995 and also refused to sign the Comprehensive Test Ban Treaty.

Picture Based Questions

1. Observe the cartoon given below carefully and answer the following questions.

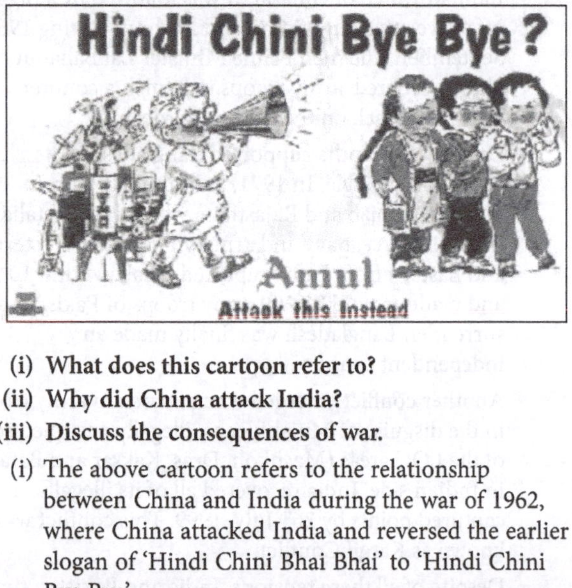

(i) What does this cartoon refer to?

(ii) Why did China attack India?

(iii) Discuss the consequences of war.

Ans. (i) The above cartoon refers to the relationship between China and India during the war of 1962, where China attacked India and reversed the earlier slogan of 'Hindi Chini Bhai Bhai' to 'Hindi Chini Bye Bye'.

(ii) China attacked India because India supported the cause of Tibet which was bitterly objected by China. India had granted asylum to Dalai Lama and his followers. China responded this with attack on Aksai-Chin and Arunachal Pradesh.

(iii) Consequences of war of 1962 were

- It caused a sense of national humiliation.
- Top army commanders resigned or retired.
- V.K. Menon left the cabinet.
- First time no confidence motion was moved and Congress lost some important by-elections to Lok Sabha.

2. Study the given cartoon and answer the questions that follow.

(i) Who are the leaders illustrated in the cartoon?

(a) Jawaharlal Nehru and Mao Tsetung
(b) Zhou Enlai and Nehru
(c) Lal Bahadur Shastri
(d) Mao Tsetung and Lal Bahadur Shastri

Ans. (a) Jawaharlal Nehru and Mao Tsetung

(ii) What does the above cartoon depicts?

(a) Sports event tournament
(b) Trade dispute between the two nations
(c) Border conflict
(d) International non co-operation on different issues

Ans. (c) Border conflict

(iii) The leaders are associated with which of the two following countries?

(a) India and Nepal
(b) Bangladesh and India
(c) India and Mongolia
(d) India and China

Ans. (d) India and China

(iv) What was the outcome of the event?

(a) Chinese invasion of Indian border and territory.
(b) Indian invasion of Nepalese territory.
(c) Trade dispute solved between the India and Bhutan.
(d) Mutual co-operation in international relation among the countries shown in the image.

Ans. (a) Chinese invasion of Indian border and territory.

SELF ASSESSMENT TEST

Objective Type Questions

1. Which article of the Indian Constitution advocates for international peace?
   (a) Article 16 (b) Article 15
   (c) Article 51 (d) Article 50
2. Choose the wrong statement from the given options.
   (a) One of the principles of Panchsheel is peaceful co-existence.
   (b) Foreign policy is designed to protect the national interests of the state.
   (c) India-China borders for a very long time were guarded under the Para-military forces instead of army.
   (d) Diplomatic relations between India and Russia were downgraded until 1976.
3. What were the three major objectives of Nehru's foreign policy?
   (a) Strengthening military alliances, expanding territory and rapid industrialisation.
   (b) Preserving sovereignty, protecting territorial integrity and promoting economic development.
   (c) Establishing global dominance, supporting communism and increasing military power.
   (d) Forming strong ties with Western countries, expanding trade and promoting democracy.
4. .... is the largest Tibetan refugee settlement in India.
   (a) Dharamashala (b) Delhi
   (c) Manali (d) Kargil

Very Short Answer Type Questions

5. Who were the leaders to support pro-US policy after independence?
6. When did India conduct its first nuclear test and why?
7. What is NPT?
8. What does Indian nuclear doctrine profess?

Short Answer Type Questions

9. How do different alliances shift in the world politics?
10. Discuss the role of NAM in the world politics of Cold War era.
11. Give a brief account of Tibet as a conflict zone for China.
12. Foreign policy has played a limited role in party politics. Explain. **Competency Based Que**

Long Answer Type Questions

13. What do you understand by Panchsheel declaration and why was it signed?
14. Describe the course of Indian's Foreign Policy after 1977.
15. Explain in detail the effects of the 1962, 1965 and 1971 war in India. **Competency Based Que**
16. Discuss India's Nuclear Policy.
17. Briefly explain about Kargil Conflict.

05
CHAPTER

This chapter discusses the challenges faced by the Congress during 1960s due to intense competition. The Congress faced splits and later revived under the leadership of Indira Gandhi.

Challenges to and Restoration of The Congress System

YOUR STUDY GOALS

5.1 Challenges of Political Succession
5.2 Fourth General Elections, 1967
5.3 Split in the Congress
5.4 Presidential Election, 1969
5.5 The 1971 Election and Restoration of Congress

YOUR PRACTICE GOAL

- Objective Type Questions (25 Qs ; MCQs, A-R, Statements, Matching, Passage Based)
- Subjective Questions (9 VSAs, 7 SAs, 5 LAs, 3 Picture Based, 4 Map Based)

5.1 Challenges of Political Succession

- After the death of Prime Minister Jawaharlal Nehru in May 1964, the debate began over the new Prime Minister.
- Another issue was that whether the democracy would be sustained in India. Just like it was under the era of Prime Minister Nehru.
- Some people were also fearful about the fact that in other newly independent countries, the army had took over the government which had uprooted the democracy.
- There were some unresolved problems as well like poverty, inequality, communal and regional divisions, which could lead to a failure of the democracy. Thus, 1960s was called a **dangerous decade.**

From Nehru to Shastri

- All of the critics were proved wrong when the Congress Party President K. Kamaraj consulted the party leaders and all of them chose **Lal Bahadur Shastri** as their new leader.
- Thus, by unity Lal Bahadur Shastri became the **second Prime Minister after Nehru.** He was from Uttar Pradesh and had been a Minister in Nehru's cabinet for many years. During his last year, Nehru was very much dependent upon Lal Bahadur Shastri.

- Lal Bahadur Shastri was known for his simplicity and commitment to principles. Earlier he had resigned from the post of Railway Minister as a moral responsibility, when a major rail accident occurred.
- During his tenure as a Prime Minister (1964-1966), India had undergone two major challenges, which are as follows
  (i) Failed monsoons caused droughts which led to **serious food crisis.** At the same time India had been recovering from the economic difficulties due to war with China in 1962.
  (ii) India faced **war with Pakistan** in 1965.
  - Shastri's famous slogan **'Jai Jawan Jai Kisan'** was a symbolic to the solution of these two problems.
  - His tenure came to end very unexpectedly, when he suddenly expired in **Tashkent, Uzbekistan.** Currently, Tashkent is the capital of Uzbekistan, which was the part of the USSR that time.

Lal Bahadur Shastri (1904-1966)

- He was the Prime Minister of India and participated in freedom movement.
- He was also a UP Cabinet Minister and General Secretary of Congress.
- He coined the famous slogan 'Jai Jawan Jai Kisan'.

From Shastri to Indira Gandhi

- After the death of Lal Bahadur Shastri, again the question of leadership emerged. There were two candidates for the position of Prime Minister.
  - **Morarji Desai** who had served as Chief Minister of Bombay state (today's Maharashtra and Gujarat) and Central Minister.
  - **Indira Gandhi**, the daughter of Jawaharlal Nehru. She had been the Union Minister for Information in Shastri's cabinet.
- The selection was made through **secret ballot** among the Congress MPs. **Indira Gandhi** was chosen as the leader by two-thirds of the MPs. It was a sign of **mature democracy** when Morarji Desai peacefully welcomed the decision and allowed Indira Gandhi to be the next Prime Minister.
- Congress leaders may have supported her because they might be thinking that Indira Gandhi is not much experienced. So she would be dependent upon them and would take decisions as per their suggestions.
- After becoming Prime Minister, Indira Gandhi faced the following challenges
  - Around this time, the economic situation of the country had further deteriorated.
  - The control of senior leaders of the Congress Party.

Indira Gandhi (1917-1984)

- She became Prime Minister from 1966 to 1977 and from 1980 to 1984.
- She was also Congress President in 1958. She has led the Congress Party to victory in 1967, 1971 and 1980 general elections.
- She gave the slogan 'Garibi Hatao' and abolished the Privy Purse.
- She is also credited for the nationalisation of banks, nuclear test and environmental protections.
- She was assassinated on 31st October, 1984.

Quick Test 1

1. By what name the decade of 1960s is known as?
2. What was the slogan given by Lal Bahadur Shastri?
3. Which two challenges were faced by Indira Gandhi, after becoming Prime Minister?

5.2 Fourth General Elections, 1967

The 1967 was a landmark year in Indian political and electoral history as it marked the end of the era of the Congress dominance.

Context of the Elections

- As the fourth general elections were approaching, the country witnessed following major challenges,
  - Death of two Prime Ministers in short span of time and the newly elected Prime Minister is also not much experienced politically.
  - Serious economic and food crisis due to droughts.
  - Depletion of foreign exchange reserves.
  - Decline in industrial production.
  - Sharp rise in military expenditure and
  - Diversion of resources from planning and economic development.
- Indira Gandhi decided to **devaluate**[1] the Indian rupee due to the pressure from the US. After devaluation, One US Dollar could be purchased for more than 7 rupees, earlier it was purchased for less than 5 rupee.
- The economic situation sparked off price rise. The devaluation of Indian rupee increased the prices of essential commodities.
- Food scarcity and the growing unemployment worsened the condition of the country. People started protesting. Bandhs and hurtals took place in the country frequently. The communists and socialist parties launched struggles for greater equality. They organised armed agrarian struggles.

Non-Congressism

- Opposition parties got together and realised that if their votes are divided, then it will favour Congress. Therefore, these parties got together and formed **anti-Congress agenda** by sharing their seats together.
- These leaders felt that **inexperience** of Indira Gandhi and **internal factionalism** of the Congress had provided them an opportunity to replace the Congress government.
- **Ram Manohar Lohia,** the socialist leader gave this strategy the name of **non-Congressism**. He also produced an argument in its defence: Congress rule was undemocratic and opposed to the interests of ordinary poor people; therefore, the coming together of the non-Congress parties was necessary for reclaiming democracy for the people.

C. Natarajan Annadurai (1909-1969)

He was the Chief Minister of Madras from 1967. He was a popular writer and journalist. Initially he was associated with the justice party, but later joined Dravid Kazagham and formed DMK as a political party in 1949. He was a proponent of Dravid culture and was opposed to imposition of Hindi and led the anti-Hindi agitations. He supported greater autonomy to states.

Ram Manohar Lohia (1910-1967)

He was a freedom fighter and a socialist leader. He also founded Congress Socialist Party with other members. He was the leader of the Socialist Party and later the Samyukta Socialist Party. He was founder editor of **Mankind** and **Jan**, known for original contribution to a non-European socialist theory. He advocated for the reservation for backward class and opposed English.

1 **Devaluate** It means to reduce the value of something.

Electoral Verdict

- The fourth general elections and state assembly elections were held in February 1967. It was for the first time that elections were being held without Nehru. Many contemporary political observer described the election results as a **'political earthquake'**. The results gave a shock to the Congress at both national and state levels.
- However, Congress managed to set majority in Lok Sabha, but it was its lowest number of seats and share since 1952. Many political experts in Indira Gandhi's cabinet were defeated. These were
  - Kamaraj in Tamil Nadu
  - S.K. Patil in Maharashtra
  - Atulya Ghosh in West Bengal
  - K.B. Sahay in Bihar
- Congress lost its majority in seven states. In two states, it could not form the government because of the defection. There were 9 states where Congress lost power
  - Punjab
  - Haryana
  - Uttar Pradesh
  - Madhya Pradesh
  - Bihar
  - West Bengal
  - Odisha
  - Kerala
  - Madras (a regional party Dravida Munnetra Kazhagam (DMK) – came to power)
- The DMK won elections by leading a massive anti- Hindi agitation by the students against the central decision of imposing Hindi as the official language.
- In other eight states, coalition governments were formed by different non-Congress parties. There was a popular saying that one could take a train from Delhi to Howrah and not pass through a single congress ruled state.

Coalitions

- The 1967 elections brought a phenomena of **coalitions**. Various non-Congress parties came together to form joint legislative parties called **Samyukta Vidhayak Dal** in Hindi. That is why these government came to be described as **SVD** government.
- For example, the SVD government in Bihar included two socialist party- SSP and the PSP along with the CPI on the left and Jana Sangh on the right.
- In Punjab, Popular United Front, comprised of two opposite Akali parties, Sant Group and the Master Group with both the communist parties, the CPI, CPI (M), the SSP, the Republican Party and the Bharatiya Jana Sangh.

Defection

- Defection means when an elected representative leaves the party on whose symbol he/she has elected and then joins another party. After 1967 general elections, the non-Congress governments were installed in three states, Haryana, Madhya Pradesh and Uttar Pradesh.
- There was constant re-alignment and shifting of the political leaders from one party to another, which gave rise to the popular expression, **'Aya Ram, Gaya Ram.'**

Story of 'Aya Ram, Gaya Ram'

- Gaya lal, was a MLA in Haryana (1967), changed his party thrice in a fortnight.
- From Congress to united front back to Congress and then joined united front again. When Gaya Ram joined Congress, than the Congress leader, Rao Birendra Singh brought him to Chandigarh press and declared "Gaya Ram was now Aya Ram". Since then it has become a joke on defections.

Quick Test 2

1. What was the value of rupee after devaluation?
2. What is non-Congressism?
3. Which regional party won the 1967 elections in Madras state (Tamil Nadu)?

5.3 Split in the Congress

- After the 1967 elections, the Congress retained power at the centre but with a reduced majority and lost power in many states.
- Most of the non-Congress coalition governments that were formed in the states could not survive for long. Either they lost the majority or new combinations were formed or President's rule had to be imposed in the states.

Indira Vs. The 'Syndicate'

- The real challenge for Indira Gandhi emerged not from the opposition, but from within the Congress. She had to deal with **Syndicate**, a group of powerful and influential leaders within the Congress.
- She faced **two challenges**
  - Needed to build her independence from the Syndicate, who were expecting her to follow their advice.
  - Needed to work on ground level to regain the Congress victory.
- To gain the lost victory, Indira Gandhi took bold strategy through the following measures
  - She chose her trusted group of advisers from outside the party and sidelined the Syndicate.
  - She converted this power struggle into an ideological struggle.
  - She launched initiatives to give the government policy a left orientation.
  - Congress Working Committee under her leadership adopted **Ten Point Programme** that included
    - Social Control of Banks
    - Nationalisation of General Insurance
    - Cap on urban property and income
    - Public distribution of food grains
    - Land reforms
    - Providing of housing sites to the rural
- Though, the Syndicate leaders formally approved these left oriented measures, but they had serious reservations about this.

The Congress 'Syndicate'

- It was the **informal name** for the **group of senior Congress leaders**. It was led by **K. Kamaraj**, former Chief Minister of Tamil Nadu and the then President of the Congress Party.
- It included powerful state leaders like S. K. Patil of Bombay city (later named as Mumbai), S. Nijalingappa of Mysore (later Karnataka), N. Sanjeeva Reddy of Andhra Pradesh and Atulya Ghosh of West Bengal.
- After the Congress split, the leaders of the Syndicate group were Congress (O) and the leaders of Indira Gandhi's Congress were Congress (R).

Important Leaders

K. Kamaraj (1903-1975)

- He was a freedom fighter and Congress President. He became the Chief Minister of Madras.
- He was deprived of the education thus, spread education in Madras province. He introduced **mid-day meal scheme** for school children.
- In 1963, he proposed that all senior Congressmen should resign from office to make way for younger party workers—this proposal is famous as the **Kamaraj plan.**

S. Nijalingappa (1902-2000)

- He was the member of the Constituent Assembly and senior Congress leader.
- He was the Chief Minister of Mysore (Karnataka) and regarded as the **maker of modern Karnataka**.
- He also served as the Congress President during 1968-71.

Karpoori Thakur (1924-1988)

- He was Chief Minister of Bihar between December, 1970 and June, 1971 and again between June, 1977 and April, 1979.
- He was the freedom fighter and socialist leader.
- He was active in labour and peasant movements and a follower of Lohia.
- He participated in the movement led by Jayaprakash Narayan.
- He introduced the **backward class reservation** in Bihar, during his second Chief Ministership and he opposed the use of English language.

V.V. Giri (1894-1980)

- President of India (1969-74). He was a labour leader from Andhra Pradesh.
- Served as the High Commissioner to Ceylon (Sri Lanka), Union Labour Minister, Governor of UP, Kerala, Mysore.
- Vice -President (1967-69) and acting President after the death of President Zakir Hussain.

5.4 Presidential Election, 1969

- The rivalry between the **Syndicate** and **Indira Gandhi** came in the open in 1969. After the death of President, **Zakir Hussain, Syndicate** managed to nominate the name of Indira Gandhi's opponent **N. Sanjeeva Reddy**. He was the then Speaker of the Lok Sabha.
- Indira Gandhi did not like this and in return, she encouraged the then **Vice-President V.V. Giri** to file his nomination as an independent candidate. She also announced big and popular policy measures like **nationalisation of 14 leading private banks** and **abolition of the privy purse.**
- During that time, **Morarji Desai** was the Deputy Prime Minister as well as Finance Minister. On both these issues, he left the government.
- The Congress President **S. Nijalingappa** issues a whip[2] to all Congress MPs to vote in favour of Sanjeeva Reddy. But, Indira Gandhi silently supported V.V. Giri and called for a **conscience vote**. Conscience vote means that the MPs could vote against the whip as per their choice. Therefore, V.V. Giri emerged as the winner for Presidential elections.
- The defeat of the official Congress candidate N. Sanjeeva Reddy led to the split in the Congress party. The Congress president expelled the Prime Minister from the party. Indira Gandhi claimed that her group was real Congress. By November 1969, the Congress group of 'Syndicate' came to be known as **Congress (Organisation)** and another group by Indira Gandhi called **Congress (Requisitionists)**.

2 Whip A whip is a legislator who acts as an 'enforcer' for their political party. Their job is to make sure the other legislators in their party vote according to the official party policy.

- Indira Gandhi projected this Congress split as a divide between the **socialist** and **conservatives, the pro-poor and the pro-rich.**

Abolition of Privy Purse

- During the integration of the Princely States following promises were done to the princes.
  - Royal families would be allowed to have private property.
  - Given the government allowance, gift, revenue etc. This was called as Privy Purse.
- It was considered against the principles of equality and justice. Thus, Indira Gandhi after winning elections in 1971 amended the Constitution and abolished the privy purse, despite many opposition.

Quick Test 3

1. Who were the Syndicates?
2. Who intcoduced mid-day meal scheme in Madras province?
3. Who was the maker of modern Karnataka?
4. What were the two Congress factions, which came into existence after the Congress split?

5.5 The 1971 Election and Restoration of Congress

- After the Congress split, Indira Gandhi remained in office with the issue-based support of some parties like **CPI** and the **DMK.** She campaigned for implementing the **land reforms** and **land ceiling legislation.** Her government recommended the Lok Sabha dissolution[3] in December 1970 and the fifth general election to the Lok Sabha were held in February 1971.

The Contest

- Now the new Congress, **Congress (R)** had to compete with the old and experienced faction of the Congress, **Congress (O).** To defeat Indira Gandhi all other major non-communist, non-Congress opposition parties also formed an alliance known as the **Grand Alliance.**
- The Samyukta Socialist Party (SSP), Praja Socialist Party (PSP), Bharatiya Jana Sangh (BJS), Swatantra Party (SWA) and the Bharatiya Kranti Dal (BKD) came together under an umbrella. The ruling party had an alliance with the Communist Party of India (CPI). The Grand Alliance did not have a coherent programme.
- Indira Gandhi spread the message to the public that the opposition party had only one common programme- **Indira Hatao (Remove Indira).** She brought the famous slogan, **Garibi Hatao (Remove Poverty)** and focused on the growth of public sector. She also tried to manage the rural support by
  - promising imposition of ceiling on rural land holdings and urban property.
  - removal of differences in income and opportunity.
  - abolition of princely privileges.
  - working for the disadvantage, specially landless labour, Dalit, Adivasi, minorities, women and unemployed youth.

The Outcome and after

- The Congress (R)- CPI alliance won more seats and votes than the Congress had ever won in the first four general elections. They combine won 375 seats in Lok Sabha and Indira Gandhi's Congress (R) won 352 seats with about 44 per cent of the popular votes on its own.

3 **Dissolution** The dissolution of a legislative assembly is the simultaneous termination of services of all the members.

- The Congress (O)–Party with so many experts could get less than one-fourth of the votes secured by Indira Gandhi's party and win only 16 seats. With this the Congress Party led by Indira Gandhi established its claim to being the **'real' Congress** and restored to it the dominant position in Indian politics. The Grand Alliance of the opposition proved a grand failure.
- Soon after the 1971, Lok Sabha elections, **Bangladesh liberation war** began which added to the popularity of Indira Gandhi. Even the opposition leader admired her **statesmanship**[4], her party won all the state assembly elections held in 1972.
- She was seen as the **protector of the poor** as well as the **strong nationalist leader**. With two successive election victories, one at the centre and other at the state level, Congress dominance was again restored.

Restoration

- Under the leadership of Indira Gandhi, the Congress Party had gained the similar popularity as it used to enjoy in the past. However, it was not the revival of the old Congress, but it was the reinvention of the old party.
- This new Congress Party now had weak organisational structure because it did not have many factions, so it could not accommodate all kinds of opinions and interest like the old Congress Party. It relied entirely on the popularity of the supreme leader.
- While, it won elections, it depended more on some social groups like the poor, the women, Dalits, adivasis and minorities. Thus, Indira Gandhi restored the Congress system by changing the nature of the Congress system itself.

Quick Test 4

1. Which parties fomed the 'Grand Alliance' against Indira Gandhi in 1971?
2. What was the result of 1971 Lok Sabha elections?
3. How did Indira Gandhi change the Congress system after her victory?

4 **Statemanship** It means the skills to manage public affairs.

Mind Map

CHALLENGES TO AND RESTORATION OF THE CONGRESS SYSTEM

1 Challenges of Political Succession

After Nehru's Death
- Debate over new Prime Minister.
- Concerns about sustaining democracy in India.
- Fear of military takeover, as seen in other newly independent countries.
- **Unresolved Issues** Poverty, inequality, communal and regional divisions.

From Nehru to Shastri
- **Lal Bahadur Shastri** chosen as new leader by Congress Party President K. Kamraj.
- Known for simplicity and moral responsibility.

Faced Two Major Challenges
- (i) Food Crisis Due to failed monsoons and droughts.
- (ii) War with Pakistan 1965.
- Coined slogan 'Jai Jawan Jai Kisan'.
- Suddenly expired in Tashkent, Uzbekistan in 1966.

From Shastri to Indira Gandhi
- **Indira Gandhi** Chosen as new leader by two-thirds of Congress MPs.
- She was daughter of Jawaharlal Nehru and former Union Minister for Information.

Faced Challenges
- Economic deterioration.
- Control of senior Congress leaders over Indira Gandhi's leadership.
- Supported by Congress leaders due to inexperience.

2 Fourth General Elections, 1967

Context
- Death of two Prime Ministers.
- Economic and food crisis.
- Devaluation of Indian rupee.
- Price rise and unemployment.

Non-Congressism
- Opposition parties united against Congress.
- Anti-Congress agenda and seat sharing.
- Rammanohar Lohiya's strategy.

Defection
- Elected representatives switching parties.
- Rise of "Aya Ram, Gaya Ram" expression.
- Instability in non-Congress governments.

Electoral Verdict
- Congress won lowest number of seats since 1952.
- Lost majority in seven states.
- Defeat of senior Congress leaders.

Coalitions
- Non-Congress parties formed joint governments.
- Samyukta Vidhayak Dal (SVD) governments.

For examples, Bihar, Punjab.

3 Split in the Congress

Indira Gandhi's Strategy Ground Level
- Chose trusted advisers from outside the party.
- Sidelined the Syndicate.
- Converted power struggle into ideological struggle.
- Launched initiatives for leftoriented policies.
- Adopted Ten Point Programme.

Indira Vs. the 'Syndicate'
- Indira Gandhi faced challenge from within the Congress.
- 'Syndicate' group of powerful leaders expected Indira to follow their advice.

Indira Gandhi's Challenges
- Build independence from the Syndicate.
- Regain Congress victory at the ground level.

After 1967 Elections
- Congress retained power at the centre with reduced majority.
- Lost power in many states.
- Non-Congress coalition governments struggled to survive.

4 Fourth General Elections, 1967

- Indira Gandhi vs 'Syndicate' rivalry became public.
- Indira Gandhi backed V.V. Giri, announcing policies like bank nationalisation.
- Congress President issued whip for Sanjeeva Reddy, but Indira Gandhi called for 'conscience vote'.
- V.V. Giri won, leading to Congress Party split.
- **Split led to two factions** Congress (Requisitionists) and Congress (Organisation).

5 The 1971 Election and Restoration of Congress

Contest
- **Congress** Indira Gandhi's faction.
- **Congress (O)** 'Syndicate' faction.
- **Grand Alliance** Opposition parties (SSP, PSP, BJS, SWA, BKD) united against Indira Gandhi.

Background
- Congress split after Indira Gandhi's disagreement with the 'Syndicate'.
- Indira Gandhi remained in office with support from CPI and DMK.

Campaign
- **Indira Gandhi's slogans** Garibi Hatao (Remove Poverty), focus on public sector growth.
- **Promises** ceiling on rural land holdings, removal of income differences, abolition of princely privileges.

Outcome
- **Congress(R)** CPI alliance won 375 Lok Sabha seats, Indira Gandhi's Congress(R) won 352 seats with 44% popular votes.
- **Congress (O)** won only 16 seats.
- Indira Gandhi established her claim as the 'real' Congress leader.

Restoration of Congress
- Under Indira Gandhi's Leadership.
- Gained popularity similar to the past.
- Reinvented the old party with a new structure.
- Weak organisational structure, reliant on support from poor, women, Dalits, adivasis and minorities.

Aftermath
- **Bangladesh liberation war (1971)** Added to Indira Gandhi's popularity.
- Congress won all state assembly elections in 1972.
- Indira Gandhi seen was as protector of the poor and strong nationalist leader.
- Congress dominance restored.

NCERT Folder

Intext Questions

1. What's so unusual in hung assemblies and coalition governments? (Pg. no. 80)

Ans. Hung assemblies and coalition governments are unusual because they happen when no single party wins enough seats to form a majority in the legislature. This means that there is no clear winner and multiple parties need to come together to form a government.

They need to work together, often making compromises and forming alliances to have enough support to govern.

2. Almost four decades after giving the slogan of 'Garibi Hatao', we still have much poverty around. Was the slogan only an election gimmick? (Pg. 86)

Ans. The slogan 'Garibi Hatao' (Remove Poverty) was given by former Prime Minister Indira Gandhi in the 1971 elections to reduce poverty. While the slogan was powerful and attracted a lot of support, the reality is that poverty is a complex issue and cannot be solved quickly or easily.

Although various programmes were launched to improve the lives of poor people, many challenges such as lack of education, job opportunities and unequal wealth distribution still exist.

Exercise

1. Which of these statements about the 1967 elections is/are correct?

(i) Congress won the Lok Sabha elections, but lost the assembly elections in many states.

(ii) Congress lost both Lok Sabha and assembly elections.

(iii) Congress lost majority in the Lok Sabha, but formed a coalition government with the support of some other parties.

(iv) Congress retained power at the centre with an increased majority.

Ans. (i) Congress won the Lok Sabha elections but lost the assembly elections in many states is the correct statement.

2. Whom would you identify with the following slogans/phrases?

(i) Jai Jawan, Jai Kisan **(ii) Indira Hatao**

(iii) Garibi Hatao

Ans. (i) Lal Bahadur Shastri → Jai Jawan, Jai Kisan

(ii) Grand Alliance → Indira Hatao

(iii) Indira Gandhi → Garibi Hatao

3. Match the following.

List I		List II
A. Syndicate	1.	An elected representative leaving the party on whose ticket she has been elected.
B. Defection	2.	A catchy phrase that attracts public attention.
C. Slogan	3.	Parties with different ideological position coming together to oppose Congress and its policies.
D. Anti-Congressism	4.	A group of powerful and influential leaders within the Congress.

Ans. A → 4, B → 1, C → 2, D → 3

4. Which of the following statement about the Grand Alliance of 1971 is correct?

The Grand Alliance

(i) was formed by non-Communist, non-Congress parties.

(ii) had a clear political and ideological programme.

(iii) was formed by all non-Congress parties.

Ans. (i) was formed by non-Communist, non-Congress parties.

5. How should a political party resolve its internal differences? Here are some suggestions. Think of each and list out their advantages and shortcomings.

(i) Follow the footsteps of the party President.

(ii) Listen to the majority group.

(iii) Secret ballot voting on every issue.

(iv) Consult the senior and experienced leaders of the party.

Ans. (i) **Advantage** If party follow the footstep of President, there will be unity and discipline in party.

Shortcoming If party follow the decision of the President without taking the opinions of the members into account, there will be no internal democracy. The members of party will feel neglected.

(ii) **Advantage** If party listen to the majority group, there will be no rebel in party and order and discipline will be maintained.

Shortcoming If party listen to the majority group and do not accommodate the minority and different groups, there is greater possibility of factionalism discontent and internal fighting in party.

(iii) **Advantage** Secret ballot voting is a most democratic method of knowing the opinion of members of party, as members will vote without any fear of fighting.

Shortcoming Secret ballot voting on every issue may result in delay in decision-making in party.

(iv) **Advantage** Consulting the senior and experienced leader of the party may help the party in tackling the challenging issue because of their rich experience and maturity.

Shortcoming Consulting the senior and experienced leader of party may keep the party away from innovative and fresh ideas of young mind of party.

6. State which of these were reasons for the defeat of the Congress in 1967. Give reasons for your answer.

(i) The absence of a charismatic leader in the Congress Party.

(ii) Split within the Congress Party.

(iii) Increased mobilisation of regional, ethnic and communal groups.

(iv) Increasing unity among non-Congress parties.

(v) Internal differences within the Congress Party.

Ans. (i) This is not the reason for the defeat because Congress had so many experienced and popular leaders during elections.

(ii) This is also not the reason for the defeat because split was not much visible during election and Syndicate, a group of powerful and influential leaders also supported Indira in early years. The split become visible only after 1967 election.

(iii) This is one factor which led to formation of non Congress government in the states. For example, in Madras, DMK formed the government through mobilisation of regional and linguistic groups.

(iv) Increasing unity among non-Congress Party was also one of the reason for Congress defeat in many states like Punjab, Haryana, Uttar Pradesh, Madhya Pradesh, Bihar, Kerala, etc.

(v) Internal differences within the Congress Party was also one of the reason for Congress defeat because Congress was somewhat unable to put itself united before the public.

7. What were the factors which led to the popularity of Indira Gandhi's government in the early 1970s?

Ans. There have been many factors which led to the popularity of Indira Gandhi's government in the early 1970s. These were

- Her socialist approach worked in her favour and her ideas like land reform and land ceiling legislation as well.
- Her slogan 'Garibi Hatao' was the need of that time. People took it positively and supported her.
- Her support for the growth of public sector, removal of inequality in income and opportunity and abolition of privy purse gained popularity.
- Through 'Garibi Hatao', she became popular among dalits, disadvantaged, women, minority, etc.
- 1971 war added to her popularity. She managed the political and economic affair of that time effectively. She was admired by opposition also.
- She was seen as a protector of poor and a strong and capable national leader.

8. What does the term 'Syndicate' mean in the context of the Congress Party of the sixties? What role did the Syndicate play in the Congress Party?

Or Analyse the issue Indira Vs. the Syndicate. What type of challenges did the issue pose before Indira Gandhi? **Competency Based Que**

Ans. Syndicate was a group of powerful and influential leaders from within the Congress. Syndicate was led by K. Kamaraj, former Chief Minister of Tamil Nadu and the then President of Congress Party. It also includes some powerful leaders like S.K. Patil, S. Nijalingappa, N. Sanjeeva Reddy and Atulya Ghosh.

The role played by Syndicate were

- Syndicate played crucial and decisive role in the making of Shastri and Indira Gandhi.
- Syndicate helped Indira Gandhi in the selection of the first Council of Ministers and formulation and implementation of socialist policies and welfare programmes. After split in the Congress, Congress (O) was led by the Syndicate and Congress (R) was led by Indira Gandhi. The rising popularity and overwhelming political authority of Indira Gandhi after 1970 election made Syndicate insignificant and uninfluential.

9. Discuss the major issues which led to the formal split of the Congress Party in 1969.

Or Explain any three causes of the split in the Congress Party in 1969.

Or Examine the three main reasons responsible for the split in the Congress Party during 1969.

Or Examine any six factors which were responsible for split of the Congress in 1969.

Or Explain the major issues which were responsible for the formal split of the Congress Party in 1969. **All India 2011**

Or Explain any three reasons that led to the split in the Congress Party in 1969. **CBSE Term II 2022**

Or Highlight any two reasons for the split in the Congress Party in 1969. **CBSE Term II 2023**

Ans. The six factors responsible for the split of the Congress in 1969 were as follows

(i) The political tension inside the Congress over the unsettled question of relation between its ministerial and organisation wings became more pronounced.

(ii) Indira Gandhi had acquired a certain control over the government but after the blow suffered by the Syndicate in 1967 elections, she had hardly any organisational base in the party. The veteran leader wanted that Indira should not interfere in party affairs.

(iii) After retirement of Kamaraj as party President at the end of 1967, the other members of party foiled Indira Gandhi's attempt to have her own men elected to succeed him. But Nijalingappa was elected and none of the Indira Gandhi's men were elected to the new working committee.

(iv) She did not want to harm the unity of the party and the existence of her government by creating a conflict with the organisational wing, as the party enjoyed only a small majority in Lok Sabha.

(v) She adopted a radical ten-point programme which included social control of banks, nationalisation of 14 private banks and abolition of the privy purse or the special privileges given to former princes.

(vi) The Congress was divided into two factions, one was right and second was left. Left attacked on Morarji Desai as the representative of big business houses.

The defeat of the Congress formalised the split in the party. The Congress President expelled the Prime Minister from the party. Indira Gandhi claimed that her group was the real Congress.

10. **Read the passage and answer the questions below.**

Indira Gandhi changed the Congress into highly centralised and undemocratic party organisation, from the earlier federal, democratic and ideological formation that Nehru had led .... But this .... could not have happened had not Indira Gandhi changed the entire nature of politics.

This new, populist politics turned political ideology....... into a mere electoral discourse, use of various slogans not meant to be translated into government policies .... During its great electoral victories in early 1970s, amidst the celebration, the Congress Party as a political organisation died.

—Sudipta Kaviraj

(i) What according to the author is the difference between the strategies of Nehru and Indira Gandhi?

(ii) Why does the author say that the Congress Party 'died' in the seventies?

(iii) In what way, did the change in the Congress Party affect other political parties also?

Ans. (i) According to author, main difference between the strategies of Nehru and Indira Gandhi is that Jawaharlal Nehru made the Congress into federal, democratic and ideological party, whereas Indira Gandhi changed it into highly centralised and undemocratic party.

(ii) According to author, Congress Party died in the seventies because Indira Gandhi changed the nature of the Congress system. This new populist politics turned political ideology into a electoral politics only for the sake of victories. The use of slogans were meant to catch the attention of public, not to be translated into government policies.

(iii) The change in the Congress Party also affected the other political parties. They formed alliance and coalition to defeat the Congress. They also adopted populist and welfare measures and slogans to counter the Congress and catch the public attention.

Exam Pattern Questions

Objective Type Questions

Multiple Choice Questions (MCQs)

1. Prime Minister Jawaharlal Nehru passed away in ....

(a) May 1965 (b) May 1964
(c) June 1960 (d) June 1964

2. Which major challenge did India face during Shastri's tenure as Prime Minister?

(a) Economic Boom (b) War with Pakistan, 1965
(c) War with China, 1962 (d) Plague

3. Where did Lal Bahadur Shatri pass away unexpectedly?

(a) Delhi, India (b) Moscow, USSR
(c) Tashkent, Uzbekistan (d) Lahore, Pakistan

4. After the death of Lal Bahadur Shashtri, there was an intense competition for the post of Prime Minister between Indira Gandhi and which one of the following? CBSE 2024

(a) Morarji Desai (b) K. Kamaraj
(c) S. Nijalingappa (d) V.V. Giri

5. When was the fourth general election held in India? Diksha App

(a) 1960 (b) 1965 (c) 1964 (d) 1967

6. Which of the following problems did India face before the fourth general elections? CBSE 2024

I. Failure of monsoon
II. Food crisis
III. Heavy Rainfall
IV. Depletion of foreign exchange reserves

Choose the correct option.

(a) I, II (b) III, IV (c) I, II, IV (d) II, III, IV

7. The elections of 1967 brought into the picture the phenomenon of ....

(a) party politics (b) Syndicate
(c) coalition (d) None of these

8. Who was the official candidate of the Congress Party in the Presidential election of 1969? Diksha App

(a) Zakir Hussain (b) N. Sanjeeva Reddy
(c) V.V. Giri (d) K. Kamaraj

9. Who was the President of the Congress Party at the time of the split in 1969? Diksha App

(a) Indira Gandhi (b) K. Kamaraj
(c) S. Nijalingappa (d) Karpoori Thakur

10. The 'Grand Alliance' formed during the 1971 elections comprised of .... Diksha App

(a) Congress (R) and Congress (O)
(b) Communist Party of India and B.J.S
(c) Congress (O) and C.P.I
(d) Major non-Communist and non-Congress opposition parties

11. Identify and write the Incorrect pair Competency Based Que

(a) K. Kamaraj – served as Chief Minister of Tamil Nadu
(b) S. Nijalingappa – served as Chief Minister of Karnataka
(c) Karpoori Thakur – introduce backward class reservations in Bihar
(d) Ram Manohar Lohia - strong opponent of socialism

12. Arrange in Sequence Competency Based Que

I. Second General Elections
II. V.V. Giri elected as the President of India
III. Fourth General Elections
IV. Congress (R)-CPI alliance won more seats in general elections

Codes

(a) I, III, II and IV (b) III, II, IV and I
(c) II, IV, I and III (d) IV, III, I and II

13. Choose the wrong statement from the given options. Competency Based Que

(a) The power structure of India after independence was dominated by the Congress Party.
(b) Congress was very well organised and had organisational presence across India.
(c) Indira Gandhi dominated the Syndicate group.
(d) Split in the Congress Party was evident during the 1969 Presidential elections.

14. Identify the false statement from the following related to Lal Bahadur Shastri. CBSE 2024

(a) He worked as the General Secretary of the Congress Party till 1966.
(b) He was in the Union Cabinet for a short period of three years.
(c) He resigned from the Union Cabinet taking responsibility for a railway accident.
(d) He gave the famous slogan 'Jai Jawan Jai Kisan'.

15. **Which of the following statements is not true?** Competency Based Que; Diksha App

(a) Indira Gandhi was unanimously elected as leader of the Congress Parliamentary Party.
(b) Indira Gandhi succeeded, Lal Bahadur Shastri as the Prime Minister of India.
(c) Initially Indira Gandhi got support from senior leaders of the Congress Party.
(d) From Pandit Jawaharlal Nehru to Lal Bahadur Shastri and Lal Bahadur Shastri to Indira Gandhi there was a peaceful transition of power.

16. **Which of the following statements is not correct?** Competency Based Que; Diksha App

(a) The 1960s were labelled as the dangerous decade.
(b) K. Kamaraj was the President of the Congress Party in 1964.
(c) Lal Bahadur Shastri was unanimously chosen as the leader of the Congress Parliamentary Party.
(d) Indira Gandhi was appointed Prime Minister in 1964.

17. **Identify the main reason for the split in Congress Party in 1969.** CBSE 2025

(a) Change in the ideology of Congress Party
(b) Dominance of the Congress Syndicate
(c) Difference of opinion among the opposition parties
(d) Opposition parties came together

18. **Identify and choose the incorrect pair** CBSE 2025

(a) Lal Bahadur Shastri	Jai Jawan Jai Kisan
(b) Indira Gandhi	Garibi Hatao
(c) Syndicate	A group of powerful opposition leaders against Indira Gandhi
(d) Grand Alliance	Formed by all Non-Congress Parties

19. **Given below are two statements** Competency Based Que

Statement I The anti-Hindi agitation in Tamil Nadu was successful in changing India's lanuage policy.

Statement II The government decided to continue using english along with Hindi for official purposes.

In the light of the above statements, choose the correct answer from the options given below

(a) Both Statement I and Statement II are true.
(b) Both Statement I and Statement II are false.
(c) Statement I is true, but Statement II is false.
(d) Statement I is false, but Statement II is true.

Assertion-Reason Questions

Directions (Q. Nos. 20-22) In the questions given below, there are two statements marked as Assertion (A) and Reason (R). Read the statements and choose the correct option.

Codes

(a) Both A and R are true and R is the correct explanation of A.
(b) Both A and R are true, but R is not the correct explanation of A.
(c) A is true, but R is false.
(d) A is false, but R is true.

20. **Assertion** (A) India faced severe food shortages during the 1950s and 60s.

Reason (R) Consecutive droughts led to a decline in agricultural production.

21. **Assertion** (A) In the election, of 1967, the Congress had to face defeat in 9 states.

Reason (R) In the election, there was a decrease in the percentage of vote obtained by the Congress and also in the number of seats.

22. **Assertion** (A) In 1969 the Congress Party faced a split.

Reason (R) Factional rivalry existed between the Congress Syndicate and Indira Gandhi.

Passage Based Questions

23. **Read the passage given below carefully and answer the questions that follow.**

Syndicate was the informal name given to a group of Congress leaders who were in control of the party's organisation. It was led by K. Kamaraj, former Chief Minister of Tamil Nadu and the then President of the Congress Party. It included powerful state leaders like S.K. Patil of Bombay city (later named as Mumbai), S. Nijalingappa of Mysore (later Karnataka), N. Sanjeeva Reddy of Andhra Pradesh and Atulya Ghosh of West Bengal. Both Lal Bahadur Shastri and later Indira Gandhi owed their position to the support received from the Syndicate.

This group had a decisive say in Indira Gandhi's First Council of Ministers and also in policy formulation and implementation. After the Congress split the leaders of the Syndicate and those owing allegiance to them stayed with the Congress (O). Since, it was Indira Gandhi's Congress (R) that won the test of popularity, all these big and powerful men of Indian politics lost their power and prestige after 1971.

(i) **Who led the Syndicate group?**

(a) S. Nijalingappa (b) S.K. Patil
(c) K. Kamaraj (d) Indira Gandhi

(ii) **What was the 'Syndicate' in the Congress Party?**

(a) A group of bureaucrats controlling the government
(b) A group of industrialists funding the Congress

(c) A group of senior Congress leaders controlling the party's organisation
(d) A faction of the opposition parties against Congress

(iii) Explain the role played by the Syndicate.

24. Read the passage carefully given below and answer the following questions.

The New Congress had something that its big opponents lacked. It has issues, an agenda and a positive slogan. The Grand Alliance did not have a coherent political programme. Indira Gandhi said that the opposition alliance had only one common programme 'Indira Hatao'. In contrast to this, she put forward a positive programme captured in the famous slogan 'Garibi Hatao'.

(i) Which Congress is referred as New Congress?
(a) Congress led by K. Kamaraj
(b) Congress led by Indira Gandhi
(c) Congress which is independent
(d) None of the above

(ii) Which common programme was highlighted by the Grand Alliance?
(a) Garibi Hatao
(b) Indira Hatao
(c) Food grains distribution
(d) Growth of public sector

(iii) Which steps were taken by Indira Gandhi to remove poverty?

25. The result of the elections dealt a blow to the congress at the national and provincial levels. Political observers of the time called the election results a 'Political earth quake'. The Congress somehow managed to get a majority in the Lok Sabha, but the percentage of votes it got and the number of seats declined drastically. Before now, the Congress had neither got so few votes nor got so few seats. Half of the ministers of Indira Gandhi's cabinet had lost the election.

(i) To which election is the above passage related?
(a) Third General Election, 1962
(b) Fourth General Election, 1967
(c) Sixth General Election, 1977
(d) Fifth General Election, 1971

(ii) By what name have political observers addressed this election?
(a) Political storm (b) Political movement
(c) Political earthquake (d) Political explosion

(iii) Which of the following big leaders of Congress lost the seat in this election?
(a) K. Kamaraj (b) Ram Manohar Lohia
(c) Neelam Sanjeeva Reddy (d) Morarji Desai

(iv) Congress lost this election due to which of the following reasons?
(a) Lack of control on inflation
(b) Better co-ordination within Congress
(c) Dispute between Indira Gandhi and the Syndicate
(d) Land reform programme

Answers

1. (b) May 1964
2. (b) War with Pakistan, 1965
3. (c) Tashkent, Uzbekistan
4. (a) Morarji Desai
5. (d) 1967
6. (c) I, II, IV
7. (c) coalition
8. (b) N. Sanjeeva Reddy
9. (c) S. Nijalingappa
10. (d) Major non-Communist and non-Congress opposition parties
11. (d) Ram Manohar Lohia - strong opponent of socialism
12. (a) I, III, II and IV
13. (c) Indira Gandhi dominated the Syndicate group.
14. (b) He was in the Union Cabinet for a short period of three years.
15. (a) Indira Gandhi was unanimously elected as leader of the Congress Parliamentary Party.
16. (d) Indira Gandhi was appointed Prime Minister in 1964.
17. (b) Dominance of the Congress Syndicate
18. (c) Syndicate — A group of powerful opposition leaders against Indira Gandhi
19. (a) Both Statement I and Statement II are true.
20. (a) Both A and R are true and R is the correct explanation of A.
21. (b) Both A and R are true, but R is not the correct explanation of A.
22. (a) Both A and R are true and R is the correct explanation of A.
23. (i) (c) K. Kamaraj

(ii) (c) A group of senior Congress leaders controlling the party's organisation

(iii) • They had a decisive say in Indira Gandhi's first Council of Ministers.
• Both Indira Gandhi and Lal Bahadur Shastri owed their position to Syndicate.
• They also had a say in policy formulation and implementation.

24. (i) (b) Congress led by Indira Gandhi
(ii) (b) Indira Hatao
(iii) Indira Gandhi took several steps to remove poverty. It includes launching public distribution of food grains, land reforms and provisions of house sites.

25. (i) (b) Fourth General elections, 1967
(ii) (c) Political earthquake
(iii) (a) K. Kamaraj
(iv) (a) Lack of control on inflation

Subjective Questions

Very Short Answer Type Questions

1. What challenges did Lal Bahadur Shastri face during his tenure as Prime Minister?

Ans. Lal Bahadur Shastri faced two major challenges during his tenure from 1964 to 1966

Economic Challenges Failed monsoons, drought and a food crisis strained the economy.

War with Pakistan In 1965, India fought a war with Pakistan. Shastri united the country with the slogan 'Jai Jawan Jai Kisan' (Hail the Soldier, Hail the Farmer) to address both military and agricultural challenges. His tenure ended abruptly due to his sudden death in Tashkent in 1966.

2. Describe any two circumstances that favoured Indira Gandhi to become Prime Minister after the death of Lal Bahadur Shastri. CBSE 2025

Ans. After the death of Lal Bahadur Shastri in 1966, the following two key circumstances favoured Indira Gandhi to became Prime Minister

- **Support from Senior Congress Leaders** The Congress syndicate, led by senior leaders like K. Kamaraj, saw Indira Gandhi as politically inexperienced and believed they could control her decisions.
- **Divided Opposition** There was no strong alternative candidate and her family legacy as Jawaharlal Nehru's daughter gave her widespread public recognition and support.

3. State the severe economic crisis prior to the Fourth General Elections of 1967. CBSE 2025

Ans. Prior to the Fourth General Elections of 1967, India faced a severe economic crisis due to consecutive droughts in 1965 and 1966. The rupee was devalued in 1966 and foreign aid dependency increased. Additionally, the wars with China (1962) and Pakistan (1965) strained the economy which caused widespread public discontent and political instability.

4. What role did the economic situation play in the political changes of the 1960s?

Ans. The 1960s saw severe economic challenges, including widespread drought and food shortages.

Devaluation of the Indian rupee, which raised the cost of living.

There were problems of rising unemployment and inflation. These issues led to public protests, strikes and discontent, which the government failed to address adequately. This unrest weakened the Congress Party's popularity, contributing to its poor performance in the 1967 elections.

5. What is meant by non-Congressism? Diksha App

Or **Highlight the importance of the strategy of 'non-Congressism' forwarded by Ram Manohar Lohia in 1967 general election.** CBSE Term II 2022

Ans. The term non-Congressism was coined by Ram Manohar Lohia. He advocated that the Congress's rule was undemocratic and opposed the interests of ordinary poor people. Thus, all other parties came and organised themselves. This system was non-Congressism. It also reclaimed the democracy for the people.

6. What was the significance of the 1967 general elections in India?

Ans. The 1967 elections were a turning point in India's political history because

The Congress Party faced its first major setback, losing power in nine states. In Tamil Nadu, the DMK became the first regional party to win a clear majority.

At the national level, the Congress retained power but with reduced seats, indicating the decline of its dominance. This marked the beginning of coalition politics and increased influence of regional parties.

7. Explain the meaning of the term defection in politics. CBSE 2024

Or **What does defection stands for in Indian politics? Highlight any two demerits of this practice.**

Or **Assess the role played by 'defections' in the Indian politics.** Competency Based Que

Ans. Defection was a factor in 1967 elections. It played an important role in formation and collapsing of government. Defection displays the behaviour of an elected representative who leaves the party on whose symbol he/she won and joins another party.

Two demerits of this practice were

(i) It causes instability within party.

(ii) It promotes political opportunism among party legislators.

8. Why did Morarji Desai left the Indira Gandhi government during his Finance Ministership?

Ans. When Indira Gandhi announced popular policies like nationalisation of 14 private banks and the abolition of privy purses. Morarji Desai, the Deputy Prime Minister and Finance Minister had sharp differences over it. Thus, he left the government.

9. How did 1971 Bangladesh military crisis impact the image of Indira Gandhi as a leader?

Ans.
- 1971 Bangladesh crisis added popularity to the image of Indira Gandhi, Even the opposition leaders admired her statesmanship.
- She seemed to be the protector of under-privileged and poor as well as a strong nationalist leader.

Short Answer Type Questions

1. Why in context of India, the 1960s were labelled as a 'dangerous decade'? Diksha App

Ans. The 1960s era was labelled as a 'dangerous decade' because

- The first Prime Minister of the country Jawaharlal Nehru died and it was a challenge for India to carry forward its democratic succession with a new leadership.
- There were several unsolved problems like poverty, inequality, communal and regional divisions which may lead to the failure of democratic project in India.

2. Describe any two advantages and two disadvantages of 'coalition' government in India.

Or **Explain any two advantages of coalition government.** CBSE 2024

Ans. The advantages of coalition government in India are

(i) Coalition government provides an alternative to form government, whenever there is a case of hung Parliament.

(ii) It gives small and regional parties, opportunities to representation in government.

The disadvantages of coalition government in India are

(i) It leads to instability in government, as different partners pull the government differently and government finds itself unable to take right decision at right time.

(ii) It reduces the credibility of office of PM/CM as their tenure depends at the pleasure of coalition partners. It produces weak government.

3. The phrase 'Aya Ram Gaya Ram' signifies which concept? Explain its impact on the Indian political system. Competency Based Que

Ans. The expression 'Aya Ram Gaya Ram' became popular in the political vocabulary in India to describe the practice of frequent floor-crossing by legislators or defection. The phrase became the subject of numerous jokes and cartoons. Ultimately, the Constitution was amended to prevent defections.

Its impacts on Indian political system were

- It leads to instability within a political party.
- It promotes political opportunism in political system.
- It erodes the faith and trust of common in political system.
- It causes instable government.

4. Highlight any four steps taken by Indira Gandhi to remove poverty. CBSE 2023

Ans. There are following steps taken by Indira Gandhi to remove poverty

(i) She got the Congress Working Committee to adopt a ten point programme in May 1967. This programme included the social control of banks, nationalisation of general insurance, ceiling on urban poverty and income.

(ii) She also promised for the public distribution of the food grains, land reforms and provision of house sites to the rural poor.

(iii) She abolished the privy purse- princely privileges in 1971 after her victory in the elections.

(iv) Before 1971 elections, she launched a massive campaign 'Garibi Hatao'. She made promises to bring popular policies for poverty eradication and bringing economic equality.

5. Examine the factors which helped V.V. Giri to become the President of India.

Ans. During 1969 Presidential election, a series of events took place which helped Shri V.V. Giri to become the President of India. These were

- The factional rivalry between the Syndicate and Indira Gandhi, the then PM became public in 1969.
- Despite Indira Gandhi's reservations, the Syndicate nominated her long time opponent and the then speaker of the Lok Sabha, N. Sanjeeva Reddy, as the official Congress candidate for Presidential elections. Smt. Indira Gandhi reacted by encouraging the then Vice-President, V.V. Giri to stand for presidential eletion as an independent candidate.
- Shri Morarji Desai was the Deputy PM and Finance Minister. On both issues, serious conflict emerged

between the old and new groups of congress due to which he left the government.

- After having silently supported to V.V. Giri, Smt. Indira Gandhi publicly called for a conscience vote which meant that the MP's and MLA's from the Congress are free to vote the way they want.
- The above factors helped in the victory of Shri V.V. Giri, the independent candidate in the presidential election. The defeat of Shri Sanjeeva Reddy, official Congress candidate formalised the split in the Congress Party.

6. What is meant by 'Privy Purse'? Why did Indira Gandhi insist on abolishing them in 1970?

Ans. At the time of dis-solution of Princely States, the rulers of Princely States had been assured that their families would get the right to retain certain private property based on heredity and government allowances would also be given by the extent of revenue and potential of the merging states. This was called as Privy Purse.

Indira Gandhi insisted on abolition of Privy Purse because

- According to Indira Gandhi such privilege to them goes against the essence of Constitution. It was against Right to Equality, even Nehru had shown his dis-satisfaction against such privilege. After she won in 1967 elections, she put her demand to abolish Privy Purse.
- This hereditary privilege was against the ideas of equality and social and economic justice, which is embedded in Indian Constitution.
- In 1970, demand to amend Privy Purse was rejected by Rajya Sabha and ordinance was put down by Supreme Court. It was in 1971 after she won with great majority, she was able to amend the Constitution to abolish Privy Purse.

7. What do the following relate to?

(i) Jai Jawan Jai Kisan **(ii) Garibi Hatao**
(iii) Indira Hatao **(iv) Grand Alliance**

Ans. (i) This was a slogan given by Lal Bahadur Shastri in 1965, when India was facing food crisis and a war with Pakistan.

(ii) Indira Gandhi gave this slogan in 1971. With this slogan, Indira Gandhi made a political strategy to build an independent nationwide political support.

(iii) This was an anti-Indira slogan during 1971 election.

(iv) This was an alliance before 1971 elections. In this alliance, non-Communist, non-Congress opposition parties formed a group known as Grand Alliance.

Long Answer Type Questions

1. Discuss the economic and political challenges faced by Indira Gandhi during her early years as Prime Minister.

Ans. Indira Gandhi faced several economic and political challenges when she became Prime Minister in 1966

- **Economic Problems** India was struggling with droughts, food shortages and inflation. In 1966, Indira Gandhi devalued the rupee to secure foreign aid, which worsened inflation and made imports costlier. This decision was widely criticised.
- **Political Rivalries** Senior Congress leaders, known as the Syndicate, believed Indira Gandhi would act under their control. However, she asserted her independence, leading to tensions within the party.
- **Decline of Congress** The Congress Party's poor performance in the 1967 elections further weakened her position, as the party lost its dominance in several states.
- **Regional Movements** Anti-Hindi agitations in Tamil Nadu and demands for state autonomy in other regions posed additional challenges to her leadership.
  Despite these challenges, Indira Gandhi gradually consolidated her power by addressing economic issues and taking bold decisions, such as nationalising banks in 1969, to strengthen her position and win public support.

2. Why was the verdict of the 1967 general election termed as a political earthquake? **Diksha App**

Ans. The verdict of 1967, general election was termed as political earthquake because

- In the 1967, general elections, the Congress Party managed to get a major majority in Lok Sabha, but with the lowest tally of seats and share of the word since 1952.
- Many political leaders and experts of Congress lost elections like K. Kamaraj, S.K. Patil, Atulya Ghosh, etc.
- Opposition parties built around non-Congressism. This strategy paid them good amount of seats.
- Congress lost majority in as many as seven states and in other two states, defection prevented it from forming a government.
- Non-Congress governments were formed in nine states which are Punjab, Haryana, Uttar Pradesh, Madhya Pradesh, Bihar, West Bengal, Odisha, Madras and Kerala.
- In most of the states, coalition governments were formed whereas in Madras DMK won with a clear majority.

This defeat of Congress led to the popular saying that a train could take from Delhi to Howrah and may not pass through even a single Congress ruled state.

3. Describe any three major events that led to the formal split in the Congress Party in 1969.

Or **Analyse any two reasons for the split of Congress in 1969.** **CBSE Term II 2022**

Ans. Three major events that led to the formal split in the Congress Party in 1969 were as follows

(i) The political tension inside the Congress over the unsettled question of relation between its ministerial and organisation wings became more pronounced.

Indira Gandhi had acquired a certain control over the government but after the blow suffered by the Syndicate in 1967 elections, she had hardly any organisational base in the party. The veteran leader wanted that Indira should not interfere in party affairs.

(ii) After retirement of Kamaraj, as party President at the end of 1967, the other members of party foiled Indira Gandhi's attempt to have her own men elected to succeed him. But Nijalingappa was elected and none of the Indira Gandhi's men were elected to the new working committee.

She did not want to harm the unity of the party and the existence of her government by creating a conflict with the organisational wing, as the party enjoyed only a small majority in Lok Sabha.

(iii) Indira Gandhi adopted a radical ten-point programme which included social control of banks, nationalisation of 14 private banks and abolition of the privy purse or the special privileges given to former princes.

The Congress divided into two factions, one was right and second was left. Left attacked on Morarji Desai as the representative of big business houses.

The defeat of the Congress formalised the split in the party. The Congress President expelled the Prime Minister from the party. Indira Gandhi claimed that her group was the real Congress.

4. Assess any three challenges that the Congress Party had to face during the period from 1964 to 1971.

Or **Explain any three factors that influenced the results of 1971 election in India.** **CBSE Term II 2022**

Ans. The three challenges that the Congress Party had to face during the period from 1964 to 1971 were

(i) **Political Succession** After Nehru, some outsiders had doubts that Indian democracy will not survive, meanwhile party President K. Kamaraj, suggested Lal Bahadur Shastri's name as the Prime Minister, thus he became the second Prime Minister of India.

An abrupt end of Shastri led to challenge of political succession. This time, there was intense competition between Morarji Desai and Indira Gandhi.

Finally, Indira Gandhi became the Prime Minister. She set out to gain control over the party and to demonstrate her leadership skills.

(ii) **Emergence of Non-Congressism** Opposition parties realised that the division of their votes kept the Congress in power. So that they joined together to form anti-Congress fronts. This strategy was named as non-Congressism by Ram Manohar Lohia.

The result of 1967 elections jolted the Congress at both centre and state levels. Many elite leaders of Congress parties came together to form joint legislative parties (Samyukt Vidhayak Dal). In most of the states, Congress lost and coalition government was formed.

(iii) **Split in the Congress** Indira Gandhi had to face internal challenge that was Syndicate, a group of influential Congress leaders who were in control of the party's organisation.

Gradually, she attempted to assert her position within the government and the party. She choose her trusted group of advisers from outside the party. Slowly and carefully she sidelined the Syndicate. Meanwhile, President of India Dr. Zakir Hussain died and the post of President fell vacant.

Despite of Mrs. Gandhi reservations, the Syndicate nominated N. Sanjeeva Reddy's name as President. But Indira Gandhi Supported V.V. Giri as an independent candidate. The election ultimately, resulted in the victory of V.V. Giri and the defeat of N. Sanjeeva Reddy, the official Congress candidate formalised the split in the party Congress (O) which was Syndicate supported party and Congress (R) which was Indira Gandhi party.

5. Describe the factors which contributed to the emergence of Indira Gandhi as the most popular leader in early 1970s. **Diksha App**

Ans. • After a split in Congress, Indira Gandhi government continued in office with the issues based support of CPI, DMK and other parties. Some left oriented policies of Indira Gandhi, like the imposition of a ceiling on rural landholdings and urban properties.

- Abolition of princely privileges and steps to remove disparities, built her positive image. A massive campaign with the slogan, 'Garibi Hatao' also caught the public attention and image.
- Indira Gandhi tried to garner the support base among landless labors, Dalit and Adivasi, minority women and unemployed youth. Her popularity resulted in a victory for the Congress (R) in 1971 Lok Sabha elections.
- The crisis in East Pakistan 1971 and the establishment of Bangladesh added to the popularity of Indira Gandhi. Even opposition leaders admired her statesmanship.

Picture Based Questions

1. Observe the cartoon given below and answer the following questions.

(i) Which of the following event has been depicted by the picture given?

(a) Victory of N.Sanjeeva Reddy in Presidential elections.
(b) Victory of V.V. Giri in 1969 Presidential elections.
(c) Victory of Indira Gandhi in 1980's elections.
(d) None of the above

Ans. (b) Victory of V.V. Giri in 1969 Presidential elections.

(ii) Whom does the person lying on the floor depict?

(a) N. Sanjeeva Reddy
(b) S. Nijalingappa
(c) K. Kamaraj
(d) None of the above

Ans. (b) N. Sanjeeva Reddy

(iii) Who proposed the name of 'N. Sanjeeva Reddy' as the President for the Presidential elections in 1969?

(a) Indira Gandhi (b) Syndicate
(c) Congress (R) (d) None of these

Ans. (b) Syndicate

(iv) Before the victory, at what post did the 'winner' candidate serve for India?

(a) President
(b) Deputy-Prime minster
(c) Vice-President
(d) Cabinet Minister

Ans. (c) Vice-President

2. Observe the cartoon given below and answer the following questions.

(i) What is the overall massage conveyed by the cartoon and how does it relate to the political challenge faced during the restoration of the congress system in India ?

Ans. The overall massage of the cartoon emphasises the need for greater unity and corporation among political parties during the periods of challenges to the Congress system. Political fragmentation and operation alliances like grand alliance failed to provide cohesive alternative to Indira Gandhi 's to leadership. This highlighted the importance of political stability and collaboration to address the nation's challenges effectively .

(ii) What do the abbreviations 'LD', 'BKS', 'SSP', and 'UTKAL' in the picture represent?

Ans. These abbreviations represent different political parties that are working together in a coalition. Each party is identified by its unique abbreviation, reflecting its individual identity, but they have come together to form a united political front for shared objectives.

(iii) What does the sign "KEEP RIGHT, NO LEFT TURN" symbolise in the context of the cartoon?

Ans. The sign symbolises an attempt to form a united front of non-communist parties in India. It indicates the collaboration of right-leaning political parties that oppose leftist ideologies, showing their collective effort to counter the influence of communist movements in the political landscape.

3. Observe the cartoon given below and answer the following questions.

(i) To which year does the cartoon refer?

(a) 1989 (b) 1967 (c) 1966 (d) 1969

Ans. (b) 1967

(ii) Name the person for whom this comment 'Aya Ram Gaya Ram' was made.

(a) Aaya lal (b) Aaya Ram (c) Gaya lal (d) None of these

Ans. (c) Gaya lal

(iii) He belongs to which state?

(a) Punjab (b) Uttar Pradesh
(c) Madhya Pradesh (d) Haryana

Ans. (d) Haryana

(iv) How many times did the person change his party within 14 days?

(a) 3 (b) 2 (c) 1 (d) 5

Ans. (a) 3

Map Based Questions

1. In the given outline map of India, four states have been marked as A, B, C and D. Identify the states on the basis of the information given below and write their correct names in the answer book. **CBSE SQP 2024**

Sr. no. of the Information used	Concerned alphabet given in the map	Name of the State
I.		
II.		
III.		
IV.		

I. The state related to the leader who coined the famous slogan, 'Jai Jawan-Jai Kisan'.
II. The state associated with the formation of 'DK, DMK and AIDMK'.
III. The state where a coalition called the 'Popular United Front' came to power after 1967 election.
IV. The official Congress candidate for the 1969 Presidential election belonged to this state.

Ans.

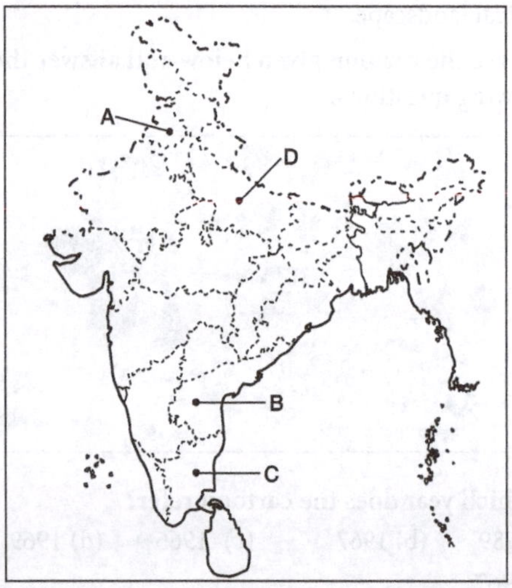

Sr. no. for the Information used	Concerned alphabet given in the map	Name of the State
I.	D	Uttar Pradesh
II.	C	Tamil Nadu
III.	A	Punjab
IV.	B	Andhra Pradesh

2. In the given outline map of India, four states have been marked as A, B, C and D. Identify the states on the basis of the information given below and write their correct names in the answer book. **CBSE 2024**

Sr. no. of the Information used	Concerned alphabet given in the map	Name of the State
I.		
II.		
III.		
IV.		

I. The state to which the former Congress President K. Kamaraj belonged.
II. The state from where the phrase 'Aya Ram, Gaya Ram' originated.
III. The state to which former Prime Minister Lal Bahadur Shastri belonged.
IV. The state where the Congress Party did not get majority in 1967 assembly election.

Ans.

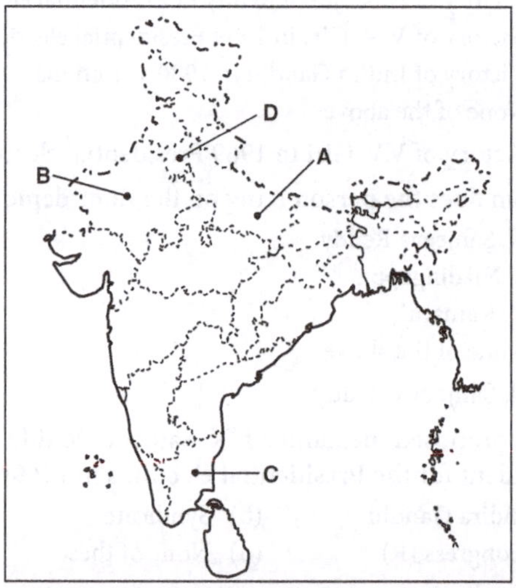

Sr. no. for the Information used	Concerned alphabet given in the map	Name of the State
I.	C	Tamil Nadu
II.	D	Haryana
III.	A	Uttar Pradesh
IV.	B	Rajasthan

3. In the given political outline map of India, four states have been marked as A, B, C and D. Identify the states on the basis of the information given below and write their correct names in your answer book along with the respective serial number and the concerned alphabet given in the map.

I. The state from which S.K. Patil lost.

II. The state to which former Chief Minister S. Nijalingappa belonged.

III. The state where DMK (Dravida Munnetra Kazhagam) came to power in 1967.

IV. The state where the Congress Party did not get majority in 1967 assembly elections.

Sr. no. for the Information used	Concerned alphabet given in the map	Name of the State
I.		
II.		
III.		
IV.		

Ans.

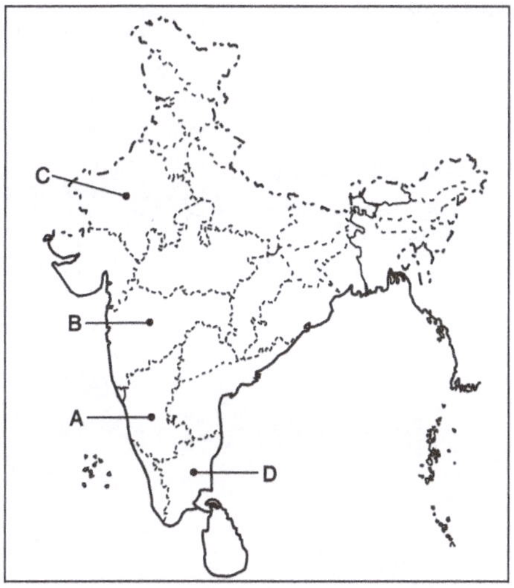

Sr. no. for the Information used	Concerned alphabet given in the map	Name of the State
I.	B	Maharashtra
II.	A	Karnataka
III.	D	Tamil Nadu
IV.	C	Rajasthan

4. In the given political outline map of India (on page 17), four States have been marked as A , B , C and D . Identify these States on the basis of the information given below and write their correct names in your answer-book along with the respective serial number of the information used and the concerned alphabets given in the map as per the following format

Serial number of the information used Concerned alphabet given in the map Name of the State **CBSE 2024 C**

Sr. no. for the Information used	Concerned alphabet given in the map	Name of the State
I.		
II.		
III.		
IV.		

I. The state to which the former Prime Minister Lal Bahadur Shastri belonged.

II. The state to which the former Chief Minister Karpoori Thakur belonged.

III. The state to which the former Chief Minister C. Natarajan Annadurai belonged.

IV. The state to which the former President of India V.V. Giri belonged.

Ans.

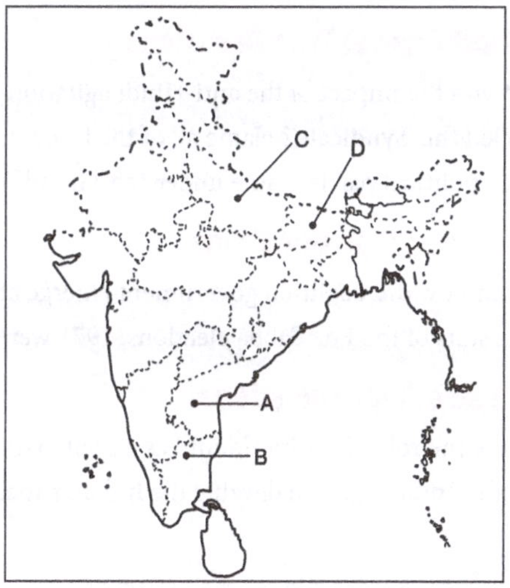

Sr. no. for the Information used	Concerned alphabet given in the map	Name of the State
I.	C	Uttar Pradesh
II.	D	Bihar
III.	B	Tamil Nadu
IV.	A	Andhra Pradesh

SELF ASSESSMENT TEST

Objective Type Questions

1. Which of the statement is/are correct about the expression 'Aya Ram Gaya Ram'?
   (a) The constant re-alignment and shifting of political loyalties.
   (b) Frequent shifting of alliance groups.
   (c) Frequent change in government.
   (d) None of the above
2. What was the price of 1 US dollar before devaluation of Indian rupee?
   (a) 7 rupees (b) 8 rupees (c) 5 rupees (d) 10 rupees
3. What did SVD stand for?
   (a) Samyukta Vidhansabha Dal (b) Samyukta Vichar Dal
   (c) Samyukta Vishwa Dal (d) Samyukta Vidhayak Dal
4. Name the state to which the former President of India V.V. Giri belonged.
   (a) Andhra Pradesh (b) Madhya Pradesh
   (c) Uttarakhand (d) Uttar Pradesh
5. What was the group of Congress called which was led by Indira Gandhi in 1969?
   (a) Congress (R) (b) Congress (O)
   (c) Congress (I) (d) Syndicate

Very Short Answer Type Questions

6. What was the impact of the anti-Hindi agitation in Tamil Nadu?
7. Who led the 'Syndicate'? Name all of the leaders.
8. Which political parties came under the 'Grand Alliance' umbrella?

Short Answer Type Questions

9. Explain how did coalition government emerge after the 1967 elections?
10. The results of the Lok Sabha elections, 1971 were dramatic. Elucidate.

Long Answer Type Questions

11. Analyse the role of Indira Gandhi as a politician.
12. Why did Indira Gandhi devalue the Indian rupee in 1966 and what was its effect on India? Explain.

06
CHAPTER

This chapter introduces the political conflict after 1967. It also highlights the conflict between the judiciary and the government and the period of emergency during 1975. The politics after emergency, formation of Janata Party and the legacy of Congress is also described.

The Crisis of Democratic Order

YOUR STUDY GOALS

6.1 Background to Emergency
6.2 Declaration of Emergency
6.3 Politics after Emergency

YOUR PRACTICE GOAL

- Objective Type Questions (28 Qs ; MCQs, A-R, Statements, Matching, Passage Based)
- Subjective Questions (8 VSAs, 7 SAs, 8 LAs) 4 Picture Based, 2 Map Based)

6.1 Background to Emergency

- After 1967, Indira Gandhi emerged as the popular leader. This period witnessed the conflict between **judiciary** and **the government** on the following issues
  - The Supreme Court declared many initiatives of the government as violative of the Constitution.
  - The Congress alleged the court that it was being against the principles of Parliamentary democracy.
  - Congress also alleged that the court was interfering in the government's implementation of pro-poor welfare schemes and becoming conservative.
- Opposition parties felt that the government has become **personal authority** because it was following very **personalised politics.**

Economic Context

- Despite of the slogan **'Garibi Hatao'** (remove poverty), the social and economic conditions in the country did not improve much after 1971-72.
- After the **Bangladesh-Pakistan War,** the **US Government** stopped all the help to India. In the international market, oil prices increased which further in turn increased the prices of commodities.
- Also, India had to deal with the population of around eight million, who came to India from East Pakistan (which is now Bangladesh).

- There was very **low growth in industries** and **unemployment** was also very high especially in the rural areas.
- In order to reduce expenditure, government had to freeze the salary of its employees which caused dissatisfaction among them.
- During 1972-73, **monsoon failed,** which caused sharp decline in the agricultural production. It further, led to the decline of food grain output by 8 per cent.
- All these problems together caused unrest among the students and they organised protests.
- During the period, Marxist groups increased their activities. These groups took arms and used revolutionary techniques to overthrow the capitalist government and established the political system. This group is known as **Marxist-leninist (Maoist)** or Naxalites. These groups were particularly strong in West Bengal.

Gujarat and Bihar Movements

- Gujarat and Bihar were the Congress ruled states. In January 1974, students in Gujarat began an agitation against the government on the following issues
  - Rising food grain prices
  - Rising prices of cooking oil and other essentials commodities
  - Corruption in high places.
- Major opposition parties also joined students protest, which leads to the **President's rule** in the state. The opposition parties demanded that the fresh elections should be held in Gujarat. **Morarji Desai** was the prominent leader of Congress(O) who was the main rival of Indira Gandhi. He announced to hold indefinite fast if fresh elections were not held in the state.
- In June 1975, fresh elections were held in Gujarat and Congress was defeated.
- In **Bihar** also, students came together to protest in the month of March 1974 against the rising prices, food scarcity and unemployment. These students invited **Jayaprakash Narayan (JP)** who had left the active politics and involved in social work.

Loknayak Jayaprakash Narayan (1902-1979)

- Marxist in his youth.
- General Secretary of the Congress Socialist Party and the Socialist Party.
- Hero of Quit India Movement, 1942.
- Declined to join Nehru's cabinet and after 1955 he quit active politics.
- Later, he became Gandhian and involved in **Bhoodan movement**.
- He also, contributed in negotiations with Naga rebels, peace in Kashmir and ensured decoits surrender in Chambal.
- He became symbol of opposition during emergency and he was also the leader of **Bihar movement.**
- He was the moving force behind the formation of **Janata Party**.

- He joined the movement on the condition that the movement should not be violent and it should not be limited to Bihar only.
- Jayaprakash Narayan demanded the dismissal of the Congress government in Bihar and gave a call for **total revolution** in the social, economic and political spheres, in order to establish **true democracy**.
- A series of bandhs, gheraos[1] and strikes were organised in protest against the Bihar government.

1 **Gheraos** Gherao is a Hindi word. It refers to a tactic used in India where protesters surround a place of work to pressure the authority from leaving until their demands are heard or met.

- The movement influenced the national politics. The employees of the railways gave a call for a **nationwide strike**. In 1975, JP led a people's march to the Parliament.
- His march was now supported by the non-Congress opposition parties such as Bharatiya Jana Sangh, Congress (O), the Bharatiya Lok Dal, the Socialist Party and others.
- But, Indira Gandhi saw these protests as anti-Congress and motivated by personal opposition to her.

Railway Strike of 1974

- Railways strike was led by a group called National **Co-ordination Committee for Railwaymen's struggle.**
- George Fernandes (the leader of the strike) gave a call for nationwide strike by all the employees of railways for pressing their demands related to bonus and working conditions.
- The government did not fulfill these demands and the employees of India's largest public sector undertaking went on strike in May 1974.
- The government declared this strike illegal and deployed army to protect railway tracks. After twenty days, the strike was called off without any settlement.

Conflict with Judiciary

- There were **three Constitutional issues** between the ruling party and the judiciary that emerged during this period, which are described in the table below.

Constitutional Question	Supreme Court Verdict
Can the Parliament take away the Fundamental Rights?	No
Can the Parliament set a limit on the right to property by amendment?	No
Parliament amended the Constitution by saying that it can take away some of the Fundamental Rights to give effect to the Directive Principles of State Policy.	Supreme Court rejected this provision.

- This increased the crisis between the judiciary and the government, which was finally balanced by the landmark verdict of the Supreme Court in the case of **Kesavananda Bharati** in 1973.
- Immediately, after the judgement of Supreme Court in the Kesavananda Bharati case (1973), government appointed **A.N. Ray** as the Chief Justice of India. His appointment become controversial because, it was against the principle of seniority. There were three senior judges, but government superseded them and appointed A.N. Ray.

Quick Test 1

1 Who emerged as a popular leader after 1967?
2 When the Students of Gujarat began the strike against the government?
3 Who gave the call for 'Total revolution'?
4 For how many days, the railway strike continued?

6.2 Declaration of Emergency

- On 12th June 1975, **Justice Jagmohan Lal Sinha** of the Allahabad High Court passed a judgement declaring Indira Gandhi's election to the Lok Sabha invalid.
- Raj Narain, a socialist leader and a candidate who had contested[2] against Indira Gandhi in 1971 elections filed an election petition[3]. This petition challenge the election of Indira Gandhi on the ground that she had used the government employees in her election campaign.

2 Contested It means to take part in competition and try to win.
3 Election Petition An election petition is a procedure for challenging the validity of the election results of Parliamentary or local government elections.

- After the judgement, **Indira Gandhi's election became illegal,** and thus she was removed as an MP. Therefore, she had to be elected again within six months to become the Prime Minister.

Crisis and Response

- The opposition political parties led by Jayaprakash Narayan pressed for Indira Gandhi's resignation and organised protests in Delhi's Ramleela ground on 25th June 1975.
- Jayaprakash Narayan announced to held a nationwide satyagraha[4] for her resignation. He even asked the army and the police not to obey **illegal and immoral orders** of the government. The political mood of the country had turned against the Congress.
- On **25th June 1975,** the government declared that there was a threat of **internal disturbances.** Therefore, it invoked **Article 352** of the Constitution.
- According to Article 352 of the Constitution, the government can declare a state of emergency on the grounds of external threat or a threat of internal disturbances. Technically, our Constitution provides some special powers to the government, once an emergency is declared.
- Under this provision of emergency, the Union Government can take away the powers of the State Government. The Union Government can also restrict any of the Fundamental Rights during the emergency. Therefore special powers are granted to the government.
- On the night of 25th June 1975, the Prime Minister recommended the imposition of emergency to President Fakhruddin Ali Ahmed. After the midnight, the electricity to all the major newspaper offices was disconnected.
- In the early morning, a large number of leaders and workers of the opposition parties were arrested and the cabinet held a special meeting at 6 a.m. on 26th June.

Consequences

- Strikes were banned, many opposition leaders were arrested, and the situation of politics became very tense.
- Government suspended, **the freedom of the press.** Newspapers had to take permission before publishing their material. This was known as **press censorship.**
- The government also banned **Rashtriya Swayamsewak Sangh (RSS)** and **Jamat-e-Islami.**
- The government extensively used preventive detention[5]. Under preventive detention, people can be arrested before they could commit any offence.
- By using **Preventive Detention Acts,** the government attempted large scale arrests. People who were arrested could not file habeas corpus[6] petitions. However, several High Courts gave judgements that even after the declaration of emergency court could listen the writ petitions of habeas corpus to challenge their arrest.

4 Satyagraha It is a form of non-violent resistance or civil disobedience that involves seeking social and political reform through peaceful action.
5 Detention The act of stopping a person leaving a place, especially by keeping him/her in prison.
6 Habeas Corpus It is a writ petition. Writ petition can be filled in the court when the Fundamental Rights of any individual is violated. When a person is arrested or detained illegally, the person has the right to file the writ petition of habeas corpus, either in the High Court or the Supreme Court.

- In April 1976, the Constitution bench of the Supreme Court overruled the High Court and accepted the government's petition that people cannot file their habeas corpus petition to challenge their detention or arrest.
- All this meant that government could take away the citizens **right to life and liberty** during the emergency and it **close the door of judiciary** for the citizens.
- Many political workers who were not arrested in the first wave went underground and organised protests. Newspapers like **the Indian express** and **the Statesmen** protested against the censorship by leaving blank spaces where news items had been censored. Magazines like **the Seminar** and **the Mainstream** chose to close down. Many journalist were arrested for writing against the emergency.
- Kannada writer, **Shivaram Karanth** awarded with Padma Bhushan and Hindi writer, **Phanishwar Nath Renu** awarded with Padma Shri returned their awards in protest against the suspension of democracy.
- During the emergency, the Parliament brought many changes in the Constitution. These changes were as follows
    - The elections of Prime Minister, President and Vice-President could not be challenged in the court.
    - The 42nd amendment was also passed during the emergency.
    - The duration of the legislature in the country was extended from five to six years.
    - During an emergency, the elections can be postponed by one year.

Lessons of the Emergency

- The emergency brought out both the weaknesses and the strengths of the Indian democracy.
- Though many observers think that democracy was completely vanished during the emergency. However, normal democratic functioning resumed within a short period of time. Thus, the **first lesson of emergency** is that it is very difficult to completely remove democracy in India.
- The **second lesson** is, it brought out some questions regarding the emergency provision in the Constitution. After this emergency, some provisions were rectified in the Constitution. Now internal emergency could be proclaimed only on the ground of **armed rebellion**. The advice to the President must be given in writing by the Union Cabinet.
- The **third lesson** is that emergency made everyone aware about the **value of civil liberties**. The courts played an active role after emergency in protecting the civil rights of the individuals. Many civil liberty organisations were also established after this experience.
- The actual implementation of the emergency rule took place through the police and the administration. These institutions could not function independently and became the political instrument of the ruling party. According to the **Shah Commission Report,** the administration and the police became vulnerable to political pressures.

Quick Test 2

1. Who had contested against Indira Gandhi in the elections of 1971?
2. Which article of the Constitution was invoked to declare emergencey in 1975?
3. Who was the President of India during the declaration of emergency?
4. What was the most controversial acts of the government during the emergency?

6.3 Politics after Emergency

Emergency was over and the Lok Sabha elections were announced. The opposition fought the elections on the slogan of **'save democracy'**.

Lok Sabha Elections, 1977

- In January 1977, after 18 months of emergency, the government decided to hold elections.
- All the leaders and activists were released from jail and elections were held in **March 1977**.
- Thus, the opposition leaders had a very little time to campaign for their election. Major opposition parties became closer during the pre-emergency period and came together on the eve of elections to form a new party called **the Janata Party**.
- Some other Congress leaders who were opposed to the emergency also came out and formed a separate party under the leadership of **Jagjivan Ram**. This party named as **Congress for democracy** later merged with the Janata Party.

Morarji Desai (1896-1995)

- He was a Gandhian freedom fighter. He was a leader who was a proponent of khadi and naturopathy.
- He was the Chief Minister of Bombay state and Deputy Prime Minister. He joined Congress after the split in the party.
- He became Prime Minister from 1977 to 1979, and also the **first Prime Minister** belonging to a **non-Congress Party**.

- The Janata Party made this election into a **'referendum on emergency'**[7]. It campaigned for saving the democracy. Jayaprakash Narayan became the popular symbol of **'restoration**[8] of democracy'. The formation of the Janata Party also ensured that non-Congress votes would not be divided.
- For the first time since independence, the **Congress Party was defeated** in the Lok Sabha elections. Given below is the tally of the election results
  - Congress- 154 seats in Lok Sabha
  - Janata Party and it's allies – 330 out of 542 seats
  - Janata Party- 295 seats
- In the North India, Congress lost every **constituency**[9] in Bihar, Uttar Pradesh, Delhi, Haryana and the Punjab. It could win only one seat in Rajasthan and Madhya Pradesh. **Indira Gandhi** was defeated from Rae Bareli and his son Sanjay Gandhi from Amethi.
- Though Congress retained many seats in Maharashtra, Gujarat, Odisha and in Southern states, it came with clear majority.
- The impact of emergency was not felt equally in all the states. The forced relocation, displacement and the forced sterilisations were mostly concentrated in the Northern states. The middle cast from North India were beginning to move away from the Congress and Janata Party became a platform for these sections. In this sense, the elections of 1977 was not only about the emergency.

---

7 **Referendum on Emergency** Referendum is an occasion in when all the people of a country can vote on a particular political question. Morarji Desai called 1977 elections as referendum on emergency because here, people had to vote on the question whether they supported emergency or not. If people would have voted for the Janata Party, it meant that they have rejected the Congress because of the emergency period.

8 **Restoration** The action of returning or making something to its former conditions.

9 **Constituency** A group of voters in a specified area who elect representative to a legislative body. Each state has many electoral constituencies.

Janata Government

- The Janata Party government came into the power after 1977 elections. After the election, there was a competition among the three leaders
  - **Morarji Desai** – who was the rival to Indira Gandhi ever since 1966-67.
  - **Charan Singh**- leader of the Bharatiya Lok Dal and farmer's leader from UP.
  - **Jagjivan Ram**- who had vast experience as a senior minister in the Congress government.
- **Morarji Desai** became the **Prime Minister,** but the power struggle did not end.
- The Janata Party could not bring a fundamental change in policies. They were together only for sometime. Some critics felt that the Janata Party lacked direction, leadership, and a common programme.
- Thus, the Janata Party split and the government led by Morarji Desai, lost its majority in **less than 28 months. Charan Singh** formed another government on the assurance of the support of Congress Party, but later Congress Party withdrew its support.
- Fresh Lok Sabha elections were held in **January 1980** in which Janata Party suffered a defeat.
- Thus, again, Congress Party led by Indira Gandhi, repeated its victory in 1971, and came back in power by winning 353 seats.
- The experience of 1977–79 taught **another lesson** in democratic politics: governments that are seen to be **unstable and quarrelsome** are severely punished by the voters.

Chaudhary Charan Singh (1902-1987)

- He was a freedom fighter and active in the politics of Uttar Pradesh.
- He was a proponent of rural and agricultural development.
- He left Congress Party and founded **Bharatiya Kranti Dal** in 1967. He also founded **Lok Dal.**
- He had served on the following positions
  - UP Chief Minister twice.
  - Deputy Prime Minister and Home Minister.
  - Prime Minister of India between July 1979 to January 1980.
- He was also one of the founders of the Janata Party.

Legacy

- Between the elections of 1977 and 1980, the party system had changed dramatically.
- The Congress Party, which initially accommodated different ideological leaders under an umbrella but later changed its ideology and claimed to be the only **socialist** and **pro-poor party.**
- With the early 1970s, the Congress political success depended only on attracting people on basis of social and ideological divisions and the personality of only one leader, Indira Gandhi.
- The opposition parties came together and relied more on what is known as **non-Congressism.** These parties realised the need to avoid a division of non-Congress votes in the election, which played a major role in the elections of 1977.
- In an indirect manner, the issue of **welfare of the backward caste** also began to dominate politics since 1977.
- Following the Lok Sabha elections, many states also held assembly elections in 1977.
- Again, the Northern states elected non-Congress governments in which the leaders of the backward classes played an important role. The issue of reservations for other backward classes became very controversial in Bihar.

- The **Mandal commission** was appointed by the Janata government to give recommendations for reservation to the OBC. The emergency and the period around it was described as the **period of Constitutional crisis**. It was also **a period of political crisis.**
- The makers of the Indian Constitution would have trusted all the political parties that they would stick to the democratic norms. However, this period saw **constant conflict between judiciary and legislature**.
- Another critical issue that emerged during this period was the role and extent of the mass protest in the Parliamentary democracy.

Jagjivan Ram (1908-1986)

- He was a freedom fighter and a Congress leader from Bihar.
- He has served as the Deputy Prime Minister of India and Labour Minister in the first ministry of free India. He has also held other ministries from 1952 to 1977.
- He was also a member of the Constituent Assembly and remained the member of Parliament since 1952, till his death.
- He was an administrator and scholar.

Democratic Upsurges

Increasing participation of the people in the democratic politics of the country is broadly characterised as democratic upsurge. Based on this principle, social scientists have characterised three democratic upsurges in post-independence history of India.

- The **First Democratic Upsurge** could be attributed from the 1950s till 1970s which was based on the participation of Indian adult voters to the democratic politics both at the centre and in states.
- The **Second Democratic Upsurge** by political experts. This participation has made Indian politics more accommodative and accessible for these classes.
- The **Third Democratic Upsurge** represents a competitive electoral market which is based not on the principle of survival of the best but rather the survival of the ablest.
- Moreover, the third democratic upsurge seeks to promote the participation of the youth who constitute a significant chunk of Indian society and have emerged as the real game changers in view of their increasing electoral preference for both development and governance in India's contemporary democratic politics.

Famous Personalities and Their Theories

Jayaprakash Narayan and Total Revolution

- Jayaprakash Narayan, popularly referred to as JP or Lok Nayak (The People's Leader), was an Indian independence activist, theorist, socialist and political leader.
- Jayaprakash Narayan is known for three key contributions
  - Fight Against Corruption.
  - Principle of Communitarian Socialism.
  - Championing of 'Total Revolution'.
- He was the first leader in post-independence India who undertook a tirade against corruption through the participation of youth, particularly in Gujarat and Bihar. He advocated the office of Lokpal against corruption.
- His principle of Communitarian Socialism views India as a society of communities encompassing three key layers, viz., community, region and rashtra– all combine together as an example of true federation.

Ram Manohar Lohia and Socialism

- Ram Manohar Lohia was a socialist leader and thinker, freedom fighter and among the founders of the Congress Socialist Party, after the split in the parent party, the leader of the Socialist Party and later Samyukta Socialist Party member. He was one of the proponents of socialism in India. He championed the idea of 'Democratic Socialism' while associating with democracy.
- Lohia considered both capitalism and communism equally irrelevant for Indian society. His principle of Democratic Socialism has two objectives
  - The economic objective in the form of food and housing.
  - The non-economic objective in the form of democracy and freedom.

Deendayal Upadhyaya and Integral Humanism

- Deendayal Upadhyaya was a philosopher, sociologist, economist and politician. He presented the philosophy which is known as 'Integral Humanism' which was intended to present an 'indigenous socio-economic model' in which human being remains at the centre of development.
- The aim of Integral Humanism is to ensure dignified life for every human being while balancing the needs of the individual and society. It supports sustainable consumption of natural resources so that those resources can be replenished. Integral Humanism enhances not only political but also economic and social democracy and freedom.
- As it seeks to promote diversity, it is best suited for a country as diverse as India. The Philosophy of Integral Humanism is based on the following three principles
  - Primacy of whole, not part
  - Supremacy of Dharma
  - Autonomy of Society
- Pandit Deendayal Upadhyaya opposed both Western 'Capitalist Individualism' and 'Marxist Socialism'. According to him, capitalist and socialist ideologies only consider the needs of the human body and mind, so they are based on materialistic purpose whereas spiritual development is equally considered important for the complete development of human being which is missing in both capitalism and socialism.
- His philosophy was based on the internal conscience, pure human soul to be called Chhitti, Deendayal Upadhyaya envisaged a classless, casteless and conflict-free social system. He advocated Indianisation of Democracy, particularly with a focus on Economic Democracy.
- For him, decentralisation and Swadeshi are the foundation of Economic Democracy. His philosophy broadly revolved around the principle of Arthayaam which states that both the absence and prominence of arths lead to the destruction and denigration of Dharma which is central to Integral Humanism.

Quick Test 3

1. From where did Sanjay Gandhi loose in 1977 elections?
2. Who were the three rivals for the post of the Prime Minister after 1977 elections?
3. Who was the first non-Congress Prime Minister of India?
4. After the elections of 1980, which ideology was adopted by the Congress Party?

Mind Map

THE CRISIS OF DEMOCRATIC ORDER

1 Background to Emergency

Conflict Between Judiciary and Government

Issues

- Supreme Court declared government initiatives as violative to the Constitution.
- Congress alleged court was against Parliamentary democracy and pro-poor welfare schemes.
- Congress claimed court was becoming conservative.

Constitutional Questions

- Can Parliament take away Fundamental Rights? (No).
- Can Parliament set a limit on the right to property by amendment? (No).
- Can Parliament amend the Constitution to give effect to Directive Principles of State Policy? (Rejected).

Economic Context

Post-1971-72

- Social and economic conditions didn't improve much.
- US stopped aid to India after Bangladesh-Pakistan War.
- High oil prices increased commodity prices.
- India dealt with 8 million refugees from East Pakistan (now Bangladesh).

Economic Issues

- Low industrial growth.
- High unemployment, especially in rural areas.
- Salary freeze for government employees.
- Failed monsoon led to 8% decline in food grain output.

Protests and Movements

Gujarat Movement (1974)

- Students protested against rising prices, corruption, and unemployment.
- Opposition parties joined, leading to President's rule.

Bihar Movement (1974)

- Students protested against rising prices, food scarcity, and unemployment.
- Jayaprakash Narayan joined, demanded dismissal of Congress government.

Railway Strike (1974)

- Led by George Fernandes, demanding bonus and better working conditions.
- Government declared strike illegal, deployed army to protect railway tracks.

2 Declaration of Emergency

Judgement and Crisis

- **Allahabad High Court Judgement** Indira Gandhi's election to Lok Sabha declared invalid due to use of government employees in her election campaign.
- **Raj Narain's Petition** Challenged Indira Gandhi's election.
- **Consequences** Indira Gandhi's election declared illegal, she was no longer an MP, and had to be re-elected within six months to remain Prime Minister.

Response and Emergency

- **Opposition Protests** Led by Jayaprakash Narayan, demanding Indira Gandhi's resignation.
- **Nationwide Satyagraha** Announced by Jayaprakash Narayan.
- **Government's Response** Declared internal disturbances based emergency under Article 352 of the Constitution.
- **Emergency Powers** Union Government took away powers of State Government and restricted Fundamental Rights.

Consequences of Emergency

- **Arrests and Bans** Opposition leaders arrested, strikes banned, freedom of press suspended.
- **Preventive Detention** People arrested before committing any offense.
- **Judiciary's Response** High Courts allowed habeas corpus petitions, later overruled by Supreme Court.

Lessons of the Emergency

- **Resilience of Democracy** Normal democratic functioning resumed after a short period.
- **Emergency Provision** Rectified to allow internal emergency only on grounds of armed rebellion.
- **Value of Civil Liberties** Emergency made people aware of the importance of civil liberties, courts played an active role in protecting individual rights.

3 Politics after Emergency

Lok Sabha Elections, 1977

- **Background** Emergency lifted, elections announced.
- **Opposition Unity** Major opposition parties formed Janata Party.
- **Campaign** Fought on slogan of "save democracy".
- **Result** Congress defeated, Janata Party won 330 seats.

Janata Government

- **Formation** Morarji Desai became Prime Minister.
- **Power Struggle** Competition among leaders (Morarji Desai, Charan Singh, Jagjivan Ram).
- **Policy** Lacked direction, leadership, and common programme.
- **Split** Janata Party split, government lost majority.

Impact of 1977 Elections

- **Non-Congressism** Opposition parties came together.
- **Backward Caste Welfare** Issue began to dominate politics.
- **State Elections** Non-Congress governments elected in Northern states.

Legacy

- **Party System Change** Dramatic change between 1977 and 1980 elections.
- **Congress Party** Claimed to be socialist and pro-poor party.
- **Mandal Commission** Appointed by Janata government to recommend reservations for OBC.

Constitutional and Political Crisis

- **Conflict between Judiciary and Legislature** Constant conflict during this period.
- **Role of Mass Protest** Critical issue emerged during this period in Parliamentary democracy.

NCERT Folder

Intext Questions

1. Do 'committed judiciary' and 'committed bureaucracy' means that the judges and government officials should be loyal to the ruling party? (Pg. no. 96)

Ans. The terms 'committed judiciary' and 'committed bureaucracy' do not mean that judges and government officials should be loyal to the ruling party. Rather, they are used to refer to a concept where the judiciary and bureaucracy are seen as being aligned or committed to the goals and values of the ruling government, often with the expectation of supporting its policies.

However, in a democratic system like India, it is essential that the judiciary and bureaucracy maintain their independence and objectivity. The judiciary should be impartial, interpreting the law without bias or influence from the ruling party. Similarly, the bureaucracy should function according to established rules and policies, serving the public and the state rather than any political party.

Thus, a truly democratic society requires both the judiciary and bureaucracy to be independent, free from political influence, and focused on serving the rule of law and the public interest.

2. Should the President have declared an emergency without any recommendation from the cabinet? (Pg. 101)

Ans. No, the President should not have declared an emergency without any recommendation from the cabinet. According to the Constitution of India, the President can only declare an emergency on the advice of the Union Cabinet, as stated in Article 352. This ensures that the decision to declare an emergency is made collectively by the government and is not a unilateral decision by the President.

The experience of the 1975–77 emergency highlighted the dangers of not following the constitutional process. During this period, emergency was declared by then-Prime Minister Indira Gandhi, and the cabinet's advice was not taken. This led to the abuse of power, as the government used emergency provisions to suppress political opposition, curtail civil liberties, and extend its rule without proper checks and balances.

After the emergency, the Constitution was amended to clarify that an emergency must be declared only with the written recommendation of the Union Cabinet. This was done to ensure that the powers of the government are exercised responsibly and in accordance with democratic principles. Thus, the President should always act on the cabinet's advice to maintain the integrity of the democratic system.

3. Read this map and identify the states where

(i) Congress lost

(ii) Congress lost very badly and

(iii) those states where Congress and its allies nearly swept the polls.

(iv) Which are the constituencies in North India that the Congress managed to win? (Pg. 106)

Ans. (i) The Congress lost in Uttarakhand, Haryana, Uttar Pradesh, Bihar, Odisha, Madhya Pradesh, Punjab, Gujarat and Rajasthan.

(ii) The Congress lost very badly in Uttarakhand, Haryana, Uttar Pradesh and Bihar.

(iii) Tamil Nadu, Kerala, Karnataka, Andhra Pradesh, West Bengal and Maharashtra.

(iv) The Congress manage to win the constituencies of Rajasthan, Gujarat and Madhya Pradesh.

Exercise

1. State whether the following statements regarding the emergency are correct or incorrect.

(i) It was declared in 1975 by Indira Gandhi.

(ii) It led to the suspension of all Fundamental Rights.

(iii) It was proclaimed due to the deteriorating economic conditions.

(iv) **Many opposition leaders were arrested during the emergency.**

(v) **CPI supported the proclamation of the emergency.**

Ans. (i) Correct (ii) Correct
(iii) Incorrect (iv) Correct
(v) Correct

2. Find the odd one out in the context of proclamation of emergency.

(a) **The call for 'Total Revolution'**
(b) **The Railway Strike of 1974**
(c) **The Naxalite Movement**
(d) **The Allahabad High court Verdict**
(e) **The findings of the Shah Commission Report**

Ans. (c) The Naxalite Movement

3. Match the following.

A.	Total Revolution	1.	Indira Gandhi
B.	Garibi Hatao	2.	Jayaprakash Narayan
C.	Student's Protest	3.	Bihar Movement
D.	Railway Strike	4.	George Fernandes

Ans. A → 2 B → 1
C → 3 D → 4

4. What were the reasons which led to the mid-term elections in 1980?

Ans. Janata Party had many differences within itself. It lacked direction, leadership and a common programme. The Janata Party could not make any fundamental change to policies. Disagreements among members prevented it to do so.

The Janata Party split after 18 months of its formation. Gaining from the scenario, Chaudhary Charan Singh formed its government with the support of Congress, but Congress withdrew its support after a short period of 4 months.

Thus, due to these reasons in 1980, fresh Lok Sabha elections were conducted in which Janata Party suffered a defeat and Congress seemed to gain its position back. Congress won 353 out of 542 seats in Lok Sabha. Congress restored itself again in 1980 Lok Sabha elections.

5. The Shah Commission was appointed in 1977 by the Janata Party government. Why was it appointed and what were its findings?

Ans. The Shah Commission was appointed in May 1977 by Janata Party government which was headed by J.C. Shah, retired Chief Justice of Supreme Court of India to look into the matters of

(i) Allegations of abuse of authority, excesses and malpractices as well as actions taken in the name of emergency proclaimed on 25th June, 1975.

(ii) The commission performed to examine various evidences to give testimonies even including Indira Gandhi to appear before commission, but she refused to answer any questions.

Findings of Shah Commission

(a) It was found that the decision to impose emergency was solely taken by Indira Gandhi. Who did not consult cabinet ministers.

(b) Emergency witnessed a large-scale displacement of people.

(c) It found many 'excesses' committed during emergency.

(d) Under preventive detention laws nearly one lakh eleven thousand people were arrested.

(e) Press censorship took place without any proper legal sanctions.

(f) Even general manager of Delhi Power Supply Corporation received verbal orders from the officers of the Lt. Governor of Delhi to cut electricity to all newspapers press at 2 a.m. on 26th June, 1975.

6. What reasons did the government give for declaring a National Emergency in 1975?

Or **Analyse the circumstances responsible for the declaration of a state of emergency in India on 25th June, 1975.**

Or **What reasons, do you think, were responsible for the declaration of emergency in 1975? Examine any two reasons.**

Or **Describe any three events that led to the imposition of emergency in 1975.** **Delhi 2019**

Ans. The circumstances which led to the proclamation of Emergency were

- Bihar and Gujarat's movement created an unrest in the country. Students were protesting against the price rise and against the established Government in the states. Congress as ruling party failed to handle these protests. Leadership by influential leaders further gave them a momentum against government.
- George Fernandes gave a call for nationwide strike to all the railwaymen. Their demands were suppressed by the government. Shutdown of such a big institution created a havoc in the country.
- Declaration of Indira Gandhi's 1971 election invalid was a last straw. Jayaprakash Narayan organised a massive demonstration demanding her resignation. The situation was tense and emergency was declared on 25th June, 1975.

- Call of total revolution by Jayaprakash Narayan and unexpected people movement in Delhi.
- Jayaprakash Narayan announced a nationwide satyagraha for resignation and asked the army, the police and government employees not to obey illegal and immoral orders.

7. 'The 1977 elections for the first time saw the opposition coming to power at the centre'. Examine any six reasons for this change.

Or **The 1977 elections for the first time saw the opposition coming into power at the centre. What would you consider as the reasons for this development?**

Or **Explain any factors responsible for the defeat of the Congress Party in 1977 elections.**

Or **'Governments that are perceived to be anti- democratic are severely punished by the voters'. Explain the statement with reference to the emergency period of 1975-77.**

Or **'Government that seem to be unstable and quarrelsome are severely punished by the voters'. Explain with reference to Janata Party rule.**

Or **Highlight any three factors which were responsible for the downfall of the Congress Party in the 1977 elections.**

Ans. In January 1977, after 18th months of emergency, government decided to hold the election. Decision was quick, parties did not have enough time for preparation. Janata Party which had formed during pre-emergency period by coalition of various anti-Congress and anti-emergency parties decided to fight against Congress.

Result of 1977 came out with a big surprise to the country. For the first time since independence, Congress had lost in centre. Janata Party won 330 out of 542 seats.

The main reasons behind Congress defeat in 1977 were

- Misuse of Constitutional provisions.
- Imposition of emergency had negative impact on the image of Congress.
- During emergency, Congress had used harsh measures like forced sterilisation, forced re-locations, displacement, etc. That is why, people decided not to elect Congress representative to next Lok Sabha election and Janata Party, which gave public a bright look of democracy and was sympathetic towards public, was elected.
- The opposition fought the election on the slogan of 'Save democracy'. People's verdict was decisively against the excesses of emergency.
- The middle class from North India, where the impact of emergency was at its peak moved away from Congress and the Janata Party became a platform for different groups of people to come together.

8. Discuss the effects of Emergency on the following aspects for our polity.
   (i) Effects on civil liberties for citizens.
   (ii) Impact on relationship between the Executive and Judiciary.
   (iii) Functioning of Mass Media.
   (iv) Working of Police and Bureaucracy.

Ans. (i) **Effect on Civil Liberties for Citizens**

- Large scale arrest of leaders and workers of the opposition parties were made under Preventive Detention Act.
- Forced re-location and sterilisation of poor.
- Suspension of Fundamental Rights and available Constitutional Remedies.

(ii) **Impact on Relationship between the Executive and Judiciary**

- Rising conflict between government and judiciary.
- In the background of the ruling of Allahabad High Court, an amendment was brought that elections of Prime Minister, President and Vice-President cannot be challenged in the court.
- 42nd amendment was also passed to bring series of changes in Constitution like duration of legislature, etc.

(iii) **Functioning of Mass Media**

- Electricity was cut on the 25th June, 1975, midnight, for all newspaper offices.
- Government imposed press censorship suspending the freedom of press, newspapers and magazine to publish anti-government contents. Newspapers were asked to get prior permission from government before publishing any content.
- Newspaper like the Indian Express and the Statesmen protested against press censorship by leaving blank spaces where news items were censored.

(iv) **Working of Police and Bureaucracy**

- Government used police and bureaucracy to commit suppression, torture and atrocities on leaders and workers of opposition parties.
- Police and bureaucracy were misused to meet agenda of ruling party.

9. In what way did the imposition of emergency affect the party system in India? Elaborate your answer with examples.

Ans. The imposition of emergency brought opposition parties together to form new party 'Janata Party' to stop the split of the non-Congress vote.

Atrocities, torture and suppression committed during the emergency helped to the opposition parties under the leadership of J.P. in mobilising and organising people against Indira Gandhi. The election of 1977 brought to an end the Congress dominance at centre first time since independence. Post-emergency brought backward caste politics into the mainstream Indian politics which played a significant role in changing the shape of party system in India.

10. Read the passage and answer the questions below.

Indian democracy was never so close to a two-party system as it was during the 1977 elections. However, the next few years saw a complete change. Soon after its defeat, the Indian National Congress split into two groups ....The Janata Party also went through major conclusions............ David Butler, Ashok Lahiri and Prannoy Roy. **—Partha Chatterjee**

(i) What made the party system in India look like a two-party system in 1977?

(ii) Many more two parties existed in 1977. Why then are the authors describing this period as close to a two-party system?

(iii) What caused splits in Congress and the Janata Party?

Ans. (i) The emergence of Janata Party as a majority winner at centre first time since independence made the party system look like a two-party system.

(ii) Although more than just two parties existed in 1977, however, author described this period as close to a two-party system because only two major parties Congress and Janata Party have mass base support and mobilisation to form majority government.

(iii) The split in Congress took over the issue of Presidential election in 1969 and in Janata Party, split occured due to internal deadlock over the post of Prime Ministership in 1979.

Exam Pattern Questions

Objective Type Questions

Multiple Choice Questions (MCQs)

1. Which of the following is the feature of politics in India since 1967? **Diksha App**

(a) Towering popularity of Indira Gandhi
(b) Tension in the relationship of the Supreme Court and the High Court
(c) Towering popularity of Bharatiya Jana Sangh
(d) More propaganda of BJP

2. Which slogan was given by Congress in the elections of 1971? **Diksha App**

(a) Garibi Hatao
(b) Save democracy
(c) No taxation without representation
(d) Equality, liberty, fraternity

3. Students of which two states started an agitation against the rising food prices in 1974? **CBSE 2024**

(a) Uttar Pradesh and Bihar
(b) Rajasthan and Bihar
(c) Bihar and Gujarat
(d) Bihar and Madhya Pradesh

4. Who led the Bihar Movement in 1974?

(a) Morarji Desai (b) George Fernandes
(c) Jayaprakash Narayan (d) Lal Bahadur Shastri

5. What was Jayaprakash Narayan's call for a 'Total Revolution' aimed at?

(a) Strengthening the Congress
(b) Reforming social, economic and political systems
(c) Establishing military rule
(d) Abolishing parliamentary democracy

6. Who gave a call for a nationwide railway strike in 1974? **CBSE 2023**

(a) Jayaprakash Narayan (b) George Fernandes
(c) Ram Manohar Lohia (d) Morarji Desai

7. Who led the ' People's march' to the Parliament in 1975? **CBSE 2024**

(a) Jagjivan Ram (b) S.K. Patil
(c) Charu Majumdar (d) Jayaprakash Narayan

8. Why did tensions arise between the judiciary and the government during 1970s?

(a) The judiciary supported the opposition.
(b) The judiciary found many government initiatives unconstitutional.

(c) The government refused to implement court orders.
(d) Judges joined opposition protests.

9. **Which High Court passed a judgment declaring Indira Gandhi election to the Lok Sabha invalid on 12th June, 1975?** Diksha App

(a) Allahabad High Court (b) Chandigarh High Court
(c) Karnataka High Court (d) Maharashtra High Court

10. **Who among the following had announced a nationwide satyagraha on 25th June, 1975 for the resignation of Prime Minister Indira Gandhi?** CBSE 2023

(a) Morarji Desai (b) Jayaprakash Narayan
(c) George Fernandes (d) Atal Bihari Vajpayee

11. **Given below are two statements**

Statement I Fundamental Rights were suspended during the emergency.

Statement II The government used special powers under Article 356 of the Constitution.

In the light of above statements, choose the correct answer from the options given below

(a) Both Statement I and Statement II are true.
(b) Both Statement I and Statement II are false.
(c) Statement I is true, but Statement II is false.
(d) Statement I is false, but Statement II is true.

12. **Which of the following steps was not done by the government after imposing an emergency on 25th June, 1975 in India?** Diksha App

(a) Protests and public agitations were prohibited.
(b) Strikes were banned.
(c) Press was censored.
(d) Social media was censored.

13. **Which of the following were the consequences of emergency imposed in 1975?**

(a) The government made large scale arrest under preventive detention.
(b) Press censorship was imposed on newspapers.
(c) Fundamental Rights were suspended.
(d) All of the above

14. **Identify the incorrect pair.** Competency Based Que

(a) Indian Express-Magazine (b) Statesman-Newspaper
(c) Seminar-Magazine (d) Mainstream-Magazine

15. **Which among the following was the slogan of opposition parties in 1977 election which took place after the emergency?** Diksha App

(a) Save democracy (b) Save India
(c) Attack dictatorship (d) Garibi Hatao

16. **Which of the following leader of Janata Party came to power after the 1977 elections?** Diksha App

(a) Charan Singh (b) Jagjivan Ram
(c) Morarji Desai (d) Jayaprakash Narayan

17. **Which of the following statement (s) is/are correct about the proclamation of emergency in 1975?**

(a) Power politics became personalised.
(b) Bitter party competition.
(c) Tensed relations between the government and judiciary.
(d) All of the above

18. **Consider the following statement(s) correct about the downfall of the Janata government.** Competency Based Que

(a) The Janata Party could not keep together due to the internal conflict.
(b) It had good leaders.
(c) It lacked common programme.
(d) Both (a) and (c)

19. **Arrange the following in the chronological order** Competency Based Que

I. Gujarat Student Agitation
II. Railway Strike led by George Fernandes 1974
III. Declaration of Emergency by President Fakhruddin Ali Ahmed 1975
IV. 'Garibi Hatao' slogan

Codes

(a) I, II, III and IV (b) IV, I, II and III
(c) II, I, IV and III (d) III, I, II and IV

20. **List I and List II select the correct answer using the codes given below.** Competency Based Que

List I	List II
A. Jagjivan Ram	1. Prime Minister of India 1966-77 and 1980-1984
B. Chaudhary Charan Singh	2. Prime Minister of India between July 1979-1980 January
C. Morarji Desai	3. Deputy Prime Minister of India in 1979
D. Indira Gandhi	4. Prime Minister 1977-79

Codes

	A	B	C	D
(a)	1	4	3	2
(b)	3	2	4	1
(c)	2	4	3	1
(d)	4	3	2	1

21. **Match the following.** Competency Based Que

List-I	List-II
A. Declaration of Emergency	1. Jayaprakash Narayan
B. Save Democracy	2. Raj Narain
C. Filed petition to challenge Indira Gandhi victory	3. Morarji Desai
D. Janata Party	4. Fakhruddin Ali Ahmad

Codes

	A	B	C	D		A	B	C	D
(a)	1	2	3	4	(b)	2	3	4	1
(c)	3	4	2	1	(d)	4	1	2	3

Assertion-Reason Questions

Directions (Q. Nos. 22-24) In the questions given below, there are two statements marked as Assertion (A) and Reason (R). Read the statements and choose the correct option.

Codes

(a) Both A and R are true and R is the correct explanation of A.
(b) Both A and R are true, but R is not the correct explanation of A.
(c) A is true, but R is false.
(d) A is false, but R is true.

22. **Assertion** (A) People started protesting against the increase in prices of essential commodities, food scarcity and growing unemployment before the fourth General Elections in India.

Reason (R) Failure of monsoons, widespread drought, decline in agricultural production and serious food shortage caused the problem. **CBSE 2023**

23. **Assertion** (A) Emergency is one of the most controversial episodes in Indian politics.

Reason (R) The Constitution simply mentioned 'Internal disturbances' as the reason for declaring emergency.

24. **Assertion** (A) In May, 1977, the Janata Party government appointed a commission of inquiry headed by Justice J.C. Shah.

Reason (R) The commission was apponted to inquire into the reasons for declaring emergency, by the Indira Gandhi government. **CBSE 2023**

Passage Based Questions

25. Read the passage given below and answer the following questions.

Once an emergency is proclaimed, the federal distribution of powers remains practically suspended and all the powers are concentrated in the hands of the Union Government. Secondly, the government also gets the power to curtail or restrict all or any of the Fundamental Rights during the emergency. It is clear that an emergency is seen as an extraordinary condition in which normal democratic politics cannot function.

(i) Who among the following was the President of India during emergency?

(a) V.V. Giri (b) Morarji Desai
(c) Fakhruddin Ali Ahmed
(d) Ram Manohar Lohia

(ii) On what grounds emergency was imposed?

(a) External threats (b) Internal disturbances
(c) Terrorist attacks (d) Both (a) and (b)

(iii) What were the implications of emergency?

26. Read the given passage carefully and answer the questions that follow.

The opposition to emergency could keep the Janata Party together only for a while. Its critics felt that Janata Party lacked direction, leadership and a common programme. The Janata Party government could not bring about a fundamental change in policies from those pursued by the Congress. The Janata Party split and the government which was led by Morarji Desai lost its majority in less than 18 months. Another government headed by Charan Singh was formed on assurance of the support of the Congress Party. **CBSE 2020**

(i) In which year did the Janata Party government came to power?

(a) 1976 (b) 1977
(c) 1978 (d) 1979

(ii) Which of the following reasons were responsible for the split of the Janata Party?

(a) It lacked direction, leadership and a common programme.
(b) A stiff competition among the leaders of the Janata Party for the post of Prime Minister.
(c) There was no fundamental change in policies from those pursued by the previous Congress government.
(d) Both (a) and (b)

(iii) Why could the Charan Singh government remain in power for just about four months only?

27. Study the following passage carefully and answer the questions that follow.

The Emergency made everyone more aware of the value of civil liberties. The courts too, have taken an active role after the emergency in protecting the civil liberties of the individuals. This is a response to the inability of the judiciary to protect civil liberties effectively during the emergency.

(i) National emergency was imposed on ....

(a) 12th June, 1975 (b) 15th June, 1975
(c) 25th June, 1975 (d) 26th June, 1975

(ii) Which Fundamental Right of the citizens was affected the most during the emergency period?

(a) Right to Equality
(b) Freedom of Speech and Expression
(c) Cultural and Educational Rights
(d) Right against Exploitation

(iii) **Why did the judiciary start taking an active role after the emergency in protecting the civil liberties of the individuals?**

28. Read the passage given below and answer the following questions

The most valuable and lasting lesson of the emergency was learnt as soon as the emergency was over and the Lok Sabha elections were announced. The 1977 elections turned into a referendum on the experience of the emergency, at least in North India where the impact of the emergency was felt most strongly. The opposition fought the election on the slogan of 'Save democracy'. The people's verdict was decisively against the emergency. The lesson was clear and has been reiterated in many state level elections thereafter–governments that are perceived to be anti-democratic are severely punished by the voters. In this sense the experience of 1975–77 ended up strengthening the foundations of democracy in India.

(i) **What was the primary issue the opposition highlighted during the 1977 elections?**

(a) Economic reforms (b) Save democracy
(c) Development projects (d) Foreign relations

(ii) **Which region of India felt the strongest impact of the emergency?**

(a) South India (b) East India
(c) North India (d) West India

(iii) **What lesson was learned from the 1977 elections?**

(a) Anti-democratic governments are often supported by voters.
(b) Economic development is more important than democracy.
(c) Anti-democratic governments are severely punished by voters.
(d) Emergency strengthens political authority.

(iv) **How did the 1977 elections strengthen democracy in India?**

(a) By removing the opposition parties.
(b) By reaffirming people's support for the emergency.
(c) By showing that voters reject anti-democratic practices.
(d) By ensuring Indira Gandhi's leadership.

Answers

1. (a) Towering popularity of Indira Gandhi
2. (a) Garibi Hatao
3. (c) Bihar and Gujarat
4. (c) Jayaprakash Narayan
5. (b) Reforming social, economic and political systems
6. (b) George Fernandes
7. (d) Jayaprakash Narayan
8. (b) The judiciary found many government initiatives unconstitutional.
9. (a) Allahabad High Court
10. (b) Jayaprakash Narayan
11. (c) Statement I is true, but Statement II is false.
12. (d) Social media was censored.
13. (d) All of the above
14. (a) Indian Express- Magazine
15. (a) Save democracy
16. (c) Morarji Desai
17. (d) All of the above
18. (d) Both (a) and (c)
19. (b) IV, I, II and III
20. (b) 3 2 4 1
21. (d) 4 1 2 3
22. (d) A is false, but R is true.
23. (b) Both A and R are true, but R is not the correct explanation of A.
24. (c) A is true, but R is false.
25. (i) (c) Fakhruddin Ali Ahmed
    (ii) (b) Internal disturbances
    (iii) • All the powers got concentrated in the hands of the Union Government.
    • Government also got the power to curtail all or any of the Fundamental Rights.
    • Federal distribution of power remained practically suspended during that time.
26. (i) (b) 1977 (ii) (d) Both (a) and (b)
    (iii) • The Charan Singh government remained in power for just about four months only because the goverment was formed on the assurance of the support given by the Congress Party.
    • The Congress Party later decided to withdraw its support from his government.
27. (i) (c) 25th June, 1975
    (ii) (b) Freedom of Speech and Expression
    (iii) The judiciary started taking an active role after the emergency to protect the civil liberties because it was unable to protect the civil liberties and Fundamental Rights during the emergency period.
28. (i) (b) Save democracy (ii) (c) North India
    (iii) (c) Anti-democratic governments are severely punished by voters.
    (iv) (c) By showing that voters reject anti-democratic practices.

Subjective Questions

Very Short Answer Type Questions

1. Identify two special Constitutional powers which the government gets once emergency is proclaimed. **Competency Based Que; CBSE 2019**

Ans. Two special Constitutional powers which the government gets during emergency are

- Once an emergency is proclaimed, the federal distribution of powers remains practically suspended and all the powers are concentrated in the hands of Union Government.
- The government gets the power to suspend the Fundamental Rights of the citizens. It can also suspend the freedom of expression through suspending the freedom of press.

2. Evaluate the impact of national emergency declared in June, 1975. **Competency Based Que; Delhi 2019**

Or **Assess the impact of national emergency, declared in 1975, on the people of India.** **CBSE Term II 2022**

Or **State any two effects of imposing national emergency.** **CBSE 2024**

Ans. Impacts of Emergency declared in June, 1975 were

(i) Fundamental Rights were suspended.

(ii) The power of judiciary were limited.

3. Why were newspapers censored during emergency?

Ans Newspapers were censored during emergency to avoid anti-government feeling among people. Government ordered the press of various newspapers to get prior permission before publishing any matter.

4. Highlight any two steps taken by Indira Gandhi to remove poverty. **CBSE 2025**

Ans. To remove poverty, Indira Gandhi took the following steps

- **Garibi Hatao (Remove Poverty) Slogan** This slogan was given during the 1971 elections, this aimed to uplift the poor through social and economic reforms.
- **Nationalization of Banks (1969)** This step ensured easier credit access for farmers and small businesses throughout the country and promoted financial inclusion and rural

5. Describe in brief any two changes made in the Constitution of 42nd Constitutional Amendment.

Ans. (i) The election for the post of Prime minister, President and Vice-President can not be challenged in the court.

(ii) The tenure of Lok Sabha was increased from 5 to 6 years.

6. What was the significance of the slogan 'Save democracy'?

Ans. The slogan 'Save democracy,' used by the opposition during the 1977 elections, highlighted the public's anger against the emergency's authoritarian actions. It symbolised the collective demand for restoring civil liberties, democratic processes and constitutional Governance.

The slogan resonated strongly with voters, leading to the Congress Party's defeat and reaffirming India's commitment to democracy.

7. Mention any two reasons due to which Janata Party won the election of 1977?

Or **Describe any two reason for the victory of Janata Party in 1977 Lok Sabha elections.** **CBSE 2025**

Ans. The two reasons were

(i) Non-democratic outlook of Congress favoured Janata Party.

(ii) Formation of the Janata Party also ensured that non-Congress votes would not be divided.

8. Why is the 'Emergency' and the period around it known as the period of Constitutional crisis? Explain.

Ans. The emergency and the period around it can be described as a period of Constitutional crisis because it had its origin in the Constitutional battle over the jurisdiction of the Parliament and the judiciary.

It was also a period of political crisis because the party in power had absolute majority and yet, its leadership decided to suspend the democratic process.

Short Answer Type Questions

1. Describe any four circumstances that led to protests against the Congress government during 1974-1975. **CBSE 2024**

Ans. The following circumstances led to the protest against the Congress government during 1974–1975

(i) In January 1974, students in Gujarat started agitation against rising food, prices, cooking oil and other essential commodities. They also protested against the corruption in high places. This protest was joined by major opposition parties.

(ii) The opposition parties demanded fresh elections to the State Legislature. Morarji Desai, who was the prominent leader of Congress (O) announced that he would go on an indefinite fast if elections are not held within the state.

(iii) In March 1974, students again protested in the state of Bihar against the rising prices, food scarcity, unemployment and corruption. Students invited Jayaprakash Narayan, who had given up the politics and involved in the social work to lead this student movement.

(iv) The government was opposed to the demand of the railway employees to increase the bonus and service conditions. This led to the nationwide railway strike by George Fernandes.

2. Explain the reasons for the students movement of 1974 in Bihar and role played by Jayaprakash Narayan in this movement. **Competency Based Que**

Ans. Reasons for the students movement of 1974 in Bihar were as follows

- Rising prices of foodgrains, cooking oil and other essential commodities and corruption in high places.
- There was a demand for fresh elections to the State Legislature.

Role played by Jayaprakash Narayan in this movement were as follows

- He demanded the dismissal of the Congress government in Bihar and gave a call for total revolution in the social, economic and political spheres.
- In 1975, he led a people's march to the Parliament.

3. Write a short note on Jayaprakash Narayan.

Or **Describe the role of Jayaprakash Narayan in Indian National Politics.** **CBSE 2025**

Ans. Jayaprakash Narayan, popularly referred to as JP or Lok Nayak (The People's Leader), was an Indian independence activist, theorist, socialist and political leader. Jayaprakash Narayan is known for three key contributions: Fight Against Corruption, Principle of Communitarian Socialism and Championing of 'Total Revolution'.

He was the first leader in post-independence India who undertook a tirade against corruption through the participation of youth, particularly in Gujarat and Bihar.

He advocated the office of Lokpal against corruption. His principle of communitarian socialism views India as a society of communities encompassing three key layers, viz. community, region and rashtra–all combine together as an example of true federation.

4. Examine the factors that led to the conflict between the judiciary and the Parliament in India, 1973. **CBSE SQP 2024**

Ans. There are following factors that was the lead to the conflict between the judiciary and the Parliament in their 1973

There were three Constitutional questions that emerged before the Supreme Court of India.

- First was that whether the Parliament can take away the Fundamental Rights which Supreme Court responded as no it cannot.
- Second question was that whether the Parliament has the right to reduce or limit the right to property through an amendment which was also rejected by the Supreme Court.

  The Supreme Court also rejected Parliaments Amendment to the Constitution to abridge the Fundamental Rights for implementing DPSP.
- This crisis ended in the famous Kesavananda Bharati case in 1973. In this judgement, Supreme Court said that Parliament can amend the Constitution. However, there are some basic features of the Constitution which it cannot amend.
- The government immediately reacted after this judgement by appointing Justice A.N. Ray as the Chief Justice of India. This was made by setting aside the principle of seniority of the justice.
- The government did not appoint any of the three senior most judges as the Chief Justice because they had given rulings against the stand of the government.

5. Discuss the views against the emergency given by the critics. **Competency Based Que**

Ans. Some of the views against the emergency are discussed below

- Critics of emergency argued that India had history of such movements including freedom movement and also people had the right to protest against government in democracy.
- As emergency was imposed to curb the law and order situation but on the other hand, the Home Ministry which was monitoring the internal situation of the country did not express any concern about law and order situation in the country.
- Even if some agitations like Bihar and Gujarat had overstepped their limits, there was no need to suspend the democratic functioning of the country.
- Critics also held that Indira Gandhi had misused Constitutional provision for saving her personal power instead of saving the country.

6. How did Janata Party make the 1977 elections into a referendum on the emergency imposed in 1975? Explain.

Ans. Janata Party made the election of 1977 into a referendum on the Emergency imposed in 1975 in the following ways

- Janata Party's campaign focussed on the non-democratic character of the rule and on the various excesses that took place during this period.
- In the backdrop of arrests of thousands of persons and the censorship of the press, the public opinion was against the Congress.
  - Jayaprakash Narayan who led the party became the popular symbol of restoration of democracy.
  - The party ensured that non-Congress votes would not be divided.

7. What were the reasons for the Janata Party's instability and eventual downfall?

Ans. The Janata Party, despite its initial success in the 1977 elections, struggled with instability and internal conflicts. The party was a coalition of various groups and leaders with differing ideologies and goals, which made it difficult to maintain unity.

One of the major issues was the leadership struggle. After the elections, there was stiff competition for the post of Prime Minister, with leaders like Morarji Desai, Charan Singh and Jagjivan Ram all vying for power. Although Morarji Desai was appointed as Prime Minister, the power struggles within the party did not end.

The Janata Party lacked a clear direction and common policies, which made it difficult for the government to function cohesively. The party was also not able to implement significant changes from the policies of the Congress, which had been in power for so long. As a result, the government lost its majority in less than two years.

Charan Singh, another prominent leader, formed a new government, but it too faced similar issues. When Congress withdrew its support, the government collapsed after just four months.

This instability led to the call for fresh elections in 1980, where the Janata Party suffered a crushing defeat.

Long Answer Type Questions

1. Describe the economic crisis through which India was passing before the emergency of 25th June, 1975 was declared. **Competency Based Que Diksha App**

Ans. The economic crisis through which India was passing before the emergency of 25th June, 1975 was as follows

- About 8 million people crossed over the East Pakistan which put a heavy strain on Indian economy. After the war, US government stopped all the aid to India.
- In the international market oil prices increased and prices of other essential food items also increased. The inflation increased from 23 per cent in 1973 to 30 per cent in 1974.
- Industrial growth was also very low and unemployment was high.
- The government had to freeze the salaries of its employees which caused dis-satisfaction among government employees. Monsoon failed in 1972-73. The agricultural growth declined.

2. How far was Indira Gandhi's government's conflict with the judiciary responsible for the proclamation of emergency of 25th January, 1975? **Diksha App**

Ans. (i) There was an ongoing conflict between the Indira Gandhi's government and Judiciary since 1973. The Supreme Court in Kesavananda Bharati case 1973 declared that the Parliament can amend the Constitution but not the basic features.

(ii) This made the government to react against the principle of seniority of justice. This ongoing conflict between the judiciary and the government reached its climax when Indira Gandhi's election victory was declared invalid.

(iii) Raj Narain who fought Lok Sabha elections in 1975 against Indira Gandhi, filed an election petition to challenge the validity of her election. He filed the petition on the grounds that she has misused the government employees for her election process and victory. The Allahabad High Court declared that Indira Gandhi's victory is invalid on 12th June, 1975.

(iv) This made Indira Gandhi's disqualification from being an MP and Prime Minister. She had to elect again within the 6th months to become the Prime Minister. All these developments led Indira Gandhi to impose an emergency on the 25th June, 1975.

3. Was the declaration of emergency in 1975 necessary? Support your answer with any three suitable arguments. **Competency Based Que CBSE Term II 2022**

Ans. The massive frequent protest, agitation and disruption led by the opposition parties under the leadership of JP and tussle between Indian Government and Judiciary Prompted Government to declare state of emergency on 25th June, 1975.

Government justified the declaration of emergency on the following three arguments

(i) There was a threat of internal disturbances which caused serious crisis which made declaration of emergency necessary.

(ii) In democracy, opposition parties must allow the elected ruling party to govern according to its policies. Frequent agitation, protest and disruption derailed government and democracy as well.

(iii) Extra-Parliamentary politics targeting government leads to instability and divert the focus of administration of law and order from development to maintenance.

4. Evaluate the consequences of declaration of emergency in 1975. Competency Based Que All India 2014

Or **Explain any four consequences of emergency declared on 25th June, 1975.**

Ans. Consequences of declaration of emergency in 1975 were as follows

(i) During emergency, democracy was suspended the federal distribution of powered remained practically suspended and all the powers were concentrated in the hands of the Union Government. It was made clear that a democratic country like India could not do away from democracy. Wide protest against emergency arose to restore democracy.

(ii) Several changes to Constitution came into existence, e.g. election of Prime Minister, President and Vice President could not be challenged in the Supreme Court. 42nd amendment came during this time and duration of legislature increased from 5 to 6 years.

(iii) The government also got the power to curtail or restrict all or any of the Fundamental Rights during the emergency.

(iv) Measures like Preventive Detention could be used by government. Right to move the court for the restoration of Fundamental Rights were taken away.

(v) Government ordered newspaper press to censor the matter. The prior approval of government was made necessary before publishing any article in newspaper to avoid anti-government feeling.

5. Describe any three major political developments that took place in India after the lifting of Emergency in 1977. Competency Based Que

Ans. Three major political developments that took place in India after the lifting of emergency in 1977 were as follows

(i) **Janata Party** It accepted the leadership of Jayaprakash Narayan. Some leaders of the Congress who opposed the emergency also joined this new party. Some other Congress leaders also came out and formed a separate party under the leadership of Jagjivan Ram. This party named as Congress for democracy which later merged with the Janata Party. Janata Party made this election into a referendum on the emergency.

Its campaign was focussed on the non-democratic character of the rule and torture, atrocities, supression, etc that took place during Emergency.

(ii) **Result of 1977 Elections** The final result of 1977 election was surprising because the Congress was defeated in the Lok Sabha elections for the first time since independence.

In North India, it was a massive electoral wave against the Congress. The Congress lost in every constituency in Bihar, Uttar Pradesh, Delhi, Haryana and the Punjab. It could hardly won any seat each in Rajasthan and Madhya Pradesh. Indira Gandhi was defeated from Rae Bareli and her son Sanjay Gandhi from Amethi.

The impact of emergency was not felt equally in all the states. The forced relocations and displacements, the forced sterilisation, were mostly concentrated in the Northern states.

The middle castes from North India were moving away from the Congress and Janata Party became a platform for many of these sections to come together.

(iii) **Split between Janata Party** Janata Party government that came to power after 1977 elections was far from unity. There was stiff competition among Morarji Desai, Charan Singh and Jagjivan Ram for the post of Prime Minister. Finally, Morarji Desai became the Prime Minister but internal power struggle within the party continued.

The Janata Party Government did not bring any fundamental change in policies that pursued by the Congress.

The Janata Party split and the government led by Morarji Desai lost its majority in less than 18th months. Another government headed by Charan Singh was formed on the assurance of the support of the Congress Party.

Fresh elections to Lok Sabha were held in January 1980 in which Janata Party lost badly, particularly in North India where it had swept the polls in 1977.

Congress Party under the leadership of Indira Gandhi repeated its great victory. It won 353 seats and formed the government.

6. Assess any three effects of emergency imposed in 1975 in strengthening the democracy in India. Competency Based Que, CBSE 2023

Or **Analyse any three lessons learnt form the emergency of 1975.** Competency Based Que

Or **Highlight any two lessons learnt from the emergency in India.** CBSE 2024

Ans. (i) The emergency has brought out both the strengths and weaknesses of the democracy in India. It was observed after the emergency that the democracy was curtailed but soon, the democratic set up was restored. Thus, is this way it was relised that it was not easy to remove the democracy from India.

(ii) Secondly, it brought out certain ambiguities in the Constitution which was later amended. After the amendment, internal disturbance could be imposed only on 'armed rebelion'. It was made necessary that if it was neassary to impose the emergency, then Union Cabinet had to suggest it in the written format to the President.

(iii) Thirdly the court had played a significant role in strengthening the civil liberties after the emergency. Many civil rights organisations were also established.

7. Explain the major outcome of 1977 Lok Sabha elections.

Ans. The major outcomes of 1977 Lok Sabha elections were

- The Janata Party successfully achieved what it desired for. The democratic outlook attracted the masses and result of 1977 Lok Sabha elections worked in its favour.
- The result of 1997 Lok Sabha elections was a big shock and surprise to Congress and Janata Party respectively.
- It was for the first time when Congress had lost the election at centre ever since the independence.
- Janata Party won 330 out of 542 seats, while Congress had to satisfy with only 154 seats.
- In North India, Congress had bitterest experience. In Bihar, Uttar Pradesh, Delhi, Haryana and Punjab, Congress rule was outrightly rejected.
- Indira Gandhi from Rae Bareli and her son Sanjay Gandhi from Amethi were defeated too.
- Congress manages to save many seats in Maharashtra, Gujarat, Odisha and Southern states and this was a great relief to the Congress.
- Congress managed to do so, because the impact of emergency was comparatively less in Southern part. North India witnessed the harshest measures like displacement of people, sterilisation, etc.

Janata Party also gave a perfect alternative to the people of North India. People began to move away from Congress, specially the middle class.

8. Analyse any three reasons for the dominance of the Congress Party in Indian politics during the initial 20 years after independence. Competency Based Que CBSE 2023

Ans. The Congress remain dominant for almost 2 decades after the independence, because of the following reasons

(i) Initially, the Congress remain a umbrella party which used to accommodate different ideologies, actions and social groups within it.

These different groups did not leave the party rather remain in the party by creating different factions among them. These factions represented different state assemblies–Congress used to remain at the centre as well as in the different states.

(ii) The Congress Party had almost all ideologies due to which the opposition could not find any relevant question.

However, when the 1967 elections were facing different challenges of economic crisis, Indira Gandhi with her charismatic leadership attracted the social basis of under privileged sections. She gained widespread support of minorities, women, labour, etc. and one 1971 elections with the slogan of 'Garibi Hatao'. She was seen as the protector of the marginalised as well as the national leader because she had been successful in liberating Bangladesh from Pakistan.

(iii) Even after emergency and very bad defeat in 1977, elections, Congress managed to win again in 1980 elections. It was because of the poor co-ordination among the leaders of the Janata government.

Critics also felt that there was a lack of direction in the Janata government.

The Indira Gandhi's statesmanship and welfare programmes for the underprivileged made a good return for the Congress again.

The Congress Party now identify itself with a particular ideology claiming to be the only socialist and pro-poor party.

Picture Based Questions

1. Study the given cartoon and answer the questions that follow.

(i) Identify and name the person holding in his hand, the placard 'Save democracy'. In your opinion, the group of five persons belongs to which political party?

(ii) According to the group of five, what are the intentions of the person sitting on 'Dharna'?

(iii) Which issues are responsible for the downfall of democracy are highlighted in the cartoon?

Ans. (i) Jayaprakash Narayan is holding the placard 'Save democracy'. In the above cartoon, the group of five persons belong to Congress Party.

(ii) The intentions of the person sitting on 'Dharna' are to create chaos and grab power.

(iii) Corruption, lawlessness, violence, etc are responsible for the downfall of democracy.

2. Study the given cartoon and answer the questions that follow.

(i) Who are the people standing and looking at the defeated Congress?

(a) Common man and Congress workers
(b) Government employees
(c) Morarji Desai and other leaders with common man
(d) All of the above

Ans. (c) Morarji Desai and other leaders with common man

(ii) What are the different weapons in the hands of the Congress depict?

(a) Emergency provisions
(b) Constitutional amendments
(c) Press censorship
(d) All of the above

Ans. (d) All of the above

(iii) Why is the speaker saying to be careful?

(a) He has a fear of losing by Congress again.
(b) People are now more aware of their rights and any strict control of Congress won't be tolerated again.
(c) He is fearful of imposing emergency by Congress again?
(d) None of the above

Ans. (b) People are now more aware of their rights and any strict control of Congress won't be tolerated again.

(iv) What does the above picture depicts?

(a) Leaders of Congress beaten by public.
(b) Defeat of Congress in 1990's General Election.
(c) Defeat of Congress in General Elections for the first time after independence.
(d) Split in Congress due to internal politics.

Ans. (c) Defeat of Congress in General Elections for the first time after independence.

3. Study the given cartoon and answer the questions that follow.

(i) What does the above image depicts?

Ans. Sense of impending political crises.

(ii) When did the cartoon appeared?

Ans. Few days before the declaration of the emergency.

(iii) Identify the person behind the leader sitting in chair.

Ans. D.K. Barooah

4. Study the given cartoon and answer the questions that follow.

(i) Identify and name the leader who toppled the Janata government. **CBSE 2024**

(a) Sarojini Naidu
(b) Indira Gandhi
(c) Mayawati
(d) None of these

Ans. (b) Indira Gandhi

(ii) Identify and name the Prime Minister of the Janata Party government shown in the cartoon.

(a) Jayaprakash Narayan
(b) Jagjivan Ram
(c) Raj Narain
(d) Morarji Desai

Ans. (d) Morarji Desai

(iii) Highlight any two reasons for the defeat of the Janata Party in 1980.

(a) Lack of dedication in the Janata government and Indira Gandhi' s interference.
(b) It could not bring significant change in the policies from the government and lacked leadership.

(c) Indira Gandhi's campaign for 'Garibi Hatao' and her personality.
(d) None of the above

Ans. (b) It could not bring significant change in the policies from the government and lacked leadership.

(iv) Why did the speaker standing behind call Indira Gandhi's credit of toppling the government as lie?
(a) The actual reason for the toppling of the Janata government was lack of leadership, common programme and party split.
(b) Congress withdrew its support from the Janata government.
(c) Lack of common programme among Congress and Janata government.
(d) All of the above

Ans. (a) The actual reason for the toppling of the Janata government was lack of leadership, common programme and party split.

Map Based Questions

1. In the given outline Political map of India, four states have been marked as A, B, C and D. With the help of the information given below, identify them and write their correct names in your answer book along with the serial number of the information used and the related alphabet in the map as per the format given below. CBSE Term II 2022

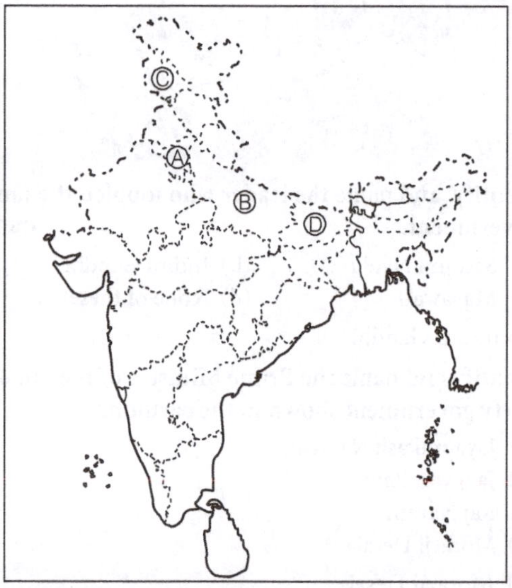

(i) The state to which Jayaprakash Narayan belonged.
(ii) The state where Indian National Congress won most of the Lok Sabha seats in 1977 elections.
(iii) The state from where Raj Narain contested the Lok Sabha seat against Indira Gandhi in 1977 election.
(iv) The state where Janata Party won all the Lok Sabha seats in 1977 elections.

Ans.

S.No. of the information used	Concerned alphabet given in the Map	Name of the State
(i)	D	Bihar
(ii)	C	Jammu & Kashmir
(iii)	B	Uttar Pradesh
(iv)	A	Haryana

2. In the given political outline map of India, four states have been marked as A, B, C and D. Identify the states on the basis of the information given below and write their correct names in your answer book along with the respective serial number and the concerned alphabet given in the map.

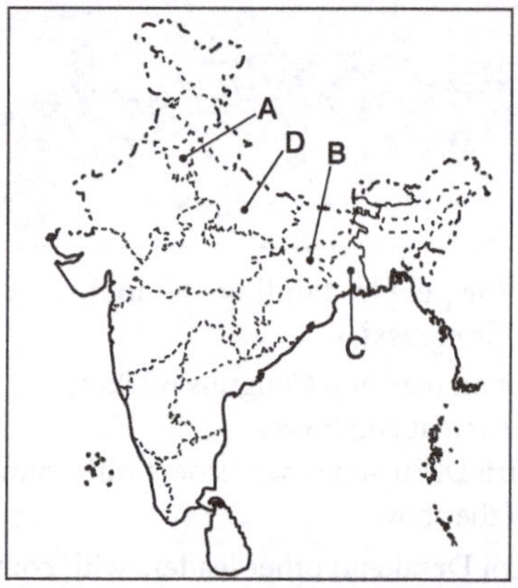

S.No. for the Information used	Concerned alphabet given in the map	Name of the State
(i)		
(ii)		
(iii)		
(iv)		

(i) The state related to former Prime Minister Chaudhary Charan Singh.
(ii) The state to which former Deputy Prime Minister Jagjivan Ram belong.
(iii) The state where the naxalites were very active.
(iv) A state where the Congress Party could not win even a single seat in the Lok Sabha elections in 1977.

S.No. for the Information used	Concerned alphabet given in the map	Name of the State
(i)	D	Uttar Pradesh
(ii)	B	Bihar
(iii)	C	West Bengal
(iv)	A	Haryana

SELF ASSESSMENT TEST

Objective Type Questions

1. Why did Bangladesh crisis put heavy strain on Indian economy?
   (a) US Government stopped all aid to India.
   (b) 8 million people came to India from Bangladesh.
   (c) Pakistan was imposing economic sanctions
   (d) Bothe (a) and (b)
2. The demand for dismissal of Congress government was demanded in Gujarat because ....
   (a) against corruption
   (b) rising prices
   (c) to conduct re-elections
   (d) All of these
3. In which year A.N. Ray was appointed as the Chief Justice and removing the seniority of three judges which generated a political controversy?
   (a) 1971 (b) 1972 (c) 1973 (d) 1974
4. In 1977 elections Congress Party won only .... seats.
   (a) 120 (b) 154 (c) 155 (d) 157
5. According to which act, a person can be detained on the apprehension that he/she may commit a crime.
   (a) Preventive Arrest
   (b) Preventive Detention
   (c) Precautionary Detention
   (d) Arms Act

Very Short Answer Type Questions

6. What was the main demand of the railwaymen during the railway strike led by George Fernandes in 1974?
7. What was Kesavananda Bharati judgement?
8. Which two organisations were banned during the emergency and why?
9. Mention any two reasons due to which Janata Party won the elections of 1977?

Short Answer Type Questions

10. What was the reason behind the invalidity of Indira's 1971 election?
11. State any two reasons which added to Indira's problems after 1971 elections.
12. Explain Preventive Detention. How was it used during emergency?
13. Who was Chaudhary Charan Singh? Explain his role in Indian politics.

Long Answer Type Questions

14. Jayaprakash Narayan announced a nationwide satyagraha on 25th June 1975 and asked the government employees not to obey "Illegal and immoral orders". Why? **Competency Based Que**
15. Analyse and compare the Constitutional features regarding the emergency before and after the 1975 emergency. **Competency Based Que**

07 CHAPTER

This chapter introduces various accords and agreements between the government of India and leaders of various movements that aimed for greater regional autonomy.

Regional Aspirations

YOUR STUDY GOALS

7.1 Region and the Nation
7.2 Jammu and Kashmir
7.3 Punjab
7.4 The North-Eastern
7.5 Accommodation and National Integration

YOUR PRACTICE GOAL

- Objective Type Questions (34 Qs ; MCQs, A-R, Statements, Matching, Passage Based)
- Subjective Questions (13 VSAs, 10 SAs, 5 LAs, 2 Picture Based, 2 Map Based)

7.1 Region and the Nation

- The period of 1980s saw the rise in demands for **regional autonomy**. These movements involved armed struggle by the people, their suppression by the government and collapse of political process.
- Some movements drew long and had to be ended up with the negotiations between the Central Government and the organisations, who leads these movements.
- The **accords**[1] between the government and the organisations were reached after a process of dialogue but this journey is marked by violence sometimes.

Indian Approach

- Our Indian Constitution and the process of nation-building follows the principle of not to deny the **rights of different regions** and **linguistic groups** to keep their own culture.
- Indian nationalism sought to balance the principles of unity and diversity.
- The Indian approach on diversity was different from the approach adopted in European countries where they saw cultural diversity as threat to the nation.

---

1 **Accord** An official agreement or treaty.

- India adopted a democratic approach to the question of diversity. Democracy allows the regional aspirations to be expressed with complete freedom. Therefore, in democratic politics regional demands or aspirations are not seen as **anti-national**.
- In fact, in a democracy, regional issues and problems receive proper attention and there is a process followed for the accommodation of various differences. But sometimes, such attention obscure the national unity.
- Sometimes demand for a particular region alone may make us to ignore the larger needs of the nation. Therefore, political conflicts over issues of power of the regions, their rights and their separate existence are common to the nations that want to respect diversity as well as maintain their unity.

Areas of Tension

- After independence, our nation had to cope up with the many problems like partition, displacement, integration of princely states, reorganisation of states and so on. On the basis of these problems many observers predicted that 'India as one unified country can not last long'.
- There were many regional issues that emerged after the independence within different states like,
  - **Jammu and Kashmir** it was not about India and Pakistan, but also about the political aspirations of the Kashmir Valley People.
  - In the North-Eastern part of India, not every region wanted to be within India. Nagaland first demanded for separation from India, which was followed by Mizoram.
  - **South India** Some groups from the **Dravid movement** had an idea for a separate country.
  - India also, witnessed some mass agitations to form the linguistic states. In some parts of Southern India, particularly Tamil Nadu, there were protests against making Hindi the official national language of the country.
  - In Northern India, there were strong pro-Hindi agitation's to make it the official language.
  - In late 1950s, **Punjabi language speaking,** people started demanding for a separate state for themselves. This demand was finally accepted and the states of **Punjab** and **Haryana** were created in 1966.
  - Later the states of **Chhattisgarh, Uttarakhand** and **Jharkhand** were created.
  - Thus, **India** has witnessed the continuous challenges of diversity which were accommodated by redrawing the internal boundaries of the country.
- Yet the regional aspirations are not fulfilled completely. Some states like Punjab, Assam, Mizoram, Kashmir and Nagaland still have some complex issues. The study of these cases are important for the study of our past as well as understanding of India's future.

Quick Test 1

1. Which principles Indian Nationalism sought to balance?
2. What was the idea of Dravidian movement?
3. Which region of the country protested against making Hindi as an official language of the country?
4. Identify the state from North East India which first demanded separation from India.

7.2 Jammu and Kashmir

- Jammu and Kashmir had a special status under **Article 370.**
- Despite of the special status, Jammu and Kashmir had faced the following problems
  - Violence
  - Cross border terrorism
  - Political instability
  - Internal and external issues.
  - Loss of lives – Innocent civilians, security officials and militants[2].

2 Militants A person who uses violent methods to fulfill his demands.

- Large scale displacements of Kashmiri Pandits from Kashmir Valley.

▲ *Union Territories of Jammu & Kashmir and Ladakh*

- There are three **social and political regions**
  - The **Jammu region** is a mix of foothills and plains. This area is mainly inhabited by Hindus. Sikhs, Muslims and other people also live there.
  - The **Kashmir region** comprises of the Kashmir Valley with mostly Muslim population. Hindus, Sikhs and Buddhists also live there.
  - The **Ladakh region** is mostly mountainous with almost equal population of Buddhists and Muslims.

Roots of the Problem

- Jammu and Kashmir was a Princely State before 1947. **Maharaja Hari Singh** did not want to join either India or Pakistan but to have an independent status for his state. Pakistan thought that Kashmir has mostly Muslim population so it belonged to Pakistan. However, Kashmiri people see themselves as Kashmiri above all. This regional aspiration is know as **Kashmiriyat.**
- **Sheikh Abdullah** of the **National Conference** wanted to free Kashmir from Maharaja, but was against joining Pakistan. The National Conference was a secular organisation and had a long connection with Congress. Sheikh Abdullah was a friend of Nehru and other leading nationalist leaders.
- In October 1947, Pakistan sent **tribal invaders** to capture Kashmir. Maharaja of Kashmir asked for military help to India. India extended its military support and drove back those invaders from the Kashmir Valley, but only after the condition if Maharaja had signed the **Instrument of Accession** with Government of India.
- However, the Pakistan continued to control some part of the state, so the issue was taken to the **United Nation Organisation.** On **21st April, 1948,** the resolution suggested a three step process,
  Step 1 Pakistan had to withdraw its people from Kashmir.
  Step 2 India have to withdraw its forces to maintain law and order.
  Step 3 A plebiscite was to be conducted in a free and impartial manner.

- This resolution could not solve the problems. **Sheikh Abdullah** became the **Prime Minister** of the State of J&K in March 1948. India agreed to give provisional autonomy to Jammu and Kashmir under **Article 370**. At that time, the head of the government in state was called the **Prime Minister**.

External and Internal Disputes

- Pakistan has always claimed that Kashmir Valley should be the part of Pakistan. It had sponsored the tribal invasion in 1947. Due to this illegal invasion, Pakistan has control in one part of the state. This Indian territorial part under illegal control of Pakistan is called **Pakistan Occupied Jammu** and **Kashmir (POJK)**.
- Internally, there is a dispute about the status of Kashmir within Indian Union. The special status under Article 370 and 371 had provoked two opposite reactions, which are as follows
  - People outside of Jammu and Kashmir feel that the special status under Article 370 did not allow the full integration of the state with India.
  - Kashmiris felt that the autonomy under **Article 370** is not enough and they had three major complaints as follows
    (i) The succession of Kashmir in India should be referred to the people of the state through plebiscite after situations become normalised. But this has not happened as Pakistan did not vacate the illegal occupation. Thus, it could not happen.
    (ii) There was a feeling among people that the special status under Article 370 has been taken away in practice. This has only been in the papers not in the reality. Therefore, there was a demand for restoration of autonomy or **Greater State Autonomy**.
    (iii) The democracy which is practised in other states of India is not practised in the state of Jammu and Kashmir.

The Kashmir Issues

- Since its integration with the Union of India, Kashmir has remained one of the burning issues in post-independence India. The problem became more complicated when it was accorded a special status in the Constitution through Article 370 and Article 35A
  - the former giving it special powers like having its separate Constitution/Constituent Assembly/Flag,
  - new nomenclature for Chief Minister as Prime Minister and Governor as Sadr-e-Riyasat, and
  - the non-enforcement of most of the union laws in the state while the later imparting it special citizenship rights prohibiting the non-Kashmiris from buying property in the state.
- It was against the special status of the state of Jammu and Kashmir that there was a clarion call (request for action) for abrogation of Articles 370 and 35A. Others equated Article 370 and 35A as 'Constitutionally recognised separatism'.
- It was against this backdrop that the NDA government presented the Jammu and Kashmir Re-organisation Bill in Rajya Sabha on 5th August, 2019 for the abolition of Section 370 and 35 A from Kashmir, which was passed by a majority. The bill was passed by the Lok Sabha on 6th August, 2019. After the President's assent on 9th August, 2019, Sections 370 and 35A were repealed and Jammu and Kashmir got divided into two union territories of Ladakh and Jammu & Kashmir.

Politics Since 1948

- After coming to power Sheikh Abdullah initiated many **land reforms** and other policies through which common people were benefited. However, the difference between Sheikh Abdullah and the Central Government started increasing because of his position on Kashmir status.

- He was dismissed in 1953 and kept in detention for number of years. After him the successive leadership could not get major support of the people. There were serious allegations of malpractices in various elections.
- The Congress Party exercised influence on the politics of the state. National Conference (without Sheikh Abdullah) remained in power with the active support of Congress for some time. Later it was merged with the Congress.
- There were many attempts to reach an agreement between Sheikh Abdullah and the Government of India. The Constitutional provisions of Jammu and Kashmir had changed in 1965 that changed the designation of the **Prime Minister** of state to the **Chief Minister**. **Ghulam Mohammed Sadiq** of the **Indian National Congress** became the **first Chief Minister of the state.**
- In 1974, Indira Gandhi reached an agreement with Sheikh Abdullah and he became the Chief Minister of the state. He revived the National Conference and elected with the majority in the elections of 1977.
- In 1982, Sheikh Abdullah died and his son **Farooq Abdullah** became Chief Minister. He was soon dismissed by the governor. This dismissal generated a feeling of resentment in Kashmir. A feeling among Kashmiris began to start that the centre was intervening in the politics of state.

Insurgency and After

- In 1987 assembly elections, Farooq Abdullah returned as Chief Minister, but it was because of the Congress and National Conference Alliance. Therefore, it was widely believed that the results did not reflect a popular choice. Therefore, there was a popular resentment among the people since early 1980s, which gave a rise to **insurgency**[3].
- By 1989, a militant movement began to mobilise to form a separate Kashmiri nation. These militants got moral, material and military support from Pakistan. For many years, the state had to undergo **President's Rule** and effective control of the armed forces.
- Throughout the period from 1990, Jammu and Kashmir experienced violence by the insurgents and through the army action. In 1996, national conference came to power with a demand for regional autonomy for Jammu and Kashmir, elections were again held in 2002. This time the national conference failed to win and a coalition government of **People's Democratic Party (PDP) and Congress** was formed.

2002 and Beyond

- As per the coalition agreement **Mufti Mohammed** headed the government for the first three years and then succeeded by **Ghulam Nabi Azad** of the Indian National Congress. President rule was imposed in the state in July, 2008. The next election was held in November-December, 2008.
- The next coalition government composed of National Conference and Indian National Congress came into power, which was headed by **Omar Abdullah** in 2009.
- However, the state witnessed disturbances by the **Hurriyat Conference.** In 2014, the state went into another election, which recorded the **highest voters** turn out in 25 years. A coalition government led by Mufti Mohammed Sayeed of the **PDP with BJP** as its partner was formed. Mufti Mohammad sayeed died and his daughter **Mehbooba Mufti** became the **first woman Chief Minister of Jammu and Kashmir** in April, 2016.
- During the tenure of Mehbooba Mufti, major acts of terrorism and internal and external tensions were seen, then, BJP withdrew its support and the President rule was imposed in June 2018.
- On **5th August, 2019,** Article 370 was abolished by the **Jammu and Kashmir Re-organisation Act 2019**. The state was constituted into two union territories, namely, Jammu & Kashmir and Ladakh.

3 **Insurgency** It is a movement within a country dedicated to overthrowing the government.

- Jammu and Kashmir and Ladakh are the living examples of plural diversity in India. These regions have all kinds of diversities – cultural, religious, linguistic, ethnic and tribal. There are also other divergent, political and developmental aspirations which are aimed to be achieved by the latest act.

Quick Test 2

1. Under which article was Jammu and Kashmir granted special status?
2. Define the term ' Kashmiriyat'.
3. Who was the first Chief Minister of Jammu and Kashmir?
4. When Mehbooba Mufti came to power, PDP had an alliance with which political party?

7.3 Punjab

- The decade of **1980s** witnessed major developments in Punjab. Punjab had changed the composition two times
  - First with partition
  - Second when Haryana and Himachal Pradesh were carved out.
- The **Akali Dal**, which was formed in 1920 as the political wing of the Sikhs, had led the movement for the formation of a **'Punjabi Suba'**.

Political Context

- After the formation of Punjab state, the Akalis came to power in 1967 then in 1977. It was the coalition government, both the times. The Akalis felt that even after the re-organisation, their power and position remained doubtful.
  - Firstly the government was dismissed by the centre in the mid term.
  - Secondly, they did not enjoy strong support among the Hindus.
  - Thirdly, the Sikh community like other religious communities was internally divided on the basis of caste and class.
- The Congress got more support among the Dalits whether Hindu or Sikh than the Akalis.
- In 1970s a section of Akalis demanded for political autonomy. A resolution was passed at **Anandpur Sahib** in 1973.
- The **Anandpur Sahib Resolution** asserted regional autonomy and wanted to redefine centre-state relationship in the country. It spoke for the aspiration of the **Sikh qaum** (community or nation).
- It declared its goal of attaining the **bolbala** (dominance or hegemony) of the Sikhs. But after few years, Akali government was dismissed.
- In 1980, the Akali Dal launched a movement on the question of the **distribution of water** between Punjab and its neighbouring states.

Cycle of Violence

- The leadership of the movement passed from the moderate Akalis to the **extremist elements and armed insurgenct**. These extremists made their headquarters inside the Sikh Holi shrine, **the Golden Temple** in **Amritsar** and turned the temple premises into the armed fortress.
- In June 1984, the Government of India carried out **'Operation Blue Star',** (code name for army action in the Golden Temple). In this operation, the government could successfully flush out the militant, but it damaged the historic temple which deeply hurt the sentiments of the Sikhs.
- A large number of Sikh in India and in foreign country saw the military operation as an attack on their faith, which gave more encouragement to the militant and extremist group.

- One tragic event complicated the problem of Punjab. Prime Minister **Indira Gandhi** was **assassinated** on 31st October, 1984 by her Sikhs bodyguards as a revenge. Entire country was shocked by this event.
- In Delhi and in many parts of Northern India, violence broke out against the Sikh community. More than two thousand Sikhs were killed in the national capital. Hundreds of Sikhs were killed in other parts of the country, especially in places like Kanpur, Bokaro and Chas.
- Many Sikh families lost their male members and suffered emotional and financial loss.
- The Sikh community was deeply hurt, when the government took a long time in restoring normalcy. Also the offenders of this violence were not punished effectively.
- Twenty years later, speaking in the Parliament in 2005, **Prime Minister Dr. Manmohan Singh** expressed regret over these killings and apologised to the nation for the anti-Sikh violence.

Road to Peace

- The new **Prime Minister Rajiv Gandhi** initiated a dialogue with moderate Akali leaders in 1984. In July 1985, he reached an agreement with **Harchand Singh Longowal,** the then President of the Akali Dal. This agreement known as the **Rajiv Gandhi – Longowal accord** or the **Punjab accord**. The Punjab accord was a step to bring normalcy in Punjab.
- It brought out the following conditions
  - Transfer of Chandigarh to Punjab.
  - A separate commission would be appointed to resolve the border dispute between the states of Punjab and Haryana.
  - A tribunal to be set up between the sharing of the Ravi–Beas river water among the states of Punjab, Haryana and Rajasthan.
  - This agreement also provided compansation for the better treatment of those, who were affected by the militancy in Punjab.
  - Withdrawl of the Armed Forces Special Powers Act in Punjab.
- The cycle of violence continued for a decade even after the acccord.
- Militancy and insurgency, violated the human rights. It also led to the fragmentation of the Akali Dal. On these issue, the Central Government imposed President rule in the state.
- In 1992, elections were held in Punjab, but only 24 per cent of the electors turned out to vote.
- Finally, militancy was eradicated by the security forces. Peace returned to Punjab by the middle of 1990s. In 1997, **the alliance of Akali Dal (Badal)** and the **BJP** scored a major victory. This was the **first normal elections** after the militancy era.
- Politics now became secular and the questions of development and social change began to occupy the state.

Quick Test 3

1. What was the Anandpur Sahib resolution?
2. What is qaum?
3. When did 'Operation Blue Star' take place?
4. Which places witnessed the large scale violence against the Sikh community in 1984?

7.4 The North-Eastern

- The North-East region comprises of eight states, namely, Arunachal Pradesh, Assam, Nagaland, Manipur, Tripura, Mizoram and Meghalaya. These states are called 'the seven sisters'. The Sikkim state is referred to as the 'brother of seven sisters'.
- The entire region has only 4 per cent of the country's population. There is a very small corridor of 22 km which connects the region to the rest of his country.
- The region shares its boundaries with **Myanmar, China and Bangladesh.** It serves as the **gateway of India to the South-East Asia.**
- Since 1947, the region has undergone various changes. Tripura, Manipur and Khasi Hills of Meghalaya were the Princely States which merged with India after the independence. But the regional aspirations were turned out in 1980s.
- **Nagaland** was created as a state in 1963. **Manipur, Tripura** and **Meghalaya** became state in 1972. **Mizoram** and **Arunachal Pradesh** became separate states in 1987.
- The partition of India affected the North-Eastern region. The North-Eastern region now became a **land locked**[4] area which affected the economy of the region.
- The politics of this region also remain isolated. Population changes began when migrants from neighbouring states and countries started coming.
- There was a complicated demand from North-Eastern regions because, of the following reasons
  - Complex Social Character of the region
  - Backwardness compared to other parts of the country
  - Vast international border
  - Weak communication between the Northeast and the rest of the India
  - Fragile nature of politics

4 **Landlocked** The area, which is surrounded by the land on all sides and not connected to any open sea or ocean.

- Three issues, which dominate the politics of Northeast are as follows
  - Demand for autonomy
  - Movement for secession[5]
  - Opposition to 'outsiders'
- In 1970s, some initiatives were taken on the first issue which led to dramatic developments. In 1980s, the initiatives were taken on the second and third issues.

Demand for Autonomy

- During independence, the state of Assam comprised the entire North-East region except Manipur and Tripura. When **non-Assamese** people felt that the Assam government was imposing Assamese language on them. It made these people to demand for the political autonomy.
- Leaders of opposition protested and there were riots throughout the state. Major tribal community leaders wanted to separate the Assam state. All these leaders founded the **Eastern India Tribal Union**. It later on converted into **All Party Hill Leaders Conference** in 1960.
- Finally instead of one tribal state, several states got carved out of Assam. The re-organisation of the North-East was completed by 1972. But this was not the end of autonomy demands in this region. There are several communities in Assam, like **the Bodos, Karbis** and **Dimasas** who wanted separate states.
- It was not possible to go on making smaller and yet smaller states. Therefore, it was decided to give some features in our federal set up[6] to satisfy their demands of autonomy, while remaining in Assam.
- The **Autonomous District Councils** were created for **Karbis** and **Dimasas** within the Assam to grant autonomy. **Bodos** were given autonomy under Autonomous Council.

Secessionist Movements

- It was easier to respond the demands for autonomy but it is very difficult to tackle when these diversities demand for a separate country. In two North-Eastern states, such demands raised and challenged the country's leadership.
- The area of **Mizo hills** was made an autonomous district within the state of Assam after the independence. But Assam government failed to respond properly during the **great famine** in 1959 in Mizo hills. This made the Mizos angry and their old belief became stronger that they were not the part of the British India so they were not the part of India. They formed **Mizo National Front (MNF)** under the leadership of Laldenga.
- In 1966, a two decade long battle began between the **Mizo insurgents** and **the Indian Army**. The MNF forces got support from the **Pakistan**. They went for guerilla war[7]. The Indian forces had to counter these insurgents and sometimes Air Force was also used.
- Laldenga came from the exile and made negotiations with the Indian Government.
- In 1986, a **Peace Agreement** was signed between Rajiv Gandhi and Laldenga. According to this accord, Mizoram was granted full fledged state hood with special powers. Laldenga took over as the Chief Minister. Today, Mizoram is one of the most peaceful places in the region and has taken big strides in literacy and development.
- The secessionist movement in **Nagaland** began much earlier but did not have a happy ending. Some Nagas under **Angami Zapu Phizo,** declared their independence from India in 1951. The **Naga National Council** launched an armed struggle for sovereignty of Nagas. An agreement was signed between the Government of India and the Council. Such agreement was not acceptable to the rebels. The problem in Nagaland has not been solved yet.

---

5 Movement for Secession A secessionist movement is a group of people, who want a region or group to become separate from a larger group of country.

6 Federal Setup It is a system of government, where power is divided.

7 Guerilla war It is a type of unconventional conflict, where small groups of fighters use irregular tactics to fight against larger and more established military forces.

Movements Against Outsiders

- A special problem occurred when large scale migration started in the North-East. **'Local'** communities did not like these 'outsiders'. They saw these migrants as the invaders and captured their land and limited resources.
- These migrants were seen as competitors to the political power and employment opportunities. This took a violent turn. The Assam movement is one such example which lasted from 1979 to 1985.
- In 1979 **All Assam Students' Union (AASU),** a students group not affiliated to any party led an **anti-foreigner movement**. It was because of the following reasons
  - There were huge numbers of illegal Bengali Muslim settlers from Bangladesh in the state of Assam.
  - It was a belief among Assamese people that these foreign people would change the Assam population and the original Assamese inhabitants would become minorities within their own country.
  - Though Assam has natural resources like oil, tea and coal, but still it had other economic issues because of poverty and unemployment in Assam.
  - Therefore, Assamese people demanded that these **illegal Bengali Muslim settlers** should be detected and deported[8] to their country.
  - The movement was against the illegal migrants, other outsiders and faulty voters' register that included the names of lakhs of immigrants.
- The movement demanded that all the outsiders who have come in Assam after 1951 should be sent back. This movement involved so many violent incidents and loss of human lives. There were train blockages and even the supply of oil from Assam to refineries in Bihar was blocked.
- In 1985, after the six years of such crisis Rajiv Gandhi led government signed an accord with the AASU leaders. It was decided that the foreigners who migrated during and after the Bangladesh war into the state of Assam would be identified and deported.
- Later, the **AASU** and the **Asom Gana Sangram Parishad** organised themselves as a regional political party called **Asom Gana Parishad (AGP)**. It came to power in 1985 with the promise to build a **golden Assam** by resolving the problem of foreign migration. The peace was established in Assam, but the problem of outsiders continues to be issue till now in the politics of Assam and other North-Eastern states. In Tripura, also, the original inhabitants have become minority in their own land. Even in the state of Mizoram and Arunachal Pradesh, the Chakma refugees create same problems for the local population.

Sikkim's Merger

- Sikkim was a **protectorate** of India at the time of independence. This means it was not a part of India, but also not a fully sovereign country. India would look after Sikkim's **defence** and **foreign relations** while the **internal administration** would be run by **The Chogyal, Sikkim's King.**
- This king was unable to keep the people happy, democratically. Most of the Sikkim population was Nepali, but the Chogyal was keen on maintaining the minority rule of elite **Lepcha-Bhutia community**. The led to the rise of Anti-Chogyal sentiments among some leaders of both the communities and they got the support from Government of India.
- Assembly elections were held in Sikkim in 1974 for the first time in democratic manner. In these elections, Sikkim Congress, which wanted greater integration with India won with all the seats.
- In the beginning, the assembly talked about the associate state, but in **April 1975,** a resolution was passed for the **full integration** of the Sikkim state in India. All this was followed by a referendum[9] that put a stamp of popular approval on assembly request.
- This request was immediately accepted by the Indian Parliament and thus Sikkim became the **22nd state of the Indian Union**. However, the King Chogyal did not accept this merger. The supporters of the King blamed the Government of India of cheating and use of force. However, this merger enjoyed the support of people and never became a divisive issue in Sikkim's politics.

---

8 Deported The process of removing illegal migrants from country.

9 Referendum A direct vote by the people on a particular policy or issue.

Quick Test 4

1. Which state is called the brother of the seven sisters?
2. What is movement for secession?
3. Who promised for golden Assam?
4. When was the resolution passed for the full integration of the Sikkim state in India?

7.5 Accommodation and National Integration

Period since 1980 has tested the capacity of democratic politics to accommodate the various economic, regional and other demands of the diverse sections of the society. We can draw some lessons from these examples.

- **The first lesson** is that the regional aspirations are very much part of the democratic politics. It is not an obstacle or abnormal process. These regional aspirations can rise even in the smaller countries like
  - In United Kingdom-Regional aspirations in Scotland, Wales and Northern Ireland.
  - Spain-Secessionist movement from the Basques.
  - Sri Lanka-Tamils

Therefore, for a large and diverse democracy, like India nation building is an ongoing process because it has to deal with the regional aspirations regularly.

- **The second lesson** is that the regional aspirations should be dealt with **democratic negotiations** rather than any violence or suppression. The Government of India reached negotiated settlement in the case of militant in Punjab, problems in Northeast and Kashmir Valley, which reduced the tensions and created the feeling of reconciliation. The political settlement in Mizoram shows how peaceful settlement can resolve the huge problem of separatism effectively.
- **The third lesson** is of power-sharing. Besides, having a formal democratic structure, the power should be shared with the regional parties and groups at the state level. Such idea of power sharing reduces the feelings of injustice and alienation.
- **The fourth lesson** is that if any particular region gets lesser economic development, it may have the feeling of discrimination as compared to the other economically developed regions. Naturally some backward states or backward region, in some states desire for the resolution on priority basis.
- These cases show the farsightedness of our Constitution makers in handling diversity. India's flexible federal system gives most states equal powers, with special provisions for some, like Jammu & Kashmir and North-East states. Article 370 for J&K was removed in 2019. The Sixth Schedule allows North-East tribes to preserve their customs, helping resolve political issues.

Dravidian Movement

- The Dravidian movement was one of the first regional movements in Indian politics. It gave a popular slogan- **'Vadakku Vaazhgiradhu; Therkku Thaeikiradhu'** [The North thrives even as the South decays].
- The Dravidian movement wanted to create a Dravid nation. It raised its demand through democratic means like public debates and electoral platform. Such strategy gained popular support and thus such movement could gain political power in the state and also became influential at the national level.
- Tamil social reformer, **E.V. Ramasami Periyar** led the formation of **Dravidar Kazhagam** [DK]. Under this movement, there was a strong opposition of Brahmin dominance, regional pride against the political, economical and cultural domination of the North.
- At the beginning, the Dravidian movement spoke on the behalf of the entire South India, but it did not get much support. Therefore, it got limited to Tamil Nadu only. The DK split and the political legacy of Dravidian movement was shifted to **Dravida Munnetra Kazhagam (DMK).**
- It demanded for three agitations in 1953–54.

  (i) **Firstly,** demanded the restoration of the original name of **Kallakudi railway station.** The original name of this station was changed from **Kallakudi to Dalmiapuram** after an industrial house from North India. This demand shows that the movement was a strong opposition to the North Indian economic as well as cultural symbols.

  (ii) **Second** demand was that Tamil cultural history should be given greater importance in the school syllabus.

  (iii) **Third** agitation was that the State Government had crafted the education in a way that Brahmanical social outlook is linked very much to the school syllabus. It also agitated against making Hindi the country's official language.
- The success of
  - Anti-Hindi agitation added to the DMK's popularity.
  - This political agitation brought the DMK in power in the elections of 1967.
- After the death of its leader, **C. Annadurai,** the DMK split. Since then the influence of Dravidian parties increased in Tamil Nadu and its politics. There were two parties that claimed Dravidian legacy, one was **DMK** and the other was **All India Anna DMK (AIADMK).**

Goa's Liberation

- During the British rule over India, the territories of Goa, Diu and Daman were under the **Portuguese** control since 16th century. Even after the Indian independence, Portuguese did not withdraw from there.
- Indian Government had tried to patiently persuade the Portuguese Government to withdraw from Indian territories. But the Portuguese suppressed the people of Goa, took away their civil rights and carried out religious conversions forcefully.
- A strong popular movement began within Goa for freedom, which was strengthened by socialist satyagrahis in Maharashtra. In **December 1961**, finally, the Government of India sent the army and liberated the territories within two days of action.
- Goa, Diu and Daman became Union Territory. However, again a problem started when the **Maharashtrawadi Gomanatak Party (MGP)** demanded that Goa (as a Marathi speaking area) should be merged with Maharashtra. But the Goans led by the **United Goan Party (UGP)** wanted to keep their Goan identity, separate, particularly their culture and Konkani language.
- In 1967, the Central Government held a **special opinion poll** in Goa. The majority of the Goan people voted in favour of remaining outside of Maharashtra. Thus, Goa remained as union territory.
- In, 1987 it became a state.

Quick Test 5

1. Which areas seek for regional aspirations in the United Kingdom?
2. In which two parties, did the DK split into?
3. Which organisation demanded that Goa should be merged within Maharashtra?
4. Who was the founder of Sikkim Praja Mandal?

Important Leaders of the Movements for Regional Aspirations

Rajiv Gandhi (1944-1991)

- He was the son of Indira Gandhi and Prime Minister of India between 1984 and 1989.
- He joined the active politics only after 1980.
- During his tenure, he reached various agreements with militants in Punjab, Mizoram and the students union in Assam.
- He encouraged for **more open economy** and **computer technology**.
- He sent Indian Army on the request of the Sri Lankan Government to sort out the **Sinhala-Tamil conflict**. He was assassinated by suspected LTTE suicide bomber.

E.V. Ramasami Naicker (Periyar) (1879-1973)

- He was popularly known as Periyar, which means the respected.
- He was a strong supporter of **atheism**, which means that not to follow any religion.
- He was famous for his anti-caste struggle and discovery of Dravidian identity. Initially, he worked as a Congress Party worker.
- He started **self-respect movement** in 1925.
- Later, he worked for Justice Party and led anti-Brahmin movement.
- He founded **Dravidar Kazhagam**, strongly opposed Hindi and North Indian domination upon the South Indians. He believed that North Indians and Brahman are Aryan and the South Indians are Dravidians.

Sheikh Muhammad Abdullah (1905-1982)

- He was the supporter of the autonomy and secularism for Jammu and Kashmir. He led the popular struggle against the princely rule and opposed Pakistan due to its non-secular nature.
- He was the leader of **National Conference** and became **Prime Minister of Jammu and Kashmir** in 1947. Later on he was dismissed and being in jail from 1953 to 1964 and again from 1965 to 1968.
- He became Chief Minister of the state after an agreement with the Indira Gandhi in 1974.

Master Tara Singh (1885-1967)

- He was a famous Sikh religious and political leader.
- He was also one of the early leaders of the **Shiromani Gurudwara Prabandhak Committee** (SGPC).
- He was the leader of Akali movement.
- Supported the freedom movement, but he was opposed to the Congress policy of negotiating only with the Muslims.
- After the Independence, he was the senior, most advocate of the formation of a separate state of Punjab.

Sant Harchand Singh Longowal (1932-1985)

- He was a Sikh political and religious leader, who began his political career in mid-sixties as an Akali leader.
- He was successful in reaching an agreement with the then Prime Minister Rajiv Gandhi on key demands of the Akalis. He was assassinated by unknown Sikh youth.

Laldenga (1937-1990)

- He was the founder and leader of the **Mizo National Front**, which turned into a rebel after the famine experience in 1959.
- He led an armed struggle against India for 20 years, but reached a settlement and signed an agreement with then Prime Minister Rajiv Gandhi 1986.
- After that, he became a Chief Minister of the newly created state of Mizoram.

Angami Zapu Phizo (1904-1990)

- He was the leader of the movement for independent Nagaland. He was the President of **Naga National Council**, who began an armed struggle against the Indian state.
- He went underground and stayed in Pakistan. He spent the last 30 years of his life in exile in UK.

Kazi Lhendup Dorji Khangsarpa (1904)

- He was the founder of **Sikkim Praja Mandal** and became the leader of Democracy movement in Sikkim.
- He became the leader of Sikkim State Congress in 1962 and founded the **Sikkim National Congress.**
- He won the elections and led the movement for the integration of Sikkim with India. After the integration, Sikkim Congress merged with the Indian National Congress.

Mind Map

REGIONAL ASPIRATIONS

1 Region and the Nation

Period of 1980s- rise in demands for regional autonomy.
- Movements involved armed struggle and negotiations between the central government and organisations who leads these movements.

Indian Approach to Diversity
- **Principle** Balance unity and diversity.
- **Constitution** Recognises rights of different regions and linguistic groups.
- **Nationalism** Seeks to accommodate regional aspirations.
- **Democracy** Allows regional issues to be expressed freely.

Areas of Tension
- **Post-Independence Issues** Partition, displacement, integration of princely states, reorganisation of states.
- **Regional Conflicts** Jammu and Kashmir, North East (Nagaland, Mizoram), South India (Dravid movement).
- **Language Issues** Hindi Vs. regional languages (Tamil Nadu), Punjabi language demand.
- **Statehood Demands** Punjab, Haryana, Chhattisgarh, Uttarakhand, Jharkhand.

2 Jammu and Kashmir

Special Status of Jammu and Kashmir
- **Article 370** Provisional autonomy granted to Jammu and Kashmir.
- **Disputes** External (Pakistan's claim) and internal (status within Indian Union).

Historical Background
- **Princely State** Jammu and Kashmir before 1947.
- **Maharaja Hari Singh** Wanted independence, but joined India after tribal invasion.
- **Sheikh Abdullah** Wanted freedom from Maharaja, but opposed joining Pakistan.

Politics Since 1948
- **Sheikh Abdullah's Rule** Land reforms, but differences with Central Government.
- **Successive Leadership** Allegations of malpractices, Congress influence in state.
- **Agreements and Dismissals** Sheikh Abdullah's agreements with Indira Gandhi, dismissals, and later becoming Chief Minister.

Insurgency and After
- **1987 Elections** Farooq Abdullah's return, but alleged rigged elections.
- **Militant Movement** Rise of insurgency, Pakistan's support.
- **President's Rule and Violence** Period of violence, army action, and President's Rule.

2002 and Beyond
- **Coalition Governments** National Conference, PDP, Congress and BJP.
- **Disturbances and Elections** Hurriyat Conference's disturbances, highest voter turnout in 25 years.
- **Abolition of Article 370** Jammu and Kashmir Reorganisation Act 2019, formation of two union territories.

3 Punjab

Historical Background
- **Formation of Punjab State** After partition and reorganisation.
- **Akali Dal** Formed in 1920, led movement for 'Punjabi Suba'.

Political Context
- **Akali Dal in Power** 1967 and 1977, coalition governments.
- **Anandpur Sahib Resolution** 1973, demanded regional autonomy.
- **Centre-State Relationship** Wanted to redefine relationship.

Cycle of Violence
- **Operation Blue Star** 1984, army action in Golden Temple.
- **Indira Gandhi's Assassination** 1984, by Sikh bodyguards.
- **Anti-Sikh Violence** 1984, widespread violence against Sikhs.

Road to Peace
- **Rajiv Gandhi-Longowal Accord** 1985, brought normalcy to Punjab.
- **Conditions** Transfer of Chandigarh, border dispute resolution, river water sharing, compensation, and withdrawal of AFSPA.
- **Elections and Peace** 1992 elections, militancy eradicated, peace returned by mid-1990s.

4 The North Easton

Demand for Autonomy
- **Assam Reorganisation** Creation of separate states for tribal communities.
- **Autonomous District Councils** Established for Karbis, Dimasas and Bodos.

North-Eastern Region
- **Comprises** 8 states (Arunachal Pradesh, Assam, Nagaland, Manipur, Tripura, Mizoram, Meghalaya and Sikkim).
- **Population** 4% of India's population.
- **Boundary** Shares borders with Myanmar, China and Bangladesh.

Historical Background
- **Princely States** Tripura, Manipur, and Khasi Hills merged with India after independence.
- **State Reorganisation** Nagaland (1963), Manipur, Tripura, and Meghalaya (1972), Mizoram and Arunachal Pradesh (1987).

Movements Against Outsiders
- **Assam Movement (1979-1985)** Anti-foreigner movement, demanded deportation of illegal migrants.
- **Asom Gana Parishad (AGP)** Regional political party, came to power in 1985.

Secessionist Movements
- **Mizo National Front (MNF)** Demanded separate country, signed peace agreement in 1986.
- **Naga National Council** Demanded sovereignty, ongoing issue.

5 Accommodation and National Integration

Lessons Learned
- Regional aspirations are normal.
- Democratic negotiations resolve issues.
- Power-sharing reduces feelings of injustice.
- Economic development reduces feelings of discrimination.

Goa's Liberation
- **Portuguese Control** 16th century to 1961.
- **Indian Independence** Goa remained under Portuguese control.
- **Liberation Movement** Popular movement and socialist satyagrahis.
- **Indian Army Action** December 1961, liberated Goa.
- **Union Territory** Goa, Daman and Diu became union territory.
- **Statehood** 1987, Goa became a state.

NCERT Folder

Intext Questions

1. Why does the challenge always come from the border states? (Pg. no. 114)

Ans. The challenge often arises from border states because of their unique geographical, cultural and historical contexts. These states are located at India's boundaries, where they interact with neighboring countries and this positioning creates specific issues and pressures.

Reasons that challenges come from border states are as follows

- **Geographical Vulnerability** Border states are prone to infiltration, cross-border terrorism and illegal migration. For example, Jammu & Kashmir has long dealt with cross-border terrorism from Pakistan.
- **Cultural and Ethnic Diversity** Many border states have distinct cultural and ethnic identities, which sometimes create a sense of alienation from mainstream India. For example, the Northeast has several tribes that feel disconnected due to differences in language, culture and traditions.
- **Historical Factors** Some border areas were disputed during or after Partition, which increased tensions.

Economic Neglect Border states are often underdeveloped due to their distance from economic hubs, fueling discontent and demands for greater autonomy.

India addresses these challenges by promoting economic development, strengthening security and respecting regional identities to ensure integration and harmony.

2. Regional aspirations of the people of North-East get expressed in different ways. These include movements against outsiders, movement for greater autonomy and movement for separate national existence. On the map of the North-East, using different shades for these three, show the states where these expressions are prominently found.

Ans. Movements against outsiders- Assam
Movements for greater autonomy- Arunachal Pradesh, Tripura
Movements for separate nations- Mizoram and Nagaland

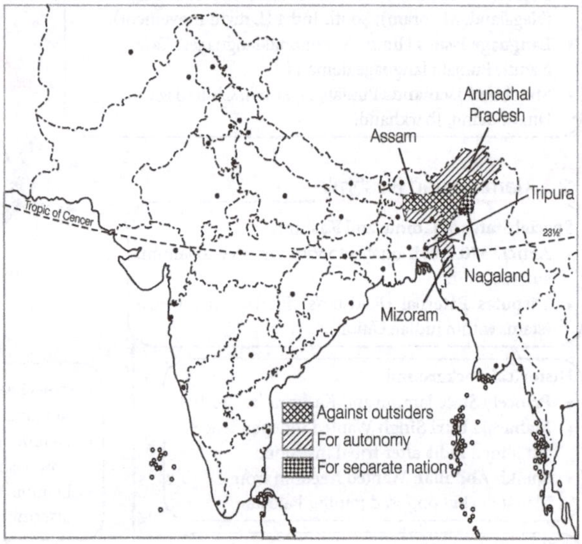

3. What were the main provisions of the Punjab Accord? In what way can they be the basis for further tensions between the Punjab and its neighbouring states?

Ans. Punjab Accord was an agreement signed between then the Prime Minister Rajiv Gandhi and Harchand Singh Longowal, then the President of Akali Dal in 1985.

The accord is also known as 'Rajiv Gandhi-Longowal Accord'. The main provisions of this accord were

- Chandigarh would be transferred to Punjab.
- A separate commission will be set-up to resolve the border dispute between Punjab and Haryana.
- A tribunal would be set up to decide the sharing of Ravi-Beas river water among Punjab, Haryana and Rajasthan.
- Compensation and better treatment of those affected by the militancy in Punjab.

Exercise

1. Match the following

Nature of Regional Aspirations	State
A. Socio-religious identity leading to statehood.	1. Nagaland/Mizoram
B. Linguistic identity and tensions with centre.	2. Jharkhand/ Chhattisgarh
C. Regional imbalance leading to demand for statehood.	3. Punjab
D. Secessionist demands on account of tribal identity.	4. Tamil Nadu

Ans. A → 3 B → 4 C → 2 D → 1

- Withdrawal of the application of Armed Forces Special Powers Act in Punjab.

But peace could not be established easily. The cycle of violence continued in Punjab. This accord can be the basis of further tension between Punjab and its neighbouring state because

- Chandigarh was transferred to Punjab which was opposed by Haryana.
- Water sharing dispute of the Ravi-Beas river among Punjab, Haryana and Rajasthan was not resolved fully.

4. Why did the Anandpur Sahib Resolution become controversial?

Ans. This resolution became controversial because

- Its limited appeal among the masses forced by the section of Akali Dal to raise the question of autonomous Sikh identity. Extremist elements in Akali started advocating secession from India.
- Akali Dal started movement over the question of water distribution between Punjab and neighbouring states.

5. Explain the internal divisions of the state of Jammu and Kashmir and describe how these lead to multiple regional aspirations in that state.

Ans. Jammu and Kashmir comprises of three social and political regions. These are

(i) **Kashmir Region** The heart of Kashmir region is the Kashmir Valley, mostly inhabitated by Kashmiri speaking Muslim with a small Kashmiri speaking Hindu minority.

(ii) **Jammu Region** It is the mix of foothills and plain. It consist of mix population of Hindus, Muslims and Sikhs who speak various languages.

(iii) **Ladakh Region** It is mountainous region having less population which is equally divided between Buddhists and Muslims.

These internal divisions of Jammu and Kashmir led to multiple regional aspirations in the state which were

- People of Kashmir region wanted to protect the identity of Kashmiriyat. Some groups demanded and fought for separate Kashmiri nation independent of India and Pakistan.
- The people of Jammu and Ladakh regions responded the idea of autonomy differently. They often complaint of neglect and backwardness. Thus, the demand for intra-state autonomy is as strong as the demand of the state autonomy.

6. What are the various positions on the issue of regional autonomy for Kashmir? Which of these do you think are justifiable? Give reasons for your answer.

Ans. Kashmir was given a special status by Article 370 in our Constitution. The view of Kashmiris about autonomy of Jammu and Kashmir is that the autonomy conferred by Article 370 is not enough.

A section of Kashmiris have expressed atleast three major grievances over the issue of autonomy. These were

(i) Government of India's promise to ascertain the view of people of Jammu and Kashmir once the situation normalised, has not been fulfilled. They demand for a plebiscite (vote).

(ii) There is a feeling that special status guaranteed by Article 370, has been eroded in practice. So, they are demanding restoration of autonomy or greater state autonomy.

(iii) Democracy has not been established in Jammu and Kashmir the way democracy is being practised in the rest of India.

The first position appears to be more justified because plebiscite will help us better to know what the people of Kashmir want and how their demands will be better accomodated under the framework of Indian Union.

7. The Assam movement was a combination of cultural pride and economic backwardness. Explain.

Ans. Assam movement was a combination of cultural pride and economic backwardness because

- The Assamese had a unique culture of their own. But the culture was suspected to be harmed because of the huge number of immigrants from Bangladesh. To tackle those immigrants and to avoid the mixing of the culture with those of outsiders, they launched Assam movement.
- There was a widespread poverty and unemployment in Assam, despite existence of natural resources like tea, coal and oil. They felt that these resources would be taken away by the outsider without giving benefit to the people of the state.

8. All regional movements need not lead to separatist demands. Explain by giving examples from this chapter.

Or **"Regional aspirations are very much a part of democratic politics". Justify the statement.**

Competency Based Que; CBSE 2024

Or **"Regional aspirations and their accommodation are an integral part of Indian democratic politics". Support the statement with any two suitable arguments.**

Competency Based Que, CBSE 2024 Set 3

Or **The issues of regional aspirations have provided valuable insights it to India democracy. State the lessons that can be drawn from this experience to pursue the future course of action.** **Competency Based Que; Diksha App**

Ans. **All regional movements need not lead to separatist demands** Regional movements in India often arise due to issues like development, cultural identity, or political rights. However, not all of these movements call for separate states. For example, in Maharashtra, the demand for a separate Vidarbha state is based on the region's economic backwardness and underdevelopment, but it does not call for separation from India. Similarly, the demand for a separate state of Telangana was about addressing regional inequalities, but after Telangana was formed, the movement shifted from separatism to focusing on regional development. Thus, regional movements may seek more autonomy or recognition, but they don't always aim for independence.

9. Regional demands from different parts of India exemplify the principle of unity with diversity. Do you agree? Give reasons.

Ans. Yes, I agree that regional demands from different parts of India show the principle of unity with diversity. India is a country with many cultures, languages, and traditions. Different regions have their own unique needs and preferences. For example, some states want to promote their local languages or have more control over their development. These regional demands are about protecting local identity and ensuring growth in each area.

However, these demands do not break the unity of India. They actually help strengthen the country by making sure each region's needs are understood and respected. The Indian Constitution allows states to have their own rights and powers, which helps in maintaining unity. Despite these differences, all regions work together for the overall development of the country. So, regional demands highlight how India can remain united while respecting its diversity.

10. Read the passage and answer the questions below.

One of Hazarika's songs ..... dwells on the unity theme; the seven states of North-Eastern India become seven sisters born of the same mother ..... 'Meghalaya went own way ..... Arunachal too separated and Mizoram appeared in Assam's gateway as a groom to marry another daughter.'

The song ends with a determination to keep the unity of the Assamese with other smaller nationalities that are left in the present-day Assam - 'the Karbis and the Mising brothers and sisters are our dear ones.' **—Sanjib Baruah**

(i) Which unity is the poet talking about?

(ii) Why were some states of North-East created separately out of the erstwhile state of Assam?

(iii) Do you think that the same theme of unity could apply to all the regions of India? Why?

Ans. (i) The poet is talking about the unity of Assamese.

(ii) Some states of North-East were created separately from the state of Assam to accommodate the regional aspirations of different tribal regions of the state.

(iii) Yes, same theme of unity could be applied to all regions of India because India is a nation where everyone is Indian first despite coming from diverse culture, religion, language and geography.

Exam Pattern Questions

Objective Type Questions

Multiple Choice Questions (MCQs)

1. Name the leader of Shiromani Gurudwara Parbandhak Committee senior most advocate of formation of a separate Punjab state. Diksha App

(a) Hari Singh
(b) Master Tara Singh
(c) Sant Harchand Singh Longowal
(d) Sant Bhindranwale

2. Which period in India can be seen as a period of rising regional aspirations for autonomy?

(a) 1970s (b) 1980s
(c) 1960s (d) 1990s

3. Which of the following are the basic principles of Indian approach to diversity in the process of nation building? Diksha App

(a) The Indian nation shall not deny the rights of different regions
(b) Various linguistic groups could retain their own culture
(c) Both (a) and (b)
(d) Neither (a) nor (b)

4. Which of the following were the issues India had to cope immediately after independence?

(a) Partition and displacement
(b) Integration of Princely States
(c) Re-organisation of states
(d) All of the above

5. Which article of Indian Constitution gave special status to Jammu and Kashmir? Diksha App

(a) Article 370 (b) Article 371
(c) Article 35 (d) Article 45

6. Who was the Hindu ruler of the Princely State of Jammu and Kashmir before 1947? Diksha App

(a) Bhupinder Singh (b) Inder Singh
(c) Hari Singh (d) None of these

7. Which slogan was given by the leaders of the Dravidian movement? Diksha App

(a) The North thrives even as the South decays
(b) Give me blood and I will give you freedom
(c) Garibi Hatao Desh Bachao
(d) Indira Lao Desh Bachao

8. Which language is being opposed as the official language of India by the people of Tamil Nadu? Diksha App

(a) Hindi (b) Tamil
(c) English (d) Oriya

9. Given below are two statements

Statement I The Dravidian movement initially aimed to create a separate Dravida nation.

Statement II It used violent methods to achieve its goals.

In the light of above statements, choose the correct answer from the options given below

(a) Both Statement I and Statement II are true.
(b) Both Statement I and Statement II are false.
(c) Statement I is true, but Statement II is false.
(d) Statement I is false, but Statement II is true.

10. After the death of C. Annadurai the permanent party the DMK splits into which parties? Diksha App

(a) DMK and AIADMK (b) MDMK and DMDK
(c) MDMK and PMK (d) None of these

11. In June 1984, the Government of India carried out an army action in the Golden Temple. What was the code name of the action? Diksha App

(a) Operation Blue Star
(b) Operation Vijay
(c) Operation Golden Temple
(d) None of the above

12. Which region of India is referred to as the 'Seven Sisters'? CBSE 2024

(a) North-East region (b) South-West region
(c) North-West region (d) South-East region

13. In which state of India are the 'Khasi Hills' located? CBSE 2024

(a) Meghalaya (b) Manipur
(c) Mizoram (d) Tripura

14. Which of the following regions of the Northeast did not become a separate state in 1972? Diksha App

(a) Manipur
(b) Tripura
(c) Meghalaya
(d) Arunachal Pradesh

15. Which of the following statement(s) can be considered as the political aspirations of the people of Assam?
(a) Secession from India
(b) Opposition to Brahmins dominance
(c) Anti-foreigners movement (To detect and deport outsiders)
(d) Both (a) and (c)

16. 'Bodo' is a community in .... state of India. CBSE SQP 2024
(a) Arunachal Pradesh (b) Assam
(c) Manipur (d) Mizoram

17. 'Karbis' community belongs to which state of India? CBSE 2024
(a) Manipur (b) Assam
(c) Arunachal Pradesh (d) Nagaland

18. To which state of India does the Dimasa Community belong? CBSE 2024
(a) Mizoram (b) Tripura
(c) Assam (d) Manipur

19. Who was the founder of Mizo National Front? Diksha App
(a) Rajiv Gandhi (b) Indira Gandhi
(c) Laldenga (d) Angami Zapu Phizo

20. Which of the following statement(s) is/are true about the reasons for the rise of and agitation violence in Assam? Competency Based Que
(a) The large scale migration into North-East.
(b) The late comers either from India or abroad were seen as encroachers on scarce resource like land.
(c) Seen as potential competitors to employment opportunities and political power.
(d) All of the above

21. Which of the following Schedules of the Constitution allows complete autonomy of different types to preserve their practises and customary laws? CBSE SQP 2024
(a) Fourth Schedule (b) Sixth Schedule
(c) Seventh Schedule (d) Eight Schedule

22. When was Goa finally liberated from Portuguese control? Diksha App
(a) December, 1961 (b) August, 1947
(c) May, 1950 (d) August, 1951

23. When did Goa finally become a state of Indian Union? Diksha App
(a) 1999 (b) 1980
(c) 1966 (d) 1987

24. Identify the incorrect pair. Competency Based Que
(a) Jammu and Kashmir Re-organisation Act- 2018
(b) Rajiv Gandhi – Longowal Agreement 1985
(c) Anandpur Sahib Resolution- 1973
(d) Resolution for Sikkim Merger into Indian Union- 1975

25. Match the following. Competency Based Que

List I	List II
A. Dravidian Movement	1. Maharashtrawadi Gomantak Party
B. Bolbala	2. Phizo
C. Naga National Council	3. Periyar
D. Goa	4. Akalis

Codes

	A	B	C	D
(a)	3	4	1	2
(b)	4	1	3	2
(c)	2	3	4	1
(d)	3	4	2	1

26. Arrange the following in the chronological order
I. Pakistan sent tribal infiltrators to Kashmir.
II. Sheikh Abdullah became Prime Minister of Jammu and Kashmir.
III. The Punjab accord was signed by Longowal and Rajiv Gandhi.
IV. Jammu and Kashmir was a Princely State.
Choose the correct option.
(a) I, II, III, IV (b) IV, I, II, III
(c) IV, II, I, III (d) II, I, IV, III

27. Choose the wrong statement from the given options Competency Based Que
(a) To protect Kashmir, Maharaja Hari Singh had to seek India's support.
(b) In the year 2009, the state witnessed higher voter turnout.
(c) Congress Party greatly influenced the politics of the state in the initial years.
(d) Jammu and Kashmir got divided into two union territories in 2019.

Assertion-Reason Questions

Directions (Q. Nos. 28-31) In the questions given below, there are two statements marked as Assertion (A) and Reason (R). Read the statements and choose the correct option.

Codes
(a) Both A and R are true and R is the correct explanation of A.
(b) Both A and R are true, but R is not the correct explanation of A.
(c) A is true, but R is false.
(d) A is false, but R is true.

28. Assertion (A) Democracy allows the political expressions of regional aspirations and does not look upon them as anti-nationals.
Reason (R) Democratic politics allows parties and groups to address the people on the basis of their regional identity, aspiration and specific regional problems.

29. **Assertion** (A) The Mizo National Front (MNF) started an armed campaign for independence.

Reason (R) After independence, the Mizo area was made an autonomous district with Assam. **CBSE 2024**

30. **Assertion** (A) In 1979, the All Assam Students' Union (AASU) led an Anti-foreigner movement.

Reason (R) The movement was against illegal migrations and against faulty voter's lists.

31. **Assertion** (A) Instead of one tribal state, several states got carved out of Assam.

Reason (R) Leaders of the major tribal communities wanted to separate from Assam.

Passage Based Questions

32. **Read the passage given below and answer the questions that follow.**

India adopted a democratic approach to the question of diversity. Democracy allows the political expressions of regional aspirations and does not look upon them as anti-national. Besides, democratic politics allows parties and groups to address the people on the basis of their regional identity, aspirations and specific regional problems. Thus, in the course of democratic politics, regional aspirations get strengthened. At the same time, democratic politics also means that regional issues and problems will receive adequate attention and accommodation in the policy making process. **CBSE 2025**

(i) **Which period in India is seen as a period of grooming regional aspirations for autonomy?**

(a) 1960s (b) 1970s (c) 1980s (d) 1990s

(ii) **Which type of diversity is dominant in India?**

(a) Social diversity (b) Political diversity
(c) Cultural diversity (d) Regional diversity

(iii) **How does democracy deal with the regional problems?**

(a) Through regular negotiations
(b) Through strong steps
(c) Through elections
(d) Through economic measures

(iv) **Which one of the following joined Indian Union in 1975?**

(a) Goa (b) Sikkim
(c) Puducherry (d) An Island

33. **Read the passage carefully given below and answer the questions that follows.**

The Assam movement from 1979 to 1985 is the best example of such movement against 'outsiders'.
The Assamese suspected that there were huge numbers of illegal Bengali Muslim setters from Bangladesh. They felt that unless these foreign nationals are detected and deported, they would reduce the indigenous Assamese into a minority. There were other economic issues too. There was widespread poverty and unemployment in Assam despite the existence of natural resources like oil, tea and coal. It was felt that these were drained out of the state without any commensurate benefit to the people.

(i) **The Assam movement was led by the group named ....**

(a) All India Students Union
(b) All Assam Students Union
(c) All Assam Sabha Unit
(d) All Assam Sabha Union

(ii) **What were the economic issues taken up as a part of the movement?**

(a) Widespread poverty (b) Unemployment
(c) Inflation (d) Both (a) and (b)

(iii) **Why did the Assamese seek the detection and deportation of the outsiders?**

34. **Read the passage given below and answer the questions that follow.**

Before 1947, Jammu and Kashmir (J&K) was a Princely State. Its ruler, Maharaja Hari Singh did not want to merge either with India or Pakistan but to have an independent status for his state. The Pakistani leaders thought that Kashmir region 'belonged' to Pakistan, since the majority population of the State was Muslim. But this is not how the people of the state themselves saw it— they thought of themselves as Kashmiris above all. This issue of regional aspiration is known as Kashmiriyat. The popular movement in the state, led by Sheikh Abdullah of the National Conference, wanted to get rid of the Maharaja, but was against joining Pakistan. The National Conference was a secular organisation and had a long association with the Congress. Sheikh Abdullah was a personal friend of some of the leading nationalist leaders including Nehru.

(i) **Who was the ruler of Jammu and Kashmir before 1947?**

(a) Sheikh Abdullah (b) Jawaharlal Nehru
(c) Maharaja Hari Singh (d) Muhammad Ali Jinnah

(ii) **Why did Pakistani leaders believe Jammu and Kashmir should join Pakistan?**

(a) The region was close to Pakistan
(b) The majority of the population was Muslim
(c) Maharaja Hari Singh wanted to join Pakistan
(d) The state was geographically small

(iii) **What was the concept of 'Kashmiriyat' and why was it important?**

Answers

1. (b) Master Tara Singh
2. (b) 1980s
3. (c) Both (a) and (b)
4. (d) All of the above
5. (a) Article 370
6. (c) Hari Singh
7. (a) The North thrives even as the South decays
8. (a) Hindi
9. (c) Statement I is true, but Statement II is false.
10. (a) DMK and AIADMK
11. (a) Operation Blue Star
12. (a) North-East region
13. (a) Meghalaya
14. (d) Arunachal Pradesh
15. (c) Anti-foreigners movement (To detect and deport outsiders)
16. (b) Assam
17. (b) Assam
18. (c) Assam
19. (c) Laldenga
20. (d) All of the above
21. (b) Sixth Schedule
22. (a) December, 1961
23. (d) 1987
24. (a) Jammu and Kashmir Re-organisation Act- 2018
25. (d) 3 4 2 1
26. (b) IV, I, II, III
27. (b) In the year 2009, the state witnessed higher voter turnout.
28. (b) Both A and R are true, but R is not the correct explanation of A.
29. (b) Both A and R are true, but R is not the correct explanation of A.
30. (a) Both A and R are true and R is the correct explanation of A.
31. (a) Both A and R are true and R is the correct explanation of A.
32. (i) (c) 1980s (ii) (c) Cultural diversity
(iii) (c) Through elections (iv) (b) Sikkim
33. (i) (b) All Assam Students Union
(ii) (d) Both (a) and (b)
(iii) The Assamese believed that illegal Muslim migrants would reduce the indigenous Assamese population to minorities. They were looking at the outsiders as competitors for the limited resources-land, water and employment opportunities.
34. (i) (c) Maharaja Hari Singh
(ii) (b) The majority of the population was Muslim
(iii) 'Kashmiriyat' refers to the idea of a unique regional identity for the people of Jammu and Kashmir that goes beyond religion. It represents a sense of cultural unity, mutual respect and co-existence among the people of different religions in the region. This concept was important because it highlighted that many people in Jammu and Kashmir valued their Kashmiri identity above religious or political divisions, which shaped their aspirations during that period.

Subjective Questions

Very Short Answer Type Questions

1. Name the original states from which the following states were carved out.

(i) Meghalaya (ii) Gujarat

Ans. (i) Meghalaya was carved out from Assam in 1972.
(ii) Gujarat was carved out from Bombay state in 1960.

2. Analyse the main reason for limiting the Dravidian Movement from the whole of South India to Tamil Nadu only. **Competency Based Que; Delhi 2019**

Ans. The Dravidian Movement led to the formation of Dravida Kazhagam (DK) under the leadership of Tamil social reformer E.V. Ramasami 'Periyar'. The organisation strongly opposed the Brahmins' dominance and affirmed regional pride against the political, economic and cultural domination of the North. Initially, the Dravidian movement spoke in terms of the whole of South India, however lack of support from other states limited the movement to Tamil Nadu. It used democratic means like public debates and the electoral platform to achieve its ends.

3. What is Anandpur Sahib Resolution?

Ans. Following were the the main demands put forward by the Anandpur Sahib Resolution passed in 1973

- It wanted regional autonomy and redefine state-centre relationship.
- It wanted to attain the hegemony of Sikh community and a separate Sikh nation.

4. Mention any two provisions of the Punjab Accord, signed by Rajiv Gandhi and Harchand Singh Longowal in 1985. **CBSE 2024**

Ans. (i) Chandigarh would be transferred to Punjab.
(ii) A separate tribunal would be set up for the water sharing of Ravi–Beas rivers between the states of Punjab, Haryana and Rajasthan.

5. How far did the Rajiv Gandhi-Longowal Accord succeed in bringing normalcy in Punjab?

Ans. The Rajiv Gandhi-Longowal Accord or the Punjab Accord, was a step towards bringing normalcy to

Punjab but peace did not come easily or immediately and the cycle of violence continued nearly for a decade.

6. Highlight any two issues that dominate the politics of North-East India.

Ans. After independence, two issues that dominate the politics of North-East India are

(i) Demands for autonomy.

(ii) Movements for secessions and opposition to outsiders.

7. How was the re-organisation of North-East India completed and by when?

Ans. The re-organisation of North-East India was completed by 1970s. In 1972, Meghalaya was carved out of Assam, Meghalaya and Tripura which became separate states in the same year.

8. Identify any two states where the Central Government had to face separate movements. Also name the leaders who let these movements. Competency Based Que; CBSE 2023

Ans. Nagaland – Angami Zapu Phizo

Mizoram- Laldenga

9. Analyse andy two reasons for the Secessionist movement in Nagaland.

Ans. Two reason for Secessionist movement in Nagaland are

- Nagas sought independence due to their distinct culture and tradition.
- Nagas claimed that they were never part of British India and declared independence post, 1947.

10. What is meant by national integration?

Ans. National integration means the feeling of oneness and unity among the people.

- The diversity within the nation is well accommodated and handled by the society.
- The feeling of oneness promote the feeling of unity and common belongingness.
- This feeling of national integration does not allow issues like regionalism, communalism to harm the unity of a nation.
- The people could work together for the security and development of the country.

11. 'Regionalism does not imply separatism'. Explain.

Ans. Regionalism is the theory or practice of emphasising the regional characteristics of local issues. Separatism advocates separation, especially essential or political separation. Thus, regionalism does not imply separatism.

12. "Regionalism is not as dangerous as communalism". Justify the statement. CBSE 2025

Ans. Regionalism and communalism both influence Indian politics, but regionalism is not as dangerous as communalism. Regionalism arises from demands for better economic development and political representation, often within the framework of democracy. It can lead to federal strengthening and regional development. However, communalism divides society based on religion, leading to hatred, violence, and national disintegration. While regionalism seeks better governance, communalism threatens India's secularism and unity. Therefore, communalism is a more serious threat to national integrity than regionalism.

13. Name any four regional parties which have ever formed the government in any state. CBSE 2023

Ans. The four regional parties formed, the government in states are as follows

(i) National Conference – Jammu and Kashmir

(ii) Akali Dal (Badal)- Punjab

(iii) Sikkim National Congress- Sikkim

(iv) Asom Gana Parishad- Assam

Short Answer Type Questions

1. "The accommodation of regional demands and the formation of linguistic states were also seen as more democratic". Justify the statement with any three suitable arguments. Competency Based Que

Ans. This statement can be justified by following three arguments

(i) Regional aspirations are very much a part of democratic politics. Expression of regional issues is not an abnormal phenomenon. A large and diverse democracy like India must deal with regional aspirations on a regular basis.

(ii) The best way to respond to regional aspirations is through democratic negotiations rather than through suppression.

(iii) Regional imbalance in economic development contributes to the feeling of regional discrimination. Regional imbalance is a fact of India's development experience.

2. While the rest of the country was re-organised on linguistic lines in 1950s, why had Punjab to wait till 1966? Competency Based Que

Ans. Punjab had to wait to be organised as a linguistic state till 1966, because there were two linguistic groups in Punjab, the first one was Hindi speaking and another one was Punjabi speaking.

The Akali Dal was formed in 1920 as the political wing of the Sikh. It led the movement for the formation of 'Punjabi Suba', but it could not enjoy the majority support of non-Punjabi speakers and other Hindus.

It was in 1966, when two states Haryana and Himachal Pradesh were carved out of Punjab. Punjab was finally created as a Punjabi speaking state.

3. What is Operation Blue Star and how did it hurt the sentiments of Sikh Community? Diksha App

Ans. (i) The Operation Blue Star was carried out by the Government of India to flush out the militants from the Holy Shrine, Golden Temple of the Sikh community. These militants were creating secessionist tendencies to create a separate country from India.

(ii) These extremist militants made their headquarters in the Holy Shrine and turned the Golden Temple into an armed fortress.

In June 1984, Government of India carried Operation Blue Star. While carrying out the military action, the Holy Shrine Golden Temple was damaged.

(iii) This damage hurt the sentiments of the Sikh community, a large proportion of Sikhs in India and foreign country, saw it as an attack on their faith.

4. Explain the rise of political violence in the North-Eastern part of India. Competency Based Que

Ans. Following reasons are responsible for the rise of political violence in the North-Eastern part of India

- The large scale migration into North-East gave rise to a special kind of problem that marked the local communities against people who were seen as outsiders or migrants.
- These latecomers, either from India or abroad are seen as encroachers on scarce resources like land and potential competitors to employment opportunities and political power.
- These issues have taken political and sometimes violent form in many states of the North-East.

5. Why did the movement for secession in the Mizo Hills area gain popular support? How was the problem resolved?

Ans. The movement for secession in the Mizo Hills area gain popular support due to following reasons

- Some Mizos believed that they were never a part of British India and therefore did not belong to the Indian union.
- The movement for secession gained popular support only after the Assam government failed to respond adequately to the great famine of 1959 in Mizo Hills.
- The Mizo's anger led to the formation of the Mizo National Front (MNF) under the leadership of Laldenga.

After a long struggle, the problem was resolved by a peace agreement, signed between Rajiv Gandhi and Laldenga.

As per this accord, Mizoram was granted full-fledged statehood with special powers and MNF agreed to give up secessionist struggle.

6. What are the two kinds of movement that were going on in North-East India?

Ans. Following two kinds of movements were going on in North-East India

(i) **Movement for Secession** It involved armed rebellions. The aim was to form a separate country. The Central Government had to make many efforts in order to tackle such demands and movements.

(ii) **Problems of Outsiders** People from nearby countries migrated to North-East region, creating troubles for them. They raised unemployment, poverty and economic imbalance. Locals had to protest in large scale against such movement of migrants.

7. Describe the events that took place in Sikkim from the time of India's independence to its merger with India. Competency Based Que; CBSE 2024

Ans. (i) At the time of independence, Sikkim was a protectorate state of India. It means that it was not a fully sovereign country because Indian Government would look its defence and foreign relations. The internal autonomy was with the King Chogyal.

(ii) The King Chogyal was not able to satisfy the people democratically. Most of the population in Sikkim was Nepali.

However, the king wanted to maintain the rule of a small elite minority of Lepcha – Bhutia community. This led to the rising of anti-Chogyal leaders from both the communities and got support from Government of India.

(iii) In 1974, first democratic elections were held to Sikkim Assembly. These elections were won by Sikkim Congress. It first wanted to maintain the status of a associate state for Sikkim but in April 1975, it passed a resolution to fully integrate with an India.

Referendum like question was organised for the public opinion. This merger enjoyed popular support.

(iv) The Indian Parliament immediately accepted the assembly's request. Sikkim became the 22nd state of Indian union. People supported this merger.

8. **Who was Kazi Lhendup Dorji Khangsarpa?** **Diksha App**

Ans. Kazi Lhendup Dorji Khangsarpa was the leader of democracy in Sikkim.

He was the founder of Sikkim Praja Mandal and Sikkim National Congress. He was the leader of Sikkim State Congress in 1962. He led the movement for integration of Sikkim in India when he won the elections in 1974.

9. **How did India address the regional aspirations of the people explain with help of any two examples?** **CBSE 2024**

Ans. (i) India has always adopted a democratic approach towards the regional aspirations of the people. It has followed the two principles mainly.

First and foremost it it believes that the nation should not deny the rights of different regions in linguistic group to retail their own culture.

This could be seen when the Assam Accord was assigned between the then Prime Minister Rajiv Gandhi and the leaders of AASU, the creation of Punjab state as a Punjabi speaking state was also an example of India's peaceful address towards the regional aspirations.

(ii) Indian Government has peacefully settled the separatist tendency in the state of Mizoram. Mizoram that has been demanding once a separate country now is the best example of one of the most peaceful and literate state in India.

It has shown that how political settlement can effectively solve the separatist ideologies.

10. **"The best way to respond to regional aspirations is through democratic negotiations rather than through suppression". Justify the statement with examples.** **Competency Based Que; CBSE 2024**

Ans.
- During the decade of 80s, India had witnessed many violent movements, separatist tendencies and regional autonomy demands.
- India has responded with negotiations and agreements rather than suppressing these movements. Take examples of the North-East movement, Punjab or Kashmir. Government of India has always found a way through peaceful settlement.
- This has produced the reconciliation and reduce the tensions in many regions. The example of Mizoram is a perfect example that how political settlement through peaceful negotiations can resolve the problem of separatism effectively.

Long Answer Type Questions

1. **Describe the role of E.V. Ramasami 'Periyar' in the Dravid movement and formation of Dravida Kazhagam (DK). Why did the DK get split and enter into politics as DMK?**

Ans. E.V. Ramasami, also known as Periyar, was a prominent leader in the Dravidian movement in Tamil Nadu. He strongly opposed the caste system, especially the dominance of Brahmins in Tamil society and fought for the rights of lower-caste people. Periyar promoted rationalism, self-respect and social equality. He was also a critic of religious practices, particularly Hinduism, which he felt perpetuated social inequalities.

In 1944, Periyar founded the 'Dravidar Kazhagam' (DK) to promote these ideas and work towards social justice. Under his leadership, the DK championed the cause of Dravidian identity and cultural pride, focusing on social reforms, including the abolition of untouchability and the promotion of Tamil language and culture.

However, the DK eventually split in the 1940s. The split happened due to differences in ideology and approach, with some leaders.This divergence led to the formation of the Dravida Munnetra Kazhagam (DMK) in 1949, a political party that aimed to bring about Dravidian ideals through active participation in electoral politics. The DMK took Periyar's ideas and turned them into a major political force in Tamil Nadu.

2. **Analyse any three main causes of unrest in Jammu and Kashmir.** **Competency Based Que; Delhi 2019**

Ans. Three main causes of unrest in Jammu and Kashmir are

(i) There is a dispute about the status of Kashmir within the Indian Union. Article 370 gives greater autonomy to Jammu and Kasmir compared to other state of India. State has its own Constitution.

The special attention provokes two opposite reactions. Kashmiris, believe that autonomy conferred by Article 370 is not enough. They should be given more autonomy.

(ii) In 1987 assembly election, the National Conference Congress alliance gained a massive victory and Farooq Abdullah returned as Chief Minister. By 1989, the state had come in grip of a militant movement mobilised around the cause of a separate Kashmir nation by Pakistan.

Throughout the period from 1990, Jammu and Kashmir experienced violence at the hands of the insurgents and through army action.

(iii) The presence of three separate social and politial areas, i.e. Jammu and Kashmir and Ladakh demand intra-state autonomy.

Some people within the state and the separatists demand for a separate nation that is not part of India.

3. Highlight any three provisions of Article 370 which provide a special status to the state of Jammu and Kashmir. Also examine the two opposite reactions provoked by this special status among the people. Competency Based Que; All India 2019

Ans. The three provisions which reflect special status to Jammu and Kashmir are

(i) Articles 370 of Indian Constitution gives greater autonomy to Jammu and Kashmir.

(ii) The state has its own Constitution.

(iii) All provisions of the Indian Constitution are not applicable to the state, law passed by the Parliament apply to Jammu and Kashmir only if the state agrees.

The two opposite reactions provoked by this special status among the people are

(i) People outside of Jammu and Kashimir believe that special status by Article 370 does not allow full integration with India. Thus they demand cancellation of Article 370, so that Jammu and Kashmir could become like any other state in India.

(ii) Most of the Kashmiris believe that the autonomy conferred under Article 370 is not enough.

4. Describe any two Secessionist movements of North-East India.

Or **Describe the Assam movement against the outsiders from 1979 to 1985.** Diksha App

Or **'Assam movement was a combination of cultural pride and economic backwardness'. Do you agree with this statement? Substantiate your answer with any three arguments.** CBSC 2020

Ans. Two Secessionist movements of North-East India are Assam movement and Mizo movement.

Assam Movement

The Assam, North-Eastern state had seen many changes since independence. States like Mizoram, Meghalaya, Arunachal Pradesh had been carved out of it.

The Assamese had a unique culture of their own. But the culture was suspected to be harmed because of the huge number of immigrants from Bangladesh.

To tackle those immigrants and to avoid the mixing of the culture with those of outsiders they launched a movement popularly known as the Assam movement.

Yes, the Assam movement was a combination of cultural pride and economic backwardness. It is justified from the following arguments

(i) The outsiders had a deep effect on the local economy. The Assam was suffering from poverty and unemployment because of these immigrants.

(ii) In spite of being a part of India, Assam was isolated and developmental work was not as functional as they were in any other part of the country.

(iii) Economy was already at stake but the immigrants made it even worse. Assamese had to face dual problem of cultural preservation and economic degradation. All Assam Students Union formed in 1979 led a struggle against these immigrates in order to save their culture.

(iv) Question of cultural pride and economic development was the major areas of concern. AASU asked Central Government to flush out the immigrants.

After a long struggle Central Government successfully deported the immigrants and the economic condition of the region was took into concern.

Mizo Movement

After independence, the Mizo hills area was made an autonomous district within Assam. According to Mizos they were never a part of British India and therefore did not belong to the Indian Union.

When Assam government failed to respond adequately to the great famine of 1959 in Mizo Hills, Mizo's anger led to formation of the Mizo National Front (MNF) under the leadership of Laldenga.

In 1966, the MNF started campaign for separate state. Two decade long battle between the Mizo insurgents and Indian army started.

The MNF fought a guerilla war and got support from Pakistan and China. Indian army had to take the repressive measure. It was only through the Rajiv-Longowal Accord in 1986, peace returned with the formation of fulfilled Mizoram state.

5. Suggest any three measures which in your opinion, are very effective to strengthen the national integrity and unity of India. Competency Based Que

Ans. Three measures which are very effective to strengthen the national integrity and unity of India are as follows

(i) **Value to Regional Aspirations** Expression of regional issues is not an abnormal phenomenon. A large and diverse democracy like India must deal with regional aspirations on a regular basis.

(ii) **Democratic Negotiation** The best way to respond to regional aspirations is through democratic negotiations rather than through suppression. In 1980, situation in Punjab, Kashmir and Assam was severely tensed. Instead of treating these law and order problems, Government of India resolved these through negotiation and discussion.

(iii) **Power Sharing among Centre and State** Formal democratic structure is not sufficient. The groups and parties from the regions must be given share in power at the state level.

Regions must have share in deciding the destiny of the nation. If they are not given share in the national level decision-making, the feeling of injustice and alienation can spread.

Regional imbalance in economic development contributes to the feeling of regional discrimination. Regional imbalance is a fact of India's development experience.

Picture Based Questions

1. Study the given cartoon and answer the questions that follow.

The Hindustan Times
KASHMIR ACCEDES TO INDIA
PLEBISCITE SOON ON RULER'S DECISION

(i) Identify the personalities in the image.
(a) Jawaharlal Nehru and Hari Singh
(b) Muhammad Ali Jinnah and Zhou Enlai
(c) Jinnah and Nehru
(d) Hari Singh and Jinnah

Ans. (a) Jawaharlal Nehru and Hari Singh

(ii) Which articles of the Indian Constitution provided special provision to Jammu and Kashmir?
(a) A-370 (b) A-356 (c) A-270 (d) A-324

Ans. (a) A-370

(iii) The agreement between the two is called ....
(a) Plebiscite Action (b) Referendum Policy
(c) Annexation Diplomacy (d) Instrument of Accession

Ans. (d) Instrument of Accession

(iv) The agreement between both the leaders led to the ....
(a) Merger of Kashmir with India
(b) Establishing Trade Relation with China
(c) Making New Budget Policy in the State
(d) Drafting Population Control Bill

Ans. (a) Merger of Kashmir with India

2. Study the given cartoon and answer the questions that follow.

(i) What wordplay is used in the title of this Amul ad?
(a) A play on the word 'armed'
(b) A play on the word 'unarmed'
(c) A play on the word 'disarmed'
(d) A play on the word 'charmed'

Ans. (a) A play on the word 'armed'

(ii) What is the primary theme of this Amul ad?
(a) Encouraging travel to Assam
(b) A take on security or conflict issues in Assam
(c) Promoting local culture in Assam
(d) A call for environmental awareness in Assam

Ans. (b) A take on security or conflict issues in Assam

(iii) For how many years, Assam witnessed the student's movement?
(a) 5 years (b) 4 years
(c) 10 years (d) 6 years

Ans. (d) 6 years

(iv) What issue in Assam during this period led to heightened security and tensions, as hinted by the people with weapons in the ad?
(a) Border disputes and ethnic conflicts
(b) Water scarcity
(c) Agricultural decline
(d) Educational reforms

Ans. (a) Border disputes and ethnic conflicts

Map Based Questions

1. In the political outline map of India given above, five states have marked as A, B, C, D and E. Identify these states on the basis of information given below and write their correct names in your answer book along with the respective serial number of the information used and the concerned alphabet in the map as per the following format. Delhi 2019

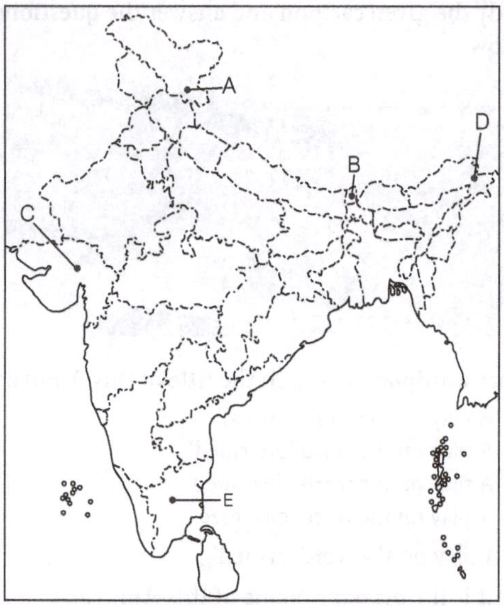

(i) The state created on linguistic Clines.
(ii) The state from where E.V. Ramasami Periyar.
(iii) The state that got statehood in 1987.
(iv) Mountainous region with equal population of Muslims and Buddhists.
(v) The state which integrated with India in 1975 as 22nd state of India.

Ans.

Sr. No. of the information used	Concerned alphabet given in the map	Name of the State
(i)	C	Gujarat
(ii)	E	Tamil Nadu
(iii)	D	Arunachal Pradesh
(iv)	A	Ladakh
(v)	B	Sikkim

2. In the given political outline map of India, four states have been marked as A, B, C and D. Identify these states on the basis of the information given below and write their correct names. Also write the concerned alphabets given in the map, as per the format that follow.

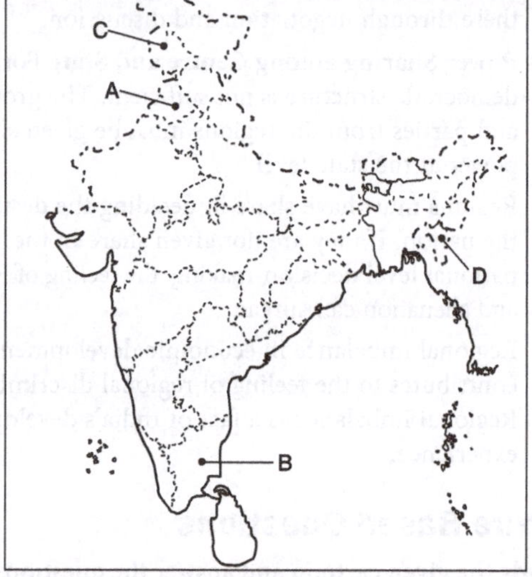

Sr. No. for the Information used	Concerned alphabet given in the map	Name of the State
(i)		
(ii)		
(iii)		
(iv)		

(i) The state, which has been bifurcated into two union territories recently.
(ii) The state, where Rajiv Gandhi – Longowal accord was signed.
(iii) The state to which Laldenga belonged.
(iv) The state from where the Dravidian movement started.

Ans.

Sr. No. for the information used	Concerned alphabet given in the map	Name of the State
(i)	C	Jammu and Kashmir
(ii)	A	Punjab
(iii)	D	Mizoram
(iv)	B	Tamil Nadu

SELF ASSESSMENT TEST

Objective Type Questions

1. Which railway station was renamed as Dalmiaparam?
   (a) Kalkaji (b) Kallakudi (c) Kakinada (d) Kasauli
2. Who was the first Chief Minister for the state of Jammu and Kashmir?
   (a) Ghulam Mohd Sadiq (b) Ghulam Nabi Azad (c) Sheikh Abdullah (d) Farooq Abdullah
3. What connects the North-East region of India with rest of the country?
   (a) Ocean (b) a narrow stream (c) a lake (d) a 22-km corridor
4. Choose the wrong statement regarding the regional parties of India.
   (a) Regional parties present greater representation of local people.
   (b) Regional political parties have emerged to fulfill the regional aspirations of the people.
   (c) In India regional parties are based on identity, statehood, autonomy and development.
   (d) Regional political parties helps in instigating riots within a particular region.
5. Arrange the following in sequence.
   I. Operation Blue Star
   II. All Party Hill Leaders Conference
   III. Famine in Mizo hills.
   IV. Self Respect Movement started by E.V. Ramasami Naicker
   Codes
   (a) I, II, III and IV (b) III, IV, I and II (c) IV, III, II and I (d) II, I, IV and III

Very Short Answer Type Questions

6. What was the Indian approach to managing regional diversity?
7. What did the demand for restoration of the name of railway station in Tamil Nadu? Signify.
8. Which areas in Assam are granted the Autonomous Councils?
9. Why was Asom Gana Parishad?

Short Answer Type Questions

10. Why Tamils opposed Hindi as national language?
11. Explain the main reason of tension between India and Pakistan.
12. Indian approach is different from other countries to solve the issue of regional aspirations? Explain.
13. Trace the journey of Goa towards the statehood.

Long Answer Type Questions

14. Explain how the Indian Government has been pursuing the path of democratic negotiation to solve the Kashmir issue.
15. Examine the major grievances of North-East region.
16. Explain the different lessons got by the various examples of regional aspirations in the 75 years of Independence.

08

CHAPTER

This chapter discusses the end of the Congress era and beginning of the coalition era along with the multi-party system. It also highlights various developments that took place during 1980s like OBC, other caste based politics and the rise of BJP.

Recent Developments in Indian Politics

YOUR STUDY GOALS

8.1 Context of the 1990s
8.2 Era of Coalitions
8.3 Political Rise of Other Backward Classes
8.4 Communalism, Secularism, Democracy
8.5 Emergence of New Consensus

YOUR PRACTICE GOAL

- Objective Type Questions (26 Qs ; MCQs, A-R, Statements, Matching, Passage Based) Subjective Questions
- (14 VSAs, 5 SAs, 6 LAs, 5 Picture Based)

8.1 Context of the 1990s

After the assassination of Prime Minister Indira Gandhi, her son Rajiv Gandhi became the Prime Minister in 1984. The Congress witnessed a huge victory in the Lok Sabha elections in 1984. During the end of 1980s, there were **five developments** which had a major impact on Indian politics which are as follows

- Firstly, the Congress was defeated in 1989 elections with only 197 seats. The Congress returned back in the mid-term elections in 1991. But the elections of 1989, marked the end of **'Congress System'**.
- The second development was the rise of **'Mandal Issue'** in national politics. Mandal commission recommended the implementation of the **reservation** for **Other Backward Classes**.
  - It led to violent anti-mandal protest.
  - It played an important role in shaping the politics of India since, 1989.
- The third development was the various economic reforms followed by different governments. Rajiv Gandhi started the new economic policy, called **structural adjustment programme**[1] **or the new economic reform**. It had changed the direction of Indian economy. Many people criticised these reforms by various movements.

1 **Structural Adjustment Programme** Structural adjustment programme is a series of economic reforms that is required for taking loans from the International Monetary Fund or the World Bank.

- Fourth, the old legal and political dispute over **Ram Janmabhoomi Temple in Ayodhya,** started influencing the Indian politics. This dispute gave birth to new political changes. This struggle ended with the construction of **Ram Temple at Ayodhya** after the landmark judgement given by the **Constitutional bench**[2] of the Supreme Court, on 9th November, 2019.
- Fifth development took place after the assassination of Rajiv Gandhi in May 1991. When he went to Tamil Nadu for his election campaign, he was assassinated by a **Sri Lankan Tamil** linked to the **LTTE.** It led to the change in leadership of the Congress Party and party chose **Narsimha Rao** as the new Prime Minister.

8.2 Era of Coalitions

- During the 1989 elections, Congress was defeated because despite of being the largest party, it could not achieve the clear majority in Lok Sabha. The **National Front government** was formed, which was an alliance of **Janata Dal** and other **regional parties**[3]. This alliance was supported by two completely different and opposite political groups, the BJP and the left front.
- The BJP and the left front were supporting the National Front government from outside. It means that they will not join the government as ministerial positions, but will support the government whenever it will need to prove its majority in the Lok Sabha.

Decline of Congress

- **During the 1960s,** the dominance of Congress Party was challenged. However, Indira Gandhi with her leadership skills, manage to re-establish the dominance of Congress in the politics.
- But in 90s, the Congress was challenged but no single party could fill its place. The era of 90s saw the **multi-party system**[4]. From 1989 to 2014, no single party could get clear majority in the Lok Sabha. Therefore, it was an era of **coalition government** at the centre.
- Under the coalition government system, many political parties come together to form the government. During this era, many regional parties played an important role in forming **ruling alliances**.
- But in **2014** and **2019, BJP** got **clear majority** on its own and won the Lok Sabha elections.

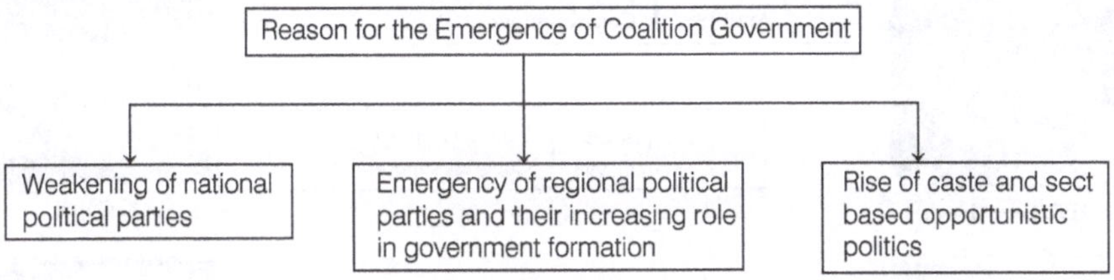

▲ *Reason for the Emergence*

Alliance Politics

- The era of 90s saw the emergence of political parties and movements that represented the interests of **Dalit and backward castes.** In 1996, **The United Front** came to power which was supported by the Congress. The BJP supported the National Front government along with the Left Front in 1989 because they wanted to keep Congress out of power. In 1996 the Congress supported the left so that BJP cannot come in power.

---

2 **Constitutional bench** A Constitutional bench is a bench of the Supreme Court of India that consist of at least five judges and is tasked with deciding cases that involve significant questions of law regarding the interpretation of the Constitution.

3 **Regional Party** A party which dominates in particular region and is based on some ethnic, social or cultural identity.

4 **Multi-party system** It is a political system in which two or more different political parties fight elections and they regularly represent the political system.

- However, these coalition governments did not last for long. This shows that the political equations are very unstable. In 1996, BJP emerged as the largest party but, it could not secure the majority support in the Lok Sabha because many parties were opposed to its policies. In 1998 Atal Bihari Vajpayee formed the coalition government which could last only a year. In **October 1999, Atal Bihari Vajpayee** was re-elected and became the Prime Minister completing its full term.
- Since 1989, a long phase of coalition politics began in India, which saw 11 governments at the centre. These governments have either been coailtion governments or minority governments supported by other parties. The different coalition formed were as follows
  - National Front in 1989
  - United Front in 1996 and 1997
  - BJP-led coalition in 1998
  - NDA in 1999
  - UPA in 2004 and 2009
- However, this trend was changed in 2014 and in 2019 when BJP came with majority.

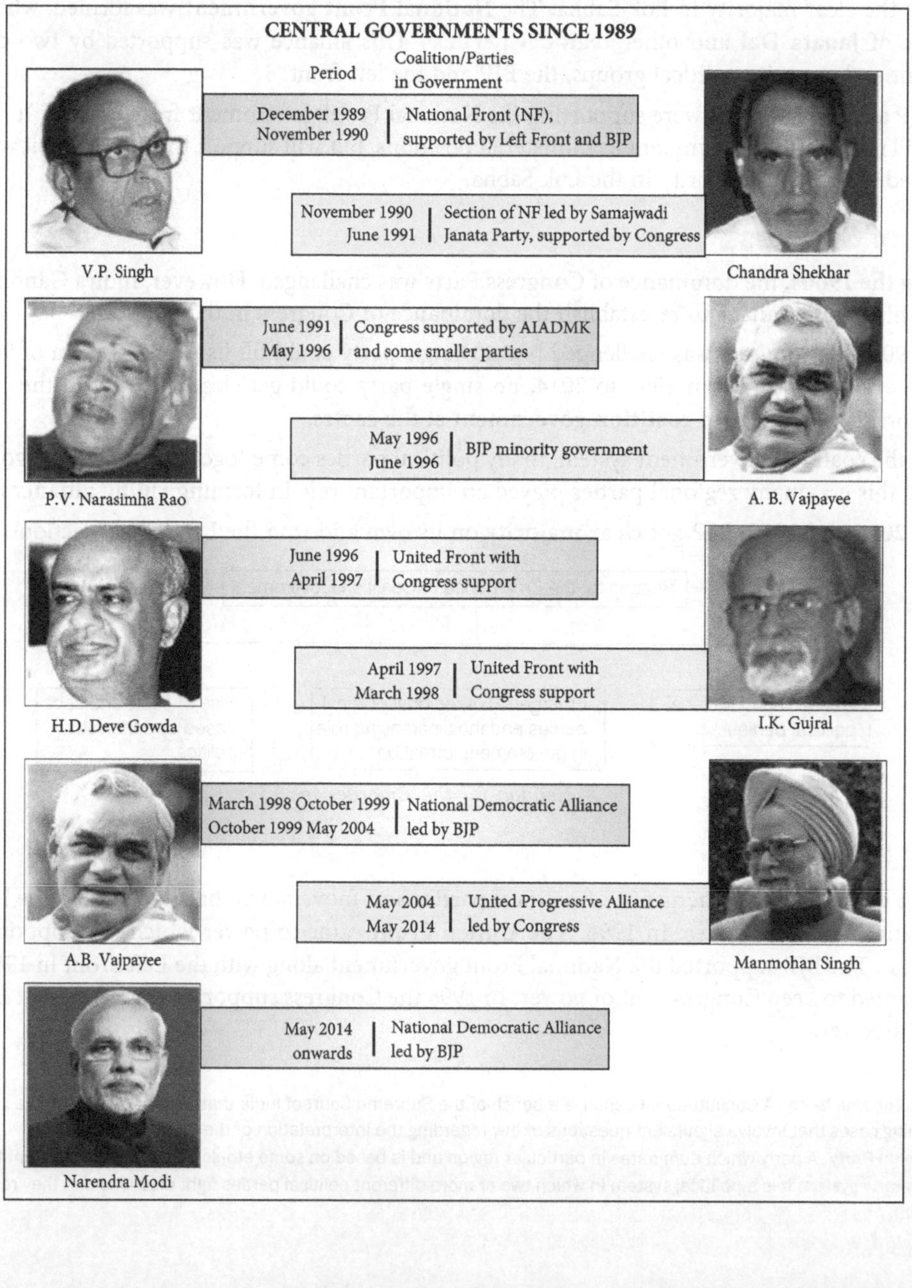

Quick Test 1

1 Who became the Prime Minister after the assassination of Indira Gandhi?
2 What was the Structural Adjustment Programme?
3 What do you understand by the term Consitutional bench?
4 Name the parties, who gave the support to National Front government from outside?
5 Write any one reason for the development of coalition government.
6 During which period, Atal Bihari Vajpayee completed his full term as Prime Minister?

8.3 Political Rise of Other Backward Classes

- During this period, the **Other Backward Classes** emerged as a new political force. These communities are other than SC and ST communities. They suffer from educational and social backwardness, therefore referred as **'backward castes'**.
- The support of backward castes for the Congress had declined. It created a space for non-Congress parties to draw more support from backward classes.
- Many parties such as **Bharatiya Kranti Dal** and the **Samyukta Socialist Party,** had a powerful rural base among the sections of the OBC.

'Mandal' Implemented

- In 1980s, **the Janata Dal** brought together many political groups with strong support among the **OBC.** When the **National Front government** decided to implement the recommendations of the mandal commission, intense debate on reservation started nationally. These debates made people more aware about their identity as OBC. This period witnessed the emergence of many parties that sought better opportunities for OBC community in education and employment.
- They also raised the questions on the share of power enjoyed by the OBCs. These parties claimed that since the OBCs are a big part of Indian society, they should get fair chances in government jobs and policies.

The Mandal Commission

- In Southern states, there was a policy of reservation for the OBC since 1960s. But this policy was not operative in north Indian states. The demand for reservation for OBC's was strongly raised during the period of Janata Party government in 1977-79.
- Karpoori Thakur, who was the Chief Minister of Bihar, introduced a new policy of reservation for OBC in Bihar. Therefore, the Union Government appointed a commission to improve the conditions of backward classes in 1978.
- This commission was known as **Second Backward Commission** because such commission was appointed second time since independence.
- The commission was named after its chairman, Bindeshwari Prasad Mandal.
- The commission gave its recommendations in 1980.
- The purpose of this commission was
  - to investigate the area of educational and social backwardness among the various sections of Indian society.
  - to recommend the ways to end the backwardness.
  - backward classes should be understood to mean 'backward castes'.
- He recommended reservation of **27 per cent** of seats in educational institutions and government jobs for these groups.
- In **August 1990,** when the **National Front government** decided to implement one of the recommendations of Mandal Commission. The entire North India witnessed agitations and violent protest. This decision was challenged in the Supreme Court. The Supreme Court gave a ruling to uphold the decision of the government through the landmark judgement, **'Indira Sawhney case'** in November 1992.

Political Fallouts

- The period of 1980s, also witnessed the rise of political organisations of the Dalits.
- In 1978, the **Backward and Minority Communities Employees Federation (BAMCEF)** was formed. It took a strong position in favour of political power to the **'Bahujan' – the SC, ST, OBC** and **minorities.**
- After sometime, **Dalit Shoshit Samaj Sangharsh Samiti** and later the **Bahujan Samaj Party (BSP)** emerged under the leadership of **Kanshi Ram** out of BAMCEF.
- The Bahujan Samaj Party (BSP), began its political career as a small party, with the support of **Dalit voters** in Punjab, Haryana and Uttar Pradesh. But in 1989 and 1991 elections, it was for the first time in independent India that a political party, with the support of Dalit voters has achieved such a big success.
- Since then, the BSP has emerged major political player in the state and has been in government on more than one occasion. Its strongest support still comes from Dalit voters, but it has expanded its support to many other social groups.

Quick Test 2

1 Name two political parties, which had powerful rural base among the Section of the OBC.
2 Which commission is known as 'Second Backward Commission'?
3 What is 'BAMCEF'?

8.4 Communalism, Secularism, Democracy

- During the period, the rise of politics based on **religious identity** developed and it lead to a debate about secularism and democracy in India.
- After the fall of Janata Party, the supporters of Jana Sangh formed the Bharatiya Janata Party (BJP) in 1980.
- BJP adopted **cultural nationalism** as its ideology and also embraced the **'Gandhian socialism'**.
- But this ideology did not help BJP to get success in the elections of 1984. After 1986, BJP emphasised on nationalism as the core of its ideology and it has also adopted the politics of **Hindutva** to gather the support of people.
- The idea of Hindutva was given by **Vinayka Damodar Savarkar** as the basis of Indian nationlism. Hindutva means to be an Indian or a person must accept India as their **'father land' (pitrubhu)** and **'holy land' (punyabhu).**
- There are two development around 1986, that became central to the politics of BJP.

Shah Bano Case

- The first issue was the **Shah Bano** case in 1985. A 62 year old divorced Muslim woman filed a case for maintenance from her former husband. The Supreme Court ruled in the favour of the Shah Bano but it was seen as an interference of court by orthodox Muslims in their personal laws.
- Due to the demand of Muslim leaders, then the government had to pass the **Muslim Women (Protection of Rights on Divorce) Act, 1986**. This act nullified the Supreme Court's judgement.
- This government act was opposed by many women organisation, Muslim groups and most of the intellectuals. The BJP criticised this action as an appeasement[5] of the minority community.

Nihang Sikhs on Janmabhoomi

There is a very interesting incident which happened on **28th November, 1858**, when **Nihang Sikhs** captured the **Janmabhoomi site** and performed **Pooja** and **Havan** rituals. But later on, they were forcibly asked to leave by colonial administration.

5 Appeasement A policy of keeping the people happy by giving them whatever they demand to avoid any anger.

Ayodhya Issue

- The second important development was the **Ayodhya issue** which find its root in socio-cultural and political history of the country.
- It involved many questions and conflicts regarding the birthplace of Lord Shri Rama.
- There is a five hundred years long history which started from 1528 and consist of many conflicts. This history is documented in district gazetteers[6] of Lucknow, Barabanki and Faizabad.
- It came to conflict because a three dome structure was built at the site of Shri Rama's birthplace in 1528. But the structure has visible display of Hindu symbols and relics in its interior as well as its exterior portion. Ayodhya, got its link to the ancient civilisation. Therefore, this place is a national pride.
- In 1949, the structure was sealed due to the court proceedings. In 1986, the Faizabad (now Ayodhya) District Court allowed the people to worship there and unlock the structure.
- It was believed that the three dome structure was built in Shri Rama's birthplace after demolishing the temple.
  - The Shilaanyas of the temple was done, but construction was prohibited. The hindu community felt their concern because it is the birthplace of Lord Shri Rama and the Muslim community believe that it belongs to them because of the three dome structure.
  - This created a conflict between both the communities. In 1992, the three dome structure was demolished which was criticised by some people as a challenge to the principles of Indian democracy.

From Legal Proceedings to Amicable Acceptance

- India is a multi-religious and multi-democratic society. Therefore, any conflict in the society is natural to happen. This conflict between the Hindu and Muslim community was resolved by the court proceedings in a democratic manner.
- On 9th November, 2019, the Ayodhya issue was resolved by the Constitutional bench of the Supreme Court with **5-0 verdict.** This meant that all the judges were in the favour of the judgement.
- The verdict allotted the disputed site to the **Shri Ram Janmabhoomi Teertha Kshetra Trust** for the construction of Ram temple. It asked the government to allot appropriate site to the Sunni Central Waqf Board for the construction of a Mosque.
- This issue was resolved with the help of the long process of archaeological excavation and historical records. Everybody including both the community celebrated the Supreme Court decision. It was a perfect example of consensus[7] building on sensitive issue which shows the maturity of democratic ethos.

Quick Test 3

1. Who captured the Ram Janmabhoomi site in November 1858?
2. What was the Shah Bano Case?
3. Which three states gazetters have documented the 500 years long history of Shri Ram Janmabhoomi?
4. When did the Supreme Court give its verdict on the Ayodhya issue?

6 Gazetteers A geographical dictionary or index, used as an important reference for information about places and place names.

7 Consensus A general agreement between various parties or people .

8.5 Emergence of a New Consensus

- The period after 1989 is sometimes regarded as the rise of BJP and decline of Congress. Let us compare the performances in elections for both the parties.

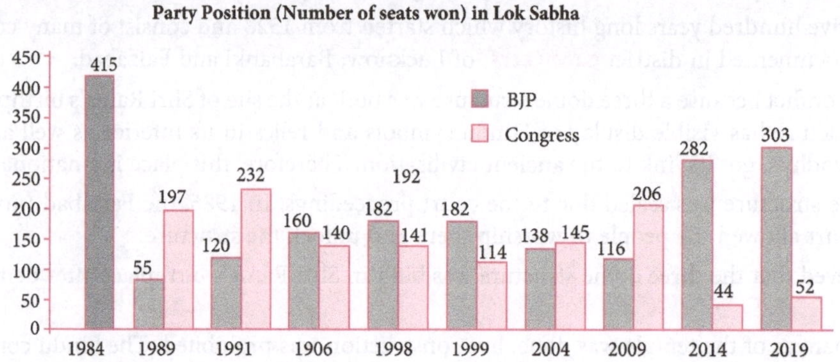

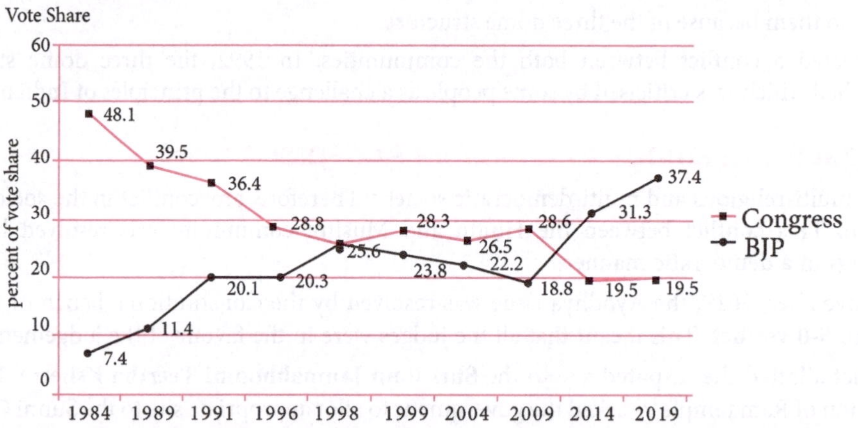

Observations of the Graphs

- There is a very tough competition between the BJP and the Congress during this period. Except for the elections in **1996, 2004** and **2009,** both the parties add up more than 50 per cent votes in their previous vote count.

Lok Sabha Elections (2004-2019)

- During the 2004 elections, the Congress entered into coalition. **The National Democratic Alliance (NDA)**[8] was defeated by the new coalition government. This new coalition government was formed by the Congress known as **United Progressive Alliance (UPA)**[9]. It was supported by the Left Front parties. This is the first time, when Congress Party could increase its number of seats in Lok Sabha since 1991.
- In 2008, the left parties withdrew their support from the UPA government on the issue of **Indo-US nuclear deal.** The 15th **Lok Sabha** elections were held in 2009. **Dr. Manmohan Singh** became the Prime Minister for the second term leading the coalition government of UPA again.

8 **NDA** It is National Democratic Alliance which is used to describe BJP-led coalition.
9 **UPA** It is United Progressive Alliance which is used to describe Congress-led alliance since 2004.

- In 2013, Bharatiya Janata Party declared **Narendra Modi**, who was the Chief Minister of Gujarat at that time as the Prime Ministerial candidate for the upcoming elections. In 2014, **BJP** won **282 seats** on its own and became the single largest party in majority after 30 years. Despite being a single party in majority, BJP choose to form the NDA government with its coalition partners.
- Narendra Modi led NDA government rapidly took decisions in **social sector, foreign policy and economic policy.** In **2019 Lok Sabha elections,** the BJP emerged winner with **303 seats** on its own. Even after the full majority victory of BJP, the recognition of coalition politics is still relevant in Indian politics.

Growing Consensus

Despite of severe competition and conflicts, there are some consensus between various political parties. This consensus consist of four elements.

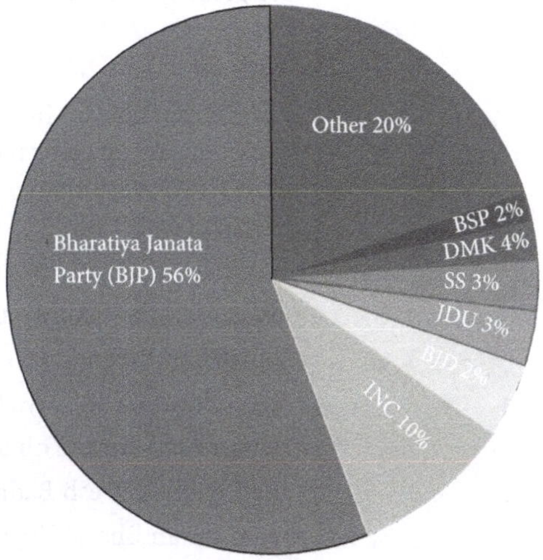

(i) The **first consensus** was on new economic policies. Most parties believe that these new policies would lead the country to prosperity.

(ii) The **second consensus** was the acceptance of the political and social claims of the backward caste.

(iii) The **third consensus** is the role of state level parties in governance of the country. State level parties have played important role in country's politics in last 20 years.

(iv) The **fourth consensus** is to shift from the ideological positions. The coalition politics has allowed the political parties to sideline their ideological differences and share the power. It is visible when many political parties who did not agree with the Hindutva ideology of the BJP, but came to share power and remained in power for the full term.

- All these momentous changes shape of the Indian politics.

B.P. Mandal (1918-1982)

- He was an MP from Bihar for 1967–1970 and 1977–1979.
- He was a socialist leader and became Chief Minister of Bihar for a month and a half in 1968.
- In 1977, he joined the Janata Party.
- He chaired the **Second Backward Classes Commission.**

Kanshi Ram (1934-2006)

- He was the founder of BAMCEF, DS-4 and Bahujan Samaj Party (1984).
- He left his Central Government job for social and political work.
- He promoted the **Bahujan empowerment** and brought **Dalit resurgence** in North Indian states.
- He was an eminent political strategist who believed that political power is the master key to attain social equality.

NDA III and IV

- The Bharatiya Janata Party led by Prime Minister Narendra Modi got an absolute majority in the Lok Sabha elections held in May, 2014 and after nearly 30 years in Indian politics; a strong government with an absolute majority was established at the centre.
- Though called NDA III, the BJP-led coalition of 2014, was largely different its predecessor coalition governments. Where the previous coalitions were led by one of the national parties, the NDA III coalition was not only steered by a national party, i.e., BJP it was also dominated by BJP with an absolute majority of its own in Lok Sabha.

- It was also called a 'surplus majority coalition'. In that sense a major transformation could be seen in the nature of coalition politics which could be seen from one party led coalition to one party dominated coalition.
- The 2019 Lok Sabha elections, the 17th since independence, once again brought back BJP led NDA [NDA IV] to the centre of power by winning more than 350 seats out of 543.
- The BJP on its own won 303 seats in Lok Sabha, the biggest number any single party has won in the lower house since 1984 when Congress swept the elections in the aftermath of Mrs. Indira Gandhi's assassination. Based on the tumultuous success of the BJP in 2019, social scientists have started equating the contemporary party system with the 'BJP system' where an era of one party dominance, like the 'Congress system' has once again started appearing on the democratic politics of India.

Issues of Development and Governance

- A major change in Indian politics after 2014 is the shift from caste and religion based politics to development and governance oriented politics. With its pre-intended goal Sabka Saath, Sabka Vikas, the NDA III Government started several socio-economic welfare schemes to make development and governance accessible to the masses such as
  - Pradhan Mantri Ujjwala Yojana,
  - Swachh Bharat Abhiyan,
  - Jan-Dhan Yojana,
  - Deendayal Upadhyaya Gram Jyoti Yojana,
  - Kisan Fasal Bima Yojna,
  - Beti Padhao, Desh Badhao,
  - Ayushman Bharat Yojana, etc.
- All these schemes intended to take administration to the doorstep of the common man by making the rural households, particularly the women, real beneficiaries of the Central Government schemes.
- The success of these schemes could be seen from the results of 2019 Lok Sabha elections where the voters across states – castes, classes, communities, gender and regions brought back the issues of development and governance to the centre stage. It was under the BJP led NDA government characterising the current change with 'Sabka Saath, Sabka Vikas and Sabka Vishwas'.

Quick Test 4

1. In which year was the Indo-US nuclear deal signed?
2. Who was B.P. Mandal?
3. Who brought the Dalit resurgence in Northern India?
4. What is the central goal behind implementing government schemes?

Mind Map

RECENT DEVELOPMENTS IN INDIAN POLITICS

1 Context of the 1990s

Assassination of Indira Gandhi and Rise of Rajiv Gandhi
- Indira Gandhi was assassinated in 1984.
- Rajiv Gandhi becomes Prime Minister.
- Congress wins huge victory in 1984 Lok Sabha elections.

Five Key Developments
(i) **End of Congress System** Congress defeated in 1989.
(ii) **Mandal Issue** Mandal Commission recommends reservation for Other Backward Classes.
(iii) **Economic Reforms** Rajiv Gandhi introduces new economic policy.
(iv) Ram Janmabhoomi Temple Dispute.
(v) Assassination of Rajiv Gandhi.

2 Era of Coalitions

Decline of Congress
- Congress dominance was challenged in 1960s.
- Indira Gandhi re-establishes dominance.
- Congress get challenged again in 1990s.

Formation of Coalition Governments
- National Front Government was formed in 1989.
- Supported by BJP and Left Front from outside.
- United Front Government was formed in 1996.
- BJP-led coalition formed in 1998.
- NDA formed in 1999.

Characteristics of Coalition Politics
- Multi-party system.
- Regional parties play important role.
- Unstable political equations.
- Coalition governments don't last long.

3 Political Rise of Other Backward Classes

Definition of OBCs
- Communities other than SC and ST.
- Suffer from educational and social backwardness.
- Referred to as 'backward castes'.

Mandal Commission Implementation
- Established in 1978.
- Recommended 27% reservation for OBCs.
- Implemented by National Front Government in 1980s.

Decline of Congress Support
- Support of backward castes for Congress declined.
- Created space for non-Congress parties.
- Parties like Bharatiya Kranti Dal and Samyukta Socialist Party gained public support.

Political Fallouts
- Rise of Dalit political organisations.
- Formation of BAMCEF, Dalit Shoshit Samaj Sangharsh Samiti and Bahujan Samaj Party (BSP).
- BSP emerged as a major political player in India, rising through politics based on social identity.

4 Communalism, Secularism, Democracy

Rise of Politics Based on Religious Identity Player in India
- Led to debate about secularism and democracy in India.
- Formation of Bharatiya Janata Party (BJP) in 1980.

BJP's Ideology
- Cultural nationalism.
- Gandhian Socialism (initially).
- Emphasis on nationalism and Hindutva after 1986.

Key Issues
- **Shah Bano Case (1985)**
  Supreme Court ruled in favour of Shah Bano.
  Government passed Muslim Women (Protection of Rights on Divorce) Act, 1986.
  Act nullified Supreme Court's judgement.
- **Ayodhya Issue** was a conflict over birthplace of Lord Shri Ram, where three-dome structure was built in (1528) and get demolished in 1992. This issue was resolved by Supreme Court in 2019.
- **Resolution of Ayodhya Issue**
  Supreme Court's verdict on November 9, 2019
  Disputed site allotted to Shri Rama Janmabhoomi Teertha Kshetra Trust.
  Government to allot site for construction of mosque to Sunni Central Waqf Board.

5 Emergence of New Consensus

Rise of BJP and Decline of Congress
- Period after 1989 marked by tough competition between BJP and Congress.
- Both parties secured more than 50% votes in most elections, except 1996, 2004, and 2009.

Lok Sabha Elections (2004-2019)
- **2004 Elections** Congress-led UPA formed government with Left Front support.
- **2009 Elections** UPA won again, with Dr. Manmohan Singh as Prime Minister.
- **2014 Elections** BJP won 282 seats, formed NDA government with its coalition partners.
- **2019 Elections** BJP won 303 seats, continued NDA government.

Growing Consensus
- Despite competition, consensus emerged among parties on
- **New Economic Policies** Most parties believed in prosperity through new policies.
- **Acceptance of Backward Castes** Recognition of political and social claim.
- **Role of State-Level Parties** Importance in governance and power-sharing.
- **Shift from Ideological Positions** Coalition politics allowed parties to sideline differences and power-sharing arrangements.

NCERT Folder

Intext Questions

1. Discuss the factors that have enabled democracy to thrive in India. (Pg. no.156)

Ans. India's democracy is often seen as a remarkable achievement, given its vast diversity, historical challenges and the scale of its population. Several factors have played a crucial role in enabling democracy to thrive in India

- **Strong Constitutional Framework** India's Constitution, adopted in 1950, provides a solid foundation for democracy. It enshrines the principles of justice, equality, liberty and fraternity, ensuring Fundamental Rights for all citizens.
- **Political Pluralism** India has a vibrant and diverse political system. With numerous political parties representing a wide array of interests, including regional, caste-based and ideological differences, political pluralism has encouraged participation from all sections of society.
- **Electoral System and Regular Elections** India holds regular, free and fair elections at the national, state and local levels. The regular transfer of power through elections has strengthened India's democratic institutions.
- **Diversity** India's rich cultural, linguistic, religious and regional diversity has not led to division but instead has encouraged the formation of various social movements and organisations that have sought to protect the rights of different communities.
- **Judicial Independence** India's judiciary is independent, which means that courts can act without interference from the executive or legislative branches.
- **Media and Freedom of Expression** India has a robust and free press, with a wide range of media outlets. The media plays an essential role in holding the government accountable and raising awareness.
- **Educational and Social Reforms** India's emphasis on education and social reforms has helped create a more politically aware and active population. Over the years, there has been significant progress in increasing literacy rates and empowering people through education.

These factors have helped democracy thrive in India and allowed it to be a beacon of hope for other democracies around the world.

Exercise

1. Unscramble a bunch of disarranged press clipping file of Unni-Munni...... and arrange the file chronologically.

(i) Mandal Recommendations and Anti-Reservation Stir.
(ii) Formation of Janata Dal.
(iii) The demolition of Babri Masjid.
(iv) Assassination of Indira Gandhi.
(v) The formation of NDA Government.
(vi) Formation of UPA Government.

Ans. (i) Assassination of Indira Gandhi (1984).
(ii) Formation of Janata Dal (1988).
(iii) Mandal Recommendations and Anti-Reservation Stir (1990).
(iv) The demolition of Babri Masjid (1992).
(v) The formation of NDA Government (1997).
(vi) Formation of UPA Government (2004).

2. Match the following.

A. Politics of Consensus	1. Shah Bano case
B. Caste based parties	2. Rise of OBCs
C. Personal Law and Gender Justice	3. Coalition government
D. Growing strength of Regional parties	4. Agreement on Economic policies

Ans. (A) → (4), (B) → (2), (C) → (1), (4) → (3)

3. State the main issues in Indian politics in the period after 1989. What different configurations of political parties these differences lead to?

Ans. Indian politics witnessed five major developments during 1980s which had a long lasting impact on politics of the country. These were
(i) End of Congress system.
(ii) Mandal issues
(iii) New economic reforms
(iv) Ayodhya dispute and rise of Hindutva politics.
(v) Assassination of Rajiv Gandhi.

The elections of 1989 marked the end of Congress dominance in the Indian Party System. This way the era of 'Multi-Party System' began where no single party secured a clear majority in any Lok Sabha election since 1989. This development started an era of coalition government in which regional parties became the king maker in government formation.

Thus, with the elections of 1989, a long phase of coalition politics began in India. Since then, there have seen nine governments at the centre. All of them have either been coalition governments or minority governments supported by other parties which did not join the government. In this new phase, any government could be formed only with the participation or support of many regional parties. For example

- National Front Government in 1989.
- The United Front Government in 1996 and 1997.
- National Democratic Alliance (NDA), BJP led coalition in 1997, 1998, 1999.
- United Progressive Alliance (UPA) in 2004.

The period after 1989 also witnesses the emergence of backward castes politics and Hindutva politics as well.

4. "In the new era of coalition politics, political parties are not aligning or re-aligning on the basis of ideology". What arguments would you put forward to support or oppose this statement? **Competency Based Que**

Ans. The statement is justified because political parties compete for political power ultimately. In the era of coalition politics, for them practical consideration rather than ideological consideration become driving factor for achieving political power.

Some arguments to support this statement are as follows

- Coalition politics has shifted the focus from ideological differences to power sharing arrangements.
- Most parties of NDA did not agree with the Hindutva ideology of BJP, still they came together to form government and remained in power for full term.

5. Trace the emergence of BJP as a significant force in post-emergency politics. **Competency Based Que**

Ans. After emergency, Bhartiya Jana Sangh had merged into the Janata Party. After the fall of the Janata Party and its break-up, the supporters of erstwhile Jana Sangh formed the Bharatiya Janata Party (BJP) in 1980. BJP adopted a broader political platform than that of the Jana Sangh. It embraced 'Gandhian socialism' as its ideology. But it did not get much success in the election of 1980 and 1984. After 1986, the party began to emphasise the Hindu nationalist element in its ideology. Thus, BJP began to pursue the politics of 'Hindutva' and adopted the strategy of mobilising the Hindus. In 1996, BJP Minority Government was formed for a short period. In June 1996, BJP failed to get majority support in the vote of confidence and thus collapsed.

From March 1998 to October 1999, BJP and others formed alliances NDA (National Democratic Alliance) under the leadership of Atal Bihari Vajpayee and his government formed in 1999 completed its full term. Again in 2014 elections, BJP under the leadership of Narendra Modi came to power with landslide victory and also formed the governments almost in more than half of the states across India. The government bought rapid changes in social and economic sectors. Thus, it emerged as the majority party with 303 seats on its own.

6. In spite of the decline of Congress dominance, the Congress Party continues to influence politics in the country. Do you agree? Give reasons. **Competency Based Que**

Ans. The defeat of Congress Party in 1989 election marked the end of Congress dominance in Indian party system. But I agree that the Congress continued to influence Indian politics because

- No other party was able to fill the space left by Congress Party.
- No single party was able to secure a clear majority in any Lok Sabha election since 1989.
- The emergence of powerful parties and movement that represented the Dalits and backward caste played important role in the formation of United Front under the support of Congress.
- Left Front started supporting Congress to curb the rise of Hindutva and communal politics of BJP.

Thus, despite the end of dominance, Congress Party continued to influence the politics of the country.

7. Many people think that a two-party system is required for successful democracy. Drawing from India's experience of last 20 years, write an essay on what advantages the present party system in India has. **Competency Based Que**

Ans. Certainly, a two-party system is relatively more stable and efficient in comparison to multi-party system. But multi-party system has its own advantages that can be seen in the functioning of present party system in India. These are

No Place for Dictatorship Even if a party enjoys full majority, it cannot function as a dictator. The multi-party system provide a democratic government. Hence if the largest party try to act like autocrat then other parties will withdraw their support.

Multiple Choice for Voters Since 1989 elections, voters have choices about whom they want to cast their votes. This is another advantage of multi-party system.

True Reflection of Public Opinion Parliament is the reflection of people. In case of multi-party system, Parliament becomes a true reflector of people because diversity in culture, language are noticeable in Parliament.

Check the Division of the Two Camp The two-party system leads to two camps. But the multi-party system checked the two hostile camps. It is rather a cementing force between groups of divergent or different loyalties.

Representation of Regional or State Parties It provides an opportunity to the different regional parties to play a significant role in decision-making process. They better represent the interests of common people.

8. Read the passage and answer the questions below.

Party politics in India has confronted numerous challenges. Not only has the Congress system destroyed itself, but the fragmentation of the Congress coalition has triggered a new emphasis on self-representation which raises questions about the party system and its capacity to accommodate diverse interests, ... An important test facing the polity is to evolve a party system or political parties that can effectively articulate and aggregate a variety of interests. —Zoya Hasan

(i) Write a short note on what the author calls challenges of the party system in the light of what you have read in this chapter?

(ii) Given an example from this chapter of the lack of accommodation and aggregation mentioned in this passage.

(iii) Why is it necessary for parties to accommodate and aggregate variety of interests?

Ans. (i) Author calls the fragmentation of political parties on the basis of caste, creed, religion, etc. a challenge to party system in India. This has caused the trend of self-representation of one's own interest through formation of new party. This poses challenge to develop a party system or political parties that can effectively accommodate and articulate different interests of society.

(ii) Lack of accommodation and aggregation of the interests and concerns of Dalits led to the formation of BAMCEF (Backward and Minority Classes Employees Federation) under the leadership of Kanshi Ram to protect interests of Dalits.

(iii) It is necessary for parties to accommodate and aggregate the variety of interests to maintain the culture of India so that there should no space for separatist movements in India.

Exam Pattern Questions

Objective Type Questions

Multiple Choice Questions (MCQs)

1. Who withdrew the support from H.D. Deve Gowda United Front government? Diksha App

(a) Congress
(b) Telugu Desam Party
(c) DMK
(d) AIADMK

2. Which coalition government decided to implement the recommendation of Mandal Commission? Diksha App

(a) United Front Government
(b) National Front Government
(c) United Progressive Alliance
(d) National Democratic Alliance

3. Which of the following statement(s) is/are correct about new economic reforms? Competency Based Que

(a) Rajiv Gandhi initiated structural adjustment programme as the new economic reforms.
(b) The changes first became visible in 1991.
(c) The new economic reforms radically changed the direction of Indian economy after independence.
(d) All of the above

4. Who among the following was the first PM to initiate economic reforms in India. CBSE 2023

(a) H.D. Deve Gowda (b) Indira Gandhi
(c) Morarji Desai (d) Rajiv Gandhi

5. Which terrorist organisation was behind the assassination of Rajiv Gandhi? Diksha App

(a) Lashkar-e-Taiba (b) ISI
(c) LTTE (d) Hizbul Mujahideen

6. Name the alliance that formed the government in march, 1998. CBSE 2025

(a) United Front (b) NDA
(c) UPA (d) National Front

7. BJP led alliance of 2010 ie. known as CBSE 2025

(a) United Progressive Alliance
(b) United Front
(c) National Democratic Alliance
(d) Democratic Coalition

8. What were the consequences of implementing Mandal Commission?

(a) There were agitations and violent protests in many cities of North India.

(b) The decision was challenged in the Supreme Court.
(c) In December 1992, the Supreme Court gave a ruling upholding the decision of the government.
(d) Both (a) and (b)

9. **Given below are two statements**

Statement I The Mandal Commission recommendations led to widespread protests in India.

Statement II The recommendations reserved 27 per cent of government jobs for Other Backward Classes (OBCs).

In the light of the above statements, choose the correct answer from the options given below

(a) Both Statement I and Statement II are true.
(b) Both Statement I and Statement II are false.
(c) Statement I is true, but Statement II is false.
(d) Statement I is false, but Statement II is true.

10. **Name is the founder of Bahujan Samaj Party?** **CBSE 2025**

(a) Kanshi Ram (b) Mayawati
(c) Mulayam Singh (d) Dr. B.R. Ambedkar

11. **The recommendations of Mandal Commission were implemented in which one of the following year?** **CBSE 2025**

(a) 1989 (b) 1990
(c) 1991 (d) 1992

12. **Who led the Central Government after the 1999 Lok Sabha Elections?** **CBSE 2025**

(a) P.V. Narasimha Rao (b) Atal Bihari Vajpayee
(c) Manmohan Singh (d) H.D. Deve Gauda

13. **New Economic Policy was adopted in India under the Prime Ministership of ………………..** **CBSE 2025**

(a) V.P. Singh (b) Manmohan Singh
(c) Narasimha Rao (d) H.D. Deve Gawda

14. **Which party gets the largest number of seats in the 16th Lok Sabha elections?** **Diksha App**

(a) BJP (b) Indian National Congress
(c) AIADMK (d) AITC

15. **Which of the following developments took place after 1980s in the country that had longlasting impact on politics?**

(a) End of Congress system
(b) Mandal Commission, New Economic reforms
(c) Ayodhya dispute, assassination of Rajiv Gandhi
(d) All of the above

16. **Identify the incorrect pair.**

(a) Mandal Issue – United Front Government
(b) Economic Reforms – Rajiv Gandhi Government
(c) Hindutva- Bharatiya Janata Party
(d) Bahujan – Kanshi Ram

17. **Arrange the following in chronological order.**

I. Formation of NDA Government
II. Appointment of Mandal Commission by Central Government
III. Janata Dal Formed
IV. New Economic Reforms

Codes

(a) II, III, IV and I (b) I, II, III and IV
(c) IV, II, III and I (d) II, III, I and IV

18. **Consider the following statement(s) about 2004, Lok Sabha elections and choose the correct option(s).** **Competency Based Que**

(a) In 2004 elections, NDA was defeated
(b) In 2004 election, there was big difference between the votes polled by the Congress and its allies and BJP and its allies.
(c) A new coalition government led by the Congress United Progressive Alliance came to power.
(d) Both (a) and (c)

19. **Arrange the following in chronological order according to their period of Prime Ministership** **Competency Based Que; CBSE 2024**

I. V.P. Singh **II. H.D. Deve Gowda**
III. Narsimha Rao **IV. Chandra Shekhar**

Codes

(a) I, II, III and IV (b) I, IV, III and II
(c) II, IV, III and I (d) IV, II, III and I

20. **Match list I with List II select the correct answer using the codes given below.** **Competency Based Que**

List-I	List-II
A. Babri demolition	1. 1998
B. NDA II	2. 1989
C. End of the Congress System	3. 1980
D. Jana Sangh formed Bharatiya Janata Party	4. 1992

Codes

	A	B	C	D
(a)	4	1	2	3
(b)	2	1	3	4
(c)	1	2	4	3
(d)	3	4	2	1

21. **Match the list I with List II and choose the correct option.** **Competency Based Que; CBSE 2024**

List-I	List-II
A. Clear majority in the 17th Lok Sabha	1. National Front Government
B. Implementation of the recommendations of the Mandal Commission	2. United Front Government
C. Prime Minister H.D. Deve Gowda	3. United Progressive Alliance Government
D. Prime Minister Manmohan Singh	4. National Democratic Alliance

Codes

	A	B	C	D		A	B	C	D
(a)	4	1	2	3	(b)	1	2	3	4
(c)	4	3	2	1	(d)	1	4	2	3

Assertion-Reason Questions

Directions (Q. Nos. 22-23) In the questions given below, there are two statements marked as Assertion (A) and Reason (R). Read the statements and choose the correct option. **Competency Based Que**

Codes

(a) Both A and R are true and R is the correct explanation of A.

(b) Both A and R are true, but R is not the correct explanation of A.

(c) A is true, but R is false.

(d) A is false, but R is true.

22. Assertion (A) The BJP continued to consolidate its position in the elections of 1991 and 1996.

Reason (R) It emerged as the largest party in the 1996 election and was invited to form the government.

23. Assertion (A) The era of multi-party system began after the election of 1989.

Reason (R) Election in 1989 led to the defeat of the Congress Party and ended its dominance over the Indian party system.

Passage Based Questions

24. Read the following passage carefully and answer the questions that follow.

Way back in the late sixties, the dominance of the Congress Party was challenged, but the Congress under the leadership of Indira Gandhi, managed to re-establish its predominant position in politics. The nineties and yet another challenge to the predominant position of the Congress. It did not, however, mean the emergence of any other single party to fill in its place.

Thus, began an era of multi-party system. To be sure, a large number of political parties always contested elections in our country. Our Parliament always had representatives from several political parties. What happened after 1989 was the emergence of several parties in such a way that one or two parties did not get most of the votes or seats. This also meant that no single party secured a clear majority of seats in any Lok Sabha election held since 1989. This development initiated an era of coalition governments at the centre, in which regional parties played a crucial role in forming ruling alliances.

(i) Multi-party system refers to ....

(a) a system where only one party compete for power.

(b) a system where two parties compete for power.

(c) a system where many parties compete for power.

(d) None of the above

(ii) In the era of coalitions which type of parties played a crucial role in forming ruling alliances?

(a) National Parties

(b) Unrecognised Parties

(c) Regional Parties

(d) None of the above

(iii) What is the reason behind the emergence of several parties?

25. Read the following passage carefully and answer the questions that follow.

The 1980s also saw the rise of political organisation of the Dalits. In 1978 the Backward and Minority Communities Employees Federation (BAMCEF) was formed. This organisation was not an ordinary trade union of government employees. It took a strong position in favour of political power to the 'Bahujan' – the SC, ST, OBC and minorities. It was out of this that the subsequent Dalit Shoshit Samaj Sangharsh Samiti and later the Bahujan Samaj Party (BSP) emerged. **CBSE 2024**

(i) Choose the correct full form of BAMCEF.

(a) Bahujan and Minority Communities Employees Federation

(b) Bahujan and Minority Comunities Employees Foundation

(c) Backward and Minority Communities Employees Federation

(d) None of the above

(ii) In which state did the Bahujan Samaj Party form its first government?

(a) 1981 (b) 1984 (c) 1989 (d) 1991

(iii) Explain the concept of BAMCEF.

26. Read the following passage carefully and answer the questions that follow

The Mandal Commission was set up to investigate the extent of educational and social backwardness among various sections of Indian society and recommend ways of identifying these 'backward classes'. It was also expected to give its recommendations on the ways in which this backwardness could be ended. The Commission gave its recommendations in 1980. By then the Janata Party government had fallen. The Commission advised that 'backward classes' should be understood to mean 'backward castes', since many castes, other than the Scheduled Castes, were also treated as low in the caste hierarchy. The commission did a survey and found that these backward castes had a very low presence in both educational institutions and in employment in public services. It therefore recommended reserving 27 per cent of seats in educational institutions and government jobs for these groups. The Mandal Commission also made many other recommendations, like, land reform, to improve the conditions of the OBCs.

(i) **What was the main objective of the Mandal Commission?**
(a) To provide financial aid to Scheduled Castes and Tribes
(b) To investigate the educational and social backwardness of various sections of society
(c) To promote industrial growth in backward areas
(d) To eliminate poverty through economic reforms

(ii) **When did the Mandal Commission submit its recommendations?**
(a) 1977 (b) 1980
(c) 1990 (d) 1985

(iii) **What percentage of seats in educational institutions and government jobs did the Mandal Commission recommend for Other Backward Classes (OBCs)?**
(a) 15 per cent (b) 27 per cent
(c) 10 per cent (d) 30 per cent

(iv) **What did the Mandal Commission mean by 'backward classes'?**
(a) Scheduled Tribes
(b) Economically weaker sections
(c) Backward castes other than Scheduled Castes and Tribes
(d) Women and children

Answers

1. (a) Congress
2. (b) National Front Government
3. (d) All of the above
4. (d) Rajiv Gandhi
5. (c) LTTE
6. (b) NDA
7. (c) National Democratic Alliance
8. (d) Both (a) and (b)
9. (a) Both Statement I and Statement II are true.
10. (a) Kanshi Ram
11. (b) 1990
12. (b) Atal Bihari Vajpayee
13. (c) Narasimha Rao
14. (a) BJP
15. (d) All of the above
16. (a) Mandal Issue – United Front Government
17. (d) II, III, I and IV
18. (d) both (a) and (c)
19. (b) I, IV, III and II
20. (a) 4 1 2 3
21. (a) 4 1 2 3
22. (a) Both A and R are true and R is the correct explanation of A.
23. (a) Both A and R are true and R is not the correct explanation of A.
24. (i) (c) a system where many parties compete for power.
(ii) (c) Regional Parties
(iii) As no single party secured a clear majority of seats in the Lok Sabha elections, so, several parties and coalition era imaged.
25. (i) (c) Backward and Minority Communities Employees Federation
(ii) (b) 1984
(iii) BAMCEF was an ordinary trade union of government employees. In fact, it took a strong position in favour of political power to the Bahujan. The term Bahujan include the SCs, STs, OBCs and minorities.
26. (i) (b) To investigate the educational and social backwardness of various sections of society
(ii) (b) 1980
(iii) (b) 27 per cent
(iv) (c) Backward castes other than Scheduled Castes and Tribes

Subjective Questions

Very Short Answer Type Questions

1. What was the Mandal issue?

Ans. Mandal issue in national politics followed the decision by the new National Front government in 1990 to implement the recommendation of the Mandal Commission, that jobs in Central Government should be reserved for OBCs. This led to violence in many parts of the country especially in North India.

This dispute between the supporters and opponents of OBC reservations was known as the mandal issue and played an important role in shaping politics since 1989.

2. How did the assassination of Rajiv Gandhi led to a change in the Congress politics? **Diksha App**

Ans. After the assassination of Rajiv Gandhi, the leadership in the Congress Party changed and the dominance of the Congress came to an end.

Although the Congress remained in power, but it lost the centrality of the power. The elections of 1989 marked an era of alliance and coalition politics.

3. Highlight any two effects of the elections of 1989 on the politics of India.

Ans. Two long lasting impact of 1989 elections were

(i) It marked the end of the dominance of the Congress Party in the party system of India.

(ii) It marked the begining of era of coalition government at the centre in which regional parties played crucial role in formation of government.

4. Why are coalition governments formed? Explain. **CBSE Term II 2022**

Ans. Coalition governments usually are a temporary alliance, being formed when no single political party gains a clear majority and competing parties instead negotiate to work together. It acts as a channel to meet the expectations and redress the grievances of different groups.

5. What do you mean by alliance politics?

Ans. During the period of 90s, many powerful political parties emerged which played an important role in the formation of government at centre.

During this period any government could be formed only with the participation or support of several regional parties. This phase of politics is called alliance politics.

6. Explain any two reasons which led to a multi-party alliance system in Indian politics since 1989. **CBSE SQP 2024**

Ans. (i) The defeat of Congress Party in 1989 elections was described as the end of Congress system by the political scientist. It marked the era of alliance and coalition politics. No single party could get the clear majority in many of the elections for Lok Sabha seats. Thus, many of the political parties had to merge together to form the government at the national level.

(ii) The era of 1980s witnessed the emergence of many political parties and groups which represented the interests of other backward classes or castes. This has impacted the nature of Indian politics.

7. Why did the first coalition governments at the centre in India not prove to be stable? Analyse the major reason.

Ans. The first coalition governments at the centre (1989-1990), was failed due to internal disagreement, especially over the implementation of the Mandal Commission Report. So, the key allies withdrew the support.

8. What does a coalition governments mean? Mention any one example of such a government.

Or **What is meant by 'coalition'? During which period did this type of government gain popularity for the first time at the centre in India.**

Ans. When two or more parties join hands together to form a government, it is known as coalition governments. For example, UPA, NDA, etc.

In 1977, coalition governments gained popularity for the first time because of the harsh emergency provisions the Congress.

9. Identify and name any two Prime Ministers of india who remained in power for less than years. **CBSE 2023**

Ans. The two Prime Ministers of India, who remained in power for less than a year.

(i) **Vishwanath Pratap Singh (Dec 1989 to Nov 1990)** his tenure was only for 11 months.

The decision of V.P. Singh's government over reservation, led to widepread protests.

(ii) **Chandra Shekhar (Nov 1990 to June 1991)** He served as Prime Minister, only for 7 months. He resigned after failing to maintain a majority in the Lok Sabha.

10. Name any four Prime Ministers of India who led the Coalition Governments at the Centre. **CBSE 2024 C**

Ans. Four Prime Ministers of India who led coalition governments at the centre are

(i) Morarji Desai

(ii) V.P. Singh

(iii) Atal Bihari Vajpayee

(iv) Manmohan Singh

11. **Who was the Chairperson of Mandal Commission? State any one recommendation made by him/her.**

Or **Highlight any two recommendations of the Mandal Commission.**

Ans. Bindeshwari Prasad Mandal was the Chairperson of Mandal Commission set-up in 1978 to investigate the extent of educational and social backwardness among various sections of society and recommended ways to identify these classes.

The two recommendations of the Mandal Commission are as follows

(i) 27 per cent of the posts in public services should be reserved for other backward classes.

(ii) Welfare programmes specially meant for OBCs should be financed by the Government of India.

12. **Give any two arguments in favour of reservation for the SCs, STs and OBCs in higher education institutions in India.**

Ans. The two arguments in favour of reservation for SCs, STs and OBCs in higher education institutions in India are as follows

(i) The backward classes had very low representation in educational institutions.

(ii) The employment in public offices also had very low representation of the backward classes.

13. **Why is National Democratic Alliance (NDA) III called a 'surplus majority coalition'? Explain.** CBSE Term II 2022

Or **Explain any two changes that came in Indian politics after 2014 as compared to the period 1989 to 2014.**
Competency Based Que; CBSE 2024

Ans. The NDA III is called 'surplus majority coalition' because in the coalition of NDA, BJP was with as absolute majority of its own in Lok Sabha.

In that sense a major transformation could be seen in the nature of coalition politics which could be seen from one party led coalition to one party dominated coalition.

14. **State any two programmes launched by the NDA government after 2014 for women's help and progress.**
CBSE 2023

Ans. NDA government under Narendra Modi's Prime Ministership took rapid decisions for women's help and progress. This includes several programmes like Beti Bachao, Beti Padhao Yojana and Ujjwala scheme.

Short Answer Type Questions

1. **Describe any two advantages and two disadvantages of coalition government in India.**

Ans. When two or more parties join hands together to form a government is known as coalition government. For example, UPA, NDA, etc. In 1977, the first coalition government was formed.

Two advantages of coalition government are as follows

(i) Dominance of one party is minimised.

(ii) More than one ideologies come together and gives strength to democracy.

Two disadvantages of coalition government are as follows

(i) It gives unstable government.

(ii) It slows the process of policy-making.

2. **Analyse the impact of political rise of Other Backward Classes in India.** Competency Based Que; CBSE 2020

Ans. The impact of political rise of Other Backward Classes (OBCs) in India is

- When the support for the Congress among many sections of the backward castes had declined, this created a space for non-Congress parties to get the support of OBCs.
- Many of the constituents of the Janata Party like the Bharatiya Kranti Dal and Samyukta Socialist Party had a powerful rural base among some sections of the OBC.
- In the 1980's, the decisions of the National Front government to implement the recommendations of the Mandal Commission further helped in shaping the politics of the OBC.
- 1980's saw the emergence of many parties like Bahujan Samaj Party (BSP) that sought better opportunities for OBCs in education, employment, adequate representation in administration.

3. **Who was the founder of Bahujan Samaj Party? Describe his political career briefly.** Diksha App

Ans.
- Kanshi Ram was the founder of Bahujan Samaj Party.
- He was the proponent of Bahujan empowerment, and he left his government job for social and political work. He was a brilliant political strategist. He believed that the social equality can be achieved through the master key of political power. He was responsible for the Dalit resurgence in the North Indian states.
- He founded the BAMCEF and DS-4.

4. **What was the change in the electoral performance of the Congress Party and BJP from 1984-2004?**

Ans. The changes in the electoral performance of the Congress Party and BJP from 1984-2004 were as follows

- The dominance of Congress declined while rise of BJP is witnessed in politics of India. From March 1998 to October 1999, BJP and other parties formed alliances NDA (National Democratic Alliance) under the leadership of Atal Bihari Vajpayee and completed full term of NDA government.

- In the elections of May 2004, Congress and its allies formed UPA (United Progressive Alliance) and came to power and Dr. Manmohan Singh became Prime Minister.

5. In the 2014 election ,why were people in favour of a stable government at the centre? Explain any two reason. CBSE 2024

Ans. In the 2014 elections, people favoured a stable government due to economic slowdown, policy paralysis, and corruption scandals under the UPA government. There was growing frustration over weak decision-making and lack of governance. Voters sought strong leadership to boost economic growth, create jobs, and ensure national security.

BJP promised decisive governance, development, and effective policy implementation. A stable, majority government was seen as essential to end coalition instability and drive reforms. As a result, the BJP secured a historic single-party majority, reflecting the public's desire for a strong and efficient Central Government.

Long Answer Type Questions

1. Describe any three recommendations of the Mandal Commission to solve the problems of the Other Backward Classes. CBSE 2025

Ans. The Mandal Commission, officially known as the Second Backward Classes Commission was established in 1979, under the chairmanship of B.P. Mandal . It was formed to identify socially and educationally Backward Classes (OBCs) and recommend measures for their upliftment. Three major recommendations of the commission were

- **Reservation in Government Jobs and Educational Institutions** The commission recommended 27 per cent reservation for Other Backward Classes (OBCs) in government services and educational institutions to improve their representation in public employment and higher education. This was aimed at reducing social and economic inequality.
- **Promotion of OBC Welfare through Development Programmes** It suggested the introduction of special programmes to enhance the economic and educational conditions of OBCs. This included access to scholarships, vocational training and financial assistance to promote self-employment and skill development.
- **Caste-based Census and Social Justice Policies** The commission emphasised the need for regular surveys and caste-based data collection to assess the socio-economic status of OBCs. It also recommended setting up institutions to monitor the implementation of reservation policies and welfare programmes.

2. Examine the impact of any three political developments that witnessed between the period, 1989 to 1999. Competency Based Que; CBSE SQP 2024

Or **Describe any three major developments that took place in Indian politics in the last decade of the 20th century.** CBSE 2024, 25

Or **Describe any four major developments in Indian politics since 1989.** CBSE 2024

Or **Analyse any three developments towards the end of 1980s that were to make along lasting impact on the politics of India.**

Or **Describe any four major political developments that took place in India from 1989 to 1999.** CBSE 2024 C

Ans. The end of the decade of 1980s witnessed many developments that had a long lasting impact on Indian politics. These are as follows

(i) The first and most crucial development was the defeat of the Congress Party in the elections of 1989. It was seen as the end of Congress system by some political scientists.

The Congress remained as an important party after that, but the centrality of the power which it used to enjoy earlier now came to an end.

(ii) The second development was the rise of the mandal issue in the national politics. Mandal Commission was appointed to look for the improvement in education and employment for the socially and educationally backward classes.

The Mandal Commission recommended for the reservation for backward classes in education as well as employment.

This became a dispute among the supporters and opponents of the OBC reservation, this issue had influenced the Indian politics since 1989.

(iii) The third development was the economic policy followed by various governments. Many of the governments took a radical shift in economic policies which was known as structural adjustment programmes. These policies have been widely criticised through various movements and organisations. However, the government that came into power, have continued to follow these policies.

(iv) The fourth was the century old legal and political dispute over the Ram Janmabhoomi Temple in Ayodhya. This issue became the central issue in Indian politics and changed the direction of secularism and democracy. It was finally ended with the construction of the Ram Temple at Ayodhya after the landmark judgement by the Constitutional bench of the Supreme Court in November 2019.

3. **From 1989 to 2004, there have been nine coalition governments in India. Analyse the rise and fall of any two such coalition governments.**

Or **"The election of 1989 marked the end of the Congress system and rise of the coalition". Support the student.**
Competency Based Que; CBSE SQP 2025

Ans. With the elections of 1989, a long phase of coalition politics began in India. Since then, there have been nine governments at the centre. All of them have either been coalition governments or minority governments supported by other parties which did not join the government.

In this new phase, any government could be formed only with the participation of support of many regional parties. For example

- Nation Front Government in 1989.
- The United Front Government in 1996 and 1997.
- National Democratic Alliance (NDA), BJP led coalition in 1997, 1998, 1999.
- United Progressive Alliance (UPA) in 2004.

United Front Government Some parties had Congress support and formed alliance in 1996 called United Front. In 1989, BJP and Left supported National Front. In 1989, BJP and Left wanted to keep the Congress out of power, hence, both supported National Front and later in 1996, Congress and Left both wanted to keep out BJP from the power. Therefore, both supported United Front in 1996.

There was a growing consensus among the political parties for power sharing arrangements. These parties sidelined their ideological positions and shifted towards alliance politics.

4. **'Coalition government is a bane or boon for democracy in India'. Explain any three arguments in support of your answer.** **Competency Based Que**

Or **How did the coalition governments prove to be a boon for democracy in India? Explain.** **CBSE 2024**

Or **Alliance politics has influenced Indian political system in recent year. Elaborate and mention at least six points to support four argument.** **Diksha App**

Or **Assess any three benefits of the coalition governments in India since 1989.**

Or **Explain any three benefits of the coalition government formed in India since 1989.** **CBSE 2024**

Ans. Coalition government is a boon because

(i) **Participation of Regional Parties at National Level** State level parties played a crucial role in the country politics for last 20 years. Therefore, the differences between state level parties and central parties is decreasing day-by-day.

(ii) **Spirit of Adaptation** Coalition politics has shifted the focus of political parties from ideological distinctions to power sharing accommodation. We can see in the government of NDA that most of the parties did not agree with the ideology of Hindutva of BJP. However, they allied with BJP to form a government for a full term.

(iii) **Inclined Towards one Consensus** Various radical parties opposed the new economic policies, but some parties came to support new economic policies because they believed that these policies would lead the country towards prosperity and raise its status all over the world.

Coalition government is a bane for democracy in India because of three reasons

(i) **Unstable Government** The coalition governments has its own interest and they fight for their own self interest. This leads to the breakup not only of various fronts but of governments as well.

(ii) **Political Opportunism** Government which is formed on the basis of coalition becomes selfish as opportunist power and unscrupulous politicians emphasise on their self interest only.

(iii) **Polarisation** The coalition governments are formed on the basis of polarisation of political forces. These are widely heterogeneous elements like CPI and BJP.

5. **Describe any three points of consensus that emerged among most political parties in India in spite of severe competition and conflicts.** **Competency Based Que**

Or **Highlight any three issues on which a broad agreement has emerged among most of the political parties in India.**

Or **Highlight any three issues of consensus to show that in midst of severe competitions and conflicts, a consensus has appeared among most political parties.** **CBSE 2018**

Or **Highlight any three areas where consensus has emerged among most of the political parties in Indian after 1989.**
CBSE Term II 2022

Or **Explain any three important issues on which a consensus has emerged among most political parties of India.** **CBSE 2024**

Or **In the midst of the severe competition and many conflicts after 1989, a consensus appeared to have emerged among most parties. Explain any three points of consensus.** **CBSE 2024**

Or **Describe any three issues on which a general consensus has emerged among most of the political parties of India.** **CBSE 2024**

Or **Describe any four issues on which consensus has emerged among most political parties of India.** **CBSE 2024 C**

Ans. Even in the midst of the severe competition and many conflicts, there are many concerns that have been emerged among the political parties. These consensus are as follows

(i) The first agreement is on the new economic policies. Despite many groups are opposed to these new economic reforms, many political parties believe that these reforms would lead the country to prosperity and a status of a strong economic power all over the world.

(ii) The second agreement among political parties is the acceptance of the political and social claims of the backward castes. Almost all the political parties believe that backward classes should be given reservations in education as well as employment.

(iii) The third agreement among the political parties is about the power sharing and the role of political alliances. Most of the political parties have shifted from the focus of ideological differences to the power-sharing arrangements.

Therefore, most parties of the NDA despite of not agreeing with the Hindu ideology of the BJP were ready to form the government as NDA and remain in power for the full term.

6. Highlight any three factors that you think are responsible for the victory of National Democratic Alliance (NDA) in 2019 election continuously for the second time. **CBSE Term II 2022**

Ans. The success of the Bharatiya Janata Party in the 2019 Lok Sabha elections was enabled by the popularity of Narendra Modi as the Prime Ministerial candidate, people's perception of the BJP being the saviour of the nation and a sense of satisfaction with the performance of its government at the centre.

Three reasons for the victory are

(i) The NDA government had taken rapid decision on social sector, foreign policy and economic reforms.

(ii) Schemes related to social issues were also one of the reasons for the second term victory of the NDA government. Schemes like building toilets, providing cooking gas connections, housing, rural electrification and banking access to power had reached to large recipients, which help the government in gaining the trust of people.

(iii) The NDA government also focused on the expansion of the formula of alliance all throughout the country, which helped them in reaching a mass level.

Picture Based Questions

1. Study the given cartoon and answer the questions that follow. **Delhi 2016, CBSE 2024**

(i) Identify any two national leaders from the above cartoon.

(a) Manmohan Singh and A.B. Vajpayee
(b) Rajiv Gandhi and A.B. Vajpayee
(c) V.P. Singh and L.K. Advani
(d) All of the above

Ans. (c) V.P. Singh and L.K. Advani

(ii) Who is holding the placard of Rath Yatra ?

(a) V.P. Singh (b) Chandra Shekhar
(c) P.V. Narasimha Rao (d) L.K. Advani

Ans. (d) L.K. Advani

(iii) What is the central theme of the cartoon ?

(a) Era of one-party dominance (b) Era of coalition politics
(c) Era of violence (d) All of these

Ans. (b) Era of coalition politics

(iv) What does the Indian Polity, roller coaster in the cartoon symbolise?

(a) The stability in Indian politics
(b) The economic growth in India
(c) The unpredictable nature of Indian politics
(d) The unity among Indian states

Ans. (c) The unpredictable nature of Indian politics

2. Observe the cartoon given below and answer the following questions.

(i) Who was head of the government formed by the National Front in 1989?

(a) V.P. Singh (b) I.K. Gujral
(c) Rajiv Gandhi (d) None of these

Ans. (a) V.P. Singh

(ii) Why was the government formed by him called a puppet government?

(a) Strings (control) of the government was in the other leaders hand.
(b) Leaders used to dance.
(c) Leader were dependent upon V.P. Singh.
(d) V.P. Singh is very rude.

Ans. (a) Strings (control) of the government was in the other leaders hand.

(iii) Identify the puppeteers pulling the strings.

(a) L.K. Advani and A.B. Vajpayee
(b) L.K. Advani and V.P. Singh
(c) Jyoti Basu and L.K. Advani
(d) V.P. Singh and Jyoti Basu

Ans. (c) Jyoti Basu and L.K. Advani

(iv) Which political ideology is reflected by Jyoti Basu ?

(a) Left (b) Right (c) Hindutva (d) None of these

Ans. (a) Left

3. Study the given cartoon and answer the questions that follow.

(i) Which party is being referred to show the dominance in 1971.

(a) Congress Party (b) Bharatiya Jana Sangh
(c) Communist Party of India (d) Bharatiya Kranti Dal

Ans. (a) Congress Party

(ii) Who is the lady shown in the first image given above?

(a) Amrit Kaur (b) Indira Gandhi
(c) Soniya Gandhi (d) Priyanka Gandhi

Ans. (b) Indira Gandhi

(iii) What does the above image depicts?

(a) Era of one-party dominance to the formation of a coalition government
(b) Condition of strong and weak leaders
(c) Strategy to topple the government
(d) None of the above

Ans. (a) Era of one-party dominance to the formation of a coalition government

(iv) Who is trying to topple the coalition government in 1999 image.

(a) Indira Gandhi (b) Soniya Gandhi
(c) Mayawati (d) None of these

Ans. (b) Soniya Gandhi

4. Observe the cartoon given below and answer the following questions. **All India 2010**

(i) Why is the girl shown in the cartoon not worried about whether it is a single-party or coalition government?

Ans. The girl is not worried about whether it is a single-party or coalition government because her main concern is whether the government is working effectively. For her, the focus is on actions and progress that benefit the country, rather than the type of government in power.

(ii) Does a coalition government involve more compromises, and can it still deliver bold and imaginative policies?

Ans. Yes, a coalition government often involves compromises because different political parties with varying ideologies come together to form a government. Despite this, it is possible for a coalition government to deliver bold and imaginative policies if the partners work collaboratively, prioritise national interests, and find common ground on critical issues.

(iii) Why do we need strong coalitions in a democratic system?

Ans. Strong coalitions are essential for

- Ensuring stability in the political system.
- Successfully implementing policies and governance initiatives.
- Maintaining and strengthening the democratic setup by fostering co-operation among diverse political parties.

5. Observe the cartoon given below and answer the following questions.

(i) What does the given picture represent, and what was the reason behind it?

Ans. The picture represents the agitation in Delhi against the Mandal Commission.

The agitation arose as a response to the recommendations of the Mandal Commission, which proposed reservations for backward castes in government jobs and educational institutions. Many people, especially students, protested against this policy, arguing that it would lead to unfair advantages and division in society.

(ii) Under which government was the demand for reservations for backward castes first raised in North India, and when were the Mandal Commission recommendations implemented?

Ans. The demand for reservations for backward castes in North India was first raised under the Janata Party government.

The recommendations of the Mandal Commission were implemented in the year 1990, during the tenure of Prime Minister V.P. Singh.

(iii) Why were there protests in the country due to the Mandal Commission's recommendations?

Ans. The protests arose because people perceived the 27 per cent reservation as an attack on the limited employment opportunities, believing it prioritised caste over merit.

SELF ASSESSMENT TEST

Objective Type Questions

1. Name the first non-Congress Prime Minister of India.

(a) V.P. Singh (b) L.K. Advani (c) A.B. Vajpayee (d) Morarji Desai

2. Name the Prime Minister who headed a coalition government from May 1996 to June 1996. **CBSE 2024 Set 1**

(a) A.B. Vajpayee (b) V.P. Singh (c) Rajiv Gandhi (d) P.V. Narasimha Rao.

3. Which of the following were the recommendations of the Mandal Commission?

(a) 27 per cent seats to be reserved in educational institutions and government jobs for OBCs.

(b) Land reform to improve the conditions of OBCs.

(c) Commission made recommendation in economic and occupational structures.

(d) All of the above

4. Who among the following introduced a policy of reservations for OBSs for the first time.

(a) Karpoori Thakur (b) B.P. Mandal (c) Indira Gandhi (d) Mayawati

5. Match the following

	List I		List II
A.	National Front Government	1.	1996
B.	The United Front Government	2.	2004
C.	National Democratic Alliance	3.	1989
D.	United Progressive Alliance	4.	1999

Codes

	A	B	C	D		A	B	C	D
(a)	3	1	4	2	(b)	1	2	3	4
(c)	2	4	3	1	(d)	1	3	2	4

Very Short Answer Type Questions

6. What finally ended the Ram Temple movement and on which date?

7. What caused the decline of Congress dominance in Indian politics after 1989?

8. On what basis was the National Front government formed?

9. Why did BJP criticse the Muslim Women (Protection of Rigts on Divorce) Act 1986?

Short Answer Type Questions

10. The 1991 economic reforms were necessary for India's growth. Analyse this statement. **Competency Based Que**

11. "Political parties are also willing to ensure that the OBC get adeqates share of power". Explain. **Competency Based Que**

Long Answer Type Questions

12. 'Ayodhya issue was deeply rooted in socio-cultural and political history of the country'. Examine this statement with examples. **Competency Based Que**

13. Explain the Mandal Commission and its significance in shaping Indian politics. **Competency Based Que**

Objective Type Questions

1. Name the first non-Congress Prime Minister of India.
   (a) V.P. Singh (b) L.K. Advani (c) A.B. Vajpayee (d) Morarji Desai
2. Name the Prime Minister who headed a coalition government from May 1996 to June 1996. CBSE 2024 Delhi
   (a) A.B. Vajpayee (b) V.P. Singh (c) Rajiv Gandhi (d) P.V. Narasimha Rao
3. Which of the following were the recommendations of the Mandal Commission?
   (a) 27 per cent seats to be reserved in educational institutions and government jobs for OBCs.
   (b) Land reform to improve the conditions of OBCs.
   (c) Commission made recommendation in economic and occupational structures.
   (d) All of the above
4. Who among the following introduced a policy of reservations for OBCs for the first time?
   (a) Karpoori Thakur (b) B.P. Mandal (c) Indira Gandhi (d) Mayawati
5. Match the following

	List I		List II
A.	National Front Government	1.	1996
B.	The United Front Government	2.	2004
C.	National Democratic Alliance	3.	1998
D.	United Progressive Alliance	4.	1989

Codes

	A	B	C	D		A	B	C	D
(a)	3	1	4	2	(b)	1	2	3	4
(c)	3	4	2	1	(d)	1	3	2	4

Very Short Answer Type Questions

6. What finally ended the Ram Temple movement and on which date?
7. What caused the decline of Congress dominance in Indian politics after 1989?
8. On what basis was the National Front government formed?
9. Why did BJP criticise the Muslim Women (Protection of Rights on Divorce) Act 1986?

Short Answer Type Questions

10. The 1991 economic reforms were necessary for India's growth. Analyse this statement. Competency Based Que
11. "Political parties are also willing to ensure that the OBC get adequate share of power." Explain.
   Competency Based Que

Long Answer Type Questions

12. Ayodhya issue was deeply rooted in socio-cultural and political history of the country. Examine this statement with examples. Competency Based Que
13. Explain the Mandal Commission and its significance in shaping Indian politics. Competency Based Que

PROJECT WORK

Emergency - A Blot on Indian Democracy

Declaration

I hereby declare that this document, titled "India Democracy," is an original work completed by me. The information presented has been gathered from various sources, including textbooks, online research, and official reports, to provide an insightful understanding of the emergency.

I affirm that this work has not been copied from any existing material, and all sources of information have been duly acknowledged.

Signature: ________________

Name: ________________

Date: ________________

Acknowledgement

I want to sincerely thank to Mr. / Mrs. .... , my Political Science instructor, for her direction and assistance with my paper. I was able to better organise and explain my ideas as a result of her insightful criticism and recommendations. Their ongoing encouragement has always encouraged me to aim high and follow my passions.

I also want to express my gratitude to the library personnel for giving me access to a variety of books on Political Science and tools. This project would not have been possible without their help.

Lastly, I appreciate the efforts of all those who work the heroes of emergency, as their dedication strengthens democracy in our country.

Date...........

....
Name of Student

Certificate

This is to Certify that the project work

.... is the bonafide

work of .... (Name of the student) who

carried out the work under my supervision

....

Name and Signature of
Teacher/Supervisor

Contents

S.No.	Particulars
1.	Introduction
2.	Historical Context and Background
3.	Economic Struggles and rise of Social Interest after the 1971 war
4.	Political Background -Movements in Gujarat -Bihar Movement or the JP Movement -Railway and Labour Strikes
5.	Conflicts with Judiciary
6.	Kesavananda Bharati Case
7.	Allahabad High Court's Verdict
8.	Declaration of Emergency -Timeline of Key Events During Emergency
9.	Consequences of Emergency -Effect on Press and Media -Preventive Detention and Social Repression
10.	Lessons of the Emergency -Lok Sabha Elections 1977 -Janata Party -Shah Commission -Legacy of th Emergency
11.	Heroes of Emergency -Jayaprakash Narayan -Morarji Desai -Chaudhary Charan Singh -Jagjivan Ram
12.	Conclusion
13.	Bibliography
14.	Viva Voce Questions

Emergency - A Blot on Indian Democracy

Introduction

Democracy is often considered the best form of government because it gives people the power to make decisions through voting. In India, democracy is a key part of the Constitution and the country follows a system where people elect their leaders. These leaders are supposed to work for the people and are held responsible for their actions.

But even though India is a democratic country, there are many problems that affect how well democracy works here. There was a time in India when democracy was put on hold, leading to one of the darkest periods in its political history. The Emergency, declared in 1975 by Prime Minister Indira Gandhi, is one of the most debated and controversial events in Indian democracy. During the Emergency, the government suspended basic rights, banned political opposition and imposed strict censorship. Many people were arrested and the government had complete control, ignoring democratic principles.

This project will look into the reasons behind the Emergency, the political situation at that time and how it affected India's democracy in the long run.

Historical Context and Background

In 1975, India was going through many problems, both politically and economically. The country faced growing inequality, high inflation, and widespread unemployment. The political situation was unstable and there was increasing opposition to the Congress Party, especially after the 1971 India-Pakistan war and the economic difficulties that followed.

In that same year, the Allahabad High Court declared that Indira Gandhi's election was invalid because of electoral misconduct. This was a major setback for her, and leaders like Jayaprakash Narayan started demanding her resignation. Feeling threatened by the growing opposition, Indira Gandhi decided to declare a state of emergency in India.

On June 25, 1975, she persuaded President Fakhruddin Ali Ahmed to declare an emergency which suspended basic rights and gave more power to the government. This started a 21 months period of authoritarian rule, which is known as the Emergency.

Economic Struggles and Rise of Social Unrest After the 1971 War

In the 1971 elections, Congress raised the slogan 'Garibi Hatao' and promised to remove poverty but the country's social and economic conditions didn't improve much after that.

The Bangladesh crisis put a heavy strain on India's economy with around 8 million refugees crossing into India. This was followed by the Indo-Pak war in 1971.

After the war, the U.S. stopped all aid to India. At the same time, oil prices rose sharply in global markets, causing prices of goods to increase. This leads to widespread hardship for the people. The country faced low industrial growth and high unemployment, especially in rural areas. To cut costs, the government froze employee salaries, which led to dissatisfaction among government workers. Poor monsoon seasons in 1972 and 1973 caused a decline in agricultural productivity with food grain output dropping by 8 per cent. This created a sense of dissatisfaction across the nation.

In this situation, opposition parties were able to organise protests and student unrest from the late 1960s intensified. Marxist-Leninist groups, also known as Naxalites, began using violence to challenge the political system, where the State Government took harsh measures against them which in turn raised social unrest.

Political Background

Movements in Gujarat

In January 1974, students in Gujarat began protesting against rising prices of essential goods and corruption. Their protest gained support from opposition parties, spreading across the state. As a result, the President's rule was imposed. The opposition demanded fresh elections, and Morarji Desai, a leader of Congress (O), threatened to go on an indefinite fast if elections were not held. Due to growing pressure from students and opposition parties, Gujarat held elections in June 1975, and the Congress Party was defeated. This movement highlighted the public dissatisfaction with the government's policies.

In 1974, as an ABVP activist, former finance minister of India late Shri Arun Jaitley ji led the statewide mass movement 'Navnirman Andolan' against massive corruption by Gujarat government.

Project Work

Bihar Movement or the JP Movement

In Bihar, in the year 1975, under the leadership of Jayaprakash Narayan, a widespread agitation erupted against corruption, mismanagement and authoritarian rule.

Jayaprakash Narayan demanded the dismissal of the Congress government in Bihar and gave a call for total revolution in the social, economic and political spheres in order to establish what he considered to be true democracy. The government, however, refused to resign.

In 1975, JP (Jayaprakash Narayan) led a huge people's march to the Parliament, he was supported by non-Congress opposition parties like the Bharatiya Jana Sangh, Congress (O) and others.

Credit: R. K. Laxman in The Times of India, 18 April 1974

The Gujarat and Bihar movements were seen as protests against Indira Gandhi's leadership rather than just opposing State Governments. Indira Gandhi believed these movements were driven by personal opposition to her.

JP Narayan speech in Gandhi Maidan, Patna on 5th June, 1974.

Railway and Labour Strikes

In 1974, India witnessed significant railway and labor strikes that added to the political and economic unrest.

- **Railway Strikes** The National Co-ordination Committee for Railwaymen's Struggle led by George Fernandes gave a call for nationwide strike by all employees of the railways for pressing their demands related to bonus and service conditions. The government was opposed to these demands. So, the employees of India's largest public sector undertaking went on a strike in May 1974.
- **Labour Strikes** Labour strikes were also widespread in 1974, with workers in various industries protesting for better wages, job security, and against poor working conditions. These strikes reflected the growing discontent among the working class due to rising inflation and economic hardships. The government's inability to address these grievances contributed to the mounting frustration among workers and the general public, fueling the growing opposition movement against Indira Gandhi's government.

Conflicts with Judiciary

During Indira Gandhi's rule, there were various conflicts between the Government and the Judiciary. One of the key conflicts arose when the Supreme Court overturned her election in 1975, declaring it invalid due to electoral malpractice. Indira Gandhi, feeling threatened, began to see the judiciary as a challenge to her authority. In response, she took steps to control the judicial system.

The tension reached a peak when the government attempted to weaken judicial review and remove legal checks on its powers, contributing to the overall authoritarian nature of her rule during the Emergency.

Kesavananda Bharati Case

The Kesavananda Bharati case (1973) was a landmark Supreme Court ruling where the court upheld the Parliament's power to amend the Constitution but declared that the "Basic structure" of the Constitution cannot be altered. This established the principle that certain fundamental features of the Constitution are beyond the reach of Parliament's amending power.

Tensions between the judiciary and executive rose after the 1973 Kesavananda Bharati case. The government bypassed seniority and appointed Justice A.N. Ray as Chief Justice, causing controversy, as the three superseded judges had opposed the government's stance. This led to calls for a judiciary aligned with the executive's vision, climaxing with the High Court declaring Indira Gandhi's election invalid.

Allahabad High Court's Verdict

On 12 June 1975, Justice Jagmohan Lal Sinha of the Allahabad High Court passed a judgement declaring Indira Gandhi's election to the Lok Sabha invalid. This order came on an election petition filed by Raj Narain, a socialist leader and a candidate who had contested against her in 1971. The court found evidence that she had used government resources to influence the election in her favour. This verdict was a severe blow to her political career and the opposition started gaining strength, calling for her resignation.

As a result, Indira Gandhi, feeling her political position was under threat, decided to declare a state of emergency across the country.

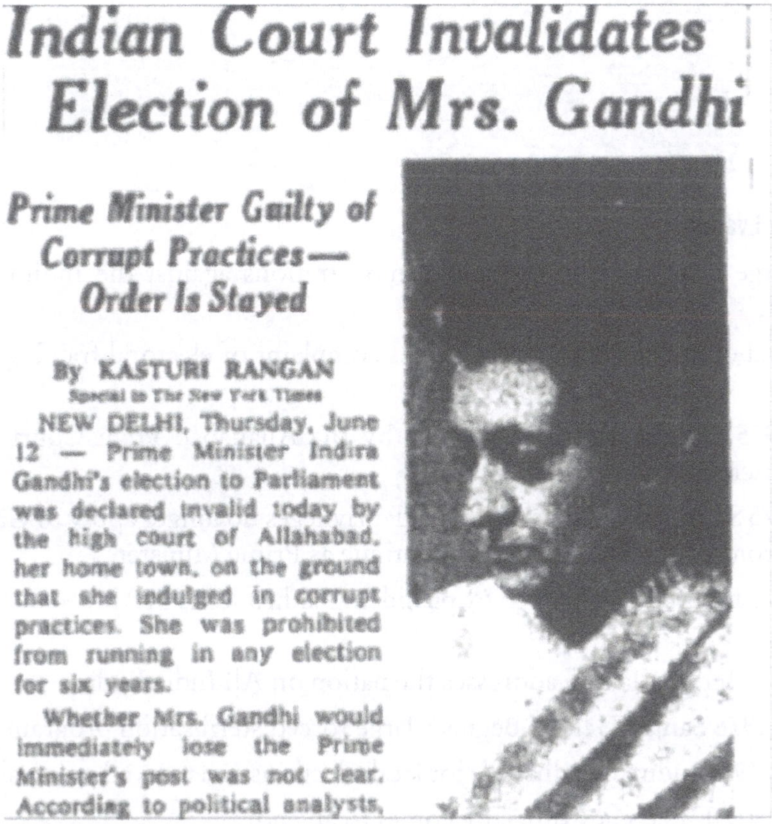

Indian Court Invalidates Election of Mrs. Gandhi

Prime Minister Guilty of Corrupt Practices— Order Is Stayed

By KASTURI RANGAN
Special to The New York Times

NEW DELHI, Thursday, June 12 — Prime Minister Indira Gandhi's election to Parliament was declared invalid today by the high court of Allahabad, her home town, on the ground that she indulged in corrupt practices. She was prohibited from running in any election for six years.

Whether Mrs. Gandhi would immediately lose the Prime Minister's post was not clear. According to political analysts,

Declaration of Emergency

The Emergency in India was declared on June 25, 1975, by Prime Minister Indira Gandhi, following the Allahabad High Court's decision that invalidated her 1971 election. Faced with growing political unrest and opposition, she suspended civil rights, imposed censorship and arrested political leaders. The Emergency lasted for 21 months, significantly limiting democratic freedoms and consolidating central power until its end in 1977. The Emergency lasted from June 25, 1975, to March 21, 1977.

INDIAN HERALD

NATIONAL ENGLISH DAILY

Founder & Editor: THAKUR V. HARI PRASAD

SPECIAL SUPPLEMENT

HYDERABAD, Thursday, June 26, 1975

EMERGENCY DECLARED
JP, Morarji, Advani, Asoka Mehta & Vajpayee arrested

Raj Narain, Mody & Chandra Sekhar held

Timeline of Key Events

- **1973-75** Surge in political unrest and demonstrations against the Indira Gandhi-led government.
- **1971** Political opponent Raj Narain lodges complaint of electoral fraud against Indira Gandhi.
- **June 12, 1975** Gandhi was found guilty by the Allahabad High Court of electoral campaign discrepancies.
- **June 24, 1975** Supreme Court rules that MP privileges no longer apply to Gandhi. She is forbidden from voting but allowed to continue as Prime Minister.
- **June 25, 1975** Emergency declared by president Fakhruddin Ali Ahmed on the advice of Indira Gandhi.
- **June 26, 1975** Indira Gandhi addresses the nation on All India Radio.
- **September 1976** Sanjay Gandhi begins a large forced sterilisation program in Delhi.
- **January 18, 1977** Indira Gandhi calls for fresh elections and frees all political prisoners.
- **March 23, 1977** Emergency officially comes to an end.

Consequences of Emergency

The Emergency in India had serious consequences. Strikes were banned, Fundamental Rights were suspended and many opposition leaders were arrested and the press was censored. Political opposition was not allowed, and the media faced strict censorship. The government had too much power and made decisions without checks. While some development projects took place, the Emergency hurt India's democracy. In 1977, elections were held and Indira Gandhi's party lost, ending the authoritarian rule.

THE HINDU

Indian National Newspaper

President Proclaims National Emergency

"Security of India Threatened by Internal Disturbances"

Preventive Arrests: Press Censorship Imposed

PM Explains Action

Effect on Press and Media During Emergency, the government controlled the press to limit criticism and control what information was shared. Strict rules were set, forcing the media to publish only pro-government stories and censor negative ones. Independent reporting was suppressed and many journalists, editors and opposition leaders were arrested or threatened.

Cartoon made by R.K. Laxman on press freedom during Emergency.

Preventive Detention and Social Repression During the Emergency, the government used preventive detention to arrest people without charges, fearing they might commit an offence. Arrested political workers couldn't challenge their arrests in court. Though some High Courts ruled that detainees could file Habeas Corpus petitions, in 1976, the Supreme Court stated that the government could deny citizens their right to life and liberty during the Emergency. This judgement is one of the most controversial in Indian legal history.

ST. PETERSBURG TIMES ■ FRIDAY, AUGUST 1, 1975

www.guruprasad.net

Maharani of Jaipur is arrested, jailed

New York Times Service (c)

NEW DELHI — The Maharani of Jaipur, one of India's wealthiest aristocrats, has been arrested under the country's Conservation of Foreign Exchange and Prevention of Smuggling Activities Act, the government announced Thursday.

The Maharani, whose name since the abolition of India's nearly 600 princely states in the 1940s has technically been Mrs. Gayatri Devi, was arrested Wednesday.

Although the government did not detail the charges, they presumably related to the disclosure last February that tax-investigators had found fabulous treasures of gold and jewelry buried under the family's palaces in Jaipur.

ALTHOUGH THE charges against the 56-year-old Maharani were economic rather than political, her arrest had been widely expected in the current crackdown on the government's political opponents. She has been an outspoken critic of Prime Minister Indira Gandhi.

A member of Parliament since 1962, representing Jaipur, the ancestral realm of her late husband, the maharani was disciple of Jayaprakash Narayan, who emerged early this year as Mrs. Gandhi's principal political opponent.

Narayan, a frail ascetic who preached "total revolution against the corruption and rottenness of the government," is also in jail, among the thousands of people rounded up in the month since the government, citing the threat of "internal chaos," declared a state of emergency.

LAST FEBRUARY the government said its investigators had found $17-million worth of currency, diamonds, emeralds and precious metals belonging to the maharani and her family, including one cache of gold coins and bullion, worth $5-million dollars, in a secret chamber under the floor of one of the palaces.

Despite her wealth and glamour, the maharani has been popular with the struggling farmers of the state of Rajasthan, where her late husband was once an absolute ruler.

AP

Maharani Gayatri Devi faces charges

Criticism censored

NEW DELHI (UPI) — The Indian press Thursday blacked out reports of strong statements by the West German government and the International Press Institute deploring the country's rigid censorship.

Both statements reached Indian news agencies through foreign wire services Wednesday but remained unpublished.

George Fernandes during Emergency, News of the Preventive detention of the queen of Jaipur Published in the St. Petersburg times

Lessons of the Emergency

The Parliament also brought in many new changes to the Constitution. In the background of the ruling of the Allahabad High Court in the Indira Gandhi case, an amendment was made declaring that elections of Prime Minister, President and Vice President could not be challenged in the Court.

Lok Sabha Elections 1977

The most valuable and lasting lesson of the Emergency was learnt as soon as the Emergency was over and the Lok Sabha elections were announced.

The 1977 elections turned into a referendum on the experience of the Emergency, at least in North India where the impact of the Emergency was felt most strongly.

The opposition fought the election on the slogan of 'Save Democracy'.

The people's verdict was decisively against the Emergency. The lesson was clear and has been reiterated in many state level elections thereafter – governments that are perceived to be anti-democratic are severely punished by the voters. In this sense the experience of 1975–77 ended up strengthening the foundations of democracy in India.

Janata Party

In the 1977 Lok Sabha elections, Janata Party formed the government and Morarji Desai became the first non congress Prime Minister.

Oath taken by the first non-Congress government at the centre in 1977. In the picture are Jayaprakash Narayan, J. B. Kriplani, Morarji Desai and Atal Behari Vajpayee.

However, the Janata Party couldn't bring about the changes it promised and couldn't move away from Congress policies. Morarji Desai's government lost its majority in less than 28 months. Another government headed by Charan Singh was formed on the assurance of the support of the Congress Party. But the Congress Party later decided to withdraw its support with the result that the Charan Singh government could remain in power for just about 4 months. In the January 1980 elections, Congress, led by Indira Gandhi, won 353 seats and came back to power.

The experience of 1977–79 taught a lesson in democratic politics

"Governments that are seen to be unstable and quarrelsome are severely punished by the voters".

Shah Commission

The Shah Commission was established in 1977 by the Janata Party government to investigate the incidents and crimes committed during the Emergency of 1975-77. It examined human rights violations, censorship, political repression and the actions of government officials. The commission's findings were critical of the Indira Gandhi government, exposing misuse of power and illegal practices. Its report raised public awareness about the undemocratic actions taken during the Emergency and contributed to the political shift that led to the Congress Party's defeat in the 1977 elections.

Legacy of the Emergency

The impact of the Emergency was felt in all areas of people's lives and politics. Between the 1977 and 1980 elections, congress positioned itself as a socialist, pro-poor party. The idea of non-Congressism was introduced among opposition parties and issues related to the welfare of backward classes started to shape politics, especially in northern states, where non-Congress leaders from backward classes were elected in 1977.

This period of emergency saw the period of Constitutional crisis lose its origin in a constitutional battle over jurisdiction of the Parliament and judiciary.

This period created a political crisis also as the party in power enjoyed absolute majority, still decided to suspend the democratic process.

The emergency tensed between institution based democracy and democracy based on spontaneous popular participation for which party system was to be blamed.

Another critical issue that emerged during this period was the role and extent of mass protests in a Parliamentary democracy. There was clearly a tension between institution-based democracy and democracy based on spontaneous popular participation.

Heroes of Emergency

Jayaprakash Narayan

Jayaprakash Narayan, often called JP, was a prominent leader in India's freedom struggle and later a key figure in the political landscape, especially during the 1975 National Emergency. JP strongly opposed the authoritarian rule of Indira Gandhi during the Emergency.

In the mid-1970s, after Indira Gandhi's government faced increasing unrest, JP became the central figure of the opposition movement. He rallied people across the country, demanding the resignation of Indira Gandhi. In 1974, he led student protests and movements against corruption, mismanagement and the authoritarian tendencies of the government.

When the Emergency was declared in June 1975, JP became one of the most outspoken critics of Indira Gandhi's government. He called for a peaceful resistance to the authoritarian rule, but many of his supporters were arrested, including JP himself. Despite his imprisonment, JP's ideas inspired many to resist the emergency rule.

His legacy as a leader committed to democracy and social justice was solidified during this period.

The Indian Government released a postage stamp in honor of Jayaprakash Narayan on October 11, 1999 to recognise his significant contributions to India's freedom movement and his role as a champion of democracy, social justice and the Total Revolution movement.

Jayaprakash Narayan *Postage stamps of Jayaprakash Narayan launched by Indian Government*

Morarji Desai

Morarji Desai was a prominent Indian politician and a key figure during the period of the National Emergency in 1975.

During the Emergency, Desai strongly opposed Indira Gandhi's authoritarian rule. He had been a vocal critic of the government even before the Emergency was declared, particularly against the centralisation of power and the curtailing of civil liberties. As a member of the opposition, he was a significant part of the movement that called for the restoration of democracy.

He was a senior leader of the Janata Party and became the first non-Congress Prime Minister of India after the Emergency ended. However, his tenure was short-lived, as his government faced internal challenges, and he lost his majority in less than 28 months. Despite his brief time as PM, Desai is remembered for his role in leading the country back to democratic governance after the Emergency.

Morarji Desai, Postage stamp of Morarji Desai issued by the Government of India

Chaudhary Charan Singh

Chaudhary Charan Singh was a significant political leader during the National Emergency in 1975. A prominent leader of the Indian Agriculturalist and Backward Classes and a key figure in the Janata Party, Charan Singh played an important role in the political developments of that time.

During the Emergency, Charan Singh was one of the strongest critics of Indira Gandhi's authoritarian rule. He opposed the suspension of democratic processes, the curtailing of civil liberties, and the suppression of the press. He was part of the broader opposition movement that sought to resist the Emergency and restore democracy in India.

Chaudhary Charan Singh

In 1977, after the Emergency ended, Charan Singh became the Deputy Prime Minister in the government formed by the Janata Party, led by Morarji Desai. He later broke away from the Janata Party and formed his own government in July 1979 with the support of the Congress Party. However, this government was short-lived, lasting only about 4 months after the Congress withdrew its support.

Charan Singh's political career was marked by his advocacy for the rights of farmers and rural communities, but his role during the Emergency highlighted his opposition to authoritarianism and his later attempts to stabilise India's political system in the post-Emergency era. His government is remembered as part of the complex political dynamics following the Emergency period.

In February 2024, the Government of India has announced to conferred him posthumously with the highest prestigious award of India "Bharat Ratna".

Jagjivan Ram

Jagjivan Ram was a prominent leader and a senior Congress politician during the National Emergency of 1975. Initially, he supported Indira Gandhi's government, holding the position of Defence Minister.

Jagjivan Ram

In 1977, after the Emergency ended, Jagjivan Ram became one of the leading figures in the opposition. He split from Indira Gandhi's Congress Party and formed the Congress (J). His new party aligned with the Janata Party in the effort to defeat Congress in the 1977 elections. This move played a key role in the downfall of Indira Gandhi's government.

He is remembered for working towards the rights of Dalits and backward classes. He also took a strong stand against the Emergency which became an important part of his political journey.

Conclusion

In conclusion, the Emergency declared in India in 1975 was a crucial event in the country's political history. It had a major impact on the functioning of democracy and governance. Prime Minister Indira Gandhi declared the Emergency, which led to the suspension of Fundamental Rights and gave the government powers to rule without checks. The government argued that it was necessary to restore order and stability, but it led to widespread political repression, censorship, and a shift in the balance of power.

During this period, political freedoms were restricted, opposition leaders were jailed, and the media was controlled. The Emergency resulted in a weakening of democratic values and raised concerns about the centralisation of power. However, after the Emergency, there was a strong push for political change, and it ultimately led to the fall of Indira Gandhi's government and a return to democracy.

The Emergency serves as an important lesson in the fragility of democracy and the need to protect individual rights and the rule of law. It reminds us of the importance of preserving democratic institutions and being vigilant in safeguarding our freedoms.

Bibliography

- https://www.indiatoday.in/india/story/when-bobby-could-not-stop-people-from-attending-a-united-opposition-rally-during-emergency-jaitley-1270090-2018-06-26
- https://www.indiatvnews.com/lifestyle/people-rip-arun-jaitley-see-rare-pictures-of-former-finance-minister-s-childhood-and-college-days-544535
- https://www.thepolisproject.com/read/constitutional-democracy-cannot-be-taken-for-granted-decoding-the-allahabad-high-courts-judgment-of-12-june-1975/
- https://thewire.in/politics/why-george-fernandes-is-a-force-to-be-reckoned-with
- https://myvoice.opindia.com/2020/06/the-truth-of-1975-emergency/
- https://www.thefamouspeople.com/profiles/jayaprakash-narayan-7121.php
- https://banknotecoinstamp.com/products/india-jaya-prakash-narayan-postage-stamp_100206
- https://newsd.in/morarji-desai/
- https://indiannerve.com/this-day-in-history-december-23-5186/chaudhary-charan-singh/
- https://www.thefamouspeople.com/banaras-hindu-university.php
- https://economictimes.indiatimes.com/news/how-to/1975-emergency-explained-a-look-back-at-indias-dark-days-of-democracy/articleshow/111248087.cms

Books

Politics in India since Independence (Class 12 NCERT)

Viva Voce Questions

1. ***When did the Emergency in India get declared?***

Ans. The Emergency in India was declared on June 25, 1975.

2. ***Who was the Prime Minister of India during the 1975 Emergency?***

Ans. Indira Gandhi was the Prime Minister of India during the 1975 Emergency.

3. ***Which article of the Indian Constitution was used to declare the Emergency?***

Ans. The Emergency was declared under Article 352 of the Indian Constitution.

4. ***What were the key reasons for the imposition of Emergency in 1975?***

Ans. The key reasons were political instability, the growing power of opposition and economic challenges.

5. ***Name some leaders that were arrested during the Emergency period in 1975?***

Ans. Several opposition leaders, including Jayaprakash Narayan, Morarji Desai and other prominent figures were arrested during the Emergency.

6. ***What were the significant outcomes of the Emergency on civil liberties in India?***

Ans. The Emergency led to the suspension of civil liberties, including freedom of speech and the right to protest.

7. ***Which movement emerged as a strong opposition to the Emergency?***

Ans. The 'Total Revolution' movement led by Jayaprakash Narayan emerged as a strong opposition to the Emergency.

8. ***What was the role of the media during the Emergency in India?***

Ans. The media was censored and could not publish any news critical of the government during the Emergency.

9. ***How did the Emergency affect the political opposition in India?***

Ans. The political opposition was severely weakened, with many leaders jailed or forced into hiding and the opposition parties were unable to function freely.

10. ***What happened to the democratic system during the Emergency in India?***

Ans. During the Emergency, democratic processes were suspended and India was ruled in an authoritarian manner by the executive.

11. ***How did the Emergency affect the judiciary in India?***

Ans. The judiciary's independence was compromised and judges who disagreed with the government's decisions were replaced or pressured.

12. ***Which party won the 1977 Lok Sabha elections and who became the first non-Congress Prime Minister?***

Ans. Janata Party won the 1977 Lok Sabha elections and Morarji Desai became the first non-Congress Prime Minister.

13. ***What do you understand about the JP Movement?***

Ans. The JP movement was a social, political and economic reform, focusing on anti-corruption and promoting democracy. It was led by Jayaprakash Narayan in the 1970s. It gained momentum as opposition to Indira Gandhi's government especially during the Emergency period.

14. ***What were the main consequences of the Emergency on individual freedoms in India?***

Ans. Individual freedoms were severely restricted, censorship was imposed on media, freedom of speech curtailed and the right to assemble suspended.

15. ***What was the Shah Commission and what were its outcomes?***

Ans. The Shah Commission was set up in 1977 to investigate human rights violations during the Emergency. It documented abuses like forced sterilisations, unlawful detentions and censorship leading to a loss of public trust in the government.

16. ***In what way did the Emergency lead to the erosion of political rights in India?***

Ans. Political rights were eroded as the government curtailed opposition activities, banned protests and suppressed freedom of expression.

17. ***How long did the Emergency in India last?***

Ans. The Emergency in India lasted from June 25, 1975 to March 21, 1977.

18. ***Which political party was in power during the Emergency in India?***

Ans. The Indian National Congress, led by Indira Gandhi was in power during the Emergency.

19. ***What were the major reforms implemented after the Emergency in India?***

Ans. After the Emergency, democratic reforms were introduced such as strengthening the Election Commission and ensuring greater political freedoms.

20. ***What role did Jayaprakash Narayan play during the Emergency?***

Ans. Jayaprakash Narayan led the opposition against the Emergency and called for a 'Total Revolution,' inspiring widespread resistance to the government.

21. ***What reasons did the Government give for declaring a National Emergency in 1975?***

Ans. In 1975, Indira Gandhi's government declared a National Emergency, saying there was unrest, political problems, and threats to national security. The court's decision against her election was the main reason, but she said the Emergency was necessary to bring back peace, control the situation, and stop the country's system from breaking down.

22. ***What were the main consequences of the emergency on democratic processes in India?***

Ans. The Emergency had severe consequences on democratic processes in India. It led to the suspension of Fundamental Rights, including the right to free speech and assembly. Political opponents were arrested, and the opposition parties were not allowed to function. The press was censored and political protests were banned.

23. ***Describe the role of the media during the 1975 Emergency in India.***

Ans. During the Emergency, the media played a restricted role. The government imposed censorship, and newspapers had to get approval before publishing any content. Any news critical of the government or discussing the opposition was banned. This created an environment of fear and limited the public's access to information, leading to the suppression of free expression.

SAMPLE QUESTION PAPERS

SAMPLE QUESTION PAPER 1

A Highly Simulated Sample Question Paper for CBSE Class XII Examination

POLITICAL SCIENCE

General Instructions

1. The question paper consists of five sections (A, B, C, D and E) with 30 questions in total.
2. All questions are compulsory.
3. Question numbers 1-12 are multiple choice questions of one mark each.
4. Question numbers 13-18 are of 2 marks each. Answers to these questions should not exceed 50-60 words each.
5. Question numbers 19-23 are of 4 marks each. Answers to these questions should not exceed 100-120 words each. There is an internal choice in two of the 4 marks questions
6. Question numbers 24-26 are passage, cartoon and map-based questions. Answer accordingly.
7. Question numbers 27-30 are of 6 marks each. Answers to these questions should not exceed 170-180 words.
8. There is an internal choice in 6 marks questions.

Time : 3 hours **Max. Marks : 80**

SECTION A

1. Identify and choose the incorrect pair (1)

(a) Lal Bahadur Shastri - Jai Jawan Jai Kisan
(b) Indira Gandhi - Garibi Hatao
(c) Syndicate - A group of powerful opposition leaders against Indira Gandhi
(d) Grand Alliance - Formed by all non-Congress parties

2. Identify the main reason for the split in Congress Party in 1969. (1)

(a) Change in the ideology of Congress Party.
(b) Dominance of the Congress Syndicate.
(c) Difference of opinion among the opposition parties.
(d) Opposition parties came together.

3. Which one among the following statements is not the objectives of NITI Aayog? (1)

(a) Provide a critical directional and strategic input to the development process of India.
(b) Serve as a think tank of the government both at the centre and state level.
(c) Arrange funds for the implementation of developmental programmes.
(d) Seek to put an end to the slow and tardy implementation of the policies.

4. Which country is not considered as a part of South-Asia region? (1)

(a) Afghanistan (b) Myanmar
(c) China (d) Sri Lanka

5. Which of the following term is all about who gets what, when, where and how? (1)

(a) Globalisation (b) Privatisation
(c) Resources geopolitics
(d) Liberalisation

6. What are the main causes of global warming? (1)

(a) Deforestation
(b) Increased use of fossil fuels
(c) Increase intensive agriculture activities
(d) All of the above

7. Which of the following are the components of traditional security? (1)

(a) Deterrence, Defence
(b) Balance of Power
(c) Alliance Building
(d) All of the above

8. How much is the tenure of the judges in the International Court of Justice? (1)

(a) Five years (b) Seven years
(c) Nine years (d) Ten years

9. Match the terms given in List I correctly with List II and choose the correct answer from the codes given below (1)

List I	List II
A. Mikhail Gorbachev elected as the General-Secretary of the Communist Party	1. 1991
B. Russian Parliament declared its independence from the Soviet Union	2. 1988
C. Independence movement began in Lithuania	3. 1985
D. Three Baltic republics Estonia, Latvia and Lithuania become republics	4. 1990

Codes

	A	B	C	D		A	B	C	D
(a)	3	4	2	1	(b)	3	2	1	4
(c)	1	2	3	4	(d)	4	3	2	1

10. In the questions given below, there are two statements marked as Assertion (A) and Reason (R). Read the statements and choose the correct option.

Assertion (A) The First Five-Year Plan addressed, mainly the agrarian sector including investment in dams and irrigation.

Reason (R) Agricultural sector was hit haldest by partition and needed urgent attention. (1)

Codes

(a) Both A and R are true and R is the correct explanation of A.

(b) Both A and R are true, but R is not the correct explanation of A.

(c) A is true, but R is false.

(d) A is false, but R is true.

11. **Statement I** SAARC was established with the signing of the SAARC Charter in Dhaka on 8th December, 1985. (1)

Statement II SAARC was established to promote the welfare of the people of South Asia and to improve their quality of life.

In the light of above statements, choose the correct answer from the options given below.

(a) Both Statement I and Statement II are true.

(b) Both Statement I and Statement II are false.

(c) Statement I is true, but Statement II is false.

(d) Statement I is false, but Statement II is true

12. Arrange the following in chronological order. (1)

I. Formation of NDA government

II. Appointment of Mandal Commission by Central Government

III. Janta Dal Formed

IV. New Economic Reforms

Codes

(a) II, III, IV, I

(b) I, II, III, IV

(c) IV, II, III, I

(d) II, III, I, IV

SECTION B

13. What were the main reasons behind the split of Congress in 1969? (2)

14. 'Emergency and the period around it known as the period of Constitutional crisis'. Explain the statement. (2)

15. What had been Afro-Asian unity? (2)

16. What is the one major distinction between the Soviet economy and the capitalist economy? (1 + 1 = 2)

17. What are the most important outcomes of the Rio Summit? (2)

18. "Regionalism is not as dangerous as communalism". Justify the statement. (1 + 1 = 2)

SECTION C

19. Describe the two reasons that led to National Jubilation (triumph) in India after the 1971 war with Pakistan. (2 + 2 = 4)

20. 'The Assam Movement from 1979 to 1985 is the best example of the movements against outsiders'. Support the statement with suitable arguments. (4)

Or Mention any four common features of European Union.

21. 'Coalition governments proved to be a boon for democracy in India'. Support this statement with the help of most suitable arguments. (2 + 2 = 4)

Or Discuss the significance of linguistic states in nation-building.

22. Explain any two effects of globalisation on the culture of a country. (2+2=4)

23. What are the objectives of military alliances? Give an example of a functioning military alliance with its specific objectives. (3 + 1 = 4)

SECTION D

24. Read the passage given below carefully and answer the questions that follow.

In the traditional view of security, then, most threats to a country's security come from outside its borders. That is because the international system is a rather brutal arena in which there is no central authority capable of controlling behaviour. Within a country, the threat of violence is regulated by an acknowledged central authority — the government. In world politics, there is no acknowledged central authority that stands above everyone else. It is tempting to think that the United Nations is such an authority or could become such an institution. (1 + 1 + 1 + 1 = 4)

(i) The concept of 'Human Security' was first introduced in which report?
- (a) Brundtland Report (1987)
- (b) UN Human Development Report (1994)
- (c) Kyoto Protocol (1997)
- (d) Rio Summit Report (1992)

(ii) Which of the following is an example of a traditional security concern?
- (a) Cross-border terrorism
- (b) Cybersecurity threats
- (c) Epidemics and pandemics
- (d) Economic recession

(iii) Which of the following is NOT a component of non-traditional security?
- (a) Terrorism
- (b) Human rights violations
- (c) Military alliances
- (d) Global warming

(iv) Human security includes which of the following aspects?
- (a) Economic and food security
- (b) Political and community security
- (c) Health and environmental security
- (d) All of the above

25. In the given political outline map of South Asia, four countries have been marked as A, B, C and D. Identify them on the basis of the information given below and write their correct names along with their respective serial number of the information used and the concerned alphabets as per the following format. (1 + 1 + 1 + 1 = 4)

Sr. No. of the Information Used	Alphabet Concerned	Name of the Country
(i)		
(ii)		
(iii)		
(iv)		

(i) An important country but it is not considered to be a part of South Asia.

(ii) The country has a successful Democratic System.

(iii) This country has had both Civilian and Military rulers.

(iv) This country had Constitutional Monarchy.

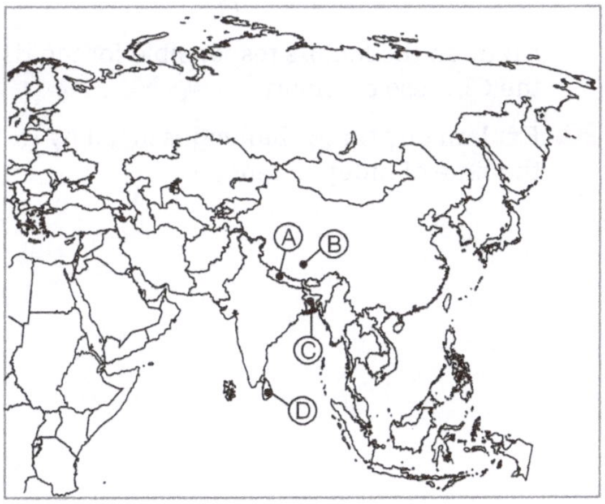

26. Observe the given picture and answer the following question given below **(1 + 1 + 1 + 1 = 4)**

(i) What broader international relations concept does this cartoon primarily criticise?
(a) Economic sanctions
(b) Preemptive military action
(c) Diplomatic negotiations
(d) Peacekeeping operations

(ii) The character with the hat represents
(a) Developing nations
(b) Powerful states/superpowers
(c) International organisations
(d) Non-state actors

(iii) The phrase "You posed a potential threat" in the cartoon critiques
(a) Legitimate self-defense
(b) Justified military intervention
(c) Rationalisation of unprovoked aggression
(d) Diplomatic failure

(iv) Which contemporary international relations principle is being questioned in this cartoon?
(a) Collective security
(b) National sovereignty
(c) Just war theory
(d) Preventive self-defense doctrine

SECTION E

27. Mention the limitations of USSR that led to its disintegration. **(6)**

Or

What do you mean by Arab Spring? Mention any four causes of Arab Spring.

28. What are the reasons being used by Nehru for keeping India secular? Do you think these reasons were only ethical and sentimental? **(3 + 3 = 6)**

Or

Mention the factors responsible for the rise of the Chinese economy.

29. Explain any three challenges faced by India at the time of independence. **(3×2=6)**

Or

"The foreign policy of independent India has pursued the dream of a peaceful world". Support the statement with three suitable examples.

30. Trace the emergence of BJP as a significant force in Indian politics since 1980's. **(6)**

Or

Since 1989, coalition politics has shifted the focus of political parties from ideological difference to power sharing arrangement within the sphere of consensus. Explain with example.

Answers

1. (c) Syndicate A group of powerful opposition leaders against Indira Gandhi
2. (b) Dominance of the Congress Syndicate.
3. (c) Arrange funds for the implementation of developmental programmes.
4. (c) China
5. (c) Resources geopolitics
6. (d) All of the above
7. (d) All of the above
8. (c) Nine years
9. (a) 3 4 2 1
10. (a) Both A and R are true and R is the correct explanation of A.
11. (a) Both Statement I and Statement II are true.
12. (d) II, III, I, IV
13. The main reasons behind the split in Congress in 1969 were
    - The factional rivalry between the Syndicate and Indira Gandhi.
    - Abolition of Privy Purse.
14. The Emergency and the period around it can be described as a period of Constitutional crisis because it had its origin in the Constitutional battle over the jurisdiction of the Parliament and the judiciary.

    It was also a period of political crisis because the party in power had absolute majority and yet, its leadership decided to suspend the democratic process.
15. The Bandung Conference in 1955 in Indonesia marked the peak point of Afro-Asian unity where nations from both Asia and Africa came together to show solidarity. This Bandung Conference later led to the beginning of Non-Alignment Movement.
16. The Soviet system was based on the principles of equality and planned economy controlled by the state.

    Whereas in capitalist economy, private ownership is dominant. Land and productive assets are owned and controlled by the capitalist.
17. The outcomes of the Rio Summit were
    - There was an agreement on combining economic growth with ecological responsibility.
    - The summit started the discussion and debate on environmental issues at global level.
18. Regionalism and communalism both influence Indian politics, but regionalism is not as dangerous as communalism. Regionalism arises from demands for better economic development and political representation, often within the framework of democracy. It can lead to federal strengthening and regional development. However, communalism divides society based on religion, leading to hatred, violence and national disintegration. While regionalism seeks better governance, communalism threatens India's secularism and unity. Therefore, communalism is a more serious threat to national integrity than regionalism.
19. India started a war with Pakistan in December 1971 for the Independence of Bangladesh. Pakistan army was forced to surrender and Bangladesh became a sovereign country. A decisive victory in the war led to National Jubilation because
    (i) Most people in India saw this as a moment of glory and clear sign of India's growing military powers.
    (ii) At that time, the Congress was in power and Indira Gandhi was the Prime Minister. Her popularity increased immensely and the people of India under the leadership of Indira Gandhi considered it to be their own victory against Pakistan.
20. The Assam Movement from 1979 to 1985 is the best example of movements against the outsiders. This can be explained in the following ways
    (i) The Assamese thought that there were large numbers of illegal Bengali Muslim settlers from Bangladesh which would reduce Assamese into minority.
    (ii) There was widespread poverty and unemployment already in Assam. It was believed that local people were deprived of its huge natural resources like oil, tea and coal. This suffering of local people also enhanced by the illegal migration.
    (iii) In 1979, the All Assam Student's Union (AASU) led an Anti-foreigner Movement. This movement was against illegal migrations, domination of Bengali, against faulty voters that included lakhs of immigrants.
    (iv) This movement against outsiders also tried to block the movement of trains and supply of oil from Assam to refineries in Bihar.

    Or

    The four common features of EU are as follows
    (i) EU's share of world trade is much larger than that of US allowing it to be more assertive in trade disputes with US and China.
    (ii) It has evolved from economic union to political one. It has its own flag, anthem, founding date and currency.
    (iii) Its economic power gives it influence over its closest neighbours and on Asia and Africa. It also functions as an important bloc in international economic organisation such as WTO.
    (iv) EU has political, economic, diplomatic and military influence. GDP of EU is slightly larger than that of US.
21. Coalition governments proved to be a boon for democracy in the following ways
    (i) A coalition government is a cabinet of a Parliamentary government in which multiple political parties co-operate, reducing the dominance of any one party within that

coalition. Coalition government provides an alternative to form government, whenever there is a case of hung Parliament.

(ii) The usual reason for this arrangement is that no party on its own can achieve a majority in the Parliament. At the time of national difficulty, it gives a government a high degree of perceived collective identity. It gives small and regional parties to have opportunities to representation in government.

Or Linguistic states has played significant role in nation-building through the following ways

- It accommodated regional demands and linguistic diversity.
- Formation of linguistic states made Indian democracy more democratic.
- Linguistic state reorganisation also gave uniform basis for drawing the boundaries of state.
- Linguistic state united the country more than divided. It made India a nation having unity in diversity.

22. The two effects of globalisation on the culture of a country are

(i) Cultural globalisation affects our food, clothes and thinking. But some times, external influence simply enlarge our choices and sometimes they modify our culture without overwhelming the traditional norms. For example, the burger is no substitute for a masala dosa and therefore, does not pose any real challenge. In the same way, blue jeans can go well with a homespun Khadi Kurta. Here the outcome of outside influences is a new combination that is unique. This clothing combination has been exported back to the country that gave us blue jeans.

(ii) The culture of the politically and economically dominant society leave its imprint on a less powerful society, and the world begins to look more like a dominant power it wishes to be. This is dangerous not only for the poor countries but for the whole of humanity, as it leads to the shrinking of the rich cultural heritage of the entire globe.

So, we can say that globalisation broadens our cultural outlook and promotes cultural homogenisation.

23. The objectives of military alliances are

- To form alliances with other countries to increase their effective power of the state entered in alliance relative to another country or alliance.
- These alliances are based on national interest which changes accordingly to the changing circumstances.
- Another objective of military alliance is to maintain balance of power in a region.

For example, USA supported the Islamic militants in Afghanistan to harm USSR in 1980s, but later attacked them when Al-Qaeda launched terrorist attack against USA on 9/11.

24. (i) (b) UN Human Development Report (1994)
(ii) (a) Cross-border terrorism
(iii) (c) Military alliances
(iv) (d) All of the above

25.

Sr. No. of the Information Used	Alphabet Concerned	Name of the Country
(i)	B	China
(ii)	D	Sri Lanka
(iii)	C	Bangladesh
(iv)	A	Nepal

26. (i) (b) Preemptive military action
(ii) (b) Powerful states/super powers
(iii) (c) Rationalisation of unprovoked aggression
(iv) (d) Preemptive self-defense doctrine.

27. Limitations of USSR that led to its disintegration

The Political Limitations and USSR

(i) The Soviet system became very bureaucratic and authoritarian making life very difficult of its citizens. Lack of democracy and the absence of freedom of speech stifled people in the country.

(ii) Most of the institutions of the Soviet State needed reform. The one party system represented by the Communist Party of the Soviet Union had strict control over all institutions and was unaccountable to the people. The party refused to recognise the urge of people in the fifteen different republics that formed the Soviet Union to manage their own affairs including their cultural affairs.

(iii) Although on paper Russia was only one of the fifteen republics that together constituted the USSR, in reality, Russia dominated everything and people from other regions felt neglected and often suppressed.

The Economic Limitations of USSR

(i) In the arms race, the Soviet Union managed to match the US from time to time but at great cost. The Soviet Union lagged behind the West in technology, infrastructure (e.g. transport, power) and most importantly in fulfilling the political or economic aspirations of the citizens.

(ii) The Soviet invasion of Afghanistan in 1979 weakened the system even further. Through wages continued to grow, productivity and technology fell considerably behind that of the West. This led to shortages in all consumer goods.

(iii) The Soviet economy used much of its resources in maintaining a nuclear and military arsenal and the development of its satellite states in Eastern Europe this led to a huge economic burden that the system could not cope with.

Or The Arab Spring was a series of pro-democracy uprisings that developed largely in the Muslim countries, including Tunisia, Morocco, Syria, Libya, Egypt and Baharain.

The event in these nations generally began in the spring of 2011, which led to the name Arab Spring.

The various causes of Arab Spring are as follows

- The rise in the global crisis, such as the downfall in the oil prices during 2008-09.
- The rise in the price of food leading to food crisis gave rise to the political unrest especially in poor countries.
- Increase in unemployment especially among the youths and females were one of the most important causes behind Arab Spring.
- The demand for political freedom and removal of economic inequalities was one of the major cause behind Arab Spring.
- Self-immolation of Mohamed Bouazizi a street hawker of Tunisia gave a sudden rise to the Arab Spring.

28. The main reasons for keeping India secular by Nehru were

- India after partition had considerable amount of Muslim minority population that needed accommodation.
- Providing rights and recognition to minorities will further help to strengthen our democratic system.
- It was essential to provide the minorities with citizenship status to strengthen the democratic polity of our country so that outbreak of conflict in the society is prevented.

The reasons provided by Pt. Jawaharlal Nehru were both both ethical and prudential in nature.

- **Ethical Reasons** The religious minorities in India is widely acknowledged by Pt. Jawaharlal Nehru and granting them rights also strengthened our democratic polity. The declaration of India as a secular nation would allow everyone to freely profess and propagate religion of their choice. Thus, it would form a basic foundation of our democratic system.
- **Prudential Reason** Pt. Jawaharlal Nehru has minimised the chances of conflict in the society as by declaring India a secular nation would ensure peace and security.

Or China is the third major alternative centre of power. It is the fastest growing economy. China at one time was based on Soviet model and at that time, it broke all the links with capitalist world.

Following are the factors responsible for rise of Chinese economy

- **Use of Soviet Model** China accepted the Soviet model and relied on its resources. China decided to substitute imports by domestic goods and create state owned heavy industries from capital produced by agriculture.
- **Development of Industrial Economy** China used all its resources to develop an industrial economy. All citizens were provided education and health programmes.
- **Relationship With USA** China established relation with USA in 1972.
- **Modernisation** Modernisation in field of agriculture, industry, military, science and technology were proposed.
- **Major Policies Announced** 'Open Door' Policy was announced by Deng Xiaoping in 1978, which aimed at generation of high productivity by investments in capital and technology from abroad.
- **Era of Privatisation** Privatisation of agriculture in 1982 and privatisation of industry in 1998 was done.
- **Establishment of SEZs** Special Economic Zones (SEZ) were set up. State had a centralised role in setting up of China's economy.

29. After independence, there were many challenges or problems and these challenges can be categorised as *(any three)*

(i) **To Shape a Nation** The first and foremost challenge was the political unification and integration of the territory. There were around 600 states of varying sizes and population. The partition of the country appeared to confirm every one's worst fears.

Hence, there was a serious question about the future of India. Sardar Vallabhbhai Patel took upon himself the task of integrating these Princely States, which was either wilfully or diplomatically to be completed in different stages.

(ii) **To Establish Democracy** Another challenge was to develop democratic practices in accordance with the Constitution, i.e. India opted for representative democracy, based on the Parliamentary form of government.

(iii) **To Ensure the Development and Well-being of the Society** The third challenge was to evolve effective policies for economic development and eradication of poverty and unemployment.

All these challenges required a deliberate effort which India put in accommodating social differences, establishing a welfare state and by democratising political institutions.

(iv) **To Accommodate Refugees** The migration of people took place in two forms

(a) Large number of people migrated from East and West Pakistan.

(b) Migration of people from the Princely States.

Or India has played a significant role in promoting Afro-Asian unity by supporting decolonisation, advocating economic co-operation and fostering political solidarity among developing nations.

(i) **Leadership in the Non-Aligned Movement (NAM)** India, under the leadership of Jawaharlal Nehru, was a founding member of NAM, which aimed to unite newly independent Asian and African nations against colonialism and Cold War power politics. This provided a platform for Afro-Asian countries to assert their sovereignty without aligning with major power blocs.

(ii) **Support for Decolonisation** India actively supported the struggles of African nations against colonial rule. It provided moral, political and diplomatic support to countries like South Africa, Kenya and Ghana in their fight for independence. India was also vocal against apartheid in South Africa and played a key role in the United Nations in imposing sanctions on the racist regime.

(iii) **Bandung Conference (1955)** India was instrumental in organising the Bandung Conference, which brought together leaders from 29 Asian and African countries. The conference promoted economic co-operation, cultural exchange and mutual respect for sovereignty, laying the foundation for Afro-Asian solidarity.

30. Since the late 1980's, BJP's political support started gaining strength. Since then its rise has been impressive indeed. The major trends in the electoral performance of BJP since 1989 have been quite significant. It's political ideology has also gained widespread support.

Electoral Performance of BJP

(i) In the elections of 1989, the National Front under V.P. Singh came to power supported by Left Front and BJP from outside because they wanted Congress out of power. This government due to coalition pressures came to an end in 1990. In 1996, BJP minority government was formed for a short period and collapsed as it bailed to generate minority of support.

(ii) From March 1998 to October 1999, BJP and others formed an alliance called NDA under the leadership of Atal Bihari Vajpayee. In 1999, mid-term elections NDA alliance led by BJP came to the power. In the sixteenth Lok Sabha elections held in 2014, BJP won 282 seats and formed the government under the leadership of Narendra Modi.

(iii) In the 2019 Lok Sabha elections, once again brought back BJP led NDA (NDA IV) to the centre of power by winning more than 350 seats out of 543. The BJP on its own won 303 seats in the Lok Sabha, the biggest number any single party has won in the lower house since 1985 when Congress swept the elections in the aftermath of Mrs. Indira Gandhi's assassination.

Hence, in that sense a major transformation could be seen in the nature of coalition politics which could be seen from one party led coalition to one party dominated coalition.

Based on the tumultous success of the BJP in 2019, social scientists have started equating the contemporary party system with the 'BJP system' where an era of one-party dominance, like the 'Congress system' has once again started appearing on the democratic politics of India.

Or Coalition politics has indeed shifted the focus of political parties from ideological differences to power sharing arrangement within the sphere of consensus. Most political parties except a few, unanimously agree to the new economic policy of globalisation as they believe that this is beneficial for India. Even on issue of socio-political claims of the backward castes, they have a consensus as they feel the need to accept these demands.

Regional parties and their role in formation of government has ensured that the political parties have regional parties as new competitors. In such a scenario, it becomes difficult to maintain an ideological divide.

Thus, coalitions are formed and alliances are made without consensus on ideology and it becomes more of a power play. It leads to political alliances and coalitions emerging as a power sharing arrangement. Some such alliances are NDA and UPA, popular United Front consisting of Akali Dal, CPI, CPI (M), SSP, Republican Party and Bharatiya Jana Sangh in Punjab (Assembly election 1967), Grand Alliance of 1971's general election, Alliances of Congress (R) with CPI etc.

SAMPLE QUESTION PAPER 2

A Highly Simulated Sample Question Paper for CBSE Class XII Examination

POLITICAL SCIENCE

General Instructions

1. The question paper consists of five sections (A, B, C, D and E) with 30 questions in total.
2. All questions are compulsory.
3. Question numbers 1-12 are multiple choice questions of one mark each.
4. Question numbers 13-18 are of 2 marks each. Answers to these questions should not exceed 50-60 words each.
5. Question numbers 19-23 are of 4 marks each. Answers to these questions should not exceed 100-120 words each. There is an internal choice in two of the 4 marks questions
6. Question numbers 24-26 are passage, cartoon and map-based questions. Answer accordingly.
7. Question numbers 27-30 are of 6 marks each. Answers to these questions should not exceed 170-180 words.
8. There is an internal choice in 6 marks questions.

Time : 3 hours **Max. Marks : 80**

SECTION A

1. Which of the following statement about Sardar Vallabhbhai Patel is incorrect? (1)

(a) Sardar Vallabhbhai Patel, emerged as a major leader of the freedom movement.
(b) He was not in favour of any compromise with the territorial integrity of India.
(c) He was not a part of Bardoli Satyagraha.
(d) He is known as an 'Iron Man' of India.

2. India has signed FTA's with two ASEAN members including .... (1)

(a) Singapore and Thailand
(b) Philippines and Thailand
(c) Sri Lanka and Russia
(d) China and Sri Lanka

3. Which of the following statements is correct regarding regional aspirations in India? (1)

(a) The demand for a separate state always leads to secession from India.
(b) The Indian Constitution does not allow the formation of new states.
(c) Regional movements in India have been accommodated within the framework of democracy.
(d) The reorganisation of states in India was done only on economic factors.

4. This country emerged as the strong successor of USSR. It is .... (1)

(a) Russia (b) Ukraine
(c) Georgia (d) None of these

5. Israel is an important centre of power due to its principle of .... (1)

(a) sustaining against diversity
(b) cultural complexity
(c) trade relations
(d) economic relations

6. The circle with golden stars on the European Union's flag signifies .... (1)

(a) solidarity and harmony between the people of Europe
(b) security and protection
(c) fraternity and Sovereignty
(d) liberty and Equality

7. The party of socialism according to Lohia should have three symbols in which spade signifies .... (1)

(a) power of voting
(b) willingness to make sacrifices
(c) prepared to make efforts
(d) None of the above

8. Who is the Chairman of National Development Council? (1)

(a) Prime Minister of India
(b) President of India
(c) Chief Ministers
(d) Vice-President of India

9. Match the terms given in List I correctly with List II and choose the correct answer from the codes given below (1)

List I	List II
A. Standstill Agreement	1. 1949
B. Maharaja of Manipur Signed Merger Agreement	2. 1972
C. State Re-organisation Act Passed	3. 1947
D. Major Re-organisation of States in North-East	4. 1956

Codes

	A	B	C	D		A	B	C	D
(a)	3	1	4	2	(b)	3	2	1	4
(c)	1	2	3	4	(d)	4	3	2	1

10. In the questions given below there are two statements marked as Assertion (A) and Reason (R). Read these statements and choose the correct option.

Assertion (A) India, China and other developing countries were exempted from the requirements of the Kyoto Protocol.

Reason (R) Their contribution to the emissions of greenhouse gases during the industrialisation period was not significant. (1)

Codes

(a) Both A and R are true and R is the correct explanation of A.
(b) Both A and R are true, but R is not the correct explanation of A.
(c) A is true, but R is false.
(d) A is false, but R is true.

11. **Statement I** In the traditional view of security, more threat to a country's security comes from outside its borders.

Statement II The international system is rather a brutal arena in which there is no central authority capable of controlling behaviour. (1)

In the light of above statements, choose the correct answer from the options given below

(a) Both Statement I and Statement II are true.
(b) Both Statement I and Statement II are false.
(c) Statement I is true, but Statement II is false.
(d) Statement I is false, but Statement II is true.

12. Arrange the following in a chronological order. (1)

I. India joins the UN.
II. Yalta Conference of the Big three i.e. Rooserelt, Churchill and Stalin.
III. Tehran Conference Declaration of three powers i.e. US, Britain and Soviet Union.
IV. Signing of the Atlantic Charter by US President Roosevelt and British Prime Minister Churchill.

Codes

(a) I, IV, II, III
(b) IV, III, II, I
(c) II, IV, III, I
(d) III, IV, II, I

SECTION B

13. Highlight any one major distinction between the soviet economy and the capitalist economy. (2)

14. Differentiate between 'one-party dominance' and 'one party system'. (2)

15. Identify any two outcomes of the partition of India into India and Pakistan. (1 + 1 = 2)

16. What prompted nationwide satyagraha against Congress? (2)

17. What are the two models of development and which of the models were adopted by India? (1 + 1 = 2)

18. Mention any two measures to have good relations with Pakistan. (1 + 1 = 2)

SECTION C

19. Enlist any four features of the Congress Party. (2 + 2 = 4)

20. What is UNICEF? Mention any four functions performed by it? (2 + 2 = 4)

Or "The Indian Government is already participating in global efforts through a number of programmes related to environmental issues". Give any four examples to support the statement.

21. Analyse the consequences of the Chinese invasion of 1962 in hampering India's image at home and abroad. (2 + 2 = 4)

22. What is the difference between refugees and migrants? (2 + 2 = 4)

Or 'Coalition governments proved to be are boon for democracy in India'. Support this statement with two suitable arguments.

23. What are the major problems of ecological issues?

(1 + 3 = 4)

SECTION D

24. Read the passage given below and answer the questions that follow. (1 + 1 + 1 + 1 = 4)

Globalisation is a multi-dimensional concept. It has political, economic and cultural manifestations, and these must be adequately distinguished. It is wrong to assume that globalisation has purely economic dimensions, just as it would also be mistaken to assume that it is a purely cultural phenomenon. The impact of globalisation is vastly uneven — it affects some societies more than others and some parts of some societies more than others — and it is important to avoid drawing general conclusions about the impact of globalisation without paying sufficient attention to specific contexts.

(i) Which international organisation promotes free trade and resolves trade disputes among countries?

a) International Monetary Fund (IMF)
b) United Nations (UN)
c) World Trade Organisation (WTO)
d) World Bank

(ii) Which of the following is the most significant impact of globalisation?

(a) Decline in international trade
(b) Reduction in cultural exchanges
(c) Increased interdependence among nations
(d) Strengthening of national barriers

(iii) Which of the following statements about globalisation is correct?

(a) It only benefits developed countries
(b) It has both positive and negative impacts on economies and societies
(c) It leads to complete cultural uniformity worldwide
(d) It has no impact on employment opportunities

(iv) What is the main role of the International Monetary Fund (IMF) in globalisation?

(a) Promoting free education worldwide
(b) Providing financial assistance to countries facing economic crises
(c) Controlling global media
(d) Restricting trade among nations

25. In the give outline political map of India four states have been marked as A, B, C and D. Identify these states on the basis of the information given below and write their correct names in your answer book with their respective serial number of the information used and the concerned alphabets as per format that follows. (1 + 1 + 1 + 1 = 4)

S. No. of the Information Used	Alphabet Concerned	Name of the State
(i)		
(ii)		
(iii)		
(iv)		

(i) The state to which Minister for Communications in the first ministry of free India belonged.

(ii) The state to which the former Prime Minister Morarji Desai was related.

(iii) The state to which S. Nijalingappa belonged.

(iv) The state related to former Congress President K. Kamaraj.

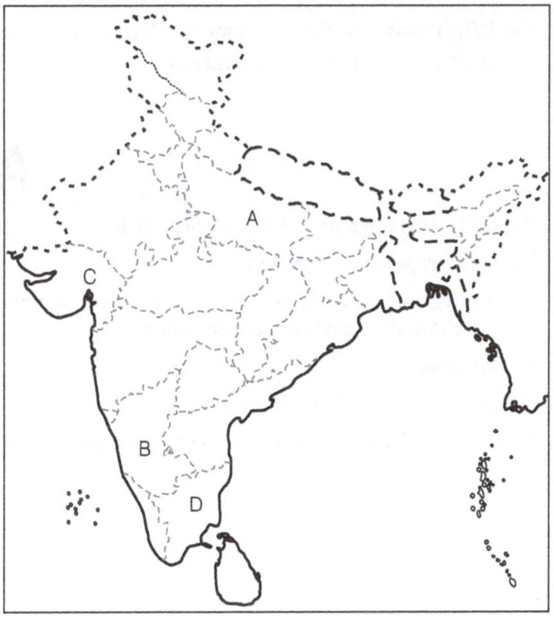

26. Observe the cartoon given below carefully and answer the questions that follow. (1+1+1+1 = 4)

(i) What aspect of democratic process is primarily depicted in this cartoon?
(a) Election campaigning
(b) Vote counting
(c) Electoral fraud
(d) Election committee's oversight function

(ii) The figure with bow and arrow in the cartoon likely symbolises.
(a) Electoral violence
(b) Democratic opposition
(c) Media scrutiny
(d) Public protest

(iii) The crowd's raised hands in the cartoon suggests.
(a) Voter intimidation
(b) Democratic participation
(c) Public protest
(d) Election fraud

(iv) Which principle of democracy is being highlighted through this cartoon?
(a) Free and fair elections
(b) Universal adult franchise
(c) Electoral transparency and accountability
(d) Secret ballot system

SECTION E

27. How Bangladesh was formed as an independent nation? (6)

Or What are the efforts which has been taken by India and Pakistan towards peace and co-operation between both the nation?

28. Highlight any three positive and three negative features each of the Soviet system in the Soviet Union. (2 + 2 + 2 = 6)

Or What was the Soviet system? Assess any four features of the Soviet system.

29. Analyse the philosophy of Integral Humanism advocated by Pandit Deendayal Upadhyay. (6)

Or What was the major outcome of 1977 Lok Sabha elections? Explain.

30. "Peace and prosperity of countries lay in the establishment and strengthening of regional economic organisations". Critically analyse the statement. (6)

Or What is Godhra riots? What were its outcomes?

Answers

1. (c) He was not a part of Bardoli Satyagraha.

2. (a) Singapore and Thailand

3. (c) Regional movements in India have been accommodated within the framework of democracy.

4. (a) Russia

5. (a) sustaining against diversity

6. (a) solidarity and harmony between the people of Europe

7. (c) prepared to make efforts

8. (a) Prime Minister of India

9. (a) 3 1 4 2

10. (a) Both A and R are true and R is the correct explanation of A.

11. (a) Both Statement I and Statement II are true.

12. (b) IV, III, II, I

SAMPLE QUESTION PAPER 3

A Highly Simulated Sample Question Paper for CBSE Class XII Examination

POLITICAL SCIENCE

General Instructions

- All questions are compulsory.
- Question numbers 1-12 are multiple choice questions of one mark each.
- Question numbers 13-18 are of 2 marks each. Answers to these questions should not exceed 50 words each.
- Question numbers 19-23 are of 4 marks each. Answer to these questions should not exceed 100 words each.
- Question numbers 24-26 are passage, cartoon and map-based questions. Answer accordingly.
- Question numbers 27-30 are of 6 marks each. Answers to these questions should not exceed 170 words.
- There is an internal choice in 6 marks questions.

Time : 3 hours **Max. Marks : 80**

SECTION A

1. Name the party that dominates the political affairs of Maldives. (1)

(a) Maldivian Dictatorship Party
(b) Maldivian Democratic Party
(c) Maldivian People's Party
(d) Maldivian Majority Party

2. In which year BRICS was founded? (1)

(a) 2000 (b) 2002 (c) 2004 (d) 2006

3. The First Summit of NAM was held in which country in September, 1961? (1)

(a) Brazil (b) Belgrade
(c) Paris (d) Philippines

4. The tenure of non-permanent members in the Security Council is of now many years? (1)

(a) One year (b) Two year
(c) Three year (d) Four year

5. Why did Russia become the successor of USSR? (1)

(a) Russia led the formation of CIS
(b) It inherited the Soviet seat in the UN
(c) It was the largest republic
(d) Boris Yeltsin was more charismatic than Gorbachev

6. In which year ASEAN established the ASEAN community comprising of three pillars? (1)

(a) 2001 (b) 2002
(c) 2003 (d) 2004

7. Who is known for the original contribution to a Non-European Socialist Theory as a political leader? (1)

(a) Deendayal Upadhyaya (b) Ram Manohar Lohia
(c) Jayaprakash Narayan (d) Indira Gandhi

8. How can we say that NITI Aayog Acts in the spirit of Co-operative Federalism? (1)

(a) As it ensures equal participation of all the states in the country.
(b) As it promotes the capability of states.
(c) As the states work maintaining their transparency level.
(d) None of the above

9. Match the terms given in List I correctly with List II and choose the correct answer from the codes given below (1)

List I		List II	
A.	Berlin wall was broken in	1.	1979
B.	Russian Revolution	2.	2001
C.	The soviet invasion of Afghanistan in	3.	1989
D.	Indo-Russian strategic Agreement	4.	1917

Codes

	A	B	C	D		A	B	C	D
(a)	1	2	4	3	(b)	3	4	1	2
(c)	3	1	2	4	(d)	2	1	3	4

10. In the questions given below there are two statements marked as Assertion (A) and Reason (R). Read these statements and choose the correct option.

Assertion (A) Global atmosphere is warming up.

Reason (R) The depletion of the stratospheric ozone layer has resulted in an increase in ultravoilet radition reaching the Earth. (1)

Codes

(a) Both A and R are true and R is the correct explanation of A.
(b) Both A and R are true, but R is not the correct explanation of A.
(c) A is true, but R is false.
(d) A is false, but R is true.

11. **Statement I** NITI Aayog was constituted with the objective of providing the necessary and technical advice to the Union Government regarding the policy-making.

Statement II NITI Aayog was formed because the National Development Council(NDC) became ineffective and irrelevant in today's era.

In the light of above statements, choose the correct answer from the options given below.

(a) Both Statement I and Statement II are true.
(b) Both Statement I and Statement II are false.
(c) Statement I is true, but Statement II is false.
(d) Statement I is false, but Statement II is true. (1)

12. Arrange the following in a chronologist order. (1)

I. Second General Elections
II. V.V. Giri elected as the President of India
III. Fourth General Elections
IV. Congress (R)-CPI alliance won more seats in general elections

Codes

(a) I, III, II, IV (b) III, II, IV, I
(c) II, IV, I, III (d) IV, III, I, II

SECTION B

13. What is economic planning and its importance in the Indian context? (2)

14. In your opinion, how far is India justified in choosing the policy of non-alignment? (2)

15. When was the reorganisation of North- East India completed and how? (1 + 1 = 2)

16. What do you mean by alliance politics? (2)

17. What is the relationship between traditional security and co-operation? (2)

18. Explain the term Environmental Movement or activism. (2)

SECTION C

19. Explain the term 'Privy Purse'? What wat the reason behind it being abolished in 1970 by Indira Gandhi? (2 + 2 = 4)

20. Explain any three lessons learnt from the Emergency of 1975. (4)

21. How can the Euro pose a danger to the US dollar? (4)

Or "European Union is a highly influential regional organisation". Justify the statement with any four suitable arguments.

22. How has globalisation enhanced the position of a state? (4)

Or "Globalisation has shifted power from nation states to global consumers". Justify the statement.

23. What is WTO? When was it set up and what are its functions? (2 + 2 = 4)

SECTION D

24. Read the passage given below and answer the questions that follow. (1 + 1 + 1 + 1 = 4)

The interim government took a firm stance against the possible division of India into smaller principalities of different sizes. The Muslim League opposed the Indian National Congress and took the view that the states should be free to adopt any course they liked. Sardar Patel, India's Deputy Prime Minister and the Home Minister during the crucial period, immediately after independence, played a historic role in negotiating with the rulers of Princely States in bringing most of them into the Indian Union.

(i) How the leader played a historic role in the integration of states?
(a) By skillfully negotiating
(b) By forcefully convincing
(c) By not trying to control through army rule
(d) None of the above

(ii) Why did the Muslim League oppose the Indian National Congress?
(a) It favoured that states should be free to adopt any course they wish.
(b) It favours the idea of secularism.
(c) It beliefs in the idea of democracy.
(d) All of the above

(iii) Which government has been referred to as the interim government?
(a) State Government
(b) Indian National Congress Government
(c) Regional Parties Government
(d) None of these

(iv) Who plays a historic role in the integration of states of India?
(a) Jawaharlal Nehru
(b) Mahatma Gandhi
(c) Sardar Vallabhbhai Patel
(d) Dr. B.R. Ambedkar

25. In the given outline political map of world, four countries have been marked as A, B, C and D. Identify these on the basis of the information given below and write the correct names in your answer book along with the respective serial number of the information used and the concerned alphabets as per format that follows. (1 + 1 + 1 + 1 = 4)

Sr. No. of the Information Used	Concerned Alphabet	Name of the Countries
(i)		
(ii)		
(iii)		
(iv)		

(i) To which country the UN Secretary-General Dag Hammarskjold Annan belonged?
(ii) To which country the UN Secretary-General Kurt Waldheim belonged?
(iii) To which country the UN Secretary-General Boutros Boutros- Ghali belonged?
(iv) To which country the UN Secretary-General Kofi Annan belonged?

26. Consider the cartoon given below and answer the questions that follow **(1 + 1 + 1 + 1 = 4)**

(i) What economic phenomenon is this cartoon primarily critiquing?
(a) International trade barriers (b) Global economic inequality
(c) Job outsourcing to developing countries (d) Child labor practices

(ii) The cartoon's 'Yesterday' and 'Today' comparison highlights.
(a) Change in dining habits (b) Educational improvements
(c) Economic hypocrisy (d) Cultural differences

(iii) What aspect of globalisation is being criticised in this cartoon?
(a) Cultural imperialism (b) Economic exploitation
(c) Environmental degradation (d) Technological advancement

(iv) The shift from 'dinner' to 'homework' context represents.
(a) Educational progress (b) Changing parental attitudes
(c) Evolution of economic arguments (d) Dietary changes

SECTION E

27. Elucidate the reasons necessary for the reforms in USSR. **(6)**

Or Explain any six outcomes of the disintegration of the Soviet Union.

28. Explain the contribution of Jawaharlal Nehru in formulating the Foreign Policy of India. **(6)**

Or Discuss the strained relationship between India and China which led to the Chinese invasion of 1962?

29. Describe any six issues of consensus to show that in the midst fo severe competitions and conflicts a consensus has appeared among most political parties. **(6)**

Or Analyse the rise and fall of any two coalition governments from the year 1989 to 2004.

30. Was the declaration of emergency in 1975 necessary? Support your answer with three suitable arguments. **(2 + 2 + 2 = 6)**

Or What are the three democratic upsurges that emersed in the post independence history of India? Explain.

Answers

1. (b) Maldivian Democratic Party
2. (d) 2006
3. (b) Belgrade
4. (b) Two year
5. (b) It inherited the Soviet seat in the UN
6. (c) 2003
7. (b) Ram Manohar Lohia
8. (a) As it ensures equal participation of all the states in the country.
9. (b) 3 4 1 2
10. (b) Both A and R are true, but R is not the correct explanation of A.
11. (c) Statement I is true, but Statement II is false.
12. (a) I, III, II, IV

CBSE
Examination Paper 2025

POLITICAL SCIENCE

Time : 3 Hours **Max. Marks : 80**

General Instructions

Read the following Instructions very carefully and follow them

(i) This question paper contains 30 question. All questions are compulsory.

(ii) Question paper is divided into five sections. Section A, B, C, D and E

(iii) Section A question numbers 1 to 12 are Multiple Choice type questions. Each question carries 1 mark.

(iv) Section B question numbers 13 to 18 are Short Answer type questions. Each question carries 2 marks. Write answer to each question in 50 to 60 words.

(v) Section C-question numbers 19 to 23 are Long Answer Type-I questions. Each question carries 4 marks. Write answer to each question in 100 to 120 words.

(vi) Section D-question numbers 24 to 26 are Passage, Cartoon/Picture and Map-based questions. Answer each question accordingly.

(vii) Section E question numbers 27 to 30 are Long Answer Type-II questions. Each question carries 6 marks. Write answer to each question in 170 to 180 words.

(viii) There is no overall choice in the question paper, However, an internal choice has been provided in few questions. Only one of the choices in such questions has to be attempted.

(ix) In addition to this, NOTE that a separate question has been provided for Visually Impaired candidates in lieu of questions having visual inputs, Map etc. Such questions are to be attempted by Visually Impaired candidates only.

Section-A

1. Given below are two statements **(1)**

Statement I Nepal was a Hindu Kingdom in the past and then a Constitutional monarchy in the modern period for many years.

Statement II The struggling pro-democracy forces achieved their first major victory in 2006 when the king was forced to restore the House of representatives.

Options

(a) Both Statement I and Statement II are true.
(b) Both Statement I and Statement II are false.
(c) Statement I is true, but Statement II is false.
(d) Statement I is false, but Statement II is true.

2. Which of the following events made the South Asian region a sudden focus of global attention after the Cold War period? **(1)**

(a) Bangladesh War of 1971
(b) Ethnic conflict of Sri Lanka
(c) India and Pakistan both became nuclear power
(d) Kargil conflict between India and Pakistan

3. Match the terms given in List I correctly with List II and choose the correct answer from the codes given below **(1)**

	List I		List II
A.	Human Rights Watch	1.	An organ of the United Nations
B.	International Monetary Fund	2.	An agency of the United Nations
C.	World Health Organisation	3.	An international organisation that oversees financial institutions
D.	General Assembly	4.	An international NGO

Codes

	A	B	C	D		A	B	C	D
(a)	3	1	4	2	(b)	4	1	3	2
(c)	4	3	2	1	(d)	2	4	3	1

4. Arrange the following in chronological order of their formation **(1)**

I. The World Trade Organisation
II. World Bank
III. The International Atomic Energy Agency
IV. United Nations Organisation
V. Choose the correct option

(a) I, II, III, IV (b) II, IV, III, I
(c) IV, I, III, II (d) III, I, II, IV

5. Institutional safeguards to minimise the negative effects of globalisation on those who are economically weak are known as **(1)**

(a) Welfare measures (b) Social safety nets
(c) Economic liberalisation (d) Voluntary services

6. In the following question, a statement of Assertion (A) is followed by a statement of Reason (R). Choose the correct option as answer. **(1)**

Assertion (A) The entry and the increased role of multinational companies all over the world leads to a reduction in the capacity of governments to take decisions on their own.

Reason (R) The state continues to discharge its essential functions and consciously withdraws from certain domains from which it wishes to.

Options

(a) Both A and R are true and R is the correct explanation of A.
(b) Both A and R are true, but R is not the correct explanation of A.
(c) A is true, but R is false.
(d) A is false, but R is true.

7. Which one among the following statements not the objective of NITI Aayog? **(1)**

(a) Provide a critical directional and strategic input to the development process of India.
(b) Serve as a think tank of the government both at the centre and state level.
(c) Arrange funds for the implementation of developmental programmes.
(d) Seek to put an end to the slow and tardy implementation of the policies.

8. Which statement among the following is correct about the planning ideology of left wing? **(1)**

(a) The Left supports a free-market economy.
(b) They support government policies which are for the benefit of poor sections.
(c) They do not want unnecessary intervention of government in the economy.
(d) They advocate for progressive policies.

9. Identify the main reason for the split in Congress Party in 1969. **(1)**

(a) Change in the ideology of Congress Party
(b) Dominance of the Congress Syndicate
(c) Difference of opinion among the opposition parties
(d) Opposition parties came together

10. Identify and choose the incorrect pair **(1)**

(a) Lal Bahadur Shastri	Jai Jawan Jai Kisan
(b) Indira Gandhi	Garibi Hatao
(c) Syndicate	A group of powerful opposition leaders against Indira Gandhi
(d) Grand Alliance	Formed by all Non-Congress Parties

11. BJP led alliance of 2010 is known as **(1)**

(a) United Progressive Alliance
(b) United Front
(c) National Democratic Alliance
(d) Democratic Coalition

12. Who led the Central Government after the 1999 Lok Sabha Elections? **(1)**

(a) P.V. Narasimha Rao
(b) Atal Bihari Vajpayee
(c) Manmohan Singh
(d) H.D. Deve Gauda

SECTION-B

13. Can Shock Therapy be called the best way to make transition from authoritarian socialist system to liberal capitalist system after the disintegration of Soviet Union? Explain. **(2)**

14. Explain any two major causes of globalisation. **(2)**

15. Explain the two commonly agreed upon goals of the national movement which were achieved after independence. **(2)**

16. Name any four global commons. **(2)**

17. State the severe economic crisis prior to the fourth general elections of 1967 . **(2)**

18. "Regionalism is not as dangerous as communalism." Justify the statement. **(2)**

Section-C

19. Explain any four reasons responsible for the economic stagnation in Soviet Union. **(4)**

20. How in the South Asian Association for Regional Co-operation (SAARC) a major regional initiative by South Asian states to evolve co-operation through multilateral means? Assess. **(4)**

Or "Despite the mixed record of democratic experiences, the people of South Asian countries share the aspiration for democracy". Justify the statement with two suitable arguments. **(4)**

21. Suggest any four steps for the Indian Government to take to check the pollution and save the environment. **(4)**

22. "One-party dominance did not affect the very essence of Indian democracy". Justify the statement with any two arguments. **(4)**

23. Describe the role of Jayaprakash Narayan in Indian National Politics. **(4)**

Or Describe any two reasons for the victory of Janata Party in 1977 Lok Sabha elections. **(4)**

Section D

24. Read the passage given below and answer the questions that follow

India adopted a democratic approach to the question of diversity Democracy allows the political expressions of regional aspirations and does not look upon them as anti-national. Besides, democratic politics allows parties and groups to address the people on the basis of their regional identity, aspiration and specific regional problems. Thus, in the course of democratic politics, regional aspirations get strengthened. At the same time, democratic politics also means that regional issues and problems will receive adequate attention and accommodation in the policy-making process. **(1+1+1+1 = 4)**

(i) Which period in India is seen as a period of grooming regional aspirations for autonomy?
(a) 1960s (b) 1970s (c) 1980s (d) 1990s

(ii) Which type of diversity is dominant in India?
(a) Social diversity (b) Political diversity
(c) Cultural diversity (d) Regional diversity

(iii) How does democracy deal with the regional problems?
(a) Through regular negotiations
(b) Through strong steps
(c) Through elections
(d) Through economic measures

(iv) Which one of the following joined Indian Union in 1975?
(a) Goa (b) Sikkim (c) Puducherry (d) An Island

25. In the given Political outline map of India, four states have been marked as (A), (B), (C) and (D). Identify these states on the basis of the information given below and write their correct names in your answer book along with the respective serial numbers of the information used and the concerned alphabets shown in the map as per the format that follows **(1+1+1+1= 4)**

SR Number for the Information used	Alphabet concerned	Name of the State
(i)		
(ii)		
(iii)		
(iv)		

(i) The Princely State whose ruler resisted its merger with India.
(ii) The State that was most affected by the partition of the country.
(iii) The State carved out from Madhya Pradesh.
(iv) The State that was formed in 1952.

26. Study the given cartoon and answer the questions that follow **(1+1+1+1 = 4)**

(i) What does the cartoon depict?
(a) Influence of UNO on the World
(b) Influence of USA on UNO
(c) Relevance of UNO
(d) Influence of USA on the World

(ii) What message is given by the cartoon ?
(a) If UN fails then the US can control the world by its military power.
(b) Economic superiority of US.
(c) Veto Power of permanent members of UN.
(d) US is the largest is not relevant today?

(iii) Why this cartoon is not relevant today?
(a) UN has become more powerful.
(b) Many new powerful international organisations have emerged.
(c) Countries are not having faith in UN.
(d) Now many new centres of power have emerged.

(iv) What is the primary objective of UNO?
(a) To foster economic ties of the developed nations
(b) To promote international peace and co-operation
(c) To eradicate terrorism
(d) To promote health care

Section E

27. Explain any two contentious issues between China and India. Suggest any two measures to resolve these issues greater co-operation. **(2×½+2×1½=6)**

Or "ASEAN took steps to establish an ASEAN community on the basis its three pillars." Explain the importance of these three pillars. **(3×2=6)**

28. Explain any three security challenges faced by the newly independent countries of Asia and Africa after the Second World War. **(3×2=6)**

Or Explain any three differences between the Non-traditional and Traditional notion of security. **(2+2+2=6)**

29. "The foreign policy of Independent India has pursued the dream of a peaceful world". Support the statement with three suitable arguments. **(3×2=6)**

Or "India played an important role in maintaining Afro-Asian Unity". Support the statement with three suitable examples.

30. Describe any three major developments that took place in Indian politics in the last decade of the 20th century. **(3×2=6)**

Or Describe any three recommendations of the Mandal Commission solve the problems of the other backward classes. **(3×2=6)**

Answers

1. (a)	**2.** (c)	**3.** (c)	**4.** (b)	**5.** (b)
6. (b)	**7.** (c)	**8.** (b)	**9.** (b)	**10.** (c)
11. (c)	**12.** (b)			

13. Shock therapy was the process of transition from an authoritarian socialist system to a democratic capitalist system, that was influenced by the World Bank and the IMF.

Shock therapy is not considered as the best way to make a transition from communism to capitalism because

- The economies were ruined and there was disaster upon the people of the entire region of the past-Soviet countries.
- The large state controlled industrial complex almost collapsed in Russia. The valuable industries were undervalued and sold at throw away prices.
- The value of the Russian currency 'Ruble' declined.
- Due to high rate of inflation people lost all their savings.
- Russia started to import food as the collective farm system disintegrated and people were left without food security.
- With no alternatives in its place the old trading structure broke down.
- Large sections of the people were put into poverty due to the withdrawal of the government subsidies.

14. The following factors are responsible for globalisation are

(i) Technology is the most important element. The invention of the telegraph, the telephone and the microchip has revolutionised communication between various global factors. The technology has made it easier to exchange ideas, capital and commodities from one place to another. The transfer of capital and commodities is a major cause of globalisation.

(ii) The increased inter-connectedness has led to migration of people in search of economic opportunities. This in turn helps in the flow of investments across the world. This has initiated globalisation on a large scale.

15. The two commonly agreed-upon goals of the national movement that were achieved after independence are

- **Democratic Government** India became an independent and sovereign nation with a democratic system based on universal adult franchise, that ensures equal political rights for all citizens.

- **Secularism** India adopted a secular Constitution which ensured freedom of religion and equal treatment to all religious communities.

16. 'Global commons' are those resources which are not owned by anyone but rather shared by a community. Four major global commons are

- **The High Seas** These are parts of the oceans that do not fall under any country's territorial control and are crucial for marine biodiversity.
- **The Atmosphere** It is essential for life and is impacted by pollution and climate change, requiring global efforts for protection.
- **Antarctica** A continent governed by the Antarctic Treaty, which prohibits military activities and promotes scientific research.
- **Outer Space** It is regulated by international treaties to prevent conflicts and ensure peaceful exploration.

Since these resources belong to all of humanity, sustainable management and international co-operation are necessary to prevent over-exploitation and environmental damage.

17. Prior to the Fourth General Elections of 1967, India faced a severe economic crisis due to consecutive droughts in 1965 and 1966. The rupee was devalued in 1966 and foreign aid dependency increased. Additionally, the wars with China (1962) and Pakistan (1965) strained the economy which caused widespread public discontent and political instability.

18. Regionalism and communalism both influence Indian politics, but regionalism is not as dangerous as communalism. Regionalism arises from demands for better economic development and political representation, often within the framework of democracy. It can lead to federal strengthening and regional development. However, communalism divides society based on religion, leading to hatred, violence, and national disintegration. While regionalism seeks better governance, communalism threatens India's secularism and unity. Therefore, communalism is a more serious threat to national integrity than regionalism.

19. The economic stagnation of the Soviet Union was driven by several structural and policy-related factors such as

- **Centralisation of the Bureaucracy** The Soviet economy was controlled by a highly centralised planning system, which led to inefficiency, delays in decision-making and widespread corruption. The lack of flexibility hindered innovation and adaptation to new economic challenges.
- **Lack of Incentives** Since industries were state-owned and profits were not a motive, workers and managers had little motivation to improve productivity or introduce technological advancements. This led to a decline in efficiency and innovation.
- **Heavy Military Expenditure** A significant portion of the Soviet budget was allocated to defense and the arms race with the United States. This diverted resources away from essential sectors like education, healthcare and consumer goods, which resulted in economic imbalance and a decline in the standard of living.
- **Collectivisation of Agriculture** The collectivisation of agriculture resulted in inefficiencies, low productivity and frequent food shortages. State-controlled farms lacked motivation to maximise output. As a result, the Soviet Union was forced to import grain despite having vast agricultural land.

20. The South Asian Association for Regional Co-operation (SAARC), established in 1985, aims to strengthen co-operation through multilateral efforts.

- One example is the South Asian Free Trade Area (SAFTA) agreement, signed in 2004 and implemented in 2006. This agreement promotes regional economic co-operation by reducing trade tariffs among SAARC countries.
- Another example is the shared interest in addressing regional challenges such as poverty, environmental issues and security. It demonstrates that despite political tensions, co-operation for mutual benefit continues to be a priority in South Asia.

Or The statement highlights that despite challenges in democratic governance, the people of South Asian countries continue to aspire for democracy. This can be justified with the following arguments

- **Struggles for Democratic Rights** In South Asia, people have consistently fought for democracy, even in countries with a history of military or authoritarian rule. For example, in Pakistan, despite military interventions, the public has repeatedly pushed for democratic elections. Similarly, in Nepal, mass movements led to the establishment of democracy in 1990 and again in 2006 after the monarchy was abolished.
- **High Voter Participation and Democratic Movements** Countries like India, Bangladesh and Sri Lanka have witnessed high voter turnout, showing people's strong belief in democratic participation. Even in nations facing political instability, such as Myanmar and the Maldives, citizens have actively supported democratic reforms. The demand for free and fair elections, civil rights and accountable governments reflects the deep-rooted aspiration for democracy in the region.

21. The Indian government can take several steps to control pollution and protect the environment

- **Improving Public Transport** Expand and promote eco-friendly public transport like metro systems and electric buses to reduce vehicular emissions and traffic congestion.

- **Promotion of Renewable Energy** Encourage the use of solar, wind and hydro energy to reduce dependence on fossil fuels, which contribute to air pollution and climate change.
- **Industrial Waste Management** Implement strict regulations for industries to treat wastewater and hazardous waste before disposal.
- **Strengthening Environmental Laws** Enforce penalties for violations of environmental laws, conduct regular pollution audits and promote eco-friendly technologies in industries.

22. No, the prevalence of one party dominance in India did not affect the democratic nature of Indian politics. It was because in India, many parties contested elections in the conditions of free and fair manner, but Congress managed to win elections democratically.

However, in some instances like Kerala elections in 1957, some decisions of Congress became controversial. But overall, the presence of the opposition parties played a crucial role in maintaining democratic character through their criticism and the process of checks and balance.

23. Jayaprakash Narayan, popularly referred to as JP or Lok Nayak (The People's Leader), was an Indian independence activist, theorist, socialist and political leader. Jayaprakash Narayan is known for three key contributions: Fight Against Corruption, Principle of Communitarian Socialism and Championing of 'Total Revolution'.
He was the first leader in post-independence India who undertook a tirade against corruption through the participation of youth, particularly in Gujarat and Bihar. He advocated the office of Lokpal against corruption. His principle of communitarian socialism views India as a society of communities en-compassing three key layers, viz. community, region and rashtra–all combine together as an example of true federation.

Or The two reasons were

(i) Non-democratic outlook of Congress favoured Janata Party.

(ii) Formation of the Janata Party also ensured that non-Congress votes would not be divided.

24. (i) (c) 1990s

(ii) (c) Cultural diversity

(iii) (c) Through elections

(iv) (b) Sikkim

25.

SR Number for the Information used	Alphabet concerned	Name of the State
(i)	C	J & K
(ii)	A	Punjab
(iii)	D	Chhattisgarh
(iv)	B	Andhra Pradesh

26. (i) (b) Influence of USA on UNO

(ii) (a) If UN fails then the US can control the world by its military power.

(iii) (b) Many new powerful international organisations have emerged.

(iv) (b) To promote international peace and co-operation

27. The contentions issues between China and India are

- In 1950, China annexed Tibet which removed a historical buffer between two countries. Initially, India didn't oppose it openly, but later it resented this issue when information regarding Tibetan culture suppression came up.
- Dalai Lama, the Tibetan spiritual leader sought and obtained political asylum in India in 1959. China opposed this move by declaring that India is supporting anti-China activities.
- China and India were involved in a border conflict in 1962 over competing territorial claims principally in Arunachal Pradesh and in the Aksai Chin region of Ladakh. The conflict of 1962, in which India suffered military reverses, had long-term implications for India–China relations.

These issues can be resolved for greater co-operation. Although attempts have been made to normalise relations between the two nations by signing border pacts and agreements and with the visits of dignitaries, both nations need to again look into their strategies, revive cordial relations and collectively tread on the path of development.
The following important suggestions can be made to improve relations between India and China.

- India and China must accelerate the pace of economic co-operation between the two nations.
- Both the countries must discover innovative and pragmatic strategies for resolving the long-standing border dispute.

- The countries must enter into bilateral agreements on trade and encourage greater cultural exchange and interaction.
- Both the countries must join hands to fight challenges confronting the world, such as terrorism, environmental degradation, etc.

Or The three pillars of ASEAN Community are

- ASEAN Security Community
- ASEAN Economic Community
- ASEAN Socio-Cultural Community

The objectives of the ASEAN Community are as follows

- To accelerate economic growth through social progress and cultural development.
- The territorial disputes should not escalate into armed confrontations.
- To promote regional peace and stability based on the rule of law.
- To establish dispute settlement mechanism for resolving economic disputes.
- Free Trade Areas will be created for investments, labour and services.

28. After the Second World War, newly independent countries in Asia and Africa faced several significant security challenges such as

(i) **Political Instability** Many of these nations emerged from colonial rule without stable political structures, leading to internal conflicts and power struggles. Ethnic and tribal divisions often flared into violence, as various groups vied for control, resulting in civil wars and prolonged unrest. Countries like Nigeria and Sudan experienced severe internal strife rooted in these divisions.

(ii) **Territorial Disputes** The arbitrary borders drawn during colonialism often grouped disparate ethnic communities together, leading to territorial disputes both within and between nations. For instance, the partition of India and Pakistan in 1947 triggered violent conflicts over Kashmir, with lasting geopolitical tensions that continue today.

(iii) **Cold War Dynamics** The global rivalry between the United States and the Soviet Union during the Cold War further complicated security. Newly independent states often found themselves pressured to align with one of the superpowers, leading to proxy wars, foreign interventions and de-stabilisation. Countries such as Vietnam and Afghanistan became battlegrounds for these larger geopolitical conflicts, severely affecting their sovereignty and security.

These challenges significantly hindered nation- building efforts and contributed to ongoing regional instability.

Or Security is a fundamental concern for nations, but its understanding has evolved over time. Traditional security mainly focuses on military aspects, while non-traditional security addresses broader concerns that impact the well-being of individuals and societies. Below is a detailed comparison of these two notions

Aspect	Traditional Security	Non-Traditional Security
Focus	Traditional security is centered around protecting the sovereignty and territorial integrity of a nation. It primarily deals with military threats and external aggression from other countries.	Non-traditional security includes a wide range of threats that are not necessarily military in nature, such as economic instability, terrorism, environmental degradation, cyber threats and pandemics.
Nature of Threats	The threats in traditional security are mostly external, involving wars, border disputes, military conflicts and arms races between nations. The primary concern is the defense of the state.	The threats in non-traditional security can be both internal and external. These include climate change, organised crime, economic crises, refugee crises, human rights violations and diseases like COVID-19.
Approach to Security	The approach relies on military preparedness, strategic alliances, deterrence policies and arms buildup. Governments invest in defense forces, nuclear weapons and military technology to maintain security.	The approach is more comprehensive and involves international cooperation, economic policies, environmental conservation, public health measures and social development programs to address security concerns.

29. India formulated its foreign policy with an aim to respe the sovereignty of all other nations and to achieve se through the maintenance of peace.

The major principles of India's Foreign Policy ar

(i) **Non-Alignment** It means not to join blocks or enter into military allian independent foreign policy and co-existence. Non-alignmen disarmament, developme democratisation of int protection of the er

(ii) **Panchsheel** It i countries th 1954. Its five p

- Respect for eac sovereignty

(ii) i ap em class

- Mutual non-aggression
- Mutual non-interference in each other's internal affairs
- Equality and mutual benefit
- Peaceful co-existence

(iii) **Opposition to Colonialism** Since we have been the victims of colonial rule and exploitation, we stand for the right of self-determination and anti-imperialism. We supported the cause of freedom of the colonies of Africa and Asia, as colonialism is a violation of Fundamental Human Rights.

India co-operated with Indonesia in its efforts for freedom and also supported the freedom struggles in Malaya, Algeria, Tansia and Namibia, etc. India's concern for Bangladesh and of Iraq's invasion of Kuwait reflects our opposition to colonialism.

Or Efforts taken by Jawaharlal Nehru for the promotion of Afro-Asian unity is as follows

- Due to India's size, location and power potential, Nehru dreamt of major role for India in world affairs specially in Asia.
- Under Nehru's leadership, India made contact with other newly emerged independent nations of Asia and Africa.
- During the 1940s and 1950s, Nehru advocated with great enthusiasm to support the Asian unity. Under his leadership, India hosted the Asian relations conference in March 1947, five months before India's independence.
- India was a staunch supporter of decolonisation and firmly opposed racism, partiaularly apartheid in South Africa.
- The Afro-Asian Conference known as the Bandung Conference was held in 1955.
- The Bandung Conference marked the climax of India's engagement with newly independent Asian and African nations.

30. The end of the decade of 1980s witnessed many developments that had a long lasting impact on Indian politics. These are as follows

(i) The first and most crucial development was the defeat of the Congress Party in the elections of 1989. It was seen as the end of Congress system by some political scientists.

The Congress remained as an important party after that, but the centrality of the power which it used to enjoy earlier now came to an end.

The second development was the rise of the mandal ...sue in the national politics. Mandal Commission was ...pointed to look for the improvement in education and ...loyment for the socially and educationally backward ...s.

The Mandal Commission recommended for the reservation for backward classes in education as well as employment.

This became a dispute among the supporters and opponents of the OBC reservation, this issue had influenced the Indian politics since 1989.

(iii) The third development was the economic policy followed by various governments. Many of the governments took a radical shift in economic policies which was known as structural adjustment programmes. These policies have been widely criticised through various movements and organisations. However, the government that came into power, have continued to follow these policies.

(iv) The fourth was the century old legal and political dispute over the Ram Janmabhoomi Temple in Ayodhya. This issue became the central issue in Indian politics and changed the direction of secularism and democracy. It was finally ended with the construction of the Ram Temple at Ayodhya after the landmark judgement by the Constitutional bench of the Supreme Court in November 2019.

Or The Mandal Commission, officially known as the Second Backward Classes Commission was established in 1979 under the chairmanship of B.P. Mandal. It was formed to identify socially and educationally backward classes (OBCs) and recommend measures for their upliftment. Three major recommendations of the commission were

- **Reservation in Government Jobs and Educational Institutions** The commission recommended 27 percent reservation for Other Backward Classes (OBCs) in government services and educational institutions to improve their representation in public employment and higher education. This was aimed at reducing social and economic inequality.
- **Promotion of OBC Welfare through Development Programmes** It suggested the introduction of special programmes to enhance the economic and educational conditions of OBCs. This included access to scholarships, vocational training and financial assistance to promote self-employment and skill development.
- **Caste-based Census and Social Justice Policies** The commission emphasised the need for regular surveys and caste-based data collection to assess the socio-economic status of OBCs. It also recommended setting up institutions to monitor the implementation of reservation policies and welfare programs.